SEAFOOD SAFETY

Committee on Evaluation of the Safety of Fishery Products

Farid E. Ahmed, Editor

Food and Nutrition Board
Institute of Medicine

NATIONAL ACADEMY PRESS
Washington, D.C. 1991

National Academy Press ● 2101 Constitution Avenue, N.W. ● Washington, D.C. 20418

NOTICE: The project that is the subject of this report was approved by the Governing Board of the National Research Council, whose members are drawn from the councils of the National Academy of Sciences, the National Academy of Engineering, and the Institute of Medicine. The members of the committee responsible for the report were chosen for their special competences and with regard for appropriate balance.

This report has been reviewed by a group other than the authors according to procedures approved by a Report Review Committee consisting of members of the National Academy of Sciences, the National Academy of Engineering, and the Institute of Medicine.

The Institute of Medicine was chartered in 1970 by the National Academy of Sciences to enlist distinguished members of the appropriate professions in the examination of policy matters pertaining to the health of the public. In this, the Institute acts under both the Academy's 1863 congressional charter responsibility to be an adviser to the federal government and its own initiative in identifying issues of medical care, research, and education. Dr. Samuel O. Thier is president of the Institute of Medicine.

This study was supported by contract no. 50-WCNF-8-060636 from the U.S. Department of Commerce, National Oceanic and Atmospheric Administration.

Library of Congress Cataloging-in-Publication Data

Seafood safety / Committee on Evaluation of the Safety of Fishery Products,
    Food and Nutrition Board, Institute of Medicine,
    National Academy of Sciences : Farid E. Ahmed, editor.
        p.   cm.
    Includes bibliographical references and index.
    ISBN 0-309-04387-5
    1. Seafood--Health aspects. 2. Seafood--Safety measures.
    3. Seafood--Contamination. I. Ahmed, Farid E. II. Institute of
    Medicine (U.S.). Committee on Evaluation of the Safety of Fishery
    Products.
    RA602.F5S43 1991
    363.19'29--dc20   90-25996

Printed in the United States of America

The serpent has been a symbol of long life, healing, and knowledge among almost all cultures and religions since the beginning of recorded history. The image adopted as a logotype by the Institute of Medicine is based on a relief carving from ancient Greece, now held by the Staatlichemuseen in Berlin.

iii

iv

Preface

The responsibility for monitoring and control of seafood safety is divided among various agencies of the federal government, primarily the Food and Drug Administration (FDA), the Environmental Protection Agency (EPA), the National Marine Fisheries Service (NMFS), and the states. In recent years, however, the effectiveness of their respective programs has been questioned.

As a result of negative public perceptions, studies, and surveys conducted by various groups interested in seafood safety, Congress appropriated funds in 1988 to the National Oceanic and Atmospheric Administration (NOAA) of the Department of Commerce (DOC). These resources were dedicated to a two-year study to design a program of certification and seafood surveillance consistent with the Hazard Analysis Critical Control Point (HACCP) program, a concept recommended in 1985 and 1987 by Food and Nutrition Board (FNB) committees for the inspection of meat and poultry. The National Marine Fisheries Service of NOAA then approached the Institute of Medicine (IOM) Food and Nutrition Board with a formal solicitation for a two-year study to be conducted as part of the agency's overall plan.

In response, a multidisciplinary committee of 13 scientists was convened under the auspices of the FNB to conduct the study. The committee consisted of experts in the fields of public health, marine pathology, marine toxicology, food science and technology, food microbiology, biostatistics, seafood safety policy and regulations, epidemiology, risk assessment, industry structure, and public interest. In addition, the committee had four consultants in the areas of trace-metal safety, environmental chemical contaminants, marine resources, and comparative risk assessment. The committee was divided into the following working groups to address contract tasks: (1) regulatory/legislative, (2) microbiology/parasitology, (3) natural toxins, (4) chemical residues/risk assessment, and (5) seafood consumption/industry structure. The committee was asked to evaluate the health effects of marine and freshwater fishery products (fresh or frozen) available to the consumer from commercial and recreational sources, and to identify options for improvement of the current system of seafood surveillance and control. The evaluation was to include an examination of the potential

v

health hazards ascribed to chemical, microbial, and parasitic contaminants of seafood (e.g., natural toxins, toxic metals, synthetic substances, microorganisms, and parasites). Existing programs conducted under the authority of federal, state, or local governments, other public bodies, and private organizations were to be evaluated to ensure the safety of seafood obtained from domestic and foreign sources. The charge to the committee was divided into nine tasks:

1. Meeting with personnel from NMFS, FDA, the U.S. Department of Agriculture (USDA), and selected state government agencies to determine the perspectives of these agencies on seafood product safety, to learn about seafood control programs under their jurisdiction, and to hear the concerns and recommendations of federal agencies currently involved in fishery products safety issues. Programs conducted under the authority of those agencies were to be evaluated and recommendations for quality control measures were to be made.

2. Collecting and examining data on sources of outbreaks of seafood-borne illnesses among U.S. consumers from 1978 to 1987 gathered by the Centers for Disease Control (CDC), the Northeast Technical Support Unit (NETSU) of FDA, and the states.

3. Evaluating the efficacy of current systems for documenting and reporting cases of seafood-borne illnesses among U.S. consumers in relation to other foods, including the prevalence and effect of underreporting by state public health authorities to CDC, and evaluating the adequacy of current mechanisms for advising the fishing industry and the public of desirable or necessary follow-up actions to ameliorate problems due to seafood-borne illnesses.

4. Identifying the cause of illness in the targeted states or territories of Hawaii, Puerto Rico, the Virgin Islands, Guam, New York, California, Washington, Connecticut, and Florida attributable to dietary exposure to fresh and frozen seafoods harvested from either commercial or recreational sources in relation to any of the following variables: the species and percentages of fishery products implicated in such illnesses, the demography of affected consumers, and the possible role of ethnic dietary habits or improper food handling by the consumer. This task includes a review of how U.S. food control systems and state programs address major health hazards associated with fishery products, as well as recommendations for improvement.

5. Examining contemporary procedures for detecting, identifying, and quantifying etiological agents in seafood-borne illness, along with the methods used, pertinent scientific research in progress, and recommendations for improvement in these areas.

6. Reviewing the role of principal imported fresh and frozen fishery products in reported outbreaks of illness among U.S. consumers, and examining the relative prevalence and significance of imported and domestic seafoods as vehicles of etiologic factors.

7. Conducting a statistical evaluation of FDA's acceptance sampling plans and associated decision criteria, evaluating the quality assurance principles and procedures used by FDA in accepting the results of private testing laboratories for blocklisted imported products, and making suggestions for improvements of these procedures.

8. Reviewing contaminants associated with seafoods that are defined by the Federal Food, Drug, and Cosmetic Act as "avoidable" or "unavoidable" and assessing how well the current regulatory framework protects public health.

9. Assessing some indices of health risk assessment already determined by FDA and EPA for selected environmental pollutants that have an impact on fisheries, and recommending future research directions in this area as appropriate.

The tasks addressed by the committee are detailed in the various chapters and in its Executive Summary.

During the two-year duration of the study, the committee met nine times: five times the first year and four times the second year. The committee hosted a public meeting, which was part of its first meeting on January 31, 1989, to provide an opportunity for interested individuals and groups to express views or to present information to the committee for consideration. Eight speakers representing consumer groups, environmental and conservation foundations, trade organizations, and international and scientific organizations gave presentations. Some of these groups also provided the committee with additional data and information for consideration in carrying out its task.

The regulatory working group held group meetings and individual interviews with federal regulatory agencies, a variety of coastal state agencies, and industry representatives involved in seafood inspection and monitoring. Meetings with respective state regulatory representatives were conducted in Massachusetts, California, Hawaii, and the state of Washington. Additional state regulatory representation was ensured through numerous meetings and conversations with individuals from Arkansas, Wisconsin, Connecticut, Rhode Island, New York, and Guam. Results from meetings in Texas, Louisiana, Massachusetts, Alabama, Florida, Georgia, South Carolina, North Carolina, and Puerto Rico were referenced from project work conducted in conjunction with the Southeastern Fisheries Association, Tallahassee, Florida. This endeavor was directed toward assessing the intermingling roles of the federal and state governments in seafood regulation.

In addition to its meetings, the committee also visited several seafood processing plants in various regions of the country (Seattle, Washington; Houma, Louisiana; and Hampton, Virginia) to observe food safety issues related to production, preparation, and processing methodologies employed in the seafood industry.

The committee held a workshop in the third quarter of the study on July 26, 1989, focusing on assessing and controlling health hazards from fishery products. Seven invited speakers gave presentations, and four guests from academia and government agencies participated in the discussion.

A summary of the committee's findings, conclusions, and recommendations appears in Chapter 1. Chapter 2 describes the demographics of the seafood industry, fishery resources, aquaculture, and consumption trends. It also elaborates on activities in other countries. Chapters 3 and 4 outline health effects due to microbiological and parasitic infections and to exposure to natural toxins. Chapter 5 details the risks from exposure to environmental chemicals in aquatic organisms. Chapter 6 critiques existing risk assessment practices and suggests recommendations for improvement. Statistical sampling methods used in control of seafood hazards and suggestions for improvement are outlined in Chapter 7. Federal, state, and international programs with impact on seafood are described in Chapter 8, as well as causes of illness in targeted states, and comparative risks for consumers from different seafood products. A glossary of terms and acronyms is presented in Appendix A. The affiliation and major research interests of committee members and staff may be found in Appendix B.

The committee thanks the following individuals for public presentations: Ellen Haas of Public Voice for Food and Health Policy; Lee Weddig of National Fisheries Institute; John Farquhar of the Food Marketing Institute; Robert Murchelano of NMFS; Eleanor Dorsey of Conservation Law Foundation of New England; Carlos Fetterolf, Jr., of the Great Lakes Fishery Commission; Mary Uva of the Natural Resources Defense Council; and Theodora Colborn of the Conservation Foundation.

The committee is grateful to the following NOAA/NMFS staff who provided it with data and information: Thomas Billy, Richard Cano, Paul Comar, Ford Cross, Melvin Eklund, Peter Eldridge, E. Spencer Garrett, Amor Lane, G. Malcolm Meaburn, Bruce Morehead, and John Pearce. The committee appreciates the help of FDA representatives (George Hoskin, Richard Ronk, Alvin Shroff, Mary Snyder, and John Taylor) and USDA representatives (Catherine Adams and Lester Crawford) for the material they provided.

The committee values and benefited from the information presented at its workshop by Harold Humphrey, Joseph Rodricks, Yoshitsugi Hokama, David Weber, John Kvenberg, David Bevan, and E. Spencer Garrett.

The committee appreciates the assistance of the following seafood plant personnel who facilitated its visits to their operations: Richard Pace of Unisea, Inc., in Redmond, Washington; Ray Clark of Sea Freeze Cold Storage in Seattle, Washington; Michael and Elgin Voisin of Motivatit Seafoods in Houma, Louisiana; Harold La Peyer of Indian Ridge Shrimp Co. in Houma, Louisiana; and Daniel Kauffman of Amory Seafood, Inc., in Hampton, Virginia.

The committee is also grateful to the numerous state regulatory officials, particularly Robert Price and Robert Ross from California; Richard Delaney and Nancy Ridley from Massachusetts; Kathryn Kendrick-Vanderpool, John Crobin, and Howard Deese from Hawaii; and John Daly and Roger deCamp from Washington State, who assisted in arrangement and participation in state regulatory meetings, and the project liaison provided by Robert P. Jones of Southeastern Fisheries Association, Inc. In addition, the committee is indebted to the the following people who provided invaluable written and oral material: G. Burton Ayles, Carl Baker, Carin Bisland, David Borgeson, Daniel Brazo, Robert Burgess, James Colquhoun, Floyd Cornelius, John Farrington, Barbara Glenn, David Goldthwaite, Robert Haddock, Richard Hassinger, Diane Heiman, Daniel Helwig, Richard Hess, John Hesse, Kimberly Hummel, Roger Kenyon, Lee Kernen, Susan M. Krebs-Smith, Thomas Lauer, Gerry LeTendre, Lee Liebenstein, Donald Lollick, James Maclean, Sally Cole-Misch, Douglas Morrisette, Dale Morse, Steve Plakas, Gerald Pollack, Judy Pratt, Ronald Preston, Gilbert Radonski, Alvin Rainosek, Aaron Rosenfield, Rosalie Schnick, Lawrence Skinner, Mitsuto Sugi, Maurice Tamura, Paulette Thompson, Alan White, Asa Wright, and Chester Zawacki.

Moreover, the committee commends the assistance, hard work, and support of FNB staff: Farid E. Ahmed for the organizational and administrative support of the committee's work, and for editing the report; Barbara Matos for typing and finalizing the documents; Robert Earl for finalizing some chapters; and Catherine Woteki, Enriqueta Bond, and Samuel Thier for their support of the committee's work. Florence Poillon and Sally Stanfield are to be commended for final manuscript editing and report preparation, and Francesca Moghari for designing the cover to the report.

The Chair also wishes to thank the committee and its consultants, who volunteered countless hours and effort to produce an objective and timely report on a controversial subject that is a small part of a major national issue, the safety of the food supply.

JOHN LISTON
Chairman
Committee on Evaluation of
Safety of Fishery Products

Contents

1

Executive Summary

OVERVIEW

Fish and shellfish are nutritious foods that constitute desirable components of a healthy diet. Most seafoods available to the U.S. public are wholesome and unlikely to cause illness in the consumer. Nevertheless, there are areas of risk. The major risk of acute disease is associated with the consumption of raw shellfish, particularly bivalve molluscs. For persons living in areas in which reef fish are consumed (Hawaii, Puerto Rico, the Virgin Islands), there is a risk of ciguatera; other natural toxins (paralytic shellfish poisoning, neurotoxic shellfish poisoning, etc.) have been associated with shellfish from endemic areas. Finally, there are less well-defined risks of acute and chronic disease related to environmental contamination of aquatic food animals. Dealing with such risks on a short-term basis requires improvements in the present system of regulatory control. In the long term, amelioration and eventual elimination of some hazards require strengthening and more effective application of control measures to prevent the disposal of human and industrial waste into offshore marine and fresh waters.

Because of the strong public interest in seafood safety and the declared intention at the congressional level to develop a new inspection system, a clear opportunity exists to introduce innovative methodologies for control that address directly the important health issues associated with seafood consumption.

This report reviews the nature and extent of public health risks associated with seafood, and examines the scope and adequacy of current seafood safety programs. The conclusions and recommendations arrived at are summarized in the following material:

- Most current health risks associated with seafood safety originate in the environment and should be dealt with by control of harvest or at the point of capture. With minor exceptions, risks cannot be identified by an organoleptic inspection system.
- Inspection at the processing level is important to maintain safety of seafoods, but there is little evidence that increased inspection activities at this level would effectively reduce the incidence of seafood-borne disease.
- With currently available data, it is possible to identify the source of much of the acute illness associated with seafood consumption, though the dimensions of the

1

problems are not always known; these data, in turn, can form the basis for national control programs.

- Chronic illness resulting from seafood consumption is associated primarily with environmental contamination; thus, control depends on improved understanding of the occurrence and distribution of the chemical agents involved, the exclusion of contaminated seafood from the market, and increased action to prevent additional pollution of the waters.

- Because well over half the nation's seafood supply is imported and environmental contamination is globally pervasive, it is important that the safety of imported seafood be ensured through equivalent control measures in exporting countries.

- One-fifth of the fish and shellfish eaten in the United States is derived from recreational or subsistence fishing, and these products are not subject to health-based control; there is need to improve protection for consumers of these products by regulation of harvest and by education concerning risks associated with their consumption.

- Because the problems are largely regional, the primary effective control – except for imports – is at the state level, and this effort should be strengthened. However, there is need for federal oversight, general rule setting, and support to ensure the effectiveness of state-based programs and to provide expert assistance and specialized facilities.

- There is a lack of understanding of the nature of seafood hazards in the food service sectors and by the consuming public and health professionals; a vigorous campaign for information dissemination and education in these matters is needed, particularly for high-risk consumers and high-risk products such as raw shellfish.

- An improved national surveillance system should be developed to provide more reliable and comprehensive information on seafood-borne disease incidence. Data will then permit meaningful risk identification and risk assessment as a basis for effective regulation of seafoods (current data on disease occurrence in seafood consumption are too fragmentary to allow reliable risk assessment of microbiological and natural toxin hazards).

A summary of hazards, risks, and their control for the major groups of hazardous seafoods in shown in Table 1-1. They are arranged in order of importance.

Among seafood consumers, the group at greatest risk appears to be consumers of raw molluscs because of environmental contamination and naturally occurring vibrios. Consumers of recreational and subsistence fishery products are the second largest constituency at risk, both from natural toxins and from environmental contaminants. Inhabitants of islands in the Caribbean and tropical Pacific Ocean, and to a lesser extent of the Gulf of Mexico States, are uniquely at risk from ciguatera due to consumption of fish that feed on or near tropical reefs and prey upon reef fish. Although U.S. mainland inhabitants have developed the disease from imported fish, ciguatera is a highly regional problem that greatly skews disease reporting because of its geographical concentration and its high visibility in affected regions. There is a more general risk to consumers from certain fresh and frozen fish due to a milder toxic disease, scombroid poisoning.

There is generally a low risk to seafood consumers of food-borne disease due to control failures during processing or at the food service level. Fish do not normally carry microorganisms such as *Salmonella* or *Campylobacter*, which are commonly found in land animal carcasses and are the major causes of reported food-borne disease (though fish may acquire bacteria from contaminated water). Some ethnic practices in the preparation of fish for eating, place a small number of people at high risk from botulism, but this is not a significant hazard for most consumers of fish.

Thus, the health risks associated with seafood – although diverse – are identifiable and, to a significant extent, controllable by innovative measures aimed at geographically restricted or species-specific problems. Some risks, particularly those associated with environmental contamination, may be increasing; their elimination will require a major commitment on the part of both government and industry to change methods of waste disposal in our society. These and the more visible hazards mentioned can be greatly mitigated by a regulatory system specifically aimed at the causes, be they natural toxins, microorganisms, or contaminants. However, this will require something other than organoleptically based inspection systems, which may be useful for quality control and grading but are essentially worthless for detecting and controlling health risks.

NATURE AND EXTENT OF PUBLIC HEALTH RISKS

General

The principal source of data on the incidence of seafood-borne illness in the United States is the Centers for Disease Control (CDC). Its compilations are accumulated passively from state reports of food-borne outbreaks. An outbreak is an incident involving two or more sick individuals, except for botulism and certain chemical poisonings in which one sick individual constitutes an outbreak. A case is a single ill person. Unfortunately, not all states report each of the major types of seafood-borne disease, and within states there is considerable underreporting of incidents for a variety of reasons. Thus, CDC data may not be representative of actual disease occurrence and may omit altogether important seafood-originated disease outside the reporting format. The CDC information is useful when supplemented by other data on the occurrence of pathogens, an understanding of the patterns of seafood harvest and processing, a knowledge of the mechanisms of disease development, and – where available – independent epidemiological data. The CDC data cannot be used to estimate risks from chemical contamination, because no disease outbreaks have yet been reported from this cause.

Seafood-borne illness reported by CDC in the 10-year period 1978-1987 totaled 558 outbreaks involving 5,980 cases. However, fish and shellfish constitute only 10.5% of all outbreaks and 3.6% of all cases when food-borne illnesses from all foods are considered. The number of people made ill from beef (4%) and turkey (3.7%) exceeds the seafood total, whereas pork (2.7%) and chicken (2.6%) are slightly lower. If shellfish (2.3%) and fish (1.2%) are considered separately, the number of reported cases from each is lower than for any animal meat category. Nevertheless, when only muscle foods (e.g., red meat, fish, poultry) are consumed, seafood-borne illness represents 56% of all outbreaks and 21% of all cases when incidents of unknown etiology are included.

TABLE 1-1 Hazards and Risks of Seafood Consumption and Their Control Arranged According to Order of Importance

Hazardous Seafood [a]	Hazard [b]	Severity of Hazard [c]	Risk to Consumers [d]	Factors Enhancing Risk
Raw bivalve molluscs (oysters, clams, mussels)	(1) Viruses, enteric bacteria (2) *Vibrio* species	(1-2) Mostly mild gastroenteritis (2) Severe for susceptible hosts	High for consumers of raw molluscs	(1) Polluted growing waters (1-2) Temperature abuse (2) Host factors
Naturally toxic finfish	(1) Ciguatera	Moderately severe	(1) High in endemic areas	(1) Recreational fishing on reefs
	(2) Scombroid poisoning	Mild	(2) High for consumption of few species	(2) Temperature abuse after capture
Molluscs	(3) PSP, NSP, DSP, ASP	Mild to severe	(3) High if harvest is uncontrolled	(3) Recreational shellfish harvest
Chemically contaminated finfish and shellfish [g] (freshwater species, specific marine areas species)	Environmental chemicals such as mercury, lead, cadmium, PCBs, dioxin, pesticides	All levels mild to severe	High for subsistence recreational fishers in certain areas, pregnant women, and children	Subsistence and recreational fishing in areas of high contamination; species and fish portions eaten
Processed seafood	(1) *Clostridium perfringens* (2) *Salmonella* (3) *Shigella* (4) *Staphylococcus aureus* (5) *Vibrio parahemolyticus* (6) *HAV* (7) *Clostridium botulinum*	(1-5) Usually mild (7) Severe	Low when adequate cooking precedes consumption	Cross-contamination; temperature abuse; processor presentation errors

NOTE: HACCP = Hazard Analysis Critical Control Point; PSP = paralytic shellfish poisoning; NSP = neurotoxic shellfish poisoning; DSP = diarrhetic shellfish poisoning; ASP = amnesic shellfish poisoning; PCBs polychlorinated biphenyls; HAV = hepatitis A virus.

[a] Fish or shellfish, the consumption of which can lead to disease.

[b] An organism, substance, or condition having the potential to cause disease.

[c] Severe: may cause disability, extended sequelae, and in some cases, death; moderate: may require medical

Factors Reducing Risk	Present Control Systems [e]	Deficiencies of Present System [f]	Proposed Corrective Measures
(1-2) Cooking (2) Rapid cooling (1-2) Irradiation	(1) Shellfish sanitation program (2) None	(1) Unreliable indicators (2) No indicators	(1) Identify reliable indicators (2) Rapid method for *Vibrio* identification; chilling molluscs; radiation (1-2) Warn consumers of dangers of eating raw seafood
— (2) Good temperature control (3) Informed consumers	(1) Voluntary harvest restriction (2) Rapid cooling; histamine testing (3) State surveillance and harvest control	(1) No widely available test (2) Limited effectiveness of control (3) Harvest closure not always effective	(1) Regulate fisheries; develop reliable, rapid test(s) (2) Enforce temperature control through HACCP system (3) Additional policing and stronger advisories
Decreased consumption (avoid during pregnancy); avoid high-risk areas and species; trim skin and fat	Local regulations and advisories; some federal tolerance and action levels	Action levels too few and too permissive; inadequate harvest management and control; noncancer effects poorly evaluated; poor contaminant data bases	Further reductions in discharges; harvest restriction by site and species; improve advisories and possibly label fish; improve risk assessment for cancer and noncancer effects
Adequate cooking; temperature control; proper processing and food service	Sanitation inspection; process control	Limited inspection; ineffective inspection methods; diverse processing	Inspection and control based on HACCP system; improved temperature control on shipboard and during distribution

intervention to avoid debilitating or life-threatening effect, rarely self-resolving; mild: symptoms are transitory, rarely lasting more than a few days, no sequelae, no threat to life, usually self-resolving.
[d] Probability that a consumer will become ill from the hazard.
[e] Mechanisms to reduce or eliminate risk form hazard(s) by government, industry, or related individual action.
[f] Aspects of control systems that reduce their effectiveness.
[g] Presence of significant levels of undesirable chemicals (causing acute or chronic effects) in edible fish or shellfish tissue derived from natural environment of anthropogenic origin.

Natural seafood toxins – mainly ciguatera and scombroid poisoning and, to a lesser extent, paralytic shellfish poisoning – were responsible for 62.5% of all seafood-borne outbreaks of illness, but constituted only 28% of all reported cases. Shellfish-related incidents, although responsible for only 31% of the seafood illness outbreaks, involved 66% of all seafood-borne cases. Most of these (55%) were registered as of unknown etiology but are believed to be due mainly to Norwalk, Norwalk-like, or human enteric virus infections, with a smaller proportion caused by *Vibrio* bacteria. Fish-borne incidents due to causes other than natural toxins were only 9% of all outbreaks and 8% of all cases. They resulted mainly from bacteria, including common food-borne disease organisms, and from unknown etiology, suspected to be primarily enteric virus or recontaminant vibrios. Botulism is a specialized but significant component of fish-borne disease. Disease due to parasites was minimal (0.4% of outbreaks and 0.6% of cases reported from seafoods).

Shellfish-borne disease occurs mostly from molluscs consumed raw or lightly heated, which constitutes the largest consumer risk. Ciguatera is a highly regionalized and intense risk for inhabitants and visitors consuming certain reef-associated fish in Caribbean and tropical Pacific islands and in adjacent mainland areas. Scombroid poisoning is widely distributed geographically but is specifically associated with consumption of certain fish species, particularly tuna, mackerel, mahimahi (dolphin), and bluefish. Botulism is a hazard for native American groups in Alaska that eat traditional fermented seafoods. Other risks are typical of food-borne disease in general and result from errors in handling, storage, or processing procedures. These are no greater than for other foods of animal origin.

Intolerance to eating certain types of seafood is rare and more typically associated with certain individuals in risk categories predisposed by other health complications. Seafood allergies, distinguished as immunological reactions rather than the inability to digest, appear to be more prevalent, but they are difficult to diagnose and document. Specific allergens in seafood have thus far been only grossly characterized in few studies. Seafood intolerances and allergies can be due to food additives (e.g., sulfites) that cause symptoms and confuse diagnoses. Additional investigation of the biochemical and immunological characteristics of seafood allergies and their significance seems warranted. In light of this level of information on the cause and occurrence of this somewhat limited form of seafood-borne illness, regulatory response must depend on proper labeling to distinguish (1) species or seafood type, (2) ingredients in formulated and fabricated seafoods [e.g., fish base surimi (a washed mince of the separated muscle tissue from fish to which cryoprotectants are added) formed to resemble crab], and (3) ingredients used in preservation and processing (e.g., sulfites to retard shrimp melanosis).

Microorganisms and Parasites

Extent of Risk

Seafoods, like any food item, have the potential to cause disease from viral, bacterial, and parasitic microorganisms under certain circumstances. These agents are acquired from three sources: (1) mainly fecal pollution of the aquatic environment, (2) the natural aquatic environment, and (3) industry, retail, restaurant, or home processing and preparation. With the exception of foods consumed raw, however, the reported incidences of seafood-related microbial diseases are low.

Available data from CDC and from the Northeast Technical Support Unit (NETSU) of the Food and Drug Administration (FDA) for 1978-1987, as well as literature reports, suggest that the greatest numbers of seafood-associated illnesses are from raw molluscan shellfish harvested in waters contaminated with raw or poorly treated human sewage. The majority of these illnesses have unknown etiologies clinically suggestive of Norwalk and Norwalk-like agents that cause human viral gastroenteritis. Although these are the most common seafood-associated illnesses, they tend to be relatively mild with no associated mortality.

Except for Guam, naturally occurring marine *Vibrio* species are responsible for fewer reported cases of infections involving the consumption of raw molluscan shellfish, but certain species such as *V. vulnificus* can be associated with high mortality (>50%) in persons who are immunocompromised or who have underlying liver disease.

The microbiological risk associated with seafood other than raw molluscan shellfish is much lower and appears to result from recontamination or cross-contamination of cooked with raw products, or to contamination during preparation followed by time/temperature abuse (e.g., holding at warm temperature long enough for microbial growth or toxin production to occur). This occurs mainly at the food service (postprocessing) level, which is common to all foods and not specific for seafood products.

Seafood-related parasitic infections are even less common than bacterial and viral infections, with anisakids and cestodes having the greatest public health significance in the United States. In general, parasitic infections are concentrated in certain ethnic groups that favor the consumption of raw or partially cooked seafoods.

Thorough cooking of seafood products would virtually eliminate all microbial and parasitic pathogens. Individuals who choose to eat raw seafood should be educated about the potential risks involved and how to avoid or mitigate them. In particular, immunocompromised individuals and those with defective liver function should be warned never to eat raw shellfish.

The greatest risks from the consumption of raw molluscan shellfish could be minimized by research to develop valid human enteric virus indicators for the proper classification of shellfish growing waters; by implementing and maintaining proper treatment and disposal of sewage to avoid human enteric pathogen contamination of harvest areas; by efforts to identify and limit the number of pathogenic *Vibrio* species in shellfish; by developing new diagnostic methods and improved processing technologies; and by applying risk-based regulatory and control measures for potential microbial pathogens in raw molluscan shellfish.

Other seafood-associated risks can be reduced by proper application of a Hazard Analysis Critical Control Point (HACCP) system. This cannot be achieved by the visual or organoleptic inspection currently used for meat and poultry. Seafood inspection should be directed toward identification of microbiological risks to consumers and the effectiveness of methods to reduce or eliminate such risks. Additional studies are necessary to determine levels of particular microorganisms that constitute a risk and that can be used as a basis for microbial guidelines. This requires appropriate epidemiological research. Inspection requirements should apply to imported as well as domestic products.

Principal Conclusions

• Most seafood-associated illness is reported from consumers of raw bivalve molluscs, and is due to unknown etiologies but is clinically suggestive of Norwalk-like viral gastroenteritis. The majority of incidents are due to consumption of shellfish from fecally polluted water. The disease is usually mild and self-resolving.

• Naturally occurring marine *Vibrio* species are responsible for fewer reported cases of infection from the consumption of raw molluscan shellfish, but species such as *V. vulnificus* can be associated with high mortality in persons who are immunocompromised or who have underlying liver disease.

• A lesser risk of microbial disease associated with other seafoods – resulting from recontamination or cross-contamination of cooked by raw product, or to contamination from other sources – is usually associated with time/temperature abuse. The etiologic agents most commonly involved, in order of reported frequency, are *V. parahaemolyticus*, hepatitis A, *Salmonella, Shigella, Clostridium perfringens,* and *C. botulinum* (mostly limited to Alaskan natives).

• Seafood-related parasitic infections are even less common than bacterial and viral infections, with anisakids and cestodes having the greatest public health significance in the United States. In general, parasitic infections have resulted from consumption of raw or partially cooked fresh- and saltwater fish of particular species (e.g., whitefish, salmon).

Principal Recommendations

• Consumers should be informed of the risks of eating raw seafoods, particularly molluscan shellfish. Individuals belonging to high-risk groups, such as cirrhotics, people with hemochromatosis, or immunosuppressed individuals, must not eat raw shellfish; this requires that health professionals be educated concerning hazards to high-risk individuals.

• Adequate and proper treatment and disposal of sewage must be implemented to avoid contamination of harvest areas by human enteric pathogens.

• Valid indicators for human pathogen contamination of growing waters must be developed. Seafood-borne infections by human enteric viruses in raw and improperly cooked molluscan shellfish could be decreased significantly by the development of valid growing water indicator(s) and of direct detection methodologies for enteric viruses.

• Effective enforcement to eliminate recreational commercial and illegal harvesting and sale of molluscan shellfish from contaminated growing areas should be developed and adequately funded.

• Means must be investigated and implemented to eliminate, or at least reduce, levels of potentially pathogenic *Vibrio* species in raw shellfish. This may necessitate restriction of harvest when water temperatures are high, rapid cool-down and continued chilling of products, and possibly irradiation of live shellstock and shucked products.

• Consideration should be given to monitoring *Vibrio* counts in molluscan shellfish during warm months.

• Because of the high risks associated with raw molluscan shellfish, the importation of live shellfish for raw consumption should not be permitted unless standards for the microbial quality of harvest waters and of harvest processing in the exporting country are fully equivalent to those in the United States.

• Consumers should be advised to cook seafood sufficiently to destroy parasites and bacterial contaminants before consumption.

• Control systems for microbiological hazards must include inspection techniques, preferably HACCP based, that specifically test for the hazard itself or for some condition that enhances or reduces hazard. Valid microbiological guidelines, established with an appropriate epidemiologic data base, are needed for seafood products.

• Special attention should be addressed to ensure the safety of seafoods processed by newer techniques, such as *sous vide* and the use of controlled atmosphere packaging, that are potentially hazardous.

• New or improved methodologies [e.g., enzyme-linked immunoabsorbent assay (ELISA), gene probe, polymerase chain reaction] should be developed that provide for the rapid identification and quantification of indicators, seafood-associated pathogens, and microbial toxins in seafoods and harvest waters.

Natural Toxins

Extent of Risk

Incidents of illness due to naturally occurring seafood toxins reported to CDC in 1978-1987 were limited to ciguatera, scombroid fish poisoning, paralytic shellfish poisoning (PSP), and neurotoxic (brevetoxic) shellfish poisoning (NSP). Other intoxications, including puffer fish poisoning (PFP), were reported earlier; diarrhetic shellfish poisoning (DSP) and amnesic shellfish poisoning (ASP) are possible risks that should be anticipated. Naturally, toxic fish and shellfish are not distinguishable from nontoxic animals by sensory inspection, and the toxins are not destroyed by normal cooking or processing. Except for scombroid fish poisoning, natural intoxications are both highly regional and species associated, and toxins are present in the fish or shellfish at the time of capture. Scombroid poisoning is due to histamine produced by bacteria multiplying on fish that are mishandled after capture; illnesses are widely reported from different states.

Ciguatera is a sometimes severe disease caused by consuming certain species of fish from tropical waters usually associated with islands or reefs. The disease is most common (endemic) in the Caribbean and Pacific islands, with some outbreaks in southern Florida and sporadic cases in other states caused by imported fish or tourist travel to endemic areas. Ciguatera was responsible for about half of all reported outbreaks of seafood intoxication in 1978-1987. The treatment is largely supportive, but mortality is low. At present, no effective control systems are in place for the prevention of ciguatera because a test for toxic fish is not generally available. Warnings and advisories concerning the hazards of ciguatera and the risks of consuming particular species of fish from ciguatera areas are issued by various states. Active control is proposed based on regulation of fishing for dangerous species, supported by testing suspect fish at dockside or on board the fishing vessel to detect and reject ciguatoxic fish. Increased education of the consuming public, sports fishers, and health professionals on the hazards and symptoms of ciguatera is also recommended.

During the same period, scombroid poisoning reportedly caused a similar number of outbreaks as ciguatera but was much more widespread in occurrence. Tuna, mahimahi, and bluefish were implicated as the major cause of scombroid poisoning in the United States. The disease is generally mild and self-resolving, and symptoms can be ameliorated by antihistamine drugs. Because the histamine that causes scombroid poisoning is produced after the fish have been caught, as a consequence of improper temperature control, the disease can be prevented by rapidly cooling fish after capture to 10°C or lower (e.g., 0°C if kept for an extended period) and holding them at or below this temperature at all times before cooking and eating. A HACCP-based system would control this poisoning for commercially handled fish, but the education of subsistence and recreational fishers is also necessary.

Paralytic shellfish poisoning was a minor cause of seafood-borne illness in 1978-1987, with only two deaths reported. This is a remarkable record in view of the annual occurrence of toxic situations among shellfish on both the East and the West coasts of the United States, which indicates that current control measures applied by coastal states are highly effective. However, the increasing occurrence of toxic dinoflagellate blooms and changing eating practices (e.g., eating whole scallops) among some sectors of the consuming public require increased surveillance and the development of more rapid and simple tests for toxic shellfish.

Although none of the other natural seafood intoxications, except for a single outbreak of NSP, have been reported recently by U.S. consumers, the potential for their occurrence either from domestically produced seafoods or from imports is real. Increased vigilance concerning imported products based on a requirement for certified nontoxicity is recommended. Moreover, both state and federal laboratories should be prepared to test for these "other" toxins, and procedures to deal with outbreaks should be in place.

Principal Conclusions

- Natural toxin risks are highly regional or species associated.
- Natural toxins are present in the environment and are not affected by procedures during or after harvest. The one exception is scombroid shellfish poisoning, which is due to postharvest mishandling.
- Reliable, rapid tests for the natural toxins are either unavailable or not fully developed.
- Although PSP is well controlled by state inspection systems and industry controls are in place for scombroid poisoning, there are no regulations for the control of ciguatera.
- Recreational and subsistence fish eaters are at particular risk from natural toxins, and there is a lack of understanding by consumers of this risk.

Principal Recommendations

- Control for natural toxins in the food chain should be at, or prior to, harvest, either by closures or by testing at the point of harvest.

● Scombroid poisoning should be controlled primarily by rapid chilling on the vessel and by maintenance of refrigeration temperatures throughout distribution.

● Major emphasis should be placed on the development of rapid assays for each of the other natural toxins; without this, control is very difficult.

● Primary regulatory authority should be at the state level, with funding, quality control, and specialized assistance from a federal seafood safety program.

● Imported seafoods must be certified to be free of natural toxins through equivalency arrangements or more effective memoranda of understanding (MOUs) with exporters. An MOU refers to a formal agreement between a U.S. government agency (e.g., FDA) and another government agency (federal, state, local), or an informal agreement with a foreign government or other foreign institution.

● Educational programs on the dangers of natural seafood toxins must be developed for recreational and subsistence fishers, and health providers must be given information to improve the identification and treatment of illness due to seafood toxins.

Chemical Residues

Extent of Risk

Fish and shellfish accumulate chemicals from the environment in which they live, but the extent of accumulation depends on such factors as geographic location, species of fish, feeding patterns, solubility and lipophilicity of the chemicals, and their persistence in the environment. Moreover, whereas land animals used for human consumption are fed mostly food of plant origin, aquatic animals that contribute to the human diet are generally predators of other animals and, in some cases, predators of predators. Because of this, chemicals have an opportunity to become more concentrated through bioaccumulation.

The most difficult area for risk evaluation is the problem of chemical residues because the health effects suspected do not take the form of obvious, distinctive, and acute illnesses. The potential risks of concern (e.g., modest changes in the overall risk of cancer; subtle impairments of neurological development in fetuses and children) are generally quite difficult to measure directly in people exposed at levels that are common for U.S. consumers. Immunoincompetence may increase cancer risk. Inferences about the potential magnitude of these problems must be based on the levels of specific chemicals present, on observations of human populations and experimental animals exposed at relatively high doses, and on reasonable theories about the likely mechanisms of action of specific toxicants and the population distributions of sensitivity and human exposure. In nearly all cases the current state of knowledge on these subjects must be regarded as quite tentative. Additionally, the number and variety of chemical residues are substantial, although a small minority constitute the bulk of the risk that can be assessed quantitatively at this time.

Overall, several chemical contaminants in some species of aquatic organisms in particular locations have the potential to pose hazards to public health that are great enough to warrant additional efforts at control. Available information suggests that these risks, in the aggregate, are not generally of a magnitude comparable to the highest environmental health hazards characterized to date; nevertheless, their control would significantly improve public health. Some examples of risks that may be

significant include reproductive effects from polychlorinated biphenyls (PCBs) and
methylmercury; carcinogenesis from selected congeners of PCBs, dioxins, and
dibenzofurans (all of which appear to act primarily by binding to a single type of
receptor); and, possibly, parkinsonism in the elderly from long-term mercury exposure.
Several other metallic and pesticide residues also warrant attention.

Principal Conclusions

• A small proportion of seafood is contaminated with appreciable
concentrations of potentially hazardous organic and inorganic chemicals from both
natural and human sources. Some examples of the risks that may be significant include
reproductive effects from PCBs and methylmercury, and carcinogenesis from selected
PCB congeners, dioxins, and chlorinated hydrocarbon pesticides.
• Consumption of some types of contaminated seafood poses enough risk that
efforts toward evaluation, education, and control of that risk must be improved.
• Present quantitative risk assessment procedures used by government agencies
should be improved and extended to noncancer effects.
• Current contaminant monitoring and surveillance programs provide an
inadequate representation of the presence of contaminants in edible portions of
domestic and imported seafood, resulting in serious difficulties in assessing both risks
and specific opportunities for control.
• Due to the unevenness of contamination among species and geographic
sources, it is feasible to narrowly target control efforts and still achieve meaningful
reductions in exposure.
• The data base for evaluating the safety of certain chemicals that find their
way into seafood via aquaculture and processing is too weak to support a conclusion
that these products are being effectively controlled.

Principal Recommendations

• Existing regulations to minimize chemical and biological contamination of the
aquatic environment should be strengthened and enforced.
• Existing FDA and state regulations should be strengthened and enforced to
reduce the human consumption of aquatic organisms with relatively high contaminant
levels (e.g., certain species from the Great Lakes with high PCB levels, swordfish and
other species with high methylmercury levels).
• Federal agencies should actively support research to determine actual risks
from the consumption of contaminants associated with seafood and to develop specific
approaches for decreasing these risks.
• Increased environmental monitoring should be initiated at the state level as
part of an overall federal exposure management system.
• States should continue to be responsible for site closures, and for issuing
health and contamination advisories tailored to the specific consumption habits,
reproductive or other special risks, and information sources of specific groups of
consumers.
• Public education on specific chemical contaminant hazards should be

expanded by government agencies and the health professions.

● For specific contaminants in particular species from high-risk domestic or foreign geographic areas, government agencies should consider the option of mandatory labeling.

● Additional study of potential chemical contamination risks associated with both domestic and imported aquaculture products is required. Because of different standards for drug or agricultural chemical use and water quality prevailing in other countries, imported aquaculture products should be effectively certified as meeting U.S. standards.

SCOPE AND ADEQUACY OF CURRENT SEAFOOD SAFETY PROGRAMS

Regulatory Guidelines, Monitoring, and Inspection

The current system of governance designed to protect the U.S. seafood consumer is composed of an intricate and complementary system of programs at the federal and state levels of government. Additional programs have been instituted in the private sector that offer a measure of industry self-regulation. At the federal level the principal responsibility for setting regulatory guidelines and for the surveillance and control of seafood safety is divided among the FDA, the Environmental Protection Agency (EPA), and the National Marine Fisheries Service (NMFS).

Within states, responsibility may lie with one or more of their health, environmental, fishery, or agricultural departments. States generally tend to adopt federal regulatory guidelines.

A primary role for the federal government is setting regulatory guidelines designed to promote inspection and enforcement activities both within and outside formal governmental programs. Existing regulatory guidelines can be divided into (1) those designed to reduce acute risk from microbial and natural toxin contaminants, and (2) those designed to reduce long-term or chronic risk due to chemical contamination. Guidelines for microorganisms and natural toxins are determined solely by the FDA and have been set primarily on an as-needed basis, that is, in response to a reported public health problem.

Properly collated and effectively presented guidelines could provide a strong basis for the production and supply of safe seafood. However, in several areas related to new processing techniques and other emerging problems, new guidelines seem both appropriate and necessary. Setting federal guidelines for residual chemical contaminants is a task shared by EPA and FDA. Their strategy has been to focus on a limited number of chemical contaminants and to set regulatory limits by means of "action levels." Results of various federal and state efforts to monitor contaminant loads in the nation's marine and freshwater environments suggest strongly that several chemicals require a more fundamental review and evaluation.

In terms of assessing and managing risks, the overall posture of relevant federal agencies, particularly FDA, appears to be almost totally reactive. In the committee's judgment, there has been less effort than would be desirable to discover and quantify hazards that are not yet on the public agenda, to evaluate options for reducing risks, and to implement policies that protect both the health of consumers and the stability of commercial markets.

One of the more important activities at both the federal and the state levels is environmental monitoring. Because the majority of seafood is from wild stocks, the quality of harvesting waters is of fundamental concern. The EPA and certain state governments [primarily by way of their involvement in the National Shellfish Sanitation Program (NSSP)] have instituted programs to establish the level of contaminants in seafood harvesting waters.

These efforts have led to important insights into general water quality but, for the most part, do not supply sufficient information on the question of seafood safety. Among other things, they lack (1) sufficient geographic scope, (2) a common methodological approach, and (3) sufficient focus on the edible portion of seafood in order to determine public health, as opposed to environmental health, impacts. This last point is an important one. Except for the monitoring of harvesting waters carried out as part of the NSSP, data evaluating contaminant levels in fish and shellfish do not consistently focus on the analysis of edible tissue. More often the focus is on whole fish or on liver and gallbladder analysis. These analyses, by their design, offer insufficient insight into contaminant levels in the edible portion of seafood products.

Inspection efforts by FDA and various state and local public health agencies are designed to ensure safety, but are insufficient to ensure in all cases that the regulatory guidelines defined by FDA and EPA are not being exceeded. The sampling strategies employed by these various agencies are designed to focus inspection and enforcement activities on areas in which the probability of a problem appears highest. Ongoing governmental efforts to develop new inspection programs, with a focus on the public health aspects of the raw product and the environment from which these products are derived, along with continued control of seafood production and processing, could provide measurable additional benefits in seafood safety.

Given many of the intrinsic attributes of seafood already discussed, it is clear that an approach recognizing the advantages of regional/local control and surveillance is essential. The question of seafood safety should continue to be one in which federal and state roles are viewed as a cooperative partnership. It is also apparent that seafood commerce is taking place within an increasingly interdependent international economy. Many of the major trading partners of the United States are developing or further refining formal regulatory programs for seafood safety. These efforts should be taken into account in designing a domestic program.

Principal Conclusions

● Federal (mostly FDA) guidelines for microbial and natural toxin contamination should be extended and updated. Those that exist have not been adequately conveyed to the fishing industry and to interested members of the public.

● Federal guidelines on chemical contaminants in seafoods are limited in scope and, in some cases, questionable as to the levels set. There is an apparent lack of coordination in the development and use of data on chemicals in the aquatic environment among FDA, EPA, the National Oceanic and Atmospheric Administration (NOAA), and the states. Better recognition is required of the importance of regional factors in the occurrence of toxic fish and shellfish and of the existence of high at-risk groups (e.g., pregnant women, children, recreational and subsistence fishers).

• The present federal monitoring and inspection system is too limited in frequency and direction to ensure enhanced safety of seafoods. The monitoring process depends too much on evaluation of the product, rather than on safety of raw materials, with the single notable exception of the NSSP. However, even NSSP is not providing adequate protection because molluscan shellfish appear to cause most seafood-borne disease.

• Recreational and subsistence fishing is largely ignored in health and safety monitoring at the federal level. Consumers of seafood from these sources can be at high risk from natural toxins and chemical pollutants in certain regions and in particular species of fish. The health risks include cancer and the subtle impairment of neurological development in fetuses and children.

• The present system of data collection on seafood-borne illness by CDC does not provide an adequate picture of the extent and causes of such disease.

• Seafood advisories warning of local or species-associated health risks are issued mostly by state authorities and vary greatly in both their content and their distribution. Nevertheless, these advisories serve a useful purpose.

• Because of the regional nature of much of the domestic fisheries problems, states seem the logical level at which to tackle seafood control problems. However, help and guidance from the federal level are required.

• State programs for monitoring, surveillance, and control of seafood safety are generally in place in coastal states that use federal guidelines and action levels where these are available. However, the quality and effectiveness of the programs vary greatly as a function of the financial and administrative support available to the responsible state units, and in accordance with the character of the resource. A greater emphasis should be placed on the development of formal arrangements with foreign producers to guarantee that imported seafood has been harvested and processed in noncontaminated environments.

• Present training and education of industry and regulatory personnel are too limited both in scope and in number. Insufficient attention is given to the education of physicians and other health professionals on seafood safety and the characteristics of seafood-borne disease. This is also true of the consuming public.

• The regulation of imported seafoods to ensure safety is largely based on end product inspection and testing, except where MOUs exist. This is ineffective because it involves a mainly reactive process.

• The regulation of imported seafood products is carried out largely without regard to other national or international programs. There is tremendous variance in both regulatory limits for contaminants and inspection protocols in various countries, which leads to excessive and cumbersome inspection strategies for the importing state, and may also lead to a general reduction in the number of countries engaged in international seafood trade in the future.

Principal Recommendations

• A more concise, comprehensive, and generally available single source for all FDA guidelines relating to seafood safety should be developed and updated on a regular basis. This information should be disseminated to industry and integrated into state regulatory processes through more routine and uniform training programs.

● The development of an interagency structure with a single focus on seafood safety could contribute significantly toward increasing communication within the federal regulatory system, but the responsibility for primary control should be with the state.

● Federal agencies should develop a set of monitoring and inspection practices focusing more strongly on environmental conditions and on contaminant levels in the edible portion of seafood at the point of capture.

● Strong consideration should be given to creating a marine recreational fishing license system that is linked to the distribution of information characterizing the level and scope of potential risk from eating recreationally caught fish. Strong consideration should also be given to the closure of recreational harvest areas deemed to pose a threat to human health.

● The CDC should develop an active and aggressive program, founded on community-based health surveys, to better determine the level and source of seafood-borne illness in the U.S. population.

● Consideration should be given to the development of agreements with foreign authorities and individual producers to ensure that imported products are treated in a manner consistent with and equivalent to domestic products.

● A more pronounced and consistently defined federal role in the risk characterizations leading to seafood health advisories should be developed. A more consistent and focused effort in determining and communicating public health risks from contaminated seafood should also be developed.

● As more countries require the equivalency of domestic and imported products, it is apparent that the time has come for the international community to begin a process that would minimize the differences existing among national regulatory guidelines and approaches.

OPTIONS FOR REDUCING PUBLIC HEALTH RISKS

Monitoring, Control, and Surveillance Measures

The current system involves (1) surveillance by federal and state agencies to identify seafood-borne disease (e.g., CDC and state health departments); (2) evaluation of risk and setting of guidelines and action levels mostly by federal agencies (e.g., EPA and FDA); (3) control of risk by inspection and testing of edible fish and shellfish (e.g., states, FDA, and NMFS); and (4) action to protect consumers by embargo, detention, seizure, or recall, and by issuance of warning advisories (e.g., states and FDA). This system needs revision and strengthening to develop a truly risk-based regulatory process.

The data base on which regulation depends is inadequate. The disease surveillance system of CDC suffers from inadequate resources and should be refocused to provide a more complete and balanced account of seafood-borne disease. More analytical data on contaminants are needed, which could be obtained by increasing FDA analyses and sponsoring broader integrated studies of marine and fresh waters by EPA and corresponding state agencies.

Inspection and testing should focus on actual problems (as in HACCP systems), and there should be increased efforts to develop rapid, reliable test methods for dangerous microorganisms, toxins, and contaminants. This will require a restructuring of inspectional systems to accommodate newer methodologies and to train personnel in their application. Emphasis on purely sensory evaluation should be decreased.

Problems of interagency jurisdiction, unclear regulations, or poor cooperation among state and federal agencies should be addressed and rectified. This will require added resources.

Characteristics of Control Requirements

Control measures should be applied initially at the earliest stage of seafood production by monitoring of water quality and condition. Such measures would apply to the molluscan shellfish problem and to most natural toxins and chemical contaminants, and would permit the exclusion of potentially dangerous fish or shellfish from markets by fishing closures and use of advisories. Rapid and simple tests should be developed and used to screen potentially hazardous fish or shellfish at the point of harvest to reduce costs to the fishermen and to protect the consumer from toxins and dangerous contaminants. Postharvest control seems likely to be most readily achieved through an HACCP-based system focusing on cross-contamination, temperature control, and the effectiveness of handling and processing methods designed to inhibit or destroy microorganisms. This system must be based on safety considerations, not solely on quality.

The extent of chemical contamination of seafood species is both species and region dependent. A few chemicals such as mercury have strong species associations (e.g., swordfish). The concentrations of most organic chemicals tend to be less species associated and more dependent on geographic region. Within aquatic organisms, bioaccumulation may be organ specific or related to fat concentrations (e.g., methylmercury in muscle tissues and PCBs in fatty tissues).

Improvement of the total data base on chemical contamination of fish could enable regulatory agencies to target their efforts on particular species of fish in specifically defined areas and, thus, lead to considerable mitigation of individual and societal health risks with minimal economic effects. Improvement of the data base could also enable consumers, especially subsistence and sport fishers, to select the least toxic fish in their waters for consumption. Clearly, however, chemical contamination is ultimately a problem of environmental degradation due to waste dumping that can be solved only by the development of systems to reduce chemical disposal in fresh and marine waters and in the atmosphere. The improvement of environmental quality will mean safer fish.

The effectiveness of current fishing controls and consumer/fisher information programs in geographic areas with greater-than-average contamination problems is uncertain. Unfortunately, contaminated areas may be pocketed within broader fishing grounds, and the precise distribution of relatively high residue levels may be difficult to determine. In areas such as the Great Lakes, steps have been taken to prevent the commercial distribution of fish that have contaminants exceeding established tolerance or action levels. However, the adequacy of some regulatory levels is open to question in light of newly available information (see Chapter 6), and the degree of protection afforded the substantial population of consumers of sport caught fish by advisories based on those tolerance/action levels is even more doubtful.

Better control is needed of imported fish products, which represent over half of the fish and shellfish consumed in the United States. Seafood imports are coming from an increasing number of countries, some of which have poor internal control systems. A significant number of supplier countries are in tropical areas where some bacteria and toxin hazards are intrinsically high. Additionally, the United States is receiving increasing numbers of fish and crustaceans from foreign aquaculture operations (see Chapters 2 and 8). In view of the often regional and species-associated nature of seafood hazards, it would be appropriate to classify suppliers into risk categories for particular species or processed seafoods. Consideration should be given to extending the scope of MOU arrangements to cover all seafoods, and unfettered import of seafood products should be permitted only from countries with whom the United States has MOUs. Testing of imports for chemical residues should be carried out systematically according to a planned program designed to provide long-term estimates of the level of contamination in particular species or in the products of different supplier countries. In view of the very complex structure of international trade in fishery products, it is desirable that a better system be established to identify the country of origin of imported seafoods. This may require international agreements.

Legislative Considerations

Education and Information Measures

Programs should be established for training regulators and seafood industry personnel to be proficient in the regulatory programs under consideration. These programs should be well-coordinated across states, with more national guidance and increased consideration of the unique attributes of various geographic regions.

States should be required to produce advisories that can be used by both commercial and recreational personnel to learn about local public health risks and protective measures. In the development of advisories for reproductive effects, due weight must be given to the persistence of different toxicants in people. A useful federal function, besides producing advisories to meet national problems, would be development—with the states—of a standardized format for written and broadcast advisories so that there will be minimum confusion due to state and local differences.

Educational programs for safe preparation and service of seafoods in commercial and home settings must also be developed and delivered as a part of an integrated seafood safety program.

Recommendations for Improved Inspection Strategies

Inspection should continue to be based on shared responsibility between state and federal agencies. The general philosophy presented here involves the concept of a federal agency (or agencies) having responsibility for identifying and characterizing risks, establishing methodologies and acceptable or actionable levels of undesirable agents, and monitoring state inspection programs. In addition, the federal agency would continue to have primary responsibility for imported products and products in interstate shipment. The agency would establish well-equipped regional laboratories to conduct tests for the federal program and—where appropriate—for state agency programs. States, with the financial support of federal sources, would carry out inspections and apply police powers to in-state fishing industry operations, by using methods and procedures that meet or exceed federal standards. Monitoring and certifying state programs to determine their eligibility for federal funding of such operations would be the responsibility of the federal agency. Results would include better use of state agencies and strengthening their role in inspection, rather than depending solely on a federal agency to perform nationwide inspection. The federal agency should have overall responsibility for coordinating the national program and carrying out those functions that states cannot or will not undertake, as well as ensuring the training of state personnel. Organoleptic inspection must be recognized as inadequate and of little value for seafood safety because it is unable to identify risks to humans.

Where new legislation is being considered in relation to the problems of seafood safety, the following important points should be considered: (1) the need to facilitate closure of harvesting areas on the basis of human health hazards, (2) the need for a strong state role in inspection that will require federal support, (3) the desirability of regulating vessels and dock facilities in relation to human health, (4) the collation of current regulations in easily available form, and (5) the need to train state and federal regulatory personnel.

POTENTIAL IMPACT OF PROPOSED OPTIONS

The proposed options outlined above will have the following impact on seafood and the consumer: (1) they will improve the general health of the public by focusing on the cause of disease, thus reducing the cases of seafood-borne diseases; (2) they will produce a quicker, more effective response when the public is subjected to unacceptable risks; (3) they will promote compliance through increased and improved communication among the involved agencies and industry, and through increased public knowledge; and (4) they will require the appropriation of funds to develop a comprehensive system incorporating the above recommendations.

DIRECTION FOR DATA COLLECTION AND FUTURE RESEARCH

Inasmuch as accurate risk identification is the first step in risk-based control programs, stronger epidemiologic data are needed to assess the extent of public health risk in terms of incidence, severity, vehicle, and setting. The two major viable data bases for seafood-borne illnesses from CDC and NETSU are too limited in scope and have discrepancies related to methods of surveillance and reporting that prevent consistent correlation of the outbreaks of some pathogens. In addition, more basic research is necessary to understand why and how certain pathogens or toxins cause illness. For example, there are bacterial pathogens, such as *Vibrio vulnificus*, or non-O1 *V. cholerae* that are commonly isolated from shellfish, that cause only a small number of clinical cases; we need to understand why only a minority of persons become ill after exposure to these organisms. Similarly, a better understanding is required of how natural toxins and chemicals are processed by fish, so that we can better predict when and where human illness will occur. Rapid, nondestructive, and easy-to-perform tests for toxins, microorganisms, and chemicals [e.g., stick test for ciguatera, deoxyribonucleic acid (DNA) probes for specific viruses and bacteria, and instrumental chemical analysis] must be developed. The current programs for testing water and seafoods for potentially dangerous chemicals should be broadened to provide a satisfactory data base for regulation and control.

2

Seafood Production, Distribution, and Consumption

ABSTRACT

Consumption of seafood has increased over the last decade, without a concomitant increase in reported illness. This increased consumption trend is expected to continue both for prepared and for fresh or frozen varieties. The 1989 consumption figure was 15.9 pounds of edible meat per person per year. Total commercial landings were a record 8.5 billion pounds in 1989, and imported edible products totaled 3.2 billion pounds. The majority of the seafood supply was harvested from wild populations. The aquaculture portion of this supply will probably increase. A substantial amount of seafood (600 million pounds of finfish and 300 million pounds of shellfish) is caught recreationally. About 70% of commercially produced seafood in the United States is sold fresh or frozen. Canned seafood constitutes approximately 25%, and smoked/cured products 5%, of the seafood consumed. The United States exported 1.4 billion pounds of edible domestic fishery products in 1989. The largest importer was Japan; Canada, the United Kingdom, France, and South Korea also provided good markets. The seafood harvest by industry is fragmented, diversified, seasonal, complex, and difficult to manage. Studies are needed to monitor changing consumption trends and patterns. The processing, distribution and merchandising of finfish and shellfish will require more emphasis to reduce cross-contamination. Attention must be given to aquaculture in order to produce high-quality, consistently available species. Attention must also be focused on the harvesting, handling, distribution, and preparation of recreationally harvested fish to ensure consumer safety. More emphasis should be placed on educating the industry and the consumer about safe handling practices that can reduce potential food-handling problems.

INTRODUCTION

As Americans become increasingly aware of the relation between diet and good health, the consumption of fishery products will most likely increase. The consumer recognizes that fish and shellfish are nutritious and wholesome foods. They are perceived as an excellent source of high-quality protein, containing lipids with high levels of unsaturated fatty acids, and perhaps contributing to the enhancement of human health by reducing the risk of cardiovascular disease. Likewise, seafood is characteristically tender, easily digested, and a good source of many important minerals

21

and vitamins (NRC, 1989).

Although the attributes of seafood attract a more health conscious consumer, they also enforce expectations for enhanced safety. Consumer consciousness of seafood safety issues has become, as a result, increasingly important. Pollution and environmental issues have further focused people's attention on contamination problems. Concurrent media coverage and public interest groups have heightened the demand for rigorous safety standards in the food industry (Haas et al., 1986; Newton, 1989).

Unlike meat and poultry, which are derived from domesticated sources, the majority of the edible seafood supply in the United States, approximately 12.0 billion pounds including domestic landings and imports in round weight equivalents, was harvested from wild populations in 1989 (NMFS, 1990). The aquacultured portion of this supply is predicted to increase from both foreign and domestic sources (Redmayne, 1989), and recorded commercial landings are further supplemented by a growing portion of recreationally caught seafood destined for consumption.

Because the supplies of many seafoods are relatively small and regional, large numbers of individuals, using a variety of vessels that range from small boats to large factory ships, are involved. The seafood harvesting industry is highly fragmented. The diversity of the industry, the seasonal nature of fishing, the complexity of fish processing operations, and the substantial amount of seafood caught recreationally (600 million pounds of finfish and 300 million pounds of shellfish) make it difficult to manage and regulate these living resources (NOAA, 1990).

Both finfish and shellfish are subjected to contamination and cross-contamination in their natural habitat, as well as at any point during handling, processing, distribution, or preparation (Haas et al., 1986; Newton, 1989; NOAA, 1990). Seafood-borne illness has been reported due to natural toxins, microbial contamination, parasites, poor seafood handling, and chemical contaminants (CDC, 1981a-c, 1983a,b, 1984, 1985, 1989; FDA, 1989). Because of the primary reliance on limited data-reporting systems via state departments of public health, and eventually the Centers for Disease Control (CDC), the extent of the public health risk due to cumulative exposure to microorganisms, natural toxins, and chemical contaminants cannot be assessed easily, especially in the context of total dietary exposure. Given this qualification, current data indicate a decrease in the reported incidents of illness from seafood relative to consumption.

The committee has critically examined and evaluated the degree of severity of illnesses, their significance, and the extent of possible health risks involved. Its findings are documented in subsequent chapters of this report.

DEMOGRAPHICS OF THE SEAFOOD INDUSTRY

In 1989, commercial and recreational fishermen harvested more than 8.5 billion pounds of fish and shellfish from U.S. waters, which includes edible and industrial products. More than 300 major species of seafood were marketed, reflecting the diversity of the resource base (NMFS, 1990). Over 4,000 processing and distribution plants handled the commercial products of the nation's 256,000 fishermen. Almost 95,000 boats and vessels constituted the fleet (NMFS, 1990).

Although commercial establishments are easily documented, the number of recreational fishermen and their support base are more difficult to quantify. Increasing numbers of anglers for fish from the nation's freshwater, estuarine, and marine waters are producing a growing share of the fresh and frozen seafood in today's diet. The number of recreational harvesters has been estimated to be in excess of 17 million individuals (NOAA, 1990).

Fresh and frozen seafood constitute about 70% of the product consumed in the United States. Canned seafood, particularly tuna, constitutes almost 25% of domestic consumption, and cured/smoked products account for the remaining 5% of per capita consumption.

FISHERY RESOURCES

Commercial landings (edible and industrial) by U.S. fishermen at ports in all the fishing states were a record 8.5 billion pounds (3.8 million metric tons) valued at $3.2 billion in 1989 (NMFS, 1990). This was an increase of 1.3 billion pounds (576,300 metric tons) in quantity, but a decrease of $281.8 million in value, compared with 1988. The total import value of edible fishery products was $5.5 billion in 1989, based on a record quantity of 3.2 billion pounds. Imports of nonedible (industrial) products set a record in 1989, with products valued at $4.1 billion, an increase of $676.1 million compared with 1988 (NMFS, 1990).

The trade deficit in fishery products has not declined. The dollar value of imports was higher in 1989 than in the previous year (NMFS, 1990). Canada is still the largest exporter to the United States, sending in more than 700 million pounds of fishery products in 1988. Ecuador was ranked second and Mexico third. Whereas Canada ships finfish products, shrimp is the primary commodity exported by Ecuador and Mexico. Imports from Thailand and China are both increasing due to rising shrimp production from their expanding aquaculture systems.

On a worldwide basis, aquaculture is becoming a major new factor in seafood production. The cultivation of high-value species, popular in the U.S. market, is a major factor in import sourcing. China, for example, along with other Asian nations, is replacing South and Central American countries as a major shrimp supplier to the United States. Aquaculture is expected to determine much of the future fisheries growth, because wild stocks are nearing full utilization (NMFS, 1990; NOAA, 1990).

The total export value of edible and nonedible fishery products of domestic origin was a record $4.7 billion in 1989, an increase of $2.4 billion compared with 1988. The United States exported 1.4 billion pounds of edible products valued at $2.3 billion, compared with 1.1 billion pounds at $2.2 billion exported in 1988. Exports of nonedible products were valued at $2.4 billion. Japan continues to be America's best export customer. Over 700 million pounds of seafood was sold to the Japanese market, with salmon, crabs, and herring the primary commodities. Canada, the United Kingdom, France, and South Korea were also good markets in 1989, but the value of their imports was small, compared to Japan's purchase of West Coast products (NMFS, 1990).

Consumers in the United States spent an estimated $28.3 billion for fishery goods in 1989, a 5% increase from 1988 (NMFS, 1990). The total included $19.1 billion in expenditures in food service establishments (e.g., restaurants, carryouts, caterers); $9.0 billion in retail stores (for home consumption); and $181.7 million for industrial fish products. In producing and marketing a variety of fishery products for domestic and foreign markets, the commercial fishing industry contributed $17.2 billion in value-added dollars to the gross national product (GNP), an increase of 5% compared to 1988.

Consumption of fish and shellfish in the United States totaled 15.9 pounds of edible meat per person in 1989 (NMFS, 1990). This total was up 0.7 pound from the 15.2 pounds consumed per capita in 1988. Per capita consumption of fresh and frozen products registered a total of 10.5 pounds, an increase of 0.3 pound from the 1988 level. Fresh and frozen finfish consumption was 7.1 pounds per capita in 1989. Fresh and frozen shellfish consumption amounted to 3.4 pounds per capita, with canned fishery products at 5.1 pounds per capita, up 0.4 pound over 1988. The per capita use of all fishery products (edible and nonedible) was 62.2 pounds (round weight), up 2.8 pounds compared with 1988 (NMFS, 1990).

Although most of the fish and shellfish consumed is from commercial production, a significant share is caught recreationally. In 1990, the National Marine Fisheries Service (NMFS) estimated that 17 million marine anglers harvested more than 600 million pounds of finfish (NOAA, 1990). Although statistics are lacking, NMFS suggests that 200-300 million live pounds of molluscs and crustaceans was harvested by recreationalists. This catch represents 3-4 live pounds or about 1-1.5 edible pounds of domestic per capita consumption (Krebs-Smith, 1989), outside the commercial figure of over 15 edible pounds per person. The source, handling, and distribution of the recreational catch are just beginning to draw attention. Indeed, because recreational anglers are not regulated as food producers/manufacturers, there is concern about the use and distribution of this "recreational" resource.

Although it is difficult to give definite numbers for either the commercial or the recreational harvesting sector, some general observations can be made. Commercially, the trend is toward more efficient activity. Consequently, the number of participants in the commercial sector is decreasing. The commercial processing industry appears headed toward consolidation, with increased dependence on imported products and aquaculture. Recreational participation remains strong. Consumption data, as suggested by both the Department of Agriculture and the Department of Commerce, indicate a continued, if not expanding, harvest of sport caught fish and shellfish. More than 20% of all fresh and frozen seafood consumed in the United States may now be attributed to noncommercial harvest and distribution.

AQUACULTURE

Aquaculture is a rapidly growing mode of production in the seafood industry. Annual production of farmed fish and shellfish in the United States has grown 305% since 1980 (TFTC, 1988). The greatest production is of catfish (Sperber, 1989). Catfish production increased 31% from 1986 to 1987. According to the Catfish Institute, farm-raised catfish increased from 5.7 million pounds in 1970 to 295 million pounds in 1988 and were expected to exceed 310 million pounds in 1989 (Sperber, 1989). Salmon production in the Pacific Northwest and Maine totaled 85 million pounds in 1987. In addition, other fish that are farmed include trout, redfish, sturgeon, hybrid striped bass, carp, and tilapia, as well as shellfish and crustaceans such as oysters and crawfish. Crawfish production acreage has increased 145% to about

160,000 acres. Overall U.S. aquaculture production of fish and shellfish increased from 203 million pounds in 1980 to some 750 million pounds in 1987. It is estimated that by the year 2000, that figure will reach 1.26 billion pounds.

Large amounts of cultured fish and shellfish are also imported annually. Approximately one-half of the 500 million pounds of shrimp imported is cultured (Schnick, 1990); 143 million pounds comes from China and Ecuador, neither of which regulates the use of chemotherapeutic agents in culture. More than 40 million pounds of salmon is also imported annually, often from countries similarly lacking tolerance levels for residues. Of special interest are the use of chloramphenicol in shrimp culture and ampicillin in yellowtail culture (Hawke et al., 1987; Manci, 1990). The Food and Drug Administration (FDA) has not examined imported seafood for drug residues, and there is no information regarding levels that might be ingested (Schnick, 1990).

Aquaculture also produces fish used to stock recreational fishing areas. This procedure is under the control of government agencies that follow FDA regulations, use only approved drugs, and abide by legal withdrawal times.

CONSUMPTION TRENDS

Today's consumer is changing rapidly. Instead of single-income households, it is increasingly more common to have both man and woman working. The size of the family is decreasing. As many as one-fourth of all households are occupied by one person. This means more shoppers and diners, most with little time for home preparation (Davis, 1989).

Most adult men and women now work outside the home. In recent surveys, 7 out of 10 new home buyers noted that they will need two incomes to pay their respective mortgages. Nevertheless, the growth in two-income couples has generally created an increase in disposable income, but with little time to spend it. With as many as 50% of new mothers working outside the home within the first year of childbirth, it is easy to see the revolutionary changes taking place among families. The working mother or single dweller does not have the time to prepare meals in the traditional sense. In recent Food Marketing Institute (FMI) surveys, more than 30% of the husbands of women who work full-time did as much cooking, cleaning, and food shopping as their wives (Davis, 1989; FMI, 1988).

The population is aging. Going into the next century, the fastest growing groups will be those aged 45 to 54, along with those over age 85. By the year 2000, the proportion of Americans over age 65 will be the same throughout the country as the proportion in Florida today. An aging population means decreased discretionary spending and more demands for healthful and nutritious foods.

Minorities are growing in America. Within 10 years, one-quarter of all Americans will be either black, Hispanic, or Asian. The city of Los Angeles illustrates the trend. At present, Los Angeles is the largest Mexican city outside Mexico, the second largest Chinese city outside China, the second largest Japanese city outside Japan, and the largest Philippine city outside the Philippines (Davis, 1989).

The consumer demand for convenience, gourmet foods, ethnic items, and other services is increasingly evident in the food service and retail food industries. As the number of working women and single dwellers increases, the consumer base continues to change. With reduced leisure time, consumers who once spent two hours per day in the kitchen now spend less than a half hour. Convenience stores, fast-food restaurants, specialty food service outlets, and prepared items in the supermarket are food industry responses (FMI, 1988; Taylor, 1989).

To illustrate the impact of less preparation time in the home, a quick review of consumer buying habits is in order. In 1973, almost 80% of the food dollar was spent on home-prepared foods. In 1988, this number had fallen to 67%. Many predict that the figure may be as low as 40% by the year 2000. As with all foods, fish and shellfish preparation must be viewed in the manner in which consumers use the product in a contemporary environment. This does not mean that the consumer will be eating at home less but, rather, that less time will be devoted to food preparation. This trend toward "cocooning," in which the family spends more time around the home but utilizes the time more prudently, is central to future consumer patterns (Davis, 1989).

Consumers want more convenience and nutrition. Value-added products, ready-to-eat items, and microwave entrees are examples. Deli departments of the supermarket may soon become food service operations, competing with fast-food and takeout restaurants (FMI, 1989; Taylor, 1989).

Seafood, like other foods, will be placed in a competitive consumer environment. Fish and shellfish must continue to taste good if they are expected to attract more consumers. Further, seafood must stay within the budget of the new consumer. If the industry can respond to the changing consumer base, the opportunity to expand per capita consumption appears good (Taylor, 1989).

The amount of imported product is not yet recognized as a potential problem by the consumer, yet it is of significant concern to regulatory officials. Rising needs place increased pressure on government to protect consumers without the ability to monitor the harvest, processing, and distribution of the hundreds of species in question. Because of the potential of ever-increasing imports, the safety issue is becoming a matter of international concern. Although agencies routinely sample and require country-of-origin labeling, the consumer is unaware of the complexity of attempting to truly safeguard these foodstuffs.

ACTIVITIES IN OTHER COUNTRIES

A number of countries have endeavored to enhance the value of their seafood products by enacting programs to ensure product quality. Canada, Denmark, and Norway have given high priority to marketing safe, quality seafood items. Canada, for example, inspects vessels, landing sites, and processing facilities on an annual basis. Vessels must meet the same exacting standards as processing facilities or risk losing their certification. Canadian plant registration requires compliance with a posted list of standards. At inspection, plants are rated by use of a Hazard Analysis Critical Control Point (HAACP) approach. Critical findings result in more frequent inspections or the possibility of noncertification.

In Europe, similar programs are in place. Denmark inspects fishing vessels. Each participant must meet certain sanitation requirements, as well as certification for activities such as on-board processing. Distribution centers receive regular inspections that monitor all products entering the marketplace. The advent of the European Economic Community (EEC) has brought forth a host of new regulations, ensuring that member nations comply with the policies of their EEC partners.

Many other countries have seafood inspection programs, but they are often not dedicated programs like those in Canada, Denmark, Norway, Iceland, and New Zealand. Consequently, they do not pay the same rigorous attention to detail. Indeed, most countries have programs centered on seafood as a food group, not as a distinct entity that requires special attention.

CONCLUSIONS AND RECOMMENDATIONS

Based on commercial sources, Americans consumed almost 23% more seafood in 1989 than they did 10 years earlier. This increase in consumption was not accompanied by a concomitant increase in reported seafood-borne illnesses. The total supply of fishery products to fulfill the domestic requirement for seafood was in excess of 8.5 billion pounds in 1989, with over 300 species involved in the catch statistics. Production and consumption trends suggest that domestic seafood demand will continue, with more emphasis on prepared convenience foods along with the traditional demand for fresh and frozen selections. Production will have to be supplemented with more imported and cultured sources. Recreational harvesting, both in the purist sense and as subsistence fishing, continues to contribute a significant portion to the annual per capita intake.

The committee recommends the following:

• Consumer information studies must be conducted to monitor the rapidly changing consumption trends in the United States. Patterns of consumer use and preparation, as well as sources of seafood products used in the home, must be evaluated. By better understanding consumption patterns, fishery managers and food regulators will be more able to influence dietary intake, and reduce potential exposure to fish from contaminated water.

• Changes in consumption patterns necessitate more attention to informing consumers on how to best handle highly perishable products such as seafood. As much as 50% of all reported, acute fish and shellfish problems might be eliminated by more careful handling and proper preparation in the home or in food service establishments. With the advent of more prepared foods, every effort should be made to ensure the safety of the product both in the manufacturing/distribution chain and for the end user.

• The retail and institutional handling of seafood products requires increased attention to control cross-contamination. A number of seafood-related illnesses can be traced to poor sanitation practices by employees or to lack of proper handling via the distribution system. More efforts will be needed to alert all users to the importance of time/temperature relationships, HACCP concepts, good manufacturing practices, and new technology (e.g., live holding tanks).

• Aquaculture promises to produce a larger share of domestically consumed fish and shellfish in the years ahead. Cultured plants and animals hold the promise of being high quality, and generally free of some of the contamination associated with wild species. Care, however, must be taken to avoid the untimely use of antibiotics and other chemicals in these closed or recirculated systems, which are often used to control pathogens in semiclosed systems.

● The safety of recreationally harvested fish and shellfish requires increased vigilance, which means increased focus on the origin, handling, and distribution of recreational products. These harvesting efforts may now account for over 20% of all fresh and frozen seafood consumed in the United States. However, this catch is not well controlled, and users may handle, distribute, and prepare the product in an unsafe manner. Further, much of this product may be harvested from areas not suited for consumption due to natural or induced contamination problems. Increased educational activity is required to protect the consumer with regard to this resource. Fishery managers will have to pay greater attention to the implications of sport caught fish and shellfish on consumer health.

REFERENCES

CDC (Centers for Disease Control). 1981a. *Salmonella* Surveillance, Annual Summary, 1978. HHS Publ. No. (CDC) 81-8219. Public Health Service, U.S. Department of Health and Human Services, Atlanta, Ga. 25 pp.

CDC (Centers for Disease Control). 1981b. Annual Summary of Foodborne Disease, 1978. HHS Publ. No. (CDC) 81-8185. Public Health Service, U.S. Department of Health and Human Services, Atlanta, Ga. 53 pp.

CDC (Centers for Disease Control). 1981c. Annual Summary of Foodborne Disease, 1979. HHS Publ. No. (CDC) 81-8185. Public Health Service, U.S. Department of Health and Human Services, Atlanta, Ga. 40 pp.

CDC (Centers for Disease Control). 1983a. Food-Borne Disease Outbreaks, Annual Summary of Foodborne Disease, 1980. HHS Publ. No. (CDC) 83-8185. Public Health Service, U.S. Department of Health and Human Services, Atlanta, Ga. 32 pp.

CDC (Centers for Disease Control). 1983b. Food-Borne Disease Outbreaks, Annual Summary of Foodborne Disease, 1981. HHS Publ. No. (CDC) 83-8185. Public Health Service, U.S. Department of Health and Human Services, Atlanta, Ga. 41 pp.

CDC (Centers for Disease Control). 1984. Food-borne disease outbreaks, Annual summary of foodborne disease, 1983: Reported morbidity and mortality in the United States. Morbid. Mortal. Weekly Rep. (annual suppl). 32 pp.

CDC (Centers for Disease Control). 1985. Annual Summary of Food-Borne Disease, 1982. HHS Publ. No. (CDC) 85-8185. U.S. Department of Health and Human Services, Atlanta, Ga. 38 pp.

CDC (Centers for Disease Control). 1989. Annual Summary of Food-Borne Disease (unpublished dates from 1983 to 1986). U.S. Department of Health and Human Services, Atlanta, Ga. 1989.

Davis, A. Dano. 1989. Remarks by A. Dano Davis at FMI Seafood Conference, Tampa, Fla.

FDA (Food and Drug Administration). 1989. Safe Seafood: An Analysis of FDA Strategy. Food and Drug Administration, Washington, D.C. 59 pp.

FMI (Food Marketing Institute). 1988. Trends: Consumer Attitudes and the Supermarket - 1988. Food Marketing Institute, Washington, D.C. 58 pp.

FMI (Food Marketing Institute). 1989. Seafood Survey. Washington, D.C. Unpublished.

Haas, E., D. Heiman, and M. Jones. 1986. The Great American Fish Scandal: Health Risks Unchecked. A report by Public Voice for Food and Health, Washington, D.C. November. 44 pp.

Hawke, J.P., S.M. Plakas, R. Vernon Minton, R.M. McPhearson, T.G. Snider, and A.M. Guarino. 1987. Fish pasteurellosis of cultured striped bass (*Morone saxatilis*) in coastal Alabama. Aquaculture 65:193-204.

Krebs-Smith, S.M. 1989. Letter report on per capita consumption and intake of fishery products dated October 25, 1989 from Dr. Susan M. Krebs-Smith, Nutritionist, Human Nutrition Information Service, U.S. Department of Agriculture, Hyattsville, Md. to Dr. Farid E. Ahmed, Project Director, Committee on Evaluation of the Safety of Fishery Products, Institute of Medicine, National Academy of Sciences, Washington, D.C.

Manci, W. 1990. Hope and caution highlight fish disease news. Catfish News/Aquaculture News 4:10.

Newton, S. 1989. Seafood safety: Industry and regulations of fish for solution. Prepared Foods (July) 96-102.

NMFS (National Marine Fisheries Service). 1990. Fisheries Statistics of the United States--1989. Current Fisheries Statistics No. 8900. Washington, D.C. 111 pp.

NOAA (National Oceanic and Atmospheric Administration). 1990. Meeting the Challenge: New Directions in Seafood Inspection. Pascagoula, Miss. 34 pp.

NRC (National Research Council). 1989. Diet and Health: Implications for Reducing Chronic Disease Risk. Committee on Diet and Health. National Academy of Sciences, Washington, D.C. 794 pp.

Redmayne, P.C. 1989. World aquaculture developments. Food Technol. 43:80-81.

Schnick, R.A. 1990. Record of meeting with FDA on the new seafood fish definition proposed by the Fish and Wildlife Service. Memorandum, National Fisheries Research Center, LaCrosse, Wisc.

Sperber, R.M. 1989. Aquaculture expands 20% annually. Food Processing 50:60-66.

Taylor, J. 1989. Better Homes and Gardens Consumer Panel, August 1989. Better Homes and Gardens, Des Moines, Ia. Unpublished.

TFTC (Task Force on Therapeutic Compounds). 1988. Report to the Joint Subcommittee on Aquaculture. August. Washington, D.C. 31 pp.

3

Microbiological and Parasitic Exposure and Health Effects

ABSTRACT

Seafood, like any food item, has the potential to cause diseases from viral, bacterial, and parasitic pathogens under certain circumstances. These agents are acquired from three sources: (1) mainly fecal pollution of the aquatic environment, (2) to a lesser extent, the natural aquatic environment, and (3) industry, retail, restaurant, or home processing and preparation. With the exception of foods consumed raw, however, the reported incidences of seafood-related disease are low.

Available data from the Centers for Disease Control and the Northeast Technical Support Unit of the Food and Drug Administration for 1978-1987, as well as literature reports, suggest that the greatest numbers of seafood-associated illnesses are from raw molluscan shellfish harvested from waters contaminated with raw or poorly treated human sewage. The vast majority of this illness is gastroenteritis of unknown etiologies clinically suggestive of human-specific Norwalk and Norwalk-like agents. Although these are the most common seafood-associated illnesses, they tend to be relatively mild with no associated mortality.

Naturally occurring marine *Vibrio* species are responsible for many fewer reported cases of infection from the consumption of raw molluscan shellfish, but certain species such as *V. vulnificus* can be associated with high mortality (>50%) in persons who are immunocompromised or have underlying liver disease.

The microbiological risk associated with seafood other than raw molluscan shellfish is much lower and appears to result from recontamination or cross-contamination of cooked by raw product, or from contamination during preparation followed by time/temperature abuse. This occurs mainly at the food service (postprocessing) level, which is common to all foods and not specific for seafood products.

Seafood-related parasitic infections are even less common than bacterial and viral infections, with *Anisakis simplex* and cestodes having the greatest public health significance in the United States. In general, parasitic infections are concentrated in certain ethnic groups that favor consumption of raw or partially cooked seafoods.

Thorough cooking of seafood products would virtually eliminate all microbial and parasitic pathogens; it will not destroy some microbial toxic metabolites (e.g., *Staphylococcus* toxins). Individuals who choose to eat raw seafood should be educated about the potential risks involved and how to avoid or mitigate them. In particular, immunocompromised individuals, those with defective liver function, people afflicted with diabetes, and the elderly should be warned never to eat raw shellfish.

The greatest risks from the consumption of raw molluscan shellfish could be minimized by research to develop valid indicators of human enteric viruses for proper classification of shellfish growing waters; by implementing and maintaining proper treatment and disposal of sewage to avoid human enteric pathogen contamination of harvest areas; by efforts to identify and limit the number of pathogenic *Vibrio* species in shellfish; by the development of new diagnostic methods and improved processing technology; and by the application of risk-based regulatory control measures for potential microbial pathogens in raw molluscan shellfish.

Other seafood-associated risks can be reduced by proper application of a Hazard Analysis Critical Control Point system. This cannot be achieved by the visual or organoleptic inspection currently used for meat and poultry. Seafood inspection requires the development of valid microbiological guidelines to accurately assess human health risk from raw and processed seafoods. Inspection system guidelines must apply to imported as well as domestic products.

INTRODUCTION

Like any food items, fish and shellfish carry a variety of bacteria, viruses, and parasites capable of causing disease in consumers (WHO, 1990). Table 3-1 lists some of the agents that occur naturally in seafood or in the marine environment, are associated with sewage contamination of harvesting areas, or can be acquired during seafood harvest or processing. Many of these microorganisms pose only a slight risk to normal human populations, but all are pathogens and some pose serious risk to specific population groups, such as persons with defects in their immune systems (Archer and Young, 1988). Because of the increasing availability of sophisticated microbiological techniques, it has become possible to identify and provide detailed characterizations of many of the microorganisms present in or on seafood. Unfortunately, epidemiological studies, which are necessary to define risk clearly, have not kept pace with microbiological advances. In many instances, only rudimentary epidemiological data are available with which to correlate the information derived from microbiological product analyses. Thus, it is very difficult to assess the risk from these microorganisms to the health of the population.

The major sources of information on seafood-associated illness are the Centers for Disease Control (CDC) Foodborne Disease Outbreak Surveillance Program and a data base on shellfish-associated food-borne cases maintained by the Food and Drug Administration (FDA) Northeast Technical Support Unit (Table 3-2). The CDC data are derived from reports of food-borne outbreaks[1] by state health departments. Reporting is passive, but data are collected in a systematic fashion. The FDA Northeast Technical Support Unit (NETSU) data come from books, news accounts, CDC reports, city and state health department files, Public Health Service regional files, case histories, and archival reports. Both collection systems have a number of inherent biases, which are discussed elsewhere in this report. Based on experience with other foods (NRC, 1987), it is likely that only a small fraction of seafood-associated disease is reported and that the two available data bases therefore reflect only a small fraction of the actual number of seafood-associated illnesses that occur. Even when outbreaks are reported, etiologic agents are frequently not identified. For example, the NETSU data base from 1978 to 1987 includes an additional 5,342 cases[2] of shellfish-associated illness for which no etiology was determined; the CDC food-borne

TABLE 3-1 Seafood-Associated Human Pathogens

Pathogens	Isolated from Seafoods	Proven Pathogen in Seafood	Pathogen Source[a]
Organisms That Can Cause Disease in Normal, Healthy Adults			
Bacteria			
Vibrio cholerae O1	Yes	Yes	1, 2
Vibrio cholerae non-O1[b]	Yes	Yes	1
Vibrio parahaemolyticus	Yes	Yes	1
Vibrio mimicus	Yes	Yes	1
Vibrio fluvialis	Yes	Yes	1
Vibrio furnissii	Yes	Yes	1
Vibrio hollisae	Yes	Yes	1
Salmonella typhi[c]	Yes	Yes	2, 3
Salmonella (nontyphoidal)	Yes	Yes	2, 3
Campylobacter jejuni	Yes	Yes	2, 3
Escherichia coli	Yes	No	2, 3
Yersinia enterocolitica	Yes	No	2, 3
Clostridium botulinum	Yes	Yes	2, 3
Shigella	Yes	Yes	2, 3
Staphylococcus aureus	Yes	Yes	3
Helminths			
Anisakis simplex	Yes	Yes	1
Other helminths	Yes	Yes	1
Viruses			
Poliovirus	Yes	No	2
Other picornaviruses	Yes	No	2
Norwalk/Snow Mountain/small round viruses (SRVs)	No	Yes	2
Enteral non-A, non-B hepatitis	No	Yes	2
Hepatitis A	Yes	Yes	2, 3
Organisms That Cause Disease Most Often in Special Population Groups			
Vibrio vulnificus[d]	Yes	Yes	1
Rotavirus[e]	Yes	No	2
Listeria	Yes	No	1, 3
Organisms with Uncertain Roles as Food-borne Pathogens			
Aeromonas hydrophila[f]	Yes	Yes	1
Plesiomonas shigelloides	Yes	Yes	1
Edwardsiella tarda	Yes	No	1

[a] (1) Harvest water/associated with naturally occurring aquatic bacteria; (2) harvest water/associated with fecal pollution; (3) associated with processing and preparation (cross-contamination or time/temperature abuse, infected food handlers).

[b] Causes gastroenteritis in normal, healthy hosts; can cause septicemia in persons in high-risk groups, as outlined in Table 3-6.

[c] Primarily of historical association in the United States, but remains a problem in some foreign countries and could affect imports.

[d] Illness usually confined to high-risk groups outlined in Table 3-6.

[e] Illness generally occurs in children under the age of 2; older persons are usually immune.

[f] Aeromonas can cause serious wound infections and septicemia; however, conclusive data on its role as a cause of gastroenteritis are lacking. Studies suggesting that it is a gastrointestinal pathogen have not implicated seafood as a risk factor for illness.

TABLE 3-2 Seafood-Associated Outbreaks and Related Cases by Pathogen, 1978-1987

Pathogen	Finfish/Other CDC Outbreaks	Finfish/Other CDC Cases	Shellfish[a] CDC Outbreaks	Shellfish[a] CDC Cases	NETSU Cases
Naturally Occurring Aquatic Agents					
Vibrio parahaemolyticus[b]	-	-	-	-	52
Vibrio cholerae O1	1	2	2	14	13
Vibrio cholerae non-O1	-	-	2	11	120
Vibrio vulnificus	-	-	-	-	100
Vibrio mimicus	-	-	-	-	5
Vibrio hollisae	-	-	-	-	5
Vibrio fluvialis	-	-	-	-	5
Plesiomonas	-	-	-	-	18
Aeromonas	-	-	-	-	7
Giardia	1	29	-	-	-
Diphyllobothrium	1	10	-	-	-
Infectious Agents Generally Associated with Fecal Pollution					
Unspecified hepatitis[b]	-	-	-	-	1,645
Hepatitis A[b]	-	-	7	33	45
Salmonella (nontyphoidal)[b]	-	-	3	80	-
Shigella	-	-	4	77	84
Campylobacter	-	-	-	-	16
Norwalk and related viruses	-	-	2	42	82
Non-A, non-B hepatitis[b]	-	-	-	-	1
Infectious Agents Generally Associated with Processing and Preparation					
Vibrio parahaemolyticus[b]			15	176	-
Clostridium perfringens	1	46	2	28	-
Hepatitis type A[b]	2	92	-	-	-
Salmonella (nontyphoidal)[b]	3	67	-	-	-
Clostridium botulinum	26	38	-	-	-
Shigella[b]	3	60	-	-	-
Staphylococcus aureus	1	3	1	9	-
Bacillus cereus	1	4	2	6	-
Total outbreaks/cases	38	351	40	476	2,198
Unknown agents[c]	16	203	88	3,271	5,098

[a] CDC reports disease from all crustacean and molluscan shellfish; NETSU reports only bivalve molluscan shellfish incidence.

[b] Pathogens that may be associated with pollution or processing/handling - most molluscan shellfish-associated cases due to pollution.

[c] Unknown etiologies are probably not all microbiological pathogens.

SOURCE: CDC (1989); Rippey and Verber (1988).

TABLE 3-3 Shellfish-Associated Outbreaks and Related Cases by Frequency of Occurrence, 1978-1987

CDC				NETSU Cases	
Outbreaks		Cases			
Etiology	Number	Etiology	Number	Etiology	Number
1. Unknown[a]	88	1. Unknown[a]	3,271	1. Unknown[a]	5,098
2. Vibrio parahaemolyticus	15	2. Vibrio parahaemolyticus	176	2. Unspecified hepatitis	1,645
3. Hepatitis A virus	7	3. Salmonella (non-typhi)	80	3. Non-O1 Vibrio cholerae	120
4. Shigella	4	4. Shigella	77	4. Vibrio vulnificus	100
5. Salmonella	3	5. Other viral	42	5. Shigella	84
6. Vibrio cholerae O1	2	6. Hepatitis A virus	33	6. Norwalk and related viruses	82
Other viral	2	7. Clostridium perfringens	28	7. Vibrio parahaemolyticus	52
Non-O1 Vibrio cholerae	2	8. Vibrio cholerae O1	14	8. Hepatitis A virus	45
Clostridium perfringens	2	9. Non-O1 Vibrio cholerae	11	9. Plesiomonas	18
Bacillus cereus	2	10. Staphylococcus aureus	9	10. Campylobacter	16
7. Staphylococcus aureus	1	11. Bacillus cereus	6	11. Vibrio cholerae O1	13
				12. Aeromonas	7
				13. Vibrio mimicus	5
				Vibrio hollisae	5
				Vibrio fluvialis	5
				14. Non-A, non-B hepatitis	1
Totals	128		3,747		7,280

[a] The unknown etiologies are probably not all microbiological pathogens.
SOURCE: CDC (1989); Rippey and Verber (1988).

34

surveillance data base reported 3,271 cases of shellfish-associated illness and 203 cases of other seafood-associated illness with unknown etiologies in the same time period (Tables 3-3 and 3-4).   Cases with unknown etiology are probably not all of microbiological origin and could include toxins or allergies, among other causes. Overall, because of the different surveillance and reporting systems, the two data bases do not consistently correlate reports of outbreaks and cases of the same pathogens (Tables 3-2 – 3-4).

Despite these limitations, they represent the only available national data bases on finfish- and shellfish-associated diseases.   In this chapter, these data bases are used as a starting point to assess the relative importance of seafood-associated pathogens and to evaluate, to the extent possible, the risk that each pathogen poses to consumers. Risk management is dictated to a large degree by where and how microorganisms contaminate seafood or where they may be most easily controlled.   For this reason, pathogens have been grouped according to their origin.   The natural marine or freshwater environment harbors specific bacterial and helminthic parasitic pathogens, whereas pollution contributes bacterial and viral pathogens from human and animal fecal sources.   Microbial agents associated with workers or the environment of processing, distribution, and food service systems include both anthropophilic microorganisms and microorganisms that populate reservoirs of infection created by processing conditions.

TABLE 3-4   Finfish and Other Seafood-Associated Outbreaks and Related Cases by Frequency of Occurrence, 1978-1987

Pathogen	Outbreaks	Pathogen	Cases
1. *Clostridium botulinum*	26	1. Unknown[a]	203
2. Unknown[a]	16	2. Hepatitis A virus[b]	92 [a]
3. *Salmonella* (nontyphoidal)	3	3. *Salmonella*	67
Shigella	3		
		4. *Shigella*	60
4. Hepatitis A virus[b]	2 [a]		
		5. *Clostridium perfringens*	46
5. *Staphylococcus aureus*	1		
Clostridium perfringens	1	6. *Clostridium botulinum*	38
Vibrio cholerae O1	1		
Bacillus cereus	1	7. *Bacillus cereus*	4
		8. *Staphylococcus aureus*	3
		9. *Vibrio cholerae* O1	2
Total outbreaks/cases	51		515

[a] Unknown etiologies are probably not all microbiological pathogens.
[b] Food handler positive for hepatitis A virus.
SOURCE: CDC (1981b,c, 1989).

   This chapter emphasizes domestic production of wild caught fish and shellfish. The same pathogens are of concern in imported seafood, although the risks of specific pathogens vary depending on conditions in the growing waters at the point of harvest, as well as subsequent handling and processing. Aquaculture presents a different set of potential concerns, which are summarized in a separate section below (also see Chapters 5 and 8).

PATHOGENS NATURALLY PRESENT IN MARINE OR FRESHWATER ENVIRONMENTS

Naturally Occurring Marine Bacteria Associated with Human Disease

   A number of free-living estuarine and freshwater bacteria may be associated with human disease. Most of these bacteria fall within the family Vibrionaceae, which includes the genera *Vibrio, Aeromonas*, and *Plesiomonas*. These bacteria are generally not associated with fecal contamination of harvest waters, and some studies suggest an inverse relationship between counts of certain species and fecal coliform levels (Kaper et al., 1979; Tamplin et al., 1982). Counts tend to be highest in warm summer months, particularly when water temperature exceeds 15-20°C (Baross and Liston, 1970).

TABLE 3-5 Vibrionaceae Identified with Shellfish-Associated Human Disease

	Clinical Features		Implicated Shellfish Vehicle	
Pathogen	Diarrhea	Septicemia	Most Common	Other
Vibrio cholerae O1	++[a]		Crab	Oyster
Vibrio cholerae non-O1	++	+[b]	Oyster	
Vibrio parahaemolyticus	++	(+)[c]	Shellfish (shrimp, crab)	
Vibrio fluvialis	++		?[e]	
Vibrio mimicus	++		Oyster	
Vibrio hollisae	++	(+)	Shellfish (unspecified)	
Vibrio furnissii	++		?	
Vibrio vulnificus	+	++	Oyster	Crab
Aeromonas hydrophila (including *Aeromonas caviae* and *Aeromonas sobria*)	?[d]		?	
Plesiomonas shigelloides	++		Oyster	

[a] Most common clinical manifestation.
[b] Occasional clinical manifestation.
[c] Rare clinical manifestation.
[d] Suspected, but not proven clinical manifestation.
[e] Unsure if shellfish can be implicated as a vehicle.

Illnesses associated with these organisms can generally be divided into two categories: disease (usually gastroenteritis) due to ingestion of seafoods containing these organisms, and wound infections related to contamination of wounds by seawater (Blake et al., 1979; Morris and Black, 1985). Cases tend to occur during late summer and early fall, when bacterial counts are highest in the water. Species of Vibrionaceae that are transmitted by eating shellfish are listed in Table 3-5 and described in detail below.

Vibrio cholerae O1.

Vibrio cholerae can be classified according to O group: strains in O group 1 (*V. cholerae* O1) cause cholera, whereas strains in other O groups (non-O1 *V. cholerae*) are generally associated with milder illness. The virulence of *V. cholerae* O1 is determined primarily by the presence of a protein enterotoxin, cholera toxin (CT). Strains that do not produce cholera toxin (i.e., are not toxigenic) tend to be avirulent or have reduced virulence (Morris et al., 1984). Persons with the most severe forms of cholera (cholera gravis) have profuse, watery diarrhea (Pierce and Mondal, 1974). The volume of diarrhea may exceed 1 liter per hour, resulting in rapid water depletion, circulatory collapse, and (if untreated) death. Fortunately, cholera gravis is relatively uncommon. In infections with *V. cholerae* O1 of the classical biotype, four or five inapparent infections or mild illnesses may occur for every apparent case. In infections with El Tor (the biotype present in the United States), 25-100 other infections may be expected for every hospitalized case (Bart et al., 1970).

It has traditionally been thought that strains of *V. cholerae* O1 were transmitted by fecal contamination of food or water, and this mode of transmission likely predominates in developing countries. However, there is increasing evidence that free-living strains of *V. cholerae* O1 have become established in the U.S. Gulf Coast environment and may be transmitted to man via consumption of raw, undercooked, or cross-contaminated shellfish (Morris and Black, 1985). The number of cases of cholera associated with these strains is relatively small (in the range of 50 cases since 1973); their significance lies in their potential for causing severe disease in otherwise healthy hosts.

Epidemiology and risk assessment

Epidemiologic investigations have associated *V. cholerae* O1 illness with eating crabs, shrimp, and raw oysters harvested along the Gulf Coast (Blake et al., 1980). The CDC (1989) reported three outbreaks of *V. cholerae* O1 involving 16 cases between 1978 and 1987 (Tables 3-2–3-4), and NETSU (Rippey and Verber, 1988) reported 13 cases in this same period (Tables 3-2 and 3-3). Based on these and other reports in the literature, at least 50 cholera cases appear to have been acquired in the United States since 1973 when the first recent indigenous U.S. case was reported (Blake et al., 1980; Lowry et al., 1989b; Morris and Black, 1985).

Toxigenic *V. cholerae* O1 has been isolated from estuarine water, from fresh shrimp, and from cooked crabs. All U.S. *V. cholerae* O1 isolates have been hemolytic, biotype El Tor, serotype Inaba, and all have had the same unique *Hind*III digest pattern on Southern blot analysis. Because of the occurrence of cases over a period of years and in a variety of locations, many authors suggest that this strain has become endemic along the Gulf Coast (Morris and Black, 1985).

Although toxigenic *V. cholerae* O1 strains are known to be present in Gulf Coast estuaries, the percentage of shellfish that carry the organism appears to be quite low. In one study conducted by the FDA, *V. cholerae* O1 was isolated from 0.9% of 790 oyster lots sampled over 12 months. None of the *V. cholerae* O1 strains isolated was able to produce cholera toxin (Twedt et al., 1981).

Seroepidemiologic studies provide an alternative means of assessing disease burden/risk of infection, particularly for microorganisms such as *V. cholerae* O1 that produce a high percentage of asymptomatic infections. In a study conducted along the Gulf Coast in Texas (Hunt et al., 1988), 0.89% of persons sampled had elevated titers of both vibriocidal and anticholera toxin antibodies, the standard serologic assays used for *V. cholerae* infections. These assays have relatively low specificity, making the interpretation of results difficult. However, these data do raise the possibility that a small percentage of persons living along the U.S. Gulf Coast has recently been infected with toxigenic strains of *V. cholerae* O1 (Hunt et al., 1988).

Disease control

Because *V. cholerae* appears to contaminate marine animals in situ, it must be destroyed by treatment of the food. For crustacean seafood, proper cooking in primary processing (crab) or at the food service level (shrimp) and avoidance of recontamination of cooked product are recommended (Shultz et al., 1984). Studies conducted by CDC indicate that large whole male crabs boiled for less than 8 minutes or steamed for less than 25 minutes may still contain viable *V. cholerae* organisms (Blake et al., 1980), an observation that has led to a series of recommended time and temperature conditions for cooking crabs.

Toxigenic *V. cholerae* O1 strains can be identified rapidly in shellfish by using deoxyribonucleic acid (DNA) probes. A monitoring system that employs such probes might be useful in identifying potential "high-risk" harvesting areas. However, without further studies it is unclear how such data should be used. Given the low frequency with which toxigenic *V. cholerae* O1 are found, it would be difficult to justify embargoing all shellfish from a given area based solely on a positive sampling result. Using probes to screen shellfish on a lot-by-lot basis would be of little value, because results from a single crab or oyster are unlikely to be representative of the lot as a whole. Finally, epidemiological data are lacking to show how changes in the frequency of isolation of *V. cholerae* O1 from shellfish correlate with changes in disease occurrence in the community.

Non-O1 *Vibrio cholerae* (*V. cholerae* of O Groups Other Than 1)

Non-O1 *V. cholerae* strains are ubiquitous in estuarine environments (including bays and estuaries of the U.S. Gulf, Atlantic, and Pacific coasts) and are commonly isolated from shellfish. In one study conducted by the FDA, non-O1 *V. cholerae* was isolated in up to 37% of U.S. oyster lots harvested during warm summer months

(Twedt et al., 1981). Non-O1 *V. cholerae* has been associated with gastroenteritis, wound and ear infections, and septicemia (Hughes et al., 1978; Safrin et al., 1988). Gastroenteritis can occur in normal, healthy persons (Morris et al., 1990). Septicemia appears to occur primarily in persons who are immunocompromised or who have underlying liver disease; the mortality rate for persons with septicemia exceeds 50% (Safrin et al., 1988). Persons who have acquired non-O1 *V. cholerae* infections in the United States have almost all given a history of having eaten raw oysters before the onset of illness (Morris et al., 1981). However, the number of reported cases of non-O1 *V. cholerae* gastroenteritis is relatively low, suggesting that only a minority of strains are able to infect humans, or that most infections result in mild or asymptomatic illness.

Epidemiology and risk assessment

In the NETSU data base (Table 3-2), non-O1 *V. cholerae* is the most common bacterial cause of molluscan shellfish-associated illness. Still, only 120 cases were reported between 1978 and 1987 (Rippey and Verber, 1988). The CDC (1989) reported only two shellfish-associated outbreaks involving 11 cases during the same period (Tables 3-2 and 3-3). Given the amount of raw shellfish consumed and the frequency with which the organism is present in shellfish, the number of reported cases of non-O1 disease in the United States is much less than might be anticipated. Seven coastal area hospitals in four southern states isolated only seven specimens of non-O1 *V. cholerae* (including five isolates from a single outbreak) from approximately 11,000 stool cultures performed with the use of thiosulfate-citrate-bile salts-sucrose (TCBS) agar, an appropriate selective culture medium (Morris and Black, 1985). Only two non-O1 *V. cholerae* specimens were isolated from over 10,000 stool cultures on TCBS performed during 14 years in a Chesapeake Bay area hospital (Hoge et al., 1989).

This small number of reported cases is probably a reflection of several factors. It is likely that the majority of environmental strains lack the necessary colonization factors, appropriate toxins, or other virulence determinants to cause human disease (Morris et al., 1990). Even when infections occur, patients may often be asymptomatic or have only mild illness and, consequently, not come to medical attention. In support of the latter hypothesis, non-O1 *V. cholerae* strains were isolated from 13 (2.7%) of 479 persons in a cohort of physicians attending a convention in New Orleans in late September; among persons eating raw oysters, 4% had non-O1 *V. cholerae* in their stool. However, despite this relatively high colonization rate, only 2 (15%) of the 13 culture-positive persons were symptomatic, comparable to the overall 14% rate of diarrhea reported in the entire cohort (Lowry et al., 1989a).

Disease control

There are currently no programs attempting to limit exposure of the general population to non-O1 *V. cholerae*, other than recommendations that persons who are immunocompromised or who have underlying liver disease avoid the consumption of raw oysters (Blake, 1983). Exposure to non-O1 strains could be reduced significantly if oyster harvesting was confined to colder months when *Vibrio* counts in water are lowest (Twedt et al., 1981).

If it is assumed that most environmental non-O1 *V. cholerae* strains are nonpathogenic, identification of these strains in oysters has limited public health utility. It would clearly be of value if pathogenic strains could be differentiated from those that are nonpathogenic. Basic research in this area should be encouraged.

Vibrio parahaemolyticus

The CDC reported *V. parahaemolyticus* as the most common cause of vibrio disease due to consumption of seafoods from 1978 to 1987, whereas NETSU reported lower incidences (Tables 3-2 and 3-3). This is a mildly halophilic vibrio commonly isolated from fish, shellfish, and other marine sources in inshore waters, which is most abundant when water temperatures exceed 15°C. It is difficult to isolate during cold winter months. The ability to cause human gastroenteritis is most highly correlated with the production of a heat-stable hemolysin (Miyamoto et al., 1969). Most strains isolated from the marine environment lack this hemolysin and are probably not pathogenic, although nonhemolytic strains have recently been associated with illness occurring along the U.S. Pacific Coast (Abbott et al., 1989; Kelly and Stroh, 1989). *V. parahaemolyticus* reproduces very rapidly at temperatures of 20°C and above, and has been shown to reach potentially infective levels [more than 10^5 colony forming units (CFU)] in shrimp and crabs held for 2-3 hours at such temperatures (Liston, 1973). However, it is heat sensitive and rapidly killed at 60°C.

Epidemiology and risk assessment

V. parahaemolyticus is a common marine isolate, with isolation reported from water, sediment, suspended particulates, plankton, fish, and shellfish (Joseph et al., 1983). However, it is likely that only a small fraction of marine isolates are potentially pathogenic. For example, in a study by Thompson and Vanderzant (1976), only 4 of 2,218 isolates from Galveston Bay were able to produce the heat-stable hemolysin generally associated with virulence.

In Japan, *V. parahaemolyticus* has been implicated as the etiologic agent in 24% of reported cases of food-borne disease (Miwatani and Takeda, 1976). In the United States, *V. parahaemolyticus* has caused several major food-borne disease outbreaks (Barker, 1974). The CDC food-borne surveillance data from 1978 to 1987 (Tables 3-2 and 3-3) reported *V. parahaemolyticus* as the cause of 15 outbreaks associated with 176 cases of mostly crustacean shellfish-associated illness (CDC, 1989). No other seafood-associated illnesses from *V. parahaemolyticus* were reported to CDC during this time; NETSU reported 52 cases in the same period (Rippey and Verber, 1988) (Tables 3-2 and 3-3).

Outbreaks of *V. parahaemolyticus* have often been associated with cross-contamination or time/temperature abuse of cooked seafood. Although sporadic cases associated with the consumption of raw oysters have occurred, there does not appear to be the same strong association with consumption of raw oysters as reported for non-O1 *V. cholerae*. As with non-O1 *V. cholerae*, estimates of incidence are complicated by the need for TCBS selective media for isolation of the organism from stool cultures. In areas and studies in the United States where TCBS has been used routinely, *V. parahaemolyticus* has been the *Vibrio* species isolated most frequently from stool samples, with an isolation rate two to three times that reported for non-O1 *V. cholerae* (Bonner et al., 1983; Hoge et al., 1989; Lowry et al., 1989a). However, the overall disease incidence remains quite low, even in communities where shellfish consumption would be expected to be high. In a hospital-based study in Annapolis, Maryland, there was estimated to be less than 0.5 case/100,000 population/year (Hoge et al., 1989).

Disease control

The impact of major food-borne outbreaks due to *V. parahaemolyticus* can be limited by emphasizing avoidance of cross-contamination and time/temperature abuse of cooked shellfish or of seafood that will be consumed raw. Illness due to *V. parahaemolyticus* is typically associated with multiplication of the organism to high numbers on the food either in the raw state or after cooking. Seafood eaten shortly after adequate cooking is generally safe (Bradshaw et al., 1974). Control has thus been aimed at ensuring good handling and processing practices whereby the seafood is held at low temperature (<5°C) and recontamination of the cooked product is avoided.

Specific counts of *V. parahaemolyticus* on seafoods have been proposed as an index of hazard, but this method has not been widely used because of cost, lack of specificity for pathogenic strains, and time lag (3-5 days) between sampling and results.

The DNA probes for identification of hemolytic (Kanagawa-positive) strains are available (Nishibuchi et al., 1985). With nonradioactively labeled oligonucleotide probes it may be possible to identify potentially pathogenic strains within a matter of hours. However, no effort has been made to make such probes commercially available or to assess their utility as public health tools.

Vibrio vulnificus

V. vulnificus is very similar to *V. parahaemolyticus* in cultural characteristics and sensitivity to processing procedures. It is widespread in estuarine waters around the U.S. coastline and is a common isolate in oysters harvested from warm (>20°C) waters. Although *V. cholerae* O1 is capable of causing severe, life-threatening disease in healthy individuals, *V. vulnificus* is potentially the most dangerous of the vibrios for persons with underlying illnesses such as cirrhosis or hemochromatosis or persons who are immunocompromised (Klontz et al., 1988; Morris et al., 1987b; Tacket et al., 1984). When such persons become infected, the mortality rate can exceed 50% (Morris, 1988). Fortunately, *V. vulnificus* infections are relatively uncommon, with an estimated annual incidence rate in the range of 0.5 case/100,000 population/year.

Epidemiology and risk assessment

Like other *Vibrio* species, *V. vulnificus* appears to be part of the normal bacterial flora of estuaries along the U.S. Gulf, Atlantic, and Pacific coasts. Although data are limited, some studies reported that close to 100% of oyster lots harvested in some areas during warm summer months have been positive for *V. vulnificus*, and in one study, 11% of the blue crabs harvested from Galveston Bay during summer months had the organism in their hemolymph (Davis and Sizemore, 1982; Tamplin, 1990).

Occurrence of *V. vulnificus*-induced primary septicemia is significantly associated with eating raw oysters (Tacket et al., 1984). However, susceptibility appears to be limited to certain high-risk groups, particularly those with hemochromatosis, cirrhosis, hematologic or other disorders associated with immunosuppression, renal failure, and diabetes (Table 3-6). Wound infections are associated with contamination of wounds with seawater. Although wound infections can occur in otherwise healthy persons, deaths associated with wound infection have occurred almost exclusively among persons in the same high-risk groups mentioned above.

TABLE 3-6 Risk Factors for Primary *Vibrio* Septicemia

Risk Factors[a]	CDC (n = 42)[b] %	Florida (n = 38)[c] %
Alcoholic cirrhosis	31	32
Hemochromatosis/cirrhosis	12	13
"Chronic hepatitis"	10	-
Postnecrotic cirrhosis	5	-
Liver disease - undetermined or unspecified cause[d]	10	21
Alcohol abuse (without liver disease)	12	16
Diabetes	10	11
Other illnesses[e]	3	3
No known underlying disease	7	5

[a] Based on report of attending physician.
[b] Includes data from national retrospective studies conducted by Blake et al. (1979) and Tacket et al. (1984) at the Centers for Disease Control.
[c] Data from a prospective study conducted in Florida by Klontz et al. (1988).
[d] May include patients with alcohol-related illness.
[e] These include renal disease, steroid-dependent rheumatoid arthritis, thalassemia, malignancies, hematologic disorders associated with immunosuppression (neutropenia and leukopenia), and acquired immune deficiency syndrome.

Between 1978 and 1987, NETSU reported 100 cases of *V. vulnificus* infections (Tables 3-2, 3-3, and 3-7) (Rippey and Verber, 1988). *V. vulnificus* infections have not been reported to CDC because outbreaks involving two or more individuals have not occurred. The increased number of cases reported to NETSU in the last two years probably reflects better isolation methods and a more rigorous screening for the organism by public health laboratories. However, the mortality rate has remained high (Table 3-7).

The incidence of *V. vulnificus* infections in coastal states appears to be 0.5 case/100,000 population/year, with primary septicemia accounting for approximately two-thirds of the cases. Based on reported cases, the incidence in the Florida panhandle was estimated to be 0.4 case/100,000/year (Klontz et al., 1988). Johnston et al. (1985) estimated an incidence of 0.8/100,000/year in Louisiana coastal parishes. The estimated incidence in a hospital-based study in Annapolis, Maryland was 0.5 case/100,000/year (Hoge et al., 1989). These estimates are clearly lower than might be

TABLE 3-7 *Vibrio vulnificus* Cases Associated with Oysters, 1978-1987

	Vibrio vulnificus Cases	Percentage of Total Oyster-Associated Cases	Deaths	Mortality (%)
1978	2	4	0	0
1979	7	14	2(?)	29
1980	2	2	1	50
1981	16	64	5	31
1982	13	2	10	77
1983	9	12	4	44
1984	9	6	4	44
1985	7	16	0	0
1986	21	14	5	23
1987	16	68	8	53

SOURCE: NETSU data base (Rippey and Verber, 1988).

expected, given the frequency with which the organism has been identified in shellfish and the amount of shellfish consumed in these areas. This may reflect differences in virulence among strains, the effect of infectious dose (i.e., the minimum number of organisms needed to cause disease), or the critical importance of host susceptibility in the disease process.

Disease control

The incidence of *V. vulnificus* infections associated with ingestion of raw oysters by high-risk individuals (Table 3-6) could be reduced by cooking the product before eating. If a dose-response relationship exists, disease incidence might also be reduced by reducing the counts of *V. vulnificus* in shellfish by restricting harvesting to times when vibrio counts in harvesting areas are low (i.e., when water temperatures are <20°C) or by monitoring vibrio counts carefully in summer months. A recent study by Cook and Ruple (1989) indicated increases of one to three orders of magnitude in subsequent storage of shellstock at above 20°C. Rapid cooling of shellfish after harvest may decrease the initial bacterial counts, and careful avoidance of time/temperature abuse during handling and shipment would limit subsequent multiplication of the organism (Cook and Ruple, 1989). Low-dose gamma irradiation of live shellstock and fresh or frozen seafood products has been shown to be extremely effective in the elimination of *Vibrio* species (Giddings, 1984; Kilgen et al., 1988). Rapid diagnostic techniques are available for *V. vulnificus*, based both on agglutination reactions with specific antisera (Simonson and Siebeling, 1986) and on DNA probes (Morris et al., 1987a). However, these techniques have not been used as regulatory tools, and their exact role in disease control remains to be determined.

An ability to differentiate potentially pathogenic strains from strains without recognized virulence would clearly be of help in designing appropriate control strategies (Simpson et al., 1987). Similarly, there is a need to better understand the interaction between the organisms and oysters, both before and after harvesting. A better understanding of the host response to *V. vulnificus* would allow more careful delineation of groups at high risk for infection (Table 3-6). An educational program defining the risks and explaining prevention by cooking and proper handling should be directed to this group through physicians, health organizations, and other public sources. Education of seafood producers, seafood processors and handlers, health professionals, and consumers regarding groups at high risk is also extremely important. Further studies in these areas must be encouraged as part of any overall plan for control of this pathogen.

Other *Vibrio* Species

Several other *Vibrio* species have been associated with human illness, including *V. mimicus* (Shandera et al., 1983), *V. hollisae* (Morris et al., 1982), *V. fluvialis* (Huq et al., 1980), and *V. furnissii* (Brenner et al., 1983) (Tables 3-2, 3-3, and 3-5). Illness from these species has generally been associated with seafood or shellfish consumption. However, the incidence of infection with these organisms appears to be quite low, and they are of much less importance as human pathogens than *V. cholerae, V. parahaemolyticus*, and *V. vulnificus*.

V. fluvialis, V. mimicus, and *V. furnissii* all appear to be naturally present in the marine environment. Infection with *V. mimicus* and *V. hollisae* has been associated with consumption of raw shellfish, especially raw oysters (Morris et al., 1982; Shandera et al., 1983). It is very difficult to estimate the incidence of infection with these organisms, because appropriate selective media for isolation are seldom used (except for *V. hollisae*, which may be best seen on blood agar) and because of difficulties with *Vibrio* taxonomy. Although they contain a number of inherent biases, data on the number of strains of each species sent to CDC for identification provide some basis for comparing relative frequencies of isolation. In a period during which CDC received 136 non-O1 *V. cholerae* isolates for identification, 39 *V. mimicus* isolates were received, 32 *V. hollisae*, 15 *V. fluvialis*, and 16 *V. furnissii* (Farmer et al., 1985). Between 1978 and 1987, NETSU (Rippey and Verber, 1988) reported five cases of *V. mimicus*, five cases of *V. hollisae*, and five cases of *V. fluvialis* (Tables 3-2 and 3-3).

The risk of infection with these organisms can likely be reduced by strategies similar to those used for other *Vibrio* species: that is, by using good manufacturing practices (GMPs) involving immediate and proper refrigeration, by possibly limiting shellfish harvesting to cooler months, by monitoring *Vibrio* counts in summer months for management purposes, by using low-dose irradiation for processing raw seafoods or live shellstock, and by advising persons in high-risk groups to avoid consumption of raw shellfish.

Aeromonas

Aeromonas species are common environmental isolates. They are ubiquitous in estuarine areas (Kaper et al., 1979) and can be isolated from a variety of foods (Palumbo et al., 1989). Their role as a pathogen remains highly controversial.

In controlled epidemiologic studies, strains within the *A. hydrophila* group have been associated with diarrheal disease in children in Australia and in travelers in Thailand (Burke et al., 1983; Pitarangsi et al., 1982). However, there are a number of studies in which no association with diarrheal disease has been established, and in which isolation rates from asymptomatic persons equal or exceed isolation rates from persons with diarrhea. In the one volunteer study performed, volunteers ingesting *Aeromonas* strains did not become ill. A small minority of strains may carry virulent characteristics that enable them to cause human disease, but there is currently no way of differentiating potentially pathogenic strains from nonpathogenic strains.

Contact with untreated surface water appears to be the major risk factor for infection with *Aeromonas* (Burke et al., 1983; Holmberg et al., 1986a). Between 1978 and 1987, only seven cases associated with shellfish consumption were reported to NETSU; CDC did not report any seafood-associated cases of *Aeromonas* in this same period (Tables 3-2–3-4). Currently, any association between eating fish or shellfish and *Aeromonas* infection is at best circumstantial.

No programs to limit exposure to *Aeromonas* currently exist. Any such program would probably be premature because of uncertainties about the role of the organism as a pathogen.

Plesiomonas

Plesiomonas shigelloides (formerly *Aeromonas shigelloides*) has been implicated as a cause of human gastroenteritis for 40 years (Miller and Koburger, 1985). Like other members of the Vibrionaceae, *P. shigelloides* is a common environmental isolate, widespread in nature, being mostly associated with fresh surface water but also found in seawater (Van Damme and Vandepitte, 1980). It shows a seasonal variation in its isolation similar to that of marine vibrios, being isolated more often during warmer months (Miller and Koburger, 1985). Isolation of *P. shigelloides* has been significantly associated with foreign travel and with the consumption of raw oysters (Holmberg et al., 1986b; Kain and Kelly, 1989). Other foods implicated as vehicles for *P. shigelloides* include cuttlefish salad and salt mackerel. In the United States, raw oysters are probably the food most commonly implicated. However, questions remain about its pathogenicity.

Controlled epidemiologic studies have not shown a clear association between isolation of *P. shigelloides* and occurrence of diarrhea (Pitarangsi et al., 1982), and volunteers ingesting the organism have not become ill (Herrington et al., 1987). It is possible that few strains carry virulent characteristics that enable them to cause human disease, but there is currently no way of differentiating potentially pathogenic strains from nonpathogenic ones.

According to the NETSU data base, *P. shigelloides* has been implicated in only 18 cases of illness in 1978-1987. This is less than 0.5% of the cases of illness associated with molluscan shellfish (Tables 3-2 and 3-3). The CDC did not report any outbreaks of seafood-associated *P. shigelloides* in the same period.

Most strains of *P. shigelloides* have a minimum growth temperature of 8°C, but at least one strain has been reported to grow at 0°C. Strains seem to survive well in shellstock oysters held at refrigeration temperature. The organism is sensitive to a pH less than 4 and to a salt concentration higher than 5% (Miller and Koburger, 1985). In addition, being a member of the family Vibrionaceae, it should be killed by relatively mild cooking temperatures.

Because of the strong association between eating oysters and human infection, *P. shigelloides* should be considered in any program to limit exposure to bacterial pathogens in shellfish. Again, there is a need to establish its pathogenicity for humans before initiating any specific control measures.

Helminthic Agents Present in Seafood

A number of helminths may be present in fish and shellfish. However, with few exceptions (Table 3-8), they are harmless to humans. Illness from these agents is most commonly associated with eating fish. However, helminths are responsible for much less illness than either bacterial or viral agents (Table 3-2). Only two outbreaks involving 39 cases of fish-associated parasitic illnesses were reported to CDC (1989) between 1978 and 1987, one outbreak each in California and Minnesota. Thus, parasitic infections from fish are rare in the United States, and there is, as yet, no evidence of a significant increase due to changed eating habits.

For many of these agents, humans are not the definitive host. Characteristics of the organism's life cycle may determine its relative importance as a human pathogen. Risk of exposure is dependent to a large degree on the geographic location of harvest. Areas endemic for specific helminth zoonoses in the United States include the Great Lakes region and Florida (*Diphyllobothrium latum*); Pacific Northwest and marine areas (*D. pacificum*); Pacific Islands, New Orleans, and Puerto Rico (*Angiostrongylus cantonensis*); the Atlantic and Pacific coasts *(Anisakis simplex)*; the Pacific coast (*Contraceacum osculatum*); the Gulf of Mexico (*Contraceacum* spp.); the Northern Atlantic and Pacific Ocean (*Pseudoterranova dicipiens*); and the Pacific islands (*Paragonimus westermani*) (Bryan, 1986; Chitwood, 1970; Healy and Juranek, 1979).

TABLE 3-8 Helminthic Agents Present in Fish and Shellfish

Imported fish and shellfish

Trematodes

Clonorchis sinensis
Heterophyes heterophyes
Metagonimus yokogawai
Opisthorchis felineus

Nematodes

Gnathostoma spinigerum

Domestic fish and shellfish

Trematodes

Paragonimus westermani

Cestodes

Diphyllobothrium latum
Diphyllobothrium pacificum

Nematodes

Angiostrongylus cantonensis
Contraceacum species *(osculatum)*
Hysterothylacium species
Pseudoterranova dicipiens
Anisakis simplex

Trematodes

Only digenetic trematodes are known to produce disease in humans, and there are no data to suggest that any of these organisms represent a substantive health problem in the United States.

Clonorchis sinensis, or the Chinese liver fluke, is transmitted by eating raw or undercooked freshwater fish containing cyst stages of the organism. The organism is endemic in east Asia in a zone extending from Japan to Vietnam. *Heterophyes*, an intestinal fluke, is transmitted by eating fresh- or brackish-water fish (frequently mullet) in a raw, salted, or dried condition. The organism is a common parasite in the lower Nile valley near the Mediterranean coastline, and has been reported in the Orient and in western India. *Metagonimus yokogawai*, which closely resembles *H. heterophyes*, may be present in freshwater trout in the Orient, the maritime provinces of the USSR, northern Siberia, and the Balkans. *Paragonimus westermani*, the oriental lung fluke, is acquired by eating freshwater crabs or crawfish that are raw or have been pickled in brine, vinegar, or rice wine. The organism is endemic in east Asia, including Japan, Korea, the Philippines, and Taiwan.

Transmission of food-borne illness due to trematodes is prevented by adequate cooking and probably by freezing seafoods (Healy and Juranek, 1979).

Cestodes

Diphyllobothrium latum and *D. pacificum* are the only cestodes associated with parasitic infections from seafoods (Table 3-8). However, there are inadequate data to estimate their incidence in the United States. Cases have been reported among Jewish cooks who sampled gefilte fish during its preparation.

D. latum is acquired by eating raw freshwater fish containing appropriate plerocercoids (Healy and Juranek, 1979). The organism is indigenous throughout many parts of the USSR; the Baltic Sea countries; central and southeastern Europe; Lake N'gami, Africa; northern Manchuria and Japan; and New South Wales, Australia. In the Americas it is found in northern Minnesota, extensive areas of Canada and Alaska, and in the lakes of southern Chile and Argentina.

Control of disease caused by cestodes is dependent on thorough cooking of fish from endemic areas; cysts are also killed by freezing at -10°C for 24 hours (Healy and Juranek, 1979).

Nematodes

Disease from *Anisakis simplex* arises in humans when improperly cooked, smoked, or raw fish are eaten (Cheng, 1976). Anisakids are usually found in herring less than 12 centimeters (cm) long. Although the medical literature contains few reports of anisakiasis in the United States, over 3,000 cases are reported annually from Japan (Fontaine, 1985).

Whitish to clear larval worms approximately 1 cm long are found in the posterior body cavity of fish, coiled and encapsulated (McGladdery, 1986; Smith and Wooten, 1975). About 2-3% of the total bore into muscle. Some of these may be loosely encapsulated. Worms are usually seen on fresh fillets or about anal areas in the round of the fish. Up to 30% of European herring may be infected in a single sample, but estimates of total numbers with actual fillet infection are as low as 0.001%. It has been suggested that the prevalence of muscle infection is related to the intensity of body cavity infection. Fish with eight or fewer organisms in the body cavity seldom show fillet infection.

From 1958 to 1980, 13 cases were reported in the United States, for a mean of 0.59 case/year; however, 37 cases have been reported since 1980 (4.1 cases/year) (Deardorff et al., 1986; McKerrow et al., 1988).

Pseudoterranova dicipiens and *Contraceacum* closely resemble *A. simplex*. Both have been identified in pinnipeds in the Atlantic and northern Pacific. Cases in the United States associated with *P. dicipiens* have been reported on the West Coast, resulting from consumption of salmon and Pacific rockfish (*Sebastes*) (Kliks, 1983; Margolis, 1977; Myers, 1979).

The risk of infection from nematodes is reduced when fish are gutted soon after capture; salting may also decrease incidence. However, neither smoking nor light salting of fish normally affects larvae. Freezing at -20°C for 72 hours or heating above 55°C for 10 seconds kills adult parasites (Khalil, 1969). Because infection of fillets may be related to body cavity burdens, subsamples that cannot be immediately frozen or gutted could be checked for numbers of parasites. If the number exceeds 15, the fish should be banned for human consumption (Bier, 1976; Bier et al., 1987).

Other Nematodes

Angiostrongylus cantonensis is acquired by eating raw snails (the intermediate host for the organism). Crabs, prawns, and fish that have eaten infective snails can serve as transport hosts. Heavy infections cause an eosinophilic meningoencephalitis. Epidemics and sporadic infections occur most commonly in the South Pacific, Southeast Asia, and Taiwan (Alicata, 1988; Kliks et al., 1982). In recent years the parasite has spread to the Caribbean, and in 1986 it was reported in rat and snail populations in Puerto Rico (Anderson et al., 1986).

Gnathostoma spinigerum is acquired by eating raw or undercooked freshwater fish. The organism presents a clinical picture of larval migrans, a granulomatous lesion, or a stationary abscess. Infections have been reported from eastern and Southeast Asia, India, and Israel (Healy and Juranek, 1979).

PATHOGENS ASSOCIATED WITH FECAL POLLUTION OF THE MARINE OR FRESHWATER ENVIRONMENT

Species of fish and shellfish harvested from inshore waters that are subject to contamination by human or terrestrial animal feces, and by other industrial/agricultural pollutants, may contain bacteria and viruses that are pathogenic for humans (Liston, 1980). This is especially true for filter feeders that concentrate bacteria and viruses present in polluted waters, and oysters harvested from growing waters contaminated with human sewage have been associated with many outbreaks of enteric disease (Son and Fleet, 1980).

Viral Human Enteric Pathogens

More than 100 enteric viruses can be found in human feces. Families of viral pathogens associated with pollution of harvesting waters include picornaviruses, reoviruses, adenoviruses, caliciviruses, astroviruses, and unclassified viruses such as Norwalk and Norwalk-like viruses, Snow Mountain agent, small round viruses, and non-A, non-B hepatitis virus (NANB). Of these enteric viruses, only hepatitis A virus (HAV), caliciviruses, astroviruses, Norwalk virus, Snow Mountain agent, and NANB enteral hepatitis virus have been documented to cause seafood-associated illness (Tables 3-1–3-4) (Bryan, 1986; CDC, 1989; Cliver, 1988; Gerba, 1988; Richards, 1985, 1987; Rippey and Verber, 1988).

These human enteric viruses are species specific and even receptor specific for certain cells. Once released into the marine environment they do not multiply, and their survival and persistence are based on many factors, including temperature, salinity, ultraviolet inactivation from sunlight, and the presence of organic solids or sediments. Of these factors, the most important are temperature lower than 10°C and the protective action of organic materials (Gerba, 1988). Human enteric viruses have been isolated in field studies only from molluscan shellfish and blue crabs taken from a sludge dump in the North Atlantic. Other marine animals, including lobsters, sandworms, detrital feeding fish, and conch, have been shown to take up enteric viruses when marine waters were experimentally seeded with these viruses, but viral uptake from naturally polluted water has not been reported in field studies. The only seafood implicated to date in the transmission of enteric virus from contaminated estuarine waters has been molluscan shellfish (Gerba, 1988).

Hepatitis Type A (Enterovirus Type 72)

Hepatitis A virus is a member of the family Picornaviridae. Of the nearly 200 human-adapted picornaviruses, 69 inhabit the enteric tract (Gerba, 1988; White and Fenner, 1986). Enteroviruses of the family Picornaviridae include the following species:

Polioviruses   (Types 1, 2, and 3)
Echoviruses   (Types 1-34; no 10 or 28)
Coxsackieviruses   (Types A1-A24 and B1-B6; no A23) (67 types)
Enteroviruses   (Types 68-71)
Enterovirus type 72 (Hepatitis A, HAV)

Of these enteroviruses, only HAV has been documented as a cause of seafood-associated illness, and has been isolated from infected seafoods and waters contaminated with human feces. For this reason, the other enteroviruses are not discussed here.

All of the enteroviruses are resistant to an acidic pH, proteolytic enzymes, and bile salts in the gut. Hepatitis A is less acid stable than other enteroviruses, but more heat stable, surviving at 60°C for 4 hours (White and Fenner, 1986). HAV is more chlorine resistant than indicator bacteria and the other enteroviruses, with the exception of Norwalk virus (Grabow et al., 1983; Keswick et al., 1985; Peterson et al., 1983). Hepatitis A is one of the most serious seafood-associated viral infections, causing a protracted and sometimes severe disease, but its mortality is only approximately 0.6%.

Hepatitis A virus is spread by the fecal-oral route. It is hyperendemic in countries that are overcrowded, and have inadequate sanitation and poor hygiene. Most infections in these communities occur in childhood and are subclinical. In more developed countries the disease is seen most often between the ages of 15 and 30 (Cliver, 1988; White and Fenner, 1986).

Contaminated food or water and person-to-person contact are the main routes of transmission of HAV. Each year, 20,000 to 30,000 cases are reported to the CDC. Of these cases, approximately 140 are known to be due to foods (0.5% of the total). Most of these food-borne outbreaks are due to inappropriate personal hygiene of infected individuals (Cliver, 1988). Outbreaks can also occur due to inadequate cooking of contaminated foods and human fecal contamination of drinking water supplies, swimming waters, and shellfish growing waters.

In the 1950s the first documented case of shellfish-associated HAV occurred in Sweden (Cliver, 1988). The first shellfish-associated case in the United States was documented in the 1960s (Cliver, 1988;, Gerba, 1988; Richards, 1985). Richards (1985) reported approximately 1,400 cases of molluscan shellfish-associated HAV from 1961 to 1984. Between 1978 and 1987, the CDC food-borne surveillance system (CDC, 1989) reported nine outbreaks involving 125 cases of seafood-related HAV (Tables 3-2–3-4); however, two of the outbreaks involving 92 cases were due to contamination from food handlers (Table 3-4); NETSU reported approximately 45 cases of shellfish-associated HAV in the same period (Rippey and Verber, 1988) (Tables 3-2 and 3-3). Richards (1985) noted that the incidence of molluscan shellfish-associated HAV has decreased in the last decade, although it is difficult to describe the trend of reported HAV infections in the United States with a single, unidirectional line. There is currently no valid indicator of human enteric viruses such as HAV in shellfish growing waters.

Caliciviruses and Astroviruses

Caliciviruses, like all enteric viruses, are found in human feces and are responsible for many cases of gastroenteritis. Transmission routes of calciviruses are the same as those discussed for other enteric viruses. Infection by calicivirus tends to cause a mild gastroenteric illness. No seafood-associated outbreaks due to these enteric viruses have been reported to CDC or NETSU (CDC, 1989; Rippey and Verber, 1988).

Unclassified Viruses

Unclassified viruses include poorly characterized agents of gastroenteritis such as Norwalk and Norwalk-like agents, Snow Mountain agent, small round viruses (SRVs), and non-A, non-B enteral hepatitis (Gerba, 1988; White and Fenner, 1986). Norwalk and Norwalk-like viruses resemble caliciviruses and are considered possible members of this family of viruses by some scientists (White and Fenner, 1986).

Outbreaks of viral gastroenteritis due to the Norwalk agent have been associated with swimming in waters contaminated with human sewage, eating food or drinking water that is fecally contaminated, and consuming uncooked or partially cooked shellfish harvested from estuaries contaminated with human fecal material. The first documented shellfish-associated outbreak of gastroenteritis involving Norwalk virus occurred in 1979 in Australia, where more than 2,000 people were involved (Gerba, 1988). Since then, many outbreaks of Norwalk or Norwalk-like viral gastroenteritis have been reported in the United States (CDC, 1989; Morse et al., 1986; Richards, 1985, 1987; Rippey and Verber, 1988). Norwalk and Norwalk-like viral illnesses associated with shellfish are a continuing problem; reported incidents have increased during the last decade (Richards, 1985). Between 1978 and 1987, NETSU reported 11 shellfish-related cases of Norwalk gastroenteritis and 71 cases of Snow Mountain agent (Rippey and Verber, 1988) (Tables 3-2 and 3-3). CDC (1989) reported two outbreaks involving 42 shellfish-associated cases of Norwalk and related viruses (Tables 3-2 and 3-3). Richards (1985) reported an outbreak of shellfish-associated gastroenteritis involving 472 cases in Louisiana. Norwalk was suspected but not serologically documented. Richards (1985) also reported more than 6,000 shellfish-associated cases of unspecified gastroenteritis during the past 50 years. It is probable that many of these are of viral etiology, possibly Norwalk or Norwalk-related agents. More than 75% of these cases have been reported since 1980, which may indicate increased awareness and reporting of shellfish-related illnesses or an actual increase in infection rates. Norwalk virus is more resistant to chlorine than bacterial indicators and other enteroviruses (poliovirus and reovirus), and there is no indicator for human enteric viruses in shellfish or their growing waters (Grabow et al., 1983; Keswick et al., 1985; Peterson et al., 1983).

The etiologic agent of enteral or epidemic NANB hepatitis is unknown and may represent a group of related viruses rather than a single agent. It has been suggested that the NANB agent could be an enterovirus – possibly a different serotype of HAV (Overby et al., 1983). Enteral NANB hepatitis can be more severe than HAV, and infection by the NANB agent is associated with a high incidence of cholestasis. However, only one case of shellfish-associated NANB was reported to NETSU from 1978 to 1987 (Tables 3-2 and 3-3); CDC did not report any seafood-associated NANB in the same period.

Enteral NANB hepatitis is transmitted mainly by sewage-contaminated water and sporadically by person-to-person contact. In the Middle East and Africa, it appears to be endemic (Overby et al., 1983). Cliver (1988) reported water-associated outbreaks in India, Africa, the USSR, and Mexico. Gerba (1988) reported enteral NANB hepatitis cases associated with consumption of raw shellfish in the United States. One incident of shellfish-associated NANB and 1,645 cases of shellfish-associated nonspecified (i.e., unknown etiology) hepatitis were reported by NETSU between 1978 and 1987 (Rippey and Verber, 1988) (Tables 3-2 and 3-3). No cases of NANB or unspecified hepatitis reported to CDC between 1978 and 1987 were associated with seafood consumption. If an unspecified type of hepatitis is accurately reported as associated with seafood consumption, it would most likely be hepatitis A or enteral NANB. However, accurate case histories for an infection with such a long incubation (4 to 6 weeks) are usually difficult to obtain.

Disease Control for Human Enteric Viruses

Proper classification of shellfish growing waters based on valid human enteric virus indicators, as well as implementation and maintenance of proper treatment and disposal of sewage to prevent human enteric virus contamination of shellfish harvesting waters, are the most effective measures to deter raw shellfish-associated infections by these viruses. New sewage treatment methods may have to be developed. Norwalk virus and HAV are more resistant to chlorine than bacterial indicators (*Escherichia coli*, *Streptococcus faecalis,* and acid-fast bacteria) and other enteroviruses (poliovirus and reovirus), and there is no indicator for human viruses in shellfish or in growing waters. The only potential viral indicator that shows similar chlorine resistance is f2 bacteriophage. The specifications for disinfection of drinking water – free chlorine residue of 1-2 milligrams per liter (mg/L) for 1-2 hours at pH less than 8 and turbidity less than 1 unit – may not be sufficient to totally inactivate all HAV and is not sufficient for Norwalk virus (Grabow et al., 1983; Keswick, 1985; Peterson et al., 1983).

Effective enforcement to eliminate recreational and illegal ("bootlegging") harvesting and sale of raw molluscan shellfish from known sewage-contaminated growing areas must be developed and adequately funded.

Hepatitis A virus could also be controlled by vaccination, because infection results in permanent immunity. Although the U.S. Army is conducting live vaccine trials for HAV at this time, no licensed vaccine is available to the general public. Passive immunization with gamma globulin following known exposure to HAV is currently the primary method of control and prevention (Cliver, 1988; White and Fenner, 1986).

PROCESSING, DISTRIBUTION, AND PREPARATION-RELATED PUBLIC HEALTH HAZARDS

In addition to bacterial, helminthic, and viral pathogens that may be present in or on seafoods because of their presence in harvest waters, certain bacterial and viral pathogens can also contaminate seafoods during processing, distribution, and preparation. Some microorganisms pose risk to consumers of seafood from both harvest and postharvest sources, for example, hepatitis A virus and *Shigella*.

Bacterial Pathogens

Salmonella

Outbreaks of seafood-borne salmonellosis were reported to CDC between 1978 and 1987 (Tables 3-2 – 3-4 and 3-9); however, no cases of salmonellosis associated with shellfish consumption were reported to NETSU in the same period (Tables 3-2 and 3-3). Typhoid fever, due to infection by *S. typhi*, is of only historic importance as a seafood-related hazard in the United States, but continues to occur in foreign countries, potentially impacting the safety of imported seafood products.

Salmonellae (nontyphoidal) have been isolated from a variety of fish and shellfish. The FDA Pathogen Surveillance Program documented sporadic *Salmonella* contamination of domestic cooked shrimp and imported raw lobster, raw shrimp, and miscellaneous fishery products in fiscal year 1988. In a study in Florida, approximately 20% of oysters, clams, and crabs were contaminated with *Salmonella*, with positives found during all seasons. However, no salmonellae were recovered from samples of mullet, the only free-swimming species studied (Fraiser and Koburger, 1984). The public health impact of these findings remains to be determined.

Salmonella contamination of foods of animal origin is not uncommon, and human infections associated with a wide range of food vehicles are frequently reported. Estimates of infectious doses for *Salmonella* range from less than 100 to more than 1,000,000 organisms; characteristics of the host, the organism, and the vehicle are all important mitigating factors in the number of *Salmonella* needed to infect and cause disease.

TABLE 3-9 Seafood-Associated *Salmonella* Outbreaks, 1978-1987

Year	State	Seafood	Location	Serotype
1978				
1979				
1980				
1981	Connecticut	Shellfish	Cafeteria	*typhimurium*
	Pennsylvania	Shellfish	Restaurant	*thompson*
1982	New Jersey	Seafood combination	Restaurant	*enteritidis*
	New York	Tuna macaroni salad	Restaurant	*enteritidis*
1983	New Jersey	Shrimp cocktail	Restaurant	Untyped
1984				
1985	Pennsylvania	Stuffed sole	Church	*enteritidis*
1986	Pennsylvania	Gefilte fish	Home	*braenderup*
1987				*sandiego*

SOURCE: CDC (1989).

Epidemiology and risk assessment

For 1973-1986, an average of 55 food-borne outbreaks of nontyphoidal *Salmonella* infections, affecting a total of 3,944 persons, were reported each year to the CDC Foodborne Disease Outbreak Surveillance Program. During the same 14 years, an annual average total of 32,957 and 35,490 total *Salmonella* cases were reported through the laboratory-based *Salmonella* surveillance system and the *Morbidity and Mortality Weekly Report* (MMWR), respectively.

From 1978 to 1987, CDC reported six seafood-borne outbreaks involving 147 cases. Three of these outbreaks involving 80 cases were shellfish associated (Tables 3-2 – 3-4 and 3-9). Two shellfish-associated outbreaks of confirmed nontyphoidal salmonellosis were reported by NETSU between 1894 and 1988: a 100-case outbreak in Florida in 1947 due to contaminated oysters, and a 22-case outbreak in New York in 1967 associated with oysters imported from England. No cases of shellfish-associated *Salmonella* infections were reported to NETSU from 1978 to 1987 (Tables 3-2 and 3-3) (Rippey and Verber, 1988). Two outbreaks of nontyphoidal salmonellosis associated with salmon prepared by a caterer have been reported (Cartwright and Evans, 1988). The salmon was epidemiologically and microbiologically implicated, and multiple food-handling errors were identified. The origin of contamination of the fish was not determined, although raw chicken prepared at the same time as the salmon was also positive for *S. montevideo*, the outbreak serotype. Consumption of raw shellfish harvested from sewage-polluted waters also has resulted in *Salmonella* infections (Flowers, 1988a). Although CDC and NETSU food-borne surveillance data and literature reports indicate that seafood is a much less common vehicle for *Salmonella* than are other foods such as chicken or red meat, fish and shellfish may be responsible for at least a small proportion of the total number of *Salmonella* cases that occur each year in the United States. However, current data are inadequate to make any attempt at estimating attributable risk.

A number of years have passed since raw molluscs were associated with an outbreak of typhoid fever in the United States (Bryan, 1980; Rippey and Verber, 1988). One seafood-associated outbreak involving 25 cases was reported to CDC in 1973, but shellfish were not implicated as the vehicle. The last shellfish-associated typhoid outbreak reported in the NETSU data base occurred in 1954 (Rippey and Verber, 1988). The risk of typhoid fever associated with imported seafood may vary, depending on the rates of infection in the country of origin and the degree of pollution of harvest waters. Recent sporadic cases have been reported in consumers of raw shellfish in the Mediterranean area (Caredda et al., 1986; Torne et al., 1988) and, based on the incidence of typhoid fever in local populations, the risk associated with products imported from emerging nations would appear to be elevated (Parker, 1984).

Disease control

The microbial quality of harvest waters does not appear to be a good predictor of nontyphoidal *Salmonella* contamination, because oysters removed from closed and open beds had the same level of contamination (4%), and no correlation was observed between the presence of *E. coli* or fecal coliforms and *Salmonella* in finfish or shellfish (D'Aoust et al., 1980; Sobsey et al., 1980). Salmonellae do not appear to grow well in oysters during storage and are not selectively retained during depuration or relaying, so contaminated oysters can be purified (Son and Fleet, 1980). As with other pathogens, the risk of infection can also be minimized by ensuring that shellfish are cooked and handled properly.

Campylobacter jejuni

One outbreak of shellfish-associated campylobacteriosis has been reported to NETSU. *Campylobacter* has been isolated from fresh and coastal waters, and Sydney rock oysters and raw clams have been implicated as the source of human campylobacteriosis (Arumugaswamy and Proudford, 1987). The infectious dose for *C. jejuni* may be as low as 500-800 organisms, according to studies of volunteers drinking contaminated milk (Black et al., 1983).

The predominant symptoms of campylobacteriosis are diarrhea, abdominal pain, fever, nausea, and vomiting (Blaser and Reller, 1981). At the mild end of the spectrum, symptoms may last for only 24 hours; conversely, *C. jejuni* may also cause relapsing colitis that mimics ulcerative colitis or Crohn's disease. Most patients have a relatively mild illness and recover without sequelae.

Since the first outbreak of food-borne campylobacteriosis was reported to the CDC in 1978, state health departments have reported an additional 50 outbreaks, affecting a total of 1,717 persons. Nationwide laboratory-based *Campylobacter* surveillance was initiated in 1982. By 1986, 39 states were enrolled and 10,066 cases reported. One domestic shellfish-associated outbreak of campylobacteriosis was reported by NETSU between 1978 and 1987, an outbreak due to contaminated hard clams that affected 16 persons in New Jersey in 1980 (Tables 3-2 and 3-3). In addition, *Campylobacter* was suspected in several outbreaks reported to NETSU in which the etiological agent was listed as unknown (Rippey and Verber, 1988). Because outbreaks of campylobacteriosis have been associated with drinking contaminated surface water, freshwater species of fish and crustaceans may also pose a risk. Thus, although the risk of *Campylobacter* infection associated with eating raw shellfish appears low, the data are inadequate to make any assessment of attributable risk.

Control of *C. jejuni* is facilitated by the organism's lack of resistance to environmental factors (Franco, 1988). It is sensitive to drying, oxygen, low pH, and heat. Its sensitivity to sodium chloride limits the importance of marine species as vehicles of campylobacteriosis (Doyle and Roman, 1981, 1982). However, packaging in modified atmospheres and long-term storage at poorly controlled refrigeration temperatures may increase the risk of seafood-borne campylobacteriosis.

Escherichia coli

There are currently no data to indicate that seafood is an important source of *E. coli* infections in this country. Most infections by *E. coli* appear to be related to contamination of food or water, with some person-to-person amplification under unhygienic conditions (Gangarosa, 1978; Gross, 1983). Pathogenic strains (with the possible exception of enterohemorrhagic *E. coli*) are a much more important cause of diarrheal disease in the developing than in the developed world; thus, imported products may present greater risk than domestic seafood.

Data are inadequate to formulate any risk management plan for diarrheagenic *E. coli* – or to say whether such a plan is needed. Because *E. coli* is not selectively retained as gut flora in oysters, depuration or relaying may be helpful in reducing the risk of raw shellfish-associated human infections (Son and Fleet, 1980).

Yersinia enterocolitica

No outbreaks of seafood-related yersiniosis have been reported to CDC or NETSU; however, *Y. entercolitica* has been isolated from finfish, mussels, oysters, and other foods (Lee, 1977; Morris and Feeley, 1976). In a study of finfish and shellfish from Puget Sound, 3.8% of fresh seafood sampled in retail markets was positive for *Y. enterocolitica* (Abeyta, 1983). Bacteria have also been isolated from oysters (13%), shrimp (4%), and blue crabs (21%) harvested from coastal waters off Texas (Peixotto et al., 1979).

Y. enterocolitica is found worldwide, not only in feces but also in food, water, and the environment (Lewis and Chattopadhyay, 1986; Morris and Feeley, 1976). It is commonly found in specimens from swine slaughterhouses, and the consumption of raw sausage made from tonsil-containing pork scraps has been associated with disease (Tauxe et al., 1987). The significance of *Y. enterocolitica* as a fish- or shellfish-associated pathogen remains to be determined. Because it can grow at refrigeration temperature (i.e., is a psychrotroph), pathogenic strains that contaminate seafood could reach an infectious dose during extended storage. No specific surveillance system is in place at CDC for yersiniosis. From 1978 to 1987, state health departments reported four food-borne outbreaks of yersiniosis to CDC; however, none was associated with seafood. Likewise, NETSU reported no shellfish-associated outbreaks of yersiniosis between 1984 and 1988 (Rippey and Verber, 1988).

There are inadequate data to formulate a risk management plan for *Yersinia*. Because most environmental strains appear to be nonpathogenic, the ability to identify potential pathogens by testing isolates for pyrazinamidase activity and plasmid-associated traits such as calcium dependence, autoagglutination, or Congo Red binding will be needed in any control programs (Stern, 1982). Recent studies suggest that pathogenic strains can also be identified by using one of several DNA probes (Cornelis et al., 1987; Miliotis et al., 1989; Robins-Browne et al., 1989).

Listeria

Listeria monocytogenes is very widespread in nature and has been observed in the feces of man, farm animals, and wild birds. For example, up to 26% of sea gulls are carriers of the organism. It has also been isolated from pond-reared trout and crustaceans. *Listeria* is also widespread in the environment and can be found in soil, vegetation, crop debris, and of course, fecal material. It appears to be part of the saprophytic microflora of grass and other plants.

Listeria monocytogenes causes a wide range of diseases in humans, the most important of which are meningitis, septicemia, and perinatal disease (Lamont et al., 1988; Newman et al., 1979). Other manifestations include brain abscess, cranial nerve palsy, diffuse encephalitis, endocarditis, pneumonia, hepatitis, and arthritis. Aside from pregnancy, other predisposing conditions include immunosuppressive disorders and extremes of age, although invasive listeriosis occasionally occurs in otherwise healthy, nonpregnant persons.

Epidemiology and risk assessment

Contaminated food is becoming increasingly recognized as an important vehicle of *L. monocytogenes* (Ciesielski et al., 1987; McLauchlin, 1987). In recent years, *Listeria* has been implicated in outbreaks involving contaminated cabbage in Nova Scotia, fresh cheese in California, and pasteurized milk in Boston (Fleming et al., 1985; Linnan et al., 1988; Schlech et al., 1988). An outbreak of perinatal listeriosis was tentatively attributed to consumption of raw finfish and shellfish in New Zealand, although it is not clear whether patients consumed raw seafood more often than persons who did not become ill (Lennon et al., 1984). Catfish fillets are often contaminated with *L. monocytogenes* from their environment, but no human cases of listeriosis have been attributed to the consumption of catfish. It has been difficult to estimate the extent of listeriosis in the United States; prior to 1986, listeriosis was not reportable. A recent study identified 229 cases from the 34 million persons living in the study areas, providing minimum estimates of 1,600 culture-confirmed cases of listeriosis and 400 deaths per year for the United States (Schwartz et al., 1988). A case control study performed in conjunction with the active surveillance project identified consumption of raw hot dogs and undercooked chicken as risk factors for listeriosis; questions on seafood consumption were not included on the questionnaire (Schwartz et al., 1988).

An active listeriosis surveillance project being conducted by CDC and selected state and local health departments includes questions on seafood consumption by cases and controls, and may help define the relative importance of seafood in the epidemiology of human listeriosis. The FDA found *L. monocytogenes* in seven of eight categories of seafood cultured in fiscal year 1988 (FDA, 1988). Therefore, *L. monocytogenes* may be an unrecognized cause of food-borne enteric disease.

Disease control

   L. monocytogenes is not easily inactivated by environmental influences, such as sunlight or freezing and thawing. It is found in soil, vegetation, sewage, and streams. Its prolonged presence in soil and on vegetation does not appear to depend on continual reintroduction but, rather, results from *Listeria's* ability to exist as free-living forms on plants and in soil.

   Temperatures for the growth of *L. monocytogenes* range from 1 to 45°C, with the optimum between 30 and 37°C. At 4-5°C its growth rate is 50 times slower than at 35-37°C, but the organism can still grow. The optimum pH for growth is near neutral to slightly alkaline pH, with a range of 5.0-9.6. *L. monocytogenes* is quite tolerant to salt and low water activity. It can grow in the presence of 10% sodium chloride and can survive at 25% sodium chloride (Bryan, 1979; Medallion Laboratories, 1987; Smith et al., 1987).

   L. monocytogenes is fairly heat resistant, having $D_{150°F}$ values ranging from 12.8 seconds in skim milk to 17.6 seconds in cream (Bradshaw et al., 1985, 1987). Internalization in phagocytes did not significantly increase heat resistance (Bunning et al., 1986). Currently, FDA requires that *L. monocytogenes* not be present in ready-to-eat seafood products such as crabmeat or smoked fish. The restriction does not apply to raw products that will be cooked before eating.

Clostridium botulinum

   Human botulism is relatively rare in the United States. However, the control and prevention of botulism are some of the most important considerations in food processing. *C. botulinum* is widely distributed in soil and in the aquatic environment (Dolman, 1964; NFPA/CMI, 1984; Sakaguchi, 1979). Botulism is generally caused by consumption of food in which *C. botulinum* has grown and produced its toxin. The onset of symptoms of botulism usually occurs within 12-36 hours after ingestion of the food, with a range of 2 hours to 14 days. In general, shorter onset times result in more severe symptoms. Early signs may include gastroenteritis, weakness, lassitude, dizziness, and vertigo. These are followed by eye problems such as blurred vision, diplopia (double vision), dilated and fixed pupils, and impaired light reflex reaction (Sakaguchi, 1979). Fever is absent and mental processes are normal. The major cause of death is respiratory failure and airway obstruction. Because of the severity of the disease, most cases are likely to be reported, although milder cases may go undiagnosed.

   Botulism is among the most serious food-borne illnesses, with a mortality among untreated patients up to 70%. Competent medical treatment can reduce this mortality rate to approximately 15%. Fortunately, botulism is a rare disease, but cases due to consumption of seafoods were reported to CDC every year from 1978 to 1987 (Tables 3-2, 3-4, and 3-10). Nearly all of the cases in this period were caused by various ethnic foods prepared under conditions of poor general hygiene by individuals who did not understand the dangers of the procedure followed.

Epidemiology and risk assessment

C. botulinum is classified into toxin types A through G based on the serological specificity of the toxin produced. Types A, B, E, and F have been reported as causal agents in human food-borne botulism resulting from the consumption of foods in which bacteria have grown and produced toxins (Hauschild, 1989). Although type E is known as the "fish botulism organism," types A and B have been implicated in botulism caused by seafood (Hobbs, 1976). Nonproteolytic strains of types E and B are readily isolated from some marine sediments. Because *C. botulinum* produces heat-resistant spores and requires anaerobic conditions for growth, botulism has been most commonly associated with improperly processed canned food (usually home canned). Among fishery products, semipreserved items including smoked, salted, and fermented fish have been identified frequently as botulism vehicles (Eklund, 1982; Lynt et al., 1982).

The CDC reported 38 cases of fish-associated botulism from 1978 to 1987 (Tables 3-2, 3-4, and 3-10). Of these cases, 23 were from ethnic foods prepared and consumed in Alaska, and only one involved improperly home-canned seafood. All cases occurred in the home or as a result of eating homemade seafood products. No domestic case of botulism from commercially prepared seafoods has been reported in the United States in recent years, although canned salmon from Alaska has caused two incidents in Europe. This suggests that for most seafood consumers the present risk is negligibly low, but it is high for particular ethnic groups. During the 1960s, several outbreaks of botulism occurred from consumption of improperly processed smoked fish stored under conditions permitting the growth of *C. botulinum* (Pace and Krumbiegel, 1973). Improved processing methods have reduced this hazard, but safety still depends largely on low-temperature (<3°C) storage of the processed product.

Disease control

Botulism may be prevented by inhibiting growth of the organism or by destroying it in the food. Canning processes are generally designed to destroy the heat-resistant spores of *C. botulinum*, and this process is very effective. Type E spores of *C. botulinum* are more heat sensitive than type A or most type B, and pasteurization processes used in seafoods are generally effective in destroying most of them. Thus, hot smoking at 82.2°C can destroy 10,000,000 spores of type E in 30 minutes (Cann and Taylor, 1979), and processes used for crabs usually eliminate type E strains. However, as a safety factor it is necessary to store such heat-treated products below 3°C to prevent germination and growth of surviving spores and production of toxin. Processes such as heavy salting or drying, which reduce water activity below 0.975 (i.e., >5% salt), and pickling to reduce pH below 5.3 are effective in preventing growth of type E *C. botulinum*.

TABLE 3-10 Seafood-Related Botulism Outbreaks and Cases, 1978-1987

Year	State	Seafood	Location	Cases
1978	Puerto Rico	Home-marinated fish	Restaurant	3
1979	Alaska	"Other" fish	Home	1
1980	Alaska	"Other" fish	Home	1
1981	California	"Other" fish	Home	2
	Idaho	"Other" fish	Home	1
	Hawaii	"Other" fish	Home	1
1982	Alaska	Fermented fish eggs	Home	2
	Washington	Home-canned salmon	Home	1
1983	Alaska	Salmon eggs	Home	1
1984	Alaska	Stink eggs[a]	Home	3
1985	Alaska	Stink eggs	Home	8
	Alaska	Stink eggs	Home	1
	Alaska	Fish eggs	Home	1
	New Jersey	Kapchunka[b]	Home	2
1986	Alaska	Fermented fish heads	Unknown	3
	Alaska	Fermented fish eggs	Unknown	1
1987	Alaska	?[c]	?[d]	1
	New Jersey	?	?	5
Total				38

[a] Alaskan fermented fish eggs produced by burial in the ground.
[b] Dry salted fish.
[c] Unsure of vehicle.
[d] Unsure of location.
SOURCE: CDC (1989).

Light salting and other mild forms of processing are ineffective in destroying *C. botulinum* spores and, if followed by vacuum packing or controlled atmosphere storage, may actually promote growth of the organism by destroying competitive bacteria. It is essential that such products be held below 3.3°C and cooked prior to eating (Emodi and Lechowich, 1969).

Shigella

Seafood-associated outbreaks and cases of shigellosis have been reported to CDC and NETSU (Tables 3-2 – 3-4). The normal habitat for shigellae is the intestinal tract of humans and nonhuman primates and, rarely, other animals. Therefore, like typhoid fever, shigellosis usually originates with a human excreter (Blake and Feldman, 1986). Human volunteer studies indicate that ingestion of fewer than 100 shigellae can cause disease (DuPont et al., 1969). An estimated 300,000 cases of shigellosis occur in the United States each year, not all of which are food borne. Case fatality rates have been as high as 20% among hospitalized patients.

For the years 1978-1987, an average of seven food-borne outbreaks affecting a total of 573 persons were reported each year to the food-borne disease surveillance system (CDC, 1989). During this time, seven outbreaks involving 137 cases were seafood borne. Four of the seven outbreaks, involving 77 cases, were shellfish associated (Tables 3-2 – 3-4). During the same period, annual averages of 14,460 and 18,498 cases were reported through the laboratory-based *Shigella* surveillance system and the MMWR, respectively. In 1978-1987, NETSU reported 84 cases of shellfish-associated shigellosis, 11 in California and 26 in Arizona in 1979, and 47 in Texas in 1986 (Tables 3-2 and 3-3).

Most outbreaks of food-borne shigellosis result from contamination of raw or previously cooked foods during preparation by an infected food handler with poor personal hygiene. In view of the ability of *Shigella* to survive in seafood, the risk of seafood as a vehicle of shigellosis should parallel that of other foods.

Although shigellae are readily killed by heat and low pH, under certain conditions they can survive for some time outside the host (Flowers, 1988b). Taylor and Nakamura (1964) reported that *S. sonnei* and *S. flexneri* could survive at 25°C in clams for more than 50 days and in oysters for more than 30 days. Because of the low infectious dose, consumption of shellfish harvested from contaminated waters can result in disease.

Staphylococcus aureus

S. aureus is a common human-associated bacterium. It is one of the most frequent causes of food poisoning in the United States and is often introduced during food preparation. The human carrier rate is 6-60%, with an average of 25-30% of the population being positive for enterotoxin-producing strains. The illness is an intoxication that results from consuming food in which the bacteria has grown and produced toxin. The bacterial population must reach high levels (usually >100,000 organisms per gram) for enough toxin to be accumulated and illness to result.

The main reservoir for *S. aureus* is human nasal passages, but it is also found on skin, hands, wounds, and cutaneous abscesses. Additionally, it can be isolated from air, dust, floors, and other environmental surfaces, and it survives well in the environment. *S. aureus* is frequently isolated from seafoods, especially those that are handled during processing.

The CDC reported two seafood-associated outbreaks of *S. aureus* involving 12 cases between 1978 and 1987 (Table 3-2). One of these outbreaks, which involved nine cases, was shellfish associated (Table 3-3). The other outbreak, involving three cases, was associated with other seafood products (Table 3-4). The outbreaks were attributed to infected food handlers (CDC, 1989).

The conditions that affect the growth of *S. aureus* are often quite different from those for toxin production. In general, the relative ranges for toxin production are narrower than those for growth. For example, the temperature range for growth of

S. aureus is 7-45°C, with an optimum of 35-37°C. Toxin production is maximum at the optimum, but very little toxin is produced at lower temperatures (<20°C). The pH range for growth of the organism is 4.5-9.3, but enterotoxin production is limited to pH 5.1-9. The optimum pH for both growth and toxin production is near neutral. The water activity (partial pressure of water in a food, divided by the partial pressure of pure water at the same temperature) minima for growth and toxin production differ, being 0.85 and 0.93, respectively (Banwart, 1989).

Good sanitary measures are necessary to prevent the contamination of seafood products with *S. aureus* because the enterotoxins are heat resistant and can withstand temperatures above boiling for long periods of time (Bergdoll, 1979). Because its presence is nearly unavoidable in products handled by humans, many states have suggested guidelines for *S. aureus*. One hundred organisms per gram is the most common upper limit in these guidelines. The symptoms of *S. aureus* food poisoning include nausea, vomiting, abdominal cramps, and diarrhea. The onset time for symptoms averages 2-4 hours but may range from 0.5 to 24 hours. The illness usually lasts only 1-2 days (Bergdoll, 1979; Jay, 1986).

Viral Pathogens

To prevent and control hepatitis A virus in processing, distribution, and preparation of foods, food handlers should be carefully educated and trained for good hygienic practices, particularly hand washing and sanitizing following defecation.

Hepatitis A virus (HAV) is a pathogen mainly transmitted by unsanitary food preparation practices. Each year 20,000 to 30,000 cases of hepatitis A are reported to the CDC. Of these cases, approximately 140 are directly attributable to contaminated foods (0.5% of the total). From 1978-1987 only two fish-associated HAV outbreaks involving a total of 92 cases were reported to CDC, 7 cases of HAV in 1980 due to tuna served in the home and 85 cases of HAV from tuna salad in a New York restaurant (Tables 3-2–3-4). There are no documented cases of transmission of human enteric viruses other than hepatitis A from seafood products contaminated at the processing, distribution, or food handling level (Bryan, 1986; CDC, 1981a-c, 1983a,b, 1984, 1985, 1989; Rippey and Verber, 1988). Viruses do not replicate in seafood products, so temperature abuse is not a factor. However, handling of products by a person infected with enteric viruses could result in transmission by the fecal-oral route if poor personal hygiene is allowed (Cliver, 1988; Matches and Abeyta, 1983).

Impact of Processing Technology

Heat Treatment

Heat treatment is frequently defined in terms of D- and F-values, with subscripts indicating temperature: D is the number of minutes at the indicated temperature necessary to reduce a microbial population by 90%, and F is the lethality of a process expressed as minutes at the indicated temperature. A third term Z is the temperature difference associated with a tenfold difference in killing rate. Whereas achievement of commercial sterility (as in canned fish) generally requires a 12 x D treatment, pasteurization may require lesser treatment (commonly 4-6D).

Nearly all canned seafoods available to the U.S. consumer are fully processed, commercially sterile products that are shelf stable in their original containers. Their production is controlled by FDA or state agencies working with FDA and following a Hazard Analysis Critical Control Point (HACCP) system that has proved very effective. Because fish and shellfish are low-acid foods, the major safety concern involves *Clostridium botulinum* whose spores are extremely heat resistant. Processors must deliver a treatment of 12D or greater, which is ensured by requiring the regulating agency's approval of process regimes and strict recordkeeping by the companies.

No cases of botulism from commercially canned seafoods have occurred in the United States in recent years. A single outbreak in Europe due to Alaska canned salmon was shown to result from improperly functioning equipment related to the use of collapsed three-piece cans. This problem has been resolved by improved maintenance and quality assurance programs and by widespread adoption of two-piece extruded cans (NFPA/CMI, 1984; Thompson, 1982).

For equal safety, imported fully processed canned seafood products must be made by processes that meet domestic FDA requirements, including process approval, adequate recordkeeping, and employment of certified retort/operator supervisors.

Semiconserved canned fishery products may contain living microorganisms because they receive milder heat treatment in pasteurization (Delmore and Crisley, 1979; Eklund, 1982; Lerke and Farber, 1971). These products, which are frequently imported, depend on acidification, use of salt, and storage at reduced temperature for their stability and are generally marketed as delicatessen items kept under refrigeration.

Pasteurization is a term that refers to a mild heating process, usually below 100°C. By definition, the term indicates that the product is not sterile and therefore may continue to harbor microorganisms. Consequently, pasteurized products must be continuously refrigerated so that surviving microorganisms will not multiply too rapidly, shortening the product's anticipated shelf life and introducing hazards. The initial microbial population greatly affects the efficiency of the process. The most important application of pasteurization in the seafood industry is the treatment of pickled crabmeat, which is packed, sealed in cans, and held under refrigeration after treatment. The National Blue Crab Industry Association has recommended a national standard that effectively provides for the destruction of potentially hazardous bacteria that could grow during refrigerator storage. The process provides the equivalent of $F_{85°C}$ in excess of 31 minutes (NBCIA, 1984).

Pasteurization has been proposed for other products including shrimp (Lerke and Farber, 1971), crawfish, and smoked fish (Eklund et al., 1988). Since the FDA dropped the GMP regulations on the processing of smoked fish, there has been increasing concern regarding the potential for a botulism outbreak associated with smoked fish. The pasteurization process described by Eklund et al. (1988) has the potential to minimize the concerns associated with this product. Pasteurization was more effective for smoked fillets and steaks than for dressed fish.

Sous vide products are minimally processed foods, including seafood, that are being introduced into the U.S. market. The products are portion controlled, vacuum packaged in plastic pouches or rigid containers that are highly impermeable to oxygen and moisture, and then cooked in either a water bath or a high-humidity oven. Cooking temperatures for *sous vide* are usually far lower than those associated with pasteurization. Cooking may involve temperatures close to the desired maximum internal temperature for the product, and thus require a long cooking time, or products may be cooked quickly at temperatures considerably above the desired internal maximum. In either case, the principles that apply to pasteurization also apply to this processing technology. Products should be cooked to a desired *F*-value and cooled quickly.

The safety of *sous vide* products has been questioned because they are processed only minimally and do not contain preservatives to prevent microbial growth. Furthermore, the cooking process does not eliminate nonproteolytic types of *C. botulinum*, and there is some question as to whether it may allow other organisms such as *Listeria* to survive. The shelf life and safety of these products depend solely on refrigeration; therefore, it is critical that psychrotrophic pathogens not survive. In the United States, these items are presented as refrigerated, ready-to-eat, or heat-and-serve products. They are produced under controlled conditions, and caution is exercised during distribution. As of late 1989, the products were being sold only to food service establishments and were not being sold retail. This will probably change in the near future as demand increases. The FDA has limited the use of *sous vide* products to approved food processing operations and currently does not allow production at retail establishments such as grocery stores. It is important that they be produced under an approved HACCP program and that the principles of pasteurization be understood and applied to their production.

Modified Atmospheres and Vacuum Packaging

Modified atmosphere packaging (MAP) is defined as a process in which air is removed and replaced with other gases, usually carbon dioxide (CO_2) or a mixture of CO_2 and other gases. The atmosphere in the package will change over time because of microbial respiration and permeability characteristics of the packaging material. Controlled atmosphere packaging (CAP) is like MAP, except that the atmosphere is monitored and kept constant. For vacuum packaging, air is removed without replacement. It is well established that modified atmosphere (MA) storage of seafood products will extend the shelf life considerably by inhibiting the normal psychrotrophic microflora and reducing the spoilage rate. There is concern about the potential growth and toxin production of nonproteolytic types of *C. botulinum* (Garcia et al., 1987). It has been demonstrated that MA packaging or vacuum packaging coupled with temperature abuse can create conditions in which toxin production occurs before sensorially detected deterioration (Genigeorgis, 1985; Post et al., 1985). The National Marine Fisheries Service (NMFS) recommends (but does not require) that fisheries products not be MA or vacuum packaged if they are to be stored under refrigeration (Post et al., 1985). Where vacuum or MA packaging is used, NMFS has set guidelines (NOAA, 1990).

PUBLIC HEALTH RISK ASSESSMENT

Available epidemiologic data are inadequate to permit quantitative assessment of the risk of illness due to infectious agents acquired by eating seafood. However, it is possible to develop some qualitative data on risk.

Risk Assessment

Hazard Identification

A variety of seafood-associated bacterial, viral, and parasitic agents cause illness in humans. These agents can generally be divided into three groups: (1) those that are known to cause disease in healthy adults; (2) those that usually do not cause disease in healthy adults but can cause illness in special population groups (children, immunosuppressed patients); and (3) those that are of uncertain pathogenicity for humans (Table 3-1). It should be kept in mind that these categories are not absolute and that agents could be moved from one category to another in response to new information and changing conditions. Pathogens such as *Salmonella, V. parahaemolyticus,* or Norwalk virus cause disease in normal, healthy hosts; however, the illness in normal hosts is generally mild and self-limited. In contrast, when persons who are immunocompromised or otherwise at high risk are infected, severe, life-threatening illness may occur (e.g., *V. vulnificus*).

Dose-Response Assessment

Viral agents such as Norwalk and some bacterial agents such as *Shigella* require a very low infectious dose to cause illness (ca. 10^2 CFU for *Shigella* and theoretically one infectious viral particle for Norwalk). These agents are often transmitted by direct fecal-oral contamination and may pose a problem if they are allowed to contaminate food items after processing. Other bacteria generally require a higher infectious dose, which may be reached by time/temperature abuse of food products. Unfortunately, in the absence of volunteer studies the infectious doses for many of the viral and bacterial pathogens discussed are unknown; and even if such studies were carried out, it could not be proved that study conditions duplicate the wide range of human responses to natural exposure. However, it is probably accurate to say that the risk of infection increases with increased dose for most pathogens and that the dose depends to a large degree on the handling of the product after harvest, during processing, and in preparation.

Exposure Assessment

The risk of exposure is dependent on a number of variables, including the type of seafood, the location, the water quality at harvest, and the way the product is handled after harvest. Risks are markedly different for each pathogen and each product, making it difficult to generalize about overall risk of exposure to infectious agents or to establish uniform water quality or product safety standards.

Infections with *Vibrio* species and other naturally occurring marine bacteria are generally associated with eating shellfish. Their numbers are dependent on salinity, temperature, and a variety of other factors, with temperature (>20°C) probably being the most important variable (Baross and Liston, 1970).

Of the enteric viruses, only hepatitis A virus, Norwalk virus, Snow Mountain agent, caliciviruses, astroviruses, NANB enteral hepatitis, and unspecified hepatitis have been documented to cause seafood-associated illness. With the exception of HAV contamination of ready-to-eat seafoods by food handlers, all reported cases of seafood-associated viral infections have been from the consumption of raw or improperly cooked molluscan shellfish (Bryan, 1986; CDC, 1989; Cliver, 1988; Gerba, 1988; Richards, 1985, 1987; Rippey and Verber, 1988). Human enteric viruses from naturally occurring contamination have been isolated in field studies only from molluscan shellfish and from blue crabs collected at a sludge dump in the North Atlantic. Other marine animals, including lobsters, sandworms, detrital feeding fish, and conch, have been shown to take up enteric viruses seeded into marine waters experimentally, but this has not been reported from field studies to occur naturally. These viruses are very species specific and even receptor specific for certain cells. Once released into the marine environment, their survival and persistence are based on many factors, including temperature, salinity, ultraviolet inactivation from sunlight, and the presence of organic solids or sediments. Of these factors, the most important appears to be a temperature below 10°C and the protective action of organic material (Gerba, 1988).

Risk Characterization

Raw or undercooked shellfish appear to carry a higher risk of disease than do other types of seafood, particularly because such shellfish constitute less than 0.1% of the seafood consumed in the United States but are responsible for a large proportion of the cases reported (CDC, 1989; Rippey and Verber, 1988).

Available surveillance data from both CDC and NETSU (Tables 3-2 – 3-4) and clinicopathophysiologic studies suggest that food-borne diseases due to unknown etiologies, unspecified (i.e., unknown etiology) hepatitis, and certain *Vibrio* species (*V. parahaemolyticus, V. vulnificus,* non-O1 *V. cholerae*) represent the greatest risk for persons consuming raw molluscan shellfish.

The largest number of reported seafood-associated illnesses have unknown etiologies (Table 3-2 – 3-4) (CDC, 1989; Rippey and Verber, 1988). Although these are probably not all of microbiological etiology, many have onset periods and symptoms consistent with the clinical pathology of Norwalk and related viruses. However, both the CDC and the NETSU data bases report relatively few cases of confirmed Norwalk or related viral infections associated with shellfish (Tables 3-2 and 3-3) because only a few specialized laboratories are able to serologically diagnose infections with Norwalk, Snow Mountain, and related viruses. Despite the low number of documented cases of Norwalk and Norwalk-like agents in shellfish, recent evidence suggests that shellfish-associated infections with these agents occur more frequently than identified (Morse et al., 1986) and that they may ultimately be the most common shellfish-associated pathogens, especially in coldwater clams.

The risk of infection by bacterial pathogens appears to be lower than that due to viruses. Although data are limited, the incidence of infection with the more common *Vibrio* species in coastal states (where shellfish consumption is probably highest) is in the range of 0.5-1.0 case/100,000 population/year (Hoge et al., 1989). Although cases of *V. vulnificus* associated with shellfish are reported with approximately the same frequency as *V. parahaemolyticus* and non-O1 *V. cholerae*, the severity of the infection and the high mortality rate in populations at risk elevate the importance of the former as a seafood-associated pathogen (Tables 3-2, 3-3, 3-6, and 3-7). Shellfish-associated infections due to *Salmonella* and *Shigella* are approximately the same, based on CDC surveillance data (Tables 3-2–3-4) (CDC, 1989). However, cases due to these latter agents are probably underdiagnosed because the vehicle for the vast majority of cases caused by these agents is never identified.

Parasitic infections are less common than bacterial and viral infections in the United States, with *Anisakis simplex* and cestodes having the greatest public health significance (Table 3-2). In general, parasitic infections are concentrated in certain ethnic groups that favor the consumption of raw or partially cooked seafood from "high-risk" geographic areas.

Risk Management

Control of the risk of infectious seafood-borne disease is generally achieved by (1) excluding the agents from food, (2) controlling their growth in food, or (3) destroying them. All three methods depend to some extent on the ability to detect the occurrence of these microorganisms and to follow procedures that achieve one or more of the objectives listed.

Pathogens in Marine or Freshwater Environments

Risks associated with Vibrionaceae can be addressed at several levels. Because these organisms are a "natural" part of the bacterial flora of bays and estuaries, their presence cannot be predicted by standard indicators such as fecal coliform counts. However, their occurrence is dependent on environmental conditions (water temperature, salinity), with counts generally peaking in the late summer and early fall. The risk of infection from Vibrionaceae could be minimized by restricting summer harvesting of oysters. More realistically, a system for monitoring shellfish and harvest waters for these organisms could be established, analogous to the current system for monitoring fecal coliforms. Rapid diagnostic techniques for identification of pathogenic vibrios are available or are being developed (Kaper et al., 1988), making such a system technically possible. Monitoring data would provide an index to times when the risk of exposure to *Vibrio* is greatest and could serve as an adjunct to other indicators for the management of harvest waters.

Efforts can also be directed toward reducing or eliminating organisms present in shellfish after harvest. The self-cleansing of some enteric viruses and marine vibrios may not proceed at the same rate as for enteric bacteria and indicators, which suggests that current techniques for depuration may be of little benefit in limiting contamination with Vibrionaceae. New technology-enhanced depuration must be developed for eliminating naturally occurring vibrios (Rodrick, 1990). Low-dose gamma irradiation of live shellstock and fresh or frozen seafood products has also been shown to be an effective means of eliminating *Vibrio* species (Giddings, 1984). Dose levels of 1.0 kilogray (kGy) (100,000 rads) to 1.5 kGy (150,000 rads) will reduce high levels (10^6) of seeded *Vibrio* spp. in live shellstock oysters to undetectable levels. The LD_{50} of live shellstock oysters is 2.25 kGy (Kilgen et al., 1988). Sensory evaluation shows no significant organoleptic differences in shellstock oysters treated with 1.5-kGy gamma irradiation (Kilgen et al., 1988). Gulf Coast summer oysters naturally infected with *V.*

vulnificus levels of 10^4 organisms per gram of oyster meat also had no detectable *V. vulnificus* levels after gamma irradiation of 1.0 kGy (M. Kilgen and M. Cole, Nicholls State University, Thibodeaux, La., personal communication, 1990).

Although data on human infectious dosages are not available for all of the Vibrionaceae, it is likely that the risk of infection can also be reduced by limiting the multiplication of organisms during handling and processing. Recent studies demonstrate that there can be a striking increase in bacterial counts (including counts of *Vibrio* species) when shellfish are left unrefrigerated on the decks of boats during warm summer days (Cook and Ruple, 1989). Similarly, bacterial counts can increase if shellfish are not adequately refrigerated during transportation to plants and subsequent distribution. Some processors are currently using rapid cool-down techniques to minimize these risks; such techniques need to be further evaluated, and if shown to be effective, their implementation should be encouraged.

Finally, the consumer can play an important role in minimizing risks. Consumers should be educated about the need for proper refrigeration of fish and shellfish, and the dangers of cross-contamination. They should be advised about the risks of eating raw shellfish. Of particular concern are persons who are at high risk for septicemia due to *V. vulnificus* (persons who are cirrhotic, who have hemochromatosis, or who are in some way immunocompromised) (Tables 3-6 and 3-7). Such persons must not eat raw or undercooked shellfish.

With the development of gene probes amplified by polymerase chain reaction and other rapid, new diagnostic techniques, shellfish can be screened for the presence of some potentially pathogenic *Vibrio* species (Kaper et al., 1988). These probes could theoretically be used as part of a national monitoring system for shellfish. However, further studies are required to determine the ways in which data of this type can be used to protect the public health.

The risk of parasitic infection depends largely on the species of fish and shellfish and the area from which they are harvested. In general, prevention of infection is dependent on limiting the harvesting of seafood from high-risk areas; informing sports fishers of regionally important risks associated with certain species and the availability of alternate control strategies (e.g., freezing fish before raw consumption); and educating consumers on the importance of proper cooking of fish and shellfish.

Some parasitic agents, such as the anisakids, are detectable by visual inspection techniques. However, these are probably the only infectious agents that would be detected by such a system, and the very low frequency of reported disease due to these agents does not justify using public resources specifically to identify parasites in seafood.

Pathogens Associated with Pollution

Control of pollution-associated agents generally translates into identifying sewage contamination of harvest areas. The only seafood products that are regulated by microbiological indicator standards for growing water quality are molluscan shellfish. The sanitary quality of shellfish is based on an allowable standard of 14 most probable number (MPN) fecal coliforms per 100 milliliters (mL) of growing water, with not more than 10% exceeding 43 MPN fecal coliforms/100 mL (FDA, 1989a). The National Shellfish Sanitation Program (NSSP) manual of operations also requires a sanitary survey of oyster growing estuaries prior to approval for shellfishing, relaying, or depuration (FDA, 1989a). The revised NSSP recommendations (FDA, 1989b) for monitoring interstate shellfish shipments state that:

> Proper growing area classification and strict adherence to good manufacturing practices (GMP's) are the principal considerations for assuring the safety of shellfish. The bacteriological market guideline of 230 MPN fecal coliforms/100 g [grams] oyster meat should no longer be used as the primary basis for embargoing or destroying shellfish shipments. Shellstock shipments should be monitored within 24 hours of entering the state, and should be considered acceptable if: shipments are properly identified (by tag, bill of lading or label) and cooled, shellstock to 50°F or less, and shucked product to 45°F or less, and if they are in compliance with all other NSSP conditions of shipment. Shellfish should be rejected if shipments are not properly identified, are inadequately cooled (shellstock shipments exceeding 60°F and shucked product shipments exceeding 50°F), or other conditions exist, e.g. decomposition and/or adulteration with poisonous and deleterious substances. Shellfish received under conditions between acceptance and rejection criteria could be examined bacteriologically, and the following guidelines applied for acceptance: fecal coliform density of not more than 230 MPN/100 g and aerobic plate count (APC) of not more than 500,000/g.

The fecal coliform standard in growing waters and the guidelines for meats were established to prevent sewage contamination of shellfish that may be consumed raw. Fecal coliforms are present in high numbers in untreated sewage and are considered "indicators" of the possible bacterial and viral human enteric pathogens that may also be found in feces. The allowable numbers of fecal coliforms in shellfish growing waters were based on the relationship between total coliform counts and the number of *Salmonella typhi* present during a typhoid fever epidemic in the 1920s (FDA, 1989a). A conference was called in 1925 to establish the basic concept of a national program for sanitary control of the molluscan shellfish industry. The first growing water standard was 70 MPN/100 mL total coliforms with no more than 10% of samples exceeding 230 MPN total coliforms/100 mL and freedom from direct contamination with fresh raw sewage. This indicator standard was established through epidemiological investigations from 1914 to 1925 by the states and the Public Health Service. It was believed at this time that typhoid fever would not normally be attributed to shellfish harvested from water in which "not more than 50 percent of the 1 cc [cubic centimeter] portions of water examined were positive for coliforms" (FDA, 1989a). This equated to 70 MPN total coliforms/100 mL, which is equivalent to the fecal material from one person diluted in 8 million cubic feet of coliform-free water. Later studies concluded that fecal coliforms were more accurate indicators of fecal contamination than total coliforms, and the allowable numbers were extrapolated to the current standard of 14 MPN fecal coliforms/100mL growing water, with no more than 10% of samples exceeding 43 MPN fecal coliforms/100 mL (FDA, 1989a). However, even the more specific fecal coliform indicator of contamination in water and seafood has been questioned (Cole et al., 1986; Elliot and Colwell, 1985; Kilgen et al., 1988; Matches and Abeyta, 1983).

TABLE 3-11   State and Federal Microbiological Standards and Guidelines

FDA	Seafood Products	Total Aerobic Plate Count	Coliform	*Escherichia coli*	*Salmonella*	Coagulase+ *Staphylococcus aureus*
Administrative guidelines	Clams, mussels oysters (fresh or frozen)	500,000/g	-	230/100 g	-	-
Compliance policy guidelines	Crabmeat (fresh or frozen)	No standard	-	3.6/g	-	-
	Langostinos (frozen, cooked)	100,000/g	20/g	3.6/g	-	3.6/g
Import alert	Seafood	-	-	-	0	-

SOURCE: Martin and Pitts (1989).

According to Garrett (1988), the United States has only three types of general regulatory microbiological indicator criteria for other seafoods:

1. Microbiological standards

   ● FDA's GMP requirement that thermally processed low-acid foods packaged in hermetically sealed containers be commercially sterile
   ● FDA's microbiological standards for "approved," "conditionally approved," "restricted," or "prohibited" molluscan shellfish growing waters, used in conjunction with a sanitary survey as described above

2. Microbiological guidelines

   ● Microbiological criteria for crabmeat and langostinos
   ● Defect action levels for raw breaded shrimp plants
   ● Bacteriological market guidelines for molluscan shellfish (revised to GMPs for proper refrigeration, handling, and tagging in 1989) (FDA, 1989b)

3. Microbiological specifications

   ● Microbiological acceptance criteria contained in federal specifications for the procurement of fish and frozen shelled oysters

The National Fisheries Institute published a draft *Handbook of State and Federal Microbiological Standards and Guidelines* (Table 3-11) (Martin and Pitts, 1989).

The basic requirements for an ideal indicator have been discussed at length (Elliot and Colwell, 1985). Some of the characteristics necessary for an indicator to accurately predict the presence of sewage-associated pathogens include:

1. specificity for the source of the pathogens (i.e., raw sewage),
2. presence in feces in sufficiently high concentrations to allow sensitivity of detection,
3. persistence in the aquatic environment at least as long as the pathogens,
4. absence of growth in the aquatic environment, and
5. availability of inexpensive methods for detection and quantification.

A number of indicator organisms have been proposed in the past for detection of fecal pollution in fresh, brackish, estuarine, and seawaters. However, no single indicator organism exists for determination of public health risk in waters or seafood (Elliot and Colwell, 1985). Some of the problems encountered with the current fecal coliform indicator standard in growing waters and the guideline for oyster meat include the following:

1. Non-*Escherichia coli* fecal coliforms and even non-sewage-related bacteria may predominate in the fecal coliform population analyzed by methods approved by the American Public Health Association (APHA, 1985a,b). These non-*E. coli* fecal coliforms can be found in shellfish, sediments, and the water column, especially at warm temperatures (Cole et al., 1986; FDA, 1989b; Kilgen et al., 1988; Paille et al., 1987). Characterization of the non-*E. coli* fecal coliform population in Louisiana oysters showed that in the warm months, *Klebsiella pneumoniae* isolates accounted for 86% of the non-*E. coli* fecal coliforms and often outnumbered *E. coli* by 1,000 to 1 (Paille et al., 1987). These *Klebsiella* oyster isolates were further characterized and compared with *K. pneumoniae* human clinical isolates by electron microscopy, guanine:cytosine ratios, and antibiotic resistance. The results suggested that *K. pneumoniae* isolates from oysters were of environmental, not sewage, origin. Their seasonal variation was typical of environmental bacteria, and they did not exhibit the multiple antibiotic resistance characteristic of the clinical strains. Similar studies by the FDA agreed that Gulf of Mexico Coast oysters harvested from approved growing waters in summer months may contain excessively high levels of non-*E. coli* fecal coliforms and not represent an excessive health hazard (FDA, 1989a). It was concluded that fecal coliforms may not be a reliable indicator of fecal contamination in Gulf Coast oysters, especially in summer months, and that *E. coli* would be a better indicator for an oyster meat guideline (FDA, 1989b; Kilgen et al., 1988; Paille et al., 1987). This resulted in the adoption of a one-year interim oyster meat guideline of 230 MPN *E. coli*/100 g instead of 230 MPN fecal coliforms/100 g by the Interstate Shellfish Sanitation Conference (ISSC) in 1983. This is still recommended in the NSSP operations manual for shellfish from approved growing waters with excessively high fecal coliform indicator levels, but it is not an officially adopted guideline (FDA, 1989b).

2. The fecal coliform indicator for waters does not indicate the presence of non-sewage-related naturally occurring aquatic bacterial pathogens, such as Vibrionaceae (Elliot and Colwell, 1985; Matches and Abeyta, 1983; Tamplin et al., 1982).

3. The fecal coliform indicator does not correlate with the presence of human enteric viruses, which are the pathogens most commonly associated with sewage contamination of waters and seafood (Cole et al., 1986; Elliot and Colwell, 1985; Gerba, 1988; Kilgen et al., 1988; Richards, 1985, 1987; Sobsey, 1980).

The human enteric pathogens of main concern from sewage contamination are now enterovirus type 72 (hepatitis type A) and Norwalk or Norwalk-like gastroenteritis viruses. However, current data also indicate that a constant and predictable relationship does not exist among fecal coliform indicators, *E. coli* and enteric viruses in estuarine waters and shellfish.

The public health risk associated with fecal material from animal sources versus human sources is also in question. The most productive shellfish growing estuaries are often those most subject to rainfall runoff from animal non-point sources. Extensive closures due to high fecal coliform indicator counts from non-point animal sources have been identified as one of the major concerns of state regulatory agencies and industry members from coastal areas; a great deal of research is required to assess human health risks from wild and domestic animal runoff (Elliot and Colwell, 1985; Kilgen, 1989). Terrestrial mammals carry bacterial species pathogenic to humans; however, these have generally not been associated with shellfish-borne illnesses. Rather, sewage-associated human illnesses appear most frequently to have a viral etiology, and viruses tend to be species specific. Therefore, an indicator of human enteric viruses in water and in seafoods is needed. Some indicators that have been proposed include poliovirus type 1, enterococci, *E. coli,* coliphages, fecal streptococci, *Clostridium perfringens, Pseudomonas aeruginosa, Bifidobacterium* species, *Rhodococcus* species, *Streptococcus bovis, Bacteroides* phages, and F+ phages (Elliot and Colwell, 1985; Kilgen, 1989; Richards, 1985). None of the suggested indicators appears to be an adequate indicator of human health risk from enteric virus pathogens in seafoods or water, and none of them would predict the presence of naturally occurring bacterial pathogens such as the Vibrionaceae. This is an area for vital research.

Depuration (controlled purification) and relaying have been used successfully to remove enteric bacterial pathogens and indicators from molluscan shellfish (Richards, 1988). However, the self-cleansing of some enteric viruses and marine vibrios may not proceed at the same rate as for enteric bacteria. Hepatitis A virus persists far longer in oysters and clams than *E. coli* or poliovirus (Sobsey, 1990). Improperly depurated shellfish have been responsible for outbreaks due to enteric viruses (Richards, 1988). Inasmuch as marine vibrios may also be present far longer than standard indicators and can multiply quickly at elevated temperatures, immunocompromised individuals should not assume that depurated shellfish are safe to consume. More research is needed both to develop indicators of adequate viral depuration and to develop enhanced depuration technology to remove naturally occurring vibrios (Rodrick, 1990).

Pathogens Associated with Processing and Distribution

Methods involved in processing can increase or decrease bacterial populations present in seafood. Processing methods are amenable to monitoring by an HACCP system. However, good data are not always available to justify currently used endpoints. Further research is needed to determine the appropriateness of current quality control criteria and to demonstrate that the use of these criteria results in a decrease in the incidence of human disease.

The major problem associated with distribution of seafood products is time/temperature abuse. Some pathogenic microorganisms can grow to dangerous numbers when exposed to prolonged temperature abuse. A bacterium that may double every 30 minutes at 25°C may require 1,200 minutes at 1°C. Therefore, it is very important that seafoods be cooled quickly to achieve maximum shelf life and to maintain safety. Only four bacterial pathogens (*Listeria monocytogenes, Yersinia enterocolitica, Aeromonas hydrophila,* and nonproteolytic *Clostridium botulinum* types E, B, and F) are considered psychrotrophs and are capable of growing at refrigeration temperatures (<4°C). Of the organisms described, only the nonproteolytic *C. botulinum* types have been definitely implicated in seafood-related illness. Time/temperature abuse during transportation was the major factor in outbreaks in the 1960s when smoked fish was transported unrefrigerated from the Great Lakes to distant markets (Pace and Krumbiegel, 1973).

Other bacterial pathogens that can grow at near-refrigeration temperatures (between 4 and 10°C) include enteropathogenic *E. coli, Staphylococcus aureus,* salmonellae, and *Vibrio parahaemolyticus.* These microorganisms may become a problem during transportation if seafoods are not cooled properly at any time after harvest.

Proper cooling of seafoods for transportation is critical for safety. The seafood must be cooled before being placed in the distribution system. Most refrigerated or frozen product transport systems are designed only to maintain a predetermined temperature and do not have the capacity to reduce the temperature of the product significantly. Cooling can be a lengthy process with large lots of fish, and temperatures can remain in the above 10°C range for many hours, permitting the growth of potentially hazardous bacteria if the warm product is loaded into transport containers. Chilled product should be loaded at internal temperatures below 4°C and frozen products at or below −18°C.

Imports

A large part of imported seafood originates in countries with a much higher incidence of enteric disease and lower levels of hygiene and sanitation than the United States. Therefore, seafoods from these countries could be contaminated more frequently or at a higher level with disease-producing organisms than our domestic fisheries product. It is important that the same principles of seafood-borne disease control be applied to these products as to domestically produced seafoods, preferably through an equivalent inspection system. This will require intelligent assessment of the microbiological hazards likely to be particularly troublesome in different exporting countries and the risks associated with in-country handling and processing practices. Because of the high risks associated with raw molluscan shellfish, the importation of shellfish for raw consumption should be prohibited unless standards for the microbial quality of harvest waters and postharvest processing in the exporting country are fully equivalent to those in the United States.

Future Risk

The fishing industry is in a period of rapid and profound change as a result of depletion of traditional stocks, development of domestic fisheries in Third World countries, exploitation of new fish resources, technological innovation, and changing consumer demands and expectations. The changes have had both beneficial and potentially adverse effects on microbiological risk to the final consumer of seafoods. Changes in canning technology, process recording equipment, temperature control, and freezing methods (leading to rapid cooling and freezing of much seafood at the point of capture) have undoubtedly improved microbiological safety for many seafood products, although this has not been definitively demonstrated. The public demand for lightly cooked and "fresh"-type products, which is satisfied by vacuum packaging and relatively long-term holding, can lead to potentially more hazardous products as discussed in relation to the *sous vide* process.

Control of temperature during the handling and storage of seafoods is widely recognized as critical for microbiological safety, but newer customer presentation systems require more stringent temperature control than those to which the industry has become accustomed. Safe storage of lightly cooked vacuum packaged products for more than a few hours requires temperatures consistently below 3°C and probably nearer to 0°C if they are to be stored for more than a few days (Post et al., 1985). These stringent conditions are necessary to prevent the growth of *Clostridium botulinum* type E, psychrotrophic pathogens such as *Listeria* and *Yersinia,* and possibly opportunistic pathogens such as *Aeromonas.*

The new seafood analogue products, which are widely used as a substitute for crab and other expensive species in seafood salads or other dishes, are manufactured from Alaskan pollock and a few other fish species. These products contain other food components such as sugars, emulsifiers, and egg white and are prepared by processes that remove most of the soluble "fishy" components from the raw material. They are heat treated so that most of the naturally present bacteria are destroyed. This provides a long shelf life under good storage conditions. These virtually sterile products provide an excellent growth medium for contaminant bacteria and do not develop the characteristically unpleasant odors associated with "bad" fish, which most consumers use as a warning not to eat the product. Therefore, care must be taken to avoid cross-contamination and warming of such products.

Ethnic foods and regional considerations

The population of the United States includes many ethnic groups with different food preferences. In coastal regions this may be reflected in the patterns of fish and shellfish consumption. From a microbiological standpoint, the most important ethnic practices involve consumption of raw and fermented seafood products. Eating raw fish is most common among Americans of Asiatic origin and presents potential problems associated with parasites and *Vibrio* infection. As noted earlier, the increasing popularity of sushi and, to a lesser extent, seviche has spread the practice more widely among the U.S. population. So far, there has not been evidence of a major microbiological problem, but this situation must be watched carefully.

Fermented products present a more acute hazard because they are normally produced in the home by using traditional procedures that are poorly controlled. Most cases of seafood-borne botulism in the United States in recent years occurred in Alaska among native Americans as a result of consuming fermented fish and marine mammal parts (Table 3-10). Little is known scientifically about the processes used, which seem to be largely proteolytic in nature; more study is clearly required in this area to identify procedures that would be safer than those presently used.

Traditional methods of producing marinated and cured fish may also present botulism problems, as evidenced by cases in Puerto Rico and New Jersey (Table 3-10). In most such cases, proper temperature control during preparation could eliminate the problem. Education of specific targeted groups is necessary to manage these risks.

Other risks arise from the practice of consuming parts of fish, particularly intestines and other viscera, common among recent immigrants from Southeast Asia. In most cases, such dishes are eaten after cooking, which may explain the absence of major infectious disease outbreaks. However, the consumption of intestines and whole scallops has caused intoxications due to paralytic shellfish poisoning (PSP). It is unusual for scallop adductor muscle tissue to become toxic for humans, but viscera and other organs readily become toxic. Control has typically been based on measurement of toxin in the adductor muscle. Regulations and control measures designed to deal with common U.S. eating practices may not adequately protect individuals with different eating customs.

Aquaculture

The microbiological safety and promising future of the aquaculture industry has been reviewed by Ward (1989). Many of the microorganisms of concern in growing waters and abusive conditions in processing, handling, or preparation of other seafood products are also of concern in aquaculture. Two different areas of concern for aquaculture are pathogens known to cause disease in both fish and humans (e.g., *Edwardsiella tarda* and *Aeromonas hydrophila*) and the potential development of antibiotic resistance in these pathogens. The use of antimicrobials in aquaculture at both therapeutic and subtherapeutic levels is widespread (Brown, 1989). The possible development of antibiotic-resistant strains of bacteria, such as *Salmonella*, resulting from these feeding practices, and the subsequent transfer of such resistant bacteria on seafood products to humans are of concern. Significant levels of resistance to tetracycline compounds, some of it transferable, have been documented in *A. hydrophila* strains isolated from farmed catfish and their environment (DePaola et al., 1988). The development of antibiotic-resistant pathogens in aquaculture products is certainly of concern to the consumer. The expansion of aquaculture in the future will warrant research on the development and better management of antimicrobials for aquaculture (Ward, 1989).

CONCLUSIONS AND RECOMMENDATIONS

Seafoods, like any food items, have the potential to cause disease from viral, bacterial, and parasitic microorganisms under certain circumstances. These disease-causing agents are acquired from three sources: (1) fecal pollution of the aquatic environment; (2) the natural aquatic environment; and (3) industry, retail, restaurant, or home processing and preparation.

Fecal pollution may contribute human viral and bacterial contaminants and is the primary source of infection. Microorganisms associated with the natural environment include bacterial pathogens of marine origin and parasites transmitted from seafood to man. Agents associated with workers and the environment in processing, distribution, food services, and home preparation include microorganisms carried by humans, as well as environmental microorganisms that become problems because of processing conditions.

Available CDC and NETSU data and literature reports suggest the following risk priorities for microbiological hazards in seafoods.

Conclusions

Raw Molluscan Shellfish

Overall, when examining the potential for seafood-associated illness from microbial pathogens, several factors must be taken into consideration, including host risk factors; sources and types of microorganisms; and seafood processing, preparation, and handling procedures that either allow microorganisms to survive and grow or destroy them before consumption. Food handlers and consumers must be made aware of all these factors. Imported products may have different levels of risk. Careful surveillance is necessary to monitor these risks adequately.

1. The greatest numbers of seafood-associated illnesses are reported from unknown etiologies clinically suggestive of Norwalk and Norwalk-like agents of human enteric viral gastroenteritis. The vast majority of these illnesses are associated with the consumption of raw molluscan shellfish taken from harvest waters contaminated with raw or poorly treated human sewage. Although these are the most common seafood-associated illnesses, they tend to be relatively mild with no associated mortality.

2. Naturally occurring marine *Vibrio* species are responsible for fewer reported cases of infections from the consumption of raw molluscan shellfish, but certain species such as *V. vulnificus* can be associated with high mortality in persons who are immunocompromised or who have underlying liver disease.

Other Seafoods

1. The greatest microbiological risk associated with seafood other than raw molluscan shellfish appears to be recontamination or cross-contamination of cooked by raw product or contamination during preparation followed by time/temperature abuse. This occurs mainly at the food service (postprocessing) level. The number of total

reported cases associated with finfish between 1978 and 1987 is much lower than reported for raw molluscan shellfish in the same period. Available data show that *Vibrio parahaemolyticus* is responsible for the largest number of other seafood-associated cases of illness, followed by hepatitis A virus, *Salmonella* (nontyphoidal), *Shigella, Clostridium perfringens,* and *C. botulinum,* with HAV and *C. botulinum* being the most potentially serious of these pathogens. However, the fish-associated HAV infections reported during this time were attributed to two outbreaks due to contamination of prepared seafood by infected food handlers. Seafood-associated illnesses due to *C. botulinum* were confined to a small geographical area (mainly Alaska) and were associated with the consumption of improperly processed noncommercial products.

2. Seafood-related parasitic infections are even less common than bacterial or viral infections, with *Anisakis simplex* and cestodes having the greatest public health impact in the United States. In general, parasitic infections are concentrated in certain ethnic groups that favor consumption of raw or partially cooked seafood harvested from high-risk geographic areas.

Recommendations

Specific Recommendations for Raw Molluscan Shellfish

• High-risk groups (cirrhotics, persons with hemochromatosis, persons who are immunosuppressed) must not eat raw shellfish. It is extremely important that health professionals, especially, be educated concerning food-borne hazards to this group. Proper and thorough cooking of all shellfish before consumption would eliminate microbiological pathogens and helminthic parasites. Individuals who choose to consume raw shellfish should be educated about the potential risks described previously, and how those risks or their effects can be mitigated.

• Adequate and proper treatment and disposal of sewage must be implemented and maintained to avoid contamination of harvest areas by human enteric pathogens. This may require the development of new technology for sewage treatment.

• Valid indicators for contamination of growing waters by human pathogens must be developed. Seafood-borne infections by human enteric viruses in raw and improperly cooked molluscan shellfish could be decreased significantly by the development of valid growing water indicator(s) or direct detection methodologies for human enteric viruses.

• Effective enforcement for elimination of recreational and illegal ("bootlegged") harvesting or sale of molluscan shellfish from known sewage-contaminated shellfish growing areas should be developed and adequately funded.

• Monitoring programs for *Vibrio* species in molluscan shellfish and growing waters during warm months, as well as support for epidemiological research, should be established.

• Means must be investigated and implemented to eliminate, or at least reduce, levels of potentially pathogenic *Vibrio* species in raw shellfish. This may necessitate restriction of harvest when water temperatures are high, rapid cool-down and continued chilling of products, and possibly irradiation of live shellstock and shucked products.

• Because of the high risks associated with raw molluscan shellfish, the importation of shellfish for raw consumption should be prohibited unless there is a clear equivalence of standards for harvest waters and for postharvest processing.

General Recommendations for All Seafoods

   • Persons consuming raw fish or shellfish should be made aware of the potential microbial risks associated with these practices. Persons in specific high-risk groups (persons with cirrhosis, or hemochromatosis, or those who are immunosuppressed) should never eat raw seafood. Proper and thorough cooking of all seafood before consumption would eliminate the microbiological pathogens and helminthic parasites. Individuals who choose to eat raw seafood should be educated about the potential risks described previously, and how those risks or their effects can be mitigated.

   • Any seafood inspection system must be designed to address microbiological hazards through the HACCP approach. This cannot be achieved by the visual or organoleptic inspection currently used for meat and poultry. Seafood inspection requires the development of valid microbiological guidelines to accurately assess potential human health risks from microbial pathogens in raw and processed seafoods; the maintenance of adequate refrigeration; the avoidance of recontamination of cooked, ready-to-eat products by raw products; and good manufacturing practices and proper sanitation. All inspection system guidelines must apply to imported as well as domestic products under memoranda of understanding.

   • More research is required to develop new technology-based processing and preservation techniques that provide for safe products. Some of the new processing methods such as *sous vide* and modified atmosphere can potentially create conditions that favor *Clostridium botulinum* type E and other pathogens such as *Listeria*. New methodologies that produce organoleptically superior products must also ensure superior microbiological safety. Certification procedures should be developed for any new processing techniques.

   • Continuous, enhanced efforts should be undertaken to educate all health professionals, food handlers, and consumers regarding the microbiological risks of seafood-borne illness and the appropriate means of minimizing such risks, including immediate and adequate refrigeration, proper cooking, avoiding recontamination of cooked products by raw products, proper sanitation, and good personal hygiene, especially at the food service level.

   • A food-borne illness surveillance system sufficient for risk identification and regulatory program planning and evaluation must be developed. This system should provide a comprehensive data base that will allow statistically valid assessments of disease incidence and food/behavior risk factors for all food-borne illnesses. It is extremely difficult to assess the relative safety of seafood products accurately, or to manage seafood-borne or other food-borne risks effectively, with the available data bases.

   • New or improved methodology [e.g., enzyme-linked immunoabsorbent assay (ELISA), gene probe, polymerase chain reaction] should be developed that provide for rapid identification and quantification of indicators, seafood-associated pathogens, and microbial toxins in seafoods and in harvest waters.

NOTES

1. Outbreak (food-borne): Two or more persons experience a similar illness after ingesting a common food and epidemiological analysis implicates the food as the source. A few exceptions exist; for example, one case of botulism, seafood toxin poisoning, or chemical poisoning constitutes an outbreak (CDC, 1981a, p. 2).

2. A case is a person who is clinically ill with a syndrome compatible with food-borne illness, and whose illness in epidemiologically associated with the consumption of food (CDC, 1981a, pp. 42-46).

REFERENCES

Abbott, S.L., C. Powers, C.A. Kaysner, Y. Takeda, M. Ishibashi, S.W. Joseph, and J.M. Janda. 1989. Emergence of a restricted bioserovar of *Vibrio parahaemolyticus* as the predominant cause of vibrio-associated gastroenteritis on the West Coast of the United States and Mexico. J. Clin. Microbiol. 27:2891-2893.

Abeyta, C. 1983. Bacteriological quality of fresh seafood products from Seattle retail markets. J. Food Protect. 46:901-909.

Alicata, J.E. 1988. *Angiostrongylus cantonensis* (eosinophilic meningitis): Historical events in its recognition as a new parasitic disease of man. J. Wash. Acad. Sci. 78:38-46.

Anderson, E., D.J. Gubler, K. Sorensen, J. Beddard, and L.R. Ash. 1986. First report of *Angiostrongylus cantonensis* in Puerto Rico. Am. J. Trop. Med. Hyg. 35:319-322.

APHA (American Public Health Association). 1985a. In A.E. Greenberg and D.A. Hunt, eds. Recommended Procedures for the Examination of Seawater and Shellfish, 5th ed. American Public Health Association, Washington, D.C. 144 pp.

APHA (American Public Health Association). 1985b. In M.L. Speck, ed. Compendium of Methods for the Microbiological Examination of Foods. American Public Health Association, Washington, D.C. 702 pp.

Archer, D.L., and F.E. Young. 1988. Contemporary issues: Diseases with a food vector. Clin. Microbiol. Rev. 1:377-398.

Arumugaswamy, R.K., and R.W. Proudford. 1987. The occurrence of *Campylobacter jejuni* and *Campylobacter coli* in Sidney rock oyster. Inter. J. Food Microbiol. 4:101-104.

Banwart, G.J. 1989. P. 58 in Basic Food Microbiology. Van Nostrand Reinhold, New York.

Barker, W.H., Jr. 1974. *Vibrio parahaemolyticus* outbreaks in the United States. Lancet 1:551-554.

Baross, J., and J. Liston. 1970. Occurrence of *Vibrio parahaemolyticus* and related hemolytic vibrios in marine environment of Washington State. Appl. Microbiol. 20:179-186.

Bart, K.J., Z. Huq, M. Khan, and W.H. Mosley. 1970. Seroepidemiologic studies during a simultaneous epidemic of infection with El Tor Ogawa and classical Inaba *Vibrio cholerae*. J. Infect. Dis. 121 (suppl.):S17-S24.

Bergdoll, M.S. 1979. Staphylococcal intoxications. Pp. 443-494 in H. Riemann and F.L. Bryan, eds. Food-Borne Infections and Intoxications. Academic Press, New York.

Bier, J.W. 1976. Experimental anisakiasis: Cultivation and temperature tolerance determinations. J. Milk Food. Tech. 39:132-137.

Bier, J.W., T.L. Deardorff, G.J. Jackson, and R.B. Raybourne. 1987. Human anisakiasis. Balliere's Clinical Tropical Medicine and Communicable Diseases 2:723-733.

Black, R.E., M.M. Levine, M.J. Blaser, M.L. Clements, and T.P. Hughes. 1983. Studies of *Campylobacter jejuni* infection in volunteers. P. 13 in A.D. Pearson, M.B. Skirrow, B. Rowe, J.R. Davis, and D.M. Jones, eds. *Campylobacter* II: Proceedings of the Second International Workshop on *Campylobacter* Infections held in Brussels, September 8-9, 1983. Public Health Laboratory Service, London, England.

Blake, P.A. 1983. Vibrios on the half shell: What the walrus and the carpenter didn't know. Ann. Intern. Med. 99:558-559.

Blake, P.A., M.H. Merson, R.E. Weaver, D.G. Hollis, and P.C. Heublein. 1979. Disease caused by a marine *Vibrio*: Clinical characteristics and epidemiology. N. Engl. J. Med. 300:1-5.

Blake, P.A., D.T. Allegra, J.D. Snyder, T.J. Barrett, L. McFarland, C.T. Caraway, J.C. Feeley, J.P. Craig, J.V. Lee, N.D. Puhr, and R.A. Feldman. 1980. Cholera–A possible endemic focus in the United States. N. Engl. J. Med. 302:305-309.

Blake, P.A., and R.A. Feldman. 1986. Shigellosis. Pp. 240-242 in J.M. Last, ed. Maxey-Rosenau Public Health and Preventive Medicine, 12th ed. Appleton-Century-Crofts, Norwalk, Connecticut.

Blaser, M.J., and L.B. Reller. 1981. *Campylobacter enteritis*. N. Engl. J. Med. 305:1444-1452.

Bonner, J.R., A.S. Coker, C.R. Berryman, and H.M. Pollock. 1983. Spectrum of *Vibrio* infections in a Gulf Coast Community. Ann. Intern. Med. 99:464-469.

Bradshaw, J.G., D. Francis, and R.M. Twedt. 1974. Survival of *Vibrio parahaemolyticus* in cooked seafood at refrigeration temperatures. Appl. Microbiol. 27:657-661.

Bradshaw, J.G., J.T. Peeler, J.J. Corwin, J.M. Hunt, J.T. Tierney, and R.M. Twedt. 1985. Thermal resistance of *Listeria monocytogenes* in milk. J. Food Protect. 48:743-745.

Bradshaw, J.G., J.T. Peeler, J.J. Corwin, J.M. Hunt, and R.M. Twedt. 1987. Thermal resistance of *Listeria monocytogenes* in dairy products. J. Food Protect. 50:543-544, 556.

Brenner, D.J., F.W. Hickman-Brenner, J.V. Lee, A.G. Steigerwalt, G.R. Fanning, D.G. Hollis, J.J. Farmer, R.E. Weaver, and S.W. Joseph. 1983. *Vibrio furnissii* (formerly aerogenic biogroup of *Vibrio fluvialis*), a new species isolated from human feces and the environment. J. Clin. Microbiol. 18:816-824.

Brown, J. 1989. Antibiotics: Their use and abuse in aquaculture. World Aqua. (June):34-43.

Bryan, F.L. 1979. Infections and intoxications caused by other bacteria. Pp. 811-877 in H. Riemann and F. Bryan, eds. Food-Borne Infections and Intoxications, 2nd ed. Academic Press, New York.

Bryan, F.L. 1980. Food-borne diseases in the United States associated with meat and poultry. J. Food Protect. 43:140-150.

Bryan, F.L. 1986. Seafood-transmitted infections and intoxications in recent years. Pp. 319-337 in D.E. Kramer and J. Liston, eds. Seafood Quality Determination. Proceedings of an International Symposium Coordinated by the University of Alaska, November 10-14, 1986. Elsiever Science Publishers, Amsterdam, The Netherlands.

Bunning, V., R. Crawford, J. Bradshaw, J. Peller, J. Tierney, and R. Twedt. 1986. Thermal resistance of intracellular *Listeria monocytogenes* suspended in bovine milk. Appl. Environ. Microbiol. 52:1398-1402.

Burke, V., M. Gracey, J. Robinson, D. Peck, J. Beaman, and C. Burdell. 1983. The microbiology of childhood gastroenteritis: *Aeromonas* species and other infective agents. J. Infect. Dis. 148:68-74.

Cann, D., and L. Taylor. 1979. The control of the botulism hazard in hot-smoked trout and mackerel. J. Food Technol. 14:123-130.

Caredda, F., S. Antinori, T. Re, C. Pastecchia, and M. Moroni. 1986. Acute non-A non-B hepatitis after typhoid fever. Br. Med. J. 292:1429.

Cartwright, K.A.V., and B.G. Evans. 1988. Salmon as a food-poisoning vehicle--Two successive salmonella outbreaks. Epidem. Inf. 101:249-257.

CDC (Centers for Disease Control). 1981a. *Salmonella* Surveillance, Annual Summary, 1978. HHS Publ. No. (CDC)81-8219. Public Health Service, U.S. Department of Health and Human Services, Atlanta, Ga. 25 pp.

CDC (Centers for Disease Control). 1981b. Annual Summary of Foodborne Disease, 1978. HHS Publ. No. (CDC)81-8185. U.S. Department of Health and Human Services, Atlanta, Ga. 53 pp.

CDC (Centers for Disease Control). 1981c. Annual Summary of Foodborne Disease, 1979. HHS Publ. No. (CDC) 81-8185. Public Health Service, U.S. Department of Health and Human Services, Atlanta, Ga. 40 pp.

CDC (Centers for Disease Control). 1983a. Food-borne Disease Outbreaks, Annual Summary 1980. HHS Publ. No. (CDC) 83-8185. Public Health Service, U.S. Department of Health and Human Services, Atlanta, Ga. 32 pp.

CDC (Centers for Disease Control). 1983b. Food-borne Disease Outbreaks, Annual Summary 1981. HHS Publ. No. (CDC) 83-8185. Public Health Service, U.S. Department of Health and Human Services, Atlanta, Ga. 41 pp.

CDC (Centers for Disease Control). 1984. Food-borne disease outbreaks, Annual summary 1983: Reported morbidity and mortality in the United States. Morbid. Mortal. Weekly Rep. (annual suppl.) 32 pp.

CDC (Centers for Disease Control). 1985. Food-borne Disease Outbreaks, Annual Summary 1982. DHHS Publ. No. (CDC) 85-8185. Public Health Service, U.S. Department of Health and Human Services, Atlanta, Ga. 38 pp.

CDC (Centers for Disease Control). 1989. Food-Borne Surveillance Data for All Pathogens in Fish/Shellfish for Years 1973-1987. Public Health Service, U.S. Department of Health and Human Services, Atlanta, Ga.

Cheng, T.C. 1976. The natural history of anisakiasis in animals. J. Milk Food Technol. 39:32-46.

Chitwood, M. 1970. Nematodes of medical significance found in market fish. Am. J. Trop. Med. Hyg. 19:599-602.

Ciesielski, C.A., B. Swaminathan, and C.V. Broome. 1987. *Listeria monocytogenes*. A food-borne pathogen. Clin. Microbiol. Newsletter 9:140-150.

Cliver, D.O. 1988. Virus transmission via foods. A scientific status summary by the Institute of Food Technologists' Expert Panel on Food Safety and Nutrition. Food Technol. 42:241-247.

Cole, M.T., M.B. Kilgen, L.A. Reily, and C.R. Hackney. 1986. Detection of enteroviruses and bacterial indicators and pathogens in Louisiana oysters and their overlying waters. J. Food Protect. 49:596-601.

Cook, D.W., and A.D. Ruple. 1989. Indicator bacteria and vibrionaceae multiplication in postharvest shellstock oysters. J. Food Protect. 52:343-349.

Cornelis, G., Y. Laroche, G. Balligand, M.P. Sory, and G. Wauters. 1987. *Yersinia enterocolitica*, a primary model for bacterial invasiveness. Rev. Infect. Dis. 9:64-86.

D'Aoust, J.Y., R. Gelinas, and C. Maishment. 1980. Presence of indicator organisms and recovery of *Salmonella* in fish and shellfish. J. Food Protect. 43:679-682.

Davis, J.W., and R.K. Sizemore. 1982. Incidence of *Vibrio* species associated with blue crabs (*Callinectes sapidus*) collected from Galveston Bay, Texas. Appl. Environ. Microbiol. 43:1092-1097.

Deardorff, T.L., T. Fukumura, and R.B. Raybourne. 1986. Invasive anisakiasis. Gastroenterol. 90:1047-1050.

Delmore, R.P., and Crisley. 1979. Thermal resistance of *Vibrio parahaemolyticus* in clam homogenate. J. Food Protect. 42:131-134.

DePaola, A., P.A. Flynn, R.M. McPhearson, and S.B. Levy. 1988. Phenotypic and genotypic characterization of tetracycline and oxytetracline-resistant *Aeromonas hydrophila* for altered channel catfish (*Ictalurus punctatus*) and their environments. Appl. Environment. Microbiol. 54:1861-1863.

Dolman, C. 1964. Botulism as a world problem. Pp. 5-32 in K. Lewis and Cassel, eds., Botulism. Public Health Service, No. 999-FP-1, U.S. Department of Health, Education and Welfare. Cincinnati, Ohio.

Doyle, M., and D. Roman. 1981. Growth and survival of *Campylobacter jejuni* as a function of temperature and pH. J. Food Protect. 44:596-601.

Doyle, M.P., and D.J. Roman. 1982. Response of *Campylobacter jejuni* to sodium chloride. Appl. Environ. Microbiol. 43:561-565.

DuPont, H.L., R.B. Hornick, A.T. Dawkins, M.J. Snyder, and S.B. Forme. 1969. The response of man to virulent *Shigella flexneri*. J. Infect. Dis. 119:296-299.

Eklund, M.W. 1982. Significance of *Clostridium botulinum* in fishery products preserved short of sterilization. Food Technol. 36:107-115.

Eklund, M., M. Peterson, R. Paranjpuke, and G. Pelroy. 1988. Feasibility of a heat-pasteurization process for the inactivation of non-proteolytic *Clostridium botulinum* types B and E in vacuum-packaged, hot-process (smoked) fish. J. Food Protect. 51:720-726.

Elliot, E.L., and R.R. Colwell. 1985. Indicator organisms for estuarine and marine waters. FEMS Micro. Rev. 32:61-79.

Emodi, A.S., and R.V. Lechowich. 1969. Low temperature growth of type E *Clostridium botulinum* spores. 1. Effects of sodium chloride, sodium nitrite and pH. J. Food Sci. 34:78-87.

Farmer, J.J., III, F.W. Hickman-Brenner, and M.T. Kelly 1985. *Vibrio*. Pp. 282-301 in Manual of Clinical Microbiology, 4th ed. American Society for Microbiology, Washington, D.C.

FDA (Food and Drug Administration). 1988. Pathogen Monitoring of High Risk Foods (FY 88/89). FDA Compliance Program Guidance Manual No. 7303030. Food and Drug Administration, Washington, D.C. 18 pp.

FDA (Food and Drug Administration). 1989a revision. Sanitation of shellfish growing areas. National Shellfish Sanitation Program Manual of Operations Part I. Center for Food Safety and Applied Nutrition, Division of Cooperative Programs, Shellfish Sanitation Branch, Washington, D.C.

FDA (Food and Drug Administration). 1989b revision. Sanitation of the harvesting, processing and distribution of shellfish. National Shellfish Sanitation Program Manual of Operations Part II. Center for Food Safety and Applied Nutrition, Division of Cooperative Programs, Shellfish Sanitation Branch, Washington, D.C.

Fleming, D.W., S.L. Cochi, K.L. MacDonald, J. Brandum, P.S. Hayes, B.D. Plikaytis, M.B. Holmes, A. Audioier, C.V. Broome, and A.L. Reingold. 1985. Pasteurized milk as a vehicle of infection in an outbreak of listeriosis. N. Engl. J. Med. 312:404-407.

Flowers, R.S. 1988a. Salmonella in "bacteria associated with foodborne disease": A scientific status summary of the Institute of Food Technologists' Expert Panel on Food Safety and Nutrition. Food Technol. 42:181-200.

Flowers, R.S. 1988b. Shigella in "bacteria associated with foodborne disease": A scientific status summary of the Institute of Food Technologists' Expert Panel on Food Safety and Nutrition. Food Technol. 42:181-200.

Fontaine, R.E. 1985. Anisakiasis from the American perspective. J. Am. Med. Assoc. 253:1024-1025.

Fraiser, M.B., and J.A. Koburger. 1984. Incidence of salmonellae in clams, oysters, crabs, and mullet. J. Food Protect. 47:343-345.

Franco, D.A. 1988. Campylobacter species: Considerations for controlling a food-borne pathogen. J. Food Protect. 51:145-153.

Gangarosa, E.J. 1978. Epidemiology of Escherichia coli in the United States. J. Infect. Dis. 137:634-638.

Garcia, G., C. Genigeorgis, and S. Lindroth. 1987. Risk of growth and toxin production by Clostridium botulinum non-proteolytic types B, E, and F in salmon fillets stored under modified atmospheres at low and abused temperatures. J. Food Protect. 50:330-336.

Garrett, E.S. 1988. Microbiological standards, guidelines, and specifications and inspection of seafood products. Food Technol. 42:90-93.

Genigeorgis, C. 1985. Microbial safety implications of the use of modified atmospheres to extend storage life of fresh meat and fish. A review. Int. J. Food Microbiol. 1:237-251.

Gerba, C.P. 1988. Viral disease transmission by seafoods. Food Technol. 42:99-101.

Giddings, G.G. 1984. Radiation processing of fishery products. Food Technol. 38:61-97.

Grabow, W.O.K., V. Gauss-Müller, O.W. Prozesky, and F. Deinhardt. 1983. Inactivation of hepatitis A virus and indicator organisms in water by free chlorine residuals. Appl. Environ. Microbiol. 46:619-624.

Gross, R.J. 1983. Escherichia coli diarrhea. J. Infect. 7:177-192.

Hauschild, A.H.W. 1989. Clostridium botulinum. Pp. 111-189 in M.P. Doyle, ed., Foodborne Bacterial Pathogens. Marcel Dekker, New York.

Healy, C.R., and D. Juranek. 1979. Parasitic infections. Pp. 343-385 in H. Riemann and F.L. Bryan, eds. Food-Borne Infections and Intoxications, 2nd ed. Academic Press, New York.

Herrington, D.A., S. Tzipori, R.M. Robins-Browne, B.D. Tall, and M.M. Levine. 1987. In vitro and in vivo pathogenicity of Plesiomonas shigelloides. Infect. Immun. 55:979-985.

Hobbs, G. 1976. Clostridium botulinum and its importance in fishery products. Adv. Food Res. 22:135-185.

Hoge, C.W., D. Watsky, R.N. Peeler, J.P. Libonati, E. Israel, and J.G. Morris, Jr. 1989. Epidemiology and spectrum of Vibrio infections in a Chesapeake Bay community. J. Infect. Dis. 160:985-993.

Holmberg, S.D., W.L. Schell, G.R. Fanning, I.K. Wachsmuth, F.W. Hickman-Brenner, P.A. Blake, D.J. Brenner, and J.J. Farmer III. 1986a. Aeromonas intestinal infections in the United States. Ann. Intern. Med. 105:683-689.

Holmberg, S.D., I.K. Wachsmuth, F.W. Hickman-Brenner, P.A. Blake, and J.J. Farmer III. 1986b. Plesiomonas enteric infections in the United States. Ann. Intern. Med. 105:690-694.

Hughes, J.M., D.G. Hollis, E.J. Gangarosa, and R.E. Weaver. 1978. Non-cholera vibrio infections in the United States–Clinical, epidemiologic, and laboratory features. Ann. Intern. Med. 88:602-606.

Hunt, M.D., W.E. Woodward, B.H. Keswick, and H.L. DuPont. 1988. Seroepidemiology of cholera in gulf coastal Texas. Appl. Environ. Microbiol. 54:1673-1677.

Huq, M.I., A.K.M.J. Alam, D.J. Brenner, and G.K. Morris. 1980. Isolation of vibrio-like group, EF-6, from patients with diarrhea. J. Clin. Microbiol. 11:621-624.

Jay, J.M. 1986. Modern Food Microbiology, 3rd ed. Van Nostrand Reinhold, New York. 642 pp.

Johnston, J.M., S.F. Becker, and L.M. McFarland. 1985. Vibrio vulnificus: Man and the sea. J. Am. Med. Assoc. 253:2050-2053.

Joseph, S.W., R.R. Colwell, and J.B. Kaper. 1983. *Vibrio parahaemolyticus* and related halophilic vibrios. CRC Crit. Rev. Microbiol. 10:77-124.

Kain, K.C., and M.T. Kelly. 1989. Clinical features, epidemiology, and treatment of *Plesiomonas shigelloides* diarrhea. J. Clin. Microbiol. 27:998-1001.

Kaper, J.B., H. Lockman, R.R. Colwell, and S.W. Joseph. 1979. Ecology, serology, and enterotoxin production of *Vibrio cholerae* in Chesapeake Bay. Appl. Environ. Microbiol. 37:91-103.

Kaper, J.B., J.G. Morris, Jr., and M. Nishibuchi. 1988. DNA probes for pathogenic *Vibrio* species. Pp. 66-77 in F.C. Tenover, ed. DNA Probes for Infectious Diseases. CRC Press, Boca Raton, Fla.

Kelly, M.T., and E.M.D. Stroh. 1989. Urease-positive, kanagawa-negative *Vibrio parahaemolyticus* from patients and the environment in the Pacific northwest. J. Clin. Microbiol. 27:2820-2822.

Keswick, B.H., T.K. Satterwhite, P.C. Johnson, H.L. Dupont, S.L. Secor, J.A. Bitsuraj, G.W. Gray, and J.C. Hoff. 1985. Inactivation of Norwalk virus in drinking water by chlorine. Appl. Environ. Microbiol. 50:261-264.

Khalil, L.F. 1969. Larval nematodes in the herring (*Clupea harengus*) from British coastal waters and adjacent territories. J. Mar. Biol. Ass. UK 49:641-659.

Kilgen, M.B. 1989. Final Report on the Current National Status of the Relationships of Indicators, Human Enteric Pathogens and Potential Health Risks Within a Total Environmental Assessment. Saltonstall-Kennedy Grant No. 37-01-79000/37500. Thibodaux, Louisiana. 41 pp.

Kilgen, M.B., M.T. Cole, and C.R. Hackney. 1988. Shellfish sanitation studies in Louisiana. J. Shellfish Res. 7:527-530.

Kliks, M.M. 1983. Anisakiasis in the western United States: Four new case reports from California. Am. J. Trop. Med. Hyg. 23:526-532.

Kliks, M.M., K. Kroenke, and J.M. Hardman. 1982. Eosinophilic radiculomyeloencephalitis: An angiostrongyliasis outbreak in America Samoa related to the ingestion of *Achatina fulica* snails. Am. J. Trop. Med. Hyg. 31:1114-1122.

Klontz, K.C., S. Lieb, M. Schreiber, H.T. Janowski, L.M. Baldy, and R.A. Gunn. 1988. Syndromes of *Vibrio vulnificus* infections: Clinical and epidemiologic features in Florida cases, 1981-1987. Ann. Intern. Med. 109:318-323.

Lamont, R.J., R. Postelthwaite, and A.P. MacGowan. 1988. *Listeria monocytogenes* and its role in human infection. J. Infect. 17:7-28.

Lee, W.H. 1977. An assessment of *Yersinia enterocolitica* and its presence in foods. J. Food Protect. 40:486-489.

Lennon, D., B. Lewis, C. Mantell, D. Becroft, B. Dove, K. Farmer, S. Tonkin, N. Yeates, R. Stamp, and K. Mickelson. 1984. Epidemic perinatal listeriosis. Pediat. Infect. Dis. 3:30-34.

Lerke, P., and L. Farber. 1971. Heat pasteurization of crab and shrimp from the Pacific coast of the United States: Public health aspects. J. Food Sci. 36:277-279.

Lewis, A.M., and B. Chattopadhyay. 1986. Faecal carriage rate of *Yersinia* species. J. Hyg. Camb. 97:281-287.

Linnan, M.J., L. Mascola, X.D. Lou, V. Goulet, S. May, C. Salminen, D.W. Hird, L. Yonekura, P. Hayes, R. Weaver, A. Andurier, B.D. Plikaytis, S.L. Fannin, A. Bleks, and C.V. Broome. 1988. Epidemic listeriosis associated with Mexican-style cheese. N. Engl. J. Med. 319:823-828.

Liston, J. 1973. Influence of U.S. seafood handling procedures on *Vibrio parahaemolyticus*. Pp. 123-128 in International Symposium on *Vibrio parahaemolyticus*. Saikon Publishing Co. Ltd., Tokyo, Japan.

Liston, J. 1980. Health and safety of seafoods. Food Technol. Aust. 32:428-436.

Liston, J., and J. Baross. 1973. Distribution of *Vibrio parahaemolyticus* in the natural environment. J. Milk Food Technol. 36:113-117.

Lowry, P.W., L.M. McFarland, B.H. Peltier, N.C. Roberts, H.B. Bradford, J.L. Herndon, D.F. Stroup, J.B. Mathison, P.A. Blake, and R.A. Gunn. 1989a. *Vibrio* gastroenteritis in Louisiana: A prospective study among attendees of a scientific congress in New Orleans. J. Infect. Dis. 160:978-984.

Lowry, P.W., A.T. Pavia, L.M. McFarland, B.H. Peltier, T.J. Barrett, H.B. Bradford, J.M. Quan, J. Lynch, J.B. Mathison, R.A. Gunn, and P.A. Blake. 1989b. Cholera in Louisiana: Widening spectrum of seafood vehicles. Arch. Intern. Med. 149:2079-2084.

Lynt, R.K., D.A. Kautter, and H.M. Solomon. 1982. Differences and similarities among proteolytic and nonproteolytic strains of *Clostridium botulinum* A, B, E and F: A review. J. Food Protect. 45:466-474.

Margolis, L. 1977. Public health aspects of "codworm" infection: A review. J. Fish Res. Board Can. 34:887-898.

Martin, R.E., and G.T. Pitts. 1989. Handbook of State and Federal Microbiological Standards and Guidelines. National Fisheries Institute, Arlington, Va. 28 pp.

Matches, J.R., and C. Abeyta. 1983. Indicator organisms in fish and shellfish. J. Food Protect. 37:114-117.

McGladdery, S.E. 1986. *Anisakis simplex* (nematode: Anisakidae) infection of the musculature and body cavity of Atlantic herring (*Clupea harengus harengus*). Can. J. Fish. Aq. Sci. 43:1312-1317.

McKerrow, J.H., J. Sakanari, and T.L. Deardorff. 1988. Anisakiasis: Revenge of the sushi parasite. N. Engl. J. Med. 319:1228-1229.

McLauchlin, J. 1987. *Listeria monocytogenes*, recent advances in taxonomy and epidemiology of listeriosis in humans. J. Appl. Bacteriol. 63:1-10.

Medallion Laboratories. 1987. Food microbiology–Examining the greater risk. Analyt. Progress 4:1-8.

Miliotis, M.D., J.E. Galen, J.B. Kaper, and J.G. Morris, Jr. 1989. Development and testing of a synthetic oligonucleotide probe for the detection of pathogenic *Yersinia* strains. J. Clin. Microbiol. 27:1667-1670.

Miller, M.L., and J.A. Koburger. 1985. *Plesiomonas shigelloides*: An opportunistic food and waterborne pathogen. J. Food Protect. 48:449-457.

Miwatani, T., and Y. Takeda. 1976. *Vibrio parahaemolyticus*: A Causative Bacterium of Food Poisoning. Saikon Publishing Co., Ltd., Tokyo. 149 pp.

Miyamoto, Y., T. Kato, Y. Obara, S. Akiyama, K. Takizawa, and S. Yamai. 1969. In vitro hemolytic characteristics of *Vibrio parahaemolyticus*: Its close correlation with human pathogenicity. J. Bacteriol. 100:1147-1149.

Morris, G.K., and J.C. Feeley. 1976. *Yersinia enterocolitica*: A review of its role in food hygiene. Bull. WHO 54:79-85.

Morris, J.G., Jr. 1988. *Vibrio vulnificus*: A new monster of the deep? Ann. Intern. Med. 109:261-263.

Morris, J.G., Jr., and R.E. Black. 1985. Cholera and other vibrioses in the United States. N. Engl. J. Med. 312:343-350.

Morris, J.G., Jr., R. Wilson, B.R. Davis, I.K. Wachsmuth, C.F. Riddle, H.G. Wathen, R.A. Pollard, and P.A. Blake. 1981. Non-O group 1 *Vibrio cholerae* gastroenteritis in the United States: Clinical, epidemiologic, and laboratory characteristics of sporadic cases. Ann. Intern. Med. 94:656-658.

Morris, J.G., Jr., H.G. Miller, R. Wilson, C.O. Tacket, D.G. Hollis, F.W. Hickman, R.E. Weaver, and P.A. Blake. 1982. Illness caused by *Vibrio damsela* and *Vibrio hollisae*. Lancet 1:1294-1297.

Morris, J.G., Jr., J.L. Picardi, S. Lieb, J.V. Lee, A. Roberts, M. Hood, R.A. Gunn, and P.A. Blake. 1984. Isolation of non-toxigenic *Vibrio cholerae* O-group 1 from a case of severe gastrointestinal disease. J. Clin. Microbiol. 19:296-297.

Morris, J.G., Jr., A.C. Wright, D.M. Roberts, P.K. Wood, L.M. Simpson, and J.D. Oliver. 1987a. Identification of environmental *Vibrio vulnificus* isolates with a DNA probe for the cytotoxin-hemolysin gene. Appl. Environ. Microbiol. 53:193-195.

Morris, J.G., Jr., A.C. Wright, L.M. Simpson, P.K. Wood, D.E. Johnson, and J.D. Oliver. 1987b. Virulence of *Vibrio vulnificus*: Association with utilization of transferrin bound iron, and lack of correlation with levels of cytotoxin or protease. FEMS Microbiol. Lett. 40:55-59.

Morris, J.G., Jr., T. Takeda, B.D. Tall, G.A. Losonsky, S.K. Bhattacharya, B.D. Forrest, B.A. Kay, and M. Nishibuchi. 1990. Experimental non-O group 1 *Vibrio cholerae* gastroenteritis in humans. J. Clin. Invest. 85:697-705.

Morse, D.L., J.J. Gugewich, J.P. Hanrahan, R. Stricof, M. Shayegani, R. Deibel, J.C. Grabau, N.A. Nowak, J.E. Herrmann, G. Cukor, and N.R. Blacklow. 1986. Widespread outbreaks of clam- and oyster-associated gastroenteritis. Role of Norwalk virus. N. Engl. J. Med. 314:678-681.

Myers, B.J. 1979. Anisakine nematodes in fresh, commercial fish from waters along the United States' Washington, Oregon and California coasts. J. Food Prot. 42:380-384.

NBCIA (National Blue Crab Industry Association). 1984. National Crabmeat Industry Pasteurization Standards. National Fisheries Institute, Arlington, Va. 8 pp.

Newman, J.J., S. Waycott, and L.M. Cooney. 1979. Arthritis due to *Listeria monocytogenes*. Arthritis Rheumatism 22:1139-1140.

NFPA/CMI Container Integrity Task Force. 1984. Botulism risk from post-processing contamination of commercially canned food in metal containers. J. Food Protect. 47:801-816.

Nishibuchi, M., M. Ishibashi, Y. Takeda, and J.B. Kaper. 1985. Detection of the thermostable direct hemolysin gene and related DNA sequences in *Vibrio parahaemolyticus* and other *Vibrio* species by the DNA colony hybridization test. Infect. Immun. 49:481-486.

NOAA (National Oceanic and Atmospheric Administration). 1990. Fishery Products Inspection Manual. Part III: Certification. Chapter 3, Section 1. Handbook No. 25. DOC/NOAA/NMFS, February.

NRC (National Research Council). 1987. Poultry Inspection: The Basis for a Risk-Assessment Approach. A report of the Food and Nutrition Board. National Academy Press, Washington, D.C. 167 pp.

Overby, L.R., F. Deinhardt, and J. Deinhardt, eds. 1983. Viral Hepatitis: Second International Max von Pettenkofer Symposium. Marcel Dekker, New York. 311 pp.

Pace, P.J., and E.R. Krumbiegel. 1973. *Clostridium botulinum* and smoked fish production 1963-1972. J. Milk Food Technol. 36:42-49.

Paille, D., C. Hackney, L. Reily, M. Cole, and M. Kilgen. 1987. Seasonal variation in the fecal coliform population of Louisiana oysters and its relationship to microbiological quality. J. Food Protect. 50:545-549.

Palumbo, S.A., M.M. Bencivengo, F. Del Corral, A.C. Williams, and R.L. Buchanan. 1989. Characterization of the *Aeromonas hydrophila* group isolated from retail foods of animal origin. J. Clin. Microbiol. 27:854-859.

Parker, M.T. 1984. Enteric infections: Typhoid and paratyphoid fever. Pp. 407-428 in G. Wilson, A. Miles, and M.T. Parker, eds. Topley and Wilson's Principles of Bacteriology, Virology and Immunology, Vol. 3, 7th ed. Williams and Wilkins, Baltimore.

Peixotto, S.S., G. Finne, M.O. Hanna, and C. Vanderzant. 1979. Presence, growth and survival of *Yersinia enterocolitica* in oysters, shrimp and crab. J. Food Protect. 42:974-981.

Peterson, D.A., T.R. Hurley, J.C. Hoff, and L.G. Wolfe. 1983. Effect of chlorine treatment on infectivity of hepatitis A virus. Appl. Environ. 45:223-227.

Pierce, N.F., and A. Mondal. 1974. Clinical features of cholera. Pp. 209-220 in D. Barua and W.Barrow, eds. Cholera. W.B. Saunders, Philadelphia.

Pitarangsi, C., P. Echeverria, R. Whitmire, C. Tirapat, S. Formal, G.J. Dammin, and M. Tingtalapong. 1982. Enteropathogenicity of *Aeromonas hydrophila* and *Plesiomonas shigelloides*: Prevalence among individuals with and without diarrhea in Thailand. Infect. Immun. 35:666-673.

Post, L.S., D.A. Lee, M. Solberg, D. Furgang, J. Specchio, and C. Graham. 1985. Development of botulinal toxin and sensory deterioration during storage of vacuum and modified atmosphere packaged fish fillets. J. Food Sci. 50:990-996.

Richards, G.P. 1985. Outbreaks of shellfish-associated enteric virus illness in the United States: Requisite for development of viral guidelines. J. Food Prot. 48:815-823.

Richards, G.P. 1987. Shellfish-associated enteric virus illness in the United States, 1934-1984. Estuaries 10:84-85.

Richards, G.P. 1988. Microbial purification of shellfish: A review of depuration and relaying. J. Food Protect. 51:218-251.

Rippey, S.R., and J.L. Verber. 1988. Shellfish borne disease outbreaks. Department of Health and Human Services, Public Health Service, Food and Drug Administration, Shellfish Sanitation Branch. NETSU, Davisville, R.I. 43 pp.

Robins-Browne, R.M., M.D. Miliotis, S. Cianciosi, V.L. Miller, S. Falkow, and J.G. Morris, Jr. 1989. Detection of virulence in *Yersinia* species by DNA colony hybridization. J. Clin. Microbiol. 27:644-650.

Rodrick, G. 1990. Indigenous bacterial pathogens. Pp. 285-301 in D. Ward and C. Hackney, eds. Microbiology of Marine Food Products. Van Nostrand Reinhold, New York.

Safrin, S., J.G. Morris, Jr., M. Adams, V. Pons, R. Jacobs, and J.E. Conte, Jr. 1988. Non-O1 *Vibrio cholerae* bacteremia: Case report and review. Rev. Infect. Dis. 10:1012-1017.

Sakaguchi, G. 1979. Botulism. Pp. 389-442 in H. Rieman and F. Bryan, eds. Food-Borne Infection and Intoxication. Academic Press, New York.

Schlech, W.F., P.M. Lavigne, R.A. Bortolussi, A.C. Allen, E.V. Haldane, A.J. Wort, A.W. Hightower, S.E. Johnson, S.H. King, E.S. Nicholls, and C.V. Broome. 1988. Epidemic listeriosis – Evidence for transmission by food. N. Engl. J. Med. 308:203-206.

Schwartz, B., C.V. Broome, G.R. Brown, A.W. Hightower, C.A. Ciesielski, S. Gaventa, B.G. Gellin, L. Mascola, and the Listeriosis Study Group. 1988. Association of sporadic listeriosis with consumption of uncooked hotdogs and undercooked chicken. Lancet 1:779-782.

Shandera, W.X., J.M. Johnston, B.R. Davis, and P.A. Blake. 1983. Disease from infection with *Vibrio mimicus*, a newly recognized *Vibrio* species. Ann. Intern. Med. 99:169-171.

Shultz, L., J. Rutledge, R. Grodner, and S. Biede. 1984. Determination of the thermal death time of *Vibrio cholerae* in blue crabs (*Callinectis sapidus*). J. Food Protect. 47:4-6.

Simonson, J., and R.J. Siebeling. 1986. Rapid serological identification of *Vibrio vulnificus* by anti-H coagglutination. Appl. Environ. Microbiol. 52:1299-1304.

Simpson, L.M., V.K. White, S.F. Zane, and J.D. Oliver. 1987. Correlation between virulence and colony morphology in *Vibrio vulnificus*. Infect. Immun. 55:269-272.

Smith, J., R. Benedict, and R. Buchanan. 1987. *Listeria monocytogenes* in meat and poultry products: Review of factors affecting its introduction and growth in these foods. Report of the Microbial Food Safety Research Unit Eastern Region Research Center, U.S. Department of Agriculture. Philadelphia, Pa. 16 pp.

Smith, J.W., and R. Wooten. 1975. Experimental studies on the migration of *Anisakis* sp. larvae (nematode: Ascaridida) into the flesh of herring (*Clupea harengus* L.). Int. J. Parasitol. 5:133-136.

Sobsey, M.D. 1990. Viruses during controlled and natural depuration. Presentation to the Gulf and South Atlantic Shellfish Sanitation Conference, Wilmington, N.C.

Sobsey, M.D., C.R. Hackney, R.J. Carrick, B. Ray, and M.L. Speck. 1980. Occurrence of enteric bacteria and viruses in oysters. J. Food Protect. 43:111-113.

Son, N.T., and G.H. Fleet. 1980. Behavior of pathogenic bacteria in the oyster, *Crassostrea commercialis*, during depuration, re-laying, and storage. Appl. Environ. Microbiol. 40:994-1002.

Stern, N. 1982. *Yersinia enterocolitica*: Recovery from foods and virulence characterization. Food Technol. 36:84-88.

Tacket, C.O., F. Brenner, and P.A. Blake. 1984. Clinical features and an epidemiological study of *Vibrio vulnificus* infections. J. Infect. Dis. 149:558-561.

Tamplin, M. 1990. The ecology of *Vibrio vulnificus* in *Crassostrea virginica*. Abstracts annual meeting, National Shellfisheries Association, April 1-6, Williamsburg, Va. 451 pp.

Tamplin, M., G.E. Rodrick, N.J. Blake, and T. Cuba. 1982. Isolation and characterization of *Vibrio vulnificus* from two Florida estuaries. Appl. Environ. Microbiol. 44:1466-1470.

Tauxe, R.V., J. Vandepitte, G. Wauters, S.M. Martin, V. Goossens, P. De Mol, R. Van Noyen, and G. Thiers. 1987. *Yersinia enterocolitica* infections and pork: The missing link. Lancet 1:1129-1132.

Taylor, B.C., and M. Nakamura. 1964. Survival of *Shigella* in food. J. Hyg. 62:303-322.

Thompson, C.A., and C. Vanderzant. 1976. Serological and hemolytic characteristics of *Vibrio parahaemolyticus* from marine sources. J. Food Sci. 41:204-205.

Thompson, R.C. 1982. A tin of salmon had but a tiny hole. FDA Consumer 16:7-9.

Torne, J., R. Miralles, S. Tomas, and P. Saballs. 1988. Typhoid fever and acute non-A non-B hepatitis after shellfish consumption. Eur. J. Clin. Microbiol. Infect. Dis. 7:581-582.

Twedt, R.M., J.M. Madden, J.M. Hunt, D.W. Francis, J.T. Peeler, A.P. Duran, W.O. Hebert, S.G. McCay, C.N. Roderick, G.T. Spite, and T.J. Wazenski. 1981. Characterization of *Vibrio cholerae* isolated from oysters. Appl. Environ. Microbiol. 41:1475-1478.

Van Damme, L.R., and J. Vandepitte. 1980. Frequent isolation of *Edwardsiella tarda* and *Plesiomonas shigelloides* from healthy Zairese freshwater fish: A possible source of sporadic diarrhea in the tropics. Appl. Environ. Microbiol. 39:475-479.

Ward, D.R. 1989. Microbiology of aquaculture products. Food Technol. 43:82-86.

White, D.O., and F. Fenner. 1986. Picornaviruses, cornaviruses and caliciviruses, and other viral diseases. Pp. 451-478 and 596-601 in Medical Virology, 3rd. ed. Academic Press, New York.

WHO (World Health Organization). 1990. Report of WHO Consultation on Public Health Aspects of Seafood-Borne Zoonotic Diseases. Proceedings of a meeting in Hanover, Federal Republic of Germany, November 14-16, 1989. WHO/CDS/VPH/90.86. 62 pp.

4

Naturally Occurring Fish and Shellfish Poisons

ABSTRACT

Incidents of illness due to naturally occurring seafood toxins reported to the Centers for Disease Control in the period 1978-1987 were limited to ciguatera, scombroid fish poisoning, and paralytic shellfish poisoning. Other intoxications, including puffer fish poisoning and neurotoxic (brevetoxic) shellfish poisoning, were reported earlier, and diarrhetic shellfish poisoning and amnesic shellfish poisoning are prospective risks that should be anticipated. Naturally, toxic fish and shellfish cannot be distinguished from nontoxic animals by sensory inspection, and the toxins are not destroyed by normal cooking or processing. Except for scombroid fish poisoning, natural intoxications are both highly regional and species associated, and toxins are present in the fish or shellfish at the time of capture. Scombroid poisoning is due to histamine produced by bacteria multiplying on certain fish that are mishandled after capture, and illnesses are widely reported from different states.

Ciguatera is a sometimes severe disease caused by consuming certain species of fish in tropical waters usually associated with islands or reefs. The disease is most common (endemic) in the Caribbean and Pacific islands, with some outbreaks in southern Florida and sporadic cases in other states due to imported fish or tourist travel to endemic areas. Ciguatera was responsible for about half of all reported outbreaks of seafood intoxications in 1978-1987. Treatments are largely supportive, but mortality is low. There are presently no effective control systems in place for prevention of ciguatera because a generally accepted test for toxic fish is not available. Warnings and advisories concerning the hazards of ciguatera and the risks of consuming particular species of fish from ciguatera areas are issued by states. Active control based on regulation of fishing dangerous species, supported by testing suspect fish at dockside or on board the catching vessel to detect and reject ciguatoxic fish, is proposed. Increased education of the consuming public, sports fishers, and health professionals on the hazards and symptoms of ciguatera is also recommended.

Scombroid poisoning reportedly caused about the same number of outbreaks as ciguatera but was much more widespread in occurrence. Tuna, mahimahi (dolphin), and bluefish were implicated as the major cause of scombroid poisoning in the United States. The disease is generally mild and self-resolving, and symptoms can be ameliorated by antihistamine drugs. Because the histamine that causes scombroid poisoning is produced after the fish have been caught as a consequence of improper temperature control, the disease can be prevented by rapidly cooling fish after capture to 10°C or lower and holding them at or below this temperature at all times before cooking and eating. A system based on the Hazard Analysis Critical Control Point would ensure this for commercially handled fish, but the education of subsistence and recreational fishers is also necessary.

Paralytic shellfish poisoning was reported as a minor cause of seafood-borne illness in 1978-1987 with only two deaths. This is a remarkable record in view of the annual occurrence of toxic situations among shellfish on both the East and the West coasts of the United States and indicates that current control measures applied by coastal states are highly effective. However, the increasing occurrence of toxic dinoflagellate blooms and changing eating practices among some sectors of the consuming public require increased surveillance and the development of more rapid and simple tests for toxic shellfish.

Although other natural seafood intoxications have not been reported recently in U.S. consumers (except for an outbreak of neurotoxic shellfish poisoning in North Carolina in 1987), the potential for their occurrence either from domestically produced seafoods or from imports is real. Increased vigilance concerning imported products, based on a requirement for certified nontoxicity, is recommended. Moreover, both state and federal laboratories should be prepared to test for these "other" toxins, and procedures should be in place to deal with outbreaks.

INTRODUCTION

The toxic diseases from fish and shellfish of importance to American consumers include ciguatera, scombroid fish poisoning, paralytic shellfish poisoning, neurotoxic (brevetoxic) shellfish poisoning, puffer fish poisoning, diarrhetic shellfish poisoning, and amnesic shellfish poisoning (Hughes and Merson, 1976; Mills and Passmore, 1988; Ragelis, 1984; Todd, 1989). In all cases, illness is due to ingestion of tissues containing heat-resistant toxins that are not destroyed by normal cooking and whose presence is undetectable by organoleptic means. Except for scombroid poisoning, toxins usually accumulate in fish or shellfish through the food chain, so that the fish or shellfish are toxic at the time of harvest. Scombroid poisoning is caused by bacterial-induced chemical changes resulting from mishandling of fish after capture, which is more readily susceptible to human control (Taylor, 1986).

Fish poisoning, principally ciguatera and scombroid fish poisoning, was responsible for 17.8% of all confirmed food-borne disease outbreaks listed by the Centers for Disease Control (CDC) in 1978-1987. Reports were approximately evenly split between the two principal toxicoses: 179 ciguatera outbreaks involving 791 cases, and 157 outbreaks of scombroid with 757 cases (Table 4-1). However, as noted elsewhere in this report, CDC data are highly skewed, in this case due to the limited area within which ciguatera occurs, which enhances the visibility of this disease, and to the different symptoms associated with scombroid poisoning. Thirteen outbreaks of paralytic shellfish poisoning (PSP), the most dangerous of the intoxications, were reported and involved 134 cases, most of which (94) were from two large California outbreaks in 1980. No cases of puffer fish or diarrhetic shellfish poisoning were reported to CDC in this period. The actual incidences of cases of ciguatera and PSP with milder symptoms are probably higher than indicated due to underreporting, as evident from a comparison of CDC data with those obtained in incidence studies in defined geographical areas (Mills and Passmore, 1988; Morris et al., 1982b; Nishitani and Chew, 1988).

TABLE 4-1 Illness Due to Natural Seafood Toxins in the United States Reported to CDC

	Ciguatera		Scombroid		PSP	
	Outbreaks	Cases	Outbreaks	Cases	Outbreaks	Cases
1978	19	56	7	30	4	10
1979	21	97	14	134	1	3
1980	15	52	28	151	5	116
1981	30	219	9	93	-	-
1982	8	37	18	58	0	5
1983	13	43	13	271	-	-
1984	18	78	12	53	-	-
1985	26	104	14	56	2	3
1986	18	70	20	60	-	0
1987	11	35	22	95	-	0
Total	179	791	157	757	13	137

SPECIFIC INTOXICATIONS

Ciguatera

Ciguatera is a clinical syndrome caused by eating the flesh of toxic fish caught in tropical reef and island waters. The toxin is believed to originate in a microscopic dinoflagellate alga *Gambierdiscus toxicus* that grows on reefs (Bagnis et al., 1980). However, other benthic algae have also been implicated. Fish eating the algae become toxic, and the effect is magnified through the food chain so that large predatory fish become the most toxic. The occurrence of toxic fish tends to be localized, but localization is not consistent and toxic fish may occur sporadically anywhere in a reef or island location (Engleberg et al., 1983). More than 400 species have been implicated in ciguatera poisoning (Randall, 1980), but the fish most commonly implicated include amberjack, snapper, grouper, barracuda, goatfish, and reef fish belonging to the Carrangidae (Table 4-2). In the United States, ciguatera occurs principally in Hawaii, Puerto Rico, the Virgin Islands, Guam, and Florida (CDC, 1989). A particularly high incidence was reported from Guam (Haddock, 1989), and a few cases have been reported in other states caused by fish shipped from Florida. Cases are frequently associated with travel to endemic ciguatera areas such as Hawaii and the Virgin Islands, and there is concern that many cases are not recognized by mainland U.S. physicians.

The disease affects both gastrointestinal and neurological systems (Bagnis et al., 1979; Morris et al., 1982a). Gastrointestinal symptoms, including diarrhea, nausea, vomiting, and abdominal pain, appear 3-5 hours after ingestion of the fish and are of short duration. Neurological symptoms begin 12-18 hours after consumption and may be moderate to severe; they commonly last for 1-82 days but may persist for several months. In rare cases, symptoms may last for years, with exacerbation associated with fish consumption or possibly alcohol (Halstead, 1967). Symptoms typically include hot-cold inversion (hot coffee tastes cold, ice cream tastes hot); muscular aches;

tingling and numbness of lips, tongue, and perioral region; metallic taste; dryness of mouth; anxiety; prostration; dizziness; chills; sweating; dilated eyes, blurred vision, and temporary blindness.   Paralysis and death may occur in a few extreme cases. Symptoms may be extremely debilitating, resulting in extended periods of disability. Intravenous mannitol may relieve acute symptoms (Palafox et al., 1988), provided it is given within several hours of consumption, with amitriptyline (Bowman, 1984) or tocainide (Lange et al., 1988) suggested for more chronic manifestations.   There is considerable individuality in patient response (Engleberg et al., 1983).

TABLE 4-2 Fish Reported as a Vehicle of Ciguatera to CDC 1978-1987 Ordered by Frequency of Reported Involvement[a]

Common Fish Name	Genus or Family Name
Amberjack	*Seriola* species
Snappers[b]	Lutjanidae
Groupers	Serranidae
Goatfish	Mullidae
Po'ou	*Cheilinus* species
Jacks	Carangidae
Barracuda	Sphyrenidae
Ulua	*Caranx* species
Wrasse	Labridae
Surgeon fish	Acantharidae
Moray eel	Muraeinidae
Papio	*Trachinotus* species
Roi	*Cephalopolis* species
Rabbit fish	*Siganus* species
Parrot fish	Scaridae
Miscellaneous reef fish	

[a] See Halstead (1967) for a more complete listing of fish species involved in Ciguatera outbreaks.
[b] These categories include a number of different species commonly referred to by the vernacular name. Not all species in each category are necessarily toxic.
SOURCE: CDC (1981a-c, 1983a,b, 1984, 1985, 1989) and Haddock (1989).

Several toxic compounds have been isolated from ciguatoxic fish and from *Gambierdiscus*. The principal toxin called "ciguatoxin" is a small lipid-soluble polyether with a molecular weight of 1,112 (Scheuer et al., 1967); this toxin has been purified and its structure determined (Murata et al., 1990). Ciguatoxin (CTX) has a molecular formula of $C_{60}H_{88}O_{19}$ and is a brevitoxin type polyether, approximately 100 times more potent than terodotoxin. Ciguatoxin opens voltage-dependent sodium channels in cell membranes (Bidard, 1984), and studies with in vitro tissue preparations suggest that the toxin causes a nerve conduction block after initial neural stimulation. In animal models, low doses of ciguatoxin cause mild hypotension and brachycardia. Higher doses give a biphasic response with an initial brachycardia/hypotension followed by tachycardia/hypertension; very high doses produce a phrenic nerve block with respiratory arrest (Gillespie et al., 1986). Another lipid-soluble neurotoxin from ciguateric fish is called "scaritoxin." This toxin has been shown to depress oxidative metabolic processes in rat brain and has a depolarizing action on excitable membranes.

Generally, the pharmacological action is close to that of ciguatoxin, and they may be related compounds (Legrand and Bagnis, 1984). Maitotoxin is a water-soluble toxin that may interfere with or modify calcium movement or calcium conductance in tissues. Other lipid-soluble toxins have been reported, but their structures and pharmacologic roles are not understood (Ragelis, 1984).

The reported incidence of ciguatera as indicated by CDC data is on the order of 15-20 outbreaks per year, involving 50 to 100 cases. Cases reported to the CDC occur almost exclusively in Hawaii, Puerto Rico, the Virgin Islands, and Florida (Table 4-3). However, these numbers appear to reflect significant underreporting. In a randomized, stratified community survey conducted in the U.S. Virgin Islands, the calculated incidence rate was 73 cases/10,000 population/year (Morris et al., 1982b). In Puerto Rico, 45 cases were reported to the Puerto Rico Poison Control Center in 1982. In an associated telephone survey, 7% of persons contacted reported that at least one family member had at one time had ciguatera (Holt et al., 1984). In Miami, 129 cases of ciguatera were reported to the Dade County Health Department between 1972 and 1976, for an annual incidence of 5 cases/100,000 population; the actual incidence was estimated to be 10-100 times this figure (i.e., 50-500 cases/100,000 population) (Lawrence et al., 1980). An incidence rate of 234.9 cases/100,000 population was reported for the Marshall Islands during 1982-1987 (Ruff, 1989). The average annual incidence in Hawaii for 1984-1988 was only 8.7 cases/100,000 population, but this varied greatly from island to island: in 1988 the rate per 100,000 population was 3.2 on Oahu, 12.5 on Kauai, 11.1 on Maui, 33.9 on Hawaii (the largest island), and 7.5 for the state (Gollop and Pon, 1991). These data emphasize the striking regional nature of this disease and its very real importance as a cause of morbidity in endemic areas. There is some evidence from the Pacific region that changes in the reef environment due to construction or other underwater activities can cause an increase in the occurrence of ciguatoxic fish (Anderson et al., 1983; Ruff, 1989).

For the vast majority of U.S. consumers, the disease can be contracted only through consumption of fish imported from endemic areas. For residents of south Florida, the Caribbean, and Hawaiian or other Pacific islands, absolute safety depends on individual abstinence from eating reef fish. The risk may be greatly reduced by

TABLE 4-3 Outbreaks and Cases of Ciguatera in the United States Reported to CDC 1978-1987

State	Outbreaks	Cases	Percentage of Outbreaks	Percentage of Cases
California	1	2	0.6	0.3
Florida	9	35	5.0	4.4
Guam[a]	60	117	56.0	48.0
Hawaii	144	560	80.0	71.0
Louisiana	1	6	0.6	0.8
Puerto Rico	13	73	7.0	9.0
Vermont	1	3	0.6	0.4
Virgin Islands	9	110	5.0	14.0
Washington	1	2	0.6	0.3
Total	179	791		

[a] From Haddock (1989). These data are not included in calculation of total outbreaks and cases.

avoidance of particular species of fish from known "hot-spot" areas (Randall, 1980). However, hot spots may persist for extended periods of time or may change (Cooper, 1964; Halstead, 1967). Voluntary action by commercial fish distributors in some areas has been quite effective. Thus amberjack (*Seriola dumerili*, Kahala) is not sold commercially in Hawaii because of the known high incidence of ciguatoxic fish of this species. Other suspect species coming to market in Hawaii may be tested by the "stick test." Also, the Hawaii Department of Health (HDH, 1988) publishes a warning pamphlet on *Fish Poisoning in Hawaii* and periodically issues advisories on dangerous species and the areas from which they have been taken.

In areas where reef fish are part of the regular diet of inhabitants or visitors, and particularly where significant quantities of fish are caught and consumed by recreational or small-boat fishermen, it seems unlikely that ciguatera can be completely prevented. The impossibility of detecting toxic fish by organoleptic inspection and the sporadic occurrence of such fish limit control options. The availability of a simple reliable test would greatly improve the situation. At present, the only ciguatera screening program in existence is that employed by the Tokyo Central Wholesale Fish Market in Japan. Hygiene inspectors examine incoming shiploads of fish that have originated in tropical island regions. Suspect specimens are removed for testing. Muscle extracts are prepared and tested on cats and mice for evidence of ciguatoxicity (Halstead, 1970). This is a lengthy and expensive screening technique that is impractical when dealing with large numbers of samples. A radioimmunoassay (RIA) was developed by Hokama and co-workers in Hawaii (Hokama et al., 1977) and then modified to a simpler, enzyme immunoassay (Hokama, 1985). The method has been further simplified to a "stick" test that has been used to screen fish landed in Hawaii and holds promise as a practical basis for control (Hokama et al., 1989b).

However, even this test costs $1 to 2 per fish, and it would not be possible to test each reef fish landed. Kits are being developed for use by sports fishers that could partly resolve the cost problem. In any case it would be desirable to limit testing to high-risk fish. Research is needed into methods for predicting the development of ciguateric conditions in reef fishing areas, perhaps by assessing *Gambierdiscus* or other toxigenic microorganism populations and somehow closing such areas to fishing when the risk is high. Reef closure would probably be feasible in discrete Pacific islands where there is limited movement of fish from one reef area to another. However, this might not be the case in the Caribbean where fish movement between reefs is easier and more common. Obviously, there should be some follow-up on the reports of a relationship between reef disturbance and increased occurrence of ciguateric fish because this may result from human activity that can be controlled (Gollop and Pon, 1991).

Estimates of the economic consequences of ciguatera are not easily made. However, they are significant for island communities largely dependent on tourism. Ragelis (1984) quoted an estimate of an annual loss to fishermen in the Caribbean region and Hawaii of $10 million as a result of restricted fishing, but this may be low.

In summary, the risks of contracting ciguatera fish poisoning are low for most consumers of seafood in the mainland United States. Risks are much higher in Hawaii, other Pacific islands, Puerto Rico, and the Virgin Islands, with more moderate risks in areas such as Miami that border endemic zones. For mainland consumers, protection could be afforded by strict control of imports and intrastate shipments. However, such an approach may be unnecessarily severe and does not address the much more significant problems that exist in endemic areas. A more reasonable (and potentially cost-effective) approach would be to emphasize development of an inexpensive but reliable assay for ciguatoxic fish, similar to the stick test proposed by Hokama (1990). The stick test measures ciguatoxin and polyether compounds including okadaic acid (Hokama et al., 1989a). In a recent outbreak in Hawaii due to Philippine fish, the test was positive for a fish that was then shown to contain palytoxin (Kodama et al., 1989). It has been suggested that palytoxin, previously reported from parrot fish and crab in Japan, is one of the toxins "under the rubric of ciguatera" (Kodama et al., 1989). Obviously, this whole area needs further research, particularly because of the concern over false-positive results from the stick test. If such an assay were widely available, it might be applied both by regulation and voluntarily to reduce the incidence of disease in endemic areas, particularly if consumers were knowledgeable and insisted on purchasing only fish that had been screened for toxicity. Similarly, interstate shipment and imports of potentially high-risk fish (grouper, jack) could be restricted to fish certified to be nontoxic. This is particularly important in view of the increased production and export of fish to the United States from Pacific islands and reef fishery areas of Southeast Asia, such as the Philippines (Miller, 1991).

Scombroid (Histamine) Fish Poisoning

Scombroid intoxication results from ingestion of fish containing high levels of free histamine. Initially, the disease was associated with consumption of scombroid fish such as tuna, mackerel, bonito, and saury. More recently, other types of fish have been identified as causing the intoxication, including mahimahi, bluefish, jack, mackerel, amberjack, herring, sardine, and anchovy. In the United States, scombroid fish poisoning has been caused dominantly by mahimahi, tuna, and bluefish (CDC, 1989) (see Table 4-4).

Scombroid food poisoning has a wider geographic occurrence in the United States than ciguatera, with incidents reported from 45 states during 1978-1988. The

TABLE 4-4 Fish Reported to CDC as Vehicles of Scombroid Poisoning in the United States, 1978-1986[a]

Common Name	Genus	Reported Outbreaks
Mahimahi	*Coryphaena*	55
Tuna	*Thunnus*	41
Bluefish	*Pomatomus*	13
Salmon (raw)	*Oncorhynchus*	2
Marlin	*Makaira*	1
Mackerel	*Scomber*	1
Blue Ulua	*Caranx*	1
Opelu	*Dicapterus*	1
Redfish	*Sebastes*	1

[a] Data not available for 1987.

highest number of outbreaks (45) and cases (171) occurred in Hawaii, but mainland states reported a total of 111 outbreaks and 582 cases (see Table 4-5). This reflects the fact that the disease, although associated with warm ambient temperatures, is not due solely to tropical or subtropical species of fish. Thus, the risk of scombroid poisoning is widespread among fish-eating consumers. Fortunately, the disease is mild, of short duration, and self-resolving without any sequelae in the vast majority of cases. Moreover, because the toxic condition is a consequence of improper handling or storage of the fish and there are effective testing methods to identify toxic fish, control and prevention are possible. The mildness and transient nature of scombroid poisoning make it likely that this disease is underreported.

Fish imported to the United States from warmwater countries, particularly mahimahi, have been implicated as a cause of scombroid poisoning; this reflects both the high ambient water and air temperatures in the originating area, and the poor handling conditions on boats and in markets permitting growth of the bacteria that convert histidine to histamine.

The disease is correctly described as histamine poisoning (Taylor, 1986); it includes gastrointestinal, neurological, hemodynamic, and cutaneous symptoms such as

TABLE 4-5 Scombroid Fish Poisoning in the United States Reported to CDC, 1978-1987

State	Outbreaks	Cases
Alaska	3	17
Arizona	3	7
California	18 (12%)	69 (9%)
Connecticut	8	47
District of Columbia	1	3
Florida	1	20
Hawaii	45 (29%)	170 (23%)
Idaho	1	4
Illinois	3	35
Indiana	1	4
Kentucky	1	7
Maine	3	54
Maryland	1	10
Michigan	3	25
Minnesota	1	24
Nebraska	1	10
New Jersey	4	42
New Mexico	1	2
New York	30 (19%)	122 (16%)
North Carolina	1	10
Pennsylvania	2	4
Texas	2	11
Vermont	3	6
Virginia	2	13
Virgin Islands	1	5
Washington	16	35
Wisconsin	1	1
Total	157	757

nausea, vomiting, diarrhea, cramping, headache, palpitations, flushing, tingling, burning, itching, hypotension, rash, urticaria, edema, and localized inflammation. The most frequent symptoms are tingling and burning sensations around the mouth ("peppery tasting"), gastrointestinal complaints, and a rash with itching. The illness is generally mild and self-resolving, with rapid onset of symptoms and duration of only a few hours. Normally, treatment is unnecessary but antihistamine drugs will provide relief.

The histamine is produced in the fish flesh by decarboxylation of free histidine, which is naturally present at high levels in species of fish implicated in scombroid fish poisoning (Lukton and Olcott, 1958). The production of histamine is due to the action of histidine decarboxylase, an enzyme produced by bacteria growing on the fish. Histidine decarboxylase production is not widespread among bacteria and is found principally among species of the Enterobacteriaceae, *Clostridium, Lactobacillus* (Taylor, 1986), and possibly *Vibrio* (Van Spreekens, 1987). The enteric bacteria *Morganella morganii, Klebsiella pneumoniae,* and *Hafnia alvei* have been isolated and identified from fish implicated in histamine poisoning (Havelka, 1967; Kawabata et al., 1956; Taylor et al., 1979). Other enteric bacteria, *Clostridium perfringens,* and halophilic vibrios have also been reported, but *M. morganii* and *K. pneumoniae* are most frequently implicated. These organisms are not commonly isolated from living fish and may be added during catching and handling (Taylor, 1986).

Bacteria must grow to a large enough population for significant production of histamine to occur. These are mesophilic bacteria that require temperatures higher than 15°C. In tropical areas of the world, fish temperatures at capture frequently exceed 20°C, and on small vessels it is not unusual for fish to be held on deck at even higher temperatures for several hours. Histamine production is optimal at 30°C (Arnold et al., 1980). Once a large population of bacteria has been established, residual enzyme activity continues slowly at refrigeration temperatures (0-5°C) though bacterial growth ceases.

Thus, histamine production in fish is a consequence of improper handling and storage of fish after capture. Indeed, histamine content may be used as an index of spoilage in certain fish. The Food and Drug Administration (FDA) considers a level of 20 milligrams (mg) of histamine per 100 grams (g) of flesh, or 200 parts per million (ppm), an indication of spoilage in tuna and 50 mg/100 g (500 ppm) an indication of hazard (Federal Register, 1982). This is close to the toxic dose estimate of 60 mg/100 g made by Simidu and Hibiku (1955). There is uncertainty regarding the threshold toxic dose because potentiators of toxicity are present in fish that lower the effective dosage compared with pure histamine.

The occurrence of scombroid fish poisoning in recent years, based on CDC reports, is between 12 and 20 outbreaks involving fewer than 100 cases per year (higher numbers were recorded in 1973, 1979, and 1980). This is, without question, a considerable underestimate because the illness is generally mild, passes rapidly with no aftereffects, and is thus not usually reported to health authorities. Good chemical tests are available for histamine in fish flesh (Taylor, 1986), which has allowed FDA to set an action level for histamine in tuna at 50 mg/100 g of flesh. Above this level the fish is considered hazardous. Fish histamine poisoning is preventable by proper handling of fish at the time of capture and during subsequent storage, processing, and distribution. Fish should be chilled as rapidly as possible after capture by using ice, refrigerated seawater or brine, or mechanical refrigeration. Flesh temperature should be brought below 15°C and preferably below 10°C within 4 hours; this should be normal practice in commercial systems.   Histamine levels should be monitored routinely by the industry in susceptible species where proper prior handling cannot be ensured.   The level at which testing is performed will depend on the species and product form (e.g., tuna for canning, hot smoked mackerel).   In the United States, the highest-risk fish commercially is probably imported fresh or frozen fish from tropical areas.   High histamine levels may be present in such fish when other overt signs of spoilage (bad odor, discoloration) are absent.   Imported fish should be subject to controls.   Domestically caught species in normal commercial channels are probably less of a problem because of the widespread use of ice and refrigeration.   Bluefish and sport caught tuna or mackerel present a more intractable control problem because they are caught by individuals and either do not enter commercial channels or do so in an unconventional way.   Some local or state control may be possible where licensed charter fishing boats are involved, perhaps by requiring that adequate facilities are provided for rapid chilling of fish and for their storage in a chilled state until landed. In the absence of a simple litmus test, control for most sports fishers and their families depends on education.   States should be encouraged to provide advisory bulletins to sports fishers.   However, it should be emphasized that this is a mild disease that is neither long lasting nor life threatening, and that symptoms can be relieved quickly by antihistamines.

Paralytic Shellfish Poisoning (PSP)

Paralytic shellfish poisoning results from ingesting bivalve molluscs (mussels, clams, oysters, scallops) that have consumed toxigenic dinoflagellates (Halstead and Schantz, 1984; Schantz, 1973).   The toxins are assimilated and temporarily stored by the shellfish.   In the United States, PSP is a problem primarily in the New England states on the East Coast and in Alaska, California, and Washington on the West Coast. Very few outbreaks have occurred in other areas of the United States from shellfish harvested in coastal states, reflecting the effectiveness of current testing and control measures for commercially produced shellfish.   Most disease incidents involve mussels, clams, and scallops gathered and eaten by recreational collectors often from closed areas.   The CDC listed 12 outbreaks involving 134 people with one death during 1978-1986 (Table 4-6).   The outbreaks occurred in Alaska, California, Massachusetts, Tennessee (due to mussels from California), and Washington (Table 4-7).   The Northeast Technical Support Unit (NETSU) compilation shows a total of 282 cases for the period, including cases from Maine, Alaska, and Massachusetts.   A report by Nishitani and Chew (1988), based on data from the West Coast, lists cases as follows: 68 from Alaska, 98 from California, 1 from Oregon, and 12 from Washington.   Thus, there is some evidence of underreporting of cases to CDC.   Although PSP is an extremely dangerous disease that can cause death, there is reason to believe that mild cases due to consumption of marginally toxic clams by recreational diggers are never reported to health authorities or are misdiagnosed.

Paralytic shellfish poisoning is potentially life threatening because the toxins involved are among the most poisonous known.   Symptoms are neurological and normally appear within an hour of eating toxic shellfish; in nonlethal cases they usually subside within a few days. Symptoms include tingling, numbness, and burning of the lips and fingertips; ataxia; giddiness; staggering; drowsiness; dry throat and skin;

TABLE 4-6 PSP Incidents in the United States Reported by CDC, 1978-1985

	Outbreaks	Cases	Deaths
Alaska	2	7	–
California	2	94	2
Massachusetts	1	15	–
Tennessee	1	5	–
Washington	7	16	–

TABLE 4-7 PSP Incidents in the United States Listed Elsewhere

	NETSU Cases	Cases Reported by Nishitani and Chew (1988)[a]
Alaska	54	75
California	132[b]	98
Maine	73	–
Massachusetts	41	–
Oregon	-	1
Tennessee	5	–
Washington	15	12

[a] 1978-1987: West Coast states only.
[b] 1969-1980.

incoherence; aphasia; rash; and fever. In severe cases, respiratory paralysis occurs, which can cause death usually during the first 24 hours, so that the prognosis for recovery is good for patients surviving this period. No antidote is known, but respiratory support is given when paralysis occurs. There are no sequelae, and patients recover completely. Immunity is not conferred by a poisonous episode and multiple incidents can occur.

The cause of PSP is a complex of toxins known as saxitoxins because all can be considered forms or derivatives of saxitoxin, whose structure was reported by Schantz et al. (1975). The 12 most commonly encountered include saxitoxin, neosaxitoxin, gonyautoxins (I, II, III, IV), B1, B2, C1, C2, C3, and C4, which vary in their toxic effects on mice (Boyer et al., 1978; Shimizu and Hsu, 1981). Saxitoxin, neosaxitoxin, and gonyautoxins II and III are roughly equal in toxicity, whereas the others are somewhat weaker (Hall and Reichardt, 1984). In the United States, the toxigenic dinoflagellates of importance are *Gonyaulax catenella* and *G. tamarenses*,[1] the first being most dominant on the West Coast and the second on the East Coast (Taylor, 1988). Strains of these microorganisms develop characteristic toxin profiles that usually contain six to eight saxitoxins. Shellfish feeding on blooms of these *Gonyaulax* ingest all toxins but seem to selectively retain or biologically modify some derivatives because the toxin profiles in clams or scallops may differ from those of the *Gonyaulax* on which they have been feeding (Schantz et al., 1975; Sullivan et al., 1983).

The saxitoxins are neurotoxins that act by blocking the flow of sodium (Na^+) ions through the sodium channels of nerves, thereby interfering with signal transmission. The lethal dose for humans is 1-4 mg expressed as saxitoxin equivalents (Schantz, 1986), and the FDA action limit is 80 micrograms (μg) of toxin per 100 g of shellfish tissue.

The classical method for analysis of saxitoxins is by mouse bioassay (Schantz et al., 1958), a standardized procedure in which the strain, size, and condition of the mouse are all important. Suitable groups of mice are challenged by injection of toxin extracts, and their responses are compared with those of mice injected with known toxin at different concentrations. This method is used by state laboratories in surveillance activities. The chemical analytical methods that have been used, mostly in research, include column separation, thin-layer chromatography, and fluorescent assays either directly or after separation by high-performance liquid chromatography (HPLC). The HPLC method is quite rapid and has been considered as a possible replacement of the mouse bioassay (Sullivan and Iwaoka, 1983). Recently, immunoassay methods have been developed and reported. These involve rabbit serum antibody preparations and monoclonal antibodies, and both radioimmunoassays and enzyme-linked immunoabsorbent assays (ELISA) have been used (Chu and Fan, 1985). However, so far these methods are not acceptable for regulatory use.

Blooms of the toxigenic dinoflagellates *Gonyaulax catenella* (West Coast) and *G. tamarensis* (East Coast) occur several times each year, primarily from April to October along the U.S. West Coast, Alaska, and the East Coast from Long Island Sound through Maine. Similar blooms occur off British Columbia and the Canadian Maritime Provinces. The occurrence of blooms is not predictable with the present state of knowledge. When these blooms occur, shellfish become toxic and remain toxic for several weeks after the bloom subsides. Some species of bivalve molluscs in a few areas remain constantly toxic (e.g., butter clams in parts of Washington State and in Alaska). Protection of the consumer is primarily the responsibility of the state in which potentially toxic shellfish originate and is achieved by closure of shellfish harvesting in affected areas. Closure may be absolute for certain species over a long period (e.g., ocean coast mussels in California) or temporary (e.g., most hard-shell clam operations in Washington and Oregon) (Nishitani and Chew, 1988). Because clam digging and oyster gathering from public beaches are popular recreational activities in coastal states, the authorities issue warnings through the media when dangerous conditions exist and post warning notices (multilingual in the West) on public beaches. Each of the affected states has a surveillance system involving regular sampling and testing of shellfish from different areas during the season for blooms (April to October). Toxicity tests are normally run in state public health laboratories by using the standardized mouse bioassay (AOAC, 1984), whereas the collection of samples and posting of beaches are frequently the responsibility of local (e.g., county) authorities. Commercial producers are required to submit samples for testing, and many voluntarily send shellfish to the state laboratories.

This system, although expensive for the states, has served the U.S. consumer well, which can be seen from the very small number of outbreaks reported to CDC in recent years. In 1977-1986, these involved only twelve outbreaks with 134 cases. Only two outbreaks, both due to mussels from the same source (California), were of commercial origin. All other outbreaks were among recreational clam diggers (shellfish gatherers). Despite the seriousness of the intoxication, there have been only two deaths in the last 10 years. West Coast state records show a somewhat higher number of outbreaks, which have typically involved recreational shellfish gatherers but with no serious consequences (Nishitani and Chew, 1988).

The present system of testing and control by the states appears to provide adequate protection to the consumer of domestically produced shellfish.

Neurotoxic Shellfish Poisoning (NSP)

Neurotoxic shellfish poisoning (sometimes referred to as brevetoxic shellfish poisoning, BSP) is caused by ingesting shellfish that have fed on the red tide organism *Gymnodinium breve* (formerly *Ptychodiscus brevis*). Red tides occur sporadically in the Gulf of Mexico and off the coast of Florida (Baden et al., 1984). They may be carried north in the Gulf Stream, occasionally affecting the coastline of adjacent states. The dinoflagellate blooms are easily observed as a red coloration of seawater, and the organisms can be detected microscopically. Red tides usually cause massive fish kills, and the carcasses wash ashore. Irritant aerosols are produced by wind and wave action, which may cause respiratory distress. Filter feeding molluscs ingest the dinoflagellates and retain the toxin in their tissues for some time. No cases of NSP were reported to CDC in the period 1978-1986, but five cases were reported from Florida in 1973-1974 according to NETSU. During a red tide incident in North Carolina in 1987-1988, 48 persons became ill with NSP (Tester and Fowler, 1990). Reports of respiratory irritation affecting people in coastal areas were received on October 29 and 30, 1987; oyster harvesting was closed on November 2. However, 35 of the reported cases occurred prior to the ban on shellfish harvesting which lasted from 3½-6 months, depending on location. The basis for closure was the occurrence of more than 5,000 *G. breve* cells per liter of seawater, and reopening of harvest was dependent on demonstrated absence of brevetoxin in 100-g samples of shellfish meat based on a mouse bioassay (DNR, 1985; FDA, 1989). Notwithstanding this incident, which occurred as a result of the first bloom of *G. breve* reported in North Carolina, the general record in recent years suggests that the surveillance and closure systems operated by the states are indeed effective.

Symptoms resulting from the ingestion of shellfish containing brevetoxins include tingling and numbness of the lips, tongue, throat, and perioral area; muscular aches; gastrointestinal upset; and dizziness. The intoxication is usually not fatal. Onset is rapid and symptoms subside within a few hours or days at most. There is no antidote.

The symptoms appear to be due to two brevetoxins produced by *G. breve* that bind to nerve cells (Baden et al., 1984). They may be analyzed chemically, but this is not done routinely. Identification of a dangerous condition is readily made by observation of red tide conditions, including characteristic fish kills, and of the organisms themselves in the water. Local authorities then routinely close shellfish harvesting to industries and the public.

Diarrhetic Shellfish Poisoning (DSP)

Diarrhetic shellfish poisoning is caused by ingestion of mussels, scallops, or clams that have been feeding on *Dinophysis fortii* or *D. acuminata* and other species of *Dinophysis* and possibly *Prorocentrum* (Edler and Hageltorn, 1990; Yasumoto and Murata, 1990). There have been no confirmed outbreaks in the United States, but the disease is common in Japan and has become a problem in Europe. One confirmed DSP episode occurred in Canada in 1990.

Symptoms include diarrhea, nausea, vomiting, and abdominal pain. Onset occurs from 30 minutes to a few hours after eating toxic shellfish, and the duration is usually short with a maximum of a few days in severe cases. The disease is not life threatening (Yasumoto et al., 1984).

At least five toxins have been isolated from dinoflagellates and shellfish. Okadaic acid is most commonly encountered in Europe where *D. acuminata* is the usual agent, and mixtures of okadaic acid, dinophysistoxins, and pectenotoxins are detected in Japanese cases usually involving *D. fortii* (Yasumoto and Murata, 1990). There is a mouse bioassay for the toxins.

For the U.S. consumer, DSP would appear, at present, to be a hazard only for imported products and should be controllable by import regulation. Shellfish should be imported only from countries with whom the United States has a memorandum of understanding (MOU). Testing for shellfish toxins should be part of the general practice under the MOU. Nevertheless, because *Dinophysis* does occur in U.S. coastal waters, regulatory agencies in the United States should be alert for the possibility of an outbreak (Freudenthal and Jijina, 1988).

Puffer Fish Poisoning (PFP)

Puffer fish poisoning results from ingestion of the flesh of certain species of fish belonging to the Tetraodontidae (Halstead, 1967). The toxin involved is called tetrodotoxin and was originally believed to be a true ichthyosarcotoxin produced by the fish itself. The toxicity of poisonous puffers fluctuates greatly (Halstead, 1988). Recent observations that cultured puffer fish are atoxic has supported a food chain origin for the toxin, but this has not yet been confirmed (Mosher and Fuhrman, 1984). It has recently been shown, however, that certain common marine vibrios can produce a form of the toxin (Narita et al., 1987), and because vibrios occur as part of the microflora of puffer fish, they may be implicated in toxicity development (Sugita et al., 1989).

Puffer fish poisoning has not been reported in mainland United States in recent years, but incidents were reported in the past. Seven cases were reported in Florida between 1951 and 1974, including three fatalities (Benson, 1956; Hemmert, 1974). They appear to have been caused by the consumption of locally caught species of *Sphoeroides.* The common puffer fish, *Arothron hispidus,* has been implicated in at least seven fatalities in Hawaii (HDH, 1988). There are 20-100 deaths from fugu poisoning in Japan each year, where various species of puffer fish are eaten as a delicacy; this occurs despite very stringent controls imposed by Japanese authorities on the marketing and restaurant preparation of the dish (Ogura, 1971).

The symptoms of puffer fish poisoning are similar to those described for paralytic shellfish poisoning, including initial tingling and numbness of lips, tongue, and fingers leading to paralysis of the extremities; ataxia; difficulty in speaking; and finally, death by asphyxiation due to respiratory paralysis. Nausea and vomiting are common early symptoms. The similarity in symptoms is not surprising because tetrodotoxin, although chemically different from the saxitoxins, also blocks sodium channels. No antidote has been identified for tetrodotoxin and treatment is supportive. The toxicity of tetrodotoxin is similar to that of saxitoxin, and 1-4 mg constitutes a lethal dose for humans.

There is disagreement concerning the toxicity of U.S. Atlantic puffer fish. A recent advisory from the National Oceanic and Atmospheric Administration (NOAA, 1988) describes the northern puffer (*Sphoeroides maculatus*) as nontoxic and notes that the fish were marketed along the Atlantic Coast as "sea squab" during World War II. However, Hemmert (1974) shows a table indicating that the viscera, skin, and some flesh of *S. maculatus* caught in the Atlantic were toxic (Lalone et al., 1963). Larson et al. (1959, 1960) also reported that *S. maculatus* is toxic. From the West Coast, Goe and Halstead (1953) reported that the Pacific species *S. annulatus* is often toxic. The species *Arothron hispidus* has been implicated in at least seven fatalities in Hawaii. The wholesaling, preparation, and selling of puffers as food in Japan, even under the most rigid public health conditions by trained and certified puffer cooks, has not eliminated the danger of eating these fish. The fugu (puffer) still remains a major cause of fatal food intoxications in Japan. In brief, eating poisonous puffers is at best a game of Russian roulette. All of the U.S. puffers may be potentially toxic. There are too many variables in the puffer business, and sale of these should be prohibited in the United States. This subject has been documented and discussed at great length by Halstead (1967, 1988).

In view of these reports, it would seem prudent to exclude puffer fish, whether domestic or imported, from U.S. commercial channels at least until a proper assessment is made of the extent of risk they may present. The FDA has recently approved the importation of the Japanese puffer for fugu restaurants in the United States. Even though very strict requirements have been imposed in an attempt to ensure that the fish are nontoxic, the continuing Japanese experience should raise questions concerning the safety of this process for the U.S. public (Halstead, 1988).

Amnesic Shellfish Poisoning (ASP)

Amnesic shellfish poisoning has been proposed by Todd (1989) as a name for the syndrome caused by domoic acid. This severe disease has been identified only in a series of outbreaks in Canada in November and December 1988 involving 103 people. The toxin is present in some varieties of the diatom *Nitzschia pungens* and accumulated in mussels and clams in Atlantic Canada during a period of blooms of the diatom. Symptoms included vomiting, abdominal cramps, diarrhea, disorientation, and memory loss (Perl et al., 1988; Teitelbaum et al., 1990). Short-term memory loss was the most persistent symptom and lasted over a year in several cases. Autopsies on three fatalities showed necrosis of the hippocampus. The disease is particularly severe among older people, some of whom died in the Canadian outbreak.

Canadian authorities now analyze mussels and clams for domoic acid and enforce closure of beds when levels in excess of 20 μg/g are detected in their tissues (Gilgan et al., 1989).

Clearly, this is a toxin to be considered in U.S. testing regimes, and there should be close cooperation between U.S. and Canadian regulatory agencies on the movement of imported Canadian shellfish into the United States. *Nitzschia pungens* and *N. pseudodelicatissima* reportedly occur in northern U.S. and Canadian waters, and there is potential for development of toxicity in shellfish growing in these areas. States in the northeastern United States are now testing mussels for domoic acid.

Other Toxins

There are sporadic reports of other intoxications from seafoods from time to time (Halstead, 1988; Wekell and Liston, 1982), but these have not been investigated sufficiently to identify the toxic agent. As noted earlier, the somewhat variable symptoms defined as ciguatera and the reported association of polyether substances and palytoxin (Hokama et al., 1989a; Kodama et al., 1989) in fish implicated in such cases raise questions about the toxicity of reef-associated fish.

One well-defined syndrome reported to occur in Hawaii is "hallucinogenic fish poisoning." This illness follows consumption of mullet and a number of reef fish and occurs seasonally, usually during summer months. Hallucinations, insomnia, intense dreaming, weakness, and burning of the throat are common soon after eating the fish (Halstead and Schantz, 1984). Terrifying nightmares have been reported and constrictive chest pains occur. The condition is short-lived and self-resolving (Halstead, 1988; HDH, 1988). There does not seem to be any analytical test for this toxin.

CONCLUSIONS AND RECOMMENDATIONS

Diseases caused by natural fish poisoning are listed in Table 4-8. Three of these are of direct significance to the U.S. consumer: ciguatera, scombroid poisoning, and paralytic shellfish poisoning. Of these three, PSP, which has potentially the most severe health consequences, is well controlled by state surveillance and harvest closure practices.

Ciguatera, for which the largest number of cases is reported, has a major public health impact in Hawaii, Guam, and Caribbean island communities and a small effect in Florida. Prevention of ciguatera can be ensured only by interdiction of the supply of potentially toxic tropical reef fish to the U.S. consumer. This is theoretically possible through banning imports to the U.S. mainland of fish known to become ciguatoxic and through strict control of fishing in dangerous areas by fishery management agencies, accompanied by rejection of suspect species at the point of landing. Such action would probably be unacceptable in the island states and possessions, where local fishing provides essential employment and is closely tied to the tourist industry. Furthermore, blanket rejection of such species as groupers, which are mostly nontoxic, would greatly reduce consumer choice and adversely affect the income of fishermen and others in areas remote from the toxin problem. Fortunately, current research at the University of Hawaii provides good promise of early development of a simple reliable test for ciguatoxic fish. Such a test is urgently needed to enable selective rejection of toxic fish by testing either on board the fishing vessel or at dockside. On a longer-term basis, research should be directed toward the prediction of developing toxic conditions so that closure of fishing areas can be applied before human intoxications occur.

Scombroid fish poisoning is unquestionably a consequence of improper handling or processing of certain types of fish. Control of this hazard at the commercial level can be ensured, to a reasonable degree, by proper application of temperature control in handling and processing fish with known high content of free histidine. Where uncertainty exists concerning the quality of primary handling, as for some imported fish, reliable analytical tests may be used to determine whether fish or fish products exceed the limit for histamine content used by FDA. There seems to be no easy solution to the problem of recreationally caught fish (mostly tuna and bluefish) because it is unlikely that a mandatory inspection and testing program could be imposed. Education on proper fish handling to avoid the hazard and warnings issued by states to their recreational anglers and to businesses supporting such activity (charter boats, gear suppliers, etc.) appear to be the only available solution. However, because imported mahimahi was reportedly responsible for 47% of identified scombroid poisoning, embargoing this fish could have a significant effect. The other intoxications discussed in this chapter are rare and apparently under control in the United States (e.g., NSP and PFP), or not reported as a cause of sickness here (e.g., DSP and ASP). Nevertheless, agencies responsible for ensuring the safety of the U.S. food supply should maintain constant vigilance to avoid the importation of such problems. Appropriate tests should be sought and laboratories prepared for their use. Importers should be required to ensure that seafood products from countries where such intoxications have occurred are not toxic. This is best done by controlling imports through an MOU that would include provisions for toxicity testing.

Organoleptic inspection systems have little value in protecting the consumer from seafood intoxications. Toxic fish and shellfish usually look and smell perfectly normal. Protection of the consumer requires a multifaceted approach involving industry practices and regulations, control of harvest and distribution, and as a last resort, testing, seizure, and detention. This requires action by states and local authorities from different departments (e.g., fisheries and health), and a national program involving a single federal agency would probably not be effective without extensive state involvement.

In the final analysis the most effective measure is likely to be education of the fish-eating public about which fish and shellfish may be naturally toxic. Except for scombroid poisoning, toxicity is a function of the normal feeding habits of wild animals and cannot be controlled. Thus, potentially toxic fish may enter the food supply. Fortunately, the serious life-threatening intoxications are controllable so that most incidents of fish poisoning are of short duration and are self-resolving. Nevertheless, research aimed at the detection and elimination of toxic fish from the food supply and at methods of treatment for intoxications such as ciguatera that can have long-lasting and even disabling effects should be encouraged.

There is a need for educational materials to be made available to the fishing industry, public health workers, divers, and sports fishers. A number of popular handbooks have been published dealing with the potential health hazards caused by marine organisms (Halstead, 1959, 1990; Halstead et al., 1990). However, much of this information does not reach regulatory, clinical public health, and poison control centers (Freudenthal, 1990). In dealing with this subject matter, it is essential that the educational materials be fully illustrated, preferably in color. More charts and informational pamphlets are required.

TABLE 4-8 Information on Diseases Caused by Natural Toxins and Poisons
Found in Fish and Shellfish

	Paralytic Shellfish Poisoning (PSP)	Puffer Fish Poisoning (PFP)	Ciguatera
Seafood Involved	Mussels, clams, some fish; poison in digestive gland, siphon	Puffer or globefish (tetrodon), poison in liver, gonads, and roe	Most common in barracuda, kahala, snapper, and grouper
Source of poison or toxin	Toxic dinoflagellates: *Gonyaulax catenella* (Pacific); *G. tamarensis* (Atlantic)	May be produced by fish, some evidence from food chain	Not definitely known, possible *Gambierdiscus toxicus*
Areas commonly found	NW and NE North America, south Chile, North Sea area, Japan	Areas of Pacific around China and Japan, rare in U.S.	Tropical areas around world, in U.S. mainly around Florida
Method of assay	Mouse unit is minimum intraperitoneal dose to kill in 15 minutes, HPLC, ELISA (specific toxicity 7 µg/kg mouse)	Use mouse assay for PSP, HPLC (specific toxicity 7 µg/kg mouse)	Mouse test (poor), RIA, ELISA, immunological stick test under development
Type of poison or toxin	Neurotoxin, purine base, very water soluble	Neurotoxin, slightly water soluble	Lipid-soluble, polyether multicomponent
Extent of U.S. and worldwide problem	Local areas worldwide, few cases now	Important seafood in Japan; 100 cases, 50 deaths per year; rare in U.S.	Largest seafood problem, 50,000 cases per year, <0.1 mortality
Stability	Stable to cooking, most stable at pH 7 and below	Stable to cooking, stable between pH 4 and 9	Stable to cooking
Symptoms of poisoning in humans	Numbness, paralysis after eating; death 2-12 hours; prognosis good after 24 hours	Very similar to PSP	Abdominal pain, diarrhea, vomiting, neurological symptoms; rarely fatal
Dangerous and lethal human dose per 100 g of edible meat	1 mg (sickness) 2 mg or more (death)	Same as for PSP	Actual dose not known; any amount is dangerous
Treatment	No antidote; artificial respiration, rest	No antidote; artificial respiration, rest	No effective antidote; mannitol may be effective in acute cases
Control measures	FDA limit 80 µg/100 g of meat, minimum cases due to good management	Education on identification of toxic species	No harvesting where toxic fish are found

Remarks: In most cases toxic shellfish are not detectable by organoleptic means. It is therefore important that practical chemical or biological tests, specific for the detection of the toxins, be developed. Although not all the listed diseases are problems in the United States, seafood inspectors and processors should always be aware that toxigenic dinoflagellates, or other microorganisms producing toxins that get into fish and

Diarrhetic Shellfish Poisoning (DSP)	Neurotoxic Shellfish Poisoning (NSP)	Scombroid Fish Poisoning	Amnesic Shellfish Poisoning (ASP)
Mussels, clams, scallops; toxin in digestive gland	Bivalves and most plankton feeders	Mahimahi, tuna, bluefish, mackerel, skipjack	Mussels and clams
Dinoflagellates: *Dinophysis fortii, D. acuminata*	Dinoflagellate: *Gymnodinium breve*	Bacterial action on fish with high levels of histidine	Diatom: *Nitzschia pungens*
Heaviest around Japan and Europe, no cases in U.S.	Mostly west coast of Florida, Caribbean	Worldwide	Eastern Canada; northeast U.S.
Mouse unit minimum intraperitoneal dose to kill in 24 hours (specific toxicity in mouse, 500 µg/kg)	Mouse test	Chemical methods for histamine	HPLC
Okadaic acid, dinophysis toxin	Brevetoxin, lipid-soluble polyether	Histamine and histamine-like substances	Neurotoxic and cytotoxic, domoic acid
High morbidity rate, potentially worldwide problem, none in U.S.	Massive fish kills, environmental problems	Japan 100-1,000 cases, some in U.S.	Canada (1987) 103 cases and 3 deaths; no known cases in U.S.
Stable to cooking	Heat stable	Heat stable	Heat stable
Abdominal pain, nausea, vomiting, severe diarrhea within 4 hours after eating; rarely fatal	Feeling of nausea from red tide spray, symptoms like ciguatera from eating bivalves	Itching, redness, allergic symptoms, headache, dizziness, diarrhea, peppery taste	Vomiting, cramps, diarrhea, memory loss and disorientation; memory loss has lasted a year
Actual dose not known	Actual dose not known	Dose varies with individual	2 mg or more per 100 g of meat
No specific treatment	No specific treatment	Unnecessary for short duration, antihistamines	Rest, symptomatic
None in U.S, close shellfish beds	No established controls, close shellfish harvest	Education on care of freshly caught fish; keep below 10°C	Close shellfish beds when domoic acid is detected

shellfish, may become established in areas where fish and shellfish are harvested for U.S. consumption. An example: diarrhetic shellfish poisoning is not a problem in the United States, but the dinoflagellate that produces the toxin may become established in shellfish areas that supply U.S. markets.

The committee recommends the following:

- Fish of species reported by health authorities to have caused ciguatera, which are to be imported to the United States from regions of high ciguatera incidence, should carry certification of nontoxicity.
- States and territories in which ciguatera is a problem should license marine sports fishers and, at the point of issuance of the license, issue clear and specific warnings regarding the dangers of ciguateric fish. Pamphlets on poisonous fish should be generally available to the public in areas where ciguatera is endemic.
- When feasible, reef fishing should be closed in areas where ciguatoxic fish are present. This closure should apply to sports fishers as well as to commercial vessels.
- Research should be accelerated on the development of simple, rapid tests for toxicity such as the Hokama stick test. Research should also be directed toward analysis of the events leading to the appearance of toxic fish in particular reef environments, with the objective of developing predictive indices that can be used to close areas to fishing before human intoxications occur.
- All imported fish of species known to be a cause of scombroid poisoning should be certified as having histamine levels of less than 20 mg/100 g of fish. This should be controlled by routine lot testing.
- Vessels fishing potentially scombrotoxic species should be required to maintain time/temperature records to ensure proper cooling and refrigerated storage of fish.
- Similar temperature records should be maintained for such species during processing and shipment on land.
- Advisory leaflets describing the causes of scombroid poisoning and providing advice on how to handle fish to minimize risk of the disease should be made widely available to sports fishers who target potentially scombrotoxic species.
- Research to develop a rapid field test for PSP toxicity in shellfish should be strongly encouraged and supported. Such a test could be applied directly by commercial growers and recreational shellfish gatherers. Nevertheless, state agencies should continue to monitor the PSP condition of local shellfish.
- The consumption of puffer fish should be strongly discouraged, and their importation to the United States should be banned.
- Regulatory agencies should maintain awareness of potential toxin problems, such as diarrhetic shellfish poisoning and amnesic shellfish poisoning, and their technical personnel should be trained and equipped to run definitive analyses on these and other toxins. Shellfish should be imported only under an MOU that includes a provision for toxicity testing.
- In view of the complexity of seafood intoxications, the federal government should establish or support two to three centers of research into such toxins to enlarge understanding of the phenomena, provide possible remedies, and develop particular tests.
- Because of the highly localized impact, primary responsibility for control of seafood toxins should reside at the state level, with funding, quality control, and specialist assistance from a federal seafood safety agency.

NOTE

1. The toxigenic strains have also been designated *Protogonyaulax*, and more recently, the genus name *Alexandrium* has been proposed.

REFERENCES

Anderson, B.S., J.K. Sims, N. Wiebenga, and M. Sugi. 1983. The epidemiology of ciguatera fish poisoning in Hawaii 1975-1982. Haw. Med. J. 42:326-334.

Arnold, S.H, R.J. Price, and W.D. Brown. 1980. Histamine formation by bacteria isolated from skipjack tuna, *Katsuwonas pelamis*. Bull. Jpn. Soc. Sci. Fish 46:991-995.

AOAC (Association of Official Analytical Chemists). 1984. P. 344 in S. Williams, ed. Official Methods of Analysis of the Association of Official Analytical Chemists, 14th ed. AOAC, Arlington, Va.

Baden, D.G., T.J. Mende, M.A. Poli, and R.E. Block. 1984. Toxins from Florida's red tide dinoflagellate *Ptychodiscus brevis*. Pp. 359-367 in E.P. Ragelis, ed. Seafood Toxins. American Chemical Society, Washington, D.C.

Bagnis, R., T. Kuberski, and S. Laugier. 1979. Clinical observations on 3009 cases of ciguatera (fish poisoning) in the South Pacific. Am. J. Trop. Med. Hyg. 28:1067-1073.

Bagnis, R., S. Chanteau, E. Chungue, J.M. Hurtel, T. Yasumoto, and A. Inoue. 1980. Origins of ciguatera fish poisoning: A new dinoflagellate *Gambierdiscus toxicus* Adachi and Fukuyo, definitely involved as a causal agent. Toxicon 18:199-208.

Benson, J. 1956. Tetradon (blowfish) poisoning. A report of two fatalities. J. Forensic Sci. 1:119-126.

Bidard, J.N., H.P.M. Vijuerbert, C. Frelin, E. Chungue, A.M. Legrand, R. Bagnis, and M. Lazdunski. 1984. Ciguatoxin is a novel type of Na^+ channel toxin. J. Biol. Chem. 359:8353-8357.

Bowman, P.B. 1984. Amitriptyline and ciguatera. Med. J. Australia 140:802.

Boyer, G.E., J. Schantz, and H.K. Schnoes. 1978. Characterization of 11-hydroxysaxitoxin sulfate. J. Chem. Soc. London Chem. Comm. 20:889-893.

CDC (Centers for Disease Control). 1981a. *Salmonella* Surveillance, Annual Summary, 1978. HHS Publ. No. (CDC)81-8219. Public Health Service, U.S. Department of Health and Human Services, Atlanta, Ga. 25 pp.

CDC (Centers for Disease Control). 1981b. Annual Summary of Foodborne Disease, 1978. HHS Publ. No. (CDC)81-8185. U.S. Department of Health and Human Services, Atlanta, Ga. 53 pp.

CDC (Centers for Disease Control). 1981c. Annual Summary of Foodborne Disease, 1979. HHS Publ. No. (CDC)8185. U.S. Department of Health and Human Services, Atlanta, Ga. 40 pp.

CDC (Centers for Disease Control). 1983a. Food-Borne Disease Outbreaks, Annual Summary, 1980. HHS Publ. No. (CDC)83-8185. Public Health Service, U.S. Department of Health and Human Services, Atlanta, Ga. 32 pp.

CDC (Centers for Disease Control). 1983b. Food-Borne Disease Outbreaks, Annual Summary, 1981. HHS Publ. No. (CDC)83-8185. Public Health Service, U.S. Department of Health and Human Services, Atlanta, Ga. 41 pp.

CDC (Centers for Disease Control). 1984. Food-Borne Disease Outbreaks, Annual Summary 1983: Reported morbidity and mortality in the United States. Morbid. Mortal. Weekly Rep. (annual suppl.). 32 pp.

CDC (Centers for Disease Control). 1985. Food-Borne Disease Outbreaks, Annual Summary 1982. HHS Publ. No. (CDC)85-8185. Public Health Service, U.S. Department of Health and Human Services, Atlanta, Ga. 38 pp.

CDC (Centers for Disease Control). 1989. Annual Summary of Foodborne Disease, unpublished dates from 1983 to 1986. U.S. Department of Health and Human Services, Atlanta, Ga. 1989.

Chu, F.S., and T.S.L. Fan. 1985. Indirect enzyme-linked immunosorbent assay for saxitoxin in shellfish. J. Assoc. Off. Anal. Chem. 68:13-16.

Cooper, M.J. 1964. Ciguatera and other marine poisonings in the Gilbert Islands. Pacific Sci. 18:411-440.

DNR (Department of Natural Resources, Florida). 1985. Pp. 1-10 in Contingency Plan for Control of Shellfish Potentially Contaminated by Marine Biotoxins. Bureau of Marine Research, St. Petersburg, Fla.

Edler, L., and M. Hageltorn. 1990. Identification of the causative organism of a DSP outbreak on the Swedish west coast. Pp. 345-349 in E. Graneli, B. Sundström, L. Edler, and D.M. Anderson, eds. Toxic Marine Phytoplankton. Elsevier, Amsterdam, The Netherlands.

Engleberg, N.C., J.G. Morris, Jr., J. Lewis, J.P. McMillan, R.A. Pollard, and P.A. Blake. 1983. Ciguatera fish poisoning: A major common source outbreak in the U.S. Virgin Islands. Ann. Intern. Med. 98:336-337.

FDA (Food and Drug Administration). 1989 revision. Sanitation of shellfish growing areas. National Shellfish Sanitation Program Manual of Operations Part I. Center for Food Safety and Applied Nutrition, Division of Cooperative Programs, Shellfish Sanitation Branch, Washington, D.C.

Federal Register. 1982. Department of Health and Human Services. Food and Drug Administration. Defect action levels for histamine in tuna: Availability of a guide. Fed. Reg. 470:40487-40488.

Freudenthal, A.R. 1990. Public health aspect of ciguatera poisoning contracted on tropical vacations by North American tourists. Pp. 463-468 in E. Graneli, B. Sundström, L. Edler, and D.M. Anderson, eds. Proceedings of the 4th International Conference on Toxic Marine Phytoplankton. Elsevier, Amsterdam, The Netherlands.

Freudenthal, A.R., and J.L. Jijina. 1988. Potential hazards of *Dinophysis* to consumers and shellfisheries. J. Shellfish Res. 7:695-701.

Gilgan, M.W., B.G. Burns, and G.J. Landry. 1989. Distribution and magnitude of domoic acid contamination of shellfish in Atlantic Canada during 1988. Pp. 469-474 in Proceedings of the 4th International Conference on Toxic Marine Phytoplankton. Elsevier, Amsterdam, The Netherlands.

Gillespie, N.C., R.J. Lewis, J.H. Pearn, A.T.C. Bourke, M.J. Holmes, J.B. Bourke, and W.J. Shields. 1986. Ciguatera in Australia: Occurrence, clinical features, pathophysiology and management. Med. J. Aust. 145:584-590.

Goe, D.R., and B.R. Halstead. 1953. A preliminary report of the toxicity of the Gulf puffer, *Sphoeroides annulatus*. Calif. Fish and Game 39:229-232.

Gollop, J.H., and E.W. Pon. 1991. Ciguatera fish poisoning: Review of pathogenesis, clinical manifestations and epidemiology in Hawaii 1984-1988. Hawaii Med. J. (in press).

Haddock, R.L. 1989. Letter report on food-borne disease incidence, dated September 8, 1989, from Dr. Robert L. Haddock, Territorial Epidemiologist, Department of Public Health and Social Services, Government of Guam to Dr. Farid E. Ahmed, Project Director, Committee on Evaluation of the Safety of Fishery Products, Institute of Medicine, National Academy of Sciences, Washington, D.C.

Hall, S., and P.B. Reichardt. 1984. Cryptic paralytic shellfish toxins. Pp. 113-124 in Ragelis, E.P. ed. Seafood Toxins. American Chemical Society, Washington, D.C.

Halstead, B.W. 1959. Dangerous Marine Animals. Cornell Maritime Press, Cambridge, 146 pp.

Halstead, B.W. 1967. Poisonous and Venomous Marine Animals of the World, Vol. I, pp. 83-87; Vol. II, pp. 679-844. U.S. Government Printing Office, Washington, D.C.

Halstead, B.W. 1970. Poisonous and Venomous Marine Animals of the World. U.S. Government Printing Office, Washington, D.C. 1006 pp.

Halstead, B.W. 1988. Poisonous and Venomous Marine Animals of the World, 2nd rev. ed. Darwin Press, Princeton, N.J. 1168 pp.

Halstead, B.W. 1990. Dangerous Aquatic Animals of the World: A Color Guide. Darwin Press, Princeton, N.J. 288 pp.

Halstead, B.W., and W.M. Lively. 1954. Poisonous fishes and ichthyosarcotoxism. Their relationship to the Armed Forces. U.S. Armed Forces Med. J. 5:157-175.

Halstead, B.W., and E.J. Schantz. 1984. Paralytic shellfish poisoning. WHO Offset Publication No. 79:1-60. Geneva, Switzerland.

Halstead, B.W., P.S. Auerbach, and D. Campbell. 1990. A Colour Atlas of Dangerous Marine Animals. Wolfe Medical Publications, Ipswich, England. 192 pp.

Havelka, B. 1967. Role of *Hafnia* bacteria in the rise of histamine in tuna fish meat. Cesk. Hyg. 12:343.

HDH (Hawaii Department of Health). 1988. Fish Poisoning in Hawaii. Advisory Leaflet. Honolulu, Hawaii.

Hemmert, C.D. 1974. Tetraodon (puffer fish) poisoning. Memorandum of Florida Department of Health, Tallahassee, Fla.

Hokama, Y. 1985. A rapid simplified enzyme immunoassay stick test for the detection of ciguatoxin and related polyethers from fish tissue. Toxicon 23:939-946.

Hokama, Y. 1990. Simplified solid-phase immunobead assay for detection of ciguatoxin and related polyethers. J. Clin. Lab. Anal. 4:213-217.

Hokama, Y., A.H. Banner, and D. Boyland. 1977. A radioimmunoassay for the detection of ciguatoxin. Toxicon 15:317-325.

Hokama, Y., S.A.A. Honda, A.Y. Asahina, J.M.L. Fong, C.M. Matsumoto, and T.S. Gallacher. 1989a. Cross-reactivity of ciguatoxin, okadaic acid, and polyethers with monoclonal antibodies. Food Agric. Immunol. 1:29-35.

Hokama, Y., S.A.A. Honda, M.N. Kobayashi, L.K. Nakagawa, A.Y. Asahina, and J.T. Miyahara. 1989b. Monoclonal antibody (MAb) in detection of ciguatoxin (CTX) and related polyethers by the stick-enzyme immunoassay (S-EIA) in fish tissues associated with ciguatera poisoning. Pp. 303-310 in S. Natori, K. Hashimoto, and Y. Ueno, eds. Mycotoxins and Phycotoxins '88. Elsevier Science Publishers, Amsterdam, The Netherlands.

Holt, R.J., G. Miro, and A. Del Valle. 1984. An analysis of poison control center reports of ciguatera toxicity in Puerto Rico for one year. Clin. Toxicol. 22:177-185.

Hughes, J.M., and M.H. Merson. 1976. Fish and shellfish poisoning. N. Engl. J. Med. 295:1117-1120.

Kawabata, T., K. Ishizaka, T. Miura, and T. Sasaki. 1956. Studies on the food poisoning associated with putrefaction of marine products. VII. An outbreak of allergy-like food poisoning caused by sashimi of *Parathunnus mebachi* and the isolation of the causative bacteria. Bull. Jpn. Soc. Sci. Fish 22:41-47.

Kodama, A.M., Y. Hokama, T. Yasumoto, M. Fukui, S.J. Manea, and N. Sutherland. 1989. Clinical and laboratory findings implicating palytoxin as cause of ciguatera poisoning due to *Decapterus macrosoma* (mackerel). Toxicon 27:1051-1053.

Lalone, R.C., E.D. DeVillez, and E. Larson. 1963. An assay of the toxicity of the Atlantic puffer fish *Sphoeroides maculatus*. Toxicon 1:159-164.

Lange, W.R., S.D. Kreider, M. Hattwick, and J. Hobbs. 1988. Potential benefit of tocainide in the treatment of ciguatera: Report of three cases. Am. J. Med. 84:1087-1088.

Larson, E., L.R. Rivas, R.C. Lalone, and S. Coward. 1959. Toxicology of the Western Atlantic Puffer Fish of the Genus *Sphoeroides*. The Pharmacologists 1:70 (Abstract).

Larson, E., R.C. Lalone, and L. Rivas. 1960. Comparative toxicity of the Atlantic pufferfishes of the genera *Sphoeroides, Lactophrys, Lagocelhalus* and *Chilomycterus*. Fed. Proc. 19:388 (Abstract).

Lawrence, D.N., M.B. Enriquez, R.M. Lumish, and A. Maceo. 1980. Ciguatera fish poisoning in Miami. J. Am. Med. Assoc. 244:254-258.

Legrand, A.M., and R. Bagnis. 1984. Mode of action of ciguatera toxins. Pp. 217 in E.P. Ragelis, ed. Seafood Toxins. American Chemical Society, Washington, D.C.

Lukton, A., and H.S. Olcott. 1958. Content of free imidazole compounds in the muscle tissue of aquatic animals. Food Res. 23:611-618.

Miller, M.D. 1991. Ciguatera Seafood Toxins. CRC Press, Boca Raton, Fla. 176 pp.

Mills, A.R., and R. Passmore. 1988. Pelagic paralysis. Lancet 1:161-164.

Morris, J.G., Jr., P. Lewin, N.T. Hargrett, C.W. Smith, P.A. Blake, and R. Schneider. 1982a. Clinical features of ciguatera fish poisoning: A study of the disease in the U.S. Virgin Islands. Arch. Intern. Med. 142:1090-1092.

Morris, J.G., Jr., P. Lewin, C.W. Smith, P.A. Blake, and R. Schneider. 1982b. Ciguatera fish poisoning: Epidemiology of the disease on St. Thomas, U.S. Virgin Islands. Am. J. Trop. Med. Hyg. 31:574-578.

Mosher, H., and F.A. Fuhrman. 1984. Occurrence and origin of tetrodotoxin. Pp. 333-334 in E.P. Ragelis, ed. Seafood Toxins. American Chemical Society, Washington, D.C.

Murata, M., A.M. Legrand, Y. Ishibashi, M. Fukui, and T. Yasumoto. 1990. Structures and configurations of ciguatoxin from the moray eel *Gymnothorax javanicus* and its likely precursor from the dinoflagellate *Gambierdiscus toxicus*. J. Am. Chem. Soc. 112:4380-4386.

Narita, H., S. Matsubara, N. Miwa, S. Akahane, M. Murakami, T. Goto, M. Nara, T. Noguchi, T. Shida, and K. Hashimoto. 1987. *Vibrio alginolyticus* a TTX-producing bacterium isolated from the starfish *Astropecten polyacanthus*. Nippon Suisan Gakk. 53:617-621.

Nishitani, L., and K. Chew. 1988. PSP toxins in the Pacific Coast states: Monitoring programs and effects on bivalve industries. J. Shellfish Res. 1:653-669.

NOAA (National Oceanic and Atmospheric Administration). 1988. Japan's "Fugu" (Puffer Fish) Market Advisory. Doc/NOAA/NMFS, Washington, D.C. 1 p.

Ogura, Y. 1971. Fugu (puffer fish) poisoning and the pharmacology of crystalline tetrodotoxin in poisoning. Pp. 139-159 in L.L. Simpson, ed. Neuropoisons, Vol. I. Plenum Press, New York.

Palafox, N.A., L.G. Jain, A.Z. Pinano, T.M. Gulick, R.K. Williams, and I.J. Schatz. 1988. Successful treatment of ciguatera fish poisoning with intravenous mannitol. J. Am. Med. Assoc. 259:2740-2742.

Perl, T.M., L. Bédard, T. Kosatsky, J.C. Hockin, E.C.D. Todd, and R.S. Remis. 1988. An outbreak of toxic encephalopathy caused by eating mussels contaminated with domoic acid. N. Engl. J. Med. 322:1775-1780.

Ragelis, E.P. 1984. Ciguatera seafood poisoning: An overview. Pp. 25-36 in E.P. Ragelis, ed. Seafood Toxins. American Chemical Society, Washington, D.C.

Randall, J.E. 1980. A survey of ciguatera at Eniwetok and Bikini Marshall Islands, with notes on the systematics and food habits of ciguatoxic fish. Fish Bull. 78:201-249.

Ruff, T.A. 1989. Ciguatera in the Pacific: A link with military activities. Lancet 1:201-205.

Schantz, E. 1973. Seafood toxicants. Pp. 424-447 in Toxicants Occurring Naturally in Foods, 2nd ed. National Academy Press, Washington, D.C.

Schantz, E. 1986. Chemistry and biology of saxitoxins and related toxins. Ann. N.Y. Acad. Sci. 479:15-23.

Schantz, E.J., E.F. McFarren, M.L. Schafer, and K. H. Lewis. 1958. Purified shellfish poison for bioassay standardization. J. Off. Agric. Chem. 41:160-170.

Schantz, E.J., V.E. Ghazarossian, H.K. Schnoes, F.M. Strong, J.P. Springer, J.D. Pezzanite, and J. Clardy. 1975. The structure of saxitoxin. J. Am. Chem. Soc. 97:1238-1239.

Scheuer, P.J., W. Takahashi, J. Tsutsumi, and T. Yoshida. 1967. Ciguatoxin: Isolation and chemical nature. Science 155:1267-1268.

Shimizu, Y., and C. Hsu. 1981. Confirmation of the structure of gonyautoxins I-IV by correlation with saxitoxin. J. Chem. Soc. Chem. Comm. pp. 314-315.

Simidu, W., and S. Hibiku. 1955. Studies on putrefaction of aquatic products. XXIII. On the critical concentration of poisoning for histamine. Bull. Jpn. Soc. Sci. Fish 21:365-367.

Sugita, H., J. Iwata, C. Miyajima, T. Kubo, T. Noguchi, K. Hashimoto, and Y. Deguchi. 1989. Changes in microflora of a puffer fish *Fugu niphobles* with different water temperatures. Marine Biology 101:299-304.

Sullivan, J.J., and W.T. Iwaoka. 1983. High pressure liquid chromatographic determination of toxins associated with paralytic shellfish poisoning. J. Assoc. Off. Anal. Chem. 66:297-303.

Sullivan, J.J., W.T. Iwaoka, and J. Liston. 1983. Enzymatic transformation of PSP toxins in the littleneck clam (*Protothacis staminea*). Biochem. Biophys. Res. Commun. 114:465-472.

Taylor, S.L. 1986. Histamine food poisoning: Toxicology and clinical aspects. C.R.C. Crit. Rev. Toxicol. 17:91-128.

Taylor, S.L. 1988. Marine toxins of microbial origin. Food Tech. 42:94-98.

Taylor, S.L., L.S. Guthertz, M. Leatherwood, and E.R. Lieber. 1979. Histamine production by *Klebsiella pneumoniae* and an incident of scombroid fish poisoning. Appl. Environ. Microbiol. 37:274-278.

Teitelbaum. J.S., R.J. Zatorre, S. Carpenter, D. Gendron. A.C. Evans, A. Gjedde, and N.R. Cashman. 1990. Neurologic sequelae of domoic acid intoxication due to the ingestion of contaminated mussels. N. Engl. J. Med. 322:1781-1787.

Tester, P.A., and P.K. Fowler. 1990. Brevetoxin contamination of *Mercenaria mercenaria* and *Crassostrea virginica*: A management issue. Pp. 499-503 in E. Graneli, B. Sundström, L. Edler, and D.M. Anderson, eds. Proceedings of the 4th International Conference on Toxic Marine Phytoplankton. Elsevier, Amsterdam, The Netherlands.

Todd, E.C.D. 1989. Amnesic shellfish poisoning--A new seafood toxin syndrome. Pp. 504-508 in E. Graneli, B. Sundström, L. Edler, and D.M. Anderson, eds. Proceedings of the 4th International Conference on Toxic Marine Phytoplankton. Elsevier, Amsterdam, The Netherlands.

Van Spreekens, K. 1987. Histamine production by the psychrophilic flora. Pp. 309-318 in D.E. Kramer and J. Liston, eds. Seafood Quality Determination. Elsevier Science Publishers, Amsterdam, The Netherlands.

Wekell, J., and J. Liston. 1982. Pp. 111-155 in P. Newberne, ed. Seafood Biotoxicants in Trace Substances and Health: A Handbook Part II. Marcel Dekker, New York.

Yasumoto, T., and M. Murata. 1990. Polyether toxins involved in seafood poisoning. Pp. 120-132 in S. Hall and G. Stricharty, eds. Marine Toxins. Origin, Structure and Molecular Pharmacology. American Chemical Society, Washington, D.C.

Yasumoto, T., M. Murata, Y. Oshima, G.K. Matsumoto, and J. Clardy. 1984. Diarrhetic shellfish poisoning. Pp. 207-216 in E.P. Ragelis, ed. Seafood Toxins. American Chemical Society, Washington, D.C.

5

Occurrence of Chemical Contaminants in Seafood and Variability of Contaminant Levels

ABSTRACT

This chapter and the following one should be considered as a unit. Although the committee has not attempted a comprehensive quantitative assessment of the risks of chemical contaminants in seafood, this chapter performs the functions of the "hazard identification" portion of a chemical risk assessment—giving a broad overview of many different potential seafood contamination problems, as well as an extensive summary of available data for characterizing contaminant concentrations in aquatic organisms in the environment. Chapter 6 provides a discussion of the directions needed to improve quantitative risk assessment in this area [including a detailed treatment of the methods used to assess two specific hazards (polychlorinated biphenyls and methylmercury)] and, more broadly, covers the issues that are usually found under the headings "dose-response assessment," "exposure assessment," and "risk characterization," as well as some risk management considerations.

The inorganic contaminants with the greatest potential for toxicity appear to be antimony, arsenic, cadmium, lead, mercury, selenium, and sulfites (used in shrimp processing). Among organic compounds, polychlorinated biphenyls, dioxins, several chlorinated hydrocarbon insecticides, certain processing-related contaminants (nitrosamines and possibly products of chlorination), and contaminants related to aquaculture pose sufficient potential risks for consumers to be worthy of additional study.

In addition to providing a broad survey of data on chemical contamination of aquatic organisms and potential risks, this chapter undertakes an extensive set of analyses of the variability of concentrations of certain contaminants across geographic areas and the implications of this variability for control. In general, lognormal distributions appear to provide good descriptions of the pattern of variation of chemical contaminant concentrations among different geographic areas, and some contaminants (mostly organics) appear to be much more variable than others. The variability of contaminant concentrations among geographic areas is important because it indicates the potential for reduction of exposure through restrictions on the harvesting of aquatic organisms from specific sites. Based on analyses of data for inshore marine waters, for the most variable contaminants/sets of species, it would be possible theoretically to reduce the population dosage delivered by more than 50% by restricting harvesting/marketing from only the 5% most intensely contaminated sites. There is, therefore, considerable potential for management of the overall population dosage of contaminants by measures that would restrict harvesting in specific ways.

INTRODUCTION

There is no area of the committee's work that poses greater challenges to both the scientific tools for understanding likely health hazards and the social tools for managing risks, than the diverse collection of chemical residues that find their way into the human diet partly by way of seafood. Moreover, the confusion between technical questions and social control problems is connected. The understanding of toxicology and environmental health has made important strides since the multitiered structure of federal food protection law was erected (principally by legislation in 1906, 1938, and 1958). Older concepts, which shaped the legislative framework within which food protection agencies attempt to function, suggested sharp distinctions between "poisons" and other substances, or between "safe" and "unsafe" levels of exposure to important categories of environmental toxicants.[1] These ideas are gradually giving way to a more quantitative (although generally still highly uncertain) conception of risks, based on more detailed information about the mechanisms by which different substances interact with intricate biological systems and the diversity of those systems in different individuals in the large and disparate human population. To the extent that increased understanding indicates that certain categories of risks cannot be eliminated entirely, the tools for social control of these risks will have to be adapted to manage toxicant exposures and risks in the light of explicitly formulated trade-offs between the costs of forgoing certain portions of our food resources and the costs of potential adverse effects.

The technical advances that have occurred in risk assessment in recent years have been applied most readily to issues of health protection by governmental institutions of relatively late vintage, operating under legislation adopted within the last 20 years – most notably, the different branches of the U.S. Environmental Protection Agency (EPA) and analogous state authorities. When the more modern techniques and assumptions for quantitatively assessing risks are applied to seafood contaminants, there are a number of areas of mismatch[2] that give the appearance of inconsistency in the social and technical judgments on risks made by different agencies.

Both this chapter and the next deal with aspects of chemical residues in aquatic organisms. In this chapter the committee focuses on the tasks that are usually thought of as part of the hazard identification portion of a quantitative chemical health risk assessment. Chapter 6 deals broadly with issues in the assessment of dose-response relationships, estimation of exposures, and characterization of risks.

The committee has not, however, attempted a formal and comprehensive assessment of the risks of chemical residues in aquatic organisms. Aside from the fact that the available data on both contaminant[3] levels and risks are inadequate for such a task at this time, the charge to the committee emphasized the review of the adequacy of current risk recognition, risk assessment, and risk management procedures in governmental agencies. In the next section of this chapter, the committee gives a broad overview of the types of toxic agents that are known or believed to be contaminants of seafood. Then, the various data bases available for characterizing the geographic and species distribution of chemical contaminants are reviewed, followed by the quantitative insights gleaned from these sources. The variability of contaminants by geography and species, which provides some of the most potentially important opportunities for reduction of exposures, is then considered. Finally, preliminary conclusions and recommendations are offered, based on the material discussed in this chapter.

Chapter 6 articulates basic concepts underlying the mechanisms of action of toxic substances and quantitative ideas about dose-time-response relationships. Then, a focused examination is provided of available Food and Drug Administration (FDA) risk assessment and risk management analyses for two types of residues – one a set of organic carcinogens, polychlorinated biphenyls (PCBs), and the other an organometallic residue with reproductive and neurological effects (methylmercury). These two important examples are used to fulfill the committee's charge to critique the adequacy of current governmental procedures for assessing risks and the opportunities for risk reduction. Finally, the balance of Chapter 6 provides a more general overview of what can be said very approximately about the quantitative risks of other contaminants in seafood.

TOXIC AGENTS AND POTENTIAL TYPES OF HEALTH EFFECTS

Metals and Other Inorganics

The human and veterinary medical literature is replete with information regarding the toxicity of heavy metals. Based on this information, different metals can be classified as having major, modest, minor, or no potential for toxicity. Those with major potential for toxicity, in the committee's view, are antimony, arsenic, cadmium, chromium, lead, mercury, and nickel. Contaminants with a modest potential for toxicity include copper, iron, manganese, selenium, and zinc. Those of minor or no toxicity are aluminum, silver, strontium, thallium, and tin. This classification is based, among other parameters, on potency for producing effects and accessibility of the toxicant. Thus, such metals as nickel and chromium, known inhalant carcinogens, are among those of greatest toxicity, whereas selenium and tin are placed in the lesser categories. When considering the same metals as contaminants of an aquatic food source, however, their relative toxicities will certainly change. Criteria for identifying contaminants (hazard assessment, hazard analysis) of public health concern in the aquatic environment may vary but have been defined (PTI, 1987). These include (1) persistence, (2) bioconcentration potential, (3) toxicity to humans (or suspected toxicity), (4) sources of contaminants in the area of interest, and (5) high concentration in fish and shellfish from the area of interest.

By applying such criteria, both nickel (except for its carbonyl form) and chromium (at least in its hexavalent form), inhalant carcinogens and elicitors of dermal hypersensitivity, would be suspect as contaminants of public health concern (Haines and Nieboer, 1988). However, both are poorly absorbed from the gastrointestinal tract, and there is little evidence that this route of exposure results in systemic toxicity (Beliles, 1978; Nieboer and Jusys, 1988). Similarly, the use of tri-n-butyltin (TBT) to control marine fouling of vessels and aquaculture sea pens has been followed by the accumulation of butyl- and elemental tins in the muscles of fish and invertebrates (Short and Thrower, 1987a,b). Organic tin compounds tend to be more toxic than inorganic salts, and organic forms in particular may be of public health concern. Although little information exists about the toxicity of tin to man, there is sufficient information regarding dosage levels without observable effect to eliminate the probability of tin poisoning from contaminated seafood (WHO, 1980). Conversely, selenium is well recognized as toxic by ingestion and, at existing levels in some seafoods, may be a source of risk (Fan et al., 1988). Antimony has been recognized as both an occupational and an iatrogenic toxicant (Anonymous, 1988a,b; Groth et al., 1986). Recent seafood residue studies, however, either have failed to sample for this metal or indicate concentrations above detectable levels in few contaminated sites (Lowe et al., 1985; NOAA, 1987). Such findings and reasoning, coupled with estimates of ingestion levels, suggest a preliminary list of heavy-metal contaminants found in the edible portions of aquatic animals that may be detrimental to human health. The metals identified in this hazard analysis include arsenic, cadmium, lead, mercury, and selenium. Some toxicity information related to antimony is given later, in the section where current dosage is compared to "acceptable daily intake" levels and other recommended standards.

Specific Trace Metals

Arsenic

Arsenic has a long history as a potent poison of humans and other animals. Previously used as a chemotherapeutic and homicidal drug, much information has been collected regarding its toxicity. It exists as the toxic trivalent form (arsenic trioxide, sodium arsenate, arsenic trichloride, etc.), as the less toxic pentavalent form (arsenic pentoxide, arsenic acid, lead arsenate, calcium arsenate, etc.), and as numerous organic forms (arsanilic acid, bimethyl arsenate, etc.). When ingested, inorganic arsenic may cause acute or chronic toxicity and is of primary concern as a carcinogen responsible for pulmonary carcinoma, hemangiosarcomas, and dermal basal cell and squamous cell carcinomas. Its toxicity is dependent on oxidation state and route of exposure. In its chronic manifestations, arsenic is responsible for gastroenteritis, nephritis, hepatomegaly, peripheral symmetrical neuropathy, and a number of lesions of the skin including plantar and palmar hyperkeratosis and generalized melanosis. Some of these lesions appear related to destruction of capillary endothelium, with consequent edema and even circulatory failure. At the molecular level the metal is known to uncouple phosphorylation; to react with sulfhydryl groups, thus upsetting cellular metabolism; to damage deoxyribonucleic acid (DNA) directly and to inhibit its repair (Buck, 1978). In addition, as sodium arsenate and arsenite it is teratogenic in lower animals (Earl and Vish, 1978). The metal, therefore, places at special risk pregnant and nursing mothers and their children.

However, the predominant form of arsenic that exists in the edible portions of aquatic animals is the organic form, either arsenobetaine or arsenocholine. These forms have been named "fish arsenic" and no toxic effects from their ingestion have been reported in animals [at doses of 10,000 milligrams (mg) per kilogram (kg)] or in humans. Furthermore, there is no evidence of mutagenicity by arsenobetaine (Penrose, 1975; Tam et al., 1982). Although arsenobetaine constitutes the bulk of arsenic in fish, available studies are inadequate to conclude that the amounts of more toxic inorganic forms of arsenic (or organic forms that can be metabolized to inorganic arsenic in humans) are negligible in all fish. It is known, however, that the trivalent form (inorganic) is toxic to man and that long-term effects include dermal hyperkeratosis, dermal melanosis and carcinoma, hepatomegaly, peripheral neuropathy, and in cases of inhalation, pulmonary carcinoma (ATSDR, 1989a; Goyer, 1986).

Arsenic is used in the manufacture of pesticides, herbicides, and other agricultural products and is a by-product of mining and smelting operations (Buck, 1978).

Cadmium

Cadmium is unique among toxic metals because it is a relatively recent (50 years) contaminant of the aquatic environment. Its sources are solid waste dumping (pigment in paint) and cadmium-containing sewage sludge, the use of phosphatic fertilizers, electroplating and galvanizing manufacture, and mining (zinc, lead) wastewater (Sherlock, 1986; Sloan and Karcher, 1985). Cadmium is commonly found in its metallic form and as sulfides and sulfates. Invertebrates, both crustacea and bivalves, tend to accumulate metallic cadmium in large amounts by binding to various high-molecular-weight metallothioneine ligands. There is a differential affinity between crustacean muscle and hepatopancreas, the latter organ containing 10-20 times the concentration of the former. Because hepatopancreas may be considered a delicacy or marketed as "brown crab meat," the potential for ingesting large amounts of cadmium when eating lobsters or crabs is increased (McKenzie-Parnell et al., 1988; Sloan and Karcher, 1985).

Cadmium may damage cells by its activity in the plasmalemma where it reacts with phosphate groups of the lipid bilayer to alter permeability, in the nucleus where it is mutagenic, on lysosomal membranes, and as an inhibitor of mitochondrial activity. Its ability to stimulate metallothioneine production in aquatic animals, however, does much to decrease its toxicity (Viarengo, 1985).

Cadmium has been responsible for major human poisoning incidents as a contaminant of wastewater used for irrigation in Japan where the illness is known as itai-itai (ouch-ouch) disease. It is a chronic osteoporotic and osteomalacic condition that primarily affects multiparous females (Kobayashi, 1978). Although the highest accumulation of cadmium is found in bone, the liver and kidney also have a propensity for accumulating the metal, and the kidney is often seriously damaged in chronic occupational exposures (Lauwerys and De Wals, 1981). Clinically, patients suffer tubular dysfunction resulting in aminoaciduria, proteinuria, and glucosuria. Although the half-life of cadmium in kidneys of humans is uncertain, it may be as long as 30 years. Under such circumstances it has been conjectured that critical concentrations [kidney = 200 micrograms (μg) per gram (g) by age 50] could be used to establish maximum levels of daily exposure (Kjellström et al., 1977). What makes cadmium of dietary concern is that ordinary background dietary exposures were estimated to yield kidney concentrations of about one-quarter the hypothesized critical level. The segment of the population at greatest risk would appear to be older adults (ATSDR, 1989b).

Studies in maternal-fetal tissues have provided evidence for accumulation and transplacental transfer of metals. In one study, placental cadmium levels were one to two times those in maternal or cord blood. It was observed also that erythrocyte cadmium levels were roughly three to five times plasma cadmium levels, and that maternal erythrocyte cadmium levels were somewhat higher (27%) than those of the fetus.

Lead

Of all the heavy metals, lead probably has the longest history of environmental contamination and toxicity to humans (Green et al., 1978). For this reason, lead poisoning, or plumbism, has been intensely studied, and a large body of information is available for examination. Sources of lead found in the environment are multiple, and the metal is truly ubiquitous, being commonly found in food, water, and air. Evidence exists that lead in the environment has increased during the past 200 years, and it is not surprising that it can be found as a contaminant of aquatic animals (Shukla and Leland, 1973). Environmental lead is a product of storage battery, ammunition, solder, pigment, pipe, brass, and red lead manufacture. Tetraethyllead is a component of gasoline antiknock additives, although in recent years this use has been drastically reduced. There are at least five pools of lead in the body, two of which reside in the skeleton (90%) in cortical and trabecular bone. Lead in cortical bone is similar in half-life to cadmium (approximately 20 years). Other body compartments for lead include the kidney, lung, and central nervous system (Goyer, 1986). It is not surprising therefore that major lesions and clinical signs in humans suffering frank plumbism are referable to the blood (anemia), brain (convulsions, paralysis), and kidney (proteinuria).

The condition in humans is best known because of its chronic toxicity to young children who ingest lead-base paint chips or lead in soil, house dust from paint, industrial dust, and automotive emissions. Oral ingestion of inorganic lead is without doubt the primary port of entry into humans. Of the lead ingested, only 5-15% is absorbed in adults but considerably more in children (Goyer, 1986). Recent studies suggest that very low levels ingested by pregnant women may result in learning and behavioral disabilities in neonates and preschool children (Waternaux et al., 1989). Excretion is primarily via the bile and the gastrointestinal tract. Organic lead compounds such as tetraethyllead may be absorbed in large quantities through the skin, but as toxicants these forms of lead are primarily a problem in the petroleum industry. All forms of lead toxicity are less frequent in adults; any occurrence is usually acute and occupationally related (Green et al., 1978).

Lead's toxicological mode of action depends on its molecular configuration, inorganic lead being less toxic than and producing clinical signs different from tetraethyllead. Inorganic lead is an inhibitor of aminolevulinic acid dehydratase (ALAD) and heme synthetase, which leads to anemia (Hammond, 1978). The metal causes necrosis of neurons, myelin sheath degeneration, and especially, brain vascular damage with increased cerebrospinal fluid (CSF) pressure. These lead to encephalopathy and eventual mental retardation in children. Lead crosses the placental barrier, and there is a good correlation between maternal and fetal blood lead values (Van Gelder, 1978). Therefore, at primary risk from contaminated seafoods are the fetus and neonates.

Mercury

Mercury exists in elemental form, as monovalent (mercurous) or divalent (mercuric) salts, and methylated. The methylated form is the most toxic to humans (Harada, 1978). Methylmercury is formed in the environment from the divalent salts by anaerobic bacteria. It is quite easily absorbed after ingestion and has a variable half-life of 60-120 days in man but is reported to have a half-life of up to 2 years in fish, where it is the predominant form (Al-Shahristani and Shihab, 1974; Stopford and Goldwater, 1975).

The metal is known to produce c-mitosis and chromosomal alterations resulting in cellular damage, with the kidney and brain as target organs. Neuronal damage and axonal demyelination result in the clinical signs and symptoms of paresthesia, incoordination, tremor, and epileptic seizures. The metal also binds strongly to sulfhydral groups (mercaptans), thereby inactivating certain enzymes (Hammond, 1978).

In its methylated form, mercury quite easily passes the placental barrier, placing the fetus at particular risk (Amin-Zaki et al., 1979). The relationship of clinical signs in humans to blood, hair, and urine mercury levels has been reviewed (Tollefson and Cordle, 1986). Children of symptom-free pregnant and nursing mothers with relatively low blood and hair levels may suffer from mental retardation.

Selenium

Selenium is an enigmatic metal because it functions both as an essential nutrient and, at slightly higher levels, as a poison. It is present in various enzymes, has been reported to possess anticarcinogenic effects in animals, is an antioxidant, and yet is a well-documented toxicant of domestic animals as well as a mutagen (Griffin, 1979; Schamberger, 1985; Schnell and Angle, 1983). As an animal toxicant it is a regional problem of the Southwest and Far West. Seleniferous (alkaline, oxidizing) soils give rise to high levels in selenium accumulator plants that are grazed by cattle, sheep, horses, and swine. Poisoned animals develop conditions known as "alkali disease" [subacute, <50 parts per million (ppm)] and "blind staggers" (acute, >100 ppm). Signs include anorexia, tooth and hair loss, watery diarrhea, lassitude, progressive paralysis, and eventual death (Harr and Muth, 1972).

Selenium levels in water from seleniferous areas are often quite high so it is not surprising that selenium has been found as a contaminant of fresh and marine aquatic animals. Its source however is not solely natural. Anthropogenic contamination occurs and is the product of fossil fuel combustion (fly ash) and of paint, alloy, photoelectric battery, and rectifier manufacture (Fishbein, 1983; Sorensen et al., 1984).

Selenium exists in a number of chemical forms, elemental selenium (Se^o), selenide (Se^{2+}), selenite (Se^{4+}), and selenate (Se^{6+}). These forms may bond with other metals or organic substances such as amino acids (Ewan, 1978). The selenates are most soluble and easily enter biological systems. In one study, approximately 15-30% of the selenium found in fish muscle was the selenate form (Cappon and Smith, 1981). The selenites and elemental selenium are relatively insoluble. This is not to say that selenite when ingested will not act as a toxicant, merely that its innate insolubility may affect its absorption and distribution within the body (Goyer, 1986). The biochemistry of selenium is poorly understood but has been reviewed recently (Reddy and Massaro, 1983).

The mode of action of selenium as a toxicant at the cellular and biochemical levels is uncertain. The metal appears to damage endothelium selectively, resulting in edema and hemorrhage in both humans and animals. It is also responsible for toxic hepatitis with eventual fibrosis (not constituting cirrhosis) in chronic exposures.

Selenosis in animals is reported to produce infertility and congenital malformations (Harr, 1978). Selenosis in man appears to be a relatively rare occurrence, most often due to acute occupational exposure or chronic exposure to contaminated water or food sources. There appears to be very little information regarding the effect on man of chronically high levels of selenium in the diet and its potential risk (Wilber, 1983). Recently, however, levels have been reached in fish that have prompted health alerts in California (Fan et al., 1988).

Organic Compounds

In this section, some of the potential contaminants of seafood that have come to the committee's attention, and about which there are at least some minimal data, are surveyed. These include the chlorinated hydrocarbon pesticides that came into widespread use in the United States and elsewhere immediately after World War II (Hansen et al., 1985). Among the chlorinated hydrocarbon pesticides detected in seafood were benzene hexachloride (BHC) or hexachlorobenzene (HCB), chlordane, dieldrin, dichlorodiphenyltrichloroethane (DDT), endrin, heptachlor, lindane, nonachlor, octachlor, and pentachlorophenol. In addition, industrial chemicals and by-products such as PCBs and dioxins are routinely detected in seafood. Less frequently detected pesticides included chlorpyrifos, dacthal (DCPA), diazinon, ethylene dibromide (EDB), malathion, mirex, omethoate, pentachloroaniline, tecnazene, and trifluralin (FDA, 1988; Gunderson, 1988). In quite specific circumstances, such as in farm ponds in heavily agricultural areas, other chemicals – even those that are not known to bioconcentrate, such as atrazine – can be found in fish (Kansas DHE, 1988). Some pesticides detected are specific to various regions. The carboxylic acid herbicide 2,4-(dichlorophenoxy)acetic acid (2,4-D) has been found in oysters from the northern Chesapeake Bay and Alaskan bivalves (NOAA, 1988). Fish from the Arroyo Colorado and adjacent lower Laguna Madre in Texas contained measurable concentrations of pesticides such as ethion, carbophenothion, ethyl parathion, and methyl parathion (NOAA, 1988). The organic compounds classified here have been reviewed by Murphy (1980).

Specific Organics

Polychlorinated biphenyls (PCBs)

Polychlorinated biphenyls include more than 200 different compounds ("congeners") that were used in various formulations as liquid insulators in electrical equipment, as encapsulating agents, in carbonless carbon paper, and in hydraulic fluids. The use of PCBs in "open" applications such as carbonless carbon paper was phased out in the early 1970s, and any new use for the remaining applications was stopped in the late 1970s with the passage of the Toxic Substances Control Act. The U.S. usage of approximately 500,000 tons of PCBs in 1930-1970 accounted for about half of the total world production. However, the unusually slow rate of environmental degradation of the more highly chlorinated PCBs in the environment and in higher organisms, and slow continued discharge of PCBs from old equipment and dump sites, have led to a relatively slow rate of decline of PCB concentrations in fish from large freshwater bodies (e.g., the Great Lakes). The PCBs are a paradigmatic case for the phenomenon of bioconcentration. The more highly chlorinated congeners in particular tend to be both highly lipophilic and very slowly degraded by most organisms. Thus, PCBs that are passed "up" the food chain tend to become much more concentrated as predators are consumed by successively larger predators. In contrast, terrestrial animals that are used for human food are generally vegetarians (first-level consumers of the primary producing organisms).

The principal potential health concerns from PCB exposure include carcinogenesis (on the basis of extensive animal evidence and some suggestive findings in human epidemiological studies), changes in human birth weights, and some loss of neurological performance in the offspring of mothers with relatively high dietary exposures or body burdens (Bertazzi et al., 1987; Brown, 1987; Cordle et al., 1982; Fein et al., 1984; Gladen et al., 1988; J.L. Jacobson et al., 1989, 1990; S.W. Jacobson et al., 1985; Rogan et al., 1986; Sunahara et al., 1987; Taylor et al., 1989).

All carcinogens – in particular, the PCBs and dioxins – are not thought to act primarily by causing DNA mutations (Safe, 1989). This subject is discussed extensively in Chapter 6. Suffice it to say here that lack of knowledge of the precise mechanisms by which PCBs cause cancers makes quantitative assessment of their cancer risk more uncertain than is usual for other chemicals.

The PCB mixtures that are delivered to humans via seafood are likely to be systematically different from the original mixtures that were used in animal testing because of more rapid degradation of some (particularly less chlorinated) congeners in the environment and in aquatic organisms. The selection for relatively persistent congeners in aquatic organisms might tend to increase human risk relative to that expected from a naive extrapolation; other factors might have the opposite effect. In any event, the numbers of cases that could be expected seem large enough to warrant exploration of further options for risk reduction.

Dioxins

2,3,7,8-Tetrachlorodibenzo-*p*-dioxin (hereafter known as TCDD) is a contaminant of products made from trichlorophenol, including some chlorophenoxy herbicides. In humans, its effect has been linked to a severe dermatitis; fetal toxicity and numerous other effects have been observed in experimental animals at very low doses. In standard animal test systems, it is one of the most potent carcinogens known. Using its standard procedures for cancer potency estimation and certain consumption estimates, EPA estimated a lifetime cancer risk of approximately 1 in 100,000 from eating fish contaminated at the nominal detection level of 1 part per trillion (EPA, 1987). Using considerably different methodology for assessing the risk, FDA has advised that, for consumption patterns and species typical to the Great Lakes area, fish consumption should be limited if concentrations in the edible portion exceed 25 parts per trillion and should be banned if concentrations exceed 50 parts per trillion (Kociba et al., 1978).[4] These profound differences in risk assessment indicate the tremendous uncertainty about the true potency of TCDD to cause human cancer.

Polycyclic aromatic hydrocarbons (PAHs)

Polycyclic aromatic hydrocarbons are common environmental contaminants found in petroleum, soot, or tar from incomplete combustion, lubricants, and domestic sewage. Many are well-established carcinogens and are highly toxic. Their pervasiveness in the environment assures widespread contamination of aquatic organisms. Because they are poorly metabolized by bivalves and are easily accessible to these animals, they may pose important potential hazards to humans.

Chlorinated hydrocarbon pesticides

Like PCBs, the broad group of relatively lipid-soluble, persistent chlorinated hydrocarbons was largely phased out of production in the United States during the 1970s because of concerns for carcinogenicity and ecological effects. Fortunately, few members of the group have proved to be as persistent as PCBs in the environment. Like PCBs, however, the precise mechanisms of action of many chlorinated hydrocarbons in causing cancer appear not to be by direct or indirect reactions with DNA; accordingly, quantitative assessments of risk for this group are more uncertain than usual.

DDT and metabolites: Both DDT and its metabolites [primarily dichlorodiphenyldichloroethane (DDE)] are persistent (slowly eliminated from organisms) lipophilic substances of uncertain health significance in humans, and are among the most widespread and frequently sampled of the chlorinated hydrocarbons. They are also persistent in ecosystems and bioaccumulate at higher levels of the food chain, resulting in toxicity to birds and aquatic organisms. The use of DDT was essentially banned in the United States in December 1972. Subacute effects of these chemicals at high doses in humans include central nervous system signs and, in rodents, liver toxicity and estrogenic effects. In addition, DDE has been observed to cause liver tumors in rodents.

Dieldrin: Dieldrin (an epoxide of aldrin) is a cyclodiene insecticide that, like DDT, affects the central nervous system, but is more toxic and has caused human fatalities. It too is lipophilic and may be released from fat stores long after exposure, to cause toxicity. It has led to increased liver tumors when fed at relatively low levels to rodents.

Chlordane: Chlordane is similar in molecular structure and mode of action to dieldrin, but is less toxic.

Heptachlor and heptachlor epoxide compounds: Heptachlor and heptachlor epoxide are also chlorinated cyclodienes, and the epoxide is known to be stored in human fat. They have toxicity similar to dieldrin.

Endosulfan: Endosulfan is a cyclodiene pesticide and a problem contaminant in estuaries near agricultural drainage areas due to its widespread use (NOAA, 1989).

Endrin: Endrin is similar in its toxic effects to other cyclodiene pesticides and is more acutely toxic than DDT.

Chlorinated benzenes and phenols: Lindane (γ-isomer of 1,2,3,4,5,6-hexachlorohexane), also known as benzene hexachloride (BHC), a mixture of α-, β-, and γ-isomers of 1,2,3,4,5,6-hexachlorocyclohexane depending on the manufacturer, is a neurotoxin but has also been found to cause aplastic anemia in humans.

Hexachlorobenzene has never been manufactured in the United States, but it is a ubiquitous fungicide and contaminant often found in other pesticides such as pentachloronitrobenzene (PCNB), which is used in the United States.

Pentachlorophenol: Also known as PCP and penta, pentachlorophenol is a wood preservative, slimicide, and metabolite of the fungicide hexachlorobenzene. Like other polychlorinated phenols, it is contaminated with carcinogenic dioxins (NOAA, 1988).

Mirex: Mirex is a pesticide used to control the fire ant in the southeastern United States. Like other organochlorine pesticides, it is lipophilic and has been reported to be a carcinogen on the basis of rodent studies. It may be a precursor of chlordecone (kepone), is persistent in the environment, and bioconcentrates in the food chain.

Kepone: Kepone has produced appreciable toxicity in exposed workers. It can cause neurological lesions, liver damage, and reproductive failure and is similar in its bioconcentration properties to mirex.

Toxaphene: Toxaphene is a very common domestically used insecticide of complex and often uncertain molecular structure. It is made by chlorinating a mixture of terpenes. It therefore may vary in toxicity from batch to batch depending on the proportion of its isomers. Fortunately, it is of relatively low persistence in the body. Carcinogenic activity is suspected.

Carboxylic herbicides: The herbicides DCPA, 2,4-D, and 2,4,5-trichlorophenoxyacetic acid (2,4,5-T) are chlorophenoxy compounds commonly used in agriculture, and by government agencies and utility companies to control woody plants in rights of way and along roadsides. Although 2,4,5-T has been found to have teratogenic activity, there has long been discussion about whether this is attributable to small amounts of dioxin contaminants. Aside from teratogenesis, these agents can affect animals by impairing neurotransmission, resulting in muscle weakness, ventricular fibrillation, and neuritis.

Atrazine: Atrazine is a herbicide commercially known as AAtrex. It is of low oral acute toxicity. However, its chronic effects are unknown. Structurally similar compounds have been shown to produce thyroid adenocarcinomas in rodents.

Contamination Problems in Aquaculture

Fish culture uses a variety of chemicals that represent potential threats to the health of the cultured animal, indigenous biota, and even the human consumer (Meyer and Schnick, 1989). A number of chemicals of potential toxicity to humans that are not registered for use in the United States are employed in other nations (Fox, 1990). These include furazolidone, nitrofurazone, carofur, chloramphenicol, and silvex – all of which are known or suspected carcinogens.

Chemicals employed in aquaculture include (1) drugs used to treat disease (chemotherapy), (2) those introduced through construction materials, (3) chemicals to treat parasites (formaldehyde), (4) hormones used to alter reproductive viability, sex, and growth rates, and (5) water quality treatments (copper compounds). Of these groups, those of greatest potential concern are the chemotherapeutic drugs. Chemicals used in construction and hormones are not considered in this section because they are relatively nontoxic or have been considered under other headings (organics, pesticides).

Disease is a limiting factor in the culture of aquatic animals. In recent years, culturists have dealt with this problem by developing rapid, immunological diagnostic tests, followed by treatment with drugs commonly used in veterinary medicine. Such chemotherapeutic drugs include, but are not limited to, the potentiated sulfonamides, antibiotics, and nitrofurans. Their widespread use, both nationally and especially internationally, may pose a threat to human health if residues persist in the edible portions of fish and shellfish. Both residue tolerance levels and withdrawal times (the period prior to slaughter during which no drug may be administered) have been determined and set by FDA for major drugs used by veterinarians in the treatment of terrestrial food producing animals. Hence, the problem of persistent residues has long been recognized by the medical profession, but only recently has it been investigated in cultured aquatic animals. The Center for Veterinary Medicine of FDA is aware of the seriousness of this problem and is actively attempting to deal with it, as evidenced by its recent requests for proposals in the April 9, 1990 issue of *Business Commerce Weekly* (Guarino et al., 1988; Mitchell, 1989). The proposals will study the pharmacokinetics and methods of monitoring some six drugs, including malachite green and chloramphenicol, presently used in fish and crustacean culture. In addition to this organization, active research is being conducted by the Fisheries Research Branch of the FDA and the Fisheries Research Center, La Crosse, Wisconsin of the U.S. Fish and Wildlife Service (Schnick, 1988). The latter organization has published a booklet entitled "A Guide to Approved Chemicals in Fish Production and Fishery Resource Management" (Schnick et al., 1989). Although there is much interest in the potential toxicity of chemotherapeutic drug residues in seafood, to date only a potentiated sulfonamide (Romet-30), oxytetracycline (Terramycin), and Formalin are approved for use in food producing aquatic animals.

The nature, use, and residues of the drugs applicable to aquaculture that are used to control disease in veterinary medicine have been reviewed (Bevill and Huber, 1977; Booth, 1977; Huber, 1977a-c; Michel, 1986).

Chemotherapeutic drugs used in aquaculture are sulfonamides, antibiotics, and drugs used in the chemotherapy of protozoal, mycotic, and helminthic infections.

In addition to these examples of deliberately used chemicals, fish raised in aquaculture are also susceptible to contamination via pesticides present in feed, agricultural runoff water, and sediments. The magnitude of human exposure to these sources has not yet been assessed and should be examined periodically in light of the growth and change in this sector of the seafood industry.

Sulfonamides

The sulfonamides are readily synthesized derivatives of sulfanilic acid. They are bacteriostatic drugs, and their efficacy may be increased by the addition of ormetoprim (Plakas et al., 1990). Commonly, sulfadimethoxine is potentiated with ormetoprim (Romet-30) and fed to cultured fish at the rate of 50 mg/kg body weight for 5 days. Similarly, sulfamethoxazole is potentiated with trimethoprim (Tribrissen) and fed at the rate of 1-4 mg/kg body weight for 10-14 days. The latter drug is not approved for use in aquaculture. The FDA tolerance level for both these drugs in cattle and chickens is 0.1 ppm (Booth, 1977).

The sulfonamides have been implicated in renal damage, urinary obstructions, and hematopoietic disorders. For that reason, FDA has set withdrawal times and residue tolerance levels to protect public health. The withdrawal period for catfish is 3 days and for trout 6 weeks (Schnick et al., 1989).

Antibiotics

The term antibiotic includes a large number of drugs inimical to the growth of microorganisms. Of greatest interest in aquaculture are oxytetracycline, ampicillin, chloramphenicol, and erythromycin.

Oxytetracycline (Terramycin) is a product of the mold *Streptomyces rimosus*. It is a broad-spectrum antibiotic used to treat a number of bacterial diseases in fish and crustaceans. It is the only antibiotic approved by the FDA for use in aquaculture. Contamination of the food supply with the drug is a public health concern because chronic exposures at low levels may lead to a higher incidence of antibiotic-resistant bacterial strains, poor growth of teeth, and the possibility of photosensitivity. The FDA tolerance level for oxytetracycline in meat is 0.25 ppm, whereas in fish it is 0.1 ppm with a withdrawal time of 21 days. Elimination time from muscle appears longer for salmonids than for catfish and is dependent on the water temperature (Plakas et al., 1988).

Ampicillin is a newer, semisynthetic penicillin that has activity against both gram-positive and gram-negative organisms. Although not approved for use in the United States and seldom used domestically, it is commonly used in Japan to control pasteurellosis in yellowtail culture (Hawke et al., 1987). Ampicillin, like its congeners, may result in severe hypersensitivity reactions in some people (Huber, 1977a). Because an initial exposure to some form of penicillin is necessary to produce an eventual drug allergy, ingestion of ampicillin as a residue in seafood is of public health interest. The FDA has set a tolerance level of 0.01 ppm and a preslaughter withdrawal time in cattle of 6 days. No information is available regarding residues or withdrawal time in fish or crustaceans.

Chloramphenicol is a product of the mold *Streptomyces venezuelae* and is a potent antibiotic that is effective against most bacteria, as well as rickettsia and the psittacosis-lymphogranuloma group of organisms. Development of resistant bacteria may follow its widespread and uncontrolled use. Chloramphenicol administered for long periods may cause blood dyscrasias such as aplastic anemia and has recently been incriminated as a carcinogen. It is not approved for use in the United States in food producing animals. The drug is used, however, with impunity to control bacterial diseases of shrimp, especially in Ecuador and in European fish culture (Manci, 1990; Meyer and Schnick, 1989). Because imported seafood is not checked for antibiotics, no information is available regarding its residue levels.

Erythromycin is a product of the mold *Streptomyces erythreus* and is primarily effective against gram-positive organisms. The drug is not approved for use in domestic fish culture but is used in Europe. The tolerance level in U.S. swine is 0.01 ppm, and the withdrawal time is 7 days. The drug is not considered an important cause of hypersensitivity in man and is relatively nontoxic.

Nitrofurans

Nitrofurans are synthetic compounds that are active against most gram-negative bacteria, some fungi, and some protozoal organisms. Because of their toxicity, their clinical use is limited and FDA has attempted unsuccessfully for over 15 years to ban their use in food producing animals and to have them withdrawn from the market (FDA, 1982). Side effects include bleeding, gastrointestinal upsets, and allergic reactions. Tolerance levels for the drug have been set at zero. In aquaculture, their use has been suggested for the treatment of *Ichthyophthirius multifillis*.

Conclusions

1. Certain drugs with potential toxicity to humans are used to control disease in cultured food producing aquatic animals.
2. There is a paucity of information regarding the withdrawal times, residue levels, and pharmacokinetics in the cultured aquatic animals receiving these drugs.
3. There is some reason for concern that large amounts of imported cultured seafood, which is routinely treated with drugs, are consumed by the American public, although the magnitude of ultimate human exposure from this source is as yet uncertain.
4. Cultured seafood imported into the United States is not presently inspected for drug residues.

Contaminants as a Result of Processing

Nitrosamines

Nitrosamines are formed in smoked fish products and in the human stomach as the result of the simultaneous presence of secondary amines and nitrite. Since the late 1960s, the use of nitrite in smoked fish has been authorized to avoid the repetition of botulism incidents in the early 1960s that resulted from the mishandling of vacuum packed smoked fish. [Earlier joint industry/FDA recommendations on the time and temperature cooking of smoked fish products were reportedly not complied with by Great Lakes producers, and the food additive petition was later granted after it was shown that nitrosamine formation in the fish itself did not exceed a specific level of sensitivity specified by FDA (Hattis, 1972).] The exact extent of the extra exposure to specific nitrosamines attributable to the use of nitrite as a food additive in smoked fish has apparently not been reappraised recently by using more sensitive analytical techniques and current risk assessment procedures.

Products of chlorination, bromination, and iodination

Chlorine and some other active halogen compounds are widely used as disinfectants in seafood processing, as well as in the treatment of drinking water and sewage effluents (Fukayama et al., 1986). This process is known to generate some levels of halogenated amines, aromatics, and methanes (e.g., chloroform), and at least one test in chiller water used in chicken processing detected mutagenic activity when the chlorination level was raised to 250 ppm (Masri, 1986). The extent of contamination of seafood with products resulting from the use of chlorine and other halogen compounds does not appear to have been assessed, and there are no relevant appraisals of the associated risks in the available literature. Some relevant information may be contained in food additive petitions for disinfectants that have been submitted to FDA, but the committee has not obtained these documents.

Residues of ozonation

Ozone treatment is frequently used in foreign settings as a method of depuration of some shellfish (Fauvel et al., 1982). This technology has also been introduced into the United States for use in icing fish (Rice et al., 1982), washing seafoods, and cleansing saltwater for use in molluscan shellfish depuration. In recent years, FDA has raised questions about the safety of this process because of the likelihood of residual reaction by-products of the resulting oxidation.[5] This concern was recently debated during the First International Molluscan Shellfish Depuration Conference, November 5-8, 1989 in Orlando, Florida (W.S. Otwell, University of Florida, Gainesville, personal communication, 1989) and later in letters from the FDA Compliance Branch (J.A. Baca, FDA, personal communication, June 22, 1990) explaining its position on the use of ozone in food manufacturing facilities. The primary concern is any ozone contact with seafood whereby the ozone could become a component of the food or affect the character of the food. The prevailing differences of opinion await more technical resolution in studies to monitor the consequences from direct and indirect (treating depuration water) applications. Cognizant of the current data, the FDA regulatory interpretations to restrict use will most likely prevail.

Sulfites

Sulfites have traditionally been used to prevent melanosis in crustaceans (Camber et al., 1956). Sanctioned procedures include a 1-minute dip in concentrations of up to 1.25% sodium bisulfite or metabisulfite. This has been shown to impart a residual sulfite level of less than 100 ppm on the edible portion of penaeid shrimp.[6] Product treated in this way must be labeled to designate prior use and residuals in excess of 10 ppm. General concern for allergic-like reactions, particularly in some asthmatic people, has given rise to concern about the continued use and appropriate labeling of sulfites (Lecos, 1985). No equally effective alternative processes have yet been developed for crustaceans.

DATA ON THE DISTRIBUTION OF CHEMICAL CONTAMINATION

Introduction

Some modest concentrations of contaminants are ubiquitous in the clean (natural, pristine, nonenhanced, unimpacted) aquatic environment. A few metals, such as copper, selenium, iron, and zinc, are essential nutrients for fish and shellfish. Contamination occurs from both natural and anthropogenic sources, and can be said to exist when there is a statistically significant increase in geometric mean levels in comparable organisms, suitably adjusted for confounders.

Evidence for such higher detectable levels may be found in a number of studies conducted by university scientists and by state and federal agencies. Of major importance are ongoing studies by the National Oceanic and Atmospheric Administration (NOAA) and the U.S. Fish and Wildlife Service (USF&WS). The NOAA data are generated by the National Status and Trends Program, which examines fish and shellfish annually from more than 145 coastal sites in the United States (NOAA, 1987, 1989). Similarly, the USF&WS conducts the National Pesticides Monitoring Program, which examines fish from 115 freshwater sites in the 50 states (Lowe et al., 1985). In addition, the FDA conducts periodic inspections of domestic and imported seafoods (FDA, 1988). These federal programs are bolstered by extensive studies and reviews conducted on a regional basis by various researchers (Capuzzo et al., 1987; Clark et al., 1984; Landolt et al., 1985, 1987; Malins et al., 1980, 1982; Murphy, 1988a-c; Rohrer et al., 1982; St. Amant et al., 1983). Further, a careful literature review reveals a large number (100+) of publications on the subject of trace-metal contamination both in peer-reviewed journals and among state documents (Duling, 1988; Sloan et al., 1987).

This data base confirms that high levels of contaminants exist in various aquatic animals in some places. It has, however, a number of shortcomings for use in risk assessment. First, the more extensive studies have considered metal levels in the nonedible portions of finfish or in the whole fish. This prevents accurate determination of dosages. Second, reports vary in the data presentation (geometric versus arithmetic means), some failing to report sample size, mean values, or animal size, thus further preventing careful statistical analysis and risk assessment.

National Status and Trends Program

The NOAA National Status and Trends (NS&T) program is an extensive federal program under the direction and management of the Ocean Assessments Division of NOAA (OAD) that monitors levels of toxicants annually (routine surveillance) in shellfish (Mussel Watch) and finfish (Benthic Surveillance) from approximately 150 coastal and estuarine sites in the continental United States, Alaska, and Hawaii (NOAA, 1989). Structured in a three-tiered design, NOAA states the objectives as:

1. to determine toxic contaminants as a basis for the identification of potential geographic differences (Mussel Watch, Tier 1);
2. to identify areas where environmental quality may be significantly compromised (Mussel Watch);

3. to determine significant temporal trends in toxic contaminant levels on a national basis (Mussel Watch); and

4. to evaluate and synthesize existing sources of information pertinent to the status of contaminants in selected areas (Historic Trend Assessment, Tier 2), and in Tier 3 (Verification) to augment the basic monitoring program as needed in areas indicated by Tier 1 results.

The NS&T has been in existence since 1984 and was an outgrowth of the previous Mussel Watch program. It produces an excellent data base from which scientists may evaluate levels of contamination and their spatial and temporal differences. Sites are numerous and evenly distributed geographically. Species of animals examined well represent the particular area monitored and, in the case of invertebrates, may be in the same genus nationally, thus decreasing physiological differences. Most important, the NOAA Quality Assurance Program used by NS&T establishes analytical protocols that ensure reliability of data.

It is unfortunate, from the point of view of human exposure assessment, that the NS&T program examines fish liver samples rather than edible portions. Extrapolation from liver to muscle contaminant levels is fraught with uncertainty, and the data are essentially useless for this purpose. In all fairness, however, it was and is not the objective of the NS&T Benthic Surveillance program to supply such information, and its design fulfills its objectives admirably.

Federal Survey of PCBs in Atlantic Coast Bluefish

A NOAA (1987) interpretative report is based on a sampling of hundreds of bluefish (*Pomatomous saltaltrix*) from New England to the Atlantic Coast of Florida that was undertaken as part of a 1984 congressional mandate resulting from the discovery of relatively high PCB contamination in bluefish from New Jersey and New York waters. The wide-ranging migratory nature of bluefish, which are found along the entire Atlantic Coast of the United States, led to speculation that this highly prized and abundant sport species could be of special concern from a public health perspective. In fact, bluefish constitute the principal recreational species in terms of landings (130-155 million pounds annually) along the Atlantic Coast.

National Contaminant Biomonitoring Program

The U.S. Fish and Wildlife Service National Contaminant Biomonitoring Program (NCBP) is a continuing survey in which freshwater fish are collected from 112 stations located throughout the United States (Lowe et al., 1985). Three composite samples of three to five fish are collected at half the stations in odd years and the other half in even years. During 1978-1981, 60 species were collected; however, a common species was collected at only 39 stations and no species were collected in common at 24 stations (Schmitt et al., 1983). Analyses are conducted on whole fish samples that are homogenized and lyophilized. Precision and accuracy of analysis are estimated by duplicate samples and by the use of reference materials from the National Bureau of Standards and FDA. Data generated by the NCBP may be used to identify geographic areas of greatest concern and temporal variations. However, although the NCBP is an excellent, synoptic, national approach to the contamination of freshwater fish, it suffers from the same inadequacy as the NS&T program with regard to human exposure assessment because the samples examined are not just edible portions but include the whole animal. Furthermore, the large variation in species among collection points and between years adds to the difficulty. In this case, however, the difficulty in projection seems much less serious than in the case of fish liver.

Regional Reports

Regional reports provide other important data for examining industrial chemical and pesticide concentrations in certain species of aquatic organisms and for estimating the intake of sport and subsistence fishers. The committee relied on reports from Quincy Bay, Massachusetts; New York; southern California; and Puget Sound, Washington.

EVIDENCE FOR TRACE-METAL AND ORGANIC CONTAMINATION

This section provides an overview of both the level and the variability of contaminant concentrations, as inferred from the data bases reviewed above. The variability of contaminant concentrations among geographic areas is important because it indicates the potential for reduction of exposure through restrictions on the harvesting of aquatic organisms from specific sites. Therefore, wherever possible, the committee summarizes geographic variability data in the form of figures that show the data analyzed as lognormal distributions. In these figures, conformance to the assumption of lognormality is indicated by the correspondence of the points to a straight line. The lognormal standard deviations (slopes of the lines in these figures) allow an approximate calculation of the percentage of the aggregate fish or shellfish dose of the contaminant that could be avoided by restricting harvesting from various proportions of the sites in order of their mean concentrations. This analysis will be pursued further below.

Molluscan Shellfish

Trace Metals

National Status and Trends data for shellfish residues are summarized in Table 5-1.

Arsenic (As)

• Mean levels: Descriptive statistics of all NS&T shellfish data are presented in Table 5-1 and Figure 5-1.[7] The arithmetic grand mean arsenic levels of all bivalves

129

TABLE 5-1   Shellfish Contaminants (ppm wet weight)[a]

Contaminant	Mean ± SD	Percentiles					Geographic Distribution and Sites Exceeding 95th Percentile	Temporal Trends 1986-1988[b] (% change)
		5th	25th	50th	75th	95th		
PCB	0.052 ± 0.102	0.003	0.008	0.017	0.047	0.200	All coastal sites. AB, H/R, NYSB, SD, BB, BH	–13
DDT	0.010 ± 0.02	0.001	0.002	0.004	0.011	0.032	All coastal sites. H/R, SPH, PV, AB, SFB, CBF, NYSB, BB	+4;–6
PAH	0.158 ± 0.354	0	0.009	0.049	0.157	0.509	All coastal sites. EB, H/R, SFB, BP, BH, LIS	+8;–10
Arsenic	1.390 ± 0.81	0.600	0.892	1.12	1.694	2.879	All coastal sites. CF, CK, CH, CRH, RB, SS, SRE	+6;–8
Cadmium	0.434 ± 0.275	0.106	0.247	0.376	0.552	0.925	All coastal sites. COP, DB, CB, H/R, BH/LIS, NBR	+4;–17
Lead	0.230 ± 0.366	0.02	0.05	0.09	0.289	0.733	All coastal sites. MD, AB, H/R, BH, LIS, NBR	+5;–1
Mercury	0.015 ± 0.01	0.004	0.008	0.012	0.020	0.036	All coastal sites. TB, H/R, BP, MB, BH, MRB, CH	+11;–4
Selenium	0.318 ± 0.122	0.15	0.244	0.304	0.360	0.523	All coastal sites. HH, BP, ABT, EST, UI, PC, COP	+12;–2

NOTE: AB Anaheim Bay, Calif.; ABT Aransas Bay, Tex.; BB Buzzards Bay, Mass.; BH Boston Harbor, Mass.; BP Barbers Pt., Hawaii; CB Chesapeake Bay, Md.; CBF Choctawatchee, Fla.; CF Cape Fear, N.C.; CH Charlotte Harbor, Fla.; CK Cedar Key, Fla.; COP Copano Bay, Tex.; CRH Charleston Harbor, S.C.; DB Delaware Bay, Del.; EST Espiritu Santo, Tex.; EB Elliot Bay, Wash.; HH Honolulu Harbor, Hawaii; H/R Hudson/Raritan Bay, N.Y.; LIS Long Island Sound, N.Y.; MB Matagorda Bay, Tex.; MD Marina Del Ray, Calif.; MRB Moriches Bay, N.Y.; NBR Narragansett Bay, R.I.; NYSB New York State Bight of New Jersey; PC Point Concepcion, Calif.; PV Palos Verdes, Calif.; RB Rookery Bay, Fla.; SD San Diego Bay, Calif.; SFB San Francisco Bay, Calif.; SPH San Pedro Harbor, Calif.; SRE Savannah River Estuary, Ga.; SS Sapelo Sound, Fla.; TB Tampa Bay, Fla.; UI Unakit Inlet, Alaska.

[a] 1987 NS&T data.

[b] + = sites increased in number; – = sites decreased.

SOURCE: NOAA (1989).

from the 25 most contaminated sites reported in the 1986 Mussel Watch Survey is 2.763 ppm wet weight with a standard deviation of 0.9340 and a range of 1.920-5.131 ppm wet weight (using a dry weight/wet weight conversion factor of 0.12). Eight of the most contaminated sites (2.9604 to 5.1312 ppm wet weight) exceed the 95th percentile (2.8794).

   • Median levels: The median of the arithmetic grand means of all bivalves from the 25 most contaminated sites reported in the 1986 Mussel Watch Survey is 2.559 ppm wet weight (range 1.920-5.1310). The 1986 Mussel Watch (145 sites) national grand median for arsenic is 1.120 ppm wet weight with a range of 0.2352-5.119 ppm (dry weight/wet weight conversion factor = 0.12).

   • Geographic distribution: Arsenic was present in both oysters and mussels from all sites examined by the 1986 Mussel Watch Survey. Of the 25 most contaminated sites, 10 were in the Southeast (North and South Carolina, Georgia, and Florida) 8 in California, 1 in the mid-Atlantic region (Chesapeake Bay), and none in the Northeast or Northwest. The eight sites exceeding the 95th percentile are Cape Fear, N.C.; Cedar Key, Fla.; Charlotte Harbor, Fla.; Charleston Harbor (CHFJ and CHSF), S.C.; Rookery Bay, Fla.; Sapelo Sound, Ga.; and Savannah River Estuary, Ga.

   • Temporal trends: The most recent NS&T data indicate increases in 6 and decreases in 8 of 177 sites studied. None of the most contaminated sites showed decreases.

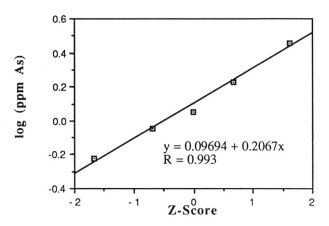

FIGURE 5-1 Lognormal distribution of wet weight concentrations of arsenic in bivalves (NS&T data set)

Cadmium (Cd)

• Mean levels: Descriptive statistics of all NS&T shellfish data are presented in Table 5-1 and Figure 5-2. The arithmetic grand mean level for cadmium of all bivalves from the 25 most contaminated sites reported in the 1986 Mussel Watch Survey is 0.9039 ppm wet weight with a standard deviation of 0.2621 and a range of 0.6276-1.560 ppm (using a dry weight/wet weight conversion factor of 0.12). Eight of the most contaminated sites (0.9324-1.56 ppm wet weight) exceed the 95th percentile (0.9252).

● Median levels: The median of the arithmetic grand means of all bivalves from the 25 most contaminated sites reported in the 1986 Mussel Watch Survey is 0.8244 ppm wet weight (range 1.920-5.1310). The 1986 Mussel Watch (145 sites) national grand median for cadmium is 0.3756 ppm wet weight with a range of 0.0240-1.5600 ppm (dry weight/wet weight conversion factor = 0.12).

● Geographic distribution: All sites examined by the NS&T program contained bivalves with tissue cadmium burdens. Of the 25 most contaminated sites, 10 were located in the Gulf of Mexico, 6 in the Chesapeake Bay area, 7 on the West Coast (6 California), and 2 in the Northeast. The eight most contaminated sites are Copano Bay, Tex.; Delaware Bay (DBAP), Del.; Chesapeake Bay, Md.; Delaware Bay (DBKI), Del.; Hudson/Raritan Estuary, N.Y.; Corpus Christi, Tex.; Mississippi Sound, Miss.; and Delaware Bay (DBBD), Del.

● Temporal trends: The most recent NS&T data indicate increases in only 4 and decreases in 17 of 177 sites studied; 4 of the sites reported as having decreased levels are sites previously listed among the 10 most contaminated.

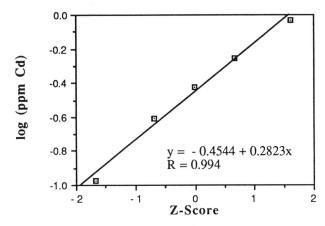

$$y = -0.4544 + 0.2823x$$
$$R = 0.994$$

FIGURE 5-2 Lognormal distribution of wet weight concentrations of cadmium in bivalves (NS&T data set)

Lead (Pb)

● Mean levels: Descriptive statistics of all NS&T shellfish data are presented in Table 5-1 and Figure 5-3. The arithmetic grand mean lead level of all bivalves from the 25 most contaminated sites reported in the 1986 Mussel Watch Survey is 0.8203 ppm wet weight with a standard deviation of 0.5684 and a range of 0.3804-2.799 ppm (using a dry weight/wet weight conversion factor of 0.12). Eight of the most contaminated sites (0.7356-2.7996 ppm wet weight) exceed the 95th percentile (0.7326).

● Median levels: The median of the arithmetic grand means of all bivalves from the 25 most contaminated sites reported in the 1986 Mussel Watch Survey is 0.6240 ppm wet weight (range 0.3804-2.799). The 1986 Mussel Watch (145 sites) national grand median for lead is 0.0900 ppm wet weight with a range of 0.0108-2.7996 ppm (dry weight/wet weight conversion factor = 0.12).

• Geographic distribution: All Mussel Watch sites reported bivalves containing lead. Of the 25 most contaminated sites, 15 were in the Northeast including the Hudson River/Raritan Estuary, Boston Harbor, Long Island Sound, New York Bight, and Narragansett Bay. Eight of the remaining sites – including the most contaminated (Marina Del Rey) – were in California. Those sites exceeding the 95th percentile are Marina Del Rey, Calif.; Anaheim Bay, Calif.; Hudson/Raritan Estuary, N.Y.; Boston Harbor (BHDB, BHBB, and BHDI), Mass.; Long Island Sound, N.Y.; and Narragansett Bay, R.I.

• Temporal trends: The most recent NS&T data indicate increases in 5 sites and decreases in only 1 of the 177 studied (Barber's Point, Hawaii). None of the increases occurred in the previously reported most contaminated sites.

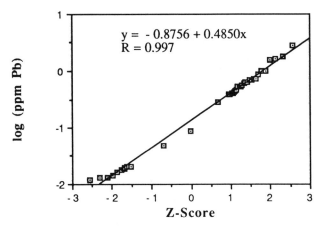

FIGURE 5-3 Lognormal distribution of wet weight concentrations of lead in bivalves (NS&T data set)

Mercury (Hg)

• Mean levels: Descriptive statistics of all NS&T shellfish data are presented in Table 5-1 and Figure 5-4. The arithmetic grand mean mercury level of all bivalves from the 25 most contaminated sites reported in the 1986 Mussel Watch Survey is 0.0351 ppm wet weight with a standard deviation of 0.0084 and a range of 0.0276-0.0576 ppm (using a dry weight/wet weight conversion factor of 0.12); 7 of the most contaminated sites (0.0372-0.0576 ppm wet weight) exceed the 95th percentile (0.0363).

• Median levels: The median of the arithmetic grand means of all bivalves from the 25 most contaminated sites reported in the 1986 Mussel Watch Survey is 0.0324 ppm wet weight (range 0.0276 to 0.0576). The 1986 Mussel Watch (145 sites) national grand median for mercury is 0.0120 ppm wet weight with a range of 0.0012-0.0576 ppm (dry weight/wet weight conversion factor = 0.12).

• Geographic distribution: Mercury was found in bivalves from all coastal sites (145) examined by the Mussel Watch Survey. Distribution of the 25 most contaminated sites included all major geographic areas; 9 sites were in the Southeast, all in Florida; 7 sites in the Northeast, most in the New York/New Jersey area; 5 in California; 2 in the Pacific Northwest; and 2 in Hawaii. The seven sites exceeding the

95th percentile are Tampa Bay, Fla.; Hudson/Raritan Estuary, N.Y.; Barber's Point, Hawaii; Matagorda Bay, Tex; Boston Harbor, Mass; Moriches Bay, N.Y.; and Charlotte Harbor, Fla.

• Temporal trends: The most recent NS&T data indicate increases in shellfish tissue mercury in 11 sites and decreases in only 4 sites of 177 studied. Of the ten most contaminated sites, one (Barber's Point, Hawaii) showed a decrease, whereas another (Hudson Raritan Estuary) had an increase. Increases occurred primarily in the northeastern and southern coastal areas.

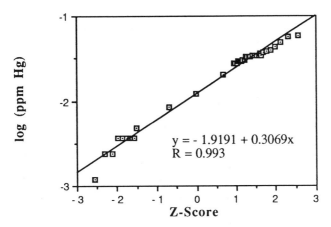

FIGURE 5-4 Lognormal distribution of wet weight concentrations of mercury in bivalves (NS&T data set)

Selenium (Se)

• Mean levels: Descriptive statistics of all NS&T shellfish data are presented in Table 5-1 and Figure 5-5. The arithmetic grand mean selenium level of all bivalves from the 25 most contaminated sites reported in the 1986 Mussel Watch Survey is 0.5145 ppm wet weight with a standard deviation of 0.1391 and a range of 0.3996-0.9800 ppm (using a dry weight/wet weight conversion factor of 0.12); 8 of the most contaminated sites (0.5364-0.9804 ppm) exceed the 95th percentile (0.5232).

• Median levels: The median of the arithmetic grand means of all bivalves from the 25 most contaminated sites reported in the 1986 Mussel Watch Survey is 0.4560 ppm wet weight (range 0.3996-0.9800). The 1986 Mussel Watch (145 sites) national grand median for selenium is 0.3036 ppm wet weight with a range of 0.1116-0.9800 ppm (dry weight/wet weight conversion factor = 0.12).

• Geographic distribution: All 145 sites examined by the NS&T program revealed selenium in indigenous bivalves; 14 of the 25 most contaminated sites were in Texas (Arkansas Bay, Espiritu Santo, Copano Bay, Matagorda Bay, San Antonio Bay, Galveston Bay, Mesquite Bay) or California (Marina Del Rey, Pt. Concepcion, Pt. Delgada, Santa Catalina Island, Bodega Bay, La Jolla, Pt. Dume). Highest levels were found in oysters in Honolulu Harbor and Barber's Pt., Hawaii. Other sites included

Chesapeake Bay and Hudson River/Raritan estuary. Sites that exceed the 95th percentile are Honolulu Harbor, Hawaii; Barber's Point, Hawaii; Arkansas Bay, Tex.; Espiritu Santo, Tex.; Marina Del Rey, Calif.; Unakwit Inlet, Alaska; Point Concepcion, Calif.; and Copano Bay, Tex.

● Temporal trends: The most recent NS&T data indicate shellfish tissue increases in 12 sites and decreases in only 2 sites (Commencement Bay, Wash., and Honolulu Harbor) of 177 sites studied. Those sites recording increases in selenium tissue content were primarily in the southern region, including four in Florida, five in Louisiana, and one each in Mississippi and Texas.

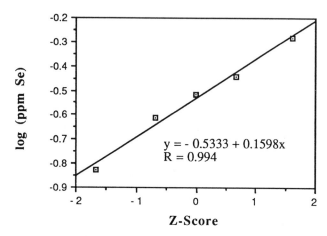

FIGURE 5-5 Lognormal distribution of wet weight concentrations of selenium in bivalves (NS&T data set)

Organics

Polychlorinated biphenyls

Polychlorinated biphenyls have been detected as contaminants in the marine environment for nearly five decades and in marine fish for nearly four decades (NOAA, 1988). Concentrations of total PCBs have ranged in fish muscle from below detection to 730 ppm wet weight in an American eel collected from New Bedford Harbor, Mass., in 1979 (NOAA, 1988). For bivalve molluscs, the most contaminated sites are located along the Northeast coast and in southern California harbors. The grand national median for PCBs calibrated against the commercial mixture Aroclor 1242[8] in the 1976 Mussel Watch Survey at 86 sites was 0.009 ppm wet weight with a range of 0.0008-2.09 ppm. Although not strictly comparable because of analytical, site, and species differences, preliminary calculations indicate that the grand national median of total PCBs in the 1986 Mussel Watch Survey at 144 sites was 0.017 ppm wet weight with a range of 0.0009-0.68 ppm (Table 5-1, Figure 5-6).

Descriptive statistics of all NS&T shellfish data are presented in Table 5-1. The arithmetic grand mean PCB levels of all bivalves from the 25 most contaminated sites reported in the 1986 Mussel Watch Survey is 0.205 ppm wet weight with a standard deviation of 0.176 (range 0.0728-0.817 ppm) using a dry weight/wet weight conversion factor of 0.12.

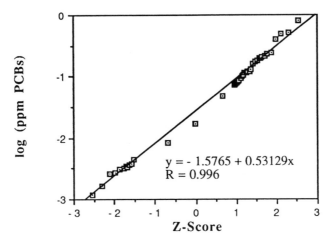

FIGURE 5-6 Lognormal distribution of wet weight concentrations of PCBs in bivalves (NS&T data set)

The median of the arithmetic grand means of all bivalves from the 25 most contaminated sites reported in the 1986 Mussel Watch Survey is 0.1287 ppm wet weight (range 0.0728-0.8169). The national grand median for total polychlorinated biphenyls (tPCBs) in 145 sites was 0.0172 ppm wet weight with a range of 0.0011-0.8170 ppm (dry weight/wet weight conversion factor, 0.12). The most contaminated sites (exceeding the 95th percentile) were Buzzards Bay, Mass.; Hudson/Raritan Estuary (HRLB), N.Y.; New York Bight (NYSR), N.J.; Hudson/Raritan Estuary (HRUB), N.Y.; San Diego Bay, Calif.; Galveston Bay, Tex.; New York Bight (NYSH), N.J.; and Boston Harbor, Mass.

Although a large body of data exists from state local programs, to date these have not been carefully analyzed. Gulf Coast sites appear undersampled. With present data it is difficult to determine if PCBs are increasing or decreasing nationally. Certain specific sites such as Whites Pt., Calif.; Escambia Bay, Fla.; Narragansett Bay, R.I.; and Chesapeake Bay, Md. have shown major decreases. However, other sites such as Boston Harbor and Beaufort, N.C. have shown no change or slight increases (Mearns et al., 1988). Most recent NS&T data (1986-1988) now including 177 sites indicate no increases in PCBs and decreases in 13 sites including 2 of the most contaminated (Boston Harbor and the Hudson River).

Polyaromatic hydrocarbons

Polyaromatic hydrocarbons contain some prominent carcinogens such as benzo[*a*]pyrene. In a recent survey of contaminants in hard-shell clams (*Mercenaria mercenaria*) in the vicinity of Alan Harbor, R.I. (the location of a military hazardous waste disposal site), PAHs were the only group of contaminants that appeared to show a gradient of increasing concentration in areas nearest the site (Hattis, 1989). Unfortunately, for purposes of risk assessment, benzo[*a*]pyrene, whose carcinogenic activity is relatively well characterized, constitutes only a minor fraction of the total PAHs found either in marine sediments or in shellfish (in the Alan Harbor data, benzo[*a*]pyrene averaged about 1% of the total PAHs measured--total PAHs in clams were about 0.8 ppm dry weight, about half of that elsewhere in Narragansett Bay). Innovative approaches to assessing the relative hazard of some other PAHs have been proposed (Rugen et al., 1989).

Very little good data exist nationwide on the extent of PAH contamination. This is of particular concern for animals lower on the food chain such as bivalves. Researchers purchased quahogs (*Mercenaria mercenaria*) from 13 markets throughout Rhode Island and analyzed them for PAHs (Pruell et al., 1984). Levels observed varied widely between stores and also between repeat visits to the same store. These data indicate clearly that shellfish consumers have the potential to purchase quahogs with elevated levels of nonregulated, carcinogenic organic contaminants.

Descriptive statistics of all the NS&T shellfish data are presented in Table 5-1 and Figure 5-7. The arithmetic grand mean of PAH levels of all bivalves from the 25 most contaminated sites reported in the 1986 Mussel Watch Survey is 0.6471 ppm wet weight with a standard deviation of 0.6458 (range 0.2400-2.760 ppm) using a dry weight/wet weight conversion factor of 0.12; 7 of the most contaminated sites (0.6360-2.7600 ppm wet weight) exceed the 95th percentile (0.5090).

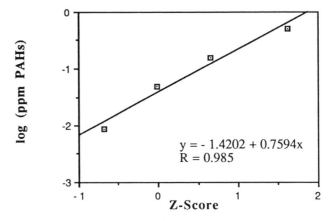

FIGURE 5-7 Lognormal distribution of wet weight concentrations of PAHs in bivalves (NS&T data set)

The median of the arithmetic grand means of all bivalves from the 25 most contaminated sites reported in the 1986 Mussel Watch Survey is 0.396 ppm wet weight (range 0.240-2.76). The national median PAH for 145 sites is 0.0492 ppm wet weight with a range of 0.0000-2.79 ppm (dry weight/wet weight conversion factor, 0.12).

The geographic distribution is widespread, from Maine to Washington including Alaska and Hawaii. The seven most heavily contaminated sites ranked from highest to lowest are Elliot Bay, Wash.; Hudson/Raritan Estuary, N.Y.; St Andrew Bay, Fla,; Barber's Point, Hawaii; Boston Harbor (BHDB and BHHB), Mass.; and Long Island Sound, N.Y.

Most recent NS&T data (1986-1988) now including 177 sites indicate increases in PAHs (high- and low-molecular-weight data combined) in 8 sites and decreases in 10 sites, including only one of the most contaminated (Hudson Raritan Estuary).

Chlorinated hydrocarbon pesticides

DDT and metabolites: According to NOAA, the pesticide DDT and its metabolites are among the most widespread and frequently sampled chlorinated hydrocarbons. In contrast with PCBs, DDT concentrations in seafood have declined dramatically in the last 15 years, perhaps as much as 100-fold nationally (NOAA, 1988). Traces of DDT have been found in marine samples from every coastal state, at many offshore and deep-water sites, and from nearly every estuary. In fact, DDT and metabolites were found in 63% of the 8,095 oysters, clams, and mussels from 180 sites sampled during the National Pesticides Monitoring Program of NOAA (NPMP) (NOAA, 1988). Mean concentrations ranged from below detection to 1.4 ppm wet weight at Iona Point in southeast Florida. When the NPMP survey resampled all sites in 1977, total DDT concentrations had fallen below the 0.01 ppm wet weight detection limit everywhere except at the Point Mugu Lagoon site near Oxnard in southern California and at sites in upper Delaware Bay. A 1976-1978 Mussel Watch Survey analyzing for DDE and using more sensitive detection limits yielded many more positive detection results (ranging from 0.001 to 0.010 ppm wet weight) from sites where there were previously no detectable levels. Still, total DDT (tDDT) concentrations in bivalves have declined nearly an order of magnitude during the past two decades.

Descriptive statistics of all NS&T shellfish DDT data are presented in Table 5-1 and Figure 5-8. The arithmetic grand mean of all bivalves from the 25 most contaminated sites reported in the 1986 Mussel Watch Survey is 0.0365 ppm wet weight with a standard deviation of 0.0353 (range 0.0570-0.1330 ppm) using a dry weight/wet weight conversion factor of 0.12. The eight most contaminated sites (0.0322-0.1330 ppm wet weight) exceed the 95th percentile (0.0321).

The median of the arithmetic grand means of all bivalves from the 25 most contaminated sites reported in the 1986 Mussel Watch Survey is 0.0229 ppm wet weight (range 0.0570-0.1330 ppm). The national grand median of tDDT for 145 sites was 0.0039 ppm wet weight with a range of 0.00002-0.133 ppm (dry weight/wet weight conversion factor, 0.12) (NOAA, 1987).

Contamination of coastal sites extends from Maine to Washington and includes Hawaii and Alaska. Of the 25 most contaminated sites, 9 are located in California (San Pedro Harbor, Palos Verdes, Anaheim Bay, San Francisco Bay, Imperial Beach),

5 in New York (Hudson/Raritan Estuary, Long Island Sound), 3 in New Jersey (New York Bight), and 1 site each in Texas, Virginia, and Massachusetts. Those exceeding the 95th percentile are Hudson/Raritan Estuary (HRLB), N.Y.; San Pedro Harbor, Palos Verdes, Anaheim Bay, and San Francisco Bay, Calif.; Choctawahatchee Bay, Fla.; New York Bight (NYSH), N.J.; and Buzzards Bay, Mass.

Since the estuarine mollusc survey of 1965-1972, the median tDDT level has decreased nationally nearly an order of magnitude from 0.024 to 0.003 ppm wet weight (Mearns et al., 1988). Most recent NS&T data (1986-1988) now including 177 sites indicate increases in DDT in 4 sites and decreases in 6 sites, including 3 of the most contaminated (Buzzards Bay, Chesapeake Bay, and HRLB).

Chlordane: According to NOAA, chlordane did not occur above the detection limit of 0.01 ppm wet weight in any of the more than 8,000 samples analyzed during the 1965-1972 or 1977 NPMP estuarine bivalve monitoring activities. However, chlordane compounds have frequently occurred in shellfish from other local and regional surveys, such as the California Mussel Watch. Chlordane was second only to DDT and PCBs in abundance in 1981-1982 samples of marine life from the Gulf of Alaska and the Bering Sea (NOAA, 1988).

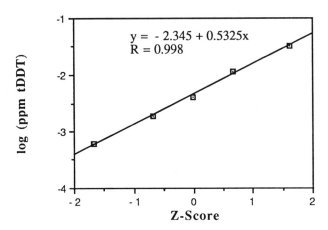

FIGURE 5-8 Lognormal distribution of wet weight concentrations of DDT and metabolites in bivalves (NS&T data set)

Heptachlor and heptachlor epoxide: Heptachlor and heptachlor epoxide did not occur above the 0.01-ppm wet weight detection limit in any of more than 8,000 shellfish samples analyzed between 1965 and 1977 during the NPMP.

Endosulfan: Endosulfan may be a problem contaminant in estuaries near agricultural drainage areas (NOAA, 1988). It should be noted that endosulfan is currently in widespread use as an agricultural pesticide and that data are clearly insufficient to judge current nationwide environmental contamination. The highest concentration of total endosulfan detected in marine shellfish is about 1.4 ppm wet weight in a 1983-1984 sample of bay mussels from Moss Landing, Monterey County, California (NOAA, 1988).

Chlorinated benzenes and phenols: Galveston Bay oysters contained penta-chlorophenol (penta) concentrations ranging from 0.003 to 0.008 ppm wet weight. In

Puget Sound, clams from Eagle Harbor, site of a wood-treatment operation, had concentrations of 0.003-0.008 ppm wet weight. Contamination has been documented from native and transplanted mussels in the northern part of Humbolt Bay. Pentachlor–anisole–a metabolite of penta–was detected in 24% of the whole fish sampled in the 1980-1981 NPMP surveys of the interior United States. Sites that produced contaminated samples include the Raritan River (New Jersey), Cape Fear River (North Carolina), Penobscott River (Maine), Mississippi River (Louisiana), and Willamette River (Oregon). It is possible that a nationwide survey of PCP and related chlorophenols would identify additional freshwater and estuarine contamination.

Kepone: By the mid-1980s, concentrations of kepone in oysters in the Virginia James River ecosystems were generally below 0.1 ppm wet weight (NOAA, 1988). This contamination is geographically limited.

Carboxylic acid herbicides: According to NOAA, the herbicide 2,4-D was documented in northern Chesapeake Bay oysters in 1979 and 1981, and there has been one confirmed occurrence in Alaska (NOAA, 1988).

Finfish

Data on contaminant levels in finfish are summarized in Table 5-2 which includes information on both the liver and the edible portions of fish (fillets), segregated according to data source.

Trace Metals

Arsenic

• Mean levels: Descriptive statistics of all data (fillet, liver) are presented in Table 5-2. The arithmetic grand mean level in the *marine edible portions* of 10 2-pound fillet samples (one sample being a within-species duplicate) from 10+ species of finfish taken from the Atlantic Ocean, the Gulf of Mexico, and the Pacific Ocean was 2.36 ppm wet weight with a standard deviation of 2.02 ppm and a range of 0.3-6.6 ppm. The arithmetic grand mean level of arsenic in *marine fish livers* from the 10 most contaminated sites reported in the 1986 NOAA NS&T is 5.20 ppm wet weight with a standard deviation of 1.94 and a range of 2.99-8.17 ppm. The grand mean level of all sites (45) is 2.34 ppm wet weight with a standard deviation of 2.06 and a range of 0.150-8.16 ppm (dry weight/wet weight conversion factor of 0.25). The geometric grand (national) mean level of arsenic in *freshwater whole fish* samples from 60 species sampled at 112 locations was, for 1978-1979, 0.16 ppm wet weight with a range of 0.04-2.08 ppm. For 1980-1981 the national mean was 0.14 ppm wet weight with a range of 0.05-1.69 ppm.

• Median levels: The arithmetic median of the grand means of arsenic in the edible portions of fish in the Zook et al. (1976) survey is 1.80 ppm wet weight. The arithmetic median of the grand means of arsenic in marine fish livers from the 10 most contaminated sites reported in the 1986 NOAA NS&T is 4.80 ppm wet weight.

TABLE 5-2   Finfish Contaminants (PPM Wet Weight)[a]

Contaminant	Mean ± SD	Percentile 5th	Percentile 50th	Percentile 90th	Geographic Distribution and Sites Exceeding 95th Percentile	Temporal Trends 1986-1988
PCB	0.420 ± 1.4[b] 0.755 ± 1.0	0.02[b]	0.10[b]	1.11[b,c]	All coastal sites. SD, EB, BH, SB	Uncertain
DDT	0.840 ± 1.78[d] 0.378 ± 0.88	0.01[d] 0.005	0.69[d] 0.06	3.04[d,e] 0.81	All coastal sites. SP, SB, SM, SD	Uncertain
Arsenic	2.355 ± 2.0d 2.335 ± 2.1 0.15[f]	0.14[e] 0.27 -	1.8[e] 1.66 -	6.11[c,e] 5.14 -	All sites examined (45). CBO, LI, NBA, DP, NBR	Uncertain
Cadmium	0.044 ± 0.01[e] 0.518 ± 0.87 0.035[c]	0.001[e] 0.02 -	0.05[e] 0.17 -	0.06[c,e] 1.31 -	All sites examined (45). SS, NRW, DP, CRO	Freshwater decline 1972-79 No change 1978-81
Lead	0.473 ± 0.11[e] 0.133 ± 0.29 0.11[f]	0.014[e] 0.002 -	0.45[e] 0.04 -	0.61[c,e] 0.27 -	All sites examined. CB, EB, CBW, BB, NBR	Like cadmium
Mercury	0.230 ± 0.16[e] 0.158 ± 0.32 0.11[f]	0.003[e] 0.003 -	0.17[e] 0.17 -	0.50[c,e] 0.22 -	All sites examined. DP, SS, SD, OH	Like cadmium
Selenium	3.22 ± 0.2 0.46[e]	0.46 -	2.52 -	5.70 -	All sites examined. SS, CC, ABF, DP, MR	Like cadmium

NOTE: ABF Appalachacola, Fla.; BB Buzzards Bay, Mass.; BH Boston Harbor, Mass.; CBO Coos Bay, Ore.; CBW Commencement Bay, Wash.; CC Corpus Christi, Tex.; CB Casco Bay, Maine; CRO Columbia River, Ore.; DP Dana Pt., Calif.; EB Elliot Bay, Wash.; LI Lutak Inlet, Alaska; MR Mississippi River, La.; NBR Narragansett Bay, R.I.; NRV Nisqually Reach, Wash.; NBA Nabhu Bay, Alaska; OH Oakland Harbor, Calif.; SB Seal Beach, Calif.; SD San Diego, Calif.; SMB Santa Monica Bay, Calif.; SP San Pedro Beach, Calif.; SS Southampton Shoal, Calif.; WLI West Long Island Sound, N.Y.

[a] NS&T (1987), livers.
[b] Fillets (Gadbois and Maney, 1983).
[c] 95th percentile.
[d] Fillets (Gosstett et al., 1983; Stout, 1980).
[e] Fillets (Zook et al., 1976).
[f] Freshwater; geometric mean; whole body (Lowe et al., 1985).
SOURCE: NOAA (1989).

140

The 1986 NS&T grand median for fish livers from all sites (45) is 1.678 ppm wet weight (NOAA, 1987).

● Geographic distribution: The five most contaminated sites (6.16-8.17 ppm wet weight) exceed the 90th percentile (5.14) and are Coos Bay, Ore.; Lutak Inlet and Nahbu Bay, Alaska; Dana Pt., Calif.; and Narragansett Bay, R.I. Freshwater sites reporting the highest individual contamination were in Lake Michigan at Saugatuck, Mich. and Sheboygan, Wisc.

● Temporal trends: Information about trends in marine fish should be available upon publication of the new NS&T data. Arsenic concentrations for freshwater fish were about midway between those reported for earlier collection periods. No increase was noted in the 1978-1981 sampling period.

Cadmium

● Mean levels: Descriptive statistics of all data (fillet, liver) are presented in Table 5-2. The arithmetic grand mean level in the *marine edible portions* of 10 2-pound fillet samples (one sample being a within-species duplicate) from 10+ species of finfish taken from the Atlantic Ocean, the Gulf of Mexico, and the Pacific Ocean was 0.0439 ppm wet weight with a standard deviation of 0.0136 ppm and a range of 0.02-0.0690 ppm. The grand mean level of cadmium in *marine fish livers* from the 10 most contaminated sites reported in the 1986 NS&T is 1.42 ppm wet weight with a standard deviation of 1.08 and a range of 0.530-3.94 ppm. The grand mean level of all sites (45) is 0.519 ppm wet weight with a standard deviation of 0.870 and a range of 0.0150-4.89 ppm (dry weight/wet weight conversion factor of 0.25). The geometric grand (national) mean level of cadmium in *freshwater whole fish* samples from 60 species sampled at 112 locations for 1978-1979 was 0.04 ppm wet weight with a range of 0.01-0.41 ppm, and for 1980-1981 was 0.03 ppm wet weight with a range of 0.01-0.35 ppm.

● Median levels: The arithmetic median of the grand means of cadmium in the edible portions of fish in the Zook et al. (1976) survey is 0.0460 ppm wet weight. The arithmetic median of the grand means of cadmium in marine fish livers from the 10 most contaminated sites reported in the 1986 NOAA NS&T is 1.310 ppm wet weight. The 1986 NS&T grand median for fish livers from all sites (45) is 0.1750 ppm wet weight.

● Geographic distribution: The five most contaminated sites (1.31-4.89 ppm wet weight) exceed the 90th percentile (1.3063) and are Southampton Shoal, Calif.; Nisqually Reach, Wash.; Dana Pt., Calif.; Columbia River, Ore.; and Dana Pt., Calif. Freshwater sites reporting the highest individual contamination were in the Columbia River Grand Coulee, Wash.; the Colorado River at Lake Powell, Ariz.; Verdigris River, Oologah, Okla.; and Kansas River at Bonner Springs, Kans.

● Temporal trends: Information about trends in marine fish should be available upon publication of the new NS&T data. Cadmium concentrations for freshwater fish declined significantly from 1972 to 1979; however, no decline was noted between 1978 and 1981.

Lead

• Mean levels: Descriptive statistics of all data (fillet, liver) are presented in Table 5-2. The arithmetic grand mean level in the *marine edible portions* of 10 2-pound fillet samples (one sample being a within-species duplicate) from 10+ species of finfish taken from the Atlantic Ocean, the Gulf of Mexico, and the Pacific Ocean was 0.474 ppm wet weight with a standard deviation of 0.111 ppm and a range of 0.320-0.630 ppm. The grand mean level of lead in *marine fish livers* from the 10 most contaminated sites reported in the 1986 NOAA NS&T is 0.414 ppm wet weight with a standard deviation of 0.523 and a range of 0.140-1.85 ppm. The grand mean level of all sites (43) is 0.133 ppm wet weight with a standard deviation of 0.294 and a range of 0.0075-1.85 ppm (dry weight/wet weight conversion factor of 0.25). The geometric grand (national) mean level of lead in *freshwater whole fish* samples from 60 species sampled at 112 locations for 1978-1979 was 0.19 ppm wet weight with a range of 0.10-6.73 ppm, and for 1980-1981 was 0.17 ppm wet weight with a range of 0.10-1.94 ppm.

• Median levels: The median of the grand means of lead in the edible portions of fish in the Zook et al. (1976) survey is 0.510 ppm wet weight. The arithmetic median of the grand means of lead in marine fish livers from the 10 most contaminated sites reported in the 1986 NS&T is 0.230 ppm wet weight. The 1986 NS&T grand median for fish livers from all sites (43) is 0.0450 ppm wet weight.

• Geographic distribution: The five most contaminated sites (0.288-1.85 ppm wet weight) exceed the 90th percentile (0.271) and are Casco Bay, Maine; Elliot Bay and Commencement Bay, Wash.; West Long Island Sound, N.Y.; Buzzards Bay, Mass.; and Narragansett Bay, R.I. Freshwater sites reporting the highest individual contamination were Manoa Stream, Honolulu, Hawaii; the Connecticut River at Windsor Locks, Conn.; and the Hudson River at Poughkeepsie, N.Y.

• Temporal trends: Information about trends in marine fish should be available upon publication of the new NS&T data. Lead concentrations for freshwater fish declined significantly from 1972 to 1979; however, no decline was noted between 1978 and 1981.

Mercury

• Mean levels: Descriptive statistics of all data (fillet, liver) are presented in Table 5-2. The arithmetic grand mean level in the *marine edible portion* of 10 2-pound fillet samples (one sample being a within-species duplicate) from 10+ species of finfish taken from the Atlantic Ocean, the Gulf of Mexico, and the Pacific Ocean was 0.230 ppm wet weight with a standard deviation of 0.160 ppm and a range of 0.070-0.600 ppm. The grand mean level of mercury in *marine fish livers* from the 10 most contaminated sites reported in the 1986 NS&T is 0.372 ppm wet weight with a standard deviation of 0.432 and a range of 0.120-1.46 ppm. The grand mean level of all sites (43) is 0.158 ppm wet weight with a standard deviation of 0.319 and a range of 0.0100-1.55 ppm (dry weight/wet weight conversion factor of 0.25). The geometric grand (national) mean level of mercury in *freshwater whole fish* samples from 60 species sampled at 112 locations for 1978-1979 was 0.11 ppm wet weight with a range of 0.01 to 1.10 ppm, and for 1980-1981 was 0.11 ppm wet weight with a range of 0.01-0.77 ppm.

• Median levels: The arithmetic median of the grand means of mercury in the edible portions of fish in the Zook et al. (1976) survey is 0.180 ppm wet weight. The arithmetic median of the grand means of mercury in marine fish livers from the 10 most contaminated sites reported in the 1986 NS&T is 0.1700 ppm wet weight. The 1986 NS&T grand median for fish livers from all sites (43) is 0.070 ppm wet weight.

• Geographic distribution: The five most contaminated sites (0.238-1.55 ppm wet weight) exceed the 90th percentile (0.215) and are Dana Pt. (bsb), Southampton Shoal, Dana Pt. (wc), San Diego Harbor, and Oakland Harbor, Calif. Freshwater sites reporting the highest individual contamination were the Columbia River, Cascades Locks, Wash.; the Red River of the North at Noyes, Minn.; the Colorado River at Imperial Reservoir, Calif.; the Truckee River at Fernley, Nev.; and the Merrimack River at Lowell, Mass.

• Temporal trends: Information about trends in marine fish should be available upon publication of the new NS&T data. Mercury concentrations for freshwater fish declined significantly from 1972 to 1977; however, no decline was noted between 1978 and 1981.

Selenium

• Mean levels: Descriptive statistics of all data (fillet, liver) are presented in Table 5-2. National data on the mean levels of selenium in the *edible portions of marine fish* were not available. The grand mean level of selenium in *marine fish livers* from the 10 most contaminated sites reported in the 1986 NS&T is 6.15 ppm wet weight with a standard deviation of 1.589 and a range of 4.79-9.05 ppm. The grand mean level of all sites (45) is 3.22 ppm wet weight with a standard deviation of 2.16 and a range of 0.292-9.05 ppm (dry weight/wet weight conversion factor of 0.25). The geometric grand (national) mean level of selenium in *freshwater whole fish* samples from 60 species sampled at 112 locations for 1978-1979 was 0.46 ppm wet weight with a range of 0.09-3.65 ppm, and for 1980-1981 was 0.47 ppm wet weight with a range of 0.09-2.47 ppm.

• Geographic distribution: The five most contaminated sites (5.96-9.05 ppm wet weight) exceed the 90th percentile (5.70) and are Southampton Shoal, Calif.; Corpus Christi Bay, Tex.; Apalachicola Bay, Fla.; Dana Pt., Calif.; and Mississippi River Delta, La. Freshwater sites reporting the highest individual contamination were the Colorado River at Imperial Reservoir, Calif.; Lake Havasu, Arizona-California; Lake Powell, Ariz.; and Yuma, Arizona-California.

• Median levels: The arithmetic median of the grand means of selenium in the edible portions of marine fish was not available. The arithmetic median of the grand means of selenium in marine fish livers from the 10 most contaminated sites reported in the 1986 NS&T is 5.28 ppm wet weight. The 1986 NS&T grand median for fish livers from all sites (45) is 2.57 ppm wet weight.

• Temporal trends: Information about trends in marine fish should be available upon publication of the new NS&T data. Selenium concentrations for freshwater fish declined significantly from 1972 to 1979; however, no decline was noted between 1980 and 1981.

Organics

Polychlorinated biphenyls

Polychlorinated biphenyl contamination varies greatly from region to region and site to site within regions. In a 1979-1980 survey of fillets of a mix of pelagic and nearshore predatory fish from sites in 15 coastal and estuarine areas, 63 of 70 samples contained PCBs with concentrations as high as 22.0 ppm wet weight in Hudson River white perch (NOAA, 1988). Sites producing the highest mean concentrations were the New York Bight Apex (1.1 ppm wet weight) and East Bay, near Panama City, Florida (0.42 ppm wet weight). Sites producing fish with the lowest PCB concentrations were at Catalina Island, offshore of Los Angeles (less than 0.04 ppm wet weight), and Chandeleur Sound, east of New Orleans (0.05 ppm wet weight in 13 species). The lognormal distribution of contaminant concentrations in edible portions of fish is illustrated in Figure 5-9. It is evident from the relatively large slope (the $\log_{10}$ of the geometric standard deviation of the distribution) that the concentrations in fish may vary greatly from site to site. Finally, data from nationwide, large-scale sampling programs confirm the fact that PCBs occur in fish and shellfish from all estuaries sampled, including remote nonindustrialized sites in Alaska, the Virgin Islands, and Hawaii. Data also indicate that the highest concentrations have occurred in fish from urban embayments on the Pacific and East coasts and near Pensacola, Florida, with lower concentrations in fish from the southeastern and Gulf of Mexico estuaries. On the basis of available comparable data, there has been no dramatic national change, or at most a minor decline, in PCB contamination of fish and shellfish over the past 10-15 years (NOAA, 1988).

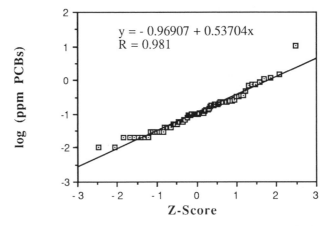

FIGURE 5-9 Lognormal distribution of wet weight concentrations of PCBs in edible portions of inshore marine fish from different locations

Descriptive statistics of all fish PCB data (fillet, liver) are presented in Table 5-2. The arithmetic grand mean PCB level in the edible portions of 188 samples (10 fillets per sample) from 32 species of finfish taken from 20 coastal sites was 0.412 ppm wet weight with a standard deviation of 0.655 ppm and a range of 0.03-2.9 ppm.

The arithmetic grand mean level of PCBs in marine fish livers from the 10 most contaminated sites reported in the 1986 NS&T is 1.90 ppm wet weight with a standard deviation of 0.90 and a range of 0.933-3.97 ppm wet weight. The grand mean level of all sites (46) is 0.755 ppm wet weight with a standard deviation of 1.03 and a range of 0.0063-4.93 ppm (dry weight/wet weight conversion factor of 0.25). The five most contaminated sites (1.99-4.93 ppm wet weight) are San Diego Harbor (bst), Calif.; Elliot Bay, Wash.; Boston Harbor, Mass.; San Diego Harbor (dt) and Seal Beach, Calif.

The arithmetic median of the grand means of the edible portions of fish in the Gadbois and Maney (1983) survey is 0.1100 ppm wet weight. The arithmetic median of the grand means of PCB in marine fish livers from the 10 most contaminated sites reported in the 1986 NS&T is 1.765 ppm wet weight. The 1986 NS&T grand median for fish livers from all sites (43) is 0.2874 ppm wet weight.

Dioxins

As part of its national dioxin strategy, EPA conducted a survey of the extent of TCDD contamination in the environment (EPA, 1987). One significant finding from this study was contamination of freshwater fish in areas of pulp and paper mills that utilize chlorine and chlorine compounds as part of that bleaching process. Dioxin contamination was discovered at approximately 85 sites throughout the country including Alaska (EPA, 1988a,b). Levels of TCDD found in whole fish were as high as 85 parts per trillion, whereas levels found in fillets ranged up to 41 parts per trillion. Two fish consumption advisories have been issued based on findings from the study. A high proportion (23 of 29) of Great Lakes fish sampling sites were found to have detectable levels of TCDD. Outside the Great Lakes, fish contamination was primarily found in major river systems, such as the Ohio and Mississippi Rivers, or in waterways with significant industry activity. Levels of TCDD in fish fillet samples may be a cause for concern at specific locations for certain consumption patterns; local exposure conditions should be evaluated to determine a level of concern for those areas. Fish and shellfish from estuarine and coastal waters were rarely contaminated with TCDD; three of the four contaminated sites were in areas heavily influenced by industrial discharge. Paper mills using chlorine bleaching are being investigated by EPA, the states, and the paper industry to determine possible sources of TCDD contamination within the mills. Because recent studies indicate that TCDD has a half-life of less than 1 year in fish, the implication is that dioxin contamination of fish is a current and continuing phenomenon.

Chlorinated hydrocarbon pesticides

DDT and metabolites: Although notable declines have occurred in DDT and metabolite concentrations in fish muscle, potentially significant concentrations of these materials continue to be found in fish from historic hot spots such as Whites Point, California. For example, the mean concentration of DDT in white croaker (a southern

California sport fish) caught from various areas in nearby Santa Monica Bay ranged from 0.22 to 0.69 ppm wet weight, but the mean was 0.6 ppm wet weight for white croaker caught from Whites Point, a site where DDT-laced waste sludge from a pesticide manufacturing plant was dumped (Gossett et al., 1982).

Descriptive statistics of all finfish DDT data (fillet, liver) are presented in Table 5-2 and Figure 5-10. The arithmetic grand mean level in the edible portions of 765 fillet samples from six species of finfish taken from the northwest Atlantic Ocean, the Gulf of Mexico, and Los Angeles Harbor was 0.841 ppm wet weight with a standard deviation of 1.78 ppm and a range of 0.008-7.6 ppm. These data come from a compilation of two studies: Stout (1980) and Gossett et al. (1983).

The grand mean level of DDT and all its metabolites in marine fish livers from the 10 most contaminated sites reported in the 1986 NS&T is 1.24 ppm wet weight with a standard deviation of 1.49 and a range of 0.2070-4.665 ppm. The grand mean level of all sites (48) is 0.3781 ppm wet weight with a standard deviation of 0.884 and a range of 0.0025-4.66 ppm (dry weight/wet weight conversion factor of 0.25). The five most contaminated sites (0.967-4.66 ppm wet weight), which exceed the 90th percentile (0.812 ppm), are San Pedro Beach, Seal Beach (wc), Seal Beach (ht), Santa Monica Beach, and San Diego Harbor, California.

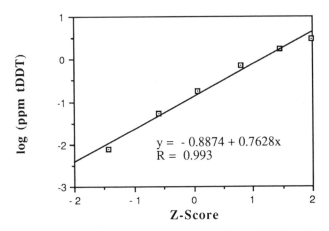

FIGURE 5-10 Lognormal distribution of wet weight concentrations of DDT and metabolites in edible portions of inshore marine fish from different locations

The arithmetic median of the grand means of tDDT in the edible portions of fish in the survey is 0.177 ppm wet weight. The arithmetic median of the grand means of tDDT in marine fish livers from the 10 most contaminated sites reported in the 1986 NS&T is 0.441 ppm wet weight. The 1986 NS&T grand median for fish livers from all sites (48) is 0.0566 ppm wet weight.

Dieldrin: According to NOAA, dieldrin has historically been the most frequently detected cyclodiene pesticide in coastal fish and shellfish (NOAA, 1988). More than 15,000 samples have been analyzed for dieldrin. Concentrations in muscle tissue ranged from below detection to a maximum of 1.56 ppm wet weight in a 1970 sample of milkfish from Ali Wai Canal, Honolulu, Hawaii. Besides milkfish, tarpon from Honolulu had levels ranging from 0.36 to 1.56 ppm wet weight or from one to five times the FDA action limit. These results, however, are approximately 20 years old. Dieldrin was a common contaminant in the 1984 NS&T Benthic Surveillance fish liver survey, occurring in fish livers in some sites at concentrations above 0.001 ppm wet weight. The range was less than 0.001 to a high of 0.104 ppm wet weight in liver of winter flounder from a site in Salem Harbor, Massachusetts (NOAA, 1989). The next highest concentrations occurred in livers of starry flounder and white croaker from two collection sites in San Francisco Bay (0.09 ppm wet weight). Urbanization does not appear to be the overriding determinant of dieldrin contamination, because some of the fish with the lowest dieldrin concentrations were in urbanized embayments such as San Diego Harbor (less than 0.0003 ppm wet weight) and Elliott Bay, Puget Sound (less than 0.01 ppm wet weight). Intermediate concentrations occurred in fish from St. Johns River, Florida; the Mississippi River Delta; San Pablo Bay, California; and Boston Harbor, Massachusetts. In summary, dieldrin is a common contaminant nationwide – particularly of inland and estuarine fish. Definite declines in concentrations can be confirmed for inland sites and some marine sites. Analyses of FDA data appear to support the hypotheses that inland fish are considerably more contaminated with dieldrin than open water marine fish and even estuarine fish. Although virtually all dieldrin uses in agriculture were restricted more than 15 years ago, its residues remain in soils and in the food web. Dieldrin was the second most frequently documented pesticide in the 1980-1981 NPMP whole composites of inland freshwater fish national surveys, occurring at 75% of the sites nationwide. Mean concentrations in whole freshwater fish on a nationwide basis declined only slightly from 0.05 ppm wet weight in 1976-1977 to 0.04 ppm wet weight in 1980-1981, but maximum concentrations over this time decreased from 5.0 to 0.72 ppm wet weight, a trend due primarily to declines in Hawaiian stream fish. In some cases, particularly with much of the freshwater harvest including farm raised fish from areas of past agricultural use, regular consumption of dieldrin-contaminated fish could be reason for concern.

Chlordane and heptachlor compounds: According to NOAA, chlordane compounds have been contaminants of fish from several estuarines for many years and are among several pesticides that contaminated coastal fish of Hawaii as well as freshwater fish from throughout the U.S. mainland. Although concentrations do not appear to be increasing, neither are they decreasing dramatically. In some states such as Kansas and New York, chlordane contamination of freshwater finfish is pervasive, based on the committee's review of data bases for these states. The contamination problem stems in part from the widespread use of chlordane as a killer of termites through 1986 and its subsequent environmental distribution and persistence.

Two chlordane compounds, alpha-chlordane and *trans*-nonachlor, were measured in livers of fish from 48 NS&T site collections made by NOAA in 1984. With the use of detection limits lower than those used in earlier national surveys of the 1970s, at least one of these compounds was detected in 95% of the site collections. To obtain a better grasp of the extent of chlordane contamination of fish and possibly bivalves, a comprehensive sampling program should be undertaken in which detection limits are 5-10 times lower than those used for regulatory purposes, along with a compilation of all available, current local and state data. Chlordane is a probable human carcinogen, but there are significant gaps in our knowledge of whether it is a teratogen, reproductive toxin, or mutagen (EPA, 1986).

Heptachlor and heptachlor epoxide: According to NOAA, heptachlor and its metabolite heptachlor epoxide have been looked for in more than 12,000 samples, mainly from the NPMP (NOAA, 1988). In contrast with shellfish, total heptachlor occurred in 39% of inland fish samples at concentrations above 0.01 ppm wet weight in the 1980-1981 NPMP surveys. Presently, heptachlor does not appear to be a prominent contaminant of marine fish anywhere.

Endosulfan: According to NOAA, the highest confirmed concentration of endosulfan in marine fish was 0.05 ppm wet weight in liver of a 1983 sample of fringehead sculpin from Elkhorn Slough near the same Moss Landing site (NOAA, 1988). Besides the Elkhorn Slough samples, endosulfan was detected in fish from an Oregon estuary and in a Pacific Coast estuary in Mexico. Fish and invertebrates from sloughs and bays of coastal Monterey County, California, were notably contaminated with endosulfan according to surveys conducted in 1980-1981, and contamination of mussels from Elkhorn Slough continued through 1984. NOAA reported that concentrations in Elkhorn Slough mussels ranged up to 0.7 ppm wet weight. Freshwater fish from the nearby Salinas River contained concentrations as high as 1.2 ppm wet weight. In 1983, seven species of marine and estuarine fish contained total endosulfan concentrations ranging from 0.021 to 0.052 ppm wet weight. Several other California sites also produced mussels containing endosulfan: Trinidad Head, Bodega Head, four San Francisco Bay sites, Bolinas Lagoon, Pacific Grove, Newport Bay, Port Hueneme, and Santa Cruz. The last two sites, plus the Elkhorn Slough site, also experienced increasing endosulfan concentrations between 1979 and 1981, and continued contamination occurred into 1986. Because California sites with significant endosulfan contamination are in heavily agricultural regions, it is important to determine the extent of recreational harvesting in such areas and the present contamination levels of endosulfan.

Lindane and benzene hexachloride: In early surveys, lindane and gamma-BHC have been looked for in nearly 12,000 marine or estuarine fish and invertebrate samples, but were found above the detection limit of 0.01 ppm wet weight in only a few samples. However, with improved detection limits in the 1984 NS&T Benthic Surveillance project, lindane occurred in 47% of the fish liver site collections at concentrations above 0.001 ppm wet weight. The nationwide average was about 0.002 ppm wet weight and the highest mean concentration was 0.014 ppm wet weight in the livers of Atlantic croaker from a site in the Chesapeake Bay (NOAA, 1988). Lindane was detected in 44% of 64 California Mussel Watch samples in 1980-1981 through 1985-1986 surveys; most of these were from San Francisco Bay and the Los Angeles area, at concentrations slightly exceeding 0.001 ppm wet weight. However, in inland waters, lindane was documented in 16% of the 1980-1981 NPMP fish samples at concentrations exceeding 0.01 ppm wet weight. Highest concentrations were in freshwater fish from a stream in Honolulu, from Lake Mead (Colorado River), and from several Great Lakes sites. The low levels observed in fish livers during the 1984 NS&T Benthic Surveillance suggest that there is no significant nationwide lindane contamination today (NOAA, 1988).

Chlorinated benzenes and phenols: According to NOAA, the highest reported concentration of hexachlorobenzene (HCB) (the fully aromatic form of benzene with 6 chlorines) used as a fungicide was about 0.7 ppm wet weight in the liver of English sole collected in 1979 from the Hylebos Waterway in Commencement Bay, Washington (NOAA, 1988). Measurable, but lower, concentrations were also reported in fish and shellfish from the New York Bight, Galveston Bay, the Upper Chesapeake Bay, and from Palos Verdes Peninsula and the Santa Monica Bay outfalls in California. However, HCB is probably a more significant inland contaminant. It was detected at concentrations above 0.01 ppm wet weight in 24% of the samples of whole fish from the 1980-1981 inland NPMP freshwater fish survey. The highest concentrations of 0.12-0.13 ppm wet weight occurred in whole fish from the Tombigbee River, Alabama and from the Mississippi River at a site in Louisiana. There is evidence that, nationwide, there has been a decline in HCB contamination since the 1976-1977 surveys.

Pentachlorophenol is a wood preservative, slimicide, metabolite of the fungicide HCB, and carrier of carcinogenic dioxins (NOAA, 1988). It has not been widely surveyed in marine and estuarine fish on a national scale. Concentrations have been found in blue crabs and brown shrimp from San Luis Pass, Texas.

Other chlorobenzenes that may be important include di- and trichlorinated benzenes as well as other monocyclic chlorinated aromatic hydrocarbons. In southern California, 1,2,4-trichlorobenzene was measured in flatfish livers near a sewage discharge site (NOAA, 1988). Monocyclic chlorinated aromatic hydrocarbons have been detected in striped bass from the San Francisco Bay-Delta region. Although none have been surveyed nationally, all are considered EPA priority pollutants. Thus, their inclusion in future national surveys is warranted.

Mirex: According to NOAA, mirex is an ant poison once thought to be a serious contaminant of Southeast U.S. estuarine organisms. Mirex was measured in inland fish NPMP surveys for the first time during the 1980-1981 surveys and occurred at 18% of the stations, mainly in the Great Lakes and the Southeast (NOAA, 1988). Because of its persistence and long term threats, fish advisories have been issued for mirex existence in Lake Ontario. Monitoring for mirex in fish from the Great Lakes, Georgia, and South Carolina waters is warranted.

Kepone: According to NOAA, since kepone was first discovered in the James River in 1973 as a result of illegal discharges from a pesticide manufacturing plant, it has since been found in thousands of samples of fish, crabs, and oysters (NOAA, 1988). By the mid-1980s, concentrations in fish and crabs were on the order of 0.2-0.8 ppm wet weight. Concentrations in some fish exceeded 7 ppm wet weight in the mid-1970s and levels above 1 ppm wet weight were common. Kepone has not been included as a target chemical in any post-1973 national or regional survey. State monitoring programs in Maryland and North Carolina included kepone, and its residues were detected at low concentration – 0.01 ppm wet weight – in the flesh of some sport fish taken near inlets in North Carolina in 1976. It is not certain whether kepone contamination is more pervasive than in the lower James River area of Virginia. Kepone levels should continue to be monitored.

Toxaphene: According to NOAA, toxaphene is possibly an important regional contaminant. Toxaphene is a mix of chlorinated camphenes and has been measured in more than 12,000 samples but was consistently present above detection limits in only a few regions including southern Georgia and southern Laguna Madre, Texas (NOAA, 1988). Secondary occurrences have been reported for fish from the San Francisco Bay-Delta area; from East Bay, Los Angeles; and from Oso Bay, Texas. The highest concentration in muscle was 35.6 ppm wet weight in both a mullet and a goatfish from the Back River near Brunswick, Georgia.

Inland sampling indicates that the chemical was recorded above detection limits of 0.01 ppm wet weight in nearly 88% of the stations in one survey. Highest concentrations were in whole fish from the Mississippi River, the Great Lakes, and the Cape Fear River in North Carolina. It is possible that toxaphene remained a significant contaminant at some estuarine sites into the 1980s and may even have increased locally or nationally. Toxaphene contamination appears to be limited to certain regions. Historically sampled sites in at least three states – Georgia, California, and Texas – should be resampled.

Carboxylic herbicides: No 2,4-D and 2,4,5-T were detected among fish in the FDA monitoring program. There was sporadic detection of DCPA. Among the most notable cases of contamination with DCPA were fish from Arroyo Colorado and adjacent areas in southern Texas.

Atrazine: The fact that surveys do not often detect atrazine may be due either to a real lack of significant bioaccumulation or to the laboratory detection limits in use. Traces of atrazine at levels ranging from 0.2-0.3 mg/kg have been found in bluegill (*Lepomis machrochirus*) in Kansas and, during periods of high use, may be found in other fish in farm ponds and nearby lakes or creeks (Kansas DHE, 1988).

Conclusions

Evidence exists that fish and shellfish from domestic freshwater and marine environments are contaminated with a number of inorganic and organic chemicals that are potentially toxic to humans. Although the contamination is widespread, it varies greatly with geographic location and species. Where adequate data are available, it appears that the distribution of contaminant levels is reasonably well described as lognormal in most cases.

POTENTIAL OPPORTUNITIES FOR REDUCING EXPOSURES

Without prejudging the need for additional controls on specific contaminant residues, it is reasonable to use the observations of contaminant variability derived in the previous sections to draw some preliminary inferences about the potential of different kinds of control measures to reduce seafood contaminant exposures in the United States. Three basic types of control measures can be considered:

1. The classical approach, now the primary control measure at the federal level, of setting maximum contaminant levels that are acceptable in seafood, analyzing a small fraction of the commercial seafood in interstate commerce, and, where excessive levels are found, seizing products with violative residues

2. Restrictions on harvesting/marketing based on relationships between contaminant levels and (1) species, (2) geographic area, and (3) size

3. Labeling and consumer information programs of various types, ranging from general advisories now issued by state health departments primarily to sport fishers, to possible programs to disclose the origin (or even average contaminant levels) for seafood sold in retail outlets.

The first type of option has obvious difficulties. Chemical analyses are both expensive and slow, relative to the usual pace of marketing fresh seafood products.

Aside from limited special programs, such as sampling for mercury compounds in imported swordfish, only a tiny fraction of product can be screened. Therefore, with the important exception of the use of analyses for detection of situations in which more intensive control efforts of other types may be indicated, direct chemical residue screening of seafood has little potential to achieve quantitative reductions in the delivery of contaminant residues to consumers.

The Food Drug and Cosmetic Act concept of "adulteration," evaluated on the basis of single items or, in practice, single-shipment lots of product, makes sense in protecting against an acute toxic hazard such as botulism or paralytic shellfish poisoning. In those cases an individual meal has a high probability of directly causing illness, and carefully excluding the tiny minority of dangerously contaminated items is an effective strategy for avoiding harm.

Many of the effects discussed in Chapter 6, however, are the products of long-term, even lifetime, levels of exposure. There simply is no neat dividing line between safety and hazard, defined on the basis of individual meals. The important risks may take the form of either a modestly increased long-term probability of cancer (in relation to the background of cancer from unrelated causes), a subtle shift in the distribution of birth weights and attained mental performance in offspring, or an increased long-term risk of a chronic cumulative condition such as Parkinson's disease. In structuring social control measures to reduce these types of risks it is important to have in mind the limitation of long-term average exposures--not simply to reduce the number of individual items that reach the market above some (arbitrarily defined) cutoff level.

The second set of options mentioned above--restrictions of various kinds on harvesting and marketing--has considerable potential to limit long-term average exposures and the exposures of selected groups for various kinds of toxic effects (e.g., women of childbearing age). This type of control measure has been utilized to some degree in closing selected areas to shellfish harvesting, particularly by state authorities, but it has not been comprehensively analyzed for the potential to reduce selected seafood-related chemical residue exposure on a national basis. Some of the existing, less-than-perfect data bases are used below to illustrate the process of analyzing the variability of residue levels by geography and size. This analysis seeks to assess the potential reduction in population doses achievable by 1-20% restrictions on harvesting/marketing. The basic concept is that the more variability there is in contaminant levels associated with geography or size, the greater is the potential for economically reducing population dosage by using those variables to control harvesting and marketing.

The advisability of expanded consumer information programs to inform people of the residual risks of different kinds of seafood products, especially people with unusual exposures (e.g., freshwater sport fishers and their families) and people of reproductive age, is discussed in Chapter 6.

Analysis of Potential Benefits from Geographic
Restrictions on Harvesting/Marketing

In one of the least utilized, best structured, and most extensive data sets on inorganic contaminants compiled during the 1970s (Hall et al., 1978), the authors write

The completion of this data report does not bring the Resource Survey to an end. No attempt has been made here, for example, to compare element levels in a particular species or to investigate possible relationships between element levels and fish location, size, or sex. The analytical values have been summarized by site only for each species and tissue, and very little of the history of the fish has been presented. . . . The complete collection of data is available for use in interpretive studies. It is also anticipated that the data will be made available to the public, in the future, through the National Oceanographic Data Center, Environmental Data Service, National Oceanic and Atmospheric Administration, Rockville, Md.

Unfortunately these hoped-for analyses of contaminant levels in relation to size, geography, and other fish characteristics readily ascertainable at harvest were never completed and published. The following illustrates what might have been done with such data.

Figures 5-1 through 5-10 are lognormal plots of the distribution of contaminant levels for geographic locations included within a few national data bases for specific contaminants in specific aquatic organisms. In general, the lognormal model appears to be reasonably accurate in describing these data, as judged by the correspondence of the points in those figures to the straight lines. In each plot there is a regression equation describing the straight line shown. The slope of those straight lines corresponds to the standard deviation of the $\log_{10}$ of the contaminant levels found at the different sites; the greater the slope (the number preceding the x), the more variability there is among geographic areas.

If, for purposes of this illustration, some simplifying assumptions are made (that the distributions are truly lognormal and that, in the absence of restrictions, all sites would make roughly equal contributions of specified seafood items to the U.S. food supply), then Table 5-3 shows how large a reduction could be made in the population aggregate dosage of specific contaminants (in specific sets of organisms) by restricting harvesting/marketing at specified percentages of the geographic sites covered in the underlying data.

The results in the top half of the table suggest that for most of the inorganics and contaminants in shellfish, the sole exception being lead, the site-to-site variability indicated in the NS&T data is small enough that even taking a relatively extreme measure (restricting harvesting from the worst 20% of locations) would be expected to reduce population aggregate dosage by less than 50%. The bottom half of the table suggests quite a different picture for organic contaminants. In each case, the indicated geographic variability is larger than the variability suggested for all five inorganics. For the most variable contaminants/sets of species, it would be theoretically possible to reduce the population dosage delivered by more than 50% through restricting harvesting/marketing from only 5% of the most intensely contaminated sites. For other cases, restrictions on slightly more than 10% of the sites would be required to achieve this goal.

TABLE 5-3 Illustrative Analysis of the Potential for Reducing the Aggregate Dosage of Specific Contaminants from Subsets of Seafood by Restricting Harvesting from the Sites with the Highest Contaminant Levels[a]

Fraction of Sites Restricted (%)	Inorganic Contaminants[b]				
	Arsenic	Cadmium	Lead	Mercury	Selenium
1	3.3	4.8	11.5	5.4	2.6
2	5.9	8.3	17.8	9.2	4.8
5	12.2	16.1	29.9	17.5	10.1
10	21.2	26.6	43.6	28.5	18.2
20	36.0	42.7	61.1	44.9	32.0
Site-to-site geometric standard deviation	1.61	1.92	3.05	2.03	1.44
Ratio arithmetic/ geometric mean	1.11	1.23	1.86	1.28	1.06

Fraction of Sites Restricted (%)	PCBs		PAHs	DDT & Metabolites	
	Bivalves	Fish, Edible Portions	Bivalves	Bivalves	Fish, Edible Portions
1	3.3	4.8	11.5	5.4	2.6
1	13.7	14.0	28.4	13.7	28.7
2	20.8	21.1	38.6	20.8	38.9
5	33.7	34.2	54.2	33.8	54.5
10	47.8	48.4	68.1	48.0	68.4
20	65.1	65.6	81.9	65.2	82.1
Site-to-site geometric standard deviation	3.40	3.44	5.75	3.41	5.79
Ratio arithmetic/ geometric mean	2.11	2.14	4.61	2.12	4.67

[a] Percentage of total population dosage contributed by highest $N\%$ if sites of equal contributions to diet are assumed from each site.
[b] Based on concentrations in bivalves, NS&T data (NOAA, 1989).

Analysis of Potential for Reducing Population Exposure to Mercury from Swordfish and PCBs from Bluefish via Size Restrictions

Size is another potentially important control parameter associated with lipophilic contaminant concentrations that may prove useful in some cases. Data obtained by FDA and Canadian authorities in the early 1970s were reviewed on swordfish mercury concentrations in relation to fish size. An association between fish size and mercury concentration can be seen in Figure 5-11, although there is quite a bit of scatter in the results for individual fish. Unfortunately, when the fish are arranged in size classes to determine the cumulative population dose reduction that could be achieved by restricting harvesting/marketing of the biggest fish, the prospects for appreciably reducing population mercury dosage by modest size restrictions appear dim. As indicated in Table 5-4, the largest fish appear to have somewhat smaller average mercury concentrations than more moderate-sized ones, and in any event, reductions in average mercury concentrations are quite modest until the fish are very small, in which case they represent a trivial proportion of the aggregate weight of the catch.

This example is provided here for illustration of the method only. If analyses of these types were extended to other species and other contaminants, it is likely that size restrictions would be found to be feasible control measures in some cases. Based on data discussed in Chapter 6 (NOAA, 1987), one promising opportunity for size-based restrictions appears to be PCB concentrations in eastern bluefish. When data for the two sexes are averaged, small bluefish (less than 11.8 inches) average about 0.21 ppm PCB; medium (11.8-19.7 inches) average 0.42 ppm; and large average somewhat over 1.4 ppm–about seven times larger than the average concentrations in the small category. Ideally, such size-based restrictions could be structured with somewhat different cut points for different geographic areas, depending on local concentration/size data.

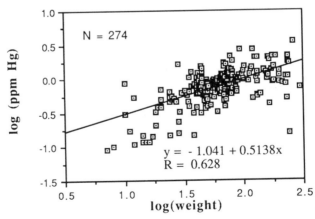

FIGURE 5-11 Mercury concentrations versus size of swordfish–log-log plot

TABLE 5-4 Potential Population Mercury Dose Reductions Achievable by Size Restrictions on Atlantic Swordfish (based on early 1970s data)

Weight Class (lb)	Number of Fish	Average Weight (lb)	Average Hg Level (ppm)	Cumulative Fish Weight (%)	Cumulative Fish Hg Dose (%)
Over 200	20	263.9	1.22	26.5	23.0
150-199	20	175.6	1.30	45.2	38.2
100-149	21	121.0	1.22	57.9	49.2
75-99	42	83.5	1.92	73.4	64.6
50-74	79	63.4	0.86	91.2	86.3
25-49	69	40.0	0.72	99.46	98.36
Under 25	23	16.4	0.32	100	100

NOTES

1. In the microbiological area, this is paralleled by the distinction between wholesome food prepared under clean conditions and food that is "adulterated" with "filth." More recently, it has become necessary for FDA to reveal that the advance of its detection capabilities for such items as rodent pellets and insect parts has required it to define finite quantitative "action levels" for these occasional food components.

2. Recently, for example, staff members of the Massachusetts Department of Environmental Quality produced a risk-based analysis of desirable levels of PCBs that might be permitted to remain in the soil of hazardous waste sites after the completion of cleanup operations. Based on an assumption that exposed individuals might ingest approximately 60 milligrams of such soil per day, and EPA's estimated "cancer potency factor" for PCBs, the authors concluded that no more than 2 parts per million of PCBs should be permitted. Ironically, this is the same level currently permitted via the U.S. Food and Drug Administration's "action level" for PCBs in fish—which is ordinarily intended for human consumption in quantities much larger than 60 milligrams per day.

3. Here and later, the use of the word "contaminant" should not be taken to imply anything about the human origin of specific residues. Particularly in the case of metallic residues in aquatic organisms, it is generally very difficult to determine the contributions of human and "natural" sources, and in any event this distinction is irrelevant for assessment of toxic potential.

4. In initially setting an advisory level for TCDD contamination in fish, FDA evidently used a no-observed effect level (NOEL)/safety factor approach to derive an "acceptable daily intake," based on the cancer findings in the two-year rodent feeding study of Kociba et al. (1978). After criticism, FDA joined other agencies in using these same data to calculate risk levels via the multistage model, but with differing results (largely attributable to the choice between surface area versus body weight scaling to project risks among species) (Michigan CEHS, 1986).

Agency	Calculated UCL Cancer Potency[a] [inductions/(mg/kg-day)]		Projected Lifetime UCL Risk	
	1 ppt TCDD[b]	20 ppt TCDD[b]	6.5 g/day	16.0 g/day
EPA/CAG[c]		1.56×10^5	1.4×10^{-5}	6.9×10^{-4}
Michigan DNR[d]		1.50×10^5	1.4×10^{-5}	6.4×10^{-4}
CDC	3.57×10^4	3.2×10^{-6}	1.6×10^{-4}	
FDA	1.75×10^4	1.6×10^{-6}	7.9×10^{-5}	

[a] UCL = upper confidence limit.
[b] ppt = parts per trillion.
[c] CAG = Carcinogen Assessment Group.
[d] DNR = Department of Natural Resources.

5. Ozone also tends to react with double bonds in organic material to create epoxides. Epoxides, to a greater or lesser extent depending on molecular weight and other factors, tend to react with DNA. Some lower-molecular-weight epoxides (such as ethylene oxide) are relatively well characterized with respect to carcinogenic activity (Hattis, 1987).

6. This is the dominant commercial species of shrimp. It is harvested particularly from warmwater regions.

7. The Z-score in Figure 5-1 is simply the number of standard deviations above or below the midpoint of a standard normal or lognormal distribution, inferred from the rank of a specific individual in a data set. The correspondence of the points to a straight line is a rough indication of the adequacy of a lognormal distribution for describing the data. In Figure 5-1 and other figures that show four or five data points, the plots were based on selected percentiles of the distribution, as shown in Table 6-1; in other plots, a more extensive sample of the available data was used. *R* is the coefficient.

8. The Aroclor family of PCB mixtures is named according to the percentage weight of chlorine that is covalently bound to biphenyls (in various positions). Thus Aroclor 1242 has about 42% chlorine, Aroclor 1254 has 54%, etc. Residues found in fish and shellfish are most similar to Aroclor 1254 and 1260, which contain mostly 5, 6, 7, or 8 chlorines per molecule (of a possible 10).

Appendix to Chapter 5

PRESENT STATUS OF DOSE-RESPONSE DATA
FOR TRACE METALS OF GREATEST POTENTIAL TOXICITY

Dose-response data used in risk assessment for trace-metal exposure are generated from animal studies and from occupational or accidental environmental exposure of humans. The uncertainty factor in the first instance (extrapolation) may be quite large, whereas data generated by occupational or accidental environmental exposures allow more accurate assessment. For four of the five metals identified as potential toxicants, arsenic, cadmium, lead, and mercury, an extensive body of literature exists documenting occupational and accidental exposure of humans. Although poisoning has been documented in humans from ingestion of selenium, far fewer dose-response data are available for accurate assessment. Dose-response data should allow the assessor to produce the following information:

1. Acceptable daily intake (ADI) or reference dose (RfD)
2. Toxic body (usually based on 70 kg) or organ burden
3. Steady daily intake for toxicity (acute/chronic)

This information can be calculated from other data obtained from controlled animal exposures or from inadvertently exposed humans. Needed for calculation are

1. human half-life of the metal (most often whole body);
2. blood LOAELs (low-observed-adverse-effect levels);
3. other tissue LOAELs (hair, nails, etc.);
4. absorption coefficient (percent absorption); and
5. age, sex, reproductive status, and interindividual variability of response.

The following are also desirable:

1. Pretoxic indicators (biomarkers)
2. Compartment kinetics (distribution within the organism)

Dose-response data used here come from three sources: the U.S. Environmental Protection Agency (EPA, 1988c) Integrated Risk Information System (IRIS); the U.S. Department of Health and Human Services (HHS) Agency for Toxic Substances and Disease Registry (ATSDR, 1989a,b); and specific papers in the world literature. These data are summarized in Table 5A-1.

TABLE 5A-1 Trace-Metal Dose-Response Data

Metal	ADI (mg/day)	Toxic Body Burden (mg)	Steady Daily Intake for Toxicity (mg/day)	Human Half-Life [a]	Blood LOAEL [b]
Arsenic	Uncertain for seafood	Uncertain for seafood	Uncertain for seafood	<20 h	Uncertain for seafood
Cadmium	51-72	Not reported	35	Three phases <200 d, +20 d, 10-30 yr	Uncertain poor monitor
Lead	429	100-400	Uncertain	Three phases 3-4 weeks, 5-30 yr	25 ppb (5-15 ppb in child)
Mercury	0.23	25	0.003 (acute)	70-110 d	0.23 ppb adult (0.1 ppb fetus)
Selenium	Uncertain for seafood	Not reported	—	Three phases 1 d, 8-20 d, 65-116 d	Uncertain (0.179 ppt)

[a] d = days; h = hours; yr = years.   [c] CNS = central nervous system.
[b] ppb = parts per billion; ppt = parts per thousand.   [d] RBC = red blood corpuscles.

Arsenic

Although seafood is a major source of arsenic in the diet, its chemical form in seafood is organic--primarily arsenobetaine and arsenocholine. This so-called fish arsenic is much less toxic than inorganic forms of arsenic and is not generally considered a threat to human health (ATSDR, 1989a). The literature concerned with arsenic in the environment and its toxicology has been reviewed by the World Health Organization (WHO, 1981), Fowler (1983), and the ATSDR (1989a,b). Inorganic forms of arsenic are established carcinogens in humans (EPA, 1988c). To the degree that inorganic forms of arsenic are either present in seafood or produced as metabolites of the organic arsenic in seafood, there would be expected to be some carcinogenic risk.

Half-life: The half-life varies according to the compound studied. For organic arsenic in seafood (fish arsenic; arsenobetaine) the best estimate in humans is less than 20 hours. Humans eliminate 50-80% of the dose from seafood within 48 hours (Tam et al., 1982). In animal studies, arsenobetaine is also rapidly eliminated in the urine; the small portion retained is found in testes, cartilage, and muscle (Vahter et al., 1983). When inorganic arsenic was force-fed (intubation) to trout it was converted to organic arsenic in the gut, and more than 95% of the arsenic found in muscle after 12 hours was the organic form (Penrose, 1975).

For inorganic arsenic the trivalent arsenite has three recorded half-lives: 2 hours, 8 hours, and 8 days. For pentavalent arsenic, half-life phases were 2.1, 9.5, and 38 days.

Gastrointestinal Absorption (%)	Dependence of Toxicity on Age, Sex, Reproductive Status	Long-Term Effects	Biomarkers	Tissue LOAEL (ppm)	Relative Priority as a Seafood Hazard
Uncertain for Seafood	Not reported for seafood	Uncertain for seafood	Uncertain for seafood	Uncertain for seafood	Very low
5	>50 years old and multi-parous female	Nephropathy	Urine retinol binding protein	Kidney, 200-285	High
10	Fetus and neonate	Anemia and CNS[c] problems	delta-Amino-levulinic acid (RBC)[d]	Poor	High
95	Fetus, neonate, and pregnant female	Retardation	Porphyrinuria	Hair, pregnant patients, 15-20	High
40-80 as the selenite	Not reported	Uncertain	Not reported	Hair, 0.828	Uncertain

Blood LOAEL: The blood LOAEL of arsenic is uncertain; levels are poor indicators of exposure. With organic arsenic, the turnover is so rapid that levels are of little value, but they do correspond to seafood in the diet.

Other Tissue LOAELs: Arsenobetaine does not accumulate in hair (Vahter et al., 1983), and inorganic arsenic hair and nail levels correlate poorly with intoxication. Furthermore, they tend to be contaminated by external factors. There is a large interindividual variability.

Percent Absorption: Both inorganic and organic forms of arsenic are similar. Absorption of inorganic form is approximately 90%; organic, reported from 70% to more than 90% (Tam et al., 1982).

Age, Sex, Reproductive Status, and Interindividual Variability: No response differences in age, sex, or reproductive status have been reported. Interindividual variability for the effects recorded may be large.

Pretoxic Indicators: Pretoxic indicators for arsenic are uncertain, with few biomonitoring options.

Long-term Effects: For inorganic arsenic in humans, the long-term effects include dermal hyperkeratosis, melanosis and carcinoma, hepatomegaly, peripheral neuropathy, and in cases of inhalation, pulmonary cancer. For the organic forms, no toxic effects have been reported in humans, and studies in animals indicate no toxic effects at an oral dose of 10,000 mg/kg. Further, there is no evidence of mutagenicity by arsenobetaine.

Kinetics: A two-compartment model is likely: initial buildup in, and clearance from, the liver, kidney, and lungs; and long-term retention in hair, skin, and skeletal system. Arsenobetaine is not biotransformed in vivo and is eliminated as such.

Acceptable Daily Intake (ADI): For inorganic arsenic trioxide the ADI is not agreed upon; it is estimated by the Food and Agriculture Organization (FAO) at 182 μg. None is reported for organic arsenic.

Toxic Body or Organ Burden: No information is available for fish arsenic.

Steady Daily Intake for Toxicity: Inorganic arsenic intake in children of 1.3-3.6 mg results in lesions in 33 days (subacute). Water levels of 0.9-3.4 mg per liter (L) result in skin lesions of adults. No information is available for fish arsenic.

Cadmium

Cadmium is both an occupational and an environmental toxicant. Occupational toxicity is, for the most part, related to inhalation, whereas environmental outbreaks are related to ingestion via contaminated food or water. Cadmium toxicity in man and animals has been extensively reviewed (ATSDR, 1989b; Friberg et al., 1985; Nriagu, 1981). Acceptable daily intake levels for cadmium may be difficult to determine for that segment of the population who are smokers. The prevalence, among cadmium-exposed individuals, of beta-2-microglobulin excretion may be three times higher in smokers than nonsmokers (Ellis et al., 1979; Hansen et al., 1985; Kjellström et al., 1977).

Half-life: Three phases are suggested. For phases 1 (<20 days) and 2 (20+ days), the half-life is estimated at 170 days. Phase 3 is estimated at 10-30 years (Friberg et al., 1974).

Blood LOAEL: Blood levels of cadmium poorly reflect the body burden but do indicate recent exposure.

Tissue LOAEL: The critical level in kidney is 200-285 ppm (effects are nephropathy and proteinuria). The LOAEL normally reaches a peak of 40-50 μg/g at age 50. Hair levels may reflect long-term exposure (Whanger, 1979).

Percent Absorption: About 2.7-5.9% is absorbed, usually considered 5% for all forms; absorption is determined by feeding humans radiolabeled cadmium (Newton et al., 1984).

Age, Sex, Reproductive Status, and Interindividual Variability of Response: Toxic effects, especially renal damage, are closely related to age, with greatest prevalence among those over 50 years (Fukushima et al., 1974). Multiparous females appear more sensitive to skeletal lesions (Kobayashi, 1978). The extent of interindividual variability is uncertain.

Pretoxic Indicator: Urine retinol binding protein (RBP) is a biomarker.

Long-term Effects: Nephropathy with tubular dysfunction results in proteinuria. There are conflicting reports regarding the production of hypertension in women. There is a significant correlation among cadmium levels in food, urine cadmium, and tubular dysfunction (Nogawa et al., 1978).

Kinetics: An eight-compartment model is used; the highest levels are found in kidney and liver (Kjellström and Nordberg, 1985).

ADI: The ADI is 57-72 μg/day; for a 70-kg individual, it is 0.0008-0.00103 mg/kg.

Toxic Body or Organ Burden: The toxic burden for kidney is 200-285 ppm.

Steady Daily Intake for Toxicity: A daily intake of 0.35 mg (0.005 mg/kg/day) at 50 years could lead to nephrosis (Friberg et al., 1974). The NOAEL is 0.2 mg/day (0.0029 mg/kg/day) (CEC, 1978).

Lead

Occupational and environmental poisoning with lead is well documented (NRC, 1972, 1980a). A plethora of dose-response information is available that has been used by risk assessors to calculate an acute ADI. Neurodevelopmental effects in children are presently being used to assess acceptable dosage and blood levels, although there is considerable skepticism that a true threshold exists. The latter is a difficult task because precise exposure doses associated with effects are not well known (Tsuchiya, 1980). Reports concerning dose-response are conflicting for similar effects, and a wide range of interindividual variability is apparent.

Half-life: The half-life is 5 years to decades for bones, depending on type and location. In blood, it is estimated at 21-28 days; in soft tissues, it is intermediate between these extremes. Lead accumulates in the skeletal system.

Blood Median Acceptable Toxicant Concentration (MATC): The Centers for Disease Control (CDC) puts the level for young children at 25 parts per billion (ppb) (but see long-term effects).

Blood LOAEL: The LOAEL is not well known in humans and varies according to the effect measured. It is a poor indicator of an individual's dose-response but is of value in assessing population exposure. Some LOAELs for varying effects are delta-aminolevulinic acid dehydratase 10-20 μg/100 mL; changes in peripheral nerve conduction velocity 51-60 μg/100 mL; chronic encephalopathy (children) 50-60 μg/100 mL; acute encephalopathy 80 μg/100 mL. Recent measurements of developmental impairment show differences between groups in the normal range (5-15 g/100 mL) (see below).

Hair LOAEL: Hair is a poor estimator; there is no LOAEL.

Percent Absorption: The absorption is very variable, with the best estimate being 10%. Children may reach 50%. True mean percentage absorption remains uncertain (Rabinowitz et al., 1974).

Age, Sex, Reproductive Status, and Interindividual Variability of Response: Recent studies indicate that the brain of the fetus may be more sensitive to lead than that of the neonate; hence, CDC levels of 25 ppb in blood may not be acceptable (Waternaux et al., 1989).

Pretoxic Indicator: delta-Aminolevulinic acid dehydratase inhibition in erythrocytes correlates negatively with lead blood levels (EPA, 1979). Free erythrocyte protoporphyrin (FEP) increases with blood lead levels but varies in relation to sex.

Long-term Effects: Anemia due to inhibition of hemoglobin production and shortened life span of erythrocytes result. There is derangement of both the peripheral and the central nervous system (CNS), especially with regard to neurobehavioral problems. Slowed mental development in neonates has been measured by the Bailey Scales of Mental Development. Children with higher blood lead levels at 6 months (7.07 μg/100 mL, SD 1.18 μg/100 mL) have poorer scores at 18 months than those with lower blood levels (4.66 μg/100 mL, SD 0.50 μg/100 mL) (Waternaux et al., 1989). Irreversible renal functional and morphological changes may occur (Tsuchiya, 1980).

Kinetics: There are essentially two compartments (three possible): blood and soft tissue (10% of burden) and skeletal system (90% of burden).

ADI: The ADI is estimated at 429 μg/day and the PTI at 6.1 μg/kg/day (FAO/WHO, 1972).

Toxic Body Burden: The body burden that would be toxic to a 70-kg individual is 100-400 mg.

Steady Daily Intake for Toxicity: The daily intake that would lead to toxicity is uncertain.

Mercury

As previously stated, the chemical form of the ingestible mercury in seafood is thought to be predominantly methylmercury. Both occupational and accidental environmental poisonings with the metal and its methyl or ethyl form have been extensively reported and reviewed in the literature. Observations of blood and other tissue LOAELs in affected individuals allow calculation of an acute ADI (Inskip and Piotrowski, 1985; Tollefson and Cordel, 1986).

Half-life: Whole body half-life values reveal an interindividual variability and differences with regard to reproductive status. The half-life is estimated at 70 days but is more than 110 days in some individuals and is 45 days for lactating females (Al-Shahristani and Shihab, 1974; Greenwood et al., 1978).

Blood LOAEL: In males and nonpregnant women the LOAEL in blood is 0.22-0.24 ppm; for pregnant women, 0.10 ppm; and due to fetal sensitivity, the maternal threshold is 0.05 ppm (Inskip and Piotrowski, 1985). A sound relationship exists between blood level and daily intake.

Hair LOAEL: The LOAEL in hair for adults is 25-50 ppm; for pregnant women, 37 ppm; maternal threshold, 15-20 ppm. The threshold may be as low as 10 ppm (10 μg/g; blood 0.03 ppm) in cases of extended periods of exposure (Inskip and Piotrowski, 1985). Hair appears to better reflect existing body mercury levels than urine or blood and is more resistant to sudden change. Hair levels also appear related to fish intake (Airey, 1983; Ohno et al., 1984). The hair/blood ratio is consistent and helpful in estimating exposure.

Percent Absorption: Gastrointestinal absorption is 95%.

Age, Sex, Reproductive Status, and Interindividual Variability of Response: There is little evidence for systematic differences in response due to age or sex of adults. Pregnant women may have a greater sensitivity; however, they deliver full-term, normal-weight children whose blood levels may be twice that of the mother. Such children develop CNS signs, including cerebral palsy, and delayed motor activity and speech. Lesions may increase in severity over long periods (Amin-Zaki et al., 1979). Effects of mild exposure are unknown.

Pretoxic Indicator: Porphyrinuria has been observed in early poisonings and is suggested as a possible indicator of exposure.

Long-term Effects: In children exposed prenatally to mercury, mental retardation can occur.

Kinetics: A single-compartment (possibly two-compartment) model is likely. There is uncertainty as to how the methyl form complexes with tissue, but studies suggest binding to glutathione in human blood and rat brain. Of the total body burden, 3-7% is found in the brain (Naganuma et al., 1980).

ADI: The ADI is 0.0033 mg/kg body weight. Estimates vary, however; even at this level there is an 8% risk of effect.

Toxic Body Burden: The toxic body burden for a 70-kg individual is calculated to be 25 mg.

Steady Daily Intake for Toxicity: The acute daily intake level is 300 μg; the chronic level is uncertain.

Selenium

Selenium as an ingestible toxicant remains enigmatic because of its known protective and deleterious effects. As previously noted, the metal may exist in a number of forms. Elemental selenium is not water soluble. The reduced form (-2) is selenide. The dioxide ($+4$) in water forms selenous acid whose salts are selenites, whereas the trioxide ($+6$) in water forms selenic acid whose salts are selenates. These substances appear to vary in toxicity and distribution in the body. Among other missing dose-response data for selenium, knowledge concerning the chemical forms found in seafood is incomplete. This lack results in an inability to calculate no-observed-adverse-effect levels (NOAELs), LOAELs, and frank effect levels (FELs). Although some dose-response data are available for inhalation toxicity in humans, very few are available concerning oral exposure. Recent studies of humans chronically exposed to selenium in endemic areas of the United States revealed no adverse health effects (Fan et al., 1988). The literature on selenium and its toxicity has been reviewed by Hogberg and Alexander (1986).

Half-life: In humans, studies reveal three phases for selenite, which are 1 day, 8-20 days, and 65-116 days.

Blood LOAEL: For nail changes the LOAEL is 0.179 μg/mL. Depending on the definition of selenosis, other reports indicate no signs with blood levels of 0.44 μg/mL.

Blood FEL: The blood FEL is 1.3-7.5 μg/mL with a mean of 3.2 μg/mL.

Tissue LOAELs: For nail changes as measured by hair concentration, the LOAEL is 0.828 μg/mL. Depending on the definition of selenosis, some report no signs with hair levels of 3.7 μg/mL.

Hair FEL: The hair FEL is 4.1-100 μg/mL with a mean of 32.2 μg/mL.

Percent Absorption: Absorption is estimated in humans to be from 40 to 80% for selenite and 75 to 97% for selenomethionine (Bopp et al., 1982).

Age, Sex, Reproductive Status, and Interindividual Variability of Response: No information is available regarding the effect of human age, sex, reproductive status, or interindividual variability of response.

Pretoxic Indicator: The use of increased glutathione peroxidase activity as an indicator of exposure is apparently of no value (Valentine et al., 1988). No biomarkers have been identified.

Long-term Effects: The long-term effects are uncertain. Pathological nail changes, loss of hair, dermatitis, icterus, mottled teeth, and caries are some of the more obvious ones. In a few instances, neurological upsets have been reported in adults. The target organ for chronic exposure in animals is the liver. This has not been documented in humans.

Kinetics: Initially, selenium is distributed to most organs, but the percentage of distribution may depend on the chemical form. Selenium in humans appears to bind to plasma lipoproteins, cross the placenta, and enter milk. Transient accumulation occurs in blood, muscle, liver, and kidney, with greater retention in the brain, thymus, and reproductive organs. Excretion in humans is primarily by urine and exhalation.

ADI: The ADI is uncertain. Yang et al. (1983) estimate 0.022 mg of organic selenium daily as a NOAEL for adult humans; the National Research Council (NRC, 1980b) gives the estimated safe and adequate daily dietary intake (ESADDI) for infants as 0.01-0.06 mg, for children 0.02-0.2 mg., and for adults 0.05-0.2 mg.

Toxic Body Burden: No information is available.

Steady Daily Intake for Toxicity: It has been estimated that 1 mg of selenium daily, as the selenite, would be toxic (Yang et al., 1983).

Conclusions

Thresholds of toxicity calculated for acute or short-term exposures, especially for mercury, may not reflect a threshold for chronic or long-term exposures. Recent assessment models have, therefore, included coefficients of cumulative toxicity (Inskip and Piotrowski, 1985; PTI, 1987). Such models, however, would be strengthened if data regarding chronic and cumulative toxicity could be generated. Models would be further strengthened by information regarding interindividual variability of response as a function of blood level. The existing dose-response data base with respect to human risk from seafoods contaminated with the trace metals arsenic, cadmium, lead, mercury, and selenium lacks sufficient information regarding the effects of chronic exposures, the sensitivity of certain subpopulations, and interindividual variability to make such an assessment. In the case of arsenic, although no sound human data exist, the primary form found in seafood is organic and appears to be of very low toxicity to animals. Therefore, identification of this trace metal as a potential hazard to humans may be premature.

REFERENCES

Airey, D. 1983. Total mercury concentrations in human hair from 13 countries in relation to fish consumptions and locations. Sci. Total Environ. 31:157-180.

Al-Shahristani, H., and K.M. Shihab. 1974. Variation of biological half-life of methylmercury in man. Arch. Environ. Health 28:342-344.

Amin-Zaki, L., M.A. Majeed, S.B. Elhassani, T.W. Clarkson, M.R. Greenwood, and R.A. Doherty. 1979. Prenatal methylmercury poisoning. Clinical observations over five years. Am. J. Dis. Child. 133:172-177.

Anonymous. 1988a. Health and environmental effects profile for antimony oxides. NTIS/PB88-175039. Government Reports Announcements and Index, Issue 12. 129 pp.

Anonymous. 1988b. Health effects assessment for antimony and compounds. NTIS/PB88-179445. Government Reports Announcements and Index, Issue 13. 46 pp.

ATSDR (Agency for Toxic Substances and Disease Registry). 1989a. Toxicological Profile for Arsenic. ATSDR/TP-88/02. Prepared by Life Systems, Inc. for ATSDR, U.S. Public Health Service in collaboration with U.S. Environmental Protection Agency. 125 pp.

ATSDR (Agency for Toxic Substances and Disease Registry). 1989b. Toxicological Profile for Cadmium. ATSDR/TP-88/08. Prepared by Life Systems, Inc. for ATSDR, U.S. Public Health Service in collaboration with U.S. Environmental Protection Agency. 107 pp.

Beliles, R.P. 1978. The lesser metals. Pp. 547-616 in F.W. Oehme, ed. Toxicity of Heavy Metals in the Environment, Part 2. Marcel Dekker, New York.

Bertazzi, P.A., L. Riboldi, A. Pesatori, L. Radice, and C. Zocchetti. 1987. Cancer mortality of capacitor manufacturing workers. Am. J. Indust. Med. 11:165-176.

Bevill, R.F., and W.G. Huber. 1977. Sulfonamides. Pp. 894-911 in L. Jones, N. Booth, and L. McDonald, eds. Veterinary Pharmacology and Therapeutics, 4th ed. Iowa State University Press, Ames.

Booth, N.H. 1977. Drug and chemical residues in the edible tissues of animals. Pp. 1299-1342 in L. Jones, N. Booth, and L. McDonald, eds. Veterinary Pharmacology and Therapeutics, 4th ed. Iowa State University Press, Ames.

Bopp, B.A., R.C. Sonders, and J.W. Kesterson. 1982. Metabolic fate of selected selenium compounds in laboratory animals and man. Drug Metab. Rev. 13:271-318.

Brown, D. P. 1987. Mortality of workers exposed to polychlorinated biphenyls: An update. Arch. Environ. Health 42:333-339.

Buck, W.B. 1978. Toxicity of inorganic and aliphatic organic arsenicals. Pp. 357-374 in F.W. Oehme, ed. Toxicity of the Heavy Metals in the Environment. Marcel Dekker, New York.

Camber, C.I., M.H. Vance, and J. Alexander. 1956. How to use sodium bisulfite to control "blackspot" on shrimp. Univ. Miami Special Bull. No. 12, 4 pp.

Cappon, C.J., and J.C. Smith. 1981. Mercury and selenium content and chemical form in fish muscle. Arch. Environ. Contam. Toxicol. 10:305-319.

Cappuzo, J., A. McElroy, and G. Wallace. 1987. Fish and shellfish contamination in New England waters: An evaluation and review of available data on the distribution of chemical contaminants. Report submitted to Coast Alliance, Washington, D.C. 85 pp.

CEC (Commission of the European Communities). 1978. Pp. 1-198 in Criteria (Dose/ Effect Relationships) for Cadmium. Pergamon Press. Oxford, England.

Clark, J.R., D. Devault, R.J. Bowden, and J.A. Weishaar. 1984. Contaminant analysis of fillets from Great Lakes coho salmon, 1980. J. Great Lakes Res. 10:38-47.

Cordle, F., R. Locke, and J. Springer. 1982. Risk assessment in a federal regulatory agency: An assessment of risk associated with the human consumption of some species of fish contaminated with polychlorinated biphenyls (PCBs). Environ. Health Perspect. 45: 171-182.

Duling, L. 1988. Fish contaminant monitoring program 1988 annual report. Report MI/DNR/SWQ-88/090. Michigan Department of Natural Resources, Surface Water Quality Division, Lansing. 300 pp.

Earl, F.L., and T.J. Vish. 1978. Teratogenicity of heavy metals. Pp. 617-640 in F.W. Oehme, ed. Toxicity of Heavy Metals in the Environment, Part 2. Marcel Dekker, New York.

Ellis, K.J., D. Vartsky, I. Zanzi, S.H. Cohn, and S. Yasumura. 1979. Cadmium: In vivo measurement in smokers and nonsmokers. Science 205:323-324.

EPA (Environmental Protection Agency). 1979. Ambient Water Quality Criteria for Lead. Water Planning and Standards. EPA 440/5-80-057. U.S. Environmental Protection Agency, Washington, D.C. 161 pp.

EPA (Environmental Protection Agency). 1986. Pesticides Fact Sheet No. 109: Chlordane. EPA 540/FS 87/143. U.S. Environmental Protection Agency, Washington, D.C. 9 pp.

EPA (Environmental Protection Agency). 1987. The National Dioxin Study: Tiers 3,5,6, and 7. EPA 440/4-87-003. Office of Water Regulations and Standards, Monitoring and Data Support Division, U.S. Environmental Protection Agency, Washington, D.C. 208 pp.

EPA (Environmental Protection Agency). 1988a. Assessment of Dioxin Contamination of Water, Sediment and Fish in the Pigeon River System (a Synoptic Study) Report No. 001. U.S. Environmental Protection Agency, Region IV, Water Management Division, Atlanta, Georgia. 75 pp.

EPA (Environmental Protection Agency). 1988b. Dioxin Levels in Fish Near Pulp and Paper Mills. Interim report dated October 25. U.S. Environmental Protection Agency, Office of Water Regulations and Standards, Washington, D.C.

EPA (Environmental Protection Agency) 1988c. Integrated Risk Information System (IRIS). As, Cd, Pb, Hg and Se. DIALCOM, Inc., Washington, D.C.

Ewan, R.C. 1978. Toxicology and adverse effects of mineral imbalance with emphasis on selenium and other minerals. Pp. 445-490 in F.W. Oehme, ed. Toxicity of Heavy Metals in the Environment, Part 2. Marcel Dekker, New York.

Fan, A.M., S.A. Book, R.R. Neutra, and D.M. Epstein. 1988. Selenium and human health implications in California's San Joaquin Valley. J. Toxicol. Environ. Health 23:539-560.

Fauvel, Y., G. Pons, and J.P. Legeron 1982. Ozonation de l'eau de mer et épuration des coquillages. Science et Peche, Nantes 320:1-16.

FDA (Food and Drug Administration). 1982. Levels for Poisonous or Deleterious Substances in Human Food and Animals Feed. U.S. Food and Drug Administration, Washington, D.C. 13 pp.

FDA (Food and Drug Administration). 1988. Compliance Program Guidance Manual. FY86 Pesticides and Industrial Chemicals in Domestic Food. Program No. 7304-004. U.S. Department of Health and Human Services, Public Health Service, U.S. Food and Drug Administration, Bureau of Foods, Washington, D.C. 48 pp.

Fein, G.G., J.L. Jacobson, S.W. Jacobson, P.M. Schwartz, and J.K. Dowler. 1984. Prenatal exposure to polychlorinated biphenyls: Effects on birth size and gestational age. J. Pediatrics 105:315-320.

Fishbein, L. 1983. Environmental selenium and its significance. Fundam. Appl. Toxicol. 3:411-419.

Fowler, B.A. 1983. Pp. 1-281 in Biological and Environmental Effects of Arsenic, Vol. 6. Elsevier Science Publishers, Amsterdam, The Netherlands.

Fox, A. 1990. Fishery chemicals used in foreign countries. Intracenter memorandum, January 16. National Fisheries Research Center, Seattle, Wash.

Friberg, L., M. Piscator, G.F. Nordberg, and T. Kjellström. 1974. Cadmium in the Environment, 2nd ed. CRC Press, Cleveland, Ohio. Vol. I, 209 pp; Vol. II, 248 pp.

Friberg, L., C.-G. Elinder, T. Kjellström, and G.F. Nordberg. 1985. Cadmium and Health. A Toxicological and Epidemiological Appraisal. CRC Press, Boca Raton, Fla. 307 pp.

Fukayama, M.Y., H. Tan, W.B. Wheeler, and C.I. Wei. 1986. Reactions of aqueous chlorine and chlorine dioxide with model food compounds. Environ. Health Perspect. 69:267-274.

Fukushima, M. A. Ishizaki, K. Nogawa, M. Sakamoto, and E. Kobayashi. 1974. Epidemiological studies on renal failure of inhabitants in "itai-itai" disease endemic district (Part 1). Some urinary findings of inhabitants living in and around the endemic district of the Jinzu River basin. Jap. J. Pub. Health 21:65-73.

Gadbois, D.F., and R.S. Maney. 1983. Survey of polychlorinated biphenyls in selected finfish species from United States coastal waters. Fish. Bull. (USFWS) 81:389-396.

Gladen, B. C., W.J. Rogan, P. Hardy, J. Thullen, J. Tingelstad, and M. Tully. 1988. Development after exposure to polychlorinated biphenyls and dichlorodiphenyl-dichloroethene transplacentally and through human milk. J. Pediatr. 113:991-995.

Gossett, R.W., H.W. Puffer, R.H. Arthur, Jr., J. Alfafara, and D.R. Young. 1982. Pp. 29-37 in W. Bascon, ed. Levels of Trace Organic Compounds in Sportfish from Southern California. Coastal Water Research Project Biennial Report. Southern California Coastal Water Research Project 1981-1982, Long Beach, Calif.

Gossett, R.W., H.W. Puffer, R.H. Arthur Jr., and D.R. Young. 1983. DDT, PCB and Benzo(a)pyrene levels in white croaker (Genyonemus lineatus) from southern California. Mar. Poll. Bull. 14:60-65.

Goyer, R.A. 1986. Toxic effects of metals. Pp. 582-635 in C. Klassen, M. Amdur, and J. Doull, eds. Casarett and Doull's Toxicology, 3rd ed. Macmillan, New York.

Green, V.A., G.W. Wise, and J.C. Callenbach. 1978. Lead poisoning. Pp. 123-141 in F.W. Oehme, ed. Toxicity of Heavy Metals in the Environment, Part 1. Marcel Dekker, New York.

Greenwood, M.R., T. W. Clarkson, R. A. Doherty, A. H. Gates, L. Amin-Zaki, S. Elhassani, and M. A. Majeed. 1978. Blood clearance half-times in lactating and non-lactating members of a population exposed to methylmercury. Environ. Res. 16:48-54.

Griffin, A.C. 1979. Role of selenium in the chemoprevention of cancer. Adv. Cancer Res. 29:419-422.

Groth, D.H., L.E. Stettler, J.R. Burg, W.M. Busey, G.C. Grant, and L. Wong. 1986. Carcinogenic effects of antimony trioxide and antimony ore concentrate in rats. J. Toxicol. Environ. Health 18: 607-626.

Guarino, A.M., S.M. Plakas, R.W. Dickey, and M. Zeeman. 1988. Principles of drug absorption and recent studies of bioavailability in aquatic species. Vet. Human Toxicol. 30:41-44.

Gunderson, E. L. 1988. FDA Total Diet Study, April 1982-April 1984, Dietary intakes of pesticides, selected elements and other chemicals. J. Assoc. Off. Anal. Chem. 71:1200-1209.

Haines, A.T., and E. Nieboer. 1988. Chromium hypersensitivity. Pp. 497-532 in J. Nrigau and E. Nieboer eds. Chromium in the Natural and Human Environment. John Wiley & Sons, New York.

Hall, R.A., E.G. Zook, and G.M. Meaburn. 1978. National Marine Fisheries Service Survey of Trace Elements in the Fishery Resource. NOAA Technical Report NMFS SSRF-721, National Technical Information Service No. PB 283 851, March. 313 pp.

Hammond, P.B. 1978. Metabolism and metabolic action of lead and other heavy metals. Pp. 87-99 in F.W. Oehme, ed. Toxicity of Heavy Metals in the Environment, Part 1. Marcel Dekker, New York.

Hansen, J.C., H.C. Wulf, N. Kromann, and K. Alboge. 1985. Cadmium concentrations in blood samples from the East Greenlandic population. Dan. Med. Bull. 32:277-279.

Harada, M. 1978. Methyl mercury poisoning due to environmental contamination (Minamata disease). Pp. 261-302 in F.W. Oehme, ed. Toxicity of Heavy Metals in the Environment, Part 1. Marcel Dekker, New York.

Harr, J.R. 1978. Biological effects of selenium. Pp. 393-426 in F.W. Oehme, ed. Toxicity of Heavy Metals in the Environment, Part 2. Marcel Dekker, New York.

Harr, J.R., and O.H. Muth. 1972. Selenium poisoning in domestic animals and its relationship to man. Clin. Toxicol. 5:175-186.

Hattis, D. 1972. The FDA and nitrite--A case study of violations of the Food, Drug, and Cosmetic Act with respect to a particular food additive. Presented in hearings before the Select Committee on Nutrition and Food Needs of the United States Senate, September 21, pp. 1692-1720.

Hattis, D. 1987. A pharmacokinetic mechanism-based analysis of the carcinogenic risk of ethylene oxide. National Technical Information Service, No. NTIS/PB88-188784. MIT Center for Technology, Policy and Industrial Development, No CTPIC 87-1, August. 176 pp.

Hattis, D. 1989. Letter report from Dr. Dale Hattis, MIT, to W. Munns, Environmental Research Laboratory, Narragansett, R.I., December 28. 4 pp.

Hawke, J.P., S.M. Plakas, R. Vernon Minton, R.M. McPhearson, T.G. Snider, and A.M. Guarino. 1987. Fish pasteurellosis of cultured striped bass (Morone saxatilis) in coastal Alabama. Aquaculture 65:193-204.

Hogberg, J., and J. Alexander. 1986. Selenium. Pp. 482-520 in L. Friberg, J. Parizek, and V. Vouk, ed. Handbook on the Toxicology of Metals, 2d end. Elsevier Science Publishers, Amsterdam, The Netherlands.

Huber, G. 1977a. Penicillins. Pp. 912-928 in L.M. Jones, N.H Booth, and L.E. McDonald, eds. Veterinary Pharmacology and Therapeutics, 4th ed. Iowa State University Press, Ames.

Huber, G. 1977b. Tetracyclines. Pp. 929-939 in L.M. Jones, N.H. Booth, and L.E. McDonald, eds. Veterinary Pharmacology and Therapeutics, 4th ed. Iowa State University Press, Ames.

Huber, G. 1977c. Streptomycin, chloramphenicol and other antibiotic agents. Pp. 940-971 in L.M. Jones, N.H. Booth, and L.E. McDonald, eds. Veterinary Pharmacology and Therapeutics, 4th ed. Iowa State University Press, Ames.

Inskip, M.J., and J.K. Piotrowski. 1985. Review of the health effects of methylmercury. J. Appl. Toxicol. 5:113-133.

Jacobson, J.L., H.E. Humphrey, S.W. Jacobson, S.L. Schantz, M.D. Mullin, and R. Welch. 1989. Determinants of polychlorinated biphenyls (PCBs), polybrominated biphenyls (PBBs), and dichlorodiphenyl trichloroethane (DDT) levels in the sera of young children. Am. J. Publ. Health 79:1401-1404.

Jacobson, J.L., S.W. Jacobson, and H.E. Humphrey. 1990. Effects of in utero exposure to polychlorinated biphenyls and related contaminants on cognitive functioning in young children. J. Pediatr. 116:38-45.

Jacobson, S.W., G.G. Fein, J.L. Jacobson, P.M. Schwartz, and J.K. Dowler. 1985. The effect of intrauterine PCB exposure on visual recognition memory. Child Develop. 56:853-860.

Kansas DHE (Department of Health and Environment). 1988. A Survey of Pesticides in Tuttle Creek Lakes, Its Tributaries and the Upper Kansas River. Water Quality Assessment Section, Bureau of Water Protection, Kansas Department of Health and Environment, Topeka, Kansas. 29 pp.

Kjellström, T., and G.F. Nordberg. 1985. Kinetic model of cadmium metabolism. Pp. 179-197 in L. Friberg, C.G. Elinder, T. Kjellström, and G.F. Nordberg, eds. Cadmium and Health: A Toxicological and Epidemiological Appraisal, Vol. 1 Exposure, Dose and Metabolism. CRC Press, Boca Raton, Fla.

Kjellström, T., P.-E. Ervin, and B. Rahnster. 1977. Dose-response relationship of cadmium-induced tubular proteinuria. Environ. Res. 13:303-317.

Kobayashi, J. 1978. Pollution by cadmium and the itai-itai disease in Japan. Pp. 199-260 in F.W. Oheme, ed. Toxicity of Heavy Metals in the Environment, Part 1. Marcel Dekker, New York.

Kociba, R.J., D.G. Keyes, J.E. Beyer, R.M. Carreon, C.E. Wade, D.A. Dittenber, R.P. Kalmins, L.E. Frauson, C.N. Park, S.D. Barnard, R.A. Hummel, and C.G. Humiston. 1978. Results of a two-year chronic toxicity and oncogenicity study of 2,3,7,8-tetrachlorodibenzo-p-dioxin in rats. Toxicol. Appl. Pharmacol. 46:279-303.

Landolt, M.L., F.R. Hafer, A. Nevissi, G. van Belle, K. Van Ness, and C. Rockwell. 1985. Potential toxicant exposures among consumers of recreationally caught fish from urban embayments of Puget Sound. NOAA Tech. Memo. NOS OMA 23. Rockville, Md. 104 pp.

Landolt, M.L., D. Kalman, A. Nevissi, G. van Belle, K. Van Ness, and F.R. Hafer. 1987. Potential toxicant exposures among consumers of recreationally caught fish from urban embayments of Puget Sound. NOAA Tech. Memo. NOS OMA 33. Rockville, Md. 111 pp.

Lauwerys, R., and Ph. De Wals. 1981. Environmental pollutions by cadmium and mortality from renal diseases. Lancet 1:383.

Lecos, C. 1985. Reacting to sulfites. FDA Consumer 19:22-25.

Lowe, T.P., T.W. May, W.G. Brumbaugh, and D.A. Kane. 1985. National contaminant biomonitoring program: Concentrations of seven elements in freshwater fish, 1978-1981. Arch. Environ. Contam. Toxicol. 14:363-388.

Malins, D.C., B.B. McCain, D.W. Brown, A.K. Sparks, and H.O. Hodgins. 1980. Chemical contaminants and biological abnormalities in central and southern Puget Sound. NOAA Tech. Memo. OMPA-2. PB 81/155/897. Boulder, Co. 312 pp.

Malins, D.C., B.B. McCain, D.W. Brown, A.K. Sparks, H.O. Hodgins, and S-L. Chan. 1982. Chemical contaminants and abnormalities in fish and invertebrates in Puget Sound. NOAA Tech. Memo. OMPA-19. PB 83/115/188. Springfield, Va. 189 pp.

Manci, W. 1990. Hope and caution highlight fish disease news. Catfish News/Aquaculture News 4:10.

Masri, M.S. 1986. Chlorinating poultry chiller water: The generation of mutagens and water reuse. Food Chem. Toxicol. 24:923-930.

McKenzie-Parnell, J.M., T.E. Kjellström, R.P. Sharma, and M.F. Robinson. 1988. Unusually high intake and fecal output of cadmium, and fecal output of other trace elements in New Zealand adults consuming dredge oysters. Environ. Res. 46:1-14.

Mearns, A.J., M.B. Matta, D. Simecek-Beatty, M.F. Buchman, G. Shigenaka, and W.A. Wert. 1988. PCB and chlorinated pesticide contamination in U.S. fish and shellfish: A historical assessment report. NOAA Tech. Memo. NOS OMA 39. Seattle, Wash. 140 pp.

Meyer, F.P., and R.A. Schnick. 1989. A review of chemicals used for the control of fish diseases. Aquat. Sci. 1:693-710.

Michel, C. 1986. Practical value, potential dangers and methods of using antibacterial drugs in fish. Rev. Sci. Tech. Off. Int. Epiz. 5:659-675.

Michigan CEHS (Center for Environmental Health Sciences). 1986. Background Document Concerning 1986 Fish Consumption Advisory for Dioxin Contaminated Fish. Prepared for the Michigan Environmental Review Board, Lansing, Mich. February. 13 pp.

Mitchell, G.A. 1989. The FDA role in aquaculture chemical and drug usage. Paper presented at Aquaculture Opportunities for Appalachia Meeting, November 13-15, 1989, Birmingham, Ala. 13 pp.

Murphy, D.L. 1988a. Basic water monitoring program. Fish tissue analysis, 1985. State of Maryland, Department of Environment, Division of Standards and Certification, Water Management Administration. Technical Report 59. Baltimore, Md. 38 pp.

Murphy, D.L. 1988b. Trace contaminants in Chesapeake Bay bluefish. Metals and organochlorine pesticides. State of Maryland, Department of the Environment, Division of Standards and Certification, Water Management Administration. Technical Report 73. Baltimore, Md. 21 pp.

Murphy, D.L. 1988c. Trace contaminants in striped bass from two Chesapeake Bay tributaries. Metals and organochlorine pesticides. State of Maryland, Department of the Environment, Division of Standards and Certification, Water Management Administration. Technical Planning and Evaluation Report 58. Baltimore, Md. 19 pp.

Murphy, S.D. 1980. Pesticides. Pp. 357-408 in J. Doull, C. Classen, and M. Amdur, eds. Casarett and Doull's Toxicology, 2nd ed. Macmillan, New York.

Naganuma, A., Y. Koyama, and N. Imura. 1980. Behaviour of methylmercury in mammalian erythrocytes. Toxicol. Appl. Pharmacol. 54:405-410.

Newton, D., P. Johnson, A.E. Lally, R.J. Pentreath, and D.J. Swift. 1984. The uptake by man of cadmium ingested in crab meat. Human Toxicol. 3:23-28.

Nieboer, E., and A.A. Jusys. 1988. Biological chemistry of chromium. Pp. 21-80in J. Nrigau and E. Nieboer, eds. Chromium in the Natural and Human Environments. John Wiley & Sons, New York.

NOAA (National Oceanic and Atmospheric Administration). 1987. A summary of selected data on chemical contaminants in tissues collected during 1984, 1985, and 1986. Progress Report. NS&T Program for Marine Environmental Quality. NOAA Technical Memorandum. NOS OMA 38. Rockville, Md. 104 pp.

NOAA (National Oceanic and Atmospheric Administration). 1988. PCB and chlorinated pesticide contamination in U.S. fish and shellfish: A historical assessment report. NOAA Technical Memorandum. NOS OMA 39. Seattle, Wash. 140 pp.

NOAA (National Oceanic and Atmospheric Administration). 1989. A summary of data on tissue contamination from the first three years (1986-1988) of the mussel watch project. Progress Report. NS&T Program for Marine Environmental Quality. NOAA Technical Memorandum. NOS OMA 49. Rockville, Md. 161 pp.

Nogawa, K., A. Ishizaki, and S. Kawano. 1978. Statistical observations of the dose-response relationships of cadmium based on epidemiological studies in the Kakehashi River basin. Environ. Res. 15:185-198.

NRC (National Research Council). 1972. Airborne Lead in Perspective. Committee on Biological Effects/Atmospheric Pollutants. National Academy Press, Washington, D.C. 333 pp.

NRC (National Research Council). 1980a. Lead in the Human Environment. Committee on Lead in Human Environment. National Academy Press, Washington, D.C. 525 pp.

NRC (National Research Council). 1980b. Recommended Dietary Allowances, 9th ed. Committee on Dietary Allowances, Food and Nutrition Board. National Academy Press, Washington, D.C. 185 pp.

Nriagu, J.O., ed. 1981. Cadmium in the Environment, Part II: Health Effects. John Wiley & Sons, New York. 908 pp.

Ohno, H., R. Doi, Y. Tani, and M. Harada. 1984. Mercury content of head hair from residents on the cost of Jakarta Bay. Bull. Env. Contamin. Toxicol. 33:382-385.

Penrose, W.R. 1975. Biosynthesis of organic arsenic compounds in the brown trout (*Salmo trutta*). J. Fish. Res. Bd. Canada 32:2385-2390.

Plakas, S.M., R.M. McPhearson, and A.M. Guarino. 1988. Disposition and bioavailability of ^{3}H-tetracycline in the channel catfish (*Ictalurus punctatus*). Xenobiotica 18:83-93.

Plakas, S.M., R.W. Dickey, M.G. Barron, and A.M. Guarino. 1990. Tissue distribution and renal excretion of ormetoprim after intravascular and oral administration in the channel catfish (*Ictalurus punctatus*). Can. J. Fish. Aquat. Sci. 47:1-6.

Pruell, R.J., E.J. Hoffman, and J.G. Quinn. 1984. Total hydrocarbons, polycyclic aromatic hydrocarbons and synthetic organic compounds in the hard shell clam, *Mercenaria mercenaria*, purchased at commercial seafood stores. Mar. Environ. Res. 11:163-181.

PTI. 1987. Guidance Manual for Assessing Human Health Risks from Chemically Contaminated Fish and Shellfish. Draft Report c737-01 submitted to Battelle New England Marine Research Laboratory, December 1987, by PTI Environmental Services, Inc., Bellevue, Wash. 64 pp.

Rabinowitz, M., G.W. Wetherill, and J.D. Kopple. 1974. Studies of human lead metabolism by use of stable isotope tracers. Environ. Health Perspect. 7:145-153.

Reddy, C.C., and E.J. Massaro. 1983. Biochemistry of selenium: A brief overview. Fundam. Appl. Toxicol. 3:431-436.

Rice, R.G., J.W. Farquhar, and L.J. Bollyky. 1982. Review of the applications of ozone for increasing storage times of perishable foods. Ozone: Science Engineer. 4:147-163.

Rogan, W.J., B.C. Gladen, J.D. McKinney, N. Carreras, P. Hardy, J. Thullen, J.Tinglestad, and M. Tully. 1986. Neonatal effects of transplacental exposure to PCBs and DDE. J. Pediatrics 109:335-341.

Rohrer, T.K., J.C. Forney, and J.H. Hartig. 1982. Organochlorine and heavy metal residues in standard fillets of coho and chinook salmon of the Great Lakes, 1980. J. Great Lakes Res. 8:623-634.

Rugen, P.J., C.D. Stern, and S.H. Lamm. 1989. Comparative carcinogenicity of the PAHs as a basis for acceptable exposure levels (AELs) in drinking water. Regul. Toxicol. Pharmacol. 9:273-283.

Safe, S. 1989. Polychlorinated biphenyls (PCBs): Mutagenicity and carcinogenicity. Mutat. Res. 220:31-47.

Schamberger, R.J. 1985. The genotoxicity of selenium. Mutation Res. 154:29-48.

Schmitt, C.J., M.A. Ribick, J.L. Ludke, and T.W. May. 1983. Organochlorine residues in freshwater fish, 1976-1979. National Pesticides Monitoring Program. Prepared by Columbia National Research Fisheries Laboratory, Columbia, Mo. 69 pp.

Schnell, R.C., and C.R. Angle. 1983. Selenium–Toxin or panacea? Fundam. Appl. Toxicol. 3:409-410.

Schnick, R.A. 1988. The impetus to register new therapeutants for aquaculture. Prog. Fish-Culturist 50:190-196.

Schnick, R.A., F.P. Meyer, and D.L. Gray. 1989. A guide to approved chemicals in fish production and fishery resource management. University of Arkansas, Cooperative Extension and U.S. Fish and Wildlife Service, Little Rock. Publication MP 241-5M-3-89RV. 27 pp.

Sherlock, J.C. 1986. Part III: Cadmium and human health. Experientia (supplement) 50:110-114.

Short, J.W., and F.P. Thrower. 1987a. Accumulations of butyltins in muscle tissue of chinook salmon reared in sea pens treated with tri-*n*-butyltin. Aquaculture 61:181-192.

Short, J.W., and F.P. Thrower. 1987b. Toxicity of tri-*n*-butyltin to chinook salmon, *Oncorhynchus tshawytscha*, adapted to seawater. Aquaculture 61:193-200.

Shukla, S.S., and H.V. Leland. 1973. Heavy metals: A review of lead. J. Water Poll. Control Fed. 45:1319-1331.

Sloan, R.J., and R. Karcher. 1985. On the origin of cadmium concentrations in Hudson River blue crab (*Callinectes sapidus* Rathbun). Northeastern Environ. Sci. 3:221-231.

Sloan, R.J., L.C. Skinner, E.G. Horn, and R. Karcher. 1987. An overview of mercury contamination in the fish of Onondaga Lake. New York State Department of Environmental Conservation, Division of Fish and Wildlife, Albany. Technical Report 87-1 (BEP). July. 44 pp.

Sorensen, E.M.B., P.M. Cumbie, T.L. Bauer, J.S. Bell, and C.W. Harlan. 1984. Histopathological, hematological, condition-factor, and organ weight changes associated with selenium accumulation in fish from Belews Lake, North Carolina. Arch. Environ. Contam. Toxicol. 13:153-162.

St. Amant, J.R., M.E. Pariso, and T.B. Sheffy. 1983. Final report on the toxic substances survey of the Lakes Michigan, Superior and tributary streams for the Wisconsin Coastal Management Program. Wisconsin Department of Natural Resources, Bureau of Water Resources Management, Water Quality Evaluation Section. Madison. 31 pp.

Stopford, W., and L.J. Goldwater. 1975. Methylmercury in the environment: A review of current understanding. Environ. Health Perspect. 12:115-118.

Stout, V.F. 1980. Organochlorine residues in fishes from the northwest Atlantic Ocean and the Gulf of Mexico. Fish. Bull. 78:51-58.

Sunahara, G.I., K.G. Nelson, T.K. Wong, and G.W. Lucier. 1987. Decreased human birth weights after in utero exposure to PCBs and PCDFs are associated with decreased placental EGF-stimulated receptor autophosphorylation capacity. Molec. Pharmacol. 32:572-578.

Tam, G.K.H., S.M. Charbonneau, F. Byrce, and E. Sandi. 1982. Excretion of a single oral dose of fish-arsenic in man. Bull. Environ. Contam. Toxicol. 28:669-673.

Taylor, P.R., J.M. Stelma, and C.E. Lawrence. 1989. The relation of polychlorinated biphenyls to birth weight and gestational age in the offspring of occupationally exposed mothers. Am. J. Epidem. 129:395-406.

Tollefson, L., and F. Cordle. 1986. Methylmercury in fish: Review of residue levels, fish consumption and regulatory action in the United States. Environ. Health Perspect. 68:203-208.

Tsuchiya, K. 1980. Lead. Pp. 451-484 in L. Friberg, G.F. Nordberg, and V.B. Vouk, eds. Handbook on the Toxicology of Metals, 2d ed. Elsevier Science Publishers, Amsterdam, The Netherlands.

Vahter, M., E. Marafante, and L. Denker. 1983. Metabolism of arsenobetaine in mice, rats and rabbits. Sci. Total Environ. 30:197-211.

Valentine, J.L., B. Faraji, and H.K. Kang. 1988. Human glutathione peroxidase activity in cases of high selenium exposures. Environ. Res. 45:16-27.

Van Gelder, G.A. 1978. Lead and the nervous system. Pp. 101-121 in F.W. Oehme, ed. Toxicity of Heavy Metals in the Environment, Part 1. Marcel Dekker, New York.

Viarengo, A. 1985. Biochemical effects of trace metals. Mar. Poll. Bull. 16:153-158.

Waternaux, C., N.M. Laird, and J.H. Ware. 1989. Methods for analysis of longitudinal data: Blood lead concentrations and cognitive development. J. Amer. Stat. Assoc. 84:33-41.

Whanger, P.D. 1979. Cadmium effects in rats on tissue iron, selenium, and blood pressure; Blood and hair cadmium in some Oregon residents. Environ. Health Perspect. 28:115-121.

WHO (World Health Organization). 1980. Tin and organotin compounds: A preliminary review.

Environmental Health Criteria 15. World Health Organization, Geneva, Switzerland. 109 pp.

WHO (World Health Organization). 1981. Pp. 1-174 in Environmental Health Criteria, Arsenic. World Health Organization, Geneva, Switzerland.

Wilber, C.G. 1983. Selenium: A potential environmental poison and a necessary food constituent. Charles C. Thomas, Springfield, Ill. 126 pp.

Yang, G., S. Wang, R. Zhou, and S. Sun. 1983. Endemic selenium intoxication of humans in China. Am. J. Clin. Nutr. 37:872-881.

Zook, E.G., J.J. Powell, B.M. Hackley, J.A. Emerson, J.R. Brooker, and G.M. Knobl, Jr. 1976. National Marine Fisheries Service preliminary survey of selected seafoods for mercury, lead, cadmium, chromium and arsenic content. J. Agric. Food Chem. 24:47-53.

6

Chemical Health Risk Assessment–Critique of Existing Practices and Suggestions for Improvement

ABSTRACT

This chapter and the previous one should be considered as a unit. A fourfold classification system of the mechanisms underlying adverse health effects is outlined below, which forms the basis for developing quantitative risk assessment approaches for both cancer and noncancer effects.

A detailed critique is then provided of existing Food and Drug Administration (FDA) risk assessments for polychlorinated biphenyls (PCBs) and methylmercury–representing the two most extensively documented examples of analyses underlying current regulatory levels for a carcinogen and a noncarcinogen in seafood, respectively. (In both cases, the committee finds considerable opportunity for improvement.)

The difficult issue of determining human intakes for a broad (though far from comprehensive) range of chemical contaminants in seafood is subsequently addressed. Estimates are made of national average daily intakes of various inorganic and organic contaminants via commercially marketed seafood, and for several organic carcinogens, upper-confidence-limit estimates of possible cancer risk are made. However, aside from the methylmercury example,[1] in the absence of better information on the population distribution of the dosage of contaminants to the U.S. population, it is impossible to make even tentative quantitative estimates of potentially significant noncancer risks. Of additional serious concern are the appreciable quantities of seafood consumed following noncommercial sport and subsistence tribal fishing.

Finally, an overview of opportunities for research on different categories of potential health impacts is presented, and conclusions are drawn from both this and the previous chapter. The principal conclusions are the following:

- From both natural and human sources, a small proportion of seafood is contaminated with appreciable concentrations of potentially hazardous organic and inorganic chemicals. Some of the risks that may be significant include reproductive effects from PCBs and methylmercury, and carcinogenesis from selected PCB congeners, dioxins, and some chlorinated hydrocarbon pesticides.
- Consumption of some types of contaminated seafood poses enough risk that efforts toward evaluation, education, and control of that risk must be improved.
- Present quantitative risk assessment procedures used by government agencies can and should be improved and extended to noncancer effects.
- Current monitoring and surveillance programs provide an inadequate representation of the presence of contaminants in edible portions of domestic and imported seafood, resulting in serious difficulties in assessing both risks and specific opportunities for control.

172

- Because of the unevenness of contamination among species and geographic areas, it is feasible to narrowly target control efforts and still achieve meaningful reductions in exposures.
- The data base for evaluating the safety of certain chemicals that find their way into seafood via aquaculture and processing is too weak to support a conclusion that these products are being effectively controlled.

The principal recommendations of the committee are as follows:

- Existing regulations to minimize chemical and biological contamination of the aquatic environment should be strengthened and enforced.
- Existing FDA and state regulations should be strengthened and enforced to reduce the human consumption of aquatic organisms with relatively high contaminant levels (e.g., certain species from the Great Lakes with high levels of PCBs, swordfish and other species with high methylmercury levels).
- Federal agencies should actively support further research to determine the actual risks from the consumption of contaminants associated with seafood and to develop specific approaches for decreasing these risks.
- Increased environmental monitoring should be initiated at the state level, as part of an overall federal exposure management system.
- States should continue to be responsible for site closures, and for issuing health and contamination advisories tailored to the specific consumption habits, reproductive or other special risks, and information sources of specific groups of consumers.
- There should be an expanded program of public education on specific chemical contaminant hazards via governmental agencies and the health professions.

INTRODUCTION

Part of the committee's charge was to review and summarize "the current status of regulations, guidelines, and advisory statements issued by Federal and State public health authorities on environmental contaminants in seafood." Its review was to specifically address contaminants defined by Food and Drug Administration (FDA) regulations as "avoidable or unavoidable." Then, based on this, the committee was asked to "assess how well the current regulatory framework protects the public health."

The committee was also charged with the task of reviewing and summarizing, specifically, the health risk assessment procedures used by FDA, the Environmental Protection Agency (EPA), and other regulatory authorities for priority environmental pollutants, including toxic metals and synthetic organic chemicals. In addition, the committee was asked to "recommend future research directions, as appropriate."

To set the stage for an examination of how current risk assessment procedures can be improved, the basic concepts underlying the mechanisms of action of toxic substances are articulated in the following section, along with quantitative ideas about dose-time-response relationships. Then an extensive critique of agency risk assessments for PCBs and methylmercury is provided. Finally, the committee addresses issues of exposure assessment and risks from other substances, and opportunities for further research on potential chemical health hazards.

BROAD CATEGORIZATION OF MECHANISMS OF DIFFERENT ADVERSE EFFECTS AND IMPLICATIONS FOR DOSE-RESPONSE RELATIONSHIPS

The concern from which much of our regulatory history has resulted is the potential carcinogenic effect of some contaminants. To a certain extent, this concern is based on the mutagenic mechanisms of cancer. For carcinogens that act by primary genetic mechanisms, there are good theoretical reasons to believe that at the limit of low dosage, the risk will be a linear function of exposure (Ehrenberg et al., 1983; Hattis, 1990a). However, as more is learned about the mechanisms of some other types of toxic effects–particularly reproductive effects and chronic degenerative neurological conditions (NRC, 1989, 1990)–concern about potential low-dose effects of other types has tended to increase. It is therefore important to clarify what the expectations should be for dose-response relationships from first principles, given the full range of causal processes that can lead to impairment of health.

Table 6-1 shows a categorization system for biological damage mechanisms that can be helpful in guiding basic choices in risk assessment modeling (Hattis, 1982, 1986). The system is intended to distinguish between different ways of looking at the likely mechanisms of disease causation that are encouraged by different groups of scientific disciplines.[2]

The focus of the scheme in Table 6-1 is to sort adverse effects according to the kinds of events that are likely to be occurring at either (1) subclinical dosage levels (doses that do not produce unusual function) or (2) preclinical stages in the development of the pathological process (i.e., the time before an overt manifestation of a latent disease, such as cancer, occurs). Under these conditions, one first asks

- Are the events occurring ordinarily fully reversible (or very nearly so), given a prolonged period with no further exposure to the hazard?

TABLE 6-1 Types of Health Hazards Requiring Fundamentally Different Risk Assessment Approaches

1. "Traditional" toxicity resulting from overwhelming body compensatory processes: below some threshold, in individuals who are not already beyond the limits of normal function without exposure, response is reversible.

- Traditional acute toxicity–Toxic action is completely reversible or proceeds to long-term damage within about three days of exposure (paralytic shellfish poisoning, puffer fish poisoning; probably many teratogenic effects).
- Traditional chronic toxicity--Toxic process typically proceeds to permanent damage over a period of several days to several months, due to either (1) reversible accumulation of a toxic agent (e.g., methylmercury, lead) or (2) accumulation of a slowly reversible toxic response (e.g., cholinesterase inhibition).

2. Effects resulting from insidious processes that are irreversible or poorly reversible at low doses or early stages of causation.

- Molecular biological (stochastic process) effects--Effects occur as a result of one or a small number of irreversible changes in information coded in DNA: mutagenesis, most carcinogenesis, and some teratogenesis.
- Chronic cumulative effects–Effects occur as a result of a chronic accumulation of many small-scale damage events: emphysema, noise-induced hearing loss, atherosclerosis, and probably hypertension; possibly depletion of mature oocytes.

If the answer to the first question is yes, then it will generally be appropriate to treat the condition within the framework of traditional toxicology.[3] Some examples of such reversible changes are the following:

- Buildup of a contaminant in blood or other tissues. It is rare for there to be a zero rate of excretion of any material. Given time and no further exposure, toxicant buildup should be reversible, although it can be quite prolonged. [Current estimates are that only about 9% of more persistent polychlorinated biphenyl (PCB) isomers may be metabolized or excreted per year in humans (Yakushiji et al., 1984).]
- Most enzyme inhibition (generally, even irreversible inactivation of enzyme molecules can be "reversed" through the synthesis of replacement molecules)
- Induction of short-term biological responses that act to maintain homeostasis (e.g., sweating in response to heat, tearing in response to eye irritation)

If the answer to the above question is no and events are likely to be occurring at subclinical exposure levels or preclinical stages that are not ordinarily reversible, the modeling of biological risks will have to be based on concepts that are fundamentally different from the homeostatic system/threshold paradigm. Examples of such irreversible or poorly reversible events include

- changes in genetic information or the heritable pattern of gene expression after these are effectively "fixed" into a cell's genome expression by replication;
- death of nonreplicating types of cells (adult neurons);
- destruction of nonregenerating structures (alveolar septa); and
- generation and buildup of incompletely repaired lesions (atherosclerotic plaques).

Appropriate modeling for conditions that are the result of irreversible or poorly reversible processes must be based fundamentally on the likely dose-response characteristics of the events that cause the basic irreversible changes. Once the primacy of such changes is established for a particular event, the analyst should then ask whether clinical manifestations are likely to be the direct result of only a few, or very many, individual irreversible damage events. If only a few events are believed to contribute directly to a particular clinical manifestation (e.g., a small number of heritable changes within a singe cell line leading to cancer), the effect can be considered a "molecular biological" disease. The risk assessment models used must follow from an understanding of the stochastic nature of the basic process. On the other hand, if thousands, millions, or billions of individual irreversible events directly contribute to a particular condition (e.g., very large numbers of individual neurons must die to cause the clinical manifestations of Alzheimer's or Parkinson's disease), the biological harm should be dealt with under the novel category of chronic cumulative conditions (see below).

Traditional Acute Toxicity

Three kinds of insights for acute toxicity risk assessment follow naturally from the homeostatic system paradigm of physiology and traditional toxicology:

1. There will be a series of toxic effects as different compensatory processes are overwhelmed and as impairment broadens from more- to less-sensitive cells and functions.

2. For each effect in each individual who is not already beyond the limits of normal functioning in the absence of exposure, there will be some subthreshold level of exposure that will be insufficient to produce the effect.

3. Individuals will differ in their thresholds.

A caveat to the general expectation of individual thresholds is that some tasks may so tax the capabilities of a system (perhaps, during fetal life, the struggle to mobilize metabolic resources to grow and differentiate as fast as possible so as to cope with the external world at birth) that any impairment of a key limiting functional parameter required for the task could compromise function to some degree. (This would also apply to reaction time for a driving task, for example.) Of particular relevance to the committee's task in this regard is the suggestion of some studies that dietary PCB exposure may be associated with either changes in birth weight (Fein et al., 1984; Sunahara et al., 1987; Taylor et al., 1989) or indices of neurological function in infants (Jacobson et al., 1985; Rogan et al., 1986).

The first job in assessing acute toxic effects is to define the series of acute responses to the disturbing influence in question. Ideally, the analysis should then attempt to determine (to whatever degree of precision is possible) the nature and magnitude of the dosage and the disturbance of physiological parameter(s) that are necessary to cause each type of acute toxic response, along with the frequency of each response in a diverse human population.[4]

Such mechanism-based analysis is, however, not common in the field. Rather, the current state of the art in those rare cases where acute toxic effects are treated quantitatively is to use probit equations (Finney, 1971) of the general form

$$\text{Probit of response} = a + b \ln (C^n T),$$

where a, b, and n are constants, C is external concentration, and T is exposure time; n represents the basic trade-off between intensity and duration of exposure, and b defines the breadth of an assumed lognormal distribution of threshold responses. Although some of the available animal data on irritant gases appear to be well summarized by equations of this form (Appelman et al., 1982), this is basically an empirical formula that does not incorporate quantitative representations of the various processes underlying toxicity. It is therefore difficult to decide what adaptations should be made in applying the empirical relationships to diverse subsets of humans.

Even more common, unfortunately, is the simple use of the no-effect level (NOEL)/"safety factor" analysis for arriving at acceptable daily intake (ADI) levels for chemical contaminants. Rather than estimate the numbers of people with specific degrees of particular effects, the general approach is to arrive at an ADI by a rule-of-thumb procedure derived from observed NOELs [or, more recently, no-adverse effect levels (NOAEL), after often contentious discussion over what effects are considered "adverse"], or sometimes low effect levels (LOELs) in animal experiments or human studies. When projections are made from animal data, generally a 100-fold "uncertainty factor" is allowed between the NOEL and the ADI (Dourson and Starra, 1983). The 100-fold factor is often decomposed as 10-fold to account for possible differences in sensitivity between humans and the most sensitive species tested and 10-fold to account for possible interindividual differences in susceptibility among humans.

This approach has a few advantages:

1. It is "quick and dirty"–relatively straightforward to apply and does not require complicated model building or analysis.

2. Through thousands of applications in the past, it is not yet known to have led to catastrophic adverse effects in humans (using Ozonoff's working definition of a "catastrophe" as an effect so large that even an epidemiological study can detect it (D. Ozonoff, Boston University School of Public Health, personal communication, 1990).

On the other hand, for the long term, the simple uncertainty factor approach has a number of disadvantages:

1. No one knows how protective it really is, either in general or in specific cases. What fraction of the diverse human population can be expected to experience adverse effects when exposed at the level calculated to be "acceptable" under the formula? (In general, there may be some finite fraction of individuals who, because of disease or other reasons, are marginal for biological functions affected by the chemical and who may be pushed beyond a functional threshold for an adverse effect by a small finite dose of the chemical.)[5]

2. The procedure incorporates one specific social policy standard for setting "acceptable" levels without making clear where technical analysis leaves off and policy/value analysis begins.

3. Effects are generally scored as either present (operationally, statistically significant) or not present (not statistically significant) at a particular dose. There is usually no quantitative analysis of the effects of sample size or the dose-response relationship for the effect in question.

4. There is no defined or obvious way to incorporate newer types of relevant data on human interindividual differences in

- rates of uptake/absorption for a constant environmental exposure ("exposure variability");
- rates of activating or detoxifying metabolism and excretion, producing differences in the concentration x time of active metabolites per unit of absorbed dose at the site of toxic action ("pharmacokinetic variability"); and
- differential risk of response ("response variability") for a given concentration x time of active metabolites at the site of toxic action.

In particular, the committee suspects that the inability of the uncertainty factor paradigm as usually formulated to incorporate newer types of relevant information into a systematic procedure for updating assessments of health hazards has tended to discourage both the collection and the analysis of potentially important data. One example of this is information on human interindividual variability in parameters that could affect susceptibility.

Table 6-2 outlines some idealized components of a full quantitative analysis of a noncancer health effect that is mediated by what is called a "functional intermediate" parameter. Such a parameter is generally a continuous variable that has a strong causal influence on performance of an important biological function (although it will not generally be the sole determinant of performance). It should, in turn, be affected by the toxin/exposure under study, and it should be reasonably likely that effects on the final health condition of concern are primarily mediated through effects on this functional intermediate parameter. For example, a key functional intermediate for some reproductive effects of PCBs may well be changes in birth weights (Fein et al., 1984; Jacobson et al., 1985; Sunahara et al., 1987; Taylor et al., 1989). Similarly, blood or tissue concentrations of lead constitute a useful intermediate parameter for lead toxicity.

TABLE 6-2 Elements of a New Analysis for Noncancer Health Effects Mediated by a "Functional Intermediate" Parameter

1.	Elucidate the quantitative relationships between internal dose/time of toxin exposure and changes in the functional intermediate parameter.
2.	Assess the preexisting "background" distribution of the functional intermediate parameter in the human population.
3.	Assess the relationship between the functional intermediate parameter and diminished physiological performance or adverse health effects.
4.	Assess the magnitude of parameter changes likely to result from specific exposures in humans (taking into account human interindividual variability in metabolism and other determinants of pharmacokinetics) and consequent changes in the incidence and severity of health effects.
5.	Do not attempt, from the biology alone, to determine "acceptable" levels of parameter change or exposure. (Let policymakers decide what changes in the incidence and severity of health effects are "acceptable" in the context of modes of exposure and in light of the feasibility of reducing or avoiding exposure.)

The illustrative calculations in Table 6-3 (from Ballew and Hattis, 1989) show how modest changes in the population distribution of a key parameter such as birth weight can be reflected in serious changes in the outcome of infant mortality. It can be seen that birth weights are very strongly related to infant mortality and that the relationship is continuous. Although very low birth weight infants are at dramatically higher risk than infants in the normal weight range, even infants weighing about 3,000 grams (g) can be expected to have their risks increased somewhat by an agent that causes a marginal change in birth weight. As indicated in the table, because there are many more infants in the 2,500-3,500-g weight range, the expected population aggregate mortality increase is as large for these categories as the population aggregate mortality increase for infants in the very low birth weight range (500-1,500 g).

TABLE 6-3   Expected Infant Mortality Effects of a 1% (33.66-g) Reduction in Birth Weight

Weight Range (g)	Fraction of Births		Mortality Risk per 1,000 Births in Category	Fraction of Births x Mortality Risks/1,000		
	Original Population	After 1% Weight Reduction		Without Birth Weight Reduction	After 1% Birth Weight Reduction	Net Change
White Infants						
Under 500	0.0006912	0.0007701	1,000	0.6912	0.7701	0.0789
500-999	0.002171	0.002335	673.31	1.4612	1.5720	0.1107
1,000-1,499	0.005249	0.005488	237.85	1.2485	1.3053	0.0568
1,500-1,999	0.009182	0.009575	76.86	0.7057	0.7360	0.0302
2,000-2,499	0.029192	0.032804	26.746	0.7808	0.8774	0.0966
2,500-2,999	0.15164	0.16568	8.3565	1.2672	1.3845	0.1174
3,000-3,499	0.36237	0.37081	4.2566	1.5424	1.5784	0.0359
3,500-3,999	0.31749	0.30337	3.0451	0.9668	0.9238	0.0430
4,000-4,499	0.10100	0.09027	3.0293	0.3060	0.2734	0.0325
4,500+	0.021021	0.01890	4.941	0.1039	0.0934	0.0105
Total	1	1		9.0736	9.5142	0.4406
Black Infants						
Under 500	0.0026095	0.0028661	1,000	2.6095	2.8661	0.2566
500-999	0.006279	0.006666	645.90	4.0558	4.3058	0.2500
1,000-1,499	0.012709	0.013154	167.98	2.1348	2.2096	0.0748
1,500-1,999	0.020673	0.02165	57.72	1.1932	1.2495	0.0563
2,000-2,499	0.067052	0.074351	21.482	1.4404	1.5972	0.1568
2,500-2,999	0.24894	0.26444	9.832	2.4476	2.6000	0.1524
3,000-3,499	0.38248	0.37936	6.636	2.5381	2.5174	0.0207
3,500-3,999	0.20683	0.19100	5.581	1.1543	1.0660	0.0883
4,000-4,499	0.04418	0.04029	5.89	0.2602	0.2373	0.0229
4,500+	0.008253	0.006226	12.33	0.1018	0.0768	0.0250
Total	1	1		17.9358	18.7257	0.7899

In principle, the use of such intermediate parameters can provide windows on the pathological processes that occur earlier in the development of toxicity, are more sensitive to the action of potential toxicants (compared with attempts to observe actual cases of illness), and are more accessible to direct comparative measurement in both animal models and humans. It is desirable, for these purposes, that the intermediate parameters chosen be as close as possible to the actual causal pathway leading to harm. However, even a parameter such as birth weight, which may not itself bear a direct causal relation to infant deaths, may be a close enough indicator of the actual causal processes to serve as a useful intermediate predictor.

Because there will generally be a series of steps in the sequence between toxin uptake and ultimate manifestation of adverse effects, the analyst may often have choices of which parameter(s) to use for assessing human risk. These choices will generally be based on the availability of measurement techniques and theory for observing or estimating the parameter(s) in question.

Traditional Chronic Toxicity

The basic principles that govern the analysis of acute toxic effects are by and large directly applicable to cases of chronic toxicity. Chronic toxic analyses tend to differ from analyses of acute toxic effects primarily in that considerable emphasis must be placed on the "slow step" of the process, which causes the effect to be chronic rather than acute. This slow step is generally either a long-term accumulation of a toxic agent that is poorly excreted under ordinary conditions (e.g., lead, mercury) or an accumulation of some slowly reversed residual effect (e.g., acrylamide).

With lead as an example, the following statements can be made:

● Appreciable information is available on the pharmacokinetics of lead absorption, transport, storage, and excretion (Barry, 1975; Bernard, 1977; Campbell et al., 1984; Chamberlain, 1985; Marcus, 1985a-c; Rabinowitz et al., 1976); and much better information could be obtained with the aid of natural experiments such as strikes among lead-exposed workers, which can give information on the rate of decrease of blood lead levels after a reduction in exposure (Hattis, 1981).

● Inhibition of heme synthesis enzymes at essentially all dose levels is well characterized (Haeger-Aronsen et al., 1974), and the inhibition of heme synthesis may be important in producing some of the neurotoxic effects of lead (Silbergeld et al., 1982), although the short- and long-term functional significance of different degrees of inhibition in different individuals is far from clear.

● Effects on some measures of neurological function and kidney function are susceptible to study in reasonably straightforward ways. Effects on higher-order development of central nervous system functions are more difficult to determine because of an ignorance of basic mechanisms; however, some good studies have become available in recent years (Baker et al., 1983; Bellinger et al., 1987, 1990; HHS, 1988; Needleman et al., 1979, 1990; Waternaux et al., 1989). The impairment of very complex neurological functions by lead raises a significant issue in the application of the traditional toxicological paradigm to risk analysis. As indicated above, the usual assumption is that there is some functional reserve capacity in "normal" individuals that maintains "adequate" performance despite a "small" degree of perturbation of a biological parameter by a "low" dose of toxic material. However, if the function is already taxed to its limit in certain situations, even in the absence of exposure (perhaps for a first grader learning to read or for a developing fetus mobilizing all its available metabolic energy to grow and differentiate), and if the biological parameter being perturbed is limiting to the performance of that function, then any level of exposure may produce at least some reduction in performance.

Addressing the issues of the population distribution of different functional reserve capacities, and the relationship of functional reserve capacities to specific biochemical parameters, is essential to the future research needs of risk assessment for classical chronic toxic agents. Also in the area of neurotoxicology, Silbergeld (1982) has written of the potential of new radioimmunoassay and functional measurement techniques to help shift the focus of research away from traditional morphological criteria of neurological damage toward more sensitive and sophisticated measures of performance.

Molecular Biological (Stochastic Process) Diseases

In addition to most carcinogenesis, molecular biological diseases include mutagenesis and at least some teratogenesis. The subject of quantitative risk assessment for carcinogenic hazards has been discussed extensively elsewhere (American Industrial Health Council, 1987; Bishop, 1987; Crump et al., 1976, 1977; EPA, 1986a; Hattis, 1982; Hattis and Smith, 1986; Moolgavkar, 1986; Rai and Ryzin, 1981; Whittemore, 1980). However, it is worth briefly recapitulating some basic features of the carcinogenic process and their implications for cancer dose-response relationships.

Science is now much closer than it was a decade ago to understanding the fundamental mechanisms involved in carcinogenic transformation. For some time it has been clear that tumors arise as a result of a series of changes or rearrangements of information coded in DNA within single cells (Cleaver and Bootsma, 1975; Fialkow, 1977; Hattis, 1982; Knudson, 1973, 1977; McCann et al., 1975; Vogel and Motulsky, 1979). These changes are often induced by electrophilic metabolites of the parent compounds to which organisms are exposed (Miller and Miller, 1981). With the identification of "oncogenes," some detailed molecular characterization is being provided of the changes resulting in DNA (Fischinger and DeVita, 1984; Hoel, 1985; Modali and Yang, 1984; Yunis, 1983).

It has also been apparent for some time that further headway cannot be made in elucidating the shapes of carcinogenesis dose-response relationships at low dosages simply by increasing the numbers of animals studied in conventional bioassays. A variety of mathematical models with dramatically different consequences for low-dose risk can always be found that fit the observations about equally well (Maugh, 1978; Whittemore, 1983). Low-dose risk projections are, therefore, inevitably much more determined by the choice of model than by the available data (Guess et al., 1977; Whittemore, 1980), if what is meant by "data" is restricted to observations of the incidence of ultimate adverse effects in small groups of animals.

Because of sample size limitations, animal carcinogenesis bioassays must be done within a limited range of relatively high dose levels. Typically, the difference between the minimum detectable response and a response that effectively saturates the system or causes interference through overt toxicity is only one to two orders of magnitude (often even less). Over this high dose range near levels where the agent produces overt toxic effects, enzyme saturation and other forms of pharmacokinetic nonlinearities are most likely. If in dose-response modeling for risk assessment, the nonlinearities of pharmacokinetic origin are not separated from the nonlinearities that may arise from the multiple mutation mechanism that is central to carcinogenesis, our ordinary curve-fitting procedures will implicitly attribute the pharmacokinetic nonlinearities to the fundamental carcinogenic process (Hoel et al., 1983). The resulting errors are particularly serious if one wishes to produce the best point estimates of carcinogenic risk in addition to upper confidence limits.

Clearly, to make real progress in modeling carcinogenic risks, knowledge of the fundamental processes involved must be used to break open the black box between external exposure levels and ultimate production of tumors. The use of pharmacokinetic models and intermediate parameters ("markers") to characterize the dose-response characteristics of small segments of the causal pathway to carcinogenesis has considerable potential to improve dose-response modeling for the process as a whole (Hattis, 1988). Such markers can include both those that may lie directly along the causal pathway, such as DNA adduct formation, and putative correlates, such as hemoglobin adduct formation, that can be good indicators of the concentration-time product of active intermediates in the systemic circulation.

One key fact must be recognized from the beginning about pharmacokinetic modeling, however. Whatever nonlinearities may be produced at high doses by the saturation of enzymes, the saturation of active transport processes, the depletion of cellular reactants for electrophilic agents, or changes in cell division rates to make up for cell killing due to overt toxicity, all of these nonlinearities must necessarily disappear as one approaches very low dose rates (Hattis, 1990a). The slope of the line relating ultimate DNA lesions in replicating cells to external dose may well be very different at low than at high doses, but it must be linear. The basic reason for this is that at low doses the rates of the transport and transformation processes that lead to DNA damage and repair depend directly on the number of collisions between molecules of an "input" chemical (or activated intermediate or DNA adduct) and a resident cellular reactant (or hole in a membrane or repair enzyme molecule). At low doses the number of resident cellular reactant molecules does not change appreciably as a function of the concentration of the input. Therefore, the number of relevant collisions and the rates of reactions and side reactions in the causal sequence at low dosage must be direct linear functions of the amounts of input chemical and its activated derivatives. Some finite fraction of the ultimate DNA lesions must escape repair before the next cell replication as long as the cells affected have a nonzero turnover rate, there are a finite number of repair enzyme molecules, and the repair molecules operate at a finite rate.

All carcinogens – in particular the PCBs and dioxins – are not thought to act primarily by causing DNA mutations (Safe, 1989). Table 6-4 lists a variety of other types of mechanisms whereby chemicals can affect carcinogenesis. There has been a tendency in some quarters to assume that if a chemical does not act via a primary genetic mechanism, one should revert to the traditional toxicological paradigm for analysis, including all of the old presumptions about thresholds and safety factors (Weisburger and Williams, 1983). As Rodericks (1989) has noted,

> There is disagreement about how to estimate risks from carcinogens. In the United States, regulatory agencies generally estimate risks in the same way for both genotoxic and non-genotoxic carcinogens. Regulatory agencies adopt this position because they believe that full knowledge of the mechanism of action of non-genotoxic agents is needed before they can be assumed to exhibit thresholds. In several foreign countries, non-genotoxic carcinogens are generally assumed to have thresholds below which there is expected to be no risk. The disagreement is not confined to official government positions; some scientists prefer to treat non-genotoxic carcinogens as having thresholds, some do not.

In the view of the committee, the quantitative implications of the many and diverse mechanisms listed in Table 6-4 must be worked out on a case by case basis. Even for specific types of mechanisms for which some data are available, as in the receptor binding studies that provide a framework for understanding the multiple effects of PCBs and dioxins, the implications for the shape of the dose-response relationship at

TABLE 6-4   "Indirect" Mechanisms of Carcinogenesis

Indirect processes that enhance the rate of "initiation" (the initial change or rearrangement of information in DNA that places a cell on a pathway to cancer):

1. Changes in basic transport processes (e.g., low-fiber diets may prolong the residence time of feces in the gut, leading to greater exposure of the intestinal epithelium to reactive agents).

2. Changes in metabolic processing (e.g., induction of enzymes such as some mixed function oxidases that convert chemicals to forms that can directly react with DNA).

3. Changes in the effective amount of target tissue available for carcinogenesis (e.g., by simple hyperplasia).

4. Changes in the efficiency of DNA repair [e.g., inhibition of DNA repair by some metals (Zakour et al., 1981) or enhancement of cell replication (leaving less time for repair before a DNA lesion can be fixed into the genome as a permanent mutation)].

Indirect processes that alter the frequency with which "initiated" cells progress through subsequent stages in the carcinogenic process:

1. Induction of subsequent genetic changes: Many promoters appear to be capable of inducing the expression of Epstein-Barr virus antigens (Takada and Zur Hausen, 1984). Additionally, some "promoters" reportedly lead to the generation of active oxygen species that may damage DNA and lead to subsequent somatic mutations along the pathway to carcinogenesis without themselves being converted to compounds that react directly with DNA (Kinsella and Radman, 1978).

2. Changes in the frequency with which initiated cells are effectively removed by terminal differentiation [e.g., effects of early and multiple pregnancies in reducing later breast cancer risk (Kampert et al., 1988; Layde et al., 1989; Moolgavkar et al., 1980)].

3. Release of initiated cells from growth control by neighboring cells
    ● Mimicry of the action of a growth regulator or hormone by an introduced substance. [Phorbol esters alter the binding and phosphorylation of epidermal growth factor receptors (Friedman et al., 1984; McCaffrey et al., 1984). The very high-affinity binding of 2,3,7,8-tetrachlorodibenzodioxin (TCDD) to the AH receptor induces an increase in transcription of the genes that code for certain P-450 isozymes, among other effects (Whitlock, 1989). Genetic studies suggest that the AH receptor is necessary but not sufficient for the activity of halogenated aryl hydrocarbons as skin tumor promoters in hairless mice (Safe, 1989).]
    ● Inhibition of the action of normal growth suppressing substances. [Phorbol esters inhibit the binding of somatostatin (Zeggari et al., 1985).]
    ● Inhibition of the passage of growth inhibitors among cells by many chlorinated aromatic compounds (Tsushimoto et al., 1983).
    ● Killing of neighboring cells responsible for repression of initiated cells.
    ● Induction of cell replication among initiated cells, interfering with the ability of repressors to pass tight junctions or isolating some daughter cells from tight junctions.

4. Changes in the rates of proliferation or survival (without terminal differentiation) of initiated cells relative to the proliferation and survival of normal cells (theoretical mechanism suggested by Moolgavkar and Knudson, 1981).

Indirect processes that might alter the survival, growth and spread of tumors, or the progression of tumors to increased malignancy:

1. Changes in hormonally mediated processes that might speed up the growth of specific cell types (e.g., estrogens and some breast cancers).

2. Changes in the efficiency of immune surveillance in destroying incipient tumors at early stages. Some observations suggest that tumor promoters may alter the functioning of "natural killer" cells (Kabelitz, 1985). Immunosuppressive effects have also been observed for some promoters in vivo (Pasquinelli et al., 1985).

3. Changes in local tissue conditions that favor colonization of new tissues by metastases (e.g., the establishment of tumor blood supplies).

SOURCE: Adapted from Hattis and Strauss (1986).

low doses will depend on some key facts that are not yet known. For receptor-binding mechanisms, the number of receptors that must be bound per relevant cell to cause or contribute to the carcinogenic transition must be known. If that number is large, and if only a few of these receptors are usually occupied by their normal substrate, then the dose-response relationship for PCB and dioxin effects might well be threshold-like, or at least highly nonlinear. On the other hand, if the occupation of only a single receptor site can lead to a relevant cellular transition, then as for a mutagenic mechanism, a linear dose-response relationship would be expected at low doses.

Generally, U.S. regulatory agencies adopt linear, no-threshold models and do not depart from them unless there is overwhelming scientific evidence to show that they are incorrect in specific cases. This is a prudent posture to take, until evidence of the details of specific nongenetic mechanisms is detailed enough for different low-dose assumptions to be indicated very clearly.

Chronic Cumulative Conditions

Chronic cumulative conditions include neurological conditions caused by the cumulative loss of neurons (e.g., Parkinsonism, Alzheimer's disease), emphysema and other chronic lung diseases, atherosclerosis, and hypertension. This new category is required because the underlying mechanism of these conditions – slow accumulation of many irreversible or poorly reversible damage steps – departs significantly from paradigmatic mechanisms that provide the basis for the three other, more traditional categories. These conditions are likely to be increasingly important as the population shifts to progressively older ages, and as continued progress is made in preventing and treating diseases that afflict younger people. For example, from 1969 to 1985, the percentage of nursing home residents with a primary diagnosis of a mental disorder rose from 11 to 22% (Hing, 1989, p. 9).

Theoretically, the approach that should be taken in developing risk assessment models for individual conditions within this new category is to

1. describe the fundamental mechanism(s) that causes individual damage events to accumulate (especially the quantitative significance of various contributory factors);
2. elucidate quantitatively the ways in which specific environmental agents enhance the production or prevent the repair of individual damage events; and
3. describe the relationships between the numbers, types, and physical distribution of individual damage events and the loss of biological function or clinical illness.

Unfortunately, no examples are known in which there has been successful quantitative modeling of any of these three types for any chronic cumulative condition. Often, the qualitative nature of individual damage events is not difficult to discern. For example, atherosclerotic lesions are thought to be produced by a sequence of events described by Ross and Glomset (1976). However, no one has yet successfully developed a predictive model that relates the frequency or severity of these events to the various internal and external causal factors that must be involved. This is clearly an area that requires basic biomedical research, as well as creative interaction between mathematical modelers and experimentalists.

A couple of consequences of importance here, however, follow from the basic nature of the cumulative irreversible processes that define this category. First, it is important to recognize that the damage processes must be proceeding continually under quite usual everyday situations. This requires viewing with some suspicion the usual presumption of the traditional toxicological paradigm that the common adaptive responses to everyday insults are harmless. For diseases such as atherosclerosis, which proceed silently and chronically in ordinary individuals throughout their lives, homeostatic protective mechanisms must be failing in subtle ways rather frequently. It is likely that there are thresholds that give rise to the small-scale damage events of chronic cardiovascular disease processes [for example, perhaps the lining of the arterial wall in a particular region only suffers appreciable damage when systolic blood pressure temporarily goes above 180 millimeters (mm) of mercury (Hg)]. However, whatever thresholds exist must be low enough to produce a sufficient accumulation of net damage to account for the observation that atherosclerosis and long-term blood pressure increases with age occur in very large numbers of "normal" people.

TABLE 6-5 Dose-Response Relationship of Parkinson's Disease Risk and Blood or Hair Mercury (Hg) Levels by Approximate Subject Tertiles

Hg Level[a]	No. of Cases	No. of Controls	Adjusted Odds Ratio[b]	95% Confidence Interval
Blood (ng/mL)				
0.0- 5.8	6	46	1.0	
5.9-14.2	20	28	8.5	2.2-33.2
≥14.3	28	21	9.4	2.5-35.9
Hair (ppm)				
0.0-4.0	10	42	1.0	
4.1-6.9	15	33	1.8	0.6-5.2
≥7.0	29	20	4.1	1.6-10.5

[a] ng = nanograms; mL = milliliters; ppm = parts per million.
[b] Odds ratio after adjustment by conditional logistic regression for cigarette smoking, alcohol consumption, seafood intake, and ethnic medication.
SOURCE: Ngim and Devathasan (1989).

Second, the basic concept of these diseases as accumulations of many small damage events implies that the number of damage events accumulated by different individuals will show a broad continuous distribution. Because of this, any agent that accelerates the production or prevents the repair of such damage events will shift all, or a very large part, of the exposed population in the direction of worse function. For example, noise exposure will cause people who would otherwise have excellent hearing to have less excellent hearing; people who might have fair hearing without noise can expect to be shifted toward poor hearing, and so forth.

Many years ago, Weiss and Spyker (1974) suggested that methylmercury might accelerate the loss of neurons in adult life and contribute to a "chronic cumulative" process that would fall within this category. Recently, an apparently very sound case control epidemiological study among people in Singapore found a strong association between blood levels of mercury and the risk of Parkinson's disease (Ngim and Devathasan, 1989) (Table 6-5). Parkinson's disease occurs when a large portion of the neurons responsible for making dopamine in the substantia nigra area of the brain is lost. Thus, if the association with mercury exposure holds and proves causal in later studies, it would be a very important basis on which to quantitatively reevaluate the long-term risks of seafood mercury consumption.

CRITIQUE OF RISK ASSESSMENTS USED IN FORMULATING CONTAMINANT GUIDELINES/TOLERANCES FOR SPECIFIC CHEMICALS AND SUGGESTIONS FOR IMPROVEMENT

One of the charges to the committee was to review and critique previous agency efforts to assess the likely human risks of chemical contaminants of aquatic organisms. The committee was asked to suggest directions for the improvement of risk assessment approaches to better serve the needs of decision making on chemical risks, but not to attempt to develop its own set of final risk numbers. The committee has chosen to focus on PCBs and methylmercury as two paradigmatic cases, representing one carcinogen and one noncarcinogen, for which there is a relatively sufficient public record of FDA efforts to assess the risks and benefits of alternative control options.

The PCBs are of special interest in light of the results presented in this chapter (Table 6-30). By using conventional carcinogenic risk assessment techniques (although these have considerable difficulties in general and especially as applied to PCBs) and available data on likely average daily intakes in the United States, PCBs are shown to pose by far the largest *potential* carcinogenic risk of any environmental contaminants for which measurements exist. According to EPA's cancer potency factor, the aggregate U.S. lifetime risk could be as high as 6×10^{-5}, corresponding to approximately 120 cancers per year. With FDA's lower estimate of the upper confidence limit (UCL) of the PCB cancer potency, the aggregate risk for the U.S. population would be considerably less, but still not insignificant, 2.7×10^{-6}, implying a maximum toll from commercial seafood of about 5 cancers per year. These risks would be much greater for the subpopulation consuming relatively large amounts of sport or subsistence caught fish near the FDA tolerance level of 2 parts per million (ppm). For someone who consumes 20 kilograms (kg) per year of 20-ppm fish [which is probably not far from the actual consumption of some individuals in some areas of Lake Michigan (Humphrey, 1983a,b)], the upper-confidence-limit lifetime risk that would be expected by using the FDA cancer potency estimates is about 5×10^{-4}; for the EPA cancer potency estimate, the lifetime upper-confidence-limit risk would be somewhat more than 1%. Perhaps in part because of the difference in cancer potency factors, there is also a great difference in the practical policies of the two agencies in regulating PCBs, with FDA generally taking a far less protective posture toward PCB exposure than EPA.[6]

Methylmercury is also of special interest because it shows the operation of the old no-effect level/safety factor paradigm in a practical case where, as it happens, an alternative type of quantitative assessment is also possible based on existing data. In this case, therefore, one can examine what levels of risk might implicitly be accepted by using FDA's rule-of-thumb procedure for dealing with noncancer effects.

In the following material, the committee will assess for both cases

• the reasonableness of the calculations that went into FDA's decision making in terms of the information available at the time; and

• the improvements that could and should be made by applying more modern analytical techniques to recently available or feasibly obtainable data on population   exposures, the nature and mechanisms of potential adverse effects, and likely   population dose-response relationships.

To briefly foreshadow the committee's conclusions, three statements can be made:

1. Both assessments (Cordle, 1983; Cordle et al., 1982; FDA, 1979; Tollefson and Cordle, 1986), even at the times they were done, suffered from ad hoc unsystematic approaches to the treatment of population heterogeneity in dosage and (for methylmercury) susceptibility to adverse effects. For mercury, the likely special susceptibility of developing fetuses was mentioned in discussion. However, a tenfold "safety factor" was applied to the lowest blood level reported to produce effects for adults (rather than to a no-effect level of intake, which would have been more consistent with established procedures) in the cited epidemiological studies, without numerical allowance for extra sensitivity of fetuses, without a quantitative dose-response treatment of the data then available for adults to gauge the potential adult risk at the blood level selected as the highest permissible for U.S. consumers, and without a quantitative treatment of the effects of pharmacokinetic differences among people that would tend to make blood levels and risks as a function of dietary intake more variable than blood levels themselves.

2. Procedures for the systematic quantitative analysis and communication of uncertainties are absent. Both analyses use the "method" of compounding a series of ad hoc allegedly "conservative" assumptions (such as the use of the consumption level of the 90th percentile consumer, the upper 99% confidence limit for the PCB animal potency calculation, but a body weight rather than a surface area scaling rule to translate animal to human dose). The difficulty in picking a single series of point estimates of uncertain parameter values is that after the first few such assumptions have been entered into an analysis, no person on earth can determine where one actually is on an overall distribution of the likelihoods of different outcomes. Monte Carlo simulation procedures are now readily available via personal computer-based software for the calculation of probability density functions of different outcomes, given uncertainties in multiple parameters affecting population risk. Such procedures have been effectively advanced in the context of risk assessment in a recent report by Finkel (1990).

3. Both assessments have been rendered substantially obsolete by the development of recent information related to PCB and to methylmercury risks, changes in the economic conditions assumed in the cost analyses, and possibly changes in residue levels and available options for population exposure reduction.

• In the case of PCBs, understanding of mechanisms has advanced to the point where there are now serious proposals for a congener-specific assessment of relative activity (Clement Associates, 1989; Jones, 1988). In the view of the committee, this congener-specific activity analysis must be coupled with a congener-specific treatment of pharmacokinetics, which now seems possible based in part on the human dietary exposure and serum concentration data being collected by Humphrey and coworkers (H. Humphrey, Michigan Department of Public Health, Lansing, personal communication, 1989). Both congener-specific activity estimates and pharmacokinetics should be used to evaluate not only existing animal carcinogenesis data, but also recently emerging epidemiological information from studies in workers.

- In the case of methylmercury, recent data allow preliminary evaluation of the population dose-response relationship for a number of long-term neurological effects from exposure during fetal development (Marsh et al., 1987). The analysis in the following section indicates that the apparent interindividual variability in susceptibility for fetal effects is much broader than that for adult effects. Consequently, although the tenfold safety factor, as applied, appears to offer a reasonable degree of protection for adult effects, projections based on an additional toxicological assumption of lognormal distribution of threshold for effects (logprobit projections) of the fetal dose-response data suggest the possibility of appreciable risk from methylmercury exposure, even at levels to which many people are exposed via the diet. Published projections applying a logistic model to the same data come to similar conclusions (Cox et al., 1989).

Polychlorinated Biphenyls (PCBs)

Background

The PCBs originally came to the attention of FDA through a series of contamination incidents in which PCB-containing oils leaked from electrical equipment directly into food substances, such as rice oil in Japan and Taiwan (the "Yusho" incidents), and by various routes found their way into U.S. livestock.[7] The initial concerns were direct overt toxicity and reproductive effects, and acceptable daily intakes were defined as 100-fold and 10-fold below the no-effect levels in animals and humans, respectively. Table 6-6 is from Scheuplein (1988).

To this day, FDA analyses continue to reflect and even emphasize calculations within the NOEL/safety factor paradigm that was initially used to interpret animal and human data on the risk of overt chronic toxicity. Thus, Scheuplein (1988) compares FDA's 1 microgram (μg)/kg/day ADI to the observations of Humphrey (1983a) that average PCB intakes in a group of heavy eaters of fish[8] from Lake Michigan were 1.75 μg/kg/day:

> No symptoms or adverse health effects clearly related to PCB ingestion could be identified in the exposed group. This suggests that FDA's acceptable intake level of 1.0 μg/kg-day provides reasonable safety, although it is possible that effects too subtle for detection are occurring or that the latency periods for cancer are very long.

From work reported to EPA (Humphrey, 1983b) and other data reported later by Humphrey (1988), it appears that the cited work had only a very small health component (major emphasis was on defining exposures). The health component seems to have been a simple medical history questionnaire administered to the participants, asking them about 18 specific conditions. Table 6-7 shows the percentage of fish eaters and the comparison group that reported various past medical complaints. This limited presentation of the data, without confidence limits or sample sizes, may not do justice to the underlying work. Clearly, however, this kind of study was not designed to be a very sensitive detector of carcinogenic risk or other types of effects (e.g., on fetal development) that are the concerns at low doses. Carcinogenic risks are traditionally studied in human populations by case control studies and detailed comparisons of the frequency of specific cancers or cancer deaths in defined cohorts, adjusted for age. Reproductive effects must clearly involve careful follow-up of offspring in groups where–through either dietary analysis or serum studies–it is possible to define prenatal exposures. The fact that the Humphrey (1983a) work is seriously cited as evidence of no effect–and that other work (e.g., Fein et al., 1984; Jacobson et al., 1985) that does suggest fetal effects from the same general Michigan fish eater population is not cited–is perhaps testimony to FDA's general lack of enthusiasm at the prospect of departing from the NOEL/safety factor paradigm.

TABLE 6-6   FDA Projection of Human Acceptable Levels for PCBs

Study	No-Effect Level (μg/kg body weight/day)[a]	Acceptable Daily Intake (μg/kg body weight/day)[a]	Reference
Subchronic (rats and dogs)	250-300	2.5-3.0	FDA file data
Yusho data (actual 50-day exposure)	200	20	Karatsune and Fukuoka, Acta Med. Med. 23(117), 1971[b]
Yusho data (assuming 1,000-day exposure)	10	1	Fed. Reg. 38(129), July 6, 1973

[a] μg = micrograms.
[b] This is the reference given by Scheuplein (1988). The Toxline data base lists a paper that seems to roughly correspond to Yamaguchi, A., T. Yoshimura, and M. Kuratsune. 1971. A survey on pregnant women having consumed rice oil contaminated with chlorobiphenyls and their babies. Fukuoka, Acta Med. 62(1):117-122 (1971).
SOURCE: Scheuplein (1988).

TABLE 6-7 Percentage of Humphrey (1983b) Study Participants Reporting Histories of Various Medical Conditions

Condition	Fish Eaters	Comparison Group
Diabetes	4.6	5.9
Heart attack	6.8	3.9
Hypertension	21.1	18.4
Kidney problems	2.2	1.2
Cancer	5.5	4.7
Liver problems	2.4	2.0
Other conditions	11.5	14.3

SOURCE: Humphrey (1988).

FDA Assessment of Costs and Risks for PCBs in Fish

The most recent detailed statements concerning FDA assessment of the carcinogenic risks of PCBs appear to be in two papers by Cordle (1983) and Cordle et al. (1982). These recapitulate and give more details of the analysis underlying the official risk assessment that appeared in the *Federal Register* (FDA, 1979) promulgating the 2-ppm tolerance (lower than the former 5-ppm guideline).

When the committee reviewed FDA's official analysis (FDA, 1979), it was surprised to find that FDA had actually calculated a series of aggregate estimates of economic costs incurred and cancer cases prevented by going to different standard levels (Table 6-8). This analysis appears to have been done in part to satisfy requirements for a balancing analysis of benefits and costs that became a government-wide requirement for regulatory action in the mid-1970s. For this purpose, however, the calculation of societal aggregate cancer risks from 90th percentile values of consumption for fish consumers is problematic because, of course, the 90th percentile overstates the average. Therefore, the committee has recalculated the balance struck by FDA in terms of the 50th percentile of fish eaters (Table 6-9). This probably results in a small error in the opposite direction, because of the likely skewed distribution of PCB consumption among fish consumers.[9] The committee's aggregate national average estimate of current PCB exposure from fish (see Table 6-31) is slightly less than 0.01 μg/kg/day. This compares quite well with the national aggregate estimate implied by Table 6-9 for the situation after implementation of the 2-ppm tolerance (0.012 μg/kg/day), if there is essentially no exposure of any but the 15% of the population covered by the FDA fish eater analysis.

It should be stressed that FDA (1979) did not juxtapose the incremental costs and benefits of different possible tolerance reductions, as has been done in Tables 6-8 and 6-9. Had it done so, FDA might at least have been led to some explicit comment on the closeness (within twofold) of the incremental cost/benefit ratio of the regulatory step it declined to take (from 2 to 1 ppm) to the incremental cost/benefit ratio of the regulatory step it did take (from 5 to 2 ppm). If FDA really intended this result, then an unusually specific insight is afforded into the value it attached implicitly to the prevention of a unit of upper-confidence-limit cancer risk.

Instead, it appears that the FDA decision was most influenced by the concentration of the regulatory impact expected for commercial harvesting of freshwater fish. Whereas the 2-ppm tolerance was expected to cause the loss of a negligible portion of the commercial marine catch (less than 0.2%), the same regulation was expected to cause the loss of 14% of the freshwater catch. For the 1-ppm standard, the loss of freshwater fish was expected to increase to 35%. In its conclusion commenting on the choice of the 2-ppm level, FDA focuses on the absolute magnitude of the losses expected from the 2-ppm and 1-ppm alternatives:

> . . .the agency estimates that under a tolerance of 1 ppm, approximately $16 million worth of the commercial fish catch would be violative and thus, presumably, removed from commerce. This is nearly triple the $5.7 million worth estimated to be violative under a 2 ppm tolerance. It is far more likely under a 1 ppm tolerance than under a 2 ppm tolerance that the more heavily contaminated species of freshwater fish would be violative in percentages high enough to put an end to their commercial exploitation and, possibly, force some segments of the freshwater fishing industry to cease operations completely. Thus, the actual loss of food resulting from the 1 ppm tolerance could

greatly exceed even the $16 million landed value (1974 dollars) estimated above. Second, for the average consumer, current exposure to PCBs in fish is at a tolerably low level, when considered in the light of the criteria of section 406 of the act [Food, Drug, and Cosmetic Act], without a 1 ppm tolerance. The average consumer eats a modest amount of fish from a variety of sources, both freshwater and marine, most of which yield fish with PCB levels below 1 ppm. Because their exposure is thus low to begin with, they are adequately protected by a 2 ppm tolerance, which ensures that they will not be exposed to the unusually high levels of PCBs found in some species of fish. The slight additional protection these average consumers might gain from a 1 ppm tolerance does not justify the significantly greater impact such a tolerance would have on the availability of food. On the other hand, atypical heavy consumers (e.g., the Great Lakes sport fisher who catches and consumes large quantities of the contaminated species) would likely not be adequately protected by even a 1 ppm tolerance because of the amount of fish they eat and because those fish are seldom affected by FDA tolerances (either because they are sport fish or are from intrastate commercial channels and, in either case, are outside FDA's jurisdiction).

TABLE 6-8   FDA Risk and Cost Calculations for PCBs

A. Incremental Health Benefits

PCB Fish Tolerance Level (ppm)	Heavy Consumers' Projected Dose (μg/day)	UCL[a] Lifetime Individual Risk for Heavy Consumers	Aggregate UCL No. of New Cancers per Year for Heavy Consumers	Incremental[b] Savings of UCL Cancers per Year
5	20.1	9.8×10^{-5}	46.8	
2	14.9	7.2×10^{-5}	34.3	12.5
1	9.1	4.4×10^{-5}	21	13.3

B. Incremental Costs and Cost/Benefit Ratios

PCB Fish Tolerance Level (ppm)	Projected Cost in Lost Landings (1974 $/yr)	Incremental[c] Cost (1974 $/yr)	Implied Incremental Cost/Benefit Ratio (1974 $/UCL cancer)
5	600,000		
2	5,700,000	5,100,000	410,000
1	16,700,000	10,300,000	770,000

[a] Upper confidence limit. The numbers in this column imply a low-dose cancer potency of about 0.34 cancer case per lifetime average mg/kg/day exposure.
[b] Numbers in this column reflect the reduction in annual UCL-estimated cancers attributable to lowering the standard from 5 to 2 ppm, and from 2 to 1 ppm.
[c] Numbers in this column reflect the increase in annual lost landings cost attributable to lowering the standard from 5 to 2 ppm, and from 2 to 1 ppm.
NOTE: Aggregate projections were apparently made by assuming that all 33 million consumers of the species of interest had intakes at the 90th percentile.
SOURCE: FDA (1979).

Table 6-8 also derives the FDA implied upper-confidence-limit cancer potency factor for PCBs of about 0.34 case/(mg/kg/day), compared to the current EPA estimate of 7.7 cases (EPA, 1989). The bulk of this difference stems from a traditional disagreement between EPA and FDA on how to perform interspecies extrapolation, with FDA favoring the translation of effective doses in mg/kg of body weight and EPA favoring the "surface area" extrapolation rule – mg/(kg body weight)$^{2/3}$. Some additional portion of the difference derives from the fact that EPA has used more recent experiments with Aroclor 1260 for its risk calculations (Norback and Weltman, 1985), whereas FDA used data on the overall tumor risk from an experiment with Aroclor 1254, which produced the highest estimate of risk from studies then available (Cordle et al., 1982).

In the context of the carcinogenic risk assessment practices of its time, the FDA quantitative analysis does not greatly depart from established principles. On the theory (discussed above) that cancer is the result of a multiple series of somatic mutations, a hypothesis of low-dose linearity in carcinogenic response is not at all unreasonable, particularly if carcinogenic transitions caused by one agent can interact with some of the processes that cause the vast number of "background" cancers in the human population. An upper-confidence-limit risk derived from the multistage theory guarantees low-dose linearity in risk estimates and thus provides a convenient benchmark for risk even though a "mean-estimate" (which would be more helpful for cost/benefit comparisons of the type shown in Table 6-9) risk is not easily produced.

TABLE 6-9 Results of Revising the Aggregate Risk Calculations to Reflect and Assumption that Consumers Had Intakes at the 50th Percentile[a]

A. Incremental Health Benefits

PCB Fish Tolerance Level (ppm)	Median Consumers' Projected Dose (μg/day)	UCL[b] Lifetime Individual Risk for Heavy Consumers	Aggregate UCL No. of New Cancers per Year for Heavy Consumers	Incremental Savings of UCL Cancers per Year
5	7.57	3.7×10^{-5}	17.6	
2	5.59	2.7×10^{-5}	12.9	4.7
1	3.3	1.6×10^{-5}	7.7	5.2

B. Incremental Costs and Cost/Benefit Ratios

PCB Fish Tolerance Level (ppm)	Projected Cost in Lost Landings (1974 $/yr)	Incremental Cost (1974 $/yr)	Implied Incremental Cost/Benefit Ratio (1974 $/UCL cancer)
5	600,000		
2	5,700,000	5,100,000	1,100,000
1	16,700,000	10,300,000	2,000,000

[a] This probably understates aggregate risks somewhat.
[b] Upper confidence limit. The numbers in this column are based on a low-dose cancer potency of 0.34 cancer case per lifetime average mg/kg/day exposure.

One can question the practice of summing up tumors from all sites in terms of the multistage theory, but this is not unusual in the context of risk assessment practices in the late 1970s and early 1980s. The choice of animal to human extrapolation formulas is open to considerable discussion in the field to this day, although in the specific case of PCBs, from some limited positive epidemiological studies in PCB-exposed workers,[10] Allen et al. (1987) have estimated a TD_{25} (the lifetime dose estimated to produce cancers in 25% of exposed people) of 0.15 mg/kg/day (for 45-year, 240-day/year occupational exposures).[11] This translates into the equivalent of a best-estimate cancer potency factor of 3.9 cases per lifetime mg/kg/day dosage – rather closer to the EPA upper confidence limit estimate of 7.7 than to the FDA estimate of 0.34 case per lifetime mg/kg/day.

Overall, FDA (1979) has been quite cautious in presenting the difficulties and uncertainties of carcinogenic risk analysis for PCBs from the data it had available:

> . . . the utility of this risk assessment for evaluating actual risk to humans from exposure to PCBs is extremely limited. This is due both to difficulties inherent in making such extrapolations from animals to humans and, perhaps more importantly in this instance, to gaps and uncertainties in the data available for this particular risk assessment. For example, the toxicity studies on which the risk assessment is based used commercial preparations of PCBs, which are chemically different from the PCB residues found in fish and which contain small amounts of highly toxic impurities (e.g., dibenzofurans) not known to be present in fish residues. [It should be noted, however, that these contaminants are also not known *not* to be present in fish.] Also, in making the exposure estimates required for the risk assessment, it was necessary to use existing data on the numerical distribution of PCB levels in fish and rely on the assumption that the effect of a given tolerance level is to remove from commerce all fish containing PCBs exceeding the tolerances. It is possible that neither the assumption nor the data precisely reflect what actually occurs.
>
> For these reasons and others . . . the risk assessment does not provide a basis for precise quantification of the amount of risk reduction accomplished by reducing the fish tolerance. Despite the limitations inherent in the risk assessment, however, the agency regards it as illustrative of the basic validity of the toxicological rationale for reducing the tolerance for PCBs in fish: Reduction of the tolerance will result in a significant reduction in risk among those who consume PCB-contaminated fish. FDA considers this risk reduction to be of significant public health value, even though it cannot be precisely quantified.

For this limited purpose, the analysis as presented may well have served an appropriate and useful function. However, there are now both an opportunity and a need to gather and analyze newer information, so that by the early to mid-1990s it will be possible to significantly improve on this 1979 effort.

Suggestions for Improved Analysis

First, a better regulatory impact analysis might evaluate *a wider range of choices* of regulatory alternatives – including not just different tolerance levels, but possible rules restricting the location of harvest, species, and size. Choices in these areas are likely to allow a more narrowly targeted regulatory action that will reduce human exposure to PCBs at less overall cost of forgone food resources. By being keyed to characteristics of fish that do not require expensive and time-consuming chemical analyses, such regulations might be much more efficiently implementable than tolerances based simply on chemical content.

Second, an improved analysis of carcinogenic risks should be based on a congener-specific assessment of (1) pharmacokinetics and (2) relative potency at the site(s) of action. The FDA analysis mentions the fact that the distribution of PCB congeners to which consumers are exposed is not the same as found in the commercial PCB preparations (e.g., Aroclor 1254) that were the subjects of carcinogenicity testing. The FDA specifically mentions the possibility of dibenzofuran contamination in the commercial mixtures used for carcinogenicity testing. Not mentioned, however, is the likely possibility that fish PCB residues may be relatively enriched in just those congeners that are more persistent in biological systems. More degradable congeners are almost by definition likely to be preferentially destroyed either in the fish themselves or in organisms that are lower on the food chain, whereas the original commercial mixtures would contain the full mix of more- and less-degradable congeners. Humphrey (1983b) noted a change over time in the distribution of PCB congeners found in human serum toward more highly chlorinated congeners, which tend to be more persistent in biological systems. Data now exist that would allow a detailed comparison of congener distributions in fish and humans with those in commercial mixtures (McFarland and Clarke, 1989).

At the same time, a long series of comparative studies by Safe (1989) and others has provided basic insights into the mechanisms of action of PCBs, dibenzofurans, and dioxins. It now appears likely that PCBs enhance carcinogenesis not by direct interaction with DNA, but through a receptor-binding mechanism (similar to dioxins) whose precise dose-response implications have not been elucidated. Receptor binding and related activities vary enormously among different congeners, with congeners that are planar in shape (and relatively highly chlorinated) appearing to have the greatest potency. Careful experiments relating tumor enhancement to the number, type, and persistence of specific PCB-receptor interactions in animal systems could yield important insights into the likely form of the dose-response relationships that should be applied to human risk assessment. There are now serious proposals for a congener-specific assessment of relative activity by using the existing data base (Clement Associates, 1989; Jones, 1988). This approach needs to be pursued and refined with additional laboratory and carcinogenesis studies.

A good opportunity may exist to reevaluate the accumulating evidence of human carcinogenic response in occupationally exposed populations with relation to serum PCB levels and to relate the human response per unit of delivered dose to the response per serum level likely to have been present in rodent bioassays. [There are two very limited but apparently positive epidemiological studies in groups of capacitor workers (Bertazzi et al., 1987; Brown, 1987) and at least one negative study at a plant in Massachusetts whose results have not yet been published in detail. In at least one case, there are measurements of serum PCB levels in the exposed group.] Harold Humphrey of the Michigan Department of Health reportedly has an extensive data set of PCB concentrations in blood in relation to dietary exposure levels. A series of congener-specific measurements is now in progress together with published measurements of metabolic rates of PCBs in humans (Buehler et al., 1988; Phillips et al., 1989; Yakushiji et al., 1984); this is likely to be useful in establishing metabolic rates of PCBs for comparison with animal models and measurements after the work by Matthews and Dedrick (1984) and Tanabe et al. (1981). Animal work, together with the newer metabolism information, appears capable of providing a basis for estimating serum PCB levels in the rats and mice that showed positive cancer responses in chronic bioassays. Projections to human risk could then be made on the basis of a more appropriate measure of "delivered dose" (weighted for different congeners by receptor binding and pharmacokinetics) rather than gross dietary intake. There already is reasonably good information on the population distribution of overall plasma PCB levels in the United States (as can be seen by the correspondence of the points to the straight line in Figure 6-1, these data are reasonably well described as lognormal).[12] Using such a distribution, if one had an estimate of cancer risk per unit of plasma PCB concentration, an inference could be made not only about the average risk to the population, but about the distribution of risk to various individuals that derives from differences in both dietary habits and PCB elimination rates. Plasma and whole body burden PCB levels could also be productively used as indicators of long-term dosage in epidemiological case control studies of cancer patients (versus other people) in communities near the Great Lakes with greater than usual numbers of people having high exposures to fish with appreciable levels of PCBs.

A better analysis should also include a quantitative assessment of the risks posed by prenatal exposure to PCBs, via such parameters as gestational period and birth weight, as well as subtle neurological measures of effect. The presence of at least modest effects on birth weight has recently been supported by an epidemiological study in workers (Taylor et al., 1989). Because birth weight is such an easy parameter to study (measurements are made routinely on nearly all newborns) and because it has a very strong relationship to infant mortality (Hogue et al., 1987), additional large population studies of birth weight and gestational period in relation to fish consumption and relevant serum PCB congener levels should be a high priority. Methodology exists to interpret birth weight changes in terms of other relevant endpoints such as infant mortality (Ballew and Hattis, 1989), but these techniques require validation with an actual case having large enough numbers of subjects to provide data on both the intermediate parameters (birth weight and gestational age) and the ultimate parameters of concern (infant mortality, impairment of neurological development, etc.).

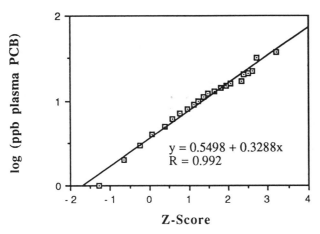

FIGURE 6-1 Plasma PCB levels in 738 Southern Californians screened prior to employment [data of Sahl et al. (1985)]

Finally, there is a need for improved and more systematic treatment of analytical uncertainties, with ultimate results in the form of cumulative probability density functions or, failing this, at least a statement of both best-estimate and upper-confidence-limit risks, under consistent and defensible theories.

Methylmercury

FDA Risk Assessment and Current Regulations

The published analysis of Tollefson and Cordle (1986) appears to be the most definitive public assessment by FDA personnel of the risks of methylmercury in fish. It is patterned after the NOEL/uncertainty factor analysis illustrated for PCBs in Table 6-6, but has distinctive elements that alter the usual risk acceptance posture somewhat.

The principal benchmark that Tollefson and Cordle (1986) use in defining an acceptable intake of methylmercury is the lowest blood methylmercury level that appeared to be associated with overt neurological symptoms of toxicity in a few studied mass poisoning incidents (two that occurred from fish taken from Minamata Bay and Niigata in Japan in the 1950s and 1960s, and one incident that arose from the consumption of contaminated seed grain in Iraq):

> A Swedish expert group evaluated data on human methylmercury toxicity derived from cases which occurred in Minamata and Niigata. The Swedish group determined (by extrapolation) that the lowest blood mercury level associated with toxic effects was 220 ppb [parts per billion] and the lowest hair mercury level associated with toxic effects was 50 ppm (Berglund et al., 1971).
>
> The Iraqi outbreak of methylmercury poisoning has been extensively studied by many investigators. The blood level of mercury at which symptoms of toxicity were first detected in the Iraqi episode was approximately 240 ppb [parts per billion] (Clarkson et al., 1976). This calculation was made on samples collected 65 days after the end of exposure, which is the approximate half-life of methylmercury in humans. Since the actual clearance times from the blood are not known, the level may lie between 240 and 480 ppb. These values are for adult exposures only.

Studies of people in Sweden who consumed relatively large amounts of fish allowed these blood levels to be related to dietary levels – at least on a population average basis (Tollefson and Cordle, 1986): "A linear relationship was found between daily ingested methylmercury and the level of methylmercury in blood, and the data indicated that a steady daily intake of approximately 300 μg Hg [mercury] as methylmercury for a 70-kg person would result in a blood concentration of roughly 200 ppb at steady state (Skerfving, 1974)."

This 300-μg/day dose rate, calculated to correspond to 200 ppb in blood *for an average person,* was interpreted by Tollefson and Cordle (1986) as

> a threshold value at which symptoms of toxicity associated with methylmercury are first noticeable. . . . Dose-response relationships below this range of intake are not known. In addition, there is concern about the relative sensitivity of the developing fetus. The question of interaction of other chemical factors such as selenium on the toxicity of methylmercury has not been conclusively demonstrated at this time, but may be a factor to be considered when more information is developed. Because of these areas of uncertainty, a safety factor of ten has been used to provide a sufficient margin of safety.

Thus a maximum tolerable level would be 30 μg methylmercury daily in the diet, resulting in 20 ppb of methylmercury in blood and 5 ppm in hair.

The following limitations to this approach were recognized: (1) it was not known to what extent particular individuals are more or less sensitive to mercury than others; (2) the estimates were based on the "lowest level that caused an effect" rather than the normal procedure of using a "no-effect dose level"; (3) paresthesia is usually the first symptom of methylmercury toxicity noted but is not sufficient to diagnose poisoning because it can be caused by many other factors (Clarkson et al., 1983); (4) questions about dose-response relationships in human fetuses and newborn infants were unanswered; and (5) there is a possibility of subclinical effects arising from exposure to very low levels of methylmercury.

Tollefson and Cordle (1986) therefore realize that they are departing from the usual procedure for the NOEL/safety factor analysis and that, in particular, risks to fetuses may not be represented adequately in the available data. However, they make no additional numerical adjustment for these uncertainties, presuming implicitly that the usual 10-fold safety factor has enough of a margin built into it to avoid an unacceptable level of risk.

In addition to these enumerated factors, there is a subtle point that makes the calculation on the basis of the average diet/blood relationship less protective than the usual calculation based on a 10-fold reduction from the dietary dose that is directly observed to be without effects. The 10-fold factor is supposed to represent the protection needed to guard against interindividual variability in the complete pathway from dietary intake to the production of biological responses. Some portion of that human interindividual variability, however, occurs in characteristics that affect individual blood levels – especially individual half-lives for elimination of methylmercury from the body. For those with relatively slow elimination rates, toxicity would be expected to be associated with lower average dietary intakes than for those with average elimination rates. Therefore, by doing the dose extrapolation in terms of blood levels, and translating the corresponding *average* dietary levels, the authors are being less protective than would have been the case had the 10-fold factor been applied to the minimum dietary dosage associated with an observed effect (or no observed effect). Later in the paper, Tollefson and Cordle (1986) discuss interindividual differences in biological half-lives for methylmercury as follows:

> Additional data developed on the biological half-life of methylmercury in humans, however, indicate a need to take into account the problem of variations among individuals. In the Iraqi episode, 90% of the individuals studied had a biological half-life of methylmercury between 60 and 70 days, but 10% showed values of 110 to 120 days (Al-Shahristani and Shihab, 1974). Individuals having a long biological half-life would accumulate much higher steady-state levels than those having short biological half-lives and would thus be at greater risk from the same level of methylmercury intake.

Tollefson and Cordle have unfortunately misread the population distribution of methylmercury half-lives presented in the cited paper. A figure in the paper is misleading in that the highest single observed biological half-life (189 days) has somehow been excluded, but there is no way that even the figure can be construed to indicate that 90% of the values are between 60 and 70 days. Had Tollefson and Cordle checked the detailed data presented in a table on the following page in the Al-Shahristani and Shihab 1974 paper, they would have seen the distribution shown in

TABLE 6-10 Biological Half-Lives for Individuals Reported
by Al-Shahristani and Shihab (1974)

Half-Life (days)	Rank Order	Percentage Score[a] [100 x (Rank - 0.5)/N]
37	1	1.04
38	2	3.13
43	3	5.21
43	4	7.29
44	5	9.38
45	6	11.46
45	7	13.54
50	8	15.63
51	9	17.71
51	10	19.79
51	11	21.88
52	12	23.96
54	13	26.04
57	14	28.13
57	15	30.21
58	16	32.29
58	17	34.38
62	18	36.46
62	19	38.54
62	20	40.63
65	21	42.71
66	22	44.79
66	23	46.88
66	24	48.96
67	25	51.04
69	26	53.13
69	27	55.21
71	28	57.29
73	29	59.38
75	30	61.46
75	31	63.54
75	32	65.63
76	33	67.71
78	34	69.79
78	35	71.88
79	36	73.96
83	37	76.04
85	38	78.13
87	39	80.21
89	40	82.29
91	41	84.38
93	42	86.46
117	43	88.54
118	44	90.63
119	45	92.71
120	46	94.79
120	47	96.88
189	48	98.96

[a] This is the percentage of an infinite sample that would be
expected to be equal to or below the stated half-life.

Table 6-10. It is apparent that overall there is a fivefold range of half-lives among the 48 people studied. Only 10 values (a little over 20%) fall between 60 and 70 days. As can be seen in Figure 6-2, the data are reasonably well described as a lognormal distribution. From the geometric standard deviation of that distribution (1.403), it would be expected that approximately 2% of the population would have half-lives more than twice the geometric mean of 68.3 days.

Tollefson and Cordle (1986) go on to support the results of their analysis by citing studies failing to find obvious methylmercury toxicity in heavy fish-eating population groups in Peru and American Samoa with average blood methylmercury concentrations in the range of 60-80 ppb (Marsh et al., 1974; Turner et al., 1980). However, without careful analysis of the distributions of thresholds implied by the earlier data, the sample sizes, and the degree of background symptoms in control groups in the negative studies cited, neither the reader nor the authors can judge the sensitivity of those studies to detect adverse effects and whatever quantitative implications there might be for the level of risk at lower doses.

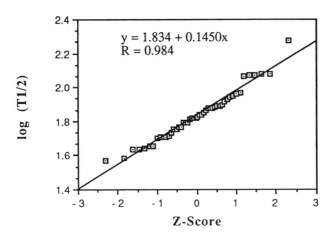

FIGURE 6-2 Lognormal plot of the distribution of methylbercury biological half-lives (data of Al-Shahristani and Shihab, 1974)

Tollefson and Cordle's apparent reluctance to construct and analyze the implications of quantitative population distributions is also seen in their treatment of the expected dietary dosage of methylmercury to consumers. They had available the results of a fairly extensive study commissioned by the Tuna Research Foundation (TRF) of one-month diary reports of consumption of different types of fish by 7,662 families, including 25,165 people, and measurements of mercury levels in different species of fish. However, instead of using these data to describe the population distribution of monthly mercury intakes from fish as a whole and the possible effects of different tolerances, Tollefson and Cordle (1986) opted for an ad hoc treatment of the data for only a few species of interest:

> Data from the TRF survey have indicated that the average consumption of all fish among the fish-eating population of the United States is 18.58 oz/month or approximately 18 g/day. Daily consumption of species containing relatively high levels

of methylmercury such as tuna, swordfish, or halibut would be considerably less. For example, the mean daily consumption of halibut is 7.2 g with two standard deviations increasing the total to 16.6 g. This would include some 97.5% of all consumers of halibut. The consumption of 16.6 g of halibut with 0.179 ppm mercury would provide a daily mercury intake of approximately 2.9 μg.

The mean daily consumption of swordfish is 6.53 g with a standard deviation of 2.5 g. If 11.53 g of swordfish with a mercury level of 1.5 ppm were consumed each day, and this would include over 95% of all swordfish eaters,[13] the daily mercury intake would be 17.3 μg, still below the ADI of 30 μg.

At the highest level of swordfish consumption shown by the NPD [National Purchase Dairy Panel, Inc.] study, i.e. 511 g in a month or 17 g per day, with a mercury residue of 1.5 ppm the daily mercury intake would be 25.5 μg, still below the ADI of 30 μg. If in addition to the highest level of consumption of swordfish in the NMFS [National Marine Fisheries Service] study, i.e. 17 g per day with a mercury residue of 1.5 ppm, the same individual consumed the average daily amounts of tuna, halibut, and salmon at the present average residue levels of mercury for each of the three species, then the total daily intake of mercury from all four species would average 31.7 μg, only 1.7 μg above the ADI. Such consumption, which would realistically be on a periodic basis to derive daily exposure, seems very unlikely, particularly since the cost of swordfish, halibut, and salmon is prohibitively high.

Tollefson and Cordle are certainly correct in concluding that very few consumers will exceed the 30-μg/day level for prolonged periods. However, this type of analysis cannot give an estimate of how many might, or how many might fall short of the 30-μg/day level by various amounts. The failure to analyze the data more rigorously is all the more unfortunate because the FDA had available an example providing statistically sophisticated treatment of these same data (NMFS, 1978).[14]

Tollefson and Cordle (1986) conclude with a somewhat unusual statement of the relevant risk issues:

> The data currently available for evaluating quantitatively the association of neurological symptoms of toxicity with exposure to methylmercury are sparse and inconsistent. Additional studies are being carried out on the prenatal effects of methylmercury to determine that this lifestage continues to be protected by the 1.0 ppm regulatory level for mercury in fish. However, even with the above-outlined uncertainties concerning the results of exposure in Japan and Iraq, where exposures were considerably higher than anything experienced in other countries, U.S. fish consumption data do not indicate any cause for concern of methylmercury poisoning for the *average American*. The majority of fish consumers could easily double their intake and still remain below the mercury ADI. The current 1.0 ppm regulatory level for marine species provides more than adequate protection *at the current average fish consumption levels in the U.S.* In addition, the enforced limit of 1.0 ppm mercury in marine fish provides a sufficient margin of safety for young children and for significant numbers of consumers exceeding the acceptable daily intake. (Emphasis added.)

The potential for a more quantitative analysis of methylmercury risks with the aid of available data on the distributions of blood methylmercury concentrations and dose-response data from the Iraqi poisoning incident is illustrated below. The aim is not to provide a definitive assessment of methylmercury risks, but to show an approach for improving the type of assessment now done by FDA.

Available Data on Blood Levels in the U.S. Population

Gathering and analyzing data on the actual distribution of blood mercury and methylmercury levels in the population allow one to bypass a great deal of the complexity of modeling individual dietary intakes over times long enough to determine biologically significant systemic exposures. Figure 6-3 shows a sample of mercury (Hg) blood levels from a fishing village in the United Kingdom (Haxton et al., 1979). Full data describing this distribution are not available; however, a plot of the median and extreme values given indicates that the distribution is well described as lognormal. The variability indicated by the $\log_{10}$ geometric standard deviation of 0.328 indicates that 95% of the population is spread out over a 20-fold range—between 4.5-fold above and 4.5-fold below the median blood level for the population. This variability includes both dietary and pharmacokinetic differences among individuals.

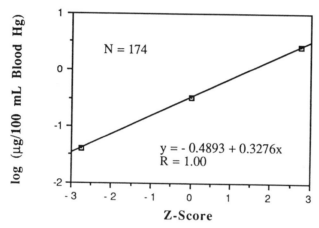

FIGURE 6-3 Lognormal plot of the Haxton et al. (1979) data on blood mercury concentrations (only the median and extreme values of the distribution were available for plotting)

Figures 6-4 – 6-6 show methylmercury (MeHg) blood level distribution data from two towns in Michigan, generously supplied to us by Harold Humphrey from unpublished data collected in the early 1970s. Algonac (population 3,684) was chosen because of its proximity to both Lake St. Clair and the St. Clair River—sites of a famous mercury contamination episode discovered by a Canadian graduate student in 1970. South Haven (population 6,471) was chosen as a control community with similar proximity to Lake Michigan. Figures 6-4 – 6-6 show the results from a portion of the study that consisted of randomly selected residents of each community. The distributions appear to be well described as lognormal (perfect lognormal distributions would appear as straight lines on this kind of plot), and the Algonac community distribution is translated distinctly upward from that of South Haven (medians at about 2.3 and 1.6 ppb, respectively). The degree of interindividual variability (the slope of the lines; the shallower the slope, the greater is the variability) is in each case similar to that inferred from the total mercury distribution observed by Haxton et al. (1979) (Figure 6-3).

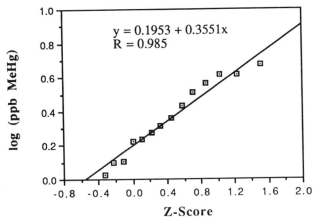

FIGURE 6-4 Lognormal plot of whole blood methylmercury levels in South Haven

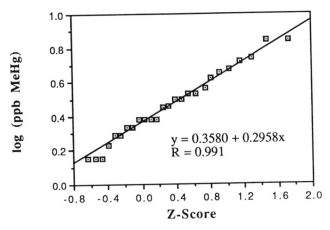

FIGURE 6-5 Lognormal plot of whole blood methylmercury levels in Algonac

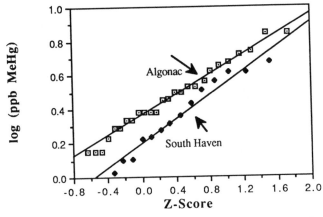

FIGURE 6-6 Comparison of blood methylmercury distribution in Algonac and South Haven

Methylmercury dose, blood levels, and population risks

Recently, Marsh et al. (1987) published detailed information on the incidence of a variety of fetal mercury effects in relation to the maximal levels of mercury found in the hair of the mothers during gestation. (The observations come from an Iraqi mass poisoning incident that resulted from the distribution of methylmercury-treated Green Revolution seed grain.) In all, 81 mother-infant pairs were studied. Table 6-11 shows the numerical results, grouped in fourfold ranges of dosage.

Figures 6-7 through 6-11 show $\log_{10}$ probit dose-response relationships for these effects. It can be seen that the $\log_{10}$ probit slopes for the five different fetal mercury effects range from 0.66 to 1.5 (the $\log_{10}$ probit slope is the number of standard deviations of the population distribution of effect thresholds per 10-fold change in dose, smaller numbers indicated a broader lognormal distribution of thresholds). These results show a very large range of variability. A slope of 1 indicates that 95% of the individual thresholds for effect would be spread over a 10,000-fold range, from 100-fold lower to 100-fold higher than the dose that would cause an effect in a median individual. Observations of the interindividual variability of human pharmacokinetic parameters indicate considerably narrower ranges of interindividual variability than suggested in this case (average chemicals giving $\log_{10}$ probit slope values on the order of 8-10, although a few chemicals are in the range of 2-3) (Hattis et al., 1987a,b).

One possible criticism of the fitting procedure represented in Figures 6-7 – 6-11 is that individual points have not been weighted for their relative degree of statistical power. Moreover, these simple probit plots necessarily exclude points at which either none or all of the subjects showed the response. To refine the analysis, therefore, the classical maximum likelihood procedure of Finney (1971) was used to fit the data in Table 6-11. This method corrects both statistical deficiencies mentioned above, provides a means to test the overall fit of the logprobit model to the data, and also measures the uncertainties of the fitted parameters (Table 6-12).[15]

By comparing these results with the regression equations given in Figures 6-7 – 6-11, it can be seen that in general the probit slopes calculated by the Finney (1971) procedure, with its fine weighing of the points and maximum likelihood estimation methods, are somewhat higher (indicating slightly less interindividual variability) than the simpler procedure without weighing. Overall, however, there is reasonably close agreement, and in any case, the conclusion appears unchanged that the Marsh et al. (1987) data indicate quite a large amount of interindividual variability. The mean $\log_{10}$ probit slope for the five effects as determined by the Finney (1971) procedure is about 1.18.

Such a conclusion, however, depends on whether the biomarker of exposure used in this case – the maximum hair mercury found at any time during gestation – is the most appropriate direct causal predictor of response that can be developed. Other possibilities might well include the concentration of mercury at a specific sensitive time during gestation or a weighted sum of concentration x duration over a specific set of sensitive periods. Accurate assessment of the degree of interindividual variability in susceptibility in humans, and consequent low-dose risks, might well depend on quantitative measurement and modeling of the causal processes involved in this case and reanalysis of the data according to the most likely causally predictive summary measure of delivered dose.

Publications by Bakir et al. (1973) and Clarkson et al. (1976) provide the basis

TABLE 6-11 Observations of Marsh et al. (1987) on the Incidence of Various Effects in Children Following in Utero Methylmercury Exposure

Effects

Maximum Hair Hg During Gestation			Late Walking (after 18 months)		Late Talking (after 24 months)		"Mental" Symptoms	
Range (ppm)	Geometric Mean	Number of Subjects	Number of Cases	Fraction Affected	Number of Cases	Fraction Affected	Number of Cases	Fraction Affected
1-3	1.37	27	0	0.000	2	0.074	1	0.037
5-19	10.00	14	2	0.143	1	0.071	0	0
20-79	52.53	13	2	0.154	3	0.231	1	0.077
80-319	163.38	12	3	0.250	4	0.333	3	0.250
Over 319	436.60	15	12	0.800	11	0.733	4	0.267

Effects

Maximum Hair Hg During Gestation			Seizures		Neurological Score over 3		Neurological Score over 4	
Range (ppm)	Geometric Mean	Number of Subjects	Number of Cases	Fraction Affected	Number of Cases	Fraction Affected	Number of Cases	Fraction Affected
1-3	1.37	27	0	0.000	3	0.111	0	0
5-19	10.00	14	0	0.000	1	0.071	1	0.071
20-79	52.53	13	1	0.077	4	0.308	2	0.154
80-319	163.38	12	2	0.167	3	0.250	2	0.167
Over 319	436.60	15	4	0.267	9	0.600	6	0.400

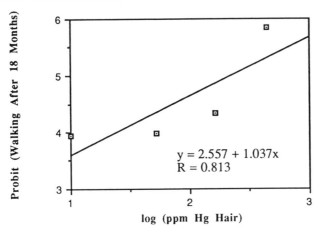

FIGURE 6-7 Logprobit dose-relationship for walking after 18 months in relation to maternal hair mercury (data of Marsh et al., 1987)

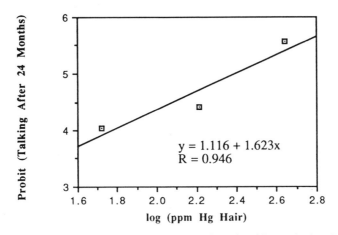

FIGURE 6-8 Logprobit dose-response relationship for talking after 24 months in reltion to maternal hair mercury (data of Marsh et al., 1987)

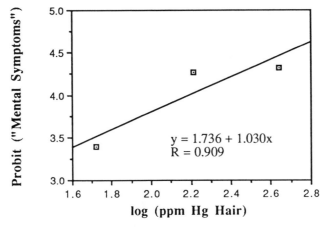

FIGURE 6-9 Logprobit dose-response relationship for "mental symptoms" in children in relation to maternal hair mercury (data of Marsh et al., 1987)

TABLE 6-12   Maximum Likelihood Fit[a] of the Marsh et al. (1987) Fetal Effects Data by Using the Method of Finney (1971)

Effect	Background Response (%)[b]	Probit Slope	Slope Standard Error	Intercept	ED$_{50}$ (ppb blood)	ED$_{50}$ Geometric Standard Error	Chi-Squared	Degrees of Freedom[c]	p[d]
Late walking	0	1.21	0.30	2.19	205	1.49	6.093	3	0.11
Late talking	7.3	1.76	0.71	0.81	244	1.38	0.689	1	0.41
Mental symptoms	2.4	0.99	0.76	1.88	1,429	4.75	0.351	1	0.55
Seizures	0	1.10	0.53	1.54	1,399	2.95	0.356	3	0.95
Neurological score >4	0	0.85	0.27	2.42	1,047	2.54	0.874	3	0.83
Average		1.18				Sum	8.363	11	0.68

[a] The equation fit is: probit of excess risk over background = intercept + (slope) x log$_{10}$ (blood Hg in ppb).

[b] Estimated from data in the lowest one to three dose groups.

[c] The number of dose groups available for analysis, less 2 for the number of parameters estimated from the data (intercept and probit slope).

[d] The probability that a deviation as large as that observed between the logprobit model and the data would have been expected by chance, even if the logprobit model were a perfect description of the underlying dose-response function.

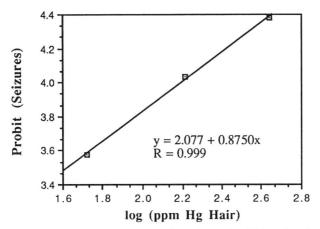

FIGURE 6-10 Logprobit dose-response relationship for seizures in children in relation to maternal hair mercury (data of Marsh et al., 1987)

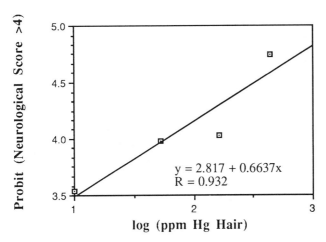

FIGURE 6-11 Logprobit dose-response relationship for adverse neurological scores in children in relation to maternal hair mercury (data of Marsh et al., 1987)

for similar treatment of the incidence of adult effects in relation to blood levels, at least as measured at a point approximately 65 days (on the order of one half-life) after the end of exposure. Table 6-13 summarizes the numerical results, and Figures 6-12–6-18 show the logprobit plots for the various effects (after subtraction of the apparent background incidence of the effects, as indicated by their observed frequencies in the lowest-dose groups). Figure 6-18 shows a plot of all the adult effects combined. The data can also

TABLE 6-13 Observations of the Incidence of Various Effects in Adults in the Iraqi Methylmercury Poisoning Incident

Observations of Various Adult Effects

ppb Blood Hg Measured About 65 Days After Exposure[a]			Paresthesias		Ataxia		"Visual Changes"	
Range	Assumed Mean	Number of Subjects	Number of Cases[b]	Fraction Affected	Number of Cases	Fraction Affected	Number of Cases	Fraction Affected
0-100	50	21	2	0.095	1	0.05	0	0
101-500	350	19	1	0.05	0	0	0	0
501-1,000	750	19	8	0.42	2	0.11	4	0.21
1,001-2,000	1,500	17	10	0.6	8	0.47	9	0.53
2,001-3,000	2,500	25	20	0.79	15	0.60	14	0.56
3,001-4,000	3,500	17	14	0.82	17	1.00	10	0.58
4,001-5,000	4,500	7	7	1.00	7	1.00	6	0.83

Observations of Various Adult Effects

ppb Blood Hg Measured About 65 Days After Exposure[a]			Disarthria		"Hearing Defects"		Deaths	
Range	Assumed Mean	Number of Subjects	Number of Cases[b]	Fraction Affected	Number of Cases	Fraction Affected	Number of Cases	Fraction Affected
0-100	50	21	1	0.05	0	0	0	0
101-500	350	19	1	0.05	0	0	0	0
501-1,000	750	19	1	0.05	1	0.05	0	0
1,001-2,000	1,500	17	4	0.24	0	0	0	0
2,001-3,000	2,500	25	6	0.25	3	0.125	0	0
3,001-4,000	3,500	17	13	0.75	6	0.36	3	0.17
4,001-5,000	4,500	7	6	0.85	5	0.66	2	0.28

[a] The numbers of cases shown here were inferred from percentages of affected subjects given in the paper and the numbers of subjects studied.
[b] The numbers of cases shown here were inferred from percentages of affected subjects given in the paper and the number of subjects studied.
NOTE: Because these measurements were done after the end of exposure, it is likely that they understate actual blood levels during exposure by about 2-fold.

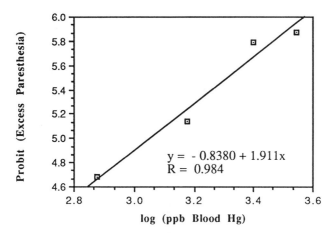

FIGURE 6-12 Logprobit dose-response relationship for "excess paresthesia"–Iraqi data

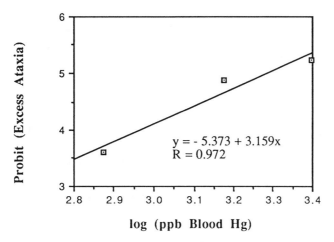

FIGURE 6-13 Logprobit dose-response relationship for "excess ataxia"–Iraqi data

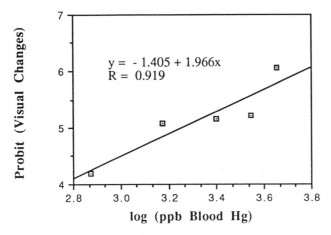

FIGURE 6-14 Logprobit dose-response relationship for "visual changes"–Iraqi data

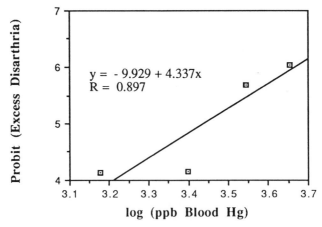

FIGURE 6-15 Logprobit dose-response relationship for "excess disarthria"–Iraqi data

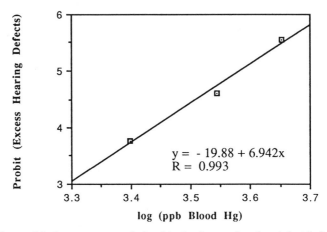

FIGURE 6-16 Logprobit dose-response relationship for "excess hearing defects"–Iraqi data

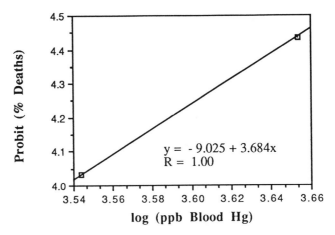

FIGURE 6-17 Logprobit dose-response relationship for percentage of deaths–Iraqi data

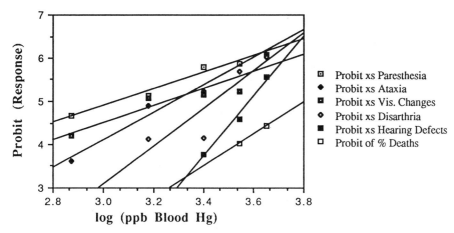

FIGURE 6-18 Logprobit dose-response relationships for all effects in adults-Iraqi data

be used to compare the probit slopes as determined by the Finney (1971) maximum likelihood fitting procedure (Table 6-15) with the simple linear regression procedure of Figures 6-7–6-11.

It can be seen that, as with fetal effects, the fuller analysis of data with the Finney (1971) procedure suggests somewhat larger probit slopes than the values determined by simple regression analysis of the points. It can also be seen that, in comparison with the fetal effects, the effects in adults tend to have larger probit slopes, indicating less interindividual variability and therefore less risk at low doses. Biologically, the implication is that the more complicated array of causal processes involved in producing fetal effects (allowing for variability in maternal mercury elimination, maternal/fetal transfer, and the time-sensitive processes of interference by methylmercury with development) tends to lead to more interindividual variability. From a social policy perspective, the implication is that the 10-fold safety factor rule, whatever its effectiveness in protecting exposed populations against the effects of interindividual variability in adults, appears likely to provide less protection for the developing organism.

Tables 6-12 and 6-14 show that the chi-squared statistical analysis indicates that the logprobit procedure provides an adequate overall fit for both the fetal and the adult data. Although this cannot be said to prove that the distribution of effect thresholds for methylmercury effects is in fact lognormal, it suggests that such an assumption is not grossly at variance with the available information. Moreover, it should be noted that logprobit analysis, as pioneered by Finney in earlier editions of his book, has been widely applied to toxicological data from animal experiments.

Tables 6-15 through 6-17 provide preliminary risk projections based on the lognormal threshold distribution model implicit in the Finney (1971) probit analysis and (for fetal effects) the same 4/1 translation of ppm hair levels into ppb blood levels used by Tollefson and Cordle (1986). Table 6-16 allows a preliminary appraisal of the difference in protection provided by the 10-fold safety factor in this case, when (as is not usual) the 10-fold factor is applied to blood levels. In part A of Tables 6-15 and 6-16, the committee has not corrected for the likely twofold underestimation of the adult blood levels associated with effects, which is related to the fact that the adult blood levels were measured 65 days after the end of exposure. The variants in part

TABLE 6-14 Maximum Likelihood Fits[a] of the Iraqi Adult Methylmercury Effects Data by Using the Method of Finney (1971)

Effects	Background Response (%)[b]	Probit Slope	Slope Standard Error	Intercept	ED_{50} (ppb blood)	ED_{50} Geometric Standard Error	Chi-Squared	Degrees of Freedom[c]	p[d]
Paresthesias	7.5	2.17	0.63	-1.64	1,145	1.24	1.155	2	0.76
Ataxias	2.5	3.92	0.76	-7.67	1,687	1.11	4.95	3	0.18
Visual changes	0	2.19	0.43	-2.24	2,006	1.16	3.695	3	0.3
Disarthria	5	4.67	1.36	-11.2	2,952	1.10	5.608	3	0.13
Hearing defects	1.3	6.42	2.17	-18.05	3,877	1.10	0.209	1	0.65
Deaths	0	7.58	3.19	-23.05	5,007	1.18	0.83	1	0.36
Sum for adult effects							16.447	13	0.22
Sum for fetal and adult effects						24.81	24	0.42	

[a] The equation fit is: probit of excess risk over background = intercept + (slope) x $\log_{10}$ (blood Hg in ppb).

[b] Estimated from data in the lowest one to three dose groups.

[c] The number of dose groups available for analysis, less 2 for the number of parameters estimated from the data (intercept and probit slope).

[d] The probability that a deviation as large as that observed between the logprobit model and the data would have been expected by chance, even if the logprobit model were a perfect description of the underlying dose-response function.

B of the tables show the results after this adjustment (no adjustment is required for fetal effects data because measurements made sequentially along hair shafts reflect methylmercury concentrations in maternal blood during pregnancy). It can be seen in Tables 6-16A and B that although a 10-fold reduction in blood level from the presumed adult LOEL is expected to reduce the incidence of adult effects to quite low rates, the greater interindividual variability associated with fetal effects suggests the possibility that very significant fetal risks may remain. The incidence of fetal effects projected by these probit risk relationships is appreciable, even for the actual population distributions of blood methylmercury levels observed in the Michigan communities (Table 6-17). It can also be seen in Table 6-17 that the bulk of the population excess fetal risk is expected to be found in portions of the population that do not have unusually high blood methylmercury levels (≤ 10 ppb).

Projections of fetal risks here, of course, are greatly affected by the assumed lognormal form of the distribution of thresholds for both adult and fetal effects. Although lognormal distributions appear to be broadly compatible with the high-dose data (see earlier figures), this is not the only statistical form that the distribution of thresholds might take. Cox et al. (1989) have applied a logit model, which assumes a different distribution of thresholds, to predict possible low-dose risks for one of the fetal effects covered here (late walking), using the same data set (Cox and coworkers also made projections based on scores for neurological impairment, but using a different cutoff for defining effect than the committee, thus rendering the risk projections noncomparable). The risk predictions are compared in Table 6-18. In the dose range of interest, it appears that the two different assumptions about the form of the population distribution of thresholds yield very similar results.

As mentioned earlier, it would be more common for a 10-fold safety factor to be applied to the dietary dosage of a toxicant, rather than to blood levels. To represent this for methylmercury, one must add to the logprobit risk equations an estimate of the interindividual variability in internal blood levels as a function of dietary intake. In principle, two factors should be considered in accomplishing this: (1) interindividual variability in absorption, and (2) interindividual variability in overall elimination of mercury from the blood. Methylmercury is relatively efficiently absorbed from food, so the influence of the first factor may well be small. For the second factor, fortunately the data of Al-Shahristani and Shihab (1974) are available, based on measurements of the decline in mercury levels with distance along hair shafts, interpreted in terms of time with the aid of measurements of individual rates of hair growth (Figure 6-2). Tables 6-19A and B (analogous to Tables 6-16A and B) show the results of translating the ED_{50}'s into equivalent daily dietary doses [ED_{50} (diet) = ED_{50} (blood) x 300/200], including the extra variability represented by the geometric standard

TABLE 6-15A Logprobit Projections of Risks of Adult and Fetal Methylmercury Effects, Based on Observations from Iraq of Effects as a Function of Blood and Hair Levels

Effects	Hair ED_{50} (ppm)	Blood ED_{50} (ppb)	Blood Levels Required for Different Degrees of Risk			
			ED_{10} (1.2816 SDs below ED_{50})	ED_{01} (2.3263 SDs below ED_{50})	$ED_{1/10,000}$ (3.719 SDs)	$ED_{1/million}$ (4.7536 SDs)
Adult						
Paresthesias		1,145	294	97	43	22
Ataxias		1,687	795	431	275	190
Visual changes		2,010	522	174	78	40
Disarthria		2,950	1,569	937	643	472
Hearing defects		3,880	2,449	1,684	1,280	1,022
Deaths		5,010	3,390	2,470	1,959	1,618
Fetal						
Late walking	205	819	72	9.9	0.71	0.10
Late talking	244	978	182	46.3	7.44	1.92
Mental symptoms	1,429	5,720	289	25.3	0.99	0.09
Seizures	1,399	5,600	383	43.0	2.33	0.27
Neurological score >4	1,047	4,190	132	7.9	0.18	0.01

NOTE: Hair ED_{50} equivalents are not given for the adult effects because the primary measurements were made in blood. Because the underlying blood mercury measurements for adults were made after the end of exposure, it is likely that they understate actual blood levels during exposure by about twofold; therefore, the blood levels associated with all the stated levels of risk should also be adjusted upward by about twofold.

TABLE 6-15B Logprobit Projections of Risks of Adult and Fetal Methylmercury Effects, Based on Observations from Iraq of Effects as a Function of Blood and Hair Levels (After a Twofold Upward Adjustment of Observed Blood Levels Because of Measurement Delay)

Effects	Hair ED_{50} (ppm)	Blood ED_{50} (ppb)	Blood Levels Required for Different Degrees of Risk			
			ED_{10} (1.2816 SDs below ED_{50})	ED_{01} (2.3263 SDs below ED_{50})	$ED_{1/10,000}$ (3.719 SDs)	$ED_{1/million}$ (4.7536 SDs)
Adult						
Paresthesias		2,290	588	194	44	15
Ataxias		3,370	1,591	862	381	208
Visual changes		4,010	1,044	348	81	27
Disarthria		5,900	3,140	1,875	944	566
Hearing defects		7,750	4,900	3,370	2,040	1,411
Deaths		10,020	6,790	4,940	3,240	2,360
Fetal						
Late walking	205	819	72	9.9	0.71	0.10
Late talking	244	978	182	46.3	7.44	1.92
Mental symptoms	1,429	5,720	289	25.3	.99	0.09
Seizures	1,399	5,600	383	43.0	2.33	0.27
Neurological score >4	1,047	4,190	132	7.9	0.18	0.01

NOTE: Hair ED_{50} equivalents are not given for the adult effects because the primary measurements were made in blood. Because the underlying blood mercury measurements for adults were made after the end of exposure, it is likely that they understate actual blood levels during exposure by about twofold; therefore, the blood levels associated with all the stated levels of risk should also be adjusted upward by about twofold.

TABLE 6-16A Projected Risks at the Presumed Adult Blood Methylmercury LOEL and at One-Tenth the Presumed Adult LOEL

Effects	Probit Slope	Blood ED_{50} (ppb)	SDs Below ED_{50} at Presumed Adult LOEL (200 ppb in blood)	Risk (expected fraction affected) at Presumed Adult LOEL	SDs Below ED_{50} at 1/10th Adult LOEL (20 ppb in blood)	Risk (expected fraction affected) at 1/10th Adult LOEL
Adult						
Paresthesias	2.170	1,145	2.64	0.050	3.81	6.8×10^{-5}
Ataxias	3.926	1,687	3.64	1.4×10^{-5}	7.56	Very small
Visual changes	2.192	2,010	2.19	0.014	4.39	5.8×10^{-6}
Disarthria	4.67	2,950	5.46	2.4×10^{-8}	10.13	Very small
Hearing defects	6.423	3,890	8.27	Very small	14.69	Very small
Deaths	7.582	5,010	10.60	Very small	18.19	Very small
Fetal						
Late walking	1.214	819	0.74	0.229	1.96	0.0251
Late talking	1.756	978	1.21	0.113	2.97	0.0015
Mental symptoms	0.988	5,720	1.44	0.075	2.43	0.0076
Seizures	1.100	5,600	1.59	0.056	2.69	0.0035
Neurological score >4	0.854	4,190	1.13	0.130	1.98	0.0237

NOTE: Because the underlying blood mercury measurements for adults were made after the end of exposure, it is likely that they understate actual blood levels during exposure by about twofold; therefore, the blood levels associated with all the stated levels of risk should also be adjusted upward by about twofold.

TABLE 6-16B Projected Risks at the Presumed Adult Blood Methylmercury LOEL, and at One-Tenth the Presumed Adult LOEL (After a Twofold Upward Adjustment of Observed Blood Levels Because of Measurement Delay)

Effects	Probit Slope	Blood ED_{50} (ppb)	SDs Below ED_{50} at Presumed Adult LOEL (200 ppb in blood)	Risk (expected fraction affected) at Presumed Adult LOEL	SDs Below ED_{50} at 1/10th Adult LOEL (20 ppb in blood)	Risk (expected fraction affected) at 1/10th Adult LOEL
Adult						
Paresthesias	2.170	2,290	2.3	0.011	4.47	4.0×10^{-6}
Ataxias	3.926	3,370	4.82	7.3×10^{-7}	8.74	Very small
Visual changes	2.192	4,010	2.85	0.0022	5.05	2.3×10^{-7}
Disarthria	4.67	5,900	6.87	Very small	11.54	Very small
Hearing defects	6.423	7,750	10.20	Very small	16.63	Very small
Deaths	7.582	10,020	12.89	Very small	20.47	Very small
Fetal						
Late walking	1.214	819	0.74	0.229	1.96	0.0251
Late Talking	1.756	978	1.21	0.113	2.97	0.0015
Mental symptoms	0.988	5,720	1.44	0.075	2.43	0.0076
Seizures	1.100	5,600	1.59	0.056	2.69	0.0035
Neurological score >4	0.854	4,190	1.13	0.130	1.98	0.0237

TABLE 6-17 Projected Effects for the Blood Methylmercury Distributions Observed in South Haven and Algonac, Michigan (Humphrey, 1974)

| Effects | Population Risk for South Haven Distribution | | | Population Risk for Algonac Distribution | | |
	Fraction of People Expected to be Affected	Population Risk (%) Due to Blood MeHg ≤10 ppb	≤20 ppb	Fraction of People Expected to be Affected	Population Risk(%) Due to Blood MeHg ≤10 ppb	≤20 ppb
Adult						
Paresthesias	1.2×10^{-7}	9	40	1.0×10^{-7}	17	61
Ataxias	Very small[a]			Very small[a]		
Visual changes	1.9×10^{-9}	3	22	1.2×10^{-9}	8	43
Disarthria	Very small[a]	Very small[a]				
Hearing defects	Very small[a]	Very small[a]				
Deaths	Very small[a]	Very small[a]				
Fetal						
Late walking	3.7×10^{-3}	88	98.2	5.3×10^{-3}	90	99.0
Late talking	1.6×10^{-5}	48	82	2.1×10^{-5}	58	91
Mental symptoms	4.5×10^{-4}	87	97.9	6.3×10^{-4}	89	98.3
Seizures	1.4×10^{-4}	82	96.6	2.0×10^{-4}	85	98.3
Neurological score >4	2.5×10^{-3}	92.2	98.9	3.4×10^{-3}	93.0	99.4

[a] Less than 10^{-10}.
SOURCE: Humphrey (1974).

TABLE 6-18 Comparison of Logit Versus Probit Risk Projections

Maternal Hair Hg Level (ppm)	Assumed Blood Hg (ppb)	Cox et al. (1989) Logit Model Risk Estimates (% excess risk)	Probit Model Risk Estimates (Table 6-16b) (% excess risk)
1	4	0.52	0.25
5	20	2.5	2.5
50	200	19	23

deviation of the blood half-lives,[16] and recalculating the risks expected at the presumed adult LOEL and 1/10th the presumed adult LOEL. The effect of this is to increase the estimate of the probit slope by a relatively greater amount for those effects that, in the absence of the adjustment, had relatively small amounts of interindividual variability (high probit slopes). The corresponding estimates of adult risks are increased, but generally not by a huge factor, for the adult effects expected to pose the numerically greatest risks.

Conclusions and Recommendations for Changes in Risk Assessment Practices

As indicated even by these two examples (PCBs and methylmercury), where FDA has devoted much more attention to two types of residues than to other potential chemical hazards of seafood consumption, the agency lags badly in the development of innovative methodology for assessing risks and evaluating the potential benefits of different options for control. This is all the more unfortunate because FDA has major technical resources available in both risk assessment and experimental toxicology (including reproductive toxicology) at the National Center for Toxicological Research in Arkansas. Neither the PCB nor the methylmercury analyses by FDA show evidence of input from this very capable group, which is under FDA's jurisdiction.

Carcinogenesis risk assessment procedures should be modified to give decision makers additional information about the uncertainties of the analysis, as well as both societal aggregate and individual risk estimates. In particular, to facilitate evaluation of the costs and benefits of measures to achieve quantitative reductions in exposure to carcinogenic inadvertent contaminants, procedures should be developed to supplement current "upper-confidence-limit" cancer potency estimates with estimates representing the central tendency of cancer risks, information on cancer risks from all available species, and comparative information on the pharmacokinetic and pharmacodynamic factors in different species.

The FDA is most conspicuously backward in the development of quantitative risk assessment approaches for noncarcinogens. The rule-of-thumb (ADI/NOEL/safety factor) procedure now universally in use has serious conceptual flaws, inappropriately mixes technical and social policy presumptions in analysis, and fails to encourage the development of better information on pharmacokinetics, human interindividual variability, and other topics that could allow better estimates to be made of human risk for noncancer effects.

TABLE 6-19A Projected Risks at the Presumed Adult Diet Methylmercury LOEL and at One-Tenth the Presumed Adult LOEL

Effects	Probit Slope	Diet ED_{50} (μg/day)	SDs Below ED_{50} at Presumed Adult LOEL (300 μg/day in diet)	Risk (expected fraction affected) at Presumed Adult LOEL	SDs Below ED_{50} at 1/10th Adult LOEL (30 μg/day in diet)	Risk (expected fraction affected) at 1/10th Adult LOEL
Adult						
Paresthesias	2.067	1,717	1.57	0.059	3.63	1.4×10^{-4}
Ataxias	3.400	2,530	3.15	8.2×10^{-4}	6.55	Very small
Visual changes	2.086	3,009	2.09	0.018	4.17	1.5×10^{-5}
Disarthria	3.850	4,427	4.50	3.4×10^{-6}	8.35	Very small
Hearing defects	4.670	5,815	6.01	9.24×10^{-10}	10.68	Very small
Deaths	5.063	7,512	7.08	Very small	12.14	Very small
Fetal						
Late walking	1.195	1,229	0.73	0.232	1.93	0.0270
Late talking	1.700	1,467	1.17	0.121	2.87	0.0020
Mental symptoms	0.978	8,574	1.42	0.077	2.40	0.0082
Seizures	1.086	8,392	1.57	0.058	2.66	0.0039
Neurological score >4	0.847	6,282	1.12	0.132	1.97	0.0246

NOTE: Because the underlying blood mercury measurements for adults were made after the end of exposure, it is likely that they understate actual blood levels during exposure by about twofold; therefore, the blood levels associated with all of the stated levels of risk should also be adjusted upward by about twofold.

TABLE 6-19B Projected Risks at the Presumed Adult Diet Methylmercury LOEL and at One-Tenth the Presumed Adult LOEL (After a Twofold Upward Adjustment of Observed Blood levels Because of Measurement Delay)

Effects	Probit Slope	Diet ED_{50} (μg/day)	SDs Below ED_{50} at Presumed Adult LOEL (300 μg/day in diet)	Risk (expected fraction affected) at Presumed Adult LOEL	SDs Below ED_{50} at 1/10th Adult LOEL (30 μg/day in diet)	Risk (expected fraction affected) at 1/10th Adult LOEL
Adult						
Paresthesias	2.067	3,430	2.19	0.014	4.26	1.0×10^{-5}
Ataxias	3.400	5,060	4.17	1.5×10^{-5}	7.57	Very small
Visual changes	2.086	6,020	2.72	0.0033	4.80	7.8×10^{-7}
Disarthria	3.850	8,860	5.66	7.6×10^{-9}	9.51	Very small
Hearing defects	4.670	11,600	7.42	Very small	12.09	Very small
Deaths	5.063	15,000	8.61	Very small	13.67	Very small
Fetal						
Late walking	1.195	1,229	0.73	0.232	1.93	0.0270
Late talking	1.700	1,467	1.17	0.121	2.87	0.0020
Mental symptoms	0.978	8,570	1.42	0.077	2.40	0.0082
Seizures	1.086	8,390	1.57	0.058	2.66	0.0039
Neurological score >4	0.847	6,280	1.12	0.132	1.97	0.0246

ESTIMATING HUMAN INTAKE OF CONTAMINANTS
FROM SEAFOOD AND SOME ASSOCIATED RISKS

In this section, the committee pursues a couple of different strategies for estimating exposures and, in some cases, risks for the array of other seafood hazards it was unable to investigate as deeply as PCBs and methylmercury. After available data bases for assessing exposures are reviewed briefly, national average intakes are estimated for various inorganic contaminants by using the FDA Total Diet Study and the Hall et al. (1978) data base, and making comparisons with regulatory levels for inorganics (similar comparisons are not presented for organic carcinogens, because the threshold assumptions implicit in the ADI methodology are not appropriate for the major effects of concern in these cases). After this, national average exposures for both organic and inorganic contaminants in commercial seafood are estimated tentatively from FDA surveillance data and, with the aid of EPA upper-confidence-limit estimates, the potential national cancer risk from organic carcinogenic contaminants is estimated. Finally, the section on exposure from sport, subsistence, and tribal fishing, and the section on the potential for reducing exposure through consumer information or labeling programs and fishing advisories, provide comments on the potential helpfulness of consumer and fisher advisories in reducing exposures.

Review of Data Bases Available for Estimating Exposures

FDA Total Diet Study

The FDA Total Diet Study provides a direct estimate of the dietary pesticide intake from a variety of foods including a limited number of seafood products (Gunderson, 1988). In the Total Diet Study, 234 different food items representing the diets of U.S. consumers are collected and analyzed four times each year throughout the United States. Each of four market basket samples is a composite of foods collected in three cities in a particular region (Gunderson, 1988). The foods are prepared table-ready and then analyzed for residues of industrial chemicals, pesticides, and metals such as cadmium and lead. The principal objective of the Total Diet Study is to develop dietary intake information on industrial chemicals and pesticides and to compare these intakes with acceptable daily intakes (ADIs). An ADI is the daily intake of a chemical which, if ingested over a lifetime, appears, according to FDA, to be without appreciable risk. The ADIs are established by scientific experts who have attended annual joint meetings of the United Nations Food and Agriculture Organization (FAO) and the World Health Organization (WHO) (Gunderson, 1988). The Total Diet Study could be a useful data base for determining the proportionate contributions of chemical and pesticide contamination of seafood and the contributions seafood makes to contamination, relative to other foods such as meat, poultry, dairy products, fruit, vegetables, grains, and oils. However, the FDA Total Diet Study included very few seafood samples among the 234 food items analyzed, and those items that were sampled – tuna, haddock, pollock, shrimp, and fish sticks – were among the products least likely to harbor significant chemical or pesticide contamination. Nonetheless, the pesticides detected in these products cast doubt on the ability of the

FDA regulatory monitoring program to detect all pesticides that may be in seafood products (Gunderson, 1988). For example, pesticides such as malathion, diazinon, penta, and chlorpropham detected in seafood products in the Total Diet Study were rarely, if ever, detected by the FDA regulatory monitoring program (Gunderson, 1988). Data from the Total Diet Study are presented later in this chapter.

FDA Pesticide Monitoring Files

The committee's use of FDA pesticide monitoring files is discussed at length in exposures from commercial seafood. Although there are appreciable concerns about the extent and representativeness of these data for specific species and areas of the country, overall they are the best source of information on organic contaminants in the commercial seafood market. However, information on inorganic contaminants in fish muscle is decidedly lacking, and the committee believes that FDA should consider bolstering its data base with measurements on edible portions of finfish for inorganic chemicals such as arsenic, cadmium, lead, and selenium.

The FDA seafood industrial pollutant and pesticide monitoring program has a tremendous potential to deliver important data about the contaminant levels in interstate seafood intended for human consumption. The committee acquired these files, numbering some 1,000 pages, for the years 1985-1988. They are rich in data, and fairly well organized and structured; yet they can also be quite superficial, with significant data gaps.

Although the full files for the most recent and the earliest years were not acquired by the committee, it is believed that complete files were acquired for 1986 and 1987. These files are among the most important sources of information about the concentration of industrial pollutants and pesticides in raw edible portions of finfish and shellfish intended to be sold in the nation's commercial markets. This monitoring effort stresses sampling of fish at the wholesale market level and is not generally useful for identifying the site of the catch and thus the exact source of the residues. However, the files are somewhat species specific. The program is designed primarily to satisfy FDA's legislative mandate of regulating shipments in interstate commerce. The fiscal year 1988 domestic monitoring program requires that a minimum of eight samples of locally produced fish or shellfish of commercial significance be collected per district as close to their origin as possible. Species selected are said to be those with the highest potential for residue contamination. In most cases, nonmigratory bottom feeders are the species of choice for pesticides and PCBs. Fresh fish are collected whenever possible. In addition to the formal domestic program requirements, several FDA district offices have ongoing cooperative programs in which samples from specific areas are submitted to a particular district laboratory for analysis.

The FDA monitoring program is divided into compliance and surveillance samples. The compliance samples are of food items the agency believes to be of special concern (i.e., to pose regulatory compliance problems). These include methylmercury in swordfish or the many freshwater fish that may contain excessive levels of pesticides and industrial chemicals such as PCBs and 2,3,7,8-tetrachlorodibenzo-p-dioxin (TCDD). The surveillance samples are representative of normal interstate seafood items for which no compliance problems are expected.

However, it is important to note that data on 80-90% of the fish selected for the committee's work were derived from FDA surveillance sampling. In only a few cases, such as tuna, swordfish, and shark, were samples listed under the compliance program. Thus, in the committee's estimation, the data should not be construed as being too heavily skewed toward the most elevated toxic concentrations. In calculations made from these data, residue levels below detection limits were considered to be zero. Because of this, in the committee's opinion, calculations based on FDA data are likely to underestimate the consumer's daily exposure to industrial chemicals, pesticides, and inorganic contaminants.

The FDA claims that the import monitoring component of this program stresses freshwater species, because strictly deep-sea species are not considered by FDA to be a significant source of pesticide residues. (However, the committee has noted that several deep-sea species such as swordfish and sablefish may indeed be sources of significant pesticide and inorganic contaminant residues.) The FDA does sample many imported saltwater species.

In fiscal year 1984, 453 samples were collected and analyzed (374 domestic and 79 imported samples), whereas in fiscal year 1985, 532 samples were analyzed (464 domestic and 68 imported). The fiscal year 1985-1986 reports appear to include a much larger number of domestic seafood samples; however these data include approximately 900 bluefish samples analyzed to fulfill the 1985-1986 congressionally mandated Atlantic Coast bluefish survey.

There are basic problems with FDA data. Among them are high detection limits for chemicals of concern, lack of monitoring for industrial pollutants such as PCBs and pesticides in interstate-trafficked bivalves, and lack of monitoring for inorganic contaminants such as arsenic, cadmium, and lead in edible portions of finfish.

National Marine Fisheries Service Survey

In 1978, the NMFS published a 300-page survey of trace elements in the fishery resource (Hall et al., 1978). This document reports trace element levels in tissues of 204 species of finfish, molluscs, and crustaceans from 198 sites around the coastal United States, including Alaska and Hawaii. Fifteen elements were determined: antimony (Sb), arsenic (As), cadmium (Cd), chromium (Cr), copper (Cu), lead (Pb), manganese (Mn), mercury (Hg), molybdenum (Mo), nickel (Ni), selenium (Se), silver (Ag), tin (Sn), vanadium (Va), and zinc (Zn). The species analyzed represented approximately 93% of the volume of the U.S. commercial and sport fish catch. It is an invaluable, well-conducted study.

Fisheries of the United States, 1987

The Fisheries of the United States, 1987 report (NMFS, 1988) details the amount of important commercial seafood species that were landed in 1987 by U.S. vessels and imported into the United States from other nations. The committee relied upon this report to estimate per capita consumption figures of important commercially caught seafood.

Exposures from Sport, Subsistence, and Tribal Fishing

Regional reports provided the principal available information for examining industrial chemical and pesticide concentrations in certain species of recreational/subsistence caught seafood and for estimating the intake of such species by anglers and their families. The committee relied on reports from Quincy Bay, Mass.; New York; southern California; and Puget Sound, Wash. These data, however, were not extensive enough to allow national estimates of exposure to be developed via this route.

Exposures from Commercial Seafood

Dietary Intake of Seafood of Various Species

Perhaps one of the most crucial tasks that the committee faced in determining the efficacy of present programs to protect the public health with regard to industrial chemicals and pesticides was determination of the daily dietary intake of specific commercial seafood species. There were several sources to which the committee had access to learn about the daily per capita intake of certain seafood species.

The NMFS *Fisheries of the United States, 1987* report was the most important resource for estimating the intake of many individual commercial seafood species (NMFS, 1988). Unfortunately, trade associations, in general, have not conducted recent consumption surveys (Konz, 1988). The committee used several regional portraits to create consumption, daily exposure, and cancer risk scenarios for typical sport fishers.

Enough information was available for the committee to make regional and national projections of seafood consumption for both commercially sold seafood and sport harvested species. In the future, because each region has different consumption patterns with different pollution problems, a variety of data sources from specific areas will play an important role in aiding risk managers to protect particular consumers, especially regional sport fishing subgroups that may concentrate their intake on certain favored but contaminated species.

The nationwide daily per capita intake of domestic and imported seafood was estimated from landing information contained in *Fisheries of the United States, 1987;* landings data for each species were given in round (live) weight, that is, the weight of the catch as aquatic animals are taken from the water before any processing (NMFS, 1988). After subtracting exports of whole uneviscerated products and annual changes in inventories (when available), the edible quantity of each species was calculated with the aid of a conversion factor supplied by NMFS. Generally, these conversion figures ranged from 0.35 to 0.59% of the live round weight. Upon application of the conversion figures, exports were subtracted under the product categories of fillets, steaks, portions, and cured products (NMFS, 1988).

Shellfish landings for univalves and bivalve molluscs, such as clams, oysters, and scallops, are reported in weight of meat, excluding the shell (NMFS, 1988, p. 2). Conversion factors were, however, applied to crabs, shrimp, squid, and the miscellaneous category of other marine and freshwater shellfish.

After applying the appropriate conversion factors and subtracting exports and year-end inventory, the amount of product remaining was divided by 242 million, the approximate U.S. population in 1987. This figure, which provided annual per capita consumption data, was then divided by 365 days to determine daily per capita consumption.

For imports, conversion factors were applied when whole or eviscerated fish were listed. Other imports were listed under fillets and steaks; canned products; balls, cakes, and puddings; and pickled or salted product; these categories, which dealt with edible portions, required no conversions. The amount imported–after the necessary conversions–was again divided by 242 million (the approximate U.S. population in 1987) and then by 365 days.

Unfortunately, the data provided for imports frequently neglected individual aquatic species. Thus, it was not possible to determine per capita consumption for certain aquatic species such as shark, swordfish, grouper, sea trout, and many others (NMFS, 1988). This is an important caveat in comparing differences between imported and U.S. seafood products, because import estimates probably underestimate the consumer's exposure to contaminants as a result of the highly generalized information provided.

The data on individual species landings, the conversion factors used, and estimates of the per capita consumption of individual categories of seafood are given in Tables 6-20 and 6-21. The resulting overall yearly per capita seafood consumption estimate, for U.S. and imported products, of about 18 pounds was a little high, but not grossly larger than the official estimate of 15.4 pounds, and well within range to offer the kind of reliability needed for a first-order appraisal of daily seafood intake patterns and exposures. (For proprietary reasons, some NMFS information that would have helped the committee further refine the per capita figures was withheld concerning year-end inventory figures underlying the data in *Fisheries of the United States, 1987*; obtaining a per capita number identical to the NMFS figure would be impossible without additional information). It can be seen that the leading contributors to U.S. per capita seafood consumption are cod, flounder, tuna, salmon, clams, shrimp, groundfish, and aquatic finfish species from two groupings of miscellaneous fish known as "other marine finfish" and "other freshwater finfish."

Inorganic Contaminant Exposures and Suggested Acceptable Intake

This section employs some of the best available data for estimating seafood-related exposure to inorganic contaminants and compares the indicated national average intakes via commercially marketed seafood with ADIs and related regulatory levels. This comparison provides a very broad indication of potential risk but is potentially misleading because the variability in exposures to different contaminants, and the variability of contaminant exposures from other nonseafood and noncommercial seafood sources, cannot be estimated from the available data. Therefore, the committee was unable to arrive at estimates of how many people are likely to exceed the stated ADI intake levels on either an acute or a chronic basis.

Mean levels and ranges of trace metals in the edible portions of certain fish and invertebrates may be obtained from combinations of the data base references previously cited in this chapter. Three agencies, the FDA, the Australian National Health and Medical Research Council (NHMRC), and the Canadian Health Protection Board (CHPB), have suggested allowable trace-metal levels for seafood and seafood

TABLE 6-20 U.S. Landings, Consumption/Live Weight Conversion Factors, and Annual Per Capita Consumption for Different Species

Species	1987 U.S. Landings (10^3 lb)	Conversion Factor (lb consumed/lb round wt)	U.S. Average Annual Per Capita Consumption (lb)[a]
Alewives	20,541		
Anchovies	12,857	1	
Bluefish	15,226	0.43	0.027
Bonito	11,420	0.43	0.020
Butterfish	10,315	0.38	0.004
Cod	229,711	0.5	0.305
Croaker	11,044	0.5	0.023
Cusk	3,064	0.5	0.006
Flounder	199,711	0.45	0.373
Grouper	9,494	0.5	0.002
Hake	56,696	Not given	0.117
Halibut	76,107	0.45	0.116
Herring, sea	207,134 [b,c]	0.59	
Jack mackerel	26,671	0.59	0.047
Lingcod	7,027	0.5	0.015
Mackerel	115,103	0.45	0.202
Mullet	30,125	0.5	0.057
Ocean perch	24,184	0.38	0.027
Pollock	597,693	0.5	1.116
Rockfish	117,881	0.5	0.244
Sablefish	102,698	0.5	0.126
Salmon	562,018	0.5	0.510
Scup or porgy	14,295	0.38	0.022
Sea bass	5,083	0.5	0.011
Sea trout	21,871	0.5	0.045
Shark	21,832	0.4	0.036
Snapper	8,908	0.42	0.015
Striped bass	431	0.5	0.001
Swordfish	9,761	0.5	0.016
Tilefish	7,950	0.5	0.016
Tuna	593,444	0.45	1.104
Whiting	34,673	0.45	0.044
Other marine finfish	199,795	0.5	0.376
Other freshwater finfish	117,880	0.5	0.244
Clams	134,357	1.0	0.550
Crabs	386,368	0.183	0.270
Lobsters	51,313	0.22	0.044
Oysters	39,807	1.0	0.164
Scallops	40,773	1	0.165
Shrimp	363,142	0.49	0.657
Squid	82,049 [c]	0.6	0.151
Other shellfish	89,702	0.4	0.116
Total	4,655,826		7.362

[a] The numbers in this column are not in all cases equal to the product of the previous two columns because of adjustments for exports and year-to-year inventory changes.
[b] Largely used for fish meal.
[c] Largely used for bait.

TABLE 6-21 Volume of Imports, Consumption/Live Weight Conversion Factors, and Annual Per Capita Consumption for Different Species

Species	1987 Imports (10^3 lb)	Conversion Factor (lb consumed/lb landed wt)	U.S. Average Annual Per Capita Consumption (lb)
Whole or eviscerated			
Cod, cusk, haddock, and flounder	105,158	0.4875	0.206
Halibut	9,295	0.45	0.017
Salmon	41,902	0.5	0.087
Tuna	787,133	0.45	1.464
Fillets and steaks			
Flounder	73,003	1	0.302
Groundfish	315,418	1	1.303
Other	232,564	1	0.961
Blocks and slabs	403,577	1	1.668
Shrimp	461,173	0.88[a]	1.677
Crabmeat	12,571	1	0.052
American lobster meat	38,974	1	0.129
Spiny lobster meat	41,949	1	0.139
Scallops (meats)	39,934	1	0.165
Analogue products with shellfish	30,539	1	0.126
Other fish and shellfish	98,996	1	0.409
Canned and other products			
Canned herring	5,617	1	0.023
Sardines	65,022	1	0.269
Tuna	211,685	1	0.875
Analogue products without shellfish	4,737	1	0.020
Other	8,797	1	0.036
Abalone	13,974	1	0.058
Crabmeat	7,967	1	0.033
American lobsters	637	1	0.003
Spiny lobsters	136	1	0.001
Oysters	32,668	1	0.135
Shrimp	17,132	1	0.071
Other fish and shellfish	57,579	1	0.238
Pickled or salted			
Cod, haddock, hake, etc.	31,893	1	0.132
Herring	9,991	1	0.041
Other fish and shellfish	16,108	1	0.067
Total	3,176,129		10.707

[a] This is the result of a weighted calculation based on the importation of 310 million pounds of shrimp with the shell on, noting that consumed weight represents 80-85% of landed weight. The rest of the shrimp is assigned a conversion factor of 1.

products (Table 6-22). The FDA has set an acceptable concentration for mercury based on per capita consumption (FDA, 1982). The Australian NHMRC has recommended maximum concentrations in seafood for arsenic, cadmium, copper, lead, and zinc (Mackay et al., 1975). The Canadian government has set action levels based on the contaminant level of edible weight for arsenic, lead, and mercury (DFO, 1989). Alert levels for trace metals in molluscs have been set by the National Shellfish Sanitation Program (NSSP) of the Interstate Shellfish Sanitation Commission. However, these have no public health significance and are based on mean survey levels in U.S. coastal waters approximately two decades ago (see Table 8-3 and the accompanying discussion in Chapter 8 of this report).

The United Nations Food and Agricultural Organization in conjunction with the World Health Organization (FAO/WHO, 1972) has suggested provisional tolerable weekly intake limits (PTWIs) for cadmium, mercury, and lead. In addition, there are estimated safe and adequate daily dietary intake (ESADDI) levels for all foods set by the National Research Council (NRC) of the National Academy of Sciences (NRC, 1980). These values are listed in the first two columns of Table 6-23. In contrast to the values quoted in Table 6-22, these suggested levels apply to all foods, not just seafood.

Below are a number of comparisons of possible intake rates with these numbers:

• The last column of Table 6-23 shows the committee's estimate of what the average daily intake of each element would be if a consumer were to eat 15 pounds of seafood per year at the weighted average concentration observed in a massive (more than 200,000 measurements) stratified survey of the U.S. marine fishery. In analyzing these data, the committee used the distribution of species-average concentrations in the NMFS survey, weighted by the percentage of the U.S. catch for each species intended for human consumption, according to the dietary patterns prevailing in 1970. (These detailed distributions are given in the discussion of individual elements following Table 6-23.) This analysis neglects freshwater species and imported seafood, but it is perhaps not an unreasonable set of provisional estimates of long-term average consumption. In comparing these numbers to the acceptable daily intake estimates and other standards, the reader should bear in mind three types of population variability that will cause some people to be at greater risk than average: (1) many people consume more seafood than the U.S. average intake of about 15 pounds per year; (2) many people may consume more of the species with higher average levels of a particular contaminant; and (3) in general, some levels of the toxicant in question can be expected to be contributed by other components of the diet (see fourth column in Table 6-23). The magnitude of these variabilities, in the context of the dynamics with which different kinds of damage may be produced by specific toxicants, will determine how many people may actually be at risk of significant harm from individual agents.

• The fourth column of Table 6-23 gives FDA estimates of overall dietary exposure to specific elements from all foods, inferred from its market basket surveys (for the adolescent male consumer).

• Finally, although most of the hazards from these inorganic elements are chronic in nature, one can get a feel for potential short-term dosage from shellfish by multiplying the ranges of contaminant levels found in different surveys by an assumed 250-g intake at a single sitting. These findings are discussed below in the separate

TABLE 6-22 Suggested Trace Metal Action Levels for Seafood and Seafood Products [μg/g (ppm)]

Metal	FDA	ANHMRC[a]	CHPB[b]
Arsenic[c]	–	1.53	3.5
Cadmium	–	2.0	–
Copper	–	30.0	–
Lead	–	2.0	0.5
Mercury	1.0	–	0.5
Zinc	–	1,000.0	–

[a] Australian National Health and Medical Research Council.
[b] Canadian Health Protection Board.
[c] As the trioxide.

TABLE 6-23 Acceptable Daily Intake Limits of Trace Metals as Suggested by FAO/WHO (PTDI) and NRC-NAS (ESADDI) Compared with Mean U.S. Daily Intake of Trace Metals Reported by FDA Total Diet Studies (μg/day)

Metal	FAO/WHO PTDI[a]	NRC-NAS ESADDI	FDA[b] Mean Daily Intake	Mean Daily Intake from 15-lb/yr U.S. Catch[c]
Antimony[d]			15	
Arsenic	182[e]	–	45	82 (43.6)[f]
Cadmium	57-72	–	15	2.0
Chromium	–	50-200	–	3.7
Copper	–	2,000-3,000	–	51
Lead	429	–	41	10[i]
Mercury[g]	33-43	–	3.9	2.1
Nickel				5.6
Selenium	–	50-200	152[h]	14
Zinc	15,000	–	17,700[h]	

[a] Calculated from the PTWI; 70-kg human.
[b] Total Diet Studies for 25-30-year-old males (FDA market basket program); Gunderson et al. (1988) except as otherwise noted.
[c] Calculated from data in Hall et al. (1978); for the breakdown of average levels for species, see Tables 6-10–6-18, which detail the distributions of species-average concentrations.
[d] EPA RfD = 4×10^{-4} mg/kg/day = 28 μg/day.
[e] Arsenic trioxide; not agreed upon but estimated.
[f] Data in parentheses are FDA seafood measurements given in Gunderson et al. (1988).
[g] Lowest value is methylmercury, highest total mercury.
[h] From the older total diet data of Gartrell et al. (1985).
[i] A study coauthor believes this result may be too high because of contamination.

subsections for each element. The data base used for this was Cappuzo et al. (1987) for the northeastern coastal region (review 1972-1983, 5 species); Landolt et al. (1985) for Puget Sound (review 1982-1985, 4 species, n = ?); Landolt et al. (1987) for Puget Sound (1985-1986, 11 species, n = 64); Murphy (1988a-c) for Chesapeake Bay (bluefish, n = 71; stripers, n = 35). Chromium is mentioned only because oral intake of amounts as small as 50 μg of potassium dichromate may exacerbate existing chromium hypersensitivity, and reported levels in finfish and squid would fulfill that criterion (Haines and Nieboer, 1988) if they were in the hexavalent form (which is probably not likely).

Use of NMFS Survey of Trace-Element Data

Available data from the NMFS survey of trace elements (Hall et al., 1978) are now examined in relation to these advisory levels.

Antimony

The committee was surprised to find that the average U.S. consumption of antimony from seafood indicated by the Hall et al. (1978) data base (Table 6-24) is within a factor of two of EPA's reference dose (RfD) value intended to protect against systemic toxicity (EPA, 1986b). It is unclear what forms of antimony are present in seafood or whether those forms have toxicity similar to the forms that gave rise to the RfD. Antimony is below arsenic on the periodic table, and antimony dust appears to be carcinogenic for the lung when tested by inhalation (Groth et al., 1986). The committee is not aware of any long-term testing by oral routes. According to the abstract of an EPA document, increases in spontaneous abortions and premature births have been reported for pregnant female workers exposed to antimony (EPA, 1981). Further investigation of antimony's potential for hazard via seafood seems warranted.

Arsenic

As can be seen in Table 6-23, the committee's calculation of the average daily intake of arsenic from seafood from the data of Hall et al. (1978) (detailed in Table 6-25) exceeded somewhat the estimated total dietary intake of arsenic from the FDA's market basket survey program. Clearly, seafood is an important source of overall arsenic exposure in the diet, although as mentioned earlier, the organic forms of arsenic that appear to predominate in the seafood species studied in detail are considerably less hazardous than inorganic forms of arsenic.

Preliminary examination of muscle levels in fish from the areas of interest from other data bases indicates a range of 0.25-20.7 ppm in finfish and up to 15.9 ppm in squid. The estimate of intake in micrograms for a 250-g serving ranges from 62.5 to 5,157. In contrasting this with the estimated FAO PTDI of 182 μg (calculated as the trioxide to be 2 μg/kg/day for a 69.1-kg human), the highest possible acute daily value exceeds the PTDI by 4,975 μg, roughly a factor of 25. No ESADDI is given by the NRC.

TABLE 6-24 Distribution of Species-Average Antimony Concentrations, Weighted by the Percentage Contribution of Each Species to 1970 Human Consumption

Range (ppm) for Species Average Consumption	Midpoint (ppm) of Range	Percentage of U.S. Catch Intended for Human Consumption
Finfish, muscle		
0.5-0.6	0.55	3.6
0.6-0.7	0.65	17.3
0.7-0.8	0.75	14.9
0.8-0.9	0.85	26
0.9-1.0	0.95	1.7
1.0-2.0	1.5	0.5
All finfish	0.764	64
Molluscs, edible tissues		
<0.1	0.05	3.4
0.5-0.6	0.55	0.4
0.6-0.7	0.65	0.6
0.7-0.8	0.75	0.1
0.8-0.9	0.85	1.9
0.9-1.0	0.95	1.1
1.0-2.0	1.5	0
All, average	0.469	7.5
Crustaceans, edible tissues		
0.2-0.3	0.25	0.1
0.8-0.9	0.85	8.7
0.9-1.0	0.95	11.7
1.0-2.0	1.50	7.8
All crustaceans	1.07	28.3
Grand weighted average (ppm)	0.83	99.8[a]
Daily dose for 15 lb/yr (μg/day)	15.4	

[a] Total is not 100% because of rounding error and because some species were excluded from the study.
SOURCE: Hall et al. (1978).

TABLE 6-25 Distribution of Species-Average Arsenic Concentrations, Weighted by the Percentage Contribution of Each Species to 1970 Human Consumption

Range (ppm) for Species Average Consumption	Midpoint (ppm) of Range	Percentage of U.S. Catch Intended for Human Consumption
Finfish, muscle		
0.6-0.7	0.65	0.2
1.0-2.0	1.5	2.6
2.0-3.0	2.5	35
3.0-4.0	3.5	13.8
4.0-5.0	4.5	3
5.0-6.0	5.5	2.8
6.0-7.0	6.5	0.3
7.0-8.0	7.5	5
8.0-9.0	8.5	0.1
9.0-10.0	9.5	0.2
10.0-20.0	15	0.7
20.0-30.0	25	0.2
All finfish	3.54	63.9
Molluscs, edible tissues		
2.0-3.0	2.5	4
3.0-4.0	3.5	3.2
4.0-5.0	4.5	0.1
10.0-20.0	15	0.1
All, average	3.13	7.4
Crustaceans, edible tissues		
3.0-4.0	3.5	1.8
4.0-5.0	4.5	14.2
5.0-6.0	5.5	2.5
6.0-7.0	6.5	5.8
9.0-10.0	9.5	2
10.0-20.0	15.0	0.5
20.0-30.0	25.0	1.5
All crustaceans	6.56	28.3
Grand weighted average (ppm)	4.37	99.6
Daily dose for 15 lb/yr (μg/day)	81.5	

SOURCE: Hall et al. (1978).

TABLE 6-26 Distribution of Species-Average Cadmium Concentrations, Weighted by the Percentage Contribution of Each Species to 1970 Human Consumption

Range (ppm) for Species Average Consumption	Midpoint (ppm) of Range	Percentage of U.S. Catch Intended for Human Consumption
Finfish, muscle		
<0.1	0.05	63.8
0.1-0.2	0.15	0.1
All finfish	0.050	63.9
Molluscs, edible tissues		
0.1-0.2	0.15	3
0.2-0.3	0.25	1.2
0.7-0.8	0.75	0.6
0.9-1.0	0.95	2
1.0-2.0	1.5	0.6
2.0-3.0	2.5	0.1
All, average	0.567	7.5
Crustaceans, edible tissues		
<0.1	0.05	9.8
0.1-0.2	0.15	17
0.2-0.3	0.25	1.5
0.3-0.4	0.35	0.1
All crustaceans	0.12	28.4
Grand weighted average (ppm)	0.11	99.8
Daily dose for 15 lb/yr (μg/day)	2.0	

SOURCE: Hall et al. (1978).

Cadmium

The overall seafood-related consumption of cadmium estimated as 2 μg/day (Table 6-26) is a modest, but not completely insignificant (6%), portion of the overall dietary exposure estimated from the total diet program. Within seafood, cadmium is relatively highly concentrated in molluscan shellfish.

Muscle levels in fish and squid from the designated data base range from 0.0006 to 0.63 ppm. For a 250-g serving, intake would vary from 0.15 to 157.5 μg. The PTDI for cadmium is 57-72 μg, approximately one-half to one-third the highest calculated intake. No estimated safe daily dietary intake is suggested by the NRC.

TABLE 6-27 Distribution of Species-Average Chromium Concentrations, Weighted by the Percentage Contribution of Each Species to 1970 Human Consumption

Range (ppm) for Species Average Consumption	Midpoint (ppm) of Range	Percentage of U.S. Catch Intended for Human Consumption
Finfish, muscle		
<0.1	0.05	0.3
0.1-0.2	0.15	51
0.2-0.3	0.250	12.5
All finfish	0.169	63.8
Molluscs, edible tissues		
0.1-0.2	0.15	0.6
0.2-0.3	0.25	0.7
0.3-0.4	0.35	6.1
All, average	0.324	7.4
Crustaceans, edible tissues		
0.1-0.2	0.15	5.4
0.2-0.3	0.25	22.9
All crustaceans	0.23	28.3
Grand weighted average (ppm)	0.20	99.5
Daily dose for 15 lb/yr (μg/day)	3.7	

SOURCE: Hall et al. (1978).

Chromium

The overall consumption of chromium from seafood indicated by the Hall et al. (1978) data (Table 6-27) appears well below the applicable ADI. Chromium levels in the muscles of finfish and squid for the areas of interest varied from 0.35 to 2.0 ppm. Calculated short-term intake levels are therefore 87.5-5,000 μg for a 250-g portion. The FAO has no suggested PTWI. There are no action levels reported for chromium in seafood. However, the ESADDI for chromium is 50-200 μg, which is far lower than the highest calculated intake (by a factor of 25). Again, whether a rare acute exposure of this magnitude is problematic is unclear.

Lead

If results from the Hall et al. (1978) data base (Table 6-28) are taken literally, seafood is contributing about one-eighth of the overall dietary exposure to lead for the general population. In the light of recent research indicating developmental toxicity even from levels of lead considered to be in the normal range, this would be worthy of further study. However, in this case, the committee has been cautioned by one of the coauthors of the Hall study (M. Meaburn) that the analyses were conducted under

TABLE 6-28 Distribution of Species-Average Lead Concentrations, Weighted by the Percentage Contribution of Each Species to 1970 Human Consumption

Range (ppm) for Species Average Consumption	Midpoint (ppm) of Range	Percentage of U.S. Catch Intended for Human Consumption
Finfish, muscle		
0.3-0.4	0.35	9.9
0.4-0.5	0.45	33.8
0.5-0.6	0.55	9.4
0.6-0.7	0.65	10.7
All finfish	0.48	63.8
Molluscs, edible tissues		
0.4-0.5	0.45	0.4
0.5-0.6	0.55	3.4
0.6-0.7	0.65	3
0.7-0.8	0.75	0.7
0.8-0.9	0.85	0.1
All, average	0.61	7.6
Crustaceans, edible tissues		
0.4-0.5	0.45	0
0.5-0.6	0.55	3.5
0.6-0.7	0.65	18.5
0.7-0.8	0.75	6.2
0.8-0.9	0.85	0.1
All crustacea	0.66	28.3
Grand weighted average (ppm)	0.54	99.7
Daily dose for 15 lb/yr (μ/day)	10.1	

NOTE: One of the coauthors of the Hall et al. (1978) study considers these analyses overstated because of contamination problems.
SOURCE: Hall et al. (1978).

conditions that, in retrospect, did not rigorously enough exclude the possibility of postcollection contamination of samples, reagents, etc. Meaburn believes that the lead results would likely prove considerably overstated, if the analyses were redone with modern methods.

Muscle levels in finfish and squid from the designated data base range from 0.008 to 12 ppm. Calculated intake for a 250-g serving would be 2.0-3,000 μg. The higher range is certainly skewed by fish taken from Boston Harbor. A more realistic range would be from 0.008 to 2.3 ppm, resulting in an intake of 2.0-575 μg. The PTDI for lead is 429 μg. In the first instance, the ADI is exceeded by a factor of 6; in the second, by 1.3. No ESADDI is given. The normal estimated daily lead intake for children is less than 0.3 μg (Green et al., 1978).

TABLE 6-29 Distribution of Species-Average Mercury Concentrations, Weighted by the Percentage Contribution of Each Species to 1970 Human Consumption

Range (ppm) for Species Average Consumption	Midpoint (ppm) of Range	Percentage of U.S. Catch Intended for Human Consumption
Finfish, muscle		
<0.1	0.05	30.7
0.1-0.2	0.15	26.1
0.2-0.3	0.25	3.9
0.3-0.4	0.35	2.2
0.4-0.5	0.45	0
0.5-0.6	0.55	0.7
0.6-0.7	0.65	0
0.7-0.8	0.75	0.1
All finfish (except swordfish)[a]	0.120	63.7
Molluscs, edible tissues		
<0.1	0.05	7.5
Crustaceans, edible tissues		
<0.1	0.05	13.7
0.1-0.2	0.15	13.2
0.2-0.3	0.25	1.4
All crustacea	0.107	28.3
Grand weighted average without swordfish (ppm)	0.111	99.5
Swordfish	0.95[b]	0.107[c]
Grand weighted average with swordfish (ppm)	0.112	
Daily dose for 15 lb/yr (μg/day)	2.09	

[a] According to one of the coauthors, for "policy reasons" swordfish was not included in the species sampled for the Hall et al. (1978) survey.
[b] Average from FDA surveillance samples.
[c] Based on total swordfish consumption of about 4 million lb/year (of about 9.7 million lb round weight landed). This represents an average of about 0.016 lb per person per year. [Landings data from NMFS (1988); consumed weight/round weight ratio taken from other NMFS data.]
SOURCE: Hall et al. (1978).

Mercury

The estimated population average consumption of mercury from aquatic animals of about 2.1 μg/day (Table 6-29) represents over half of the mercury estimated to be in the diet as a whole for the age and sex group (25-50-year-old males) with the highest daily mercury consumption in the FDA Total Diet Study. Aquatic organisms probably make a larger aggregate contribution to the methylated portion of total mercury (total mercury, of course, includes inorganic mercury, which has very different risks) (Gunderson, 1988). The 2.1-μg/day average is more than an order of magnitude below the official ADI of 33 μg/day (as methylmercury). As indicated earlier in this chapter, in one of its specific studies of FDA regulations the committee attempted to assess the degree of actual protection offered by this spread (and the degree of "safety" incorporated into the ADI itself) by analysis of data on the population distributions of internal dosage (as measured in blood or hair) and the interindividual variation in susceptibility to different effects in adults and developing fetuses.

Swordfish can routinely achieve even higher concentrations than the official 1-ppm guideline (which reportedly is not enforced in Massachusetts and perhaps elsewhere). The suggested PTDI for total mercury is 43 μg, which is exceeded by a factor of 6 in a serving containing 1 ppm. The FDA allowable level is 1.0 ppm and the Canadian action level is 0.5 ppm. The NRC has not suggested an estimated safe daily dietary intake level.

Selenium

The committee's overall average calculated selenium daily intake of slightly less than 14 μg/day (Table 6-30) represents somewhat less than 10% of the estimate of total dietary loading, and between 7 and 30% of NRC's ESADDI.

Selenium levels in teleosts (fish with bones) seldom exceed 1 ppm (Sorensen et al., 1984). The range of selenium levels from this data base was 0.0-0.49 ppm and came from determinations in Puget Sound animals only. Selenium is very much a regional, freshwater problem (most notably in a wildlife refuge that receives extensive irrigation tile drainage in California), and the chosen data base for this preliminary report does not reflect the apparent regional risk. Calculated intake levels are therefore somewhat lower than found in problem areas and range from 0.0 to 122.5 μg. This is less than the high range of the NRC ESADDI of 50-200 μg. When the data base includes site-specific studies, values for skeletal muscle may vary from 0.5 to 12.9 ppm (Cumbie and Van Horn, 1978; Sorensen et al., 1984). Calculated values of intake using this data base are 125-3,225 μg, the highest value exceeding the PTDI by a factor of 15. The Fish and Wildlife Service (F&WS) National Pesticide Monitoring Program (1980-1981) also reports higher values for selenium, which range from 0.09 to 2.47 ppm; however, these values are for the whole fish and not specifically for skeletal muscle. Thus, their use in assessing risk is devalued. The FAO/WHO Joint Committee has not suggested a PTWI for selenium. The toxic chronic dose of selenium for man is estimated as 2,400 to 3,000 μg/day (Wilber, 1983).

TABLE 6-30 Distribution of Species-Average Selenium Concentrations, Weighted by the Percentage Contribution of Each Species to 1970 Human Consumption

Range (ppm) for Species Average Consumption	Midpoint (ppm) of Range	Percentage of U.S. Catch Intended for Human Consumption
Finfish, muscle		
0.1-0.2	0.15	0.5
0.3-0.4	0.35	2.3
0.4-0.5	0.45	21.2
0.5-0.6	0.55	8.3
0.6-0.7	0.65	4.9
0.7-0.8	0.75	2.1
0.8-0.9	0.85	5.4
0.9-1.0	0.95	1.5
1.0-2.0	1.50	17.7
All finfish	0.819	63.9
Molluscs, edible tissues		
0.3-0.4	0.35	3.2
0.4-0.5	0.45	0.8
0.5-0.6	0.55	0.7
0.7-0.8	0.75	2.3
0.8-0.9	0.85	0.5
All, average	0.54	7.5
Crustaceans, edible tissues		
0.2-0.3	0.25	0.4
0.3-0.4	0.35	5.1
0.4-0.5	0.45	2.1
0.5-0.6	0.55	1.1
0.6-0.7	0.65	11.9
0.7-0.8	0.75	6.2
0.8-0.9	0.85	1.4
1.0-2.0	1.50	0.1
All crustacea	0.61	28.3
Grand weighted average (ppm)	0.737	99.7
Daily dose for 15 lb/yr (μg/day)	13.75	

SOURCE: Hall et al. (1978).

Estimates of Cancer Risks from Organic Contaminants

Once the committee established per capita consumption patterns for a variety of seafood species as outlined earlier (Tables 6-20 and 6-21), average concentrations of contaminants calculated from the available FDA surveillance and compliance data were used to estimate the average amounts of industrial organic chemicals, pesticides, and selected inorganics delivered to U.S. consumers via commercially marketed seafood.

As discussed earlier, these FDA surveillance and compliance data have quite a few weaknesses. Improvements in monitoring can be made by the responsible agencies. Yet, despite these weaknesses, the committee believes that the data provide a realistic picture of national aggregate organic chemical exposure from commercially marketed seafood. These are the only data that enable even a preliminary estimate of national aggregate cancer risks from organic carcinogens.

Among the weaknesses in the FDA data are the following:

● The detection limits used by FDA regulatory laboratories result in a generally gross underestimate of actual contaminant concentrations in seafood. For example, fish shown by other studies to be contaminated with low-level PCBs appeared to have no contamination in the FDA data set. This is true of California species such as bonito, mackerel, squid, and white croaker, which probably do have consistently low levels of PCBs according to studies performed by the Southern California Coastal Water Research Organization (Gossett et al., 1982). The committee believes that because of their frequency in the aquatic food chain and in some areas of the seafood supply, PCBs constitute an important contaminant even at levels below the present regulatory detection limits. Many contaminants probably go undetected by the FDA regulatory monitoring program because the laboratory detection limits used for enforcement of regulations have levels 5-10 times higher than the limits used in the Total Diet Study analyses (Gunderson, 1988, pp. 1200-1209).

● There are significant problems of misidentifying some fish species. The FDA lists the Great Lakes chub under whitefish; yet according to the 1988 *Fish List* (FDA, 1988), chub and whitefish are not the same species. This has added a great deal of confusion to the FDA data base.

● There is a decided lack of precise identification of species. In the FDA data base, there is only one classification of "mullet." In fact, however, 11 different species of mullet may be sold for food in interstate commerce. It would be helpful to know the precise species being sampled by FDA. In that way, it could be determined whether certain species of mullet have greater contamination than others. Another example is FDA's sampling of "croaker." There are more than 20 species of croaker that are sold for food fish according to the 1988 *Fish List* (FDA, 1988); yet it is unclear which croakers are actually being sampled and from which of the nation's coastlines. Because contaminant levels among different croaker species may vary dramatically, the committee believes that such information would prove extremely helpful in refining the understanding of which fish species, in particular, contribute the highest dietary exposure to toxic chemicals.

● There is also a tremendous need for precise geographic information. The FDA should determine where each sample has been caught.

• Because of the limited number of samples, FDA data are clearly inadequate and present absolutely no meaningful overall information on contamination of many species. Some aquatic organisms are sampled sporadically.

• Many aquatic species are never analyzed for mercury concentrations.

• Many finfish are never analyzed for inorganic contaminants, such as arsenic, cadmium, lead, and selenium, in edible portions.

• Very few shellfish are analyzed for organic chemical contamination or for other contaminants of concern such as organotins and polycyclic aromatic hydrocarbons (PAHs) even though it is known that bivalves may well be contaminated with such chemicals.

• It is uncertain for which pollutants FDA routinely tests, and at what laboratory detection limits. For example, the FDA Total Diet Study was able to detect pesticides such as chlorpropham, dacthal, diazinon and malathion on 45 occasions when analyzing 48 composite samples of seafood dishes such as cod and haddock fillets, canned tuna, and shrimp – pesticides that the FDA industrial chemical and pesticide monitoring program rarely, if ever, detected among these seafood items in some five years of sampling (Gunderson, 1988). This may occur because these pesticides are applied to the food product after harvest and during processing, because the analytical methods in use are not designed to detect these particular chemicals, or because the laboratory detection limits in the Total Diet Study have quantitation levels that are 5-10 times lower than the limits used in FDA enforcement of regulatory limits (Gunderson, 1988). In any event, FDA regulatory data appear to underestimate consumers' exposure to a variety of organic and inorganic contaminants including pesticides, metals, and PAHs.

The disparity in sampling detection limits between the Total Diet Study and regular FDA seafood monitoring programs raises serious doubts as to whether the FDA sampling program is accurately estimating the actual concentrations of industrial chemicals and pesticides in the seafood supply. Indeed, the FDA laboratories' relatively high detection levels – particularly for PCBs and dieldrin, which can occur in seafood at levels below the current detection limits – lead to so-called nondetected zero values when the PCB concentration might actually be several parts per billion. Because of the relatively high carcinogenic potency of dieldrin and PCBs, and their frequency in the seafood supply, findings of several parts per billion in widely consumed aquatic species might add appreciably to overall exposure and risk.

Nevertheless, FDA data can be used to provide a rough estimate of daily dietary exposure and at least a highly tentative indication of potential risk. Table 6-31 presents the committee's estimates of U.S. daily dietary exposure to selected organic and inorganic chemicals in terms of milligrams per kilogram of body weight per day, the form that is best suited to calculation of upper-confidence-limit cancer risks. These calculations assume a standard body weight of 70 kg. Table 6-31 also provides EPA upper-confidence-limit cancer potency estimates (where they exist) and the indicated upper-confidence-limit estimates of national aggregate lifetime cancer risk based on the committee's estimation of daily exposure to carcinogenic organic chemicals.[17]

TABLE 6-31 Dietary Exposures Estimated from Selected FDA Surveillance Data, 1984-1988

Chemical	Estimated Aggregate Exposure (mg/kg/day)				EPA Cancer Potency (mg/kg/day)$^{-1}$ [a]	Indicated Upper-Confidence-Limit Cancer Risk
	U.S. Finfish	U.S. Shellfish	All Imported	Total		
Organics						
Benzene hexachloride	2.9×10^{-8}	1.2×10^{-8}	1.0×10^{-8}	5.1×10^{-8}	6.3	3.2×10^{-7}
Chlordane	2.3×10^{-7}		5.1×10^{-8}	2.8×10^{-7}	1.3	3.6×10^{-7}
Dacthal (DCPA)	4.0×10^{-8}			4.0×10^{-8}		
tDDT	8.8×10^{-6}	2.1×10^{-8}	2.5×10^{-7}	9.0×10^{-6}	0.34	3.1×10^{-6}
Dieldrin	4.9×10^{-7}		2.5×10^{-8}	5.1×10^{-7}	16	8.2×10^{-6}
Endrin	1.7×10^{-8}			1.7×10^{-8}		
Heptachlor	4.3×10^{-8}		3.1×10^{-8}	7.4×10^{-8}	4.5	3.3×10^{-7}
Lindane			1.5×10^{-9}	1.5×10^{-9}	1.3	2.0×10^{-9}
Mirex	8.7×10^{-8}		1.5×10^{-8}	8.7×10^{-8}		
Nonachlor	2.4×10^{-7}			2.6×10^{-7}		
Octachlor	1.0×10^{-7}			1.0×10^{-7}		
Omethoate	1.2×10^{-8}			1.2×10^{-8}		
Pentachlorophenol		2.0×10^{-9}		1.5×10^{-9}		
Pentachloroaniline	1.5×10^{-9}			2.0×10^{-9}		
PCBs	6.9×10^{-6}	6.3×10^{-7}	3.7×10^{-7}	7.9×10^{-6}	7.7	6.0×10^{-5}
2,3,7,8-TCDD	1.5×10^{-11}			1.5×10^{-11}	1.6×10^{5}	2.3×10^{-6}
Tecnazene			1.5×10^{-9}	1.5×10^{-9}		
Total						7.5×10^{-5} [b]
Metals					Total in μg/day	
Aluminum		5.3×10^{-4}		5.3×10^{-4}	37	
Arsenic	5.3×10^{-7}	1.1×10^{-5}	1.1×10^{-7}	5.4×10^{-4}	38	
Beryllium		1.1×10^{-7}		1.1×10^{-7}	0.0	
Cadmium	9.6×10^{-7}	1.4×10^{-5}	9.5×10^{-6}	2.4×10^{-5}	1.7	
Chromium		8.2×10^{-6}		9.0×10^{-6}	0.6	
Lead	2.6×10^{-6}	2.8×10^{-6}	5.9×10^{-6}	1.1×10^{-5}	0.8	
Mercury	1.1×10^{-5}	1.2×10^{-5}	1.2×10^{-5}	3.5×10^{-5}	2.5	
Selenium		1.5×10^{-6}		1.5×10^{-6}	0.1	

[a] This level is an upper estimate or the actual risk may be as low as zero.

[b] ... to add them. However, the statistical error in this case is not large

Using such calculations to determine the nationwide daily per capita intake of seafood species may well tend to obscure individual risks associated with industrial chemicals. Certain consumer subgroups probably favor certain seafood over others, whether their reasons be cultural, taste, health, or simply economic. Thus, any one individual or group of individuals may have a handful of favorite seafood items that are eaten repeatedly, which means that exposure is not spread evenly throughout the population but tends to be concentrated among certain subgroups. Based on landings data, a significant amount of freshwater fish, classified under the NMFS data as "other freshwater finfish," is being eaten; consumers of freshwater finfish probably are not spread out among the approximately 242 million citizens. Also, this category contains many of the most contaminated finfish.

It can be seen that the overall estimated cancer risk is dominated by the (highly uncertain) estimate for PCBs, dieldrin, DDT, and dioxin. Nevertheless, the overall risk as assessed here is clearly not negligible, if these cancer potency estimates are at all close to the mark, and there is no way to know at present that they are not.

As for metals, the set of exposure estimates in the second part of Table 6-31 can be usefully compared with estimates made from the much more extensive and statistically representative Hall et al. (1978) data set (for the U.S. catch) in Tables 6-23 through 6-30. In the case of mercury, the two data sets provide essentially identical estimates (2.5 and 2.2 μg/day). For arsenic and cadmium, the estimates from the FDA surveillance data are lower than the Hall et al. (1978) data set but are generally within twofold. This is probably because of the lack of monitoring data for these inorganic contaminants in the edible portions of finfish. For chromium, lead, and especially selenium, there are larger differences, with the FDA data set in all cases providing the lower estimates. It is quite possible that the paucity of coverage of some important species in the FDA data set, the probably higher detection limits, and the committee's practice of assigning zero contaminant values to both samples below detection limits and species that were not sampled for a particular contaminant, lead to a downward biasing of the exposure estimates from the FDA data. It would therefore not be surprising to find that some of the estimates of organic contaminants in Table 6-31 may have a similar downward bias.

Based on the FDA data set, the six U.S. commercially caught seafood products that appear to present the greatest daily per capita aggregate PCB exposures and their upper-confidence-limit cancer risks are other freshwater finfish (5.4 x 10^{-6}), bluefish (6.3 x 10^{-7}), mackerel (2.5 x 10^{-7}), and sea trout, mullet, and scup or porgy (each 1.1 x 10^{-7}). The reader should be cautioned that these data are not adequate to fully characterize PCB levels for individual species in a nationally representative way. Nevertheless, the result that probably does have some significance is that the bulk of the PCB risk is concentrated in a relatively obscure category of "other freshwater fish." This group includes fishery products from the Great Lakes and other inland waterways. To the extent that PCBs are considered to be a problem, the bulk of contamination comes from a minor, identifiable fraction of the overall seafood in commerce.

The U.S. commercially caught seafood species presenting the greatest daily per capita dieldrin exposures and upper-confidence-limit cancer risks to the general population are other freshwater fish (4.7 x 10^{-7}), and mullet (1.0 x 10^{-8}).

Comparison of Imported and Domestic Seafood

This analysis is also based on FDA monitoring data. Information on individual imported fish is statistically insignificant, but when taken as a whole the FDA monitoring program appears to suggest some relevant differences in terms of contamination of the domestic supply versus that of the imported supply. Imported seafood, overall, appears less contaminated than domestically landed seafood. The committee believes that this overall difference is largely the result of contamination of U.S. freshwater finfish products. If freshwater finfish were not part of the U.S. seafood supply, U.S. saltwater fish probably would not differ much from imported fish. This could be established with greater precision by a more directed and well-designed sampling effort. Such an effort would be valuable in protecting the consumer and more cost effective than a visual inspection program. In fact, the hypothesis that significant differences in contamination exist between species of fish, as well as between domestically landed and imported seafood, offers a rationale to help consumers reduce toxic exposures by accurately identifying species and the geographic origin of seafood products offered for sale. This could aid consumers in choosing the least contaminated products.

Overall, in only a few cases of contaminated finfish, did imports provide a greater exposure for the consumer than the domestic catch. The committee realizes, however, that this observation may be due to the fact that import consumption patterns were not narrowed down to individual species, that many imported species were not always identified, and that many were not analyzed.

Those cases in which imports had higher contaminant levels included chemicals such as lindane, tecnazene, cadmium, and mercury.

As for cadmium, canned tuna accounts for much of the consumer's exposure. Other, lesser contributors of cadmium include imported scallops. For mercury, the biggest contributors are shark, swordfish, and tuna. An estimation of the total mercury exposure from these imports could not be determined because NMFS import data do not detail specific consumption figures for imported shark and swordfish.

Among imports, salmon and herring accounted for primary sources of PCBs in the diet. Yet, only four samples of herring were taken by the FDA monitoring program to be sampled for organic contamination between 1983 and 1987. This lack of data for individual species is disconcerting, especially when there are definite warning signals indicating that more data gathering would be warranted. The PCB concentration in imported sea herring ranged from nondetectable to 0.36 ppm with three positive detections out of the four samples – a significant positive percentage and range. Furthermore, 11 different industrial pollutants and pesticides were found in these four imported sea herring samples, and although the levels were below FDA action guidelines, these four samples with 27 individual industrial chemicals and pesticide residues warrant further sampling.

Approximately 12 samples of imported salmon were analyzed for organic contaminants between 1986 and 1988. Two of the nine samples from Norway were positive for PCBs, tecnazene, and lindane. Because so little is known about noncancer long-term health consequences of PCBs and other toxic exposures, it seems prudent to reduce PCB exposure in any way possible, and with farm-raised products, the reduction of PCB and other organic chemical contamination should be possible.

Import data are virtually comprised entirely of finfish samples. Very few samples of the imported seafood examined consisted of shellfish. There simply is not enough information available for the committee or anyone to determine the extent of contamination of imported shellfish.

Based on the data available, the biggest single potential risk to consumers in seafood is posed by exposure to PCBs. Yet, whereas the upper-confidence-limit risk per capita from PCBs alone (not counting DDT, dieldrin, and dioxin) is 5.8×10^{-5} for domestically landed finfish, the risk from imports appears significantly lower, slightly less than 3×10^{-6}. For the next highest cancer risk chemical, dieldrin, the U.S. catch typically provides a risk to the average consumer of approximately 1×10^{-5}. The risk per capita from dieldrin in imported fish also appears much smaller, less than 1×10^{-6}. These findings should not be overgeneralized nor, based on present knowledge, can one assume that imported seafood is safer than domestically landed seafood.

Exposures from Sport, Subsistence, and Tribal Fishing

Noncommercial fishing is a significant source of overall fish for human consumption in the United States – estimated at 3-4 pounds per person on the average. It is even more significant as a vehicle for the delivery of bioaccumulating chemicals for the following reasons:

1. Noncommercial seafood harvesters often concentrate their fish/shellfish harvesting within specific areas, some of which may be heavily contaminated.
2. A minority of recreational and subsistence seafood harvesters engage in this activity very frequently and consume relatively large amounts of fish (Humphrey, 1983a,b).
3. Some of the most significant recreational/subsistence caught species also happen to be among those with the largest concentrations of contaminants (e.g., northeastern bluefish; southern California white croaker; Great Lakes trout, walleye, and salmon).
4. In some states (e.g., New York), relatively uncontaminated areas appear to be difficult to find (New York State DEC, 1987).

The primary mechanism by which state governments have alerted consumers about the potential risk of contaminated finfish is the fish consumption advisory (Zeitlin, 1989). In fact, among the 30 U.S. coastal and Great Lakes states, Hawaii, and Alaska (with the exception of Georgia, which did not respond to the survey), 2,094 advisories were issued for coastal marine water, estuaries, rivers, and inland waters. Overall, the vast majority of the advisories (87%) were issued for freshwater fish. Among the states indicated, Alaska, Alabama, New Hampshire, and Oregon each issued one advisory between 1984 and 1987. On the other hand, Minnesota issued 665. As Zeitlin (1989) notes

Consistently high numbers of advisories were issued by the Great Lakes states. Even if advisories are posted to warn anglers, some persons may not heed these warnings because they do not get sick immediately from the consumption of contaminated seafood. There is no way of knowing how effective they are.

The effectiveness of advisories in convincing the general public to voluntarily alter their preparation and consumption habits is, for the most part, unknown. Very few epidemiological or social studies have been conducted. The inherent difficulty in changing pleasurable human behavior is not a novel concept and public perception of risk is often difficult to measure. Adherence to hazard warnings often depends on how much confidence the public has in the credibility of the agency issuing the warnings.

Thus, anglers may be constantly re-exposed to contaminants. Further, many of the nation's most contaminated areas are relatively accessible to the recreational seafood gatherer (e.g., estuarine regions and freshwater bodies). In addition, many "recreational" anglers may actually be subsistence anglers who fish as an important means of supplementing their diet, and they may share their catch with family members and friends.

According to Zeitlin, methods used to communicate potential risks include media announcements, printed brochures, posting notices in public places, and information in fishing license applications. Members of the medical community were contacted to disseminate information to patients in New York, Maine, Michigan, Minnesota, and Wisconsin. Indiana, New York, New Jersey, Michigan, Minnesota, Washington, and South Carolina have organized public outreach and education programs. Finally, contamination of the nation's recreational fishery appears to be pervasive, and although extensively documented as well as possible to date, the contamination is probably not very thoroughly documented – particularly for freshwater fishing.

Examination indicated that PCBs accounted for 43% of all advisories issued. Mercury accounted for 40%, followed by chlordane and dioxin at 8% and 2%, respectively. The remaining 7% was issued for chemicals such as dieldrin, kepone, DDT, PAHs, heptachlor epoxide, petroleum compounds, selenium, and chlorinated benzenes (Zeitlin, 1989).

Advisories issued according to families of freshwater fish were Percidae, including yellow perch and walleye, 21%; Salmonidae, 16% (trout, 11%; salmon, 5%); Centrachidae (sunfish and bass), 13%; Esocidae (pike), 12%; and Cyprinidae (carp), 11%. The remaining advisories were divided among Ictularidae (bullhead catfish), 10%; Catostomiae (suckers), 5%; Anguillidae (freshwater eels), 4%; striped bass and white perch, 4%; and other species, 4%. Based on regional case studies, recreational anglers probably eat far more seafood than nonrecreational seafood consumers. In the Puget Sound study, average daily consumption was 12.3 g (Landolt et al., 1987). The highest consumption rate for a smaller number of fishermen and women was estimated to be 95.1 g/day. These amounts are somewhat similar to findings for Los Angeles area recreational anglers.

Puget Sound Contaminated Recreational Fish Study

During 1986-1987 a broad-scale survey was sponsored by EPA Region X and supported by the Washington State Department of Ecology and the Department of Social and Health Services (DSHS) to characterize potential human health risks associated with chemical contaminants in Puget Sound seafood (Landolt et al., 1987). Research focused entirely on recreational harvesters who frequently collect fish, shellfish, or edible seaweed for use in personal consumption. Data were available for chemical contaminants in fish, shellfish, and macroalgae from 22 locations in Puget Sound. Fish, shellfish, and macroalgae evaluated in the risk assessments of chemically contaminated seafood included pelagic species such as coho salmon, chinook salmon, Pacific hake, striped perch, rockfish, and sablefish; bottom-feeding species such as Pacific cod, walleye, pollock, and tomcod; bottom fish such as English sole, starry flounder, Pacific sanddab, rock sole, flathead sole, and buffalo sculpin; shellfish such as Dungeness crab and rock crab; bivalves including heart cockles, bent nose clams, sand clams, soft-shell clams, littleneck clams, butter clams, Manila clams, and horseneck clams; also examined were market squid, brown algae (kelp), green algae (also known as sea lettuce), and red algae (also known as nori). Thus, the study was both very thorough and very complete.

The chemicals of highest concern included carcinogens such as arsenic, PAHs including benz[a]anthracene, benzo[a]pyrene, benzo[b]fluoranthene, and chrysene; PCBs, alpha-hexachlorocyclohexane (HCH); and DDTs. Noncarcinogenic chemicals of concern included cadmium, lead, and mercury. Interestingly, FDA tolerances or action levels existed for only three of the eight chemicals of highest concern: mercury, PCBs, and DDTs. Overall, the average concentrations of these substances in the various species and categories of seafood were lower than the FDA tolerances or action levels for all locations in Puget Sound, with the notable exception of the concentration of PCBs (2.06 ppm) in English sole from Elliott Bay.

The average consumption rate for Puget Sound recreational anglers was 12.3 g daily. The highest consumption rate for a smaller number of anglers was estimated to be 95.1 g of fish per day from Puget Sound. In this study, upper-confidence-limit cancer risks for cumulative exposure to arsenic and the four organic chemicals of concern ranged from 2×10^{-4} for average anglers to 4×10^{-3} for those most highly exposed. The relatively high, assessed upper-confidence-limit cancer risk derived primarily from potential exposure to PCBs in fish from specific locations in Puget Sound such as Commencement Bay, Elliott Bay, Manchester and Sinclair Inlet. If the contribution of PCBs is excluded, the remaining risk is less than 10^{-5}. No effort was made in this study to quantitatively evaluate the potential for noncancer risks.

It is also quite apparent from this study that recreational anglers have favorite spots and that this is important information for the distribution of risks among the community. As Landolt et al. (1987) note, "the potential cumulative health risks associated with the consumption of chemically contaminated seafood may exceed [one in 10,000 cancers in excess[18]] for certain locations in Puget Sound."

Regional Studies of Contaminants

Regional studies conducted in New York, Massachusetts, the District of Columbia, Alabama, Kansas, California, and Wisconsin indicate levels of inorganic and organic chemicals in recreationally important fish species (EPA, 1983, 1987; Kansas, 1988; New York State DEC, 1987; Rosen, 1989).

Using data generated by these regional studies, one can tentatively estimate upper-confidence-limit cancer risks that might be attributable to dioxin contamination of fish in selected areas. Given an average-size serving (based on recommendations of the Tolerance Assessment System in the EPA Office of Pesticide Programs) of approximately 114 g (0.25 pound) (PTI, 1987), if one were to eat a one-quarter pound serving of large-mouth bass with an average of 11.3 parts per trillion dioxin once a month for a lifetime, the upper-confidence-limit cancer risk implied by the EPA cancer potency factor would be 1×10^{-4}. Therefore, cases may exist in which contamination with dioxin could be a potentially serious hazard for recreational or subsistence anglers.[19]

As suggested earlier, another potential problem residue is methylmercury. Michigan's 1989 fish consumption advisory for anglers suggested that consumption of certain fish from inland lakes statewide be restricted because of mercury found in fish from Upper and Lower Peninsula lakes; approximately 60 of Michigan's inland lakes were tested since 1983, which indicated that about three out of four had at least some fish with mercury exceeding the Michigan Department of Public Health (MDPH) level of concern for state citizens (Michigan, 1988).[20] Pregnant women, nursing mothers, women who intend to have children, and children age 15 or under were advised to eat no more than one meal per month of rock bass, crappie, and yellow perch over 9 inches in length. They were advised not to eat any large-mouth bass, small-mouth bass, walleye, northern pike, or muskie from inland lakes. Others were advised to eat no more than one meal per week of these fish.

Atlantic Coast Bluefish Contamination

Bluefish is the principal recreational species along the Atlantic Coast, with 130-155 million pounds landed annually (NOAA, 1987). Contaminant levels appear to correlate with geographic site of origin and size (fork length).

Small- and medium-sized bluefish tend to have, with few exceptions, lower PCB concentrations than large bluefish. For small and medium bluefish, no samples exceeded 2 ppm PCBs at any of the sampling sites, and no statistically significant differences were noted among the site percentages in these classes. Large bluefish did exceed 2 ppm PCBs.

The arithmetic mean concentration of PCBs in medium-size bluefish taken in January-February 1985 from North Carolina was 0.20 ppm in males and 0.53 in females, whereas large bluefish had concentrations of 1.94 ppm in males and 1.61 ppm in females. The arithmetic mean concentration of PCBs in small bluefish taken from New York Bight in May-June 1985 was 0.13 ppm in males and 0.20 ppm in females. The arithmetic mean concentration of PCBs in medium bluefish was 0.38 ppm in males and 0.37 ppm in females. The arithmetic mean concentration of PCBs in large bluefish was 1.00 ppm in males and 1.58 ppm in females.

In New England for May-June 1985, small bluefish averaged 0.20 ppm PCBs in males and 0.65 ppm in females. Medium bluefish averaged 0.39 ppm in males and 0.44 ppm in females. Large bluefish averaged 1.10 ppm in males and 0.99 ppm in females. In New England for October 1985, although no small bluefish were sampled, medium bluefish averaged 0.55 ppm PCBs in males and 0.50 ppm in females. Large bluefish averaged 1.35 ppm PCBs in males and 1.11 ppm in females.

When all sampling sites were combined, the differences continued to appear significant. Small male bluefish averaged 0.15 ppm PCBs, and small females averaged 0.27 ppm. Medium male bluefish and medium female bluefish each averaged 0.42 ppm. Large male bluefish averaged 1.40 ppm, and large female bluefish averaged 1.45 ppm PCBs.

The study divided bluefish into three size groupings: Small bluefish were less than or equal to 300 mm (11.8 inches). Medium-sized bluefish ranged from 301 to 500 mm (11.8-19.7 inches). Large bluefish were more than 500 mm (19.7 inches).

Mean PCBs were compared for each fork length class to assess possible differences due to sampling site. For small bluefish, the sample PCB means did not statistically differ among sites, whereas for medium-sized bluefish, the sample PCB means formed two statistically significant site groupings. The sample mean for New England in October was 0.94 ppm, which significantly exceeded the January-February mean for North Carolina, 0.71 ppm.

However, even small bluefish may not be perfectly safe for the recreational fisher to consume constantly. The FDA tolerance of 2 ppm in fish is frequently cited as a criterion for evaluating the significance of PCB residues. However, as shown earlier, the risks associated with this level of PCB contamination could be appreciable.

Southern California Sport Fishery

A 1978 southern California sport fishing survey carried out by the California Department of Fish and Game found that 75% of the catch was composed of 20 species and that one in three fish was a white croaker, a fish known to contain significant amounts of DDT and PCBs. Another report on Los Angeles metropolitan area recreational fishers during 1980 assessed the consumption rates of potentially hazardous marine fish and shellfish by local, nonprofessional anglers; identified subgroups with a significantly large consumption rate; and estimated the size of the population potentially exposed.

The median consumption rate was found to be 37 g/day, much higher than the average fish consumption for the U.S. population as a whole (estimated at about 18.7 g/day). At the 90th percentile the average consumption rate was 225 g/day. The results of this study also demonstrated that there exists a regular fishing population along the southern California shoreline: 14% of the subjects surveyed fished three to seven times per week, even at sites likely to be contaminated by waste discharge. Furthermore, fish caught by frequent as well as infrequent fishermen are generally shared and consumed among an estimated 342,000 family members.

The fish caught are dominated by a few species, including white croaker and Pacific bonito which have been found to accumulate both PCBs and DDT. At the median, the recreational fishers surveyed consumed 14.8 g of white croaker daily and 63.6 g of bonito daily. At the 90th percentile, those surveyed consumed 85.2 g of white croaker and 334 of bonito daily.

According to analyses performed by the Southern California Coastal Water Research Project and published in 1981-1982, white croaker sampled in Los Angeles harbor in the vicinity of Cabrillo pier, a popular fishing spot, averaged 1.7 ppm DDT and 0.18 ppm PCBs. Bonito sampled in the program averaged 0.184 ppm DDT and 0.029 ppm PCBs (Gossett et al., 1982).

By using the EPA upper-confidence-limit cancer potency factors for oral administration in conjunction with median consumption rates, the potential cancer risk for consumption of white croakers from Cabrillo pier would be approximately 4×10^{-4}; the cancer risk for DDT would be 1.5×10^{-4}. The total upper-confidence-limit cancer risk for average consumers of white croaker would be 5×10^{-4}.

The results of this study suggest that certain subpopulations, characterized by age and ethnic group, may be at higher risk, including individuals over 65 years of age, Orientals, and Samoans.

In April 1985, warnings were issued by the California Department of Health Services that advised against eating white croakers and recommended reduced consumption of other fish to no more than once a week, particularly at the most contaminated sites in the Los Angeles Harbor area and near the Whites Point sewage outfall.

Posting signs is one means for advising people of some potential health threat from eating locally gathered seafood. It is not the whole answer, but it is an honest attempt to provide information and no doubt gives some fishers pause to consider whether to change their fishing locale.

Conclusions

1. Based on the committee's tentative analysis of FDA survey data, it appears that in the aggregate, freshwater fish tend to be more contaminated than open ocean saltwater fish. Past studies have reached a similar conclusion (GAO, 1988).

2. Many freshwater sport fish have levels of contamination with toxins such as chlordane, dieldrin, and PCBs that, based on current risk assessment numbers, may present an appreciable risk.

3. The health effects of concern go well beyond cancer and include reproductive effects and possibly other chronic conditions. For example, it is known that PCBs cross the placenta in women exposed to ordinary dietary levels (Fein et al., 1984). In one study of mothers who ate contaminated lake fish, PCB exposure, determined both in contaminated fish consumption and in cord serum PCB levels, predicted lower birth weight and smaller head circumference.

4. Serum monitoring of recreational anglers who frequent contaminated areas (and appropriate controls) should be conducted to ascertain the extent of recreational exposure in comparison to people who do not consume recreationally caught fish.

5. Although some problems, such as PCB contamination, result from historically poor public pollution control policy, continuing contamination with some pollutants is ongoing—most notably pesticide, PAH, and dioxin contamination of saltwater and freshwater fish—throughout the country. An active environmental stance aimed at pollution prevention (rather than mitigation after the damage has been done) should be implemented at the federal level to prevent future pollution disasters on the level of the PCB decimation of much of the nation's freshwater fishery.

6. One of the biggest weaknesses of present seafood monitoring programs is that only a certain group of chemicals, suspected to be unsafe, is monitored. However, the number of chemicals so classified is extremely small compared with the number of chemicals being added to the environment whose long-term effects are generally unknown (GAO, 1988). One researcher stated that he found 340 chemical compounds in the Chesapeake Bay, most of which have not been assessed for safety. As a result, he believes that oysters coming even from approved harvest areas are not necessarily safe to eat because of the long-term effects of accumulating toxic chemicals in humans.

7. Sampling programs are very limited—sampling too few species, too few contaminants, and too few sites (Zeitlin, 1989).

8. Exposure data, consumption estimates, and risk assessment models differ among state agencies and from state to state (Zeitlin, 1989).

9. Guidelines and criteria supplied by the federal government are rare and sometimes contradictory (Zeitlin, 1989).

10. Although different methods have been used to disseminate information concerning advisories, the most effective methods have not been identified through controlled testing (Zeitlin, 1989). Other questions relating to risk management must be considered in the development of fish consumption advisories based on quantitative health assessments. Many of these questions were discussed at a National Wildlife Federation workshop (NWF, 1989).

Consumer Information and
Labeling Programs, and Fishing Advisories

Unfortunately, as noted in the discussion of sport fishing, there appears to have been relatively little systematic study of the efficacy of state advisory programs in reducing population exposures to chemical contaminants in seafood from areas known to have higher than usual levels. Consumer information programs do, nevertheless, have features that have attracted the strong support of some members of the committee.

Advisories and other information programs represent the least coercive type of governmental intervention in the marketplace. Such programs theoretically allow the diverse set of consumers to use their individual assessment of the importance of possible risks versus costs to choose appropriate risk control policies for themselves. Moreover, advisories represent a way governmental entities can take at least some action on problems that would be difficult to attack by more rigorous measures (e.g., sport fishers may tend to resist efforts to directly limit harvesting in some areas, and enforcement of those restrictions may involve more effort and expense than public authorities can exert in some cases). Some members of the committee have advocated that retail displays of seafood be accompanied by a score based on the assessed quantitative risk of the species being offered for sale and the geographic location from which it was taken.

On the other hand, placing the burden of choice with respect to risks on the individual consumer (or individual sport fisher) may require people to devote more time and effort than they consider reasonable, in light of competing needs to evaluate other health and economic choices. Even with additional public education, there is room for doubt about how accurate consumer perceptions would be in evaluating supermarket-delivered risk information. Public agencies have a clear advantage of scale in gathering information and evaluating risks that apply to their constituencies as a whole (or to significant subsections). Public health authorities can evaluate risks much more easily than individual consumers and are in a unique position of trust to take preventive action, in light of widely shared attitudes toward risk and risk control options. A measure of the disenchantment of many consumers with agencies who hold such trust is that public demands for direct consumer information programs (such as California's Proposition 65) seem to have expanded in recent years.

PROBABLE HEALTH RISKS FROM FISH AND SHELLFISH CONSUMPTION – RECOMMENDATIONS FOR RESEARCH

Classic Acute and Chronic Toxic Effects

There seems to be little potential for important classic acute toxic effects from the types and levels of chemical contaminants in U.S. seafood. Some classic chronic effects may be of significance, however, particularly the effects of cadmium on kidney function and of lead in impairing cognitive development in early childhood. Biomarkers of lead exposure (e.g., blood and bone lead levels) should be assessed in relation to the consumption of selected seafood items to assess the potential for control and the significance of the hazard in relation to other sources of exposure to these contaminants.

Reproductive Effects

Reproductive effects constitute a seriously understudied area, in which the information available gives appreciable cause for concern. The analysis in the mercury case study discussion above indicates that low-dose developmental risks from fetal exposures to methylmercury may be appreciable. Good case control studies using hair and other biomarkers of methylmercury exposure should be pursued. More generally, markers of modestly impaired status, such as the population distribution of birth weights, should be used to assess the potential effects of other contaminants in people with unusually high in utero exposures to PCBs and related contaminants. Alternative measures of PCB concentration need to be developed that will be better indices of the potential activity of different PCB congeners in producing both reproductive and other effects.

Carcinogenesis

The committee's analyses, using conventional approaches to carcinogenic risk assessment, indicate an appreciable potential of carcinogenic risk from some freshwater locations (e.g., Lake Michigan) and species (e.g., bluefish harvested in some locations in the eastern United States) and, to a lesser extent, from general commercial seafood (Table 6-31). Assessments of this risk will benefit from further research on the mechanisms whereby some PCB and dioxin congeners enhance carcinogenesis in animal systems, and from follow-up of human populations with relatively high exposure to both seafood and nonseafood sources of different PCB mixtures.

Chronic Cumulative Toxic Effects

Studies of chronic cumulative toxic effects are in their infancy. As mentioned earlier, a recent, apparently sound case control epidemiological study among people in Singapore has found a strong association between blood levels of mercury and risk of Parkinson's disease (Ngim and Devathasan, 1989). Similar studies, using both biomarkers of exposure of selected seafood-borne toxicants and early biomarkers of progressive damage, may ultimately prove fruitful for prevention of this increasingly important area of health damage.

CONCLUSIONS AND RECOMMENDATIONS

Significance of the Risk

Seafood generally provides an important source of protein in the diet and has lower saturated fat content than most other high-protein foods. Because of this, seafood as a whole undoubtedly makes an important positive contribution to a healthy diet. Several different chemical contaminants of seafood have the potential to pose large enough hazards to public health to warrant additional societal efforts at control. However, they are not generally of such magnitude, in the aggregate, as to be comparable to the largest environmental health hazards characterized to date (e.g., indoor exposure to radon progeny). Some examples of the risks that may be significant include reproductive effects from PCBs and methylmercury; carcinogenesis from selected congeners of PCBs, dioxins, and dibenzofurans (all of which appear to act primarily by binding to a single type of receptor); and, based on a very recent and as yet unconfirmed epidemiological study from Singapore, parkinsonism in old age from very long-term mercury exposure. Several other metallic and pesticide residues also warrant attention.

Part of the reason some aquatic animals pose particular chemical contamination problems derives from their position in the food chain. Whereas the land animals used for human food are generally vegetarians, most of the aquatic animals that contribute to our diet are themselves predators of other animals – and, in some cases, predators of predators. Because of this, there is an opportunity for substances that are both poorly metabolized and poorly excreted by living organisms to become more concentrated through several successive sets of flesh consumers. Substances that tend to "bioconcentrate" in this way include chlorinated aromatic compounds such as PCBs, DDT, and related pesticides, and some metallic compounds such as methylmercury.

When these same chemical residues are consumed by humans, they also tend to persist in the body and to build up over prolonged periods. Some PCB congeners, cadmium, and lead have biological half-lives measured in several years or decades. Because of this, changes in risks from these substances will generally be manifest only long after changes have been made in exposures.

Potential for Control

Contaminant levels in aquatic animals are distributed very unevenly. The fact that some geographic areas (e.g., fresh versus salt water), some species, and some size classes of aquatic animals have much higher residue levels than others means that important quantitative reductions can be made in individual and societal aggregate health risks with measures that would restrict the overall commercial availability of fresh and marine seafood to only a modest degree. If the available data bases are improved, there is a potential for regulatory agencies to better target their efforts and for interested consumers to modify individual risks by altering their consumption of specific species, and of fresh and marine seafood originating in specific areas. Such targeting should include efforts not only to close or reduce harvesting of high-risk species from high-risk areas, but also to reduce the input of contaminants to the local marine environment. A strong effort should be made to develop systems for containment of waste that do not involve atmospheric or aquatic dumping. Coordination of efforts to improve the health of aquatic ecosystems with efforts to improve the safe management of seafood resources will have benefits for both types of social objectives.

Performance of Current Federal Regulatory Authorities in Assessing and Managing Risks

The overall posture of relevant federal agencies, particularly FDA, appears to be almost totally reactive. Whether due to inadequate resources, priorities implicit in the relevant enabling legislation, or an ideological disinclination to raise issues that might run counter to the prevailing trend toward deregulation, it is the committee's overall judgment that there has been less effort than would be desirable to discover and quantify hazards, to evaluate options for the reduction of risks, and to implement prudent policies that protect both the health of consumers and the stability of commercial markets.

Data Gathering for Risk and Control Analysis

With the notable exception of a data base created by Hall et al. (1978) for inorganic elements and never completely analyzed, the data bases available for quantifying human exposure to seafood-borne toxicants, setting priorities for control measures, and appropriately advising consumers of risks are grossly inadequate. Even though 90% of FDA's analytical samples are classified as having been taken for "surveillance" rather than "compliance" purposes, the data do not adequately represent national seafood consumption. Several extensively consumed species have not been analyzed at all, and others have received minimal effort. There has been virtually no monitoring by FDA for PCBs or pesticides in bivalves.

Some of the available sampling data are difficult to interpret or entirely useless because of inaccuracies in classification of the species concerned and inadequate recording of the geographic areas of harvest. Relatively high detection limits have been tolerated for some analytical tests, probably because the agency has focused primarily on determining the incidence of residues over a certain level that would violate current standards, rather than quantifying the overall dose delivered to consumers.

Risk Assessment Practices

Carcinogenesis risk assessment procedures should be modified to give decision makers additional information about the uncertainties of analysis, as well as both aggregate and individual risk estimates. In particular, to facilitate evaluation of the costs and benefits of measures to achieve quantitative reductions in exposure to inadvertent carcinogenic contaminants, procedures should be developed to supplement current upper-confidence-limit cancer potency estimates with estimates representing the central tendency of cancer risks, incorporating information on cancer risks from all available species, as well as comparative information on the pharmacokinetic and pharmacodynamic factors in different species.

The FDA is most conspicuously backward in the development of quantitative risk assessment approaches for noncarcinogens. The rule-of-thumb (ADI/NOEL/safety factor) procedure now universally in use has serious conceptual flaws, inappropriately mixes technical and social policy presumptions in analysis, and fails to encourage the development of additional information on pharmacokinetics, human interindividual variability, and other topics that could enable better estimates of human risk for noncancer effects.

Risk Management

The relevant federal enabling legislation is the product of a long and complex history in which different criteria and authorities have been layered on top of one another. It would be desirable to direct increased agency attention to problems involving inadvertent contaminants and natural toxins. To do this, Congress should consider a fundamental restructuring of food and fisheries management legislation. Designated federal authorities should be encouraged to evaluate the opportunities to achieve feasible reductions in risk by quantitatively analyzing the benefits and costs of control opportunities, ranging from the restriction of harvesting fish and shellfish in particular areas, through restricting the species harvested, to determining the size of fish that can be brought to market. In selected rare cases where contaminants are known to concentrate in particular organs of seafood species, such as the hepatopancreas ("tomalley") of lobsters and the gonads or roe of scallops, the relevant governmental authorities should promulgate organ-specific restrictions on marketing and consumer advisories. In light of the fact that most seafood commerce is interstate, the current restriction of FDA authority to items between states appears to be an unproductive complication. One federal agency should be given overall responsibility for managing the risk from chemical residues in seafood, to ensure at least the minimum performance of state programs, while allowing the states flexibility to implement more effective programs tailored to local hazards and consumption practices.

Despite repeated requests from the states for additional guidance on appropriate residue levels, FDA's output of contaminant standards is minuscule, although the committee understands that several informal shellfish guidance documents are expected to be completed in the summer of 1990; unfortunately these documents are not yet available (P. Lombardo, FDA, personal communication, 1991). Even the tolerances that have been promulgated were based – in at least two cases (PCBs and methylmercury) – on reasoning that was questionable at the time and has been rendered obsolete by more recent scientific information. Advances in understanding the likely mechanisms involved in PCB carcinogenesis, the relative potency of different PCB congeners, the findings of subtle noncancer risks at relatively low dose levels (via fetal exposure), and data on the uneven distribution of residue levels suggest substantial unexploited opportunities to reduce risks. Information on the fetal and chronic neurological risks of methylmercury further suggests the need to reevaluate the current tolerance in that case.

In the development of advisories for reproductive effects, due weight must be given to the persistence of different toxicants in people. For methylmercury, with an elimination half-life averaging about 70 days, it may well be sufficient to direct advice to couples who intend to have children in the near future. For PCBs on the other hand, with half-lives measured in several years or even decades, reductions in intake only in the months prior to and during pregnancy can be expected to have little impact on effective body burdens and fetal exposure. In that case, cautionary advice may need to extend to the entire population of reproductive and prereproductive ages.

NOTES

1. In the methylmercury case, the committee was able to infer the distribution of effective internal dosage and risk to the population by using some fragmentary data on blood levels. Similar blood level population distribution data were also cited in the polychlorinated biphenyl (PCB) case study, although a translation into intake distributions or risks was not possible there because of the incompleteness of information about the pharmacokinetics of different PCB congeners.

2. A major theme, if not the central organizing principle of traditional physiology and toxicology, is the concept of the "homeostatic system." Biological processes are seen as part of a complex interacting web, exquisitely designed so that modest changes in any parameter will automatically give rise to compensating processes to restore optimal functioning (e.g., too much heat input automatically induces sweating so that temperature is kept within a normal range). In this view, as long as a toxic material or any other disturbing stimulus does not push one or more parameters beyond a specified limit ("threshold"), adaptive processes will repair any damage that may have been temporarily produced and completely restore the system to its normal functional state. This paradigm has enjoyed great success in guiding the design and interpretation of a wide range of experimental findings on acute responses to toxic chemicals, heat, cold, and other agents in which the mechanism of damage, does, in fact, consist of grossly overwhelming a particular set of bodily defenses.

Another type of damage mechanism dominates thinking in molecular biology and genetics. At the molecular level, some fundamental life processes are basically fragile, in particular, the integrity of the information coded within the deoxyribonucleic acid (DNA) of each cell. An unrepaired error ("mutation") in copying will usually be passed on to all descendants of the mutated cell, and even if the mistake is confined to a single DNA base, massive adverse consequences may result if important genetic information has been altered in a way that affects its function. For the molecular biologist it is intuitively obvious that even a single molecule of a substance that reacts with DNA has some chance of producing a biologically significant result if it happens to interact with the right DNA site. For the traditional toxicologist, basic intuition leads to the opposite expectation: for any substance there is some level of exposure that will have no significant effect on a given biological system. Clearly, application of either intuition to a particular biological response is appropriate only to the degree that the causal mechanism for that response resembles the paradigmatic damage-producing process that is the basis for the intuition.

3. It should be stressed that there is no necessary association between the reversibility or irreversibility of processes causing impairment and the social significance of the impairment itself. For example, many thousands of people are killed each year in automobile accidents because of the fully reversible impairments of judgment and reaction time produced by alcohol.

4. Quantifying human interindividual differences in pharmacokinetic or other parameters that are likely to produce different susceptibilities to adverse effects is a key enterprise if risk assessment for traditional categories of toxic effects is to move from the gross no-effect level (NOEL)/"uncertainty factor" approach to more quantitative treatments of the likely incidence and severity of adverse effects. Hattis et al. (1987a,b) have compiled some preliminary data on the interindividual variability of systemic pharmacokinetic parameters for chemicals in general and of parameters that are likely to contribute to individual susceptibility to anticholinesterase agents.

5. For example, for healthy workers there may indeed be a functional reserve capacity for oxygen delivery to the myocardium and hence a finite tolerance for a small impairment of oxygen-delivering capacity for the blood due to carbon monoxide. However, for a worker who has just begun to experience a myocardial infarction, oxygen delivery to portions of the myocardium is known to be seriously compromised, and a small difference in oxygen-delivering capacity due to a modest blood carboxyhemoglobin concentration could prove the difference between life and death for portions of the heart muscle that are suddenly forced to rely on collateral arterial vessels for oxygen supply.

6. Witness FDA's 2-ppm limit in fish versus extensive EPA efforts to prevent further release of PCBs by mandating collection and destruction of PCBs from used electrical equipment, cleanup of soil contaminated by PCB spills, and even serious consideration of dredging PCB-contaminated sediment from areas such as New Bedford Harbor, Massachusetts.

7. According to R.J. Scheuplein (1988), Deputy Director of the Office of Toxicological Sciences at FDA,

> in 1969 the FDA identified PCB residues in milk from several dairy farms in West Virginia. Eventually, the source of contamination was traced to spent transformer fluid that was used as a vehicle for a herbicide; dairy cattle grazing nearby had become contaminated. FDA established an action level of 5.00 ppm on PCBs in milk (fat basis). This represented the first U.S. regulatory action taken because of PCB contamination of food. During the next two years, seven other major incidents of PCB contamination of food occurred in the United States. In New York State in 1970, 140,000 chickens were destroyed because testing showed PCBs in excess of an FDA 5 ppm action level. The alleged source of contamination was believed to be plastic bakery wrappers which were ground up with the bakery goods fed to the chickens. In April of 1970 FDA investigated the contamination of milk in Ohio and determined that some farmers were using a PCB-containing sealant in their silos that migrated to the silage. By late 1971, it was quite apparent the spillage or leakage of PCBs from equipment or contact with PCB-containing materials could directly contaminate food and feed. Spills and leaks are sporadic episodes of direct food contamination and it was in response to these potential "Yusho-like" incidents that FDA first intervened with action levels and with controls on distribution. But it was also becoming clear by 1971 that PCBs had become ubiquitous environmental contaminants capable of indirectly, unavoidably and persistently contaminating many types of food.

8. This group was defined as those consuming more than 24 pounds per year (average consumption was 38.5 pounds). If they indeed received an average of 1.75 μg/kg/day, then the average concentration of PCBs in their fish would have been approximately 2.6 ppm; 70-kg average body weights are assumed.

9. Unfortunately, a number of other difficulties with the calculation as presented are not so easily quantified. For example, on the cost side, FDA appears to have used landed weights of fish subject to seizure to estimate the economic losses expected from various policies. The assumption is thus that (1) every violative fish caught and presented to market is detected, and yet (2) fishermen make no changes in the locations they fish, species they fish for, and sizes of fish they bring in, in response to the assumed strict enforcement system. The shifting of fishing resources (people, equipment) to locations and species with fewer contamination problems would tend to reduce the long-term economic cost of the tolerance reduction.

10. Not all such studies are positive, it should be noted, and the human evidence of PCB carcinogenicity is still not regarded as definitive.

11. Note that the uncertainty bounds on this estimate extend to values that are higher and lower than the estimate by at least 10-fold; thus, the FDA potency factor is by no means ruled out by current epidemiological results.

12. The Z-score in Figure 6-1 is simply the number of standard deviations above or below the midpoint of a standard normal or lognormal distribution, inferred from the rank of a specific individual value in a data set. To create this type of plot, measurements are first arranged in order and given ranks i (1 through N). Then, a "percentage score" is calculated for each ordered value as 100 x $(i - 0.5)/N$. (This is simply the percentage of an infinite sample that would be expected to be less than or equal to the observed value. It differs from the usual definition of a "percentile" in which the highest observation is assigned a score of 100.) Finally, from tables of probits in Finney (1971) or areas under a cumulative normal distribution, one calculates the number of standard deviations above or below the median of a normal distribution that would be expected to be associated with each "percentage score," if the distribution of values were in fact normal (Gaussian). In the regression line calculated from this type of plot, the intercept ($Z = 0$) represents the expected median, and the slope represents the standard deviation; R is regression coefficient.

13. From the two preceding sentences, it can be inferred that Tollefson and Cordle (1986) are treating the distributions of consumption rates for individual species as normal (Gaussian), rather than lognormal, which may be more accurate.

14. Unfortunately, although the NMFS (1978) report is statistically sophisticated it appears to be biologically naive, in that is seems to focus on the distribution of daily intake, rather than periods of a month or more to be as comparable as possible to the long biological half-life of methylmercury in humans. The report is unclear enough in its methodology and end product results that the committee is unable to effectively utilize its contents, but it provides at least an illustration of the kind of distributional treatment that, if based on appropriate periods of exposure, could be toxicologically informative.

15. In other work (not shown) these data were fit to the lognormal risk model in Clement Associates ToxRisk2 statistical package (Crump et al., 1989). This model differs slightly from the classic probit model in that it is essentially a one-hit dose-response function, incorporating a lognormal distribution of susceptibilities. Despite

this difference, the results obtained by this procedure were very similar to those shown for the classical Finney (1971) procedure.

16. If the distributions of biological half-lives and thresholds for effect in terms of blood levels are in fact lognormal, if among individuals the two distributions are independent (uncorrelated), and if the two factors each act multiplicatively in affecting individuals' thresholds for effect in terms of long-term dietary dose, then the corresponding $\log_{10}$ variances can simply be added. Thus, the probit slope for dietary exposure =

$$1/\{(1/\text{blood probit slope})^2 + [\log_{10}(\text{half-life geometric standard deviation})^2]\}^{0.5}$$

The $\log_{10}$ (half-life geometric standard deviation) calculated from the data in Figure 6-2 is 0.147016.

17. The FDA does not publish a list of cancer potency estimates for these compounds using its own methodology, which differs from that of EPA (discussed earlier). As a standard practice, EPA accompanies the use of these cancer potency estimates with the following: "This level is an upper estimate and the actual risk may be as low as zero." Exactly how much, as a rule, these numbers are likely to overstate actual risks is the subject of much current controversy in the regulatory and toxicological communities. For a comparison of best estimates of cancer risk and EPA upper confidence limits in three cases with the aid of physiologically based pharmacokinetic analyses, see Hattis (1990b).

18. This is in excess of the background cancer risk, which is about 1 in 5 for the U.S. population.

19. For example, in the Alabama River, near Claiborne, Alabama, fillets sampled from large-mouth bass average 16.1 parts per trillion dioxin. If the consumption rate is 18 g daily, which is equivalent to about one-third of a pound per week, the cancer risk would be 6.7×10^{-4}.

20. Unlike the federal regulation, MDPH uses a concentration of 0.5 ppm of mercury in fish tissue as a trigger for issuance of fish consumption advisories. This level is based on a WHO recommendation that daily consumption of mercury not exceed 35 μg. This would result in a body burden approximately 10 times lower than that observed to cause effects in humans in mercury poisoning incidents in Japan and Iraq (Michigan, 1989). At the 0.5-ppm contamination level, a person could eat nearly a pound of fish per week without exceeding the WHO recommended maximum daily intake. Larger, older fish in many inland lakes throughout Michigan may have concentrations of mercury in the 0.5- to 1.5-ppm range. This discovery of mercury in fish from inland lakes is not limited to Michigan. Wisconsin, Minnesota, and Ontario have all experienced similar findings. The EPA and the upper Midwest states are currently evaluating whether factors such as acid rain may contribute to this problem. As for warning anglers about all sources of contamination, that task appears to be impossible. Michigan alone has approximately 10,000 inland lakes within its boundaries, and the state readily concedes that it will never be feasible for fish from all lakes to be tested for contaminants.

REFERENCES

AIHC (American Industrial Health Council). 1987. A Discussion Memorandum of the Vinyl Chloride Decision: Improving the Science Base for Health Assessment. Submitted to EPA for consideration in its Carcinogen Risk Assessment Guidelines: Proposed Updating. September. AIHC, Washington, D.C. 19 pp.

Allen, B.C., A.M. Shipp, K.S. Crump, B. Killian, M.L. Hogg, and B.K. Tudor. 1987. Investigation of Cancer Risk Assessment Methods (four volumes). Report by Clement Associates, Inc. to the U.S. Environmental Protection Agency, EPA Report No. EPA/600/6-87/007a-d, September.

Al-Shahristani, H., and K. Shihab. 1974. Variation of biological half-life of methylmercury in man. Arch. Environ. Health 28:342-344.

Appelman, L.M., W.F. ten Berge, and P.G.J. Reuzel. 1982. Acute inhalation toxicity study of ammonia in rats with variable exposure periods, Am. Ind. Hyg. Assoc. J. 43:662-665.

Baker, E.L., R.G. Feldman, R.F. White, and J.P. Harley. 1983. The role of occupational lead exposure in the genesis of psychiatric and behavioral disturbances. Acta Psychiat. Scand. 67(Suppl. 303):38-48.

Bakir, F., S.F. Damluji, L. Amin-Zaki, M. Murtadha, A. Khalidi, N.Y. al-Rawi, S. Tikriti, H.I. Dahahir, T.W. Clarkson, J.C. Smith, and R.A. Doherty. 1973. Methylmercury poisoning in Iraq. Science 181:230-241.

Ballew, M., and D. Hattis. 1989. Reproductive Effects of Glycol Ethers in Females–A Quantitative Analysis. M.I.T. Center for Technology, Policy, and Industrial Development, CTPID 89-7, July.

Barry, P.S.I. 1975. A comparison of concentrations of lead in human tissues. Brit. J. Ind. Med. 32:119-139.

Bellinger, D., A. Leviton, C. Waternaux, H. Needleman, and M. Rabinowitz. 1987. Longitudinal analyses of prenatal and postnatal lead exposure and early cognitive development. N. Engl. J. Med. 316:1037-1043.

Bellinger, D., A. Leviton, and J. Sloman. 1990. Antecedents and correlates of improved cognitive performance in children exposed in utero to low levels of lead. Environ. Health Perspect. 89:5-11.

Berglund, F., M. Berlin, G. Birke, U. von Euler, L. Friberg, B. Holmstedt, E. Jonsson, C. Ramel, S. Skerfving, A. Swensson, and S. Tejning. 1971. Methylmercury in fish: A toxicological-epidemiologic evaluation of risks. Report from an expert group. Nord. Hyg. Tidskr. 4(Suppl.):19-290.

Bernard, S.R. 1977. Dosimetric data and metabolic model for lead. Health Physics 32:44-46.

Bertazzi, P.A., L. Riboldi, A. Pesatori, L. Radice, and C. Zocchetti. 1987. Cancer mortality of capacitor manufacturing workers. Am. J. Ind. Med. 11:165-76.

Bishop, J.M. 1987. The molecular genetics of cancer. Science 235:305-311.

Brown, D.P. 1987. Mortality of workers exposed to polychlorinated biphenyls: An update. Arch. Environ. Health 42:333-339.

Buehler, F., P. Schmid, and C. Schlatter. 1988. Kinetics of PCB elimination in man. Chemosphere 17:1717-1726.

Campbell, B.C., P.A. Meredith, M.R. Moore, and W.S. Watson. 1984. Kinetics of lead following intravenous administration in man. Toxicol. Lett. 21:231-235.

Cappuzo, J., A. McElroy, and G. Wallace. 1987. Fish and shellfish contamination in New England waters: An evaluation and review of available data on the distribution of chemical contaminants. Report submitted to Coast Alliance, Washington, D.C.

Chamberlain, A.C. 1985. Prediction of response of blood lead to airborne and dietary lead from volunteer experiments with lead isotopes. Proc. Roy. Soc. London B 224:149-182.

Clarkson, T.W., L. Amin-Zaki, and S.K. Al-Tikriti. 1976. An outbreak of methylmercury poisoning due to consumption of contaminated grain. Fed. Proc. 35:2395-2399.

Clarkson, T.W., B. Weiss, and C. Cox. 1983. Public health consequences of heavy metals in dump sites. Environ. Health Perspect. 48:113-127.

Cleaver, J.E., and D. Bootsma. 1975. Xeroderma pigmentosum: Biochemical and genetic characteristics. Ann. Rev. Genet. 9:19-38.

Clement Associates, Inc. 1989. Issues in Setting Drinking Water Standards for Polychlorinated Biphenyls–Alternative Approaches to Estimates of Risk for Polychlorinated Biphenyls. Clement Associates, Inc., Ruston, La.

Cordle, F. 1983. Use of epidemiology and clinical toxicology to determine human risk in regulating polychlorinated biphenyls in the food supply. Regul. Toxicol. Pharmacol. 3:252-274.

Cordle, F., R. Locke, and J. Springer. 1982. Risk assessment in a federal regulatory agency: An assessment of risk associated with the human consumption of some species of fish contaminated with polychlorinated biphenyls (PCBs). Environ. Health Perspect. 45:171-182.

Cox, C., T.W. Clarkson, D.O. Marsh, L. Amin-Zaki, S. Tikriti, and G.G. Myers. 1989. Dose-response analysis of infants prenatally exposed to methylmercury: An application of a single compartment model to single-strand hair analysis. Environmental Research 49:318-332.

Crump, K., D. Hoel, and R. Peto. 1976. Fundamental carcinogenic processes and their implications for low dose risk assessment. Cancer Research 36:2973-2979.

Crump, K., H. Guess, and K. Deal. 1977. Confidence intervals and test of hypotheses concerning dose response relations inferred from animal carcinogenicity data. Biometrics 33:437-451.

Crump, K.S., R.B. Howe, and C. Van Landingham. 1989. Tox-Risk-Toxicology Risk Assessment Program. Clement Associates, Inc., Ruston, La.

Cumbie, P.M., and S.L. Van Horn. 1978. Selenium accumulation associated with fish mortality and reproductive failure. Proc. Am. Conf. S.E. Assoc. Fish Wildlife Agencies 32:612.

DFO (Canadian Department of Fisheries and Oceans). 1989. Canadian Guidelines for Chemical Contaminants in Fish and Fish Products. Government of Canada, Ottawa.

Dourson, M.L., and J.F. Stara. 1983. Regulatory history and experimental support of uncertainty (safety) factors. Reg. Toxicol. Pharmacol. 3:224-238.

Ehrenberg, L., E. Moustacchi, and S. Osterman-Golkar. 1983. International Commission for Protection Against Environmental Mutagens and Carcinogens. Dosimetry of genotoxic agents and dose-response relationships of their effects. Mutat. Res. 123:121-182.

EPA (Environmental Protection Agency). 1981. Chemical Hazard Information Profile Draft Report. Antimony Trioxide, CAS No. 1309-64-4. Office of Toxic Substances, U.S. Environmental Protection Agency, Washington, D.C. 41 pp.

EPA (Environmental Protection Agency). 1983. Lower Meramec River Water Quality Intensive Survey. EPA Region VII, Environmental Services Division, Environmental Monitoring and Compliance Branch, Environmental Evaluation Section.

EPA (Environmental Protection Agency). 1986a. Guidelines for carcinogen risk assessment, Parts II-VI. Federal Register 51(185):33992-34012.

EPA (Environmental Protection Agency). 1986b. Superfund Public Health Evaluation Manual EPA/540/1-86/060. Office of Emergency and Remedial Response, U.S. Environmental Protection Agency, Washington, D.C., October. 186 pp.

EPA (Environmental Protection Agency). 1987. The National Dioxin Study: Tiers 3, 5, 6, and 7. EPA 440/4-87-003. Office of Water Regulations and Standards, Monitoring and Data Support Division (WH-553), U.S. Environmental Protection Agency, Washington, D.C.

EPA (Environmental Protection Agency). 1989. Health Assessment Survey Tables - Third Quarter 1989. U.S. Environmental Protection Agency. Publication OERR 9200.6/303/(89-3), July.

FAO/WHO (Food and Agriculture Organization/World Health Organization). 1972. Evaluation of certain food additives and of the contaminants mercury, lead, and cadmium. Joint FAO/WHO Expert Committee on Food Additives. FAO Nutrition Meetings Report Series No. 51, Rome. 32 pp.

FDA (Food and Drug Administration). 1979. Polychlorinated biphenyls (PCB's); Reduction of tolerance. Federal Register 44(June 29):38330-38340.

FDA (Food and Drug Administration). 1982. Levels for poisonous or deleterious substances in human food and animals feed. Food and Drug Administration, Washington, D.C. 13 pp.

FDA (Food and Drug Administration). 1988. Fish List: Guide to Acceptable Market Names for Food Fish Sold in Interstate Commerce. U.S. Government Printing Office, Washington, D.C. 50 pp.

Fein, G.G., J.L. Jacobson, S.W. Jacobson, P.M. Schwartz, and J.K. Dowler. 1984. Prenatal exposure to polychlorinated biphenyls: Effects on birth size and gestational age. J. Pediatrics 105:315-320.

Fialkow, P.J. 1977. Clonal origin and stem cell evolution of human tumors. Pp. 439-453 in J.J. Mulvihill, R.W. Miller, and J.F. Fraumeni, Jr., eds. Genetics of Human Cancer. Raven Press, New York.

Finkel, A.M. 1990. Confronting Uncertainty in Risk Management-A Guide for Decision Makers. Resources for the Future, Washington, D.C. 68 pp.

Finney, D.J. 1971. Probit Analysis, 3rd ed. Cambridge University Press, Cambridge, England. 333 pp.

Fischinger, P.J., and V.T. DeVita, Jr. 1984. Governance of science at the National Cancer Institute: Perceptions and opportunities in oncogene research. Cancer Res. 44:4693-4696.

Friedman, B., A.R. Frackelton, Jr., A.H. Ross, J.M. Connors, H. Fujiki, T. Sugimura, and M.R. Rosner.

1984. Tumor promoters block tyrosine-specific phosphorylation of the epidermal growth factor receptor. Proc. Natl. Acad. Sci. 81:3034-3038.

GAO (General Accounting Office). 1988. Seafood Safety: Seriousness of Problems and Efforts to Protect Consumers, RCED-88-135. Report to the Chairman, Subcommittee on Commerce, Consumer and Monetary Affairs, Committee on Government Operations, House of Representatives. U.S. Government Printing Office, Washington, D.C.

Gartrell, M.J., J.C. Craun, D.S. Podrebarac, and E.L. Gunderson. 1985. Pesticides, selected elements, and other chemicals in adult total diet samples, October 1978-September 1979. J. Assoc. Off. Anal. Chem. 68:862-873.

Gossett, R., H. Puffer, R. Arthur, J. Alfafara, and D. Young. 1982. Levels of Trace Organic Compounds in Sportfish from Southern California. Coastal Water Research Project Biennial Report. Southern California Coastal Water Research Project, Long Beach, Calif.

Green, V.A., G.W. Wise, and J.C. Callenbach. 1978. Lead poisoning. Pp. 123-141 in F. Oehme, ed. Toxicity of Heavy Metals in the Environment, Part 1. Marcel Dekker, New York.

Groth, D.H., L.E. Stettler, J.R. Burg, W.M. Busey, G.C. Grant, and L. Wong. 1986. Carcinogenic effects of antimony trioxide and antimony ore concentrate in rats. J. Toxicol. Environ. Health 18:607-626.

Guess, H., K. Crump, and R. Peto. 1977. Uncertainty estimates from low-dose extrapolations of animal carcinogenicity data. Cancer Res. 37:3475-3483.

Gunderson, E.L. 1988. FDA Total Diet Study, April 1982-April 1984, Dietary intakes of pesticides, selected elements and other chemicals. J. Assoc. Off. Anal. Chem. 71:1200-1209.

Haeger-Aronsen, B., M. Abdulla, and B.I. Fristedt. 1974. Effect of lead on delta-aminolevulinic acid dehydratase activity in red blood cells. II. Regeneration of enzyme after cessation of lead exposure. Arch. Environ. Health 29:150-153.

Haines, A.T., and E. Nieboer. 1988. Chromium hypersensitivity. Pp. 497-532 in J. Nrigau and E. Nieboer, eds. Chromium in the Natural and Human Environment. John Wiley and Sons, New York.

Hall, R.A., E.G. Zook, and G.M. Meaburn. 1978. National Marine Fisheries Service Survey of Trace Elements in the Fishery Resource. NOAA Technical Report NMFS SSRF-721, National Technical Information Service No. PB 283 851, March. U.S. Government Printing Office, Washington, D.C.

Hattis, D. 1981. Dynamics of medical removal protection for lead – A reappraisal. Report to the National Institute for Occupational Safety and Health. M.I.T. Center for Policy Alternatives Report No. CPA-81-25. Cambridge, Mass. 47 pp.

Hattis, D. 1982. From presence to health impact: Models for relating presence to exposure to damage. Pp. 1-66 in N.A. Ashford and C.T. Hill, eds. Analyzing the Benefits of Health, Safety, and Environmental Regulations. M.I.T. Center for Policy Alternatives, Report No. CPA-82-16. Cambridge, Mass.

Hattis, D. 1986. The promise of molecular epidemiology for quantitative risk assessment. Risk Analysis 6:181-193.

Hattis, D. 1988. The use of biological markers in risk assessment. Statistical Science 3:358-366.

Hattis, D. 1990a. Pharmacokinetic principles for dose rate extrapolation of carcinogenic risk from genetically active agents. Risk Analysis 10:303-316.

Hattis, D. 1990b. Use of biological markers and pharmacokinetics in human health risk assessment. Environmental Health Perspectives (in press).

Hattis, D., and A. Smith. 1986. What's wrong with quantitative risk assessment? Pp. 57-79 in R. Almeder and J. Humber, eds. Biomedical Ethics Reviews 1986. The Humana Press, Clifton, N.J.

Hattis, D., and H. Strauss. 1986. Potential Indirect Mechanisms of Carcinogenesis, A Preliminary Taxonomy. National Technical Information Service No. NTIS/PB89-120513. Center for Technology, Policy, and Industrial Development, Report No. CTPID 86-3, Massachusetts Institute of Technology, Cambridge, Mass. 12 pp.

Hattis, D., L. Erdreich, and M. Ballew. 1987a. Human variability in susceptibility to toxic chemicals – A preliminary analysis of pharmacokinetic data from normal volunteers. Risk Anal. 7:415-426.

Hattis, D., S. Bird, and L. Erdreich. 1987b. Human Variability in Susceptibility to Anticholinesterase Agents. M.I.T. Center for Technology, Policy and Industrial Development, Report No. CTPID 87-4. Cambridge, Mass.

Haxton, J., D.G. Lindsay, J.S. Hislop, L. Salmon, E.J. Dixon, W.H. Evans, J.R. Reid, C.J. Hewitt, and D.F. Jeffries. 1979. Duplicate diet study on fishing communities in the United Kingdom:

Mercury exposure in a "critical group". Environ. Res. 18:351-368.

HHS (Department of Health and Human Services), Agency for Toxic Substances and Disease Registry. 1988. The Nature and Extent of Lead Poisoning in Children in the United States: A Report to Congress. July. U.S. Government Printing Office, Washington, D.C.

Hing, E. 1989. Nursing Home Utilization by Current Residents: United States, 1985. National Center for Health Statistics, Vital Health Stat. 13(102), DHHS Publication No. (PHS) 89-1763, October. U.S. Government Printing Office, Washington, D.C.

Hoel, D.G. 1985. Epidemiology and the inference of cancer mechanisms. Natl. Cancer Inst. Monogr. 67:199-203.

Hoel, D.G., N.L. Kaplan, and M.W. Anderson. 1983. Implications of non-linear kinetics on risk estimation in carcinogenesis. Science 219:1032-1037.

Hogue, C.J.R, J.W. Buehler, M.A. Strauss, and J.C. Smith. 1987. Overview of the national infant mortality surveillance (NIMS) project–Design, methods, results. Public Hlth. Reports 102:126-138.

Humphrey, H.E.B. 1974. Mercury concentrations in humans and consumption of fish containing methylmercury. Mercury Project Progress Report. Michigan Department of Public Health, Lansing. 6 pp.

Humphrey, H. 1983a. Population studies of PCBs in Michigan residents. Pp. 299-310 in F.M. D'Itri and M.A. Kamrin, eds. PCBs: Human and Environmental Hazards. Butterworth, Boston, Mass.

Humphrey, H. 1983b. Evaluation of Humans Exposed to Water-Borne Chemicals in the Great Lakes. Final Report to the Environmental Protection Agency, Cooperative Agreement CR-807192. U.S. Environmental Protection Agency, Washington, D.C. 205 pp.

Humphrey, H.E.B. 1988. Chemical contaminants in the Great Lakes: The human health aspect. Pp. 153-165 in M.S. Evans, ed. Toxic Contaminants and Ecosystem Health: A Great Lakes Focus. John Wiley & Sons, New York.

Jacobson, S.W., G.G. Fein, J.L. Jacobson, P.M. Schwartz, and J.K. Dowler. 1985. The effect of intrauterine PCB exposure on visual recognition memory. Child Develop. 56:853-860.

Jones, K.C. 1988. Determination of polychlorinated biphenyls in human foodstuffs and tissues: Suggestions for a selective congener analytical approach. Science Total Environ. 68:141-159.

Kabelitz, D. 1985. Modulation of natural killing by tumor promoters. The regulatory influence of adherent cells varies with the type of target cell. Immunobiology 169:436-446.

Kampert, J.B., A.S. Whittemore, and R.S. Paffenbarger, Jr. 1988. Combined effect of childbearing, menstrual events, and body size on age-specific breast cancer risk, Am. J. Epidemiol. 128:962-979.

Kansas DHE (Department of Health and Environment). 1988. A Survey of Pesticides in Tuttle Creek Lakes, Its Tributaries and the Upper Kansas River. Water Quality Assessment Section, Bureau of Water Protection, Kansas Department of Health and Environment, Topeka.

Kinsella, A.R., and M. Radman. 1978. Tumor promoter induces sister chromatid exchanges. Proc. Natl. Acad. Sci. 75:6149-6153.

Konz, J. 1988. Fish intake study. A memo report dated September 19, 1988 from Jim Konz of Versar, Inc. to Jacqueline Moya of the Environmental Protection Agency. Versar, Inc., Springfield, Va.

Knudson, A.G. 1973. Mutation and human cancer. Adv. Cancer Res. 17:317-352.

Knudson, A.G. 1977. Genetics and etiology of human cancer. Adv. Hum. Genet. 8:1-66.

Landolt, M.L., F.R. Hafer, A. Nevissi, G. Van Belle, K. Van Ness, and C. Rockwell. 1985. Potential toxicant exposures among consumers of recreationally caught fish from urban embankments of Puget Sound. NOAA Tech. Memo, NOS OMA 23. Rockville, Md. 104 pp.

Landolt, M.L., D. Kalman, A. Nevissi, G. van Belle, K. Van Ness, and F.R. Hafer. 1987. Potential toxicant exposures among consumers of recreationally caught fish from urban embayments of Puget Sound. NOAA Tech. Memo, NOS OMA 33. Rockville, Md. 111 pp.

Layde, P.M., L.A. Webster, A.L. Baughman, P.A. Wingo, G.L. Rubin, and H.W. Ory. 1989. The independent associations of parity, age at first full term pregnancy, and duration of breastfeeding with the risk of breast cancer. Cancer and Steroid Hormone Study Group. J. Clin. Epidemiol. 42:963-973.

Mackay, N.J., R.J. Williams, J.L. Kacprzac, M.N. Kazacos, A.J. Collins, and E.H. Auty. 1975. Heavy metals in cultivated oysters (*Crassostrea commercialis = Saccostrea cucullata*) from the estuaries of New South Wales. Aust. J. Mar. Freshwater Res. 26:31-46.

Marcus, A.H. 1985a. Multicompartment kinetic models for lead. I. Bone diffusion models for long-term retention. Environ. Res. 36:441-458.

Marcus, A.H. 1985b. Multicompartment kinetic models for lead. II. Linear kinetics and variable absorption in humans without excessive lead exposures. Environ. Res. 36:459-472.

Marcus, A.H. 1985c. Multicompartment kinetic models for lead. III. Lead in blood plasma and erythrocytes. Environ. Res. 36:473-489.

Marsh, D.O., M.D. Turner, J.C. Smith, J.W. Choe, and T.W. Clarkson. 1974. Methylmercury in human populations eating large quantities of marine fish. I. Northern Peru. Pp. 235-239 in Proceedings of the 1st International Mercury Congress, May 6-10, 1974. Barcelona, Spain.

Marsh, D.O., T.W. Clarkson, C. Cox, G.J. Myers, L. Amin-Zaki, and S. Al-Tikriti. 1987. Fetal methylmercury poisoning. Relationship between concentration in single strands of maternal hair and child effects. Arch. Neurol. 44:1017-1022.

Matthews, H.B., and R.L. Dedrick. 1984. Pharmacokinetics of PCBs. Rev. Pharmacol. Toxicol. 24:85-103.

Maugh, T.H. 1978. Chemical carcinogens: How dangerous are low doses? Science 202:37.

McCaffrey, P.G., B. Friedman, and M.R. Rosner. 1984. Diacylglycerol modulates binding and phosphorylation of the epidermal growth factor receptor. J. Biol. Chem. 259:12502-12507.

McCann, J., E. Choi, E. Yamasaki, and B.N. Ames. 1975. Detection of carcinogens as mutagens in the salmonella/microsome test: Assay of 300 chemicals. Proc. Natl. Acad. Sci. 72:5135-5139.

McFarland, V.A., and J.U. Clarke. 1989. Environmental occurrence, abundance, and potential toxicity of polychlorinated biphenyl congeners: Considerations for a congener-specific analysis. Environ. Health Perspect. 81:225-239.

Michigan DPH (Department of Public Health). 1988. Fish Consumption Advisory Issued by State Health Department. Michigan Department of Public Health, Center for Environmental Health Sciences, December 14, 1988. Lansing. 8 pp.

Miller, E.C., and J.A. Miller. 1981. Mechanisms of chemical carcinogens. Cancer 47:1055-1064.

Modali, R., and S. S. Yang. 1986. Specificity of Aflatoxin B1 binding on human proto-oncogene nucleotide sequence. Pp. 147-158 in M. Sorsa and H. Norppa, eds. Monitoring of Occupational Genotoxicants. Proceedings of a Satellite Symposium to the Fourth International Conference on Environmental Mutagens, Helsinki, Finland, June 30-July 2, 1985. Alan R. Liss, New York.

Moolgavkar, S. 1986. Carcinogenesis modeling: From molecular biology to epidemiology, Ann. Rev. Public Hlth. 7:151-169.

Moolgavkar, S.H., and A.G. Knudson, Jr. 1981. Mutation and cancer: A model for human carcinogenesis. J. Natl. Cancer Inst. 66:1037-1052.

Moolgavkar, S.H., N.E. Day, and R.G. Stevens. 1980. Two-stage model for carcinogenesis: Epidemiology of breast cancer in females, J. Natl. Cancer Inst. 65:559-569.

Murphy, D.L. 1988a. Basic water monitoring program. Fish tissue analysis, 1985. Water Management Admin. Tech. Report 59. State of Maryland, Department of the Environment, Baltimore. 38 pp.

Murphy, D.L. 1988b. Trace contaminants in Chesapeake Bay bluefish. Metals and organochlorine pesticides. Water Management Admin. Tech. Report 73. State of Maryland, Department of the Environment, Divisions of Standards and Certification, Baltimore. 21 pp.

Murphy, D.L. 1988c. Trace contaminants in striped bass from two Chesapeake Bay tributaries. Metals and organochlorine pesticides. Technical Report 58. State of Maryland, Department of the Environment, Divisions of Standards and Certification, Water Management Administration, Baltimore. 19 pp.

Needleman, H.L., C. Gunnoe, A. Leviton, R. Reed, H. Peresie, C. Maher, and P. Barrett. 1979. Deficits in psychologic and classroom performance of children with elevated dentine lead levels. N. Engl. J. Med. 300:689-695.

Needleman, H., A. Schell, D. Bellinger A. Leviton, and E. Allred. 1990. Long-term effect of childhood exposure to lead at low doses: An eleven-year follow-up report. N. Engl. J. Med. 322:83-88.

Ngim, C.N., and G. Devathasan. 1989. Epidemiologic study on the association between body burden mercury level and idiopathic Parkinson's disease. Neuroepidemiol. 8:128-141.

NMFS (National Marine Fisheries Service). 1978. On the Chance of U.S. Seafood Consumers Exceeding the Current Acceptable Daily Intake for Mercury: Recommendations, Regulatory Controls. Seafood Quality and Inspection Division, Office of Fisheries Development, National Marine Fisheries Service. 198 pp.

NMFS (National Marine Fisheries Service). 1988. Fisheries of the United States, 1987. Current Fisheries Statistics, No. 8700. U.S. Government Printing Office, Washington D.C. 115 pp.

NOAA (National Oceanic and Atmospheric Administration). 1987. Report on 1984-86 Federal Survey of PCBs in Atlantic Coast Bluefish. Interpretive Report. NOAA in cooperation with the Food and Drug Administration and Environmental Protection Agency. U.S. Government Printing

Office, Washington, D.C. March. 75 pp.

Norback, D.H., and R.H. Weltman. 1985. Polychlorinated biphenyl induction of hepatocellular carcinoma in the Sprague-Dawley rat. Environ. Health Perspect. 60:97-105.

NRC (National Research Council). 1980. Recommended Dietary Allowances, 9th ed. Committee on Dietary Allowances, Food and Nutrition Board. National Academy Press, Washington, D.C. 185 pp.

NRC (National Research Council). 1989. Biologic Markers in Reproductive Toxicology. Board on Environmental Studies and Toxicology. National Academy Press, Washington, D.C. 416 pp.

NRC (National Research Council). 1990. Managing Troubled Waters. Committee on a Systems Assessment of Marine Environmental Monitoring, Marine Board. National Academy Press, Washington, D.C. 125 pp.

NRC (National Research Council). 1991. Neurotoxicology and Models for Assessing Risk. Board on Environmental Studies and Epidemiology. National Academy Press, Washington, D.C. (in press).

NWF (National Wildlife Federation). 1989. Abbreviated summary of quantitative health assessments for PCB, dieldrin, DDT, and chlordane. Developed for the 13 April 1989 workshop on Managing the Health Risks of Consuming Contaminated Great Lakes Sport Fish. Great Lakes Natural Resource Center, National Wildlife Federation, Ann Arbor, Mich. 16 pp.

Pasquinelli, P., F. Bruschi, F. Saviozzi, and G. Malvaldi. 1985. Immunosuppressive effects and promotion of hepatic carcinogenesis by thiobenzamide. Bull. Soc. Ital. Biol. Sper. 61:61-66.

Phillips, D.L., A.B. Smith, V.W. Burse, G.K. Steele, L.L. Heedham, and W.H. Hannon. 1989. Half-life of polychlorinated biphenyls in occupationally exposed workers. Arch. Environ. Hlth. 44:351-354.

PTI. 1987. Guidance Manual for Assessing Human Health Risks from Chemically Contaminated Fish and Shellfish. Draft Report C737-2. Submitted to Batelle New England Marine Research Laboratory by TI Environmental Services, Inc., Bellevue, Wash., December. 64 pp.

Rabinowitz, M.B., G.W. Wetherill, and J.D. Kopple. 1976. Kinetic analysis of lead metabolism in healthy humans. J. Clin. Invest. 58:260-271.

Rai, K., and J. van Ryzin. 1981. A generalized multihit dose response model for low dose extrapolation. Biometrics 37:341-352.

Rodericks, J. 1989. Assessing and managing risks associated with the consumption of chemically contaminated seafoods. Paper presented at the Workshop on Assessing and Controlling Health Hazards from Fishery Products conducted by the Committee on Evaluation of the Safety of Fishery Products, Food and Nutrition Board, Institute of Medicine, National Academy of Sciences Study Center, Woods Hole, Mass., July 26. 49 pp.

Rogan, W.J., B.C. Gladen, J.D. McKinney, N. Carreras, P. Hardy, J. Thullen, J. Tinglestad, and M. Tully. 1986. Neonatal effects of transplacental exposure to PCBs and DDE. J. Pediatrics 109:335-341.

Ross, R., and J.A. Glomset. 1976. The pathogenesis of atherosclerosis (second of two parts). N. Engl. J. Med. 295:420-425.

Safe, S. 1989. Polychlorinated biphenyls (PCBs): Mutagenicity and carcinogenicity. Mutat. Res. 220:31-47.

Sahl, J.D., T.T. Crocker, R.J. Gordon, and E. J. Faeder. 1985. Polychlorinated biphenyl concentrations in the blood plasma of a selected sample of non-occupationally exposed southern California (U.S.A.) working adults. Sci. Total. Environ. 46:9-18.

Scheuplein, R.J. 1988. Risk assessment and risk management of environmental food contaminants by FDA. Pp. 109-122 in C.R. Cothern, M.A. Mehlman, and W.L. Marcus, eds. Advances in Modern Environmental Toxicology, Vol. 15: Risk Assessment and Risk Management of Industrial and Environmental Chemicals. Princeton Scientific Publishing Co., Princeton, N.J.

Silbergeld, E.K. 1982. Current status of neurotoxicology, basic and applied. Trends Neurosci. 5:291-294.

Silbergeld, E.K., R.E. Hruska, D. Bradley, J.M. Lamon, and B.C. Frykholm. 1982. Neurotoxic aspects of porphyrinopathies: Lead and succinylacetone. Environ. Res. 29:459-471.

Skerfving, S. 1974. Methylmercury exposure, mercury levels in blood and hair, and health status in Swedes consuming contaminated fish. Toxicology 2:3-23.

Sloan, R., E. O'Connell, and R. Diana. 1987. Toxic Substances in Fish and Wildlife–Analyses since May 1, 1982, Vol. 6. Technical Report 87-4 (BEP), September. New York State Department of Environmental Conservation, Division of Fish and Wildlife, Albany. 182 pp.

Sorensen, E.M.B., P.M. Cumbie, T.L. Bauer, J.S. Bell, and C.W. Harlan. 1984. Histopathological, hematological, condition-factor, and organ weight changes associated with selenium accumulation in fish from Belews Lake, North Carolina. Arch. Environ. Contam. Toxicol. 13:153-162.

Sunahara, G.I., K.G. Nelson, T.K. Wong, and G.W. Lucier. 1987. Decreased human birth weights after in utero exposure to PCBs and PCDFs are associated with decreased placental EGF-stimulated receptor autophosphorylation capacity. Molecular Pharmacol. 32:572-578.

Takada, K., and H. Zur Hausen. 1984. Induction of Epstein-Barr virus antigens by tumor promoters for epidermal and nonepidermal tissues. Int. J. Cancer 33:491-496.

Tanabe, S., Y. Nakagawa, and R. Tatsukawa. 1981. Absorption efficiency and biological half-life of individual chlorobiphenyls in rats treated with Kanechlor products. Agricult. Biol. Chemist. 45:717-726.

Taylor, P.R., J.M. Stelma, and C.E. Lawrence. 1989. The relation of polychlorinated biphenyls to birth weight and gestational age in the offspring of occupationally exposed mothers. Am. J. Epidem. 129:395-406.

Tollefson, L., and F. Cordle. 1986. Methylmercury in fish: A review of residue levels, fish consumption and regulatory action in the United States. Environ. Hlth. Perspect. 68:203-208.

Tsushimoto, G., C.C. Chang, J.E. Trosko, and F. Matsumura. 1983. Cytotoxic, mutagenic, and cell-cell communication inhibitory properties of DDT, lindane, and chlordane on Chinese hamster cells in vitro. Arch. Environ. Contam. Toxicol. 12:721-729.

Turner, M.D., D.O. Marsh, J.C. Smith, J.B. Inglis, T.W. Clarkson, C.E. Rubio, J. Chiriboga, and C.C. Chiriboga. 1980. Methylmercury in populations eating large quantities of marine fish. Arch. Environ. Health. 35:367-378.

Vogel, F., and A.G. Motulsky. 1979. Pp. 326-329 in Human Genetics–Problems and Approaches. Springer-Verlag, New York.

Waternaux, C., N.M. Laird, and J.H. Ware. 1989. Methods for analysis of longitudinal data: Blood lead concentrations and cognitive development. J. Am. Stat. Assoc. 84:33-41.

Weisburger, J.H., and G.M. Williams. 1983. The distinct health risk analyses required for genotoxic carcinogens and promoting agents. Environ. Health Perspect. 50:233-245.

Weiss, B., and J.M. Spyker. 1974. Behavioral implications of prenatal and early postnatal exposure to chemical pollutants. Pediatrics 53:851-859.

Whitlock, J.P., Jr. 1989. The control of cytochrome P-450 gene expression by dioxin. Trends Pharmacol. Sci. 10:285-288.

Whittemore, A.S. 1980. Mathematical models of cancer and their use in risk assessment, J. Environ. Pathol. Toxicol. 3:353-362.

Whittemore, A.S. 1983. Facts and values in risk assessment for environmental toxicants. Risk Anal. 3:23-33.

Wilber, C.F. 1983. Selenium: A Potential Environmental Poison and a Necessary Food Constituent. Charles C. Thomas, Springfield, Ill. 126 pp.

Yakushiji, T., I. Watanabe, K. Kuwabara, R. Tanaka, T. Kashimoto, N. Kunita, and I. Hara. 1984. Rate of decrease and half-life of polychlorinated biphenyls (PCBs) in the blood of mothers and their children occupationally exposed to PCBs, Arch. Environ. Contam. Toxicol. 13:341-345.

Yunis, J.J. 1983. The chromosomal basis of human neoplasia. Science 221:227-236.

Zakour, R.A., T.A. Kunkel, and L.A. Loeb. 1981. Metal-induced infidelity of DNA synthesis. Environ. Health Perspect. 40:197-206.

Zeggari, M., C. Susini, N. Viguerie, J.P. Esteve, N. Vaysse, and A. Ribet. 1985. Tumor promoter inhibition of cellular binding of somatostatin. Biochem. Biophys. Res. Commun. 128:850-857.

Zeitlin, D. 1989. State-Issued Fish Consumption Advisories: A National Perspective. National Ocean Pollution Program Office, National Oceanic and Atmospheric Administration, Washington, D.C. November. 73 pp.

7

Statistical Sampling Issues in the Control of Seafood Hazards

ABSTRACT

A statistical evaluation of Food and Drug Administration acceptance sampling plans was made by the committee. This chapter contains that evaluation for each of the published plans.

Based on this evaluation, the committee concludes that seafood safety should be controlled by instituting requirements for the suppliers, rather than by more frequent testing or larger sample sizes. Suppliers should be required to employ a Hazard Analysis Critical Control Point system that takes into consideration the source and condition of live animals and focuses on public health issues in handling and processing, rather than on quality control concerns.

INTRODUCTION

The committee reviewed the Food and Drug Administration (FDA) sampling inspection procedures for seafood to evaluate the statistical methods used and their appropriateness for public health. Because more than 50% of the seafood consumed in the United States is imported, it likely comes from many parts of the world and therefore is very heterogeneous in nature. This poses a number of problems in terms of sample selection and inspection. The purpose of this chapter is to address these problems and to make recommendations regarding their solution.

Because of the large volume of seafood consumed, any inspection system would have to involve sampling. Even if each boatload of fish were inspected, it would still not be reasonable to inspect each fish. Furthermore, much of the inspection is of a destructive nature. Therefore, it is important to investigate the statistical properties of the sampling procedures being used, as well as of any proposed procedures.

Development of an appropriate safety/quality control plan requires at the outset a set of difficult decisions. The planner must acknowledge that no sampling plan requiring less than 100% inspection can provide 100% assurance that no nonconforming items will pass the inspection process. The definitions of nonconformance and appropriate quality/safety goals involve careful balancing of the costs and utility of two types of errors:

1. A type I error occurs if a lot that is satisfactory is erroneously rejected, causing an economic loss to the supplier.

2. A type II error occurs if a lot that is unsatisfactory is erroneously accepted, causing economic and safety risks for both the supplier and the consumer.

As indicated by this phrasing, the two types of errors are not of equivalent value. A decision on their relative values and its consequences for sampling involve serious questions of social policy. The failure to develop formal sampling plans based on these risks may, in some cases, result from the reluctance to face these questions explicitly.

SURVEILLANCE AND COMPLIANCE SAMPLING

Two types of sampling procedures, which are named for their application, are currently used by the FDA in its inspection of fishery products: surveillance samples and compliance samples. The purpose of surveillance samples is to ascertain the overall characteristics of seafood, whereas the purpose of compliance samples is to determine whether a suspected lot meets regulatory requirements.

For either type of sample, there is a danger that many contaminated fish will pass unnoticed because most lots are not inspected at all, and for those that are, the sample is extremely small. Large samples are not practical because of the destructive nature of most testing.

In many tests, the samples must be sent to a laboratory for evaluation. In these cases, unless the product is frozen, the lot may be consumed before the results are obtained. Thus, a possible health hazard may be discovered only in time to prevent the distribution of future lots from the same source.

If sufficient control could be maintained on the suppliers of seafood, there would be little need to inspect their products. Such control is not feasible, however, because of the diversity of producers and raw products. In spite of this, the committee recommends that the responsible agency develop a procedure that will enable it to gain enough confidence in certain suppliers for inspection of their products to be virtually eliminated, or at least made with reduced frequency. This would enable compliance inspection to concentrate on a smaller population of seafood producers. Some efforts are currently underway to develop such a procedure.

For surveillance inspection, which is performed to obtain an estimate of the overall safety of fishery products, samples of incoming lots must first be made. To be representative, these samples should be random. A stratified random sampling procedure is recommended to select lots for sampling. Stratification would be based on harvesting areas and would ensure that lots selected are representative. Once the lots have been selected, random samples of fish should be chosen from each lot for inspection. Details of this procedure may be found in Cochran (1977) or Eberhardt (1990).

The FDA in the past has done very little surveillance sampling except for organic compounds, as discussed in Chapter 5. Estimates of overall seafood safety that are based primarily on compliance samples, made only when a problem is suspected, are usually biased.

ATTRIBUTES AND VARIABLES SAMPLING PLANS

Sampling plans are either attributes plans or variables plans. Attributes plans are those for which the item inspected is classified acceptable or nonacceptable and the statistics tallied are the number of unacceptable items in the sample. Fish may be classified unacceptable for any number of reasons, not all of which are linked to seafood safety. However, the basis for classifying a fish unacceptable must be stated prior to inspection. Usually, the reasons for the unacceptable conditions are listed along with the tally of the number of unacceptable fish in the inspection reports.

Variables plans are those for which a quality characteristic is measured on each item inspected and the average measurement is used for the acceptability decision. Such sampling plans have a much greater ability to distinguish between good and bad lots. However, only a single characteristic may be measured with each sampling plan. Also, some characteristics are not measurable on a continuous scale, such as appearance, texture of meat, color, or odor. Virtually all FDA plans are attributes plans of either the two-class or the three-class type. The committee did not find any other types of sampling plans in use.

Two-Class Attributes Plans

Two-class plans are discussed first. Each fish inspected falls into one of two classes--conforming or nonconforming. The statistical properties of such plans are usually described by means of an operating characteristic curve. This shows the probability of acceptance of a lot versus its quality in terms of fraction or percent nonconforming. Acceptability decisions with two-class plans may be based on a single sampling plan, a double plan, or a multiple plan. A single sampling plan specifies a sample size and an acceptability criterion. A typical single sampling plan might be $n = 13$, $c = 2$. This means that the inspector takes a sample of 13 fish and accepts the lot or lots if 2 or fewer do not conform to the specifications for safety.

A double plan that has approximately the same properties is sample size $n_1 = 8$, $n_2 = 8$; acceptance numbers $c_1 = 0$, $c_2 = 3$; rejection numbers $r_1 = 3$, $r_2 = 4$. This means the inspector takes an initial sample of 8 items; the lot is accepted if there are no nonconforming items and rejected if there are 3 or more. If there are 1 or 2, a second sample of 8 items is taken. If from the entire 16 fish, there are 3 or fewer nonconforming fish, the lot is accepted; otherwise, it is not. Such a plan would be feasible only if additional fish are available to the inspector. Often this is not true.

A multiple plan that has the same statistical properties as these two plans is presented in Table 7-1. For this plan, the inspector inspects 3 items from a lot. If 2 or more of them are nonconforming the lot is rejected; otherwise, another sample of 3 items is selected. If none of the 6 items is nonconforming the lot is accepted; if 3 or more are nonconforming it is rejected; otherwise, another 3 are selected. The acceptance (Ac) and rejection (Re) numbers for the next stage (9 items) are also 0 and 3. The process continues in this fashion until either an acceptability decision is made or the seventh stage is reached. At the seventh stage, the lot is either accepted or rejected.

TABLE 7-1 Multiple Sampling Plan

Stage	n_i	Σn_i	Ac	Re
1	3	3	_[a]	2
2	3	6	0	3
3	3	9	0	3
4	3	12	1	4
5	3	15	2	4
6	3	18	3	5
7	3	21	4	5

[a]Cannot accept the first stage.

For the above single sampling plan, $n = 13$, $c = 2$; if 5% of the lot is nonconforming, the probability of acceptance is 0.972. That is, 97.2% of such lots would be passed by this procedure. Similarly, if 10% are nonconforming, the probability of acceptance is 0.857 or 85.7% If 20% are nonconforming, the probability of acceptance is 0.518 or 51.8%. If 50% of the fish in the lot are nonconforming, there is a 4.4% chance of acceptance. The double and multiple plans have operating characteristics that are approximately the same as those of the single plan. The advantage of the double and multiple plans is that, on the average, smaller numbers of items need be inspected before a decision is made. Thus, for example, if a lot is 20% nonconforming, the single plan requires 13 items, and the double plan requires 11.5 items on the average. The multiple plan requires an average of approximately 9 items. The disadvantage is that the inspector does not know in advance how many fish to select for inspection. Multiple plans are thus much more difficult to administer and are frequently avoided for that reason.

The above single sampling plan ($n = 13$, $c = 2$) could be changed by reducing the acceptance number. This, however, would also affect the risk to the supplier of acceptable lots being rejected. The effects of such changes are indicated in Table 7-2. Assume that a 2% nonconforming lot should be accepted, whereas a 10% nonconforming lot should be rejected. Table 7-2 shows the probabilities of acceptance for acceptance numbers 0, 1, 2, and 3 for samples of size 13 and various percentages nonconforming.

Table 7-2 indicates that, by using an acceptance number of 2, virtually all 2% nonconforming lots would be passed, but most (86%) of the 10% nonconforming ones would also be passed. To reduce the latter probability, the acceptance number could be reduced to 0. Then only 27% of such lots would be accepted. However, 13% of the good (2%) lots would be rejected. By increasing the sample size while keeping the acceptance number greater than zero, this problem can be solved. Probabilities for two-class plans are calculated by using the binomial distribution. Similar probabilities for three-class plans, discussed below, are based on the multinomial distribution.

TABLE 7-2 Acceptance Probabilities for Various
Acceptance Numbers and Samples of Size 13

Nonconforming (%)	$c = 0$	$c = 1$	$c = 2$	$c = 3$
2	0.77	0.97	0.998	1.000
5	0.52	0.86	0.97	0.996
10	0.27	0.63	0.86	0.96
20	0.074	0.27	0.52	0.74

Three-Class Attributes Plans

The three-class plan is used chiefly for compliance with microbiological standards. A three-class plan has two specification values (m and M): m represents a target value, or limit of microorganisms present for products manufactured under good manufacturing practices (GMPs); M represents the limit of the same microorganisms considered to be acceptable. That is, any number more than M is unacceptable, and a lot should be rejected if any sample unit contains M or more of the microorganisms.

As an example of such a plan, for *Staphylococcus aureus* a sample of 5 is used. No sample unit may exceed 1,000 per gram (g) and 1 of the 5 items may exceed 500/g but not 1,000/g. Thus, $m = 500/g$ and $M = 1,000/g$. This plan would be described as $n = 5$, $c = 1$, $m = 500/g$, and $M = 1,000/g$.

Description of the performance of this type of plan would have to be done by means of a two-way table, where P represents the actual percentage of all items in the lot exceeding 500/g (m) but not exceeding 1,000/g (M), and Q represents the actual percentage of all items in the lot exceeding 1,000/g. The probabilities of such lots being accepted are shown in Table 7-3. Thus, if a lot of 40,000 pounds (lb) of seafood is submitted to this inspection containing $P = 20\%$ (8,000 pounds) exceeding 500/g but not 1,000/g, and $Q = 10\%$ (4,000 pounds) exceeding 1,000/g, respectively, the probability of acceptance is 41%. Similar two-way tables can be prepared that describe all of the three-class attributes plans.

TABLE 7-3 Percentages of Lots Accepted

P (%)	Q (%)				
	0	10	20	30	40
0	100	59	33	17	8
10	92	53	29	14	6
20	74	41	21	9	4
30	53	27	12	5	1
40	34	16	6	2	<1

A list of FDA sampling plans follows, which indicates acceptance probabilities for various qualities for comparison purposes. Such qualities are usually stated in terms of acceptable quality level (AQL), which is defined as the quality that has a 95% chance of acceptance. Another pertinent level is the indifference quality level (IQL), which has a 50% chance of acceptance. A third is the limiting quality level (LQL), which has only a 10% chance of acceptance. These three quality levels are given for the two-class FDA plans to be presented.

An organization responsible for compliance sampling procedures should make a decision regarding appropriate values of these quality levels before setting a plan. These decisions are policy decisions and should be based on risk assessment as described in Chapter 6.

Most Probable Number (MPN)

Some FDA plans make use of the most probable number (MPN) as a means of estimating bacterial densities. This number is based on the dilution method of estimation, which is a method for estimating, without directly counting, the number of organisms in a liquid. The dilution method consists of taking samples from the liquid, incubating each in a suitable culture medium, and observing any growth in the number of organisms present.

The MPN estimation of density is based on two assumptions: (1) that the organisms are distributed randomly throughout the liquid medium, and (2) that the incubated medium is certain to show growth whenever the sample contains an organism. If the second assumption is not met, the MPN method will underestimate the density.

If there are k organisms in a volume of liquid V, and if a sample of volume v is taken from V, the probability that none of the organisms will be found in the sample is $(1 - v/V)^k = a^k$. If n such samples are taken, the probability that s of them will contain no organisms is

$$\frac{n!}{s!(n - s)!} \, (a^k)^s \, (1 - a^k)^{n-s}$$

where $n! = n(n - 1)...(2)(1)$.

For example, if 10 samples of 2 milliliters (mL) each are taken from a total volume of 100 mL, the probability that 6 of the 10 samples will contain no organisms (and thus no growth) is

$$\frac{10!}{6!4!} \, (0.98^k)^6 \, (1 - 0.98^k)^4 = 210 \, (0.98^k)^6 \, (1 - 0.98^k)^4$$

Recall that the purpose of this analysis is to determine k, the number of organisms in the total liquid.

The MPN procedure determines the value of k that gives the largest probability of obtaining s sterile samples. For the present example, $s = 6$, and if $k = 40$, the probability of 6 sterile samples is $210 \, (0.98^{40})^6 \, (1 - 0.98^{40})^4 = 0.155$. Similarly, if $k = 50$, the probability p of 6 sterile samples is 0.080. Table 7-4 indicates the values of

p for various values of k. As indicated in the table, if 6 of the 10 samples are to be sterile, the most probable number of organisms in the total volume is 25, with a probability equal to 0.251. Even though 25 is the most probable value, the probability is only 0.251, not very high. The procedure could be improved by using a dilution series, for example, three 1:10 dilutions of 5 samples per dilution.

TABLE 7-4 Probabilities for Various Sizes of k

k	p
20	0.227
22	0.242
24	0.250
25	0.251
26	0.250
27	0.249
28	0.246
30	0.236
40	0.155
50	0.080

The MPN is a very imprecise estimate of the actual number of organisms present. To illustrate this imprecision, 95% confidence limits are listed in Table 7-5. That is, if the MPN is as shown and 5 samples per dilution for a series of three 1:10 dilutions are taken, the confidence is 95% that the true number of organisms lies between the two limits. As indicated in Table 7-5, the MPN becomes less precise as it becomes larger.

TABLE 7-5 95% Confidence Limits

MPN/100 mL	Lower	Upper
14	6	35
70	30	210
140	60	360
220	100	580
540	220	2,000

SURVEY OF CURRENT SAMPLING PLANS

Salmonella Sampling Plans

In sampling plans for *Salmonella*, three categories of food are identified by the FDA Inspection Operations Manual, chart 1 (FDA, 1980b):

I. Foods that would normally be in category II, except they are intended for consumption by the aged, infirm, or infants

II. Foods that would not normally be subjected to a process lethal to *Salmonella* between the time of sampling and consumption

III. Foods that would normally be subjected to a process lethal to *Salmonella* between the time of sampling and consumption (most seafood, except molluscan shellfish, is in food category III)

For all categories, a sample unit consists of a minimum of 100 g selected at random from a lot. A 25-g analytical unit is analyzed for *Salmonella* from each 100-g sample unit. The analytical units may be condensed with the maximum composite size of 375 g or 15 analytical units.

Table 7-6 describes the sampling plans for each of the food categories. The plans are all two-class plans. In the table, n refers to the number of sample units to be selected from each lot. If the analytical units are composited, 60 sample units would mean 4 composite units. It is assumed here that if one or more analytical units contain *Salmonella*, the composite will test positive. The c values refer to the acceptable number of positive tests. For these plans, no positive tests are allowed.

TABLE 7-6 Sampling Plan Characteristics for *Salmonella*

Food Category	n	c	AQL (%)	IQL (%)	LQL (%)
I	60	0	0.086	1.16	3.84
II	30	0	0.171	2.31	7.68
III	15	0	0.342	4.62	15.35

The AQL is the percent nonconforming that has a 95% probability of acceptance. That is, for category II, 95% of the lots for which 0.171% of the units contain *Salmonella* will be accepted in the long run. In a 40,000-pound lot, 68 pounds would contain *Salmonella*.

Similarly, the IQL is the percent nonconforming that has a 50% probability of acceptance. For category II, this means that 50% of the lots for which 2.31% of the meat contains *Salmonella* will be accepted. For a 40,000-pound lot, this would be 924 pounds.

The LQL is the percent nonconforming that has a 10% probability of acceptance. For category II, this means that 10% of the lots for which 7.68% of the meat contains *Salmonella* will be accepted. For a 40,000-pound lot, this represents 3,072 pounds.

The Food and Agriculture Organization/World Health Organization (FAO/WHO, 1969) sampling plan for *Salmonella* calls for a sample of 5 units with acceptance number 0. For this plan, the AQL is 1%, the IQL is 13%, and the LQL is 37%. The FDA plans are considerably tighter than the FAO/WHO plan.

Staphylococcus aureus **Plans**

The FAO/WHO (1969) plan for *Staphylococcus aureus* is a three-class plan. The sample size is still 5 with $c = 2$, $m = 500/g$, and $M = 5,000/g$. That is, for 5 sample units analyzed, no unit should exceed 5,000/g and no more than 2 units should exceed 500/g for the lot to be accepted. Because this plan is a three-class plan, simple descriptions such as AQL, IQL, and LQL do not apply. Instead, a two-way table describing the plan has been developed by the National Marine Fisheries Service. In Table 7-7, P is the percentage of units in the lot exceeding m (500/g) but not exceeding M (5,000/g) and Q is the percentage of units exceeding M. The percentage of lots that will be accepted is found in Table 7-7 for each P-Q combination.

TABLE 7-7 Percentages of Lots Accepted for Several P and Q Combinations

P (%)	Q (%) 0	10	20	30	40
0	100	59	33	17	8
10	99	58	32	16	7
20	94	54	29	14	6
30	83	47	24	11	4
40	68	36	16	6	2
50	50	23	9	2	<1

Plans for Fish, Fresh or Frozen

The following FDA (1980a,b) sampling procedure applies to fish, fresh or frozen, for adulteration involving decomposition and can be found in both the Inspection Operation Manual 616.12 and the Compliance Policy Guides (CPG) 7108.05. The procedure is based on a lot of fish, each weighing up to 3 pounds. The sample size is 50 fish. A lot will be cited if it has decomposed fish in 2 or more cases and if any of the following occurs:

- 5% or more fish show class 3 decomposition over 25% or more of their bodies,[1]
- 20% or more show class 2 decomposition over 25% or more of their bodies,[2] or
- % class 2 + 4(% class 3) $\geq 20\%$.

(See Table 7-8.)

TABLE 7-8 Chance of Acceptance (%)

	Class 3 (%)			
Class 2 (%)	1	3	5	10
1	99	95	83	32
3	98	84	62	21
5	94	75	48	14
10	81	47	22	3

Fish – Adulteration by Parasites

Action levels for parasites in fish (CPG 7108.06, Inspection Operation Manual chart 5) are as follows:

1. Tullibees, ciscoes, inconnus, chubs, and whitefish: 50 cysts/100 pounds and 20% of fish are infested.
2. Bluefin and other freshwater herring:

- Averaging 1 pound or less: 60 cysts/100 fish and 20% of fish examined are infested.
- Over 1 pound: 60 cysts/100 pounds of fish and 20% of fish examined are infested.
- Rosefish (redfish and ocean perch): 3% of the fillets contain one or more copepods with pus pockets.

The sample sizes are as follows:

1. Single plan (Table 7-9)

TABLE 7-9 Number of Pounds in a Single Sampling Plan

| No. of Boxes in Lot | Sample Weight (lb) | | |
	Jumbo or Large	Medium	Small
5-19	28	23	16
20-100	53	45	33
100 or over	70	56	39

SOURCE: CPG 7108.06 (FDA, 1980a).

2. Double plan (for lots of 20-100 boxes; Table 7-10)

TABLE 7-10 Number of Pounds in a Double Sampling Plan

| Size of Fish | Cysts/100 | | | Cysts/100 lb (combined samples) | | |
	n_1 (lb)	Ac (1)	Re (1)	n_2 (lb)	Ac	Re
Large or jumbo	35	30	70	63	49	50
Medium	27	26	67	43	49	50
Small	18	38	61	26	49	50

SOURCE: CPG 7108.06 (FDA, 1980a).

3. Sequential plans (for lots over 100 boxes; also listed in Inspection Operation Manual chart 5). For imported fish the FDA may use any of these plans; for domestic fish the double plan based on 25 fish is to be used. See Tables 7-9 and 7-10.

Crabmeat – Adulteration with Filth Containing *Escherichia coli*

Section 7108.02 of the CPG requires a two-class plan as follows:

For a sample of size 6, take legal action if any fish indicates adulteration. Seize the lot if 2 or more contain *Escherichia coli*. The performance of these plans is indicated in Table 7-11.

TABLE 7-11 Sampling Plan Characteristics of Crabmeat

n	Ac	Re	AQL (%)	IQL (%)	LQL (%)
6	0	1	0.85	11	32
6	1	2	6.3	26	51

Langostinos – Adulteration by Bacterial Contamination

A sample size of 10 is required. The criteria for seizure are the existence of any of the following (CPG 7108.09):

1. Coliform density greater than 20/g (by MPN method) in 20% of the samples
2. *E. coli* density greater than 3.6/g (MPN) in 20% of the samples
3. Coagulase-positive staphylococci density greater than 3.6/g (MPN) in 20% of the samples
4. Aerobic plate count (at 35°C) greater than 100,000/g as a geometric average of all the subsamples

For this plan, the sample size is 10 and the acceptance number is 0. It is understood, however, that a change is expected that will increase the acceptance number to 1. The statistics in Table 7-12 apply to these two sampling procedures.

TABLE 7-12 Sampling Plan Characteristics for Langostinos

n	Ac	Re	AQL (%)	IQL (%)	LQL (%)
10	0	1	0.5	6.7	21
10	1	2	3.7	16	34

Canned Salmon – Adulteration Involving Decomposition

For canned salmon adulteration involving decomposition, seizure is authorized if examination by two analysts in accordance with the sampling procedures shows either (CPG 7108.10)

- number of defective (class II or III) cans equal to or exceeding the action numbers,
  or
- two or more class III cans in either the first or the total sample.

The plans in this Compliance Policy Guide are double three-class plans. Different plans are required for different lot sizes. The various plans for ¼-pound through 1-

pound cans are shown in Table 7-13, with acceptance probabilities for various combinations of class II and class III defective cans in Table 7-14. Lot sizes are for cases of 48 cans each.

TABLE 7-13 Sampling Plans for Canned Salmon for ¼-lb Through 1-lb Cans

Lot Size (cases)	n_1	c_1	r_1	n_2	n_1+n_2	c_2	r_2
<100	18	0	3	32	50	4	5
100-199	20	0	3	48	68	8	9
200-499	24	1	4	64	88	10	11
500-799	30	1	4	80	110	16	17
800-999	36	1	5	96	132	22	23
1,000-1,499	42	1	6	112	154	25	26
1,500 and up	48	1	6	128	170	29	30

SOURCE: CPG 7108.10 (FDA, 1980a).

TABLE 7-14 Percentage of Lots Accepted (<100 cans/lot)

Class III Cans in Lot (%)	Class II Cans in Lot (%)							
	0	1	3	5	10	15	20	25
0	100	100	98.4	90.8	50.2	16.9	4.1	0.5
1	94.9	93.7	89.2	78.5	38.5	12.0	2.9	0.6
3	70.2	67.2	60.3	49.7	21.0	6.0	1.4	0.3
5	47.1	43.5	36.5	28.6	11.0	3.0	0.7	0.2
10	16.0	13.7	9.9	6.9	2.3	0.7	0.2	0.04
15	5.4	4.4	2.9	1.9	0.6	0.2	0.04	0.01
20	1.8	1.4	0.9	0.6	0.2	0.04	0.01	0.00
25	0.6	0.4	0.3	0.2	0.0	0.01	0.00	0.00

TABLE 7-15 Sampling Plans for Canned Sampling for ¼-lb Cans

Lot Size (cases)	n_1	c_1	r_1	n_2	n_1+n_2	c_2	r_2
<100	6	0	2	12	8	1	2
100-199	7	0	2	16	23	1	2
200-499	8	0	2	22	30	1	2
500-799	10	0	2	27	37	2	3
800-999	11	0	3	30	41	3	4
1,000-1,499	12	0	3	32	44	4	5
1,500 and up	16	0	3	38	54	5	6

SOURCE: CPG 7108.10 (FDA, 1980a).

For 1- to 4-pound cans, the sampling plans in (Table 7-15) apply. Several comparisons of these plans are shown in Tables 7-16 through 7-21.

TABLE 7-16 Percentage of Lots Accepted for 1% Class II and 1% Class III Cans (1/4-1 lb)

Lot Size	Percentage of Lots Accepted	Lot Size	Percentage of Lots Accepted
<100	93.7	800-999	78.4
100-199	90.5	1,000-1,499	73.2
200-499	91.0	1,500 and up	68.1
500-799	83.4		

TABLE 7-17 Percentage of Lots Accepted for 1% Class II and 1% Class III Cans (1-4 lb)

Lot Size	Percentage of Lots Accepted	Lot Size	Percentage of Lots Accepted
<100	97.1	800-999	96.3
100-199	95.8	1,000-1,499	95.9
200-499	94.0	1,500 and up	93.7
500-799	95.4		

TABLE 7-18 Percentage of Lots Accepted for 5% Class II and 5% Class III Cans (1/4-1 lb)

Lot Size	Percentage of Lots Accepted	Lot Size	Percentage of Lots Accepted
<100	28.6	800-999	7.31
100-199	20.6	1,000-1,499	4.23
200-499	21.4	1,500 and up	2.42
500-799	12.5		

TABLE 7-19 Percentage of Lots Accepted for 5% Class II and 5% Class III Cans (1-4 lb)

Lot size	Percentage of Lots Accepted	Lot Size	Percentage of Lots Accepted
<100	63.1	800-999	43.6
100-199	54.7	1,000-1,499	43.4
200-499	46.8	1,500 and up	31.1
500-799	42.2		

TABLE 7-20 Percentage of Lots Accepted for 15% Class II and 10% Class III Cans (¼-1 lb)

Lot Size	Percentage of Lots Accepted	Lot Size	Percentage of Lots Accepted
<100	0.65	800-999	0.03
100-199	0.36	1,000-1,499	0.00
200-499	0.59	1,500 and up	0.00
500-799	0.13		

TABLE 7-21 Percentage of Lots Accepted for 15% Class II and 10% Class III Cans (1-4 lb)

Lot Size	Percentage of Lots Accepted	Lot Size	Percentage of Lots Accepted
<100	18.8	800-999	4.36
100-199	13.6	1,000-1,499	3.44
200-499	10.0	1,500 and up	1.10
500-799	5.69		

SOURCE: CPG 7108.110 (FDA, 1980a).

Considerable variation can be seen in the percentage of lots accepted among lot sizes for each of the can sizes. The percentage of lots accepted decreases with lot size. However, the decrease is more marked for smaller cans. Also, the percentage of lots accepted is higher for the larger cans than for the smaller ones for any lot size and quality.

Shrimp – Adulteration Involving Decomposition

Shrimp are classified as follows (CPG 7108.11):

Class 1. Very fresh to fishy odor characteristic of the product
Class 2. Slight odor persistent and perceptible to an experienced examiner as pertaining to decomposition
Class 3. Strong odor of decomposition that is distinct and unmistakable

In terms of the criteria for decomposition, a subsample of 100 shrimp is classed as decomposed if

- 5% or more shrimp are class 3,
- 0% or more shrimp are class 2,
  or
- % class 2 + 4 (% class 3) ≥20%.

The sample sizes are listed in Table 7-22.

TABLE 7-22   Single Sampling Plans for
Shrimp Inspection

Number of Cases	Lot Size		
	n	Ac	Re
1-20	6	1	2
21-100	12	2	3
101 or more	18	3	4

SOURCE: CPG 7108.11 (FDA, 1980a).

The acceptance and rejection numbers refer to number of subsamples of 100 shrimp each. That is, for the first plan ($n = 6$, Ac $= 1$), 6 subsamples of 100 shrimp each are selected. If 2 or more subsamples are classed as decomposed for any of the above three criteria, the lot will not be accepted. The percentage of lots accepted will depend on a combination of class 2 and class 3 decomposition. These percentages are given in Tables 7-23 through 7-25.

TABLE 7-23 Percentage of Lots Accepted
for Lot Size 1-20, $n = 6$, $c = 1$

Class 2 (%)	Class 3 (%)		
	1	3	5
1	100	63	4
5	99	33	1
10	76	9	0

TABLE 7-24 Percentage of Lots Accepted
for Lot Size 21-100, $n = 12$, $c = 2$

Class 2 (%)	Class 3 (%)		
	1	3	5
1	100	52	0
5	100	16	0
10	71	1	0

TABLE 7-25 Percentage of Lots Accepted for
Lot Size 101 or more, $n = 18$, $c = 3$

Class 2 (%)	Class 3 (%)		
	1	3	5
1	100	45	0
5	100	9	0
10	69	0	0

As can be seen, the probability of acceptance decreases with lot size for constant quality because it would be more serious to accept a large lot of poor quality than a small one. It should also be noted, for example, that in a lot having 3% class 3 decomposition and 5% class 2 decomposition, the percentage of lots accepted will range from 9 to 33. The numbers in these tables could be reduced by either increasing the sample sizes or decreasing the acceptance numbers. However, if this is done the probability of accepting reasonably good lots will also be reduced.

As an example of this, suppose the acceptance numbers are changed from 1, 2, and 3 to 0, 1, and 2, but the same sample sizes are retained (6, 12, 18). The percentage of lots accepted for 5% class 2 and 3% class 3 lots will go from 33, 16, and 9 for the present plans to 8, 5, and 3; the percentage of lots that have 1% class 2 and 5% class 3 will go from 99, 100, and 100 to 86, 97, and 99, respectively.

CONCLUSIONS AND RECOMMENDATIONS

The above discussion of current sampling plans indicates that they provide relatively little protection to the public. Fortunately, most lots contain little contaminated seafood and most of the contaminants are removed by cooking. However, in view of the serious health hazards discussed in other chapters, it is necessary to improve seafood safety with regard to these hazards.

Safety should be improved by means of controls on the process rather than by reliance on sampling inspection. As indicated in this section, unless the sample size increases significantly, very little consumer protection is provided. None of the sampling procedures described above provides much protection to the consumer, and increasing the sample size is not a reasonable solution.

As indicated, the statistical uncertainties associated with lot sampling make this an unreliable method for ensuring the safety of food products even if testing methods for dangerous microorganisms, toxins, and contaminant chemicals were fully available and completely reliable. This is well recognized by scientists and administrators involved in food regulation, many of whom are strongly supportive of the Hazard Analysis Critical Control Point (HACCP) system. The HACCP system provides on-line, real-time control at the processing level and has worked well in the low-acid canned food industry. General procedures for this type of system have been discussed in a number of publications (ICMSF, 1988; NRC, 1985) and laid out in more detail by the Interagency Advisory Committee. Effective application of the HACCP system requires that both industry and regulatory agency personnel understand its various components and that the two groups work closely together in the development and implementation of HACCP plans. The focus must be set clearly on consumer safety in the assessment of hazards and the identification of critical control points (CCPs). The purpose of the HACCP system is to provide as high a level of assurance as possible that the food product reaching the consumer is safe and wholesome; it is not a quality control plan, though CCPs may coincide with quality control points in a process. There is a potential danger in attempting to incorporate quality control considerations, such as weight control, workmanship, or breading levels, into the HACCP plan because these may then become the focus of attention at CCPs, when they have no impact on the safety of the food. Cluttering up an HACCP plan with such considerations detracts from the essential simplicity and specificity of the system and unnecessarily complicates control and testing procedures without adding to safety. Indeed, confounding workmanship with safety controls can lead to a false sense of security by unsophisticated operators who confuse positive control signals on workmanship with safety indicators.

Application of a well-designed HACCP plan will provide greater assurance of safety for the consumer and may be readily assessed by the regulatory agencies. It is essential for fisheries products that such plans take into account the quality and condition of the water from which animals are harvested and the intrinsic condition of the animal at harvest because natural toxins, contaminant chemicals, or sewage contamination are significant risks for certain fish and shellfish.

NOTES

1. The decomposed product has an odor that is distinct and unmistakable.
2. First stage of identifiable decomposition. The product produces an odor, which while not intense, is persistent and perceptible by an experienced examiner. On the other hand, class 1 include fishery products ranging from fresh to those having odor characteristics of that product, that is not identifiable as decomposition.

REFERENCES

Cochran, W.G. 1977. Sampling Techniques, 3rd ed. John Wiley & Sons, New York. 428 pp.

Eberhardt, K.R. 1990. Survey sampling methods. Pp. 91-940 in H.M. Wadsworth, ed. Handbook of Statistical Methods for Engineers and Scientists. McGraw-Hill, New York.

FAO/WHO (Food and Agriculture Organization/World Health Organization). 1969. Codex Alimentarius. Sampling Plans for Packaged Foods, CAC/RM42-1969. Food and Agricultural Organization of the United Nations and World Health Organization, Geneva, Switzerland.

FDA (Food and Drug Administration). 1980a. Fish and seafood. Compliance Policy Guides (CPG) 7108.02-7108.25, Chap. 8. Food and Drug Administration, Public Health Service, Washington, D.C.

FDA (Food and Drug Administration). 1980b. Inspections Operations Manual 616.12. Food and Drug Administration, Public Health Service, Washington, D.C.

ICMSF (International Commission on Microbiological Specifications for Foods). 1988. Microorganisms in Foods. 4. Application of the Hazard Analysis Critical Control Point (HACCP) System to Ensure Microbiological Safety and Quality. Blackwell Scientific Publishers, Oxford, England. 357 pp.

NFI (National Fisheries Institute). 1989. Shrimp/Fish Statistical Sampling HACCP Industry Workshop Report, Atlanta, Ga., August 16. Prepared by NFI in collaboration with National Marine Fisheries Service, Arlington, Va. 82 pp.

NRC (National Research Council). 1985. An Evaluation of the Role of Microbiological Criteria for Foods and Food Ingredients. Subcommittee on Microbiological Criteria in Foods and Food Ingredients, Food and Nutrition Board. National Academy Press, Washington, D.C. 436 pp.

Schilling, E.G. 1982. Acceptance Sampling in Quality Control. Marcel Dekker, New York. 775 pp.

Wadsworth, H.M., K.S. Stephens, and A.B. Godfrey. 1986. Modern Methods for Quality Control and Improvement, John Wiley & Sons, New York. 690 pp.

8

Seafood Surveillance and Control Programs

ABSTRACT

This chapter considers the questions of how well existing governance efforts address and move to mitigate the risks in consuming seafood that have been identified thus far in this report. The chapter describes and evaluates efforts by federal and state regulatory authorities and private industry to minimize the level of seafood risk.

At the federal level, seafood safety falls primarily under the authority of the Food and Drug Administration (FDA). The FDA serves as the lead agency in setting and enforcing regulatory limits for seafood products. However, other federal agencies also play an important role. The Environmental Protection Agency is responsible for setting or recommending pesticide limits in seafood, and the National Marine Fisheries Service operates the Voluntary Seafood Inspection Program. The Centers for Disease Control is responsible for the collection and evaluation of data characterizing the source of seafood-borne illness.

Individual states play a dominant role in the control of seafood-borne risk. State public health, environmental protection, and resource management agencies have developed programs designed to mitigate that risk. The actions of state governments are fundamental to seafood safety because of the important differences in consumption and contaminant levels across regions of the country.

Furthermore, the international community, as well as individual foreign states, have developed practices and protocols impacting the regulation of seafood safety in the United States. The impacts of all these governance efforts are described and evaluated in this chapter.

INTRODUCTION

The purpose of this chapter is twofold. An initial effort is made to describe and characterize existing programs under the authority of federal, state, and local governments; other public bodies; and private organizations designed to ensure the safety of seafood consumed by the U.S. public. Based on an analysis of those programs, this report provides an overall evaluation of their effectiveness. Such a broad-based evaluation is necessary to ensure a reasonable understanding of all governance and management programs currently in place, as well as some measure of protection for the U.S. seafood consuming public. This report recognizes that the question of seafood safety is being addressed by a network of governmental and nongovernmental efforts. The committee's evaluation attempts to incorporate as comprehensive an approach as possible in order to develop a realistic characterization of seafood safety.

The organization of this evaluation is designed to reflect as reasonably as possible this complex programmatic effort. The effort addresses both those programs carried out by federal administrative agencies and the responsibilities taken on by various state or local governments and the seafood industry. Further, in recognition of the international and interdependent nature of seafood commerce, efforts related to seafood safety carried out by other countries and by international economic and scientific organizations are also characterized.

RESPONSIBILITIES AND PROGRAMS OF THE FEDERAL GOVERNMENT

A number of federal agencies are involved in regulation of seafood (Martin, 1990). The primary federal agency with responsibility for the assurance of seafood safety is the U.S. Department of Health and Human Services' Food and Drug Administration (FDA). The agency houses a wide range of programs devoted to the research and management of seafood product safety. The FDA derives its authority over such programs primarily through two statutes: (1) the Federal Food, Drug and Cosmetic Act (FFDCA: 21 U.S.C. 301 et seq.), and (2) the Public Health Service Act (PHSA: 42 U.S.C. 262, 294 et seq.). Under the FFDCA, the FDA is assigned responsibility to ensure that seafood shipped or received in interstate commerce is "safe, wholesome, and not misbranded or deceptively packaged" (FDA, 1988d). Under the PHSA, FDA is empowered to control the spread of communicable disease from one state, territory, or possession to another. To carry out these statutory mandates, FDA has developed a series of regulatory and research programs described below.

Regulatory authority for seafood safety is partially shared, within the present federal system, with two other regulatory actors. The Environmental Protection Agency (EPA) is most fundamentally involved in setting and recommending regulatory guidelines for pesticides. The EPA also provides assistance to FDA in identifying the range of residual chemical contaminants that pose a human health risk and are most likely to accumulate in seafood. The National Marine Fisheries Service of the Department of Commerce conducts the Voluntary Seafood Inspection Program. The role and responsibilities of both these agencies are detailed further below. Other federal regulators are also responsible for seafood promotion and quality. However, although programs in the Departments of Agriculture, Interior, and Defense may enhance seafood safety, such efforts should be viewed as ancillary to the larger federal efforts described below.

Standards and Guidelines

The FDA is granted primary authority to set and enforce allowable levels of contaminants and pathogenic microorganisms in seafood, and has developed a number of regulatory guidelines designed to reduce public health risk. Section 402(a) of the FFDCA provides the FDA with its most broad-based power in controlling contaminants in seafood. Under this provision, FDA may control the production and trade of any "adulterated" seafood product. Under the FFDCA [Sec. 402(a)(1)] a food is deemed adulterated if "it bears or contains any poisonous or deleterious substance which may render it injurious to health. . . ."

The FDA has historically used three related strategies to determine whether or not a seafood product should be deemed adulterated. If significant and reliable toxicological data are available, the agency will set a formal "tolerance" that identifies a limit above which the food is deemed to be injurious (FFDCA, Sec. 406). A formal tolerance identifies the amount of a given substance or organism that must be present for an enforcement action or seizure to be initiated. If a product contaminant exceeds a tolerance level, FDA may automatically remove that product from interstate commerce. However, when toxicological data are scanty or conflicting, when additional data are being developed, or when other conditions are changing rapidly, the promulgation of formal tolerance may be deemed inappropriate. In such instances the agency can promulgate "action levels" [the authority to set such levels is defined in FDCA, Sections 306, 402(a) and 406] which, according to the agency, are designed to provide prosecutorial guidance. Action levels are not binding on the agency or industry, and FDA can recommend prosecution regardless of whether the action level is exceeded. If FDA recommends prosecution, then it must establish in court that the product is injurious to health.

Although the primary authority for the designation of formal tolerances and action levels resides with FDA, the agency shares authority with EPA regarding the regulatory limits for pesticides. With the creation of EPA, and by way of the Presidential Reorganization Order No. 3 of 1970 (DOC, 1970), primary responsibility for the regulation of pesticides in food was transferred to EPA. Under present agreements, EPA holds sole responsibility for setting formal tolerances in seafood that are then enforced by FDA. For pesticide action levels, EPA submits a recommendation to FDA for enforcement.

However, lacking a formal tolerance or action level, FDA may still act on an adulterated product by providing sufficient evidence that the product constitutes a problem for public health. These three approaches are detailed below.

Tolerances

According to FDA policy and a general interpretation of the U.S. Administrative Procedures Act (APA: 5 U.S.C. 551 et seq.), the setting of a formal tolerance requires (1) significant and reliable scientific evidence of the public health impacts of the specified tolerance level, and (2) a formal application of the notice-and-comment procedures enumerated in the APA. To date, FDA has specified only one formal tolerance designed specifically to mitigate human health impacts in seafood, that is, the 2.0-parts-per-million (ppm) tolerance for total polychlorinated biphenyls (PCBs). The

FDA has developed other tolerances for food, but none that are directly related to seafood safety.

Action Levels

Although FDA has used the vehicle of formal tolerances, setting regulatory guidelines for food, including seafood, has most often proceeded through the use of action levels. Unlike the establishment of tolerances, action levels do not require FDA to proceed through formal notice-and-comment rule making. Thus, setting seafood regulatory guidelines most often occurs via action levels.

However, action levels have been the focus of significant controversy in recent years. Until recently, FDA had developed a set of enforcement practices wherein tolerances and action levels were enforced with equivalent rigor. In fact, there was little difference in the certitude with which the agency would characterize and respond to an adulterated product. Indeed, the equivalence of these two types of regulatory limits was articulated by FDA. For example, FDA published a regulation [21 CFR 109.4 (1986)] that stated

> [A]n action level for an added poisonous or deleterious substance . . . may be established to define the level of contamination at which food will be deemed adulterated. An action level may prohibit any detectable amount of substance in food.

Thus, in practice, there was no functional difference between an action level and a tolerance. However, in 1987 the legal status of FDA action levels was refined and clarified by the U.S. Court of Appeals for the District of Columbia Circuit. A suit was brought against FDA by a consortium of consumer groups and private organizations, known collectively as the Community Nutrition Institute (CNI), that challenged FDA regulation of aflatoxin in corn [Community Nutrition Institute vs. Young: 818 F. 2d 943 (D.C. Cir. 1987)]. FDA had set an action level for corn at 20 parts per billion (ppb). In addition, the agency allowed aflatoxin-contaminated and noncontaminated corn to be mixed, provided the mixture did not exceed the 20-ppb action level. The court did recognize that action levels have the benefit of apprising the regulated community of the agency's intention, as well as informing the exercise of discretion by agents and officers in the field; however, the court held [818 F. 2d 949 (D.C. Cir. 1987)] that

> [o]ur limited holding is that the current action levels are treated as substantive rules by FDA and, as such, can only be permitted if notice-and-comment procedures are employed. If it so chooses, FDA could proceed by action levels that are purely policy statements. But in order to do so, FDA must avoid giving action levels the kind of substantive significance that it now so plainly attaches to them.

Because of the Community Nutrition Institute decision, FDA reevaluated its action level policy. The FDA has also published a new regulation that allows substantive rules, called regulatory limits, to be established by formal notice-and-comment rule making [55 Fed. Reg. 20,782 (May 21, 1990)].

The regulatory limit will establish the level of an unavoidable added poisonous or deleterious substance that renders a food adulterated within the meaning of the FFDCA. A regulatory limit will be established when (1) the substance cannot be avoided by current good manufacturing practices (GMPs); (2) there is no tolerance established for the substance in the particular food; and (3) there is insufficient information by which a tolerance may be established for the substance, or technology changes that may affect the appropriateness of a tolerance appear reasonably possible [55 Fed. Reg. 20,782 (May 21, 1990)].

Although FDA has established a formal mechanism for creating regulatory limits for unavoidable deleterious or poisonous contaminants, the agency also recognizes that it will maintain the action levels. However, FDA has stressed that action levels are not binding on the agency or industry [55 Fed. Reg. 20,782 (May 21, 1990)]. As such, FDA has the discretion to recommend court enforcement regardless of whether the product is within the action level. Likewise, FDA can forgo recommending court action when a product exceeds an action level.

Although action levels are no longer binding on the FDA, they are valuable because they provide significant guidance and focus to field personnel who direct monitoring and inspection programs that contribute to the identification of adulterated seafood products. Specific action levels have been developed for several contaminants in seafoods and seafood products. The list of action levels for microbial and natural toxin contaminants includes *Escherichia coli* in fresh and frozen crabmeat, parasites in finfish, and paralytic shellfish poison in clams, mussels, and oysters. A complete list of current action levels for microbial and natural toxin contaminants, and of the measurement methods used to determine them, is presented as Table 8-1.

Additionally, FDA has published a set of action levels for residual chemical contaminants, including pesticides. As noted earlier, the list of 12 chlorinated pesticides represents a cooperative effort between FDA and EPA. Although EPA retains the right to generate formal tolerances for pesticides, its strategy has been to communicate pesticide limits in terms of action levels. According to EPA personnel, this approach allows the agency to continue to monitor pesticide levels in the environment and to modify the action level based on monitoring results. Although a broad-based reevaluation of current pesticide action levels is underway by EPA, they provide guidance for acceptable levels in seafood products. The complete list of FDA action levels for residual chemical contaminants is presented in Table 8-2.

Seafood Deemed Injurious to Public Health

The FDA need not avail itself of either a formal tolerance or an action level to make a determination of adulteration. It may monitor for any contaminant that might produce a product injurious to public health.

The most effective statement of existing FDA strategy addressing the development of regulatory guidelines was that recently presented by the agency's Acting Commissioner, during a hearing before Congress on February 7, 1990:

> In the absence of a national standard, FDA brings individual enforcement actions to establish that the amount of the contaminant present in the food may render it injurious to health. This broad legal standard in the Federal Food, Drug, and Cosmetic Act applies across the board to all foods under FDA's jurisdiction and its application is the norm in food adulteration cases. Whether a national standard does or does not exist, the Agency can still take action against potentially unsafe products. This is an

TABLE 8-1 Food and Drug Administration Compliance Policy Guides (CPG) Relating to Seafood Safety

Microbiological Contamination

Title: **Crabmeat** - Fresh and Frozen - Adulteration with Filth, Involving the Presence of the Organism *Escherichia coli.*
Action Level: *E. coli* of at least 3.6 per gram (g). Calculation by most probable number (MPN) methodology.
CPG 7108.02. Effective October 1, 1982.

Title: **Langostinos** - Frozen, Cooked - Adulteration by Bacteriological Contamination.
Action Level: (1) Coliform density greater than 20/g (MPN) in 20% of samples; (2) *E. coli* density greater than 3.6/g (MPN) in 20% of the subsamples; or, (3) coagulase-positive staphylococci density greater than 3.6/g in 20% of the subsamples or, aerobic plate count (at 35°C) greater than 100,000/g as a geometric average of all the subsamples.
CPG 7108.09. Effective October 1, 1980.

Title: **Raw Breaded Shrimp** - Microbiological Defect Action Levels
Action Level: Actionable if one or more of the following conditions are met:
1. Aerobic Plate Counts (35°C) - The mean log of 16 units of finished product breaded shrimp collected prior to freezing is greater than 5.00 (i.e., geometric mean greater than 100,000/g) and exceeds the mean log of 16 units of stock shrimp by more than twice the standard error of their difference (2 SED). 2. *E. coli* - The mean log of 16 units of finished product breaded shrimp collected prior to freezing is greater than 0.56 (i.e., geometric mean greater than 3.6/g)and exceeds the mean log of 16 units of stock shrimp by more than twice the standard error of their differences.
3. *Staphylococcus aureus* - The mean log of 16 units of finished product breaded shrimp collected prior to freezing is greater than 2.00 (i.e., geometric mean greater than 100/g) and exceeds the mean log of 16 units of stock shrimp by more than twice the standard error of their difference (2 SED).
CPG 7108.25. Effective August 1, 1983.

Title: **Fish - Fresh and Frozen, as Listed** - Adulteration by Parasites
Action Level: For tullibees, ciscoes, inconnus, chubs, and whitefish: 50 cysts per 100 pounds (lbs.) provided that 20% of the fish examined are infested. For bluefish and other freshwater herring: fish averaging 1 lb or less, 60 cysts per 100 fish, provided that 20% of the fish examined are infested. For fish averaging over 1 lb, 60 cysts per 100 lbs of fish, provided that 20% of the fish examined are infested. For rosefish (redfish and ocean perch), 3% of the fillets examined contain one or more Copepoda accompanied by pus pockets.
CPG 7108.06. Effective October 1, 1980

Natural Toxins

Title: **Clams, Mussels, Oysters, Fresh or Canned** - Paralytic Shellfish Poison (PSP)
Action Level: PSP at 80 micrograms (μg) per 100 g of meat.
CPG 7108.20. Effective October 1, 1980

Title: **Decomposition and Histamine in Canned Albacore, Skipjack, and Yellowfin Tuna**
Action Level: Histamine content at 50 milligrams (mg) per 100 g of meat.
CPG 7108.25. Effective July 1, 1981

SOURCE: FDA (1985).

TABLE 8-2 FDA Action Levels for Chemical Contaminants

Substance	Action Level (ppm)	Type of Food
Methylmercury	1.0	Fish, shellfish, crustaceans, and other aquatics
PCBs	2.0	Fish and shellfish
Aldrin	0.3	Fish and shellfish
Chlordane	0.3	Fish
Dieldrin	0.3	Fish and shellfish
DDT, DDE, and TDE[a]	5.0	Fish
Endrin	0.3	Fish and shellfish
Heptachlor and heptachlor epoxide	0.3	Fish and shellfish
Kepone	0.3	Fish and shellfish
	0.4	Crabmeat
Mirex	0.1	Fish
Toxaphene	5.0	Fish

[a]DDT = dichlorodiphenyltrichloroethane;
 DDE = dichlorodiphenyldichloroethane;
 TDE (DDD) = diphenylethanedichlorophenylethane.
SOURCE: FDA (1987).

> important point. Standards are not an essential prerequisite to Agency action.
> We regularly use an internal health hazard evaluation process to determine
> whether a contaminant in a particular sample would be likely to render that
> food injurious to public health (Benson, 1990).

Indeed, it is by way of these broad-based responsibilities to control deleterious substances in food that the agency controls microbiological pathogens in seafood. In certain instances the mere measurable presence of a pathogen will signify an adulterated product. The agency treats *Shigella dysenteriae*, *Vibrio cholerae* O-1, *Salmonella*, and *Listeria*, among others, in this fashion. The effective regulatory limit for these pathogens is equivalent to the ability of the measurement methodology to detect them. For others, the mere measurable presence of a pathogen does not constitute an automatic hazard, but significant populations would. For this class of pathogens the agency has developed a reactive strategy that allows for a broad-ranging and flexible approach to determine adulteration. Indeed, a majority of FDA enforcement actions for microbial pathogens are determined on the basis of this less formal, flexible response (John Kvenberg, FDA, personal communication, 1990).

However, this flexible system is presently under review by the National Advisory Committee on Microbiological Criteria for Food (NACMCF). The NACMCF was established and jointly funded by the Departments of Defense, Agriculture, Commerce, and Health and Human Services to provide advice on the further development of microbiological action levels in food. The committee recently proposed new criteria for cooked, ready-to-eat shrimp and cooked, ready-to-eat crabmeat.

In general, the present system for setting regulatory limits could be both adequate and appropriate if such guidelines were effectively implemented. However, several critical points must be raised. First, there are areas in which guidelines are either inappropriate or nonexistent. For example, as noted in the section of this report addressing the question of chemical contaminants in seafood, the appropriateness of the present 2.0-ppm tolerance for PCBs, and the lack of specific regulatory limits for certain other chemical contaminants such as polycyclic aromatic hydrocarbons (PAHs), cadmium, lead, and dioxin, are questionable. Further, as noted elsewhere in this report, there remains a persistent concern about certain natural toxins for which the FDA has yet to determine a discernible regulatory strategy. Specifically, the committee suggests that the agency more fundamentally address the question of regulatory guidelines for domoic acid and ciguatera.

Product concepts are emerging, both in processing and in retail settings, that may pose safety questions as yet unaddressed by specific FDA guidelines (e.g., *sous vide*, modified atmosphere packaging, custom smoking techniques, and further processing in the retail setting). Finally, it should be noted that FDA has not communicated these regulatory limits effectively to intended parties. The regulatory limits thus far determined by the agency are communicated by way of FDA Compliance Policy Guides (FDA, 1985), notices in the *Federal Register*, and even in various FDA memoranda. It can be difficult to locate these regulations because FDA publishes in such a wide variety of sources. A more concerted effort to publish in a generally available, single-source, regularly updated volume would provide for more effective communication of these limits.

National Shellfish Sanitation Program

One of the primary seafood safety responsibilities of the FDA is its role as federal representative on the Interstate Shellfish Sanitation Conference (ISSC)–the organization that implements the National Shellfish Sanitation Program. The NSSP is a cooperative program in which FDA, state agencies, and private industry work to control the quality and safety of oysters, clams, and mussels sold in interstate commerce (FDA, 1989a,b). Within this program the agency is required to (1) set certain product guidelines and standards, (2) evaluate state compliance with those rules, and (3) certify continued state participation in the ISSC. The principal objective of the NSSP is to "provide a mechanism for certifying that shellfish shipped in interstate commerce meet agreed upon, specific sanitation and quality criteria" (FDA, 1989b).

The sanitary quality of shellfish is based on both growing water and wholesale market strategies. The most significant contribution of the program has been the creation of classification and monitoring strategies designed to ensure that shellfish are taken from harvesting waters significantly free of microbial contaminants. For a state to continue as a certified member of the program, it is required to survey all growing waters within its jurisdiction and classify those waters as to their acceptability for harvesting shellfish. Waters that have not been surveyed and classified must be closed. The microbiological requirements in this program are discussed in Chapter 3. The state must then test the sample within 24 hours of the shipment entering the state. If two successive samples from the same shipper are found to be in violation of both GMPs and microbiological criteria, "the shellfish regulatory authority at the source should be requested to supply information to the receiving jurisdiction concerning the source of the product and the shipper's status may be subject to rejection by the receiving state shellfish regulatory authority. Acceptance of future shipments should depend upon satisfactory reports by shellfish regulatory authorities at the point of origin" (FDA, 1989b). These regulations have been the focus of some controversy. The move away from the independent use of microbiological criteria is viewed by some with concern. Others remain convinced that the use of fecal coliform as a broad-based indicator organism is inappropriate. Additionally, there remains a measure of concern because the NSSP is a voluntary program in which both the shipper and the receiver retain a significant amount of discretion in using the safety and quality information generated by program participation.

One contribution of the NSSP has been the characterization of a list of alert levels for several trace metal contaminants. These are listed in Table 8-3 (Ratcliffe and Wilt, 1971).

TABLE 8-3 NSSP Alert Levels for Trace Metals (ppm wet weight)

Metal	Oysters	Hard-Shell Clams	Soft-Shell Clams
Cadmium	3.5	0.5	0.5
Lead	2.0	4.0	5.0
Chromium	2.0	1.0	5.0
Zinc	2,000.0	65.0	30.0
Copper	175.0	10.0	25.0

SOURCE: Ratcliffe and Wilt (1971).

It is worth noting that these alert levels for metals were not formulated on the basis of toxicity assessment, but rather are based on a 20-year-old survey of average concentrations of metals in U.S. coastal waters (Isaac and Delany, 1975). The alert levels do not constitute a formal regulatory limit and require further, more rigorous analysis. Indeed, these levels were never formally accepted by the NSSP, but are being used by certain states to control trace-metal levels in shellfish (Robert Wetherell, FDA, personal communication, 1990).

Inspection and Enforcement

The setting of limits by an agency, however, is only an initial step in regulating contaminants in seafood. The agency must then determine the current levels in seafoods and the proportion of seafood products that exceeds the regulatory limit. To characterize the success of federal efforts in reasonably protecting the U.S. seafood consumer, the degree to which such regulations are being implemented by way of monitoring, inspection, and enforcement must also be characterized. At the federal level, several programmatic efforts are currently in place to inspect and survey seafood for public health-related contaminants.

U.S. Environmental Protection Agency

Because seafood is most typically harvested from the natural environment, considerations of monitoring in support of seafood safety should necessarily include EPA programs to monitor general water quality. The agency carries out several programs as part of its responsibilities under the Federal Water Pollution Control Act (hereafter referred to as the Clean Water Act) (CWA: 33 U.S.C. 1,251 et seq.) and the Marine Protection, Research and Sanctuaries Act (MPRSA: 33 U.S.C. 1,401 et seq.). Under the CWA, the agency is mandated to regulate all discharges into navigable waters of the United States (Sec. 520), including the territorial sea [Sec. 106(a)]. The MPRSA regulates the transportation and dumping of waste into federal waters seaward of the territorial sea (and dredged material within the territorial sea) (Sec. 502). The EPA has the authority, particularly under the CWA, to regulate a broad suite of environmental contaminants. Under Section 304(a)(4) the CWA identifies a list of "conventional pollutants," including oil and fecal coliform bacteria. The chemical toxins examined in the present study are addressed in Section 307(a)(1). The agency currently lists and regulates a total of 126 "priority pollutants" (40 CFR 122, App. D), which include both organic chemicals and metals. The identification of critical contaminants characterizes the initial effort of EPA both to monitor environmental quality in coastal areas and to assess the toxicity of chemical contaminants in seafood.

The importance of these strategies resides in the fact that a critical control point for ensuring the safety of the U.S. seafood product is the quality of the environment in which the fish are harvested. For the most part, subsequent safety assurance strategies (apart from cooking) are designed to ensure that contaminant levels are not further elevated. Therefore, any effective control strategy should begin with efforts to reduce the probability that contaminated seafood enters the processing and retail system. Further, by focusing on the quality of harvesting environments, one fundamentally achieves an opportunity to restrict products at the point of least added value.

However, current environmental monitoring programs do not focus directly on the question of seafood safety. Rather, they are designed to assess the general health of our marine and aquatic environments. Efforts to use such data directly for consideration of seafood safety suffer because most of the available environmental data (1) do not focus on seafood harvesting areas, (2) lack a common methodological approach, and (3) do not focus on the edible portion of seafood in order to determine public health hazards, as opposed to environmental health aspects. This last point is raised because most evaluations of contaminants in fish are done not on edible tissue but rather on the whole fish or on specific internal organs.

U.S. Food and Drug Administration

The Food and Drug Administration serves as the agency with primary authority for seafood product inspection. Seafood inspection within the FDA falls generally into four major categories: (1) general plant and product inspection, (2) import control inspection, (3) routine and periodic surveys for residual chemicals, and (4) compliance inspection for the National Shellfish Sanitation Program.

Any evaluation of such a monitoring and inspection program should address three related questions. First, are the inspections carried out with sufficient frequency to ensure compliance with regulatory guidelines? Second, is the sampling plan used by the program sufficient to develop a reliable estimate of the results? Third, is the program sufficiently broad to ensure that the regulatory guidelines provide a sufficient measure of protection to the public? This third point is a rather important one: that is, are contaminants being found in seafood for which the agency has not developed a sufficient regulatory response and for which there is evidence of public health concern? An effort is made here to address each of these questions in the characterization of federal monitoring, inspection, and enforcement programs.

As part of its general responsibilities under the FFDCA, FDA carries out a general inspection program involving periodic visits of its inspectors to processing facilities that prepare products destined for interstate commerce. The frequency and type of inspection are determined by the nature of plant operation, the volume of product produced, the record of previous compliance with regulations, the existence of consumer complaints, or other evidence of a problem (ICF, 1986). These inspections involve the entire suite of issues for which FDA has statutory authority. That is, they address overall plant sanitation and economic fraud (among other things), in addition to issues relating directly to seafood safety. Given the mandate of this study, the committee's effort is directed solely at programs developed to mitigate problems related to seafood safety.

Inspections directed at domestic products and processing are oriented primarily toward the maintenance of plant sanitation by way of enforcing good manufacturing practices. Although there is an acknowledged relationship between compliance with GMPs and seafood safety, the most direct impact of these inspections is on product quality. During the past several years, sanitation inspection has constituted a majority of the FDA's inspection effort. However, product evaluations for potential seafood contaminants also play a role. Data characterizing the agency's efforts to inspect for biological and chemical contaminants in both domestic and import programs are contained in Table 8-4.

In this program, biological hazards are limited almost exclusively to microbiological contaminants and parasites. Paralytic shellfish poison (PSP) and other natural toxins are more fundamentally monitored in other programs (i.e., the NSSP or state programs). Table 8-4 highlights two obvious issues: (1) that there has been a slight increase in the number of products evaluated in recent years, and (2) that most of the program effort is directed at imported products. The results of these evaluations are contained in Table 8-5. It should be noted here that individual states also carry out additional plant inspections that provide a substantial complementary contribution to this federal inspection effort.

Those data taken alone suggest that a significant proportion of both domestic and imported products are in violation of FDA regulations. However, they are derived from samples of a small proportion of seafoods that were selected as potentially troublesome lots because of previous experience or other information. It is questionable and probably unlikely that random sampling would yield such high violation rates. However, the precise relationship between directed and random inspections cannot be effectively calculated and therefore a general violation rate cannot be known.

TABLE 8-4 General FDA Seafood Inspection Program Product Evaluations

	1987	1988	1989
Domestic samples analyzed			
Biological hazards	797	1,137	1,109
Chemical contaminants	1,007	715	541
Imported samples analyzed			
Biological hazards	4,147	4,428	4,939
Chemical contaminants	881	1,204	1,063
Annual totals	6,832	7,484	7,652

SOURCE: FDA (1990).

TABLE 8-5 General FDA Seafood Inspection Program Results, 1989

Inspection	Biological Hazards	Chemical Contaminants
Domestic samples analyzed	1,109	541
Adverse	231 (21%)	20 (4%)
Regulatory action not taken	134 (12%)	12 (2%)
In compliance	744 (67%)	509 (94%)
Import samples analyzed	4,939	1,063
Adverse	1,864 (38%)	510 (48%)
Regulatory action not taken	194 (4%)	12 (1%)
In compliance	2,881 (58%)	541 (51%)

SOURCE: FDA (1990).

Import control program

The FFDCA requires all imported products to meet the same criteria for wholesomeness and safety imposed on U.S. products destined for interstate commerce. As shown in Table 8-4, a majority of the FDA inspection effort is, in fact, directed at imported products, partly because imports constitute a majority of the seafood products consumed in the United States. However, the predominance of imports in inspection is more fundamentally a result of FDA policy to direct resources toward areas suspected of safety problems. As part of its import program, and based on the results of past evaluations, the FDA has developed a strategy of automatic detention and evaluation of certain products with a history of violations. A program of automatic detention is currently in place for swordfish (evaluated for mercury/methylmercury content), mahimahi (evaluated for scombrotoxin), and raw in-shell or peeled frozen shrimp (evaluated for filth and the presence of *Salmonella* or *Listeria*) (FDA, 1986-1987). These products are detained at the point of entry and held until the importer can provide assurance, typically by using private laboratory testing, that the product is safe. The FDA reserves the right to retest private laboratory results. In 1989, 3,150 imported lots with a value of approximately $223 million were detained. This constituted about 4% of the total value of seafood imports ($5.6 billion for the year). It should be noted that neither private nor state laboratory evaluations are included in the total analyses for imported products described in Table 8-5.

The FDA also regularly releases import alert notices to communicate potential hazards. However, one difficulty with this strategy has been that the identification of specific import lots is often lost during subsequent product processing, which may reduce the impact of such alerts.

In addition to the general import strategy described above, FDA has recently developed a limited number of programs designed to focus and guide its efforts. These include the following:

- Processed Seafood Program – This program is designed to offer a comparative evaluation for microbiological contamination of domestic and imported processed seafood. Seafoods included in the survey were crabmeat, shrimp, surimi,[1] crawfish, smoked salmon, and lobster meat. The program evaluated a total of 369 domestic samples and 270 imported samples. Results indicated an adverse finding in 14.4% of the domestic samples and 11.1% of the imported products. In almost all instances the contaminant was identified as *Listeria monocytogenes* (FDA, 1988a; Matches et al., 1986).

- Imported and Domestic Shrimp Program – This program was designed to compare problems associated with imported and domestic frozen raw shrimp. A total of 183 samples of imported products from 34 countries and 30 domestic samples were taken for evaluation. Results suggested that approximately 7% of the imports were clearly in violation, whereas only one domestic sample was (John Kvenberg, FDA, personal communication, 1989).

- • Imported <u>Molluscan Shellfish Assignment</u> – This assignment was
  designed to analyze and audit samples of shellfish for use by the
  FDA in refining its general inspection program and for use by
  states in their inspection and enforcement practices.   On
  completion, the program will have evaluated 240 imported samples
  (FDA, 1989c).

These and other programs are used to periodically update and refine FDA
inspection practices and to further direct the general inspection program so as to
maximize the effectiveness of the limited resources dedicated to seafood inspection.

Routine and periodic surveys for residual chemicals

As noted in recent congressional testimony by FDA Acting Commissioner James
Benson, the agency carries out – in addition to the general inspection program – an
ongoing surveillance program for residual chemicals in seafood (Benson, 1990).   The
program is located in the Division of Contaminants Chemistry (DCC) of the FDA
Center for Food Safety and Applied Nutrition.   According to FDA personnel, agency
field officers are required to collect a specified minimum number of seafood samples
harvested or processed in that region.   The general sampling protocol for this program
has been articulated in the following way (Lombardo and Yess, 1989): Sampling for
chemical contaminants is based on a variety of factors, including inspectional findings,
historical problem areas, new toxicological concerns, changes in growing/harvesting
techniques, new sources of food, and review of state/local shellfish control programs.
     During the past three years, DCC has evaluated 2,214 seafood products for
approximately 60 pesticides and industrial chemicals.   This suite of residual chemicals
represents, according to FDA, approximately 75% of the chemicals deemed by EPA
to have the highest tendency to bioaccumulate in finfish and shellfish (George Hoskin,
FDA, personal communication, 1990).   The results of these evaluations have not been
published, nor has this committee carried out independent analysis of the data.
Therefore, the reliability of these analyses cannot be verified independently.
     The DCC also carries out periodic evaluations of trace-metal contamination in
shellfish.   The last of these surveys was done during fiscal year 1985-1986.
Approximately 300 samples were taken from 20 coastal states and evaluated for 18
trace metals (FDA, 1988c).   The DCC also carries out additional evaluations of lead
and cadmium in fresh shellfish and other seafood products; of mercury/methylmercury
in swordfish, shark, and tuna; and of dioxins in fish.   These data have led FDA to
assert that its current regulatory effort to control exposure to chemical contaminants
is sufficient.   The agency argues that the current set of action levels, designed to guide
the general inspection program, reflect current concerns over residual contaminants.
This policy was recently expressed in the following terms (Benson, 1990):

> Occasionally, there are good candidates for the establishment of national standards.
> . . . Generally speaking, a candidate for a binding standard is one that would warrant
> a national policy based on what is known about its toxicity, the amounts being found,
> and geographic factors such as how widespread or localized the problem may be.
> Various metals of potential concern for seafood, such as lead, cadmium and arsenic,

have not shown up in the sample surveys that we have taken in amounts that would warrant a national standard. Similarly, pesticides newer than the 13 for which action levels were originally set tend to break down quickly and thus are not generally found in samples. We continue to conduct surveys, however, to update our knowledge.

The committee's assessment of these programs is contained in Chapter 5.

National Marine Fisheries Service

The Inspection Services Division of the National Marine Fisheries Service (NMFS) conducts a voluntary, fee-for-service National Seafood Inspection Program of seafood destined for domestic consumption and for export. The program's regulatory authority derives primarily from the Agricultural Marketing Act of 1946, which allows for the creation of a voluntary inspection and certification program for products in interstate commerce. The Presidential Reorganization Plan No. 3 of 1970 (DOC, 1970) transferred the voluntary inspection program to the U.S. Department of Commerce (DOC), in which NMFS resides. The service is constituted by three general programmatic elements: programs designed to develop product standards and specifications; the voluntary fee-for-service inspection program; and a training and industry/consumer liaison effort.

A primary effort within the inspection program is to inspect and certify seafood processing plants and to issue a "Packed Under Federal Inspection" (PUFI) mark or a U.S. Grade mark to seafood products. Efforts in standard setting and product specification include the "development of product grade standards, Federal purchase specifications, cooperation and compliance with FDA regulations and policies, and the participation in the activities of international organizations (e.g., Codex Alimentarius Commission) as they relate to the development and implementation of international standards and codes of practice" (DOC, 1989). These product specifications are designed primarily to ensure product quality, as opposed to product safety, but do address safety issues to the degree to which they consider FDA seafood safety policies and to which assurances of product quality also provide a means to increase product safety.

The inspection service carries out a wide range of inspection activities including vessel and plant sanitation inspection and seafood product evaluation (which includes a limited number of laboratory evaluations, typically fewer than 100 per year, for biological and chemical contaminants). These inspections are carried out by DOC inspectors, inspectors cross-licensed with the U.S. Department of Agriculture (USDA), and inspectors cross-licensed with DOC-trained state inspectors. Two general types of inspections are carried out under the program: type I in-plant inspections, and type II product lot inspections. In-plant inspections are primarily designed to ensure compliance with minimum sanitation practices and with product-grade standards. A product may be certified U.S. Grade A, B, or C; be certified by a PUFI designation; or be inspected and graded by means of a "no mark" certification. PUFI and "no mark" certifications are driven and limited by the contractual agreement signed between the DOC and the processor (NOAA, 1988a,b). Such agreements may include product-grade specifications (particularly for PUFI certification), but may also be limited to such issues as a contractual assurance that minimum counts (such as the number of shrimp in a box) are being met.

The DOC also conducts product lot inspections for both domestic and exported products. These inspections are generally not carried out for product safety purposes; rather, they are almost exclusively designed to ensure product quality and condition.

General participation in the Voluntary Seafood Inspection Program has increased in recent years. The total amount of reimbursable contract activity increased from $4.4 million in fiscal year 1988 to a projected level of $7.6 million for fiscal year 1990. However, the total number of pounds inspected under the program has decreased significantly over the past decade. For example, in fiscal year 1981 a total of 625 million pounds was inspected, whereas for fiscal year 1988 that total had dropped to 495 million pounds. The reasons for this drop are somewhat unclear. One reason is that the cost of the program to the processor has increased significantly and some participants have dropped out. However, there has also been an apparent shift in the kind of processor contracting with the program. In recent years, more firms processing fresh fish products have been brought into the program, and fewer firms processing large lots of breaded fish have continued in the program. One consequence of this shift has been that although the program has been growing in terms of total contract reimbursement and personnel (the Northeast Inspection Office witnessed nearly a 100% increase in the number of inspectors in the past year), the amount of product (as measured in pounds annually inspected) has decreased. The reasoning here is that for an equivalent effort, an inspector will certify fewer pounds of a fresh or fresh frozen product than in large lots of processed product.

It should be reiterated that this voluntary program is not directed primarily at seafood safety. Rather, the program is directed almost exclusively at plant sanitation and product quality and condition. However, it does impact on the safety of seafood in two nontrivial ways. First, there is a strong correlation between product quality and safety. Although there are many safety questions in which the quality of the product does not play a role (e.g., residual chemical contaminants, natural toxins such as ciguatera and PSP, and certain microbial pathogens), a number of safety issues can be mitigated by a sanitary processing environment and the application of GMPs. Second, the program does provide that a trained inspector be in the plant on a regular basis, and if the product being processed is suspected of being unsafe, the inspector can collect a sample for further analysis or alert the FDA of a potential safety problem.

Training and Educational Programs

The final set of activities to be considered here that are carried out by the federal government in support of seafood safety are related to training and education. In general, these programs and efforts are designed to educate relevant state officials and industry representatives about the risks from various seafood contaminants and about the development of strategies to mitigate those risks. These programs are addressed later in this chapter.

Public Health Monitoring

Some of the more relevant and fundamental governmental monitoring responsibilities are those relating to the compilation and evaluation of data characterizing the number of people who become ill from eating contaminated seafood. The issue of public health and food has, in recent years, occupied a central place on the nation's political agenda. With this increased emphasis has come an attendant rise in the expectations for, and emphasis on, the role of government reporting of food-borne and – in the context of the present study – seafood-borne illness. The Centers for Disease Control (CDC) of the U.S. Public Health Service (PHS) is the lead agency providing technical support and direction for a range of programs, including the surveillance and investigation of food-borne diseases.

The CDC (1985b) collects and analyzes data on reportable diseases from states and territories. These data are distributed in the *Morbidity and Mortality Weekly Report* (MMWR) and published in an annual summary (CDC, 1985b). The legislative authority for collecting and disseminating morbidity and mortality statistics goes back to an 1878 act authorizing the collection of morbidity reports by the PHS for quarantine purposes against such pestilential diseases as cholera and yellow fever; however, it was not until 1925 that all states began to submit reports routinely. State and territorial health officers established the Conference of State Epidemiologists in 1950 to determine which diseases should be reported to the PHS by states and what procedures should be followed in submitting weekly reports and annual summaries. This group, currently known as the Conference of State and Territorial Epidemiologists (CSTE), continues to determine the procedures for nationwide morbidity and mortality reporting.

In addition to routine disease-specific reporting, CDC administers other surveillance systems and has conducted national food-borne disease surveillance since 1967. This system also is based primarily on reports from local and state health departments. Reports of each outbreak are submitted on a standard questionnaire, which covers the number of cases, persons hospitalized, and fatalities; clinical characterization of diseases; incubation period and duration of illness; results of epidemiologic investigation, including information on the vehicle incriminated by the epidemiological evidence; the place of preparation and consumption of the suspect food; the manner in which the incriminated food was marketed; factors, such as improper food handling, that are believed to have contributed to the outbreak; and pertinent laboratory data. All questionnaires received are reviewed by CDC staff; missing information is added if possible; and the preliminary diagnosis is reevaluated by using established guidelines. During 1973-1987, 3,699 food-borne outbreaks of disease with known vehicles were reported through the food-borne disease surveillance system. These outbreaks affected 164,695 persons; shellfish accounted for 5.8%, and finfish for 14.6%, of the reported outbreaks.

Food-borne cases and outbreaks are reported to CDC by all states; however, a legal requirement to report is not universal. As with epidemics of other communicable diseases, prompt telephone or electronic notification of food-borne disease outbreaks involving commercially available food products or potential interstate consumption is important for control purposes. However, the quality and completeness of routine surveillance data collected by local or county public health officials and forwarded to state or territorial health departments for transmission to CDC are not uniform and are inadequate for planning and evaluating food safety programs. More important, reporting to CDC does not identify sufficiently the species of fish or shellfish deemed to be the source of disease. Likewise, species verification relies on menu listings (which may not be accurate) or on inexperienced opinion.

In a poll of food-borne disease cases reported in 13 selected states and territories that was conducted by the committee, the general consensus was that reporting was "good" only for outbreaks of those diseases for which an etiologic agent could be identified and for which reporting by the laboratory was required by state regulation. This last point is by no means trivial. The data collected by CDC represent efforts by state health officers, whose resources are largely directed toward the investigation and reporting of illnesses that are officially reportable by that state. The two major sources of seafood-related illness, viruses and vibrios, are not consistently reported by states (Chorba et al., 1989). Indeed, vibriosis is a reportable illness in only 10 of the 56 U.S. jurisdictions (states and affiliated areas). The impact of this point was articulated by a senior public health official in Florida (Karl Klontz, Disease Control Epidemiology Section, Florida Department of Health and Rehabilitation Services, Tallahassee, personal communication, 1989) who suggested that "food-borne outbreaks in Florida are reported if the etiological agent is on the list of reportable diseases."

For those cases in which the disease was mild or had nonspecific symptoms, no specific diagnostic test was available, or a specific food vehicle was not readily apparent, especially when occurrence was mainly restricted to single cases or to small clusters, reporting tended to be very poor. All state health departments that were questioned reported that local, county, or state personnel attempted to identify and trace implicated food vehicles but acknowledged that the success rate was low.

Therefore, it is crucial to understand the limitations of the data gathered by the national food-borne disease surveillance system before attempting to analyze or interpret them. The number of outbreaks may bear little relationship to the total number of outbreak-associated and sporadic cases that occur. For example, *Campylobacter* infections are at least as common as *Salmonella*, but many more *Salmonella* outbreaks are reported. Individual cases of illness caused by seafoods are unlikely to be linked to the responsible seafood unless the illness is typically seafood-related, such as ciguatera or scombroid fish poisoning; the illness is severe enough to lead the victim to seek medical attention; and the doctor recognizes the disease and is one of the few who report faithfully to the local health department. Outbreaks may not be recognized because only a small number of people are ill or because people eating the food disperse after the meal and do not know that others became ill. Even when victims realize that an outbreak has occurred, only a small proportion of recognized outbreaks are investigated thoroughly enough to incriminate a food and determine the pathogen or toxin that caused the illness. A second reason for the inadequacy of reported outbreaks alone in defining the burden of food-borne disease on society is that most such disease, including that transmitted by seafood, occurs as sporadic cases rather than as part of recognized outbreaks. As already noted, the cases reported by CDC are outbreak-related cases rather than a characterization of all seafood-related cases. For example, persons with liver disease who eat raw oysters can get a devastating, frequently fatal infection with *Vibrio vulnificus*, but no outbreaks caused by this bacterium have ever been reported. Thus, data in addition to those from reported outbreaks are needed to assess the magnitude of the problem.

By using CDC food-borne disease outbreak and reportable disease surveillance data bases, various attempts have been made to estimate the total societal burden posed by food-borne disease. It has been estimated that more than 6 million cases of food-borne disease (excluding *V. vulnificus* and fish parasite infections, and scombroid, ciguatera, or shellfish poisons) occur each year in the United States (Bennett et al., 1987). Todd (1989) estimated that 12.6 million cases of seafood-borne diseases annually are not considered in the report by Bennett et al. (1987). An attempt was made to rank various food vehicles by the risk they posed to public health, based on CDC data and published reports from small-scale community health surveys (Douglas Archer, FDA, personal communication, 1990). By those calculations, the consumption of raw molluscan shellfish represented a 1-2 $\log_{10}$ greater risk than cooked chicken, and consumption of cooked chicken represented a 1-2 $\log_{10}$ greater risk than cooked seafood. Clearly, existing data reporting the level and source of seafood-borne illness do not represent accurately either the level or the source of disease. Data currently available are too limited to lead to fully effective, scientifically valid, risk-based control programs, or even to valid comparisons of the hazards posed by different food vehicles. The CDC outbreak data indicate that illness due to seafood is a public health problem and provide information on the characteristics of these illnesses. However, they do not provide reliable information on the magnitude of the problem or its importance relative to that posed by other foods.

RESPONSIBILITIES AND PROGRAMS OF STATE AGENCIES

As noted earlier, the effort to enhance seafood safety in the United States consists of a set of highly integrated programs within the federal government, various state agencies, and private industry. In this section, the committee considers that suite of programs not focused exclusively within the federal environment.

The information used to develop this characterization was compiled by way of discussions from group meetings and individual interviews with a variety of coastal state regulatory agencies and respective industries in an effort to better assess the "typical" state role in assuring seafood safety (see appendix to this chapter). The selection of states for review was directed by contractual obligations referencing locations, historical seafood commerce, and prior reported seafood-related illnesses. Garrett (1988) summarized annual CDC data indicating that 81% of all seafood-related illness in the United States is reported from only nine states or territories: California, Connecticut, Florida, Guam, Hawaii, New York, Puerto Rico, the Virgin Islands, and Washington State, and that the listed territories alone account for more than 49% of all seafood-borne illnesses reported annually.

Group meetings in Hawaii, California, Washington, and Massachusetts were conducted by committee members and staff, and supplemented by results from a similar project conducted by the Southeastern Fisheries Association (Tallahassee, Florida) in Texas, Louisiana, Mississippi, Alabama, Florida, Georgia, South Carolina, North Carolina, and Puerto Rico. The meetings involved actual visits to the respective state or territory, and subsequent reviews for additional information. Information from other states and territories (Alaska, Wisconsin, Connecticut, New York, the U.S. Virgin Islands, and Guam) was obtained through individual interviews. The following observations are based on a collective assessment for all these states. Such condensed observations cannot represent all states; nor are they intended to represent, rate, or rank any individual state program. The committee's intention is to provide some initial indications on how state regulations and practices address seafood safety and how state regulations characterize the source and level of seafood risk.

State regulatory authorities pertinent to seafood safety are typically structured and directed to address the prevalent concerns particular to their regional environments, production schemes, and product types. A review of current state regulatory jurisdictions and programs reveals that efforts are segmented with respect to environments (freshwater and saltwater sources), species (shellfish and finfish), product forms (raw and cooked), and stage of product handling (production, processing, retail, etc). In most instances the respective state regulatory organizations are justified by efficient use of resources and expertise, but this inherent diversity can confuse public and industry perception and may hamper intergovernmental cooperation.

In general, seafood safety assurance requires three areas of regulatory focus: (1) harvesting, (2) processing, and (3) distribution and marketing. The remainder of this chapter is organized around these themes. Each of these categories presents attributes unique to specific regions, states, and – in some instances – local sites and species. For example, the adverse health consequence from consumption of raw oysters harboring *Vibrio vulnificus* is primarily a problem in warmer waters typical of the coastal regions of the Gulf of Mexico. Similarly, ciguatera is more prevalent in tropical regions. The increasing popularity in fresh markets of certain pelagic fish species (e.g., mahimahi, mackerel, tuna) has led to concern about regional incidents of histamine poisoning. Although the less acute health concerns related to environmental contaminants may appear more ubiquitous in distribution, their occurrence and reasons for concern are usually site and species specific. The point to be made is that seafood diversity, in type and distribution, and the association of harvest environment warrant more "customized" state and local regulatory attention than currently practiced for many other foods.

Harvest

Seafood safety at harvest must consider the initial condition of the resource prior to capture and the immediate consequences of handling on the vessel during delivery to the dock. These considerations are similar for the harvest from natural resources or from a cultured stock in fresh- or saltwater environments.

Microbial Contaminants

State efforts in environmental monitoring to protect public health from microbial contaminants are primarily carried out under the auspices of the NSSP and addressed elsewhere in this chapter.

Although molluscan shellfish-borne illnesses remain the dominant, immediate regulatory concern for most states, many felt their molluscan shellfish monitoring programs were adequate and appreciated the guidance provided by NSSP. Of particular concern is law enforcement vulnerability to adequate field staffing to enforce closures for water quality and subsequent legal consequences. The geographic distribution of the resource, surface distinction of waters, and variable harvest time complicate field enforcement. Likewise, in some instances, consequences for illegal harvest have been compromised by court delays, limited penalties, and political influence.

Natural Toxins

State regulatory monitoring for natural toxins in seafoods is largely the responsibility of the departments of health and, in some instances, agriculture – in concert with the equivalent departments of natural resources or fisheries. The role of the latter is usually necessary due to their "on the water" access for resource management. Program activities are distinctly customized to toxins of regional concern. For example, red tides vary in occurrence, duration, toxicity, and public health significance, depending on the causative dinoflagellates. Species in coastal regions of New England and states along the Pacific Coast require closer monitoring for public health reasons than do species more typical of the Gulf of Mexico and south Atlantic regions. For all occurrences, public warnings are appropriate and effective, but the toxigenicity of the northern varieties can be more threatening to public health (see Chapter 4). Epidemiology and pertinent state interviews confirm that current state regulatory programs are adequately protecting public health from toxins associated with red tide. Recreational harvesting carried out by individuals unaware of PSP risks is the major reason for continued warnings. These programs should be continued and expanded through additional public education. Further consideration should be given to future federal assistance because red tides can originate in federal waters and involve adjacent states. As suggested elsewhere in this report, serious consideration should be given to the general development of marine recreational fishing licenses to serve as a vehicle to communicate risk information.

In contrast, ciguatera is a natural toxin of historical occurrence in regions of the United States that still defies state or federal efforts, beyond education, to curb the level of incidents. The lack of a reliable method for detection and the randomness of occurrence among fish samples limit prevention. Fortunately, occurrence is somewhat localized within certain states (Florida, Hawaii) and territories (Puerto Rico, the Virgin Islands, Guam). This situation could change with the expanding demand for fresh tropical fish and recent documented increases of fish imports from tropical regions (Adams and Lawlor, 1989). Likewise, increasing recreational fishing means more harvesting effort in likely ciguatoxic areas. Although extensive research continues to attempt to define and identify the toxins involved, adequate controls have yet to be implemented by the respective states. Given the many sources of suspect fish and the complexity in documenting more accurate occurrence data (from the fish habitat or as a consequence of consumption), state regulatory authorities alone should not be expected to resolve the ciguatera problem. Cooperative federal and state approaches should be considered to restrict the harvesting and marketing of particular species and of fish from particular areas. It should be noted, however, that in some instances, notably Hawaii, the state lacks the legal authority to close ciguatoxic areas to recreational fishing. In many cases the ability to restrict fishing is limited to scientific concerns relating to the health of the stock, not to the human health of seafood consumers.

Chemical Contaminants

State monitoring for potential chemical contaminants in the harvest environments is most often the responsibility of an equivalent department of environmental regulation. The principal objective in state waters is ensuring environmental quality, which often does not include assessment of the safety of edible resources for consumption. Data on potential contaminants in edible portions of fish or shellfish are usually derived from studies directed by probable cause relative to constituents, species, or locations of concern. Edible product assessments are usually the responsibility of the departments of health or agriculture. Some routine product assessments are conducted for fish and shellfish in the environment, where there is probable cause of risk.

Most state authorities agree that additional edible product assessments should be conducted in a more continuous and expanded manner. Prior hesitancy in state programs was explained by a collection of reasons, presented here in no particular order:

- Lack of sufficient funds for appropriate sampling, and the need for more analytical equipment and personnel
- Lack of federal guidance in criteria, common risk assessments, and cooperative encouragement through shared expertise and funds
- Insufficient evidence to rank environmental contaminants higher than other more prevalent food safety concerns
- Fear of public misinterpretation and initiation of costly "witch-hunts"
- A general, professional opinion that environmental contaminants pose no significant threat in most domestic sources of seafoods

States indicated plans for environmental and seafood product assessments in the future. The impact of these assessments could be greatly enhanced by a more coordinated and effective federal-state relationship. This kind of cooperation will be more readily accessible through a recently formed Federal-State Standing Committee on Residues in Fish. These intentions could lead to a more solid foundation for action within and among states if accompanied by agreement on analytical and risk assessment methodologies, more complete listings for constituents of concern, and compilation of and screening for a national data base.

Vessels and Recreational Fishing

If state waters yield safe products, the next harvest segment for regulatory surveillance is the vessel or fishing activity. This commercial activity receives the least amount of regulatory surveillance relative to product safety. States justify their regulatory posture with the assertion that little evidence exists to support, with the exception of molluscan shellfish, direct regulatory action for seafood product safety on commercial vessels. State officials and various segments of the commercial industry contend that fishing vessels can have a profound effect on product quality. This position recognizes that thermal abuse or cross-contamination from unsanitary conditions or chemical spills could result in products compromised by microbial contaminants, elevated histamines, or exposure to sanitizing agents, petrochemicals, or other chemicals. These potential safety issues, however, have not yet been fully recognized as justifying expanded vessel regulations. Thus, many state regulations do not specify the jurisdiction or responsible authority for inspection of fishing vessels. Where states do specify or assume this regulatory role, their efforts have been minimal and typically in response to a recurrent or highly suspicious activity (such as Maryland regulation of shellfish vessels).

State regulatory agencies realize that steps to initiate more vessel seafood safety surveillance would be quite complicated and time-consuming due to the diversity of vessel types, variable harvest schedules, numerous dockside landings, and multiple products. A least-cost effort that also offers potential educational benefits, might involve initial orientation and certification for newly licensed vessels, annual certification linked to licensing, and a "terminal" inspection program based on unannounced inspections at dockside. These approaches require careful consideration to take into account vessels licensed in other states, variable handling methods per vessel and fishery, multipurpose fishing vessels, ownership of product at dockside, off-loading requirements, and additional harvest variables unique to different fisheries.

Offshore processing vessels present additional confusion for the state with such activity. In most instances, federal versus state jurisdiction would have to be resolved relative to the waters of harvest and the location when processing. Current federal efforts include processing vessels working in U.S. waters. States have not developed discrete regulatory responses to offshore processing in state waters, largely because of the limited amount of activity under their jurisdiction.

A dockside preharvest and postprocessing inspection of processing vessels to include access to records that reflect process conditions is the most plausible approach. In effect, the processing vessel would be subject to inspection similar to that used for shore-based facilities, but regulatory access during actual processing would be limited.

Because many states condone commercialization of a recreational catch, this type of vessel or shoreside harvest activity also requires regulatory consideration for product safety. In some state regulations, recreational and commercial fish harvests are distinguished by licensing, declared intent with permits, and harvest restrictions. These regulations are typically within the jurisdiction of the state agency protecting the aquatic resources and attempting to resolve recreational and commercial conflicts. Seafood product safety is rarely considered.

Whether commercial or recreational activities, all boat or shore-based seafood harvests should be made mindful of restricted areas and species, and should be properly equipped to preserve the catch. Again, certification with licensing and dockside surveillance could apply to recreational vessels, but additional requirements should be considered to ensure product safety in commercialization of the recreational harvest. State efforts to prevent seafood-borne illnesses associated with a recreational catch are typically limited to public warnings to restrict certain harvest sites, species, and consumption. Recreational closures are not common. Indeed, many states lack the legal competence to close recreational fisheries for reasons of public health. Many state-based institutions and agencies continue to issue information to encourage proper seafood handling and preparation. Public awareness and practice suggest that these state-based educational activities should continue and be more focused on prevalent seafood safety concerns.

Processing

Seafood processing is any postharvest handling of the catch or cultured product in preparation for distribution through retail or institutional settings. This activity is defined differently by fisheries and agencies of concern. It may begin with dockside off-loading and repacking firms, progress through established commercial processing firms that alter the form and appearance of the domestically harvested or imported products, and continue into retail firms that are instituting more innovative processing programs at the store level. These variable levels of seafood processing, in combination with the diversity of seafoods, complicate state regulatory responsibilities.

Organization of state regulatory authority for seafood safety during processing is less uniform among states than that for harvesting, distribution, and marketing. State health departments are most often responsible for product safety in seafood processing. In some states this responsibility is shared with the department of agriculture, with jurisdictions delineated by species and product forms (e.g., Florida, North Carolina, Alabama, Wisconsin), or geographic setting (e.g., South Carolina). Likewise, in some states, processing authority for certain species is housed in the equivalent departments for natural resources or fisheries that justify their role through linking with resource access and "on the water" enforcement capability. Shellfish (oysters and clams) and blue crab processing are the usual candidates for such regulatory distinction in the southeastern United States. A state department of agriculture with sole authority for seafood safety during processing is the exception among states and, when present, usually includes a division of health. This array of state regulatory organizations for seafood safety in processing must be considered in decisions that mandate concomitant federal authority. The alignment of jurisdictions, programs, and regulatory philosophy is essential to fostering more cooperative, responsive, and uniform programs.

In general, most state regulatory officials believe that seafood processing does not present a major food safety problem and that, where potential problems exist, they are being addressed. Therefore, limited state-based resources are directed at inspection and control of commercial processing. The four most prevalent recorded seafood-borne illnesses–ciguatera, histamine poisoning, microbial infections from raw molluscan shellfish consumption, and cross-contamination with *Vibrio parahaemolyticus* (Garrett, 1988)–occur primarily from consequences outside the processing sector. Thus, state regulatory attention to seafood safety during processing has focused on the critical points of product procurement and entry that initiate processing. This preprocessing consideration complements state recommendations to expand environmental monitoring efforts that ensure product safety prior to processing. These recommendations are supported further by the fact that imported products destined for further processing constitute the major portion of seafood consumption in the United States. Likewise, to support postprocessing concerns, states emphasize the importance of increased education for proper product handling in retail institutions and in the home because seafood product safety can be significantly compromised in these settings.

State records for common seafood processing violations usually involve GMPs and adulteration or mislabeling that constitutes economic fraud. These quality problems can be resolved by existing state authorities. State access to permitted processing firms and point-of-sale transactions represents the first and most immediate regulatory influence. The effectiveness depends on frequency of inspection and more education to direct compliance. Most state process inspections are directed by prior firm performance, probable cause, and complaints. In many instances, regulatory state and industry representatives recommend additional, routine inspections but do not expect regulatory activity to serve as a quality control program.

Certain seafood processing quality violations could constitute potential product safety problems. For example, excessive and improper application of sulfiting agents to prevent crustacean melanosis could pose a health threat for consumers in asthmatic risk groups. Fish species substitution, intentionally or by error, could present a natural toxin not common to the intended fish product. Such adverse events are possible, yet in terms of food safety reports they are rarely if ever recorded, even in states more prone to these processing considerations.

Raw molluscan shellfish production and processing were considered the most dominant seafood safety concerns for most states. Prior state concern culminated in the development of the ISSC, which helped strengthen shellfish processing guidelines specified in the federal NSSP manuals (FDA, 1989b). In addition to basic GMPs, states enforce stringent tagging and labeling requirements that identify the source and time of harvest for live shellstock and shucked meats. The tagging requirement extends the processor's responsibility to the point of harvest and through all forms of marketing. Processors remain liable for 90 days posttagging. This product identification system represents one of the most tedious forms of inter- and intrastate seafood safety regulation. In addition, specified durations for in-plant processing and terminal sale-by-date requirements can be imposed for additional public protection. Combined with the commitment to monitor shellfish growing waters, state regulatory attention to ensure safe, raw molluscan shellfish often represents the most extensive regulatory effort per single seafood commodity. Continuing raw molluscan-related illnesses justify this commitment, along with the realization that monitoring for harvestable waters represents a stalwart effort to prevent coastal pollution in producer states.

In most instances the continued level of state regulatory attention for all seafood processing will require more manpower, additional support funds, and better analytical capability. States typically lack sufficient administrators and inspectors experienced with seafoods and with the subtleties of pertinent regulations. There is interagency confusion about certain regulatory interpretations and authority. A common industry complaint is lack of knowledge of the applicable regulations and authorities. Industry processors complain of the absence of a single, condensed, and instructive manual delineating the regulations and regulators. A single source booklet would undoubtedly improve both understanding of, and compliance with, state regulations on seafood. Interestingly, many processing firms have experienced and appreciate a more "instructive" form of state inspection and regulation than evident in federal activity. In some instances, state regulations are criticized by the respective authorities and the seafood industry for lacking specificity and the ability to adapt to innovative processing concepts. Dependence on federal guidance and difficulties in changing or amending statutes are common excuses for this lack of flexibility and adaptivity in state seafood safety regulations. In general, state regulations concerning seafood quality and safety – from harvest through processing, distribution, and retail – should be reviewed periodically for changes and supplements to take into account evolving practices and better industry guidance.

Distribution and Marketing

Seafood safety in distribution and marketing usually involves the regulatory responsibility of county and city health departments inspecting restaurants, retail outlets, and institutions. Following guidelines from their respective state departments of health, and in some instances agriculture or natural resources and fisheries, these more localized authorities combine unannounced inspections with periodic training to ensure compliance with basic food safety practices. Additional guidance for food safety in retail has been provided through the national Food Retail Code Programs (AFDO/FDA, 1982) and a federal initiative to establish a Unicode that offers more uniform standards for sanitation in all retail practice (Anonymous, 1989a). These codes are basically GMPs and list critical points for control, including some specific concerns for seafoods.

Localized regulatory authority is more general, to account for the variety of food types and markets in cities and counties. Responsibilities can also include mobile retail units. The authorities are not commodity specific, rely on more specialized state-based seafood authority and training, and encourage additional and continuous training that addresses seafood safety and quality issues. This request is of particular concern in counties and cities that have a higher proportion of seafood marketing activity or experience a disruptive amount of annual inspector turnover.

The importance of localized regulation of seafood safety should be considered more in decisions to improve or expand state and federal regulatory programs. Combatting the high proportion of seafood-borne illness that occurs in restaurant settings and dealing with health concerns related to recreational fishing activities require more localized attention. Cross-contamination of ready-to-eat seafoods is a common consequence of poor handling and thermal abuse in restaurants, retail stores, or homes (Bryan, 1986). Sale of a potentially ciguatoxic or scombrotoxic fish can result from a local recreational activity. Similarly, prevention of uninformed recreational shellfish harvest from closed, contaminated waters requires local, accessible advice.

Although some county programs are extensive and may be more seafood specific, as exemplified by the King County Health Department in Washington, most county and city health authorities lack sufficient personnel and funds to afford more seafood-specific attention. Their impact on seafood safety must depend on public and institutional education available through cooperation with state authorities and academically based programs (e.g., Agricultural Cooperative Extension Services and Sea Grant Marine Advisory Services).

Additional State Considerations

Meetings and interviews with state groups revealed a number of common concerns that warrant additional consideration in evaluating state regulatory roles in ensuring seafood safety. These concerns vary by state but essentially involve every coastal state. Currently, these concerns are not considered major problems but are discussed as points for future consideration.

Aquaculture

Freshwater and marine-based culture of aquatic foods (cultured seafood) is increasing significantly in amount and diversity in domestic settings and imported products (Redmayne, 1989). Domestic aquaculture is currently estimated at more than 790 million pounds, valued at approximately $700 million and expected to surpass 2 billion pounds by the year 2000 (Anonymous, 1989b). Initially, state regulatory agencies are faced with this evolving industry through decisions for land and water use relative to zoning, quality, and public use conflicts. Most of these decisions, viewed as constraints, involve production but public health questions will eventually arise. Anticipating this situation, most states have initiated discussions of jurisdictions and the necessary aquacultured food safety priorities.

Fortunately, aquaculture offers a more controlled form of seafood production that is less prone to common seafood-borne illnesses (Fong and Brooks, 1989; Otwell, 1989; Rodrick and Cheng, 1989; Ward, 1989), but its safety can be compromised by environmental contaminants and mishandling during processing or marketing. Basic food safety considerations suggest that cultured seafoods simply represent another protein-based aquatic food that can be addressed by the existing scheme of state regulations. What is contrary to logic is the jurisdictional confusion due to the production environment (natural versus man-made, freshwater versus saltwater), the distinction between product types (traditional harvesting versus cultured), and state and federal assistance programs established to promote aquaculture. All of these issue were evident in discussions with state authorities and respective industry representatives.

The existing situation may offer a favorable incentive for all states to reevaluate their current seafood regulatory programs. Careful deliberation and federal guidance are necessary to ensure uniformity and to avoid regulatory dichotomy that could dilute and further confuse the necessary authorities for food safety and quality. There are no aquatic food safety distinctions relative to chemical or microbial contaminants to justify separate aquacultured food safety regulatory authorities, and food safety concerns should not be compromised by efforts properly aligned to direct and promote production and market development.

Admittedly, federal and state regulatory attention for safety in aquacultured products lags behind culture development, but there has been little research to characterize food safety problems with such products. Concerns for chemical and microbial contaminants in the culture water, and the use of therapeutic drugs, which are being addressed by FDA efforts, should be expanded to include more state involvement.

Recreational Fisheries

Recreational fishing activities involve public seafood safety concerns that require state scrutiny relative to the harvest and the point of sale. The catch destined for personal use or commercialization must be taken from approved waters and properly handled prior to consumption. Safety for individual use is best ensured through public education and controlling resource access. Public protection through commercialization of the recreational catch presents more challenges. Current licensing of recreational activity as a commercial practice does not address seafood safety.

State authorities have difficulty in determining when a recreational harvest becomes a wholesale or retail item. Except for dockside sales to tourists, contemplated sales to licensed firms for further seafood marketing should constitute a commercial transaction. Certain states require some form of permit for declared harvest intent or an equivalent form of "wholesale" dealers license to cover this event. These permits and licenses are usually intended to resolve recreational and commercial conflicts and to protect resources through harvest restrictions and information obtained for resource assessment. The buyer assumes responsibility for the safety of the catch.

For most recreational harvest a subsequent commercial event does not present a seafood safety problem, but states must prepare to address certain real and previously violated concerns. For example, the sale of recreationally caught fish harvested with a commercially licensed party boat from known or suspected ciguatoxic areas has resulted in ciguatera in Palm Beach County, Florida (PBCHD, 1988). Histamine poisoning is possible from the sale of certain scombroid-type fish that are popular recreational targets. Similar situations could arise from the sale of molluscan shellfish taken from local, unapproved waters. In each event, liability would rest with the initial buyer, but subsequent buyers, be they commercial or public, may not be aware of the source. If states continue to allow commercialization of recreational catch, they must consider some controls to license the event in a manner that identifies the product and the source. This situation may also involve federal authorities responsible for any harvest in federal or foreign waters.

Imports

Regulatory scrutiny for product safety of imported seafoods is the primary and initial responsibility of the FDA, but eventual domestic distribution can evoke additional state responsibility. Concerns for foreign product identification, country of origin declarations, certified sources, adulteration, and other seafood safety-related attributes become a state regulatory responsibility after the imports enter state commerce. By design, FDA attempts to alert states when specific products may pose problems, but the effectiveness of this system is compromised by limited federal surveillance of imports. Indeed, difficulties in identifying final product destination further complicate state-FDA communications. For example, as previously noted, the importation of shellfish from countries without formal NSSP memoranda of understanding[2] is currently controlled by reference to state regulations requiring purchase and handling of shellfish from approved harvesting grounds. Clearly, state regulations can have little direct impact on the certification of foreign sources. These issues are generally appropriate to a rather broad set of seafood products.

Training and Education

Recommendations solicited during state group meetings and interviews were unanimous in calling for additional employee training with orientation to seafood safety and similar continuing education for the industry. Periodic programs are currently provided by the NSSP to ensure uniformity among state molluscan shellfish regulatory programs, and FDA workshops are occasionally offered for a variety of topics (e.g., retail sanitation, importing requirements, labeling issues). Some of these programs include seafood-related training for inspectors and industry. Likewise, the USDA conducts workshops to ensure better aquacultured products. The USDA has conducted extensive work in sensory evaluation of pond-cultured catfish (Johnsen, 1989). The states acknowledge and appreciate these federal efforts, and suggest they be increased and made more convenient for regional and field staff.

Similar concerns are noted for the variety of state-based educational efforts provided through regulatory agencies or in the complementary extension and advisory programs offered by state universities and community colleges. In many programs, education for seafood safety has focused on critical points of concern for the vessel harvest through processing and retail. A few programs have included guidance in recordkeeping as an introduction to the Hazard Analysis Critical Control Point (HACCP) concept for product quality and safety. Despite these prior and ongoing efforts, most seafood industry representatives were not familiar with HACCP in a seafood processing or retail setting, yet their daily practice intuitively employs the critical point assessments without necessarily recording the daily events.

Innovative recommendations have suggested that more educational efforts should combine regulatory and seafood industry personnel in the same audience. Subsequent field education could be arranged to orient the inspector and the industry personnel to each of the respective settings. An industry-based internship for future inspectors could be instituted by trade associations to enhance regulators' appreciation of daily processing procedures. Standardized educational programs could be used to initiate a "certification" program with mandatory seafood training for plant employees, particularly managerial staff.

Despite the excellence of most programs, most seafood safety training efforts have not been well coordinated across regions (a group of states) or with respect to more national guidance for uniform content. Again, the unique attributes of a region or state require a certain seafood-specific orientation, but there needs to be greater consideration of uniformity, especially in the education of seafood inspectors and process managers.

CAUSE OF ILLNESS IN TARGETED STATES AND TERRITORIES

The situation regarding seafood-borne illness was examined specifically in a number of states identified by NMFS as having particular importance. In general, the examination confirmed conclusions of the broad national study that such illness is strongly geographic in incidence and that shellfish eaten raw are the principal cause of individual sickness in most coastal states. Data on outbreaks reported to CDC by the states under consideration for the period 1978-1987 are listed in Table 8-6 (CDC 1981a-c, 1983a,b, 1984, 1985a, 1989). Large differences are apparent in the relative importance of seafood-related illness among the states and territories. Hawaii, Puerto Rico, and the Virgin Islands report that seafood(s) are responsible for the majority of outbreaks of food-borne illness; this is due dominantly to seafood toxins. The other states report 15-33% (mean 26%). Cases per outbreak are relatively low so that the average for the nine states and territories represents only 7% of all food-borne illnesses. Nevertheless, Hawaii and New York report 39 and 23%, respectively, whereas Virgin Islands report 100% of cases. Discussions with state health department personnel and perusal of state food-borne disease reports have revealed discrepancies between CDC tabulations and in-state reported incidents of seafood-related illness. In part, these are a consequence of the limited range of diseases reported (e.g., *Vibrio vulnificus* was not reported) and the widespread occurrence of single-case incidents that are not reported. Thus, in most cases, the incidence of seafood-related illness is underreported, but this is also true for other food-borne illnesses. State health officials provided estimates for actual incidence of seafood-borne disease ranging from 8 to 25% of all food-borne illness.

It is clear, as noted elsewhere in this report (see Chapter 3), that special circumstances influence the number and type of seafood-borne illnesses reported. These include the source and condition of the seafood supply, the eating and food preparation practices of the local population, and actions by state or local authorities. Officials from coastal states in the Northeast including Massachusetts, New York, and Connecticut indicated that the seafood of major concern was raw molluscan shellfish and the causal agents were viruses. This reflects concerns over both domestically produced and imported molluscs, mostly clams, and the prevalence of local consumption of uncooked or very lightly cooked shellfish. One factor in this situation is the difficulty in controlling distribution of clams illegally harvested from areas closed because of contaminated growing waters. However, there is a question concerning the reliability of fecal indicator bacteria as an index of viral contamination because of the somewhat greater persistence of contaminant viruses. It is also known that depuration procedures used in some supplier countries are not fully effective in eliminating viruses

TABLE 8-6   CDC Food-borne Disease Outbreak Surveillance Data, 1978-1987[a]

State or Territory	Seafood-related Incidents				All Other Known Vehicles			
	Outbreaks		Cases		Outbreaks		Cases	
California	27	(15)	195	(3)	156	(85)	6,310	(97)
Connecticut	25	(27)	215	(7)	66	(73)	2,777	(93)
Florida	19	(33)	90	(4)	39	(67)	2,332	(96)
Guam	9	(64)	51	(5)	5	(36)	970	(95)
Hawaii	196	(88)	821	(39)	27	(12)	1,266	(61)
New York	113	(33)	2,681	(23)	227	(67)	8,929	(77)
Puerto Rico	14	(78)	76	(19)	4	(22)	325	(81)
Virgin Islands	11	(100)	117	(100)				
Washington	33	(21)	121	(4)	124	(79)	2,960	(96)
Median (%)		(33)		(7)		(67)		(93)

[a] Figures in parentheses indicate percentage of total number of outbreaks or cases.

from clams. There is evidence that both these deficiencies have been factors in shellfish-related incidents in the Northeast during the past 10 years. These states are also concerned with paralytic shellfish poisoning and scombroid fish poisoning. There is general satisfaction with present PSP control measures, but more rapid test methods are desired. The scombroid problem is not a major health hazard but is seen primarily as a result of poor industry practices, usually occurring outside state jurisdiction. Disease due to vibrios is not considered a major problem in these states, though sporadic illness due to *V. parahaemolyticus* does occur. Northeastern states are concerned about (industrial) chemical contamination of inshore waters and have closed areas to fishing for this reason.

Michigan was the only inland state reviewed, and health personnel indicated that on the basis of recorded illness, hepatitis A virus (HAV) and scombroid poisoning were the major concerns for seafoods. However, it was emphasized that hepatitis A was most commonly transmitted by food handlers. Thus, it is not a specific seafood-associated disease. Michigan has effected closures and warnings in its freshwater lake and river fisheries because of chemical contaminants. The West Coast states California and Washington also indicated shellfish as the major public health concern, and in both cases vibrios and PSP were identified as significant problems. *V. parahaemolyticus* is a consistent cause of sporadic seafood-related illness in both states, and *V. vulnificus* has been encountered in California. Health officials in both states expressed concern over imports, particularly from Pacific Islands and Southeast Asia. This concern is related to the large number of recent immigrants from these areas and the associated increase in production and consumption of ethnic foods. This includes different species of marine animals and consumption of parts of the animal (e.g., intestines) normally discarded by more traditional U.S. consumers. There is also concern over scombroid fish poisoning which is relatively common, and ciguatera, which is still relatively rare but expected to increase due to importation of Pacific Island fish.

A third Pacific Coast state, Alaska, shares the PSP concern, but has a unique problem of botulism associated with consumption of fish and marine animals. The occurrence of botulism is an ethnic food problem of native Alaskans resulting from consumption of "fermented" products held under conditions that encourage the growth of *Clostridium botulinum*. Scombroid fish poisoning from imported fish also occurs in Alaska.

The island states and territories Hawaii, Puerto Rico, Virgin Islands, and Guam show disease patterns that are a consequence of both the major local fish supply and local eating customs. In all areas, seafood constitutes a major part of the diet and is the cause of significant food-borne disease dominated by ciguatera and, to a lesser extent, scombroid fish poisoning. The ciguatera problem is intractable. All health officials emphasized the need for development of rapid test(s) for ciguatera toxins. Without such tests, it is impossible to ensure the safety of fish consumers in these areas. At present, the only available procedures involve warnings issued by health authorities and, in Hawaii, some voluntary control of commercial distribution of dangerous species by the industry. Ciguatera is of particular importance in the islands because fish is a major source of protein for permanent inhabitants and because tourism is a major industry. Tourists in the Caribbean are increasingly at risk from ciguatera (Morris et al., 1982; F. Quevedo, Regional Advisor for Pan American Health Organization, Washington, D.C., personal communication, 1989), although this problem does not seem to be a significant cause of illness among visitors to Hawaii (M. Sugi, Epidemiology Branch, Department of Health, State of Hawaii, personal communication, 1990).

Guam presents a somewhat different set of circumstances. Apparently, seafoods are commonly eaten raw or lightly processed so that in addition to the typical ciguatera problem, there is a significant incidence of vibrio disease. This is illustrated in Table 8-7, which tabulates seafood-related disease incidents reported by the territorial epidemiologist Dr. Robert L. Haddock (Haddock, 1989). Guam has experienced small outbreaks of true cholera related to consumption of seafoods, but most cases have been caused by *V. parahaemolyticus* or *V. cholerae* non-O1. The large number of single-case incidents are the principal reason that the data in Table 8-7 are at variance with the CDC report in Table 8-6. Although the high incidence of illness from *Vibrio* is certainly due in part to eating patterns in the territory, this cannot be the only factor. Consumption of raw seafood is also quite high in Hawaii. The territorial epidemiologist in Guam notes the importance of actually testing for vibrios in suspected seafood-related illness by the use of thiosulfate-citrate-bile salts-sucrose (TCBS) selective agar medium. The differences and similarities between patterns of seafood-related illness in the various island states and territories underscore both the commonality of problems in tropical areas and the unique features that distinguish one area from another. This supports the view that problems must be dealt with at the state and local levels.

Florida is a mainland state that abuts a tropical ocean; it is not surprising therefore that ciguatera is a concern of health officials in that state. The state is an importation point for fish from the Caribbean area, including potentially scombrotoxic fish, and is also subject to periodic red tides due to *Gymnodinium breve* that make local shellfish toxic. However, the major seafood-related health concern is vibrio disease related to raw shellfish consumption. High water temperatures encourage vibrio growth including that of *V. vulnificus,* and if oysters are not cooled quickly after harvest, vibrios will multiply and present a hazard to people eating shellfish raw. Vibrios (*V. parahaemolyticus, cholerae* non-O1, and *vulnificus*) seem to present the greatest hazard for consumers of raw molluscs harvested in states such as Florida and Louisiana, whereas viruses are more significant in the Northeast. Of course, cases due to vibrios also occur in the North, and viruses have caused mollusc-related illness in warmwater states. In West Coast states, shellfish problems appear to be PSP and vibrios, with lesser incidence of virus-related disease.

One conclusion that can be drawn from this fragmentary review of the status of seafood-related illness in selected states and territories is that the particular circumstances of each state requires that control systems be tailored – at least in emphasis – to local conditions. However, it is also obvious that states need help in developing procedures and methods of analysis that will be effective. They also lack the skilled personnel, technical facilities, and money to undertake this development themselves.

Allergies and Intolerances

This report does not directly address illnesses caused by seafood intolerance or allergies in the sense of reported occurrences and regulatory responses. Intolerance to eating certain types of seafoods is rare and more typically associated with certain individuals in risk categories predisposed by other health complications. Seafood allergies, distinguished as immunological reactions rather than the inability to digest, appear to be more prevalent, but they are difficult to diagnose and document. Specific allergens in seafood have thus far been only grossly characterized in few studies. In most seafoods of concern (e.g., certain crustaceans and "pink flesh" fish), very little has been done to identify the chemical offender (Kilara, 1982). In some cases a food

TABLE 8-7 Food-borne Illness in Guam

Year	Fish and Shellfish										All Foods and Etiologies	
	Salmonella		Vibrio cholerae		Vibrio parahaemolyticus		Ciguatera		Unknown			
	Outbreaks	Cases	Outbreaks	Cases	Outbreaks	Cases	Outbreaks	Cases	Outbreaks	Cases	Outbreaks	Cases
1978					3	22	4	6	1	2	10	56
1979					2	14	6	10			12	50
1980					2	6	5	10			13	37
1981			1	4			3	3			10	38
1982			2	9			3	3			9	31
1983					1	4	11	21	2	2	22	42
1984					6	8	8	22	2	5	40	70
1985			3	3	15	22	13	28	9	16	65	107
1986	1	2	2	4	16	24	3	9	4	5	50	121
1987	1	5			9	15	4	5	1	1	23	57
Totals	2	7	8	20	54	115	60	117	19	31	254	609

Totals		
Seafoods:	Outbreaks 143 (124)[a]	Cases 290 (259)[a]
All Foods	254	609
% Seafoods[b]	56%	48%

[a] Number in parentheses indicates total for confirmed etiologies.
[b] Indicates outbreaks or cases as a percentage of total food-borne incidents.
SOURCE: Haddock (1989).

additive (e.g., sulfiting agents on shrimp) or contaminants may cause the symptoms and confuse the diagnosis. In light of this level of information on cause and occurrence of this somewhat limited form of seafood-borne illness, regulatory response must depend on proper labeling to distinguish (1) species or types of seafood, (2) ingredients in formulated and fabricated seafoods (e.g., fish base surimi formed to resemble crab), and (3) ingredients used in preservation and processing (e.g., sulfites to retard shrimp melanosis). Future responses will require additional investigations of the biochemical and immunological characteristics of seafood allergens and their significance in producing illnesses.

STATE-FEDERAL REGULATORY LIAISON

Because seafood diversity poses region-specific concerns in monitoring coastal waters, in addressing species unique to local harvests and process settings, and in accessing point-of-sale transactions and recreational fishing, state regulations have played the more immediate and dominant role in surveillance of seafood safety and quality. However, federal cooperation and support is essential. All pertinent federal authorities are represented by an equivalent agency at the state level that, in most states, models and adopts regulations in accordance with its federal counterpart.

In most states the primary enforcing agency for seafood safety is the state department of health equivalent to the U.S. Food and Drug Administration (Hui, 1986). In some states this authority is shared across species or commercial settings by the departments of health, agriculture, and equivalent divisions within a department of natural resources. In a few states the department of agriculture maintains sole authority over all seafood, usually in a division or bureau of health. This diversity among states reflects the unique attributes of seafood and the challenge for state-federal liaisons.

The FDA exerts a significant effort to support state-based seafood safety surveillance through (1) maintaining inspection procedures and directives, (2) commissioning state officials to perform federal regulatory activities, (3) issuing contracts for routine and specific investigations, (4) advising actions and policy, and (5) administering training and education programs. In an effort to direct inspection activities, FDA maintains and, for retail programs, assists the Association of Food and Drug Officials (AFDO) and regional AFDO affiliates in preparing various retail sanitation codes (AFDO/FDA, 1982). "Unicode" is an ongoing FDA attempt to eventually combine the variety of food store codes into a single retail code (Anonymous, 1989a). Similar attempts at regulatory standardization are evident in FDA's manuals being developed for the HACCP approach in molluscan shellfish sanitation, smoked fish guidelines, course outlines on modified atmosphere packaging, and the comprehensive Fish List to designate the official nomenclature for all fish and, eventually, for molluscs and crustaceans (FDA, 1988a,b). Immediate FDA-state liaison is possible through electronic linkage now available in over 125 metropolitan centers. Periodic liaison is possible through federal contractual obligations for production or food processing and retail surveys. In 1988-1989, Colorado, Florida, Oregon, and Wisconsin participated in seafood-specific contractual surveys for microbial consequences in commerce.

Further, the Environmental Protection Agency plays an active and often aggressive liaison role. For example, a recently formed Fish Contaminants Advisory Committee combines FDA and EPA efforts to direct and encourage states to use more uniform methods of risk assessment and to advise on analytical methods and decisions concerning potential waterborne seafood contaminants. The EPA National Estuary Program can be viewed as a useful effort to work with states to determine sources and levels of contaminants in coastal waters that serve as both spawning and harvesting areas for important commercial species. Clearly, these programs are not specifically designed to deal solely with issues of seafood safety; however, the results of this sponsored research are essential to a comprehensive evaluation of the quality of the nation's harvesting environments.

The Interstate Shellfish Sanitation Conference represents the most comprehensive, routine state-federal liaison specifically established to address seafood safety concerns. This national organization ensures cooperation among state authorities, NSSP, and respective molluscan industries in sharing the responsibility to establish federal and state regulations for molluscan shellfish product safety.

Cooperative voluntary inspection services have been established between requesting states and the National Marine Fisheries Service. Under specific agreements, NMFS provides state inspector training and certification to perform DOC inspections on a per-fee basis paid by the industry user. States with varying degrees of prior participation include Alabama, Alaska, Colorado, Florida, Michigan, Minnesota, New Jersey, New York, Oregon, and Tennessee. The lack of DOC fish inspectors, particularly in certain areas, encourages continuation of these coinspectional agreements.

Efforts to promote domestic aquaculture have been enhanced by USDA's cooperative programs in regional training, research services, and extension services. The 1980 National Aquaculture Act designated USDA as the lead federal agency in promoting aquaculture. The USDA offers specific programs to improve marketing (Federal-State Marketing Program) and to resolve quality problems such as the occurrence of off-flavors in catfish (Johnsen, 1989). Likewise, USDA's Animal and Plant Health Inspection Service provides diagnostic assistance for identification and treatment of fish disease. These activities relate to cultured product quality and safety; however, FDA is still the primary food safety regulatory authority, and it maintains open cooperation with USDA and the states on all pertinent aquaculture issues.

Overall, the advantages and necessity of federal-state liaison for seafood safety could be enhanced with better and more routine communications focused on more seafood-specific issues as evidenced for molluscan shellfish. The ISSC, in design, exemplifies the mode of cooperation that can improve surveillance for seafood safety. The ISSC strength lies in equal state participation, direct industry involvement, and eventually national implementation through federal guidance. Similar efforts should be explored through established associations that offer the same essential participation and could be restructured to allow a more regulatory development forum. Candidate associations include AFDO and regional affiliates of the International Association of Milk, Food and Environmental Sanitarians (IAMFES). These groups of experts have not traditionally featured or excluded seafoods, and although they may not be amenable to new mandates, they certainly represent collective talent to initiate better seafood regulatory liaison between state and federal authorities. Recent seafood-specific concerns of the AFDO and its southern affiliate, the Association of Food and

Drug Officials of Southern States (AFDOSS), were voiced in a national letter dated September 9, 1989 of state regulatory position on seafood inspection mandates and a resolution calling for a federal position on new GMPs for smoked fish (AFDO, 1989). These actions reflect a concerned organization that can be channeled to better facilitate federal-state liaison for seafood safety.

STATE AND INDUSTRY INITIATIVES

Initiatives to foster better seafood quality and safety come in a variety of forms, both state and industry based, that are developed primarily to promote a particular product or seafoods in general. The focus is usually on product quality, and efforts are structured to direct industry compliance or to offer general operating guidelines and product specifications. Most of these efforts are based on voluntary participation.

The most structured industry initiative is the Canned Salmon Control Plan initiated in the early 1920s and formalized in 1936 (NFPA, 1989). Today the plan includes participation for nearly 99% of all domestic canned salmon, which in 1989 represented over 50% of domestic salmon consumption. Basically, the plan provides routine, uniform surveillance for particular product quality concerns, in addition to the paramount processing requirements to prevent botulism. This program is a voluntary cooperative agreement among participating packers of canned salmon, the National Food Processors Association (NFPA), and FDA; it is based in NFPA's northwest regional laboratory in Seattle. The plan incorporates all the appropriate federal regulations and clearly specifies all procedures from raw product procurement through each stage in processing. Records for operations and coding of the production lots exemplify the basic HACCP concept used for other low-acid, canned food industries. A firm's voluntary participation is confirmed by an authorized company signature that subjects the company to inspection, frequent product sampling, and detention or product destruction in the event of adverse findings. The plan requirements do not exempt products or packers from established legal action. The inspections can be conducted by NFPA or FDA staff. Every packer must designate a fully authorized person for communication in surveillance and other provisions of the plan. Production lots are specifically defined and subject to mandatory sampling per lot. Sample evaluations involve destructive laboratory analysis to judge the can seam, container integrity, and product wholesomeness. These routine lot samplings can be supplemented with random, unannounced checks. Participating firms are listed for buyer reference, including firms that may have been suspended pending any necessary corrective action.

A similar state-directed plan to ensure fish quality, and possibly safety, is the Maine Fresh Groundfish Quality Control Program initiated in 1980. This plan also requires signed agreements to participate. Currently, the program includes 12 fish processing firms that represent over 85% of Maine's fresh fillet production (Griffen, 1986). These firms have volunteered to be subject to periodic, usually weekly, unannounced inspections by trained inspectors from the Maine Department of Marine Resources. Inspections include lot assessments and rating of the facilities' operations. Program criteria for facilities and products are specified in Maine Department of Marine Resources statutes (Maine DMR, 1989). Continued compliance is denoted by a listing of participants and use of the program logo "Maine Certified Fresh Fish." The entire program is financed by the state and supplemented by additional state marketing promotions that focus on the program and logo. Lack of compliance can result in a three- to six-month suspension and possibly permanent removal from the list of certified participants. The Maine program does not evaluate or monitor for safety concerns but could alert responsible authorities in the Maine Department of Agriculture in the event of any adverse finding or suspicion. Interagency agreements have recognized the program as an effective quality assessment program, such that the Maine Department of Agriculture recognizes and does not intend to duplicate inspection efforts. Most recently, the State of Maine resolved to specify that the Maine Department of Marine Resources would do all seafood inspections if federal authority of seafood inspections is shifted to the USDA. Continued efforts in the current program, and especially in consideration of additional species (e.g., cultured trout, mussels), could be threatened by its dependence on state funds and available manpower.

The Catfish Institute (TCI) in Belzoni, Mississippi, initiated the Mississippi Prime program in 1986. The intent was to promote product quality by all participants and to build consumer confidence in cultured catfish. Since 1988, all participating firms have been obligated to maintain satisfactory sanitary status as determined by NMFS voluntary inspections in accordance with 50 CFR Part 267 (United States Standards for Grade of North American Freshwater Catfish and Products Made Therefrom). This inspection service qualifies the firm for participation and establishes its listing on DOC's Sanitary Fish Establishment List. Subsequent weekly DOC lot inspections are contracted through TCI such that the confidential results are compiled and reported by TCI to ensure compliance and encourage improvements by individual companies. Program standards include sampling procedures for flavor evaluations and product conditions. Firms maintaining a satisfactory rating based on a standard DOC inspection score can use the Mississippi Prime seal. Failure to meet standards or make necessary corrections can lead to probations or suspensions that disallow use of the program seal. The seal designates quality commitment, backed by federal TCI inspection and promoted by extensive marketing efforts.

In 1986 the Southeastern Fisheries Association (SFA, 1990a) in Tallahassee, Florida introduced a seafood Product Quality Code program. The premise of the code was to improve seafood product quality and safety through buyer education. The intended audience was any wholesale or retail seafood buyer in the nation. The code was simply a loose-leaf binder of seafood products or species as produced and processed in the southeastern coastal states, from Texas through North Carolina. Each species represented a code entry developed by selected SFA members experienced with the specific product forms and processing requirements. Each product entry was drafted to explain product quality attributes, different product forms and types, packaging recommendations, and labeling requirements. The final draft was subject to a majority vote of SFA's standing Quality Control Committee. As of July 1990, SFA had completed 14 entries: raw (headless) shrimp, rock shrimp, breaded shrimp, spiny lobster, blue crab, stone crab, oysters, hard clams, calico scallops, mullet, tuna, catfish, grouper, and snapper, and had initiated 5 new entries: swordfish, Spanish mackerel, crawfish, shark, and king mackerel. This entire effort was made possible by federal grants provided through the Saltonstall-Kennedy Fisheries Funds administered by DOC. Initial acceptance and use has exceeded expectations, and the Food Marketing Institute (FMI) representing all major supermarket chains in North America has promised extended distribution.

In 1984, the National Blue Crab Industry Association (NBCIA), in affiliation with the National Fisheries Institute (NFI), introduced recommended standards for blue crab pasteurization (NBCIA, 1984). The manual, developed by experienced members in reviews and actual field tests with various federal and state authorities, was offered for regulatory adoption by the respective states. The standards specify requirements for all processing procedures from initial raw product quality through cooking, packaging, thermal treatment, labeling, and recordkeeping. States have referenced these standards in regulatory practice, and some authorities have recodified regulations to adopt portions of these industry recommendations.

Recently, some industry- and state-based marketing efforts have used reference to advancing seafood technology and inspections in an effort to combat negative publicity and to promote consumer confidence. The Virginia Marine Products Board advertises and distributes flyers about the "fingerprinting" system available to monitor potential chemical hazards in Virginia seafood. Similarly, many state trade associations promote the extensive regulatory efforts in monitoring water quality and processing requirements to ensure safe molluscan shellfish. Their shellfish message includes definitive cooking recommendations for consumers in certain potential health risk categories. Some supermarket advertising has adopted these same approaches to promote consumer confidence; use of the DOC voluntary inspection is a common boast.

Industry initiatives and concomitant government-based promotional efforts to encourage seafood product quality and safety are all well intended and can be helpful, but they must remain aware of possible legal requirements and risks. Greenberg's (1985) review of prior legislative and Federal Trade Commission attempts to stipulate requirements for establishing voluntary standards and certifications suggests that these efforts should be referenced. Nonprofit trade associations engaged in standard setting can be subject to antitrust laws for anticompetitive action. Greenberg (1985) recommends

> In order to protect itself against potential liability in standard setting, associations should follow certain minimum procedural steps, including notification to interested parties, opportunity to participate in standard setting proceedings, complaint mechanisms, recordkeeping, and disclosure of intended scope, indicating any products or product attributes not covered by the standard that users of the standard would reasonably presume were covered . . . [and] any serious risks or limitations associated with the use of products that conform to the standard, when such risks or limitations would not be apparent to reasonable buyers. [See proposed 16 CFR 457.10, 43 Fed. Reg. 57,269 (Dec. 7, 1978).]

Furthermore, associations should adhere to certain minimum substantive requirements:

- Standards should have logical and technical justification in light of their stated or implied policy goals.
- Standards should not exclude products that are equivalent to those products that are included.
- Standards should not exclude products if there is a less restrictive alternative (i.e., one that preserves or increases buyer options and the opportunity of sellers to compete).

- Standards should not promote false assumptions that two or more conforming products are identical in performance or safety.
- Standards should not lead to misplaced buyer confidence that results in economic loss or unforeseen or unreasonable risk.

Risks beyond establishing standards involve fewer legal concerns. Again, although helpful in intent, seafood product quality and safety declarations can result in confusion and false warnings. Statement accuracy and clarity, particularly from the buyer's perspective, are essential. A seal awarded for quality may not ensure product safety. An acknowledged quality processing firm conforming to programs issuing logos or seals cannot always control the handling consequences for its products in subsequent distribution. These concerns do not preclude the necessity and value of industry and marketing initiatives, but they do give reason for scrutiny of promotional assurances.

Health Advisories

Public health advisories, warnings, and related educational activities are commonly used by state agencies to better inform choices for seafood harvest and consumption. The majority of these advisories address abiotic contaminants that may pose problems in freshwater sources and microbial concerns related to the consumption of raw molluscan shellfish. Additional issues can involve particular species or products (i.e., improperly prepared items), problematic sources (i.e., suspect ciguatoxic region), and particular constituents (e.g., mercury in certain species or locations, or PCB contamination of striped bass in New York). These advisories are deemed appropriate in terms of responsibility for public health, yet their effectiveness has typically received no assessment.

The need for such warnings for raw molluscan shellfish has recently been reinforced by legal actions in defense of clients from particular health risk categories, who have experienced severe consequences from ingestion of *Vibrio vulnificus* on raw oysters. State concern for such liability prompted the Louisiana Department of Public Health to propose a requirement for labels and public displays to deter raw molluscan consumption by persons with liver, stomach, blood, or immune system disorders (J.C. Nitzkin, Director of Office of Public Health, Louisiana Department of Public Health, New Orleans, personal communication, 1990).

In most states, criteria and authority are established to clear and direct public health advisories, but the perceived urgency of some problems, the magnitude of local situations, and media pressure or entrapment can short-circuit the system. City- and county-based authorities have released warnings, intentionally and through media coverage, that have not been addressed through official channels. The results can be confusion, mistargeted messages, and questioned credibility. Similar mishaps can occur among the variety of state agencies sharing authority over aquatic resources.

Typically, official state authorization for public health warnings rests with a department of health or equivalent public health agency housing the state's public health officer. This authority relies on the advice of state-based technical expertise and federal guidance. In many instances involving seafood, the consistency and clarity of federal advice have been questioned, particularly relating to guidelines for levels of exposure, analytical procedures, risk assessments, and mode of public notification.

Because of the diversity among seafoods and their increasing association with environmental factors that come under state jurisdiction, a more formalized national seafood health advisory program should be considered for uniform assurance of public health and confidence.

SEAFOOD SAFETY IN THE INTERNATIONAL ENVIRONMENT

The active interest in seafood safety so robustly manifest in the United States is not limited to domestic markets. Indeed, the question of seafood safety is one of increasing prominence in the policy debates of several international organizations and countries. The potential importance of this international debate exists for one rather straightforward reason. That is, the commerce of seafood products is conducted in a strongly interdependent, international market. However, international regulation of seafood is both complex and, at present, rather inconsistent.

The international program with the most direct competence in seafood safety is the Joint Food Standards Program implemented by the Codex Alimentarius Commission, which is composed of member states and associate members of the Food and Agricultural Organization (FAO) and the World Health Organization (WHO), who have notified the commission of their wish to become members. As of late 1981, the commission was comprised of 121 members. The purpose of the commission (FAO, 1983) is

> to protect the health of consumers and to ensure fair practices in the food trade; to promote coordination of all food standards work undertaken by international governmental and non-governmental organizations; to determine priorities and initiate and guide the preparation of draft standards through and with aid of appropriate organizations; to finalize standards and after acceptance by governments, publish them in a Codex Alimentarius either as regional or world-wide standards.

Upon promulgation of standards, each member state is provided a measure of latitude in accepting them. A member may (1) accept the standard fully, (2) accept it with specified deviations, or (3) target an acceptance to specific foods or food groups. Volume V of the *Codex Alimentarius* (FAO, 1983) sets the standards for 13 fish and fishery products. These are primarily standards of quality and identity criteria. However, a limited suite of microbiological and chemical limits has been agreed upon. Those addressing residual chemical contaminants are presented as Table 8-8 (with equivalent standards from the United States and Canada included for comparison). The United States has completed action on approximately one-third of the existing Codex standards. Food safety regulations by major importing countries have been tabulated and published by the Food and Agriculture Organization of the United Nations (FAO, 1989).

Perhaps a more important international influence on the U.S. seafood industry is the standards and inspection practices developed by the Canadian government (DFO, 1988). The Canadian seafood inspection program is based on an HACCP-type approach, and includes quality- and safety-oriented plant inspection, vessel and landing site inspection, and compliance with a broad list of contaminant action levels (which include the regulation of all agricultural chemicals and their derivatives). The list of Canadian regulatory limits appears in Table 8-8.

TABLE 8-8 Regulatory Limits for Toxic Contaminants in Seafood Extracted from United Nations, United States, and Canadian Regulations

Contaminant	FAO/WHO (ppm)[a]	FDA Action Level (ppm)	Canada Health and Welfare Action Level (ppm)
Arsenic	-	-	-
Cadmium	3.6-4.4	-	-
Lead	26.7	-	0.5
Mercury	2.7	1.0	0.5
Methylmercury	1.8	-	-
Fluoride	-	-	150
Dioxin	-	-	20[b]
DDT/metabolites	1.9	5.0	5.0
Heptachlor/ heptachlor epoxide	1.9	0.3	0.1[b]
Endrin	-	-	0.1[c]
Aldrin/dieldrin	-	0.3	0.1[c]
Chlordane	-	0.3	0.1[c]
Mirex	-	0.1	0.1[c]
PCBs	-	2.0	2.0
Toxaphene	-	5.0	0.1[c]
All other agricultural chemicals	-	-	0.1[c]

[a] Based on conversion of FAO/WHO provisional tolerable weekly intake (PTWI) to U.S. population assuming average per capita seafood consumption to be 18.7 grams per 70 kilogram adult body weight per day.
[b] Parts per trillion.
[c] Characterized by way of "All Other Agricultural Chemicals" in Canadian regulations.
SOURCE: DFO (1988); FAO (1989); FDA (1987).

The existing Canadian program derives from the Fish Inspection Act passed in 1970 and amended most recently in 1985 (DFO, 1985). The inspection system mandated by that legislation is designed to be comprehensive and includes all fish imported to Canada, or exported from one province to another or out of the country. Complementary legislation exists at the provincial level that effectively includes within the same regulatory structure all intraprovincial trade in seafood. The Department of Fisheries and Oceans (DFO) has primary authority to implement the program, although some authority is shared with Agriculture Canada (which has limited oversight and auditing competence), Consumer and Corporate Affairs, and Health and Welfare Canada (which sets regulatory limits for seafood contaminants). However, in recognizing the potential confusion for both industry and consumers in such a shared regulatory environment, memoranda have been signed by the agencies involved specifying a single federal contact for each regulated industry.

The decision to develop a multifaceted seafood safety program that includes programmatic efforts from harvesting through wholesale distribution was based on several assumptions about seafood commerce. First, a program limited to product sampling plans "has limitations and cannot by itself perform adequately to deliver the levels of assurance demanded by the public and buyers at a reasonable cost." Second, limiting a program to product or plant inspection detects problems only after value has been added to the product. Third, final product evaluation for any contaminant is expensive and would demand higher inspection costs than measures designed to prevent contaminated products from entering the processing system or to prevent the processing system from introducing or elevating contaminants in the product. As recently noted by a senior administrator in DFO, "this type of system will prevent problems in the final product rather than inspect problems out of final product in an attempt to reduce the incidence of problems or unacceptable lots reaching the marketplace." The frequency of the various inspection activities mandated by the Canadian program is generally described in Table 8-9 and further detailed in Table 8-10.

The cost of the entire DFO inspection was approximately Canadian $35 million in 1988 which, distributed across the amount of total seafood production, provides an estimated cost per pound of approximately $0.01 (David Bevan, Canadian Department of Fisheries and Oceans, personal communication, 1989).

TABLE 8-9 Frequency Totals for Various Inspection Classes in Canada

Total site inspections	37,500
Total field product inspections	93,000
Total laboratory product inspections	40,600
Total inspections for export certification	18,900

SOURCE: Bevan (1989).

An additional aspect of the Canadian inspection program worthy of note is that relating to imported products. The focus of the import inspection program is on importing plants or producers, rather than importing countries. The first time a producer attempts to import a product that product is inspected. If the product fails inspection, the producer is placed on the "Mandatory Inspection List" and required to pay for all subsequent inspections until the product passes four consecutive inspections, at which time the producer is removed from the list. If a producer is not listed for mandatory inspection, it is still subject to periodic inspection.

To date, the existence of the Canadian seafood inspection program has not had a particularly significant impact on U.S.-Canadian trade, but the situation may be in the process of changing. The recent Canada-U.S. Free Trade Agreement addresses the question of a consistent approach in regulations and standards to "protect human, animal and plant life and to facilitate commerce between the Parties." Section 708:1(a) calls for the harmonization of "technical regulatory requirements and inspection procedures, taking into account appropriate international standards, or, where harmonization is not feasible, to make equivalent their respective technical regulatory requirements and inspection procedures" (DEA, 1988).

According to the current Canadian interpretation of this provision, the Free Trade Agreement calls for an equivalence in U.S. and Canadian seafood inspection systems and regulatory guidelines. At present, the United States does not appear to meet the criteria of equivalence. The potential for impact on U.S. seafood exports is not limited to trade with Canada. Ongoing negotiations within the European Economic Community, directed at further uniting European economies in 1992, suggest that similar provisions relating to programmatic harmonization may be imposed on seafood imports within the next few years (CEC, 1987a,b). Indeed, the question of harmonization of national seafood safety programs is one that is taking an increasingly

TABLE 8-10 Canadian Seafood Inspections

Facility Inspection

Approximate no. of fishing vessels	39,800
Approximate no. of fishing vessel inspections/year	13,200
Approximate no. of fish processing plants	1,400
Approximate no. of fish processing plant inspections/year	18,000
Approximate no. of unloading sites	2,000
Approximate no. of unloading site inspections/year	3,300
Approximate no. of transport vehicle inspections/year	3,300

Product Inspection

Field inspections/year	
Raw material	13,200
Domestic final product	65,200
Imported product	14,600
Lab inspections/year	
Domestic product	
(chemical, bacteriological,	
and sensory analyses)	25,900
Imported product	14,700
Inspections/year for export certification	18,900

SOURCE: Bevan (1989).

prominent place in international trade and in the domestic policy debate to refine the U.S. program. However, as illustrated in Table 8-5, there is a lack of consistency in the generation and specification of regulatory guidelines. Indeed, a recent study carried out by the EPA revealed that differences in regulatory limits for individual contaminants vary as much as two orders of magnitude between countries. Clearly, present and future efforts to make regulatory practices equivalent must take these variances into account.

COMPARATIVE RISKS FOR CONSUMERS OF VARIOUS SEAFOOD PRODUCTS

A clearer view of the actual risks faced by seafood consumers can be obtained by looking at the fish and seafood products most widely and frequently consumed by Americans. Consumption and supply data (USDA, 1985a,b; NMFS, 1989, 1990) indicate that the most widely consumed item is shrimp, either produced domestically or imported from all over the world. Only the muscle of the tail of shrimp is eaten and generally after cooking, but a considerable amount is eaten cold without further cooking after a cooking operation at the processing level. The most common problem with shrimp seems to be postprocessing contamination, but the reported incidents of disease are relatively few. This is probably due to the fact that shrimp are usually frozen quickly after cooking and sold in this form to the consumer. Imported shrimp receive particular scrutiny by FDA because of periodic problems with *Salmonella* contamination, and this may also reduce the level of risk to the consumer. There is no evidence of exceptionally high levels of contaminant chemicals in shrimp tail meat, although the data are scanty. In general, therefore, unless there is a failure of process control or contamination at the food service level, shrimp is a relatively safe diet item.

The second most commonly eaten seafood products are fillets of bottom-living white-fleshed species of fish such as cod, haddock, and pollock, formed into compressed blocks, frozen, and cut to produce fish sticks, fish portions, fish nuggets, and similar products. These may be breaded, battered, and precooked before refreezing and distribution. The disease record of these products is good, with incidents of sickness mostly being due (as with shrimp) to contamination at the food service level. The fish used to manufacture these products are generally harvested from deep offshore waters and, consequently, carry low levels of chemical contamination.

Most tuna is eaten as canned fish, and this is rarely a cause of food-borne illness unless mishandled during preparation for eating. However, unprocessed tuna has been implicated as a major cause of scombroid fish poisoning. Canned tuna is protected by an aggressive preprocess sampling and histamine analysis program by canners, who also exert pressure on catchers to chill the fish rapidly. Scombroid poisoning comes mainly from improperly handled fresh or frozen tuna, which is a minor component of tuna consumption in most parts of the United States. As a pelagic, high-seas fish, tuna generally has low levels of environmental contamination, but in a few ocean regions tuna may carry marginally high levels of mercury. This is controlled by analysis and rejection of such fish by both processors and regulators. Canned tuna must fall below the FDA action levels. For most consumers this is probably safe, but there are some questions in relation to sensitive groups such as babies and young children. Thus, in tuna products targeted for these groups, much lower levels of mercury should be maintained.

Marine and cultured freshwater fish purchased as fillets or whole fish in a fresh or frozen state probably are the next most abundantly consumed items. Microbiological risks from these products when eaten cooked seem to be minor, but potential hazards from toxins or environmental chemicals vary depending on species and origin. Fish associated with tropical reef communities present a risk of ciguatera, but these fish are rarely eaten outside of tropical islands and southern Florida. Certain other marine species besides tuna present a risk of scombroid poisoning when they are mishandled. The greatest risk would seem to come from mahimahi, with a lesser risk from bluefish and mackerel (see Chapter 4). Fortunately, this is a mild disease of short duration, and the hazard is not serious. Nevertheless, consumers should be aware of it. Bluefish from certain regions and a variety of fresh fish species taken from "hot-spot" regions, including the Great Lakes and adjacent river systems, other lakes and rivers, and specific inshore marine areas along both Pacific and Atlantic coastlines, may carry undesirable levels of chemical contaminants. Such species should be thoroughly screened and excluded from commercial channels if chemical contaminant levels are higher than FDA/EPA limits. Consumers should be made aware of the risk of eating sport caught fish of this type. Naturally high mercury levels may occur in species of shark, swordfish, and halibut, but these are quite closely regulated (especially swordfish) by state agencies and FDA, so it is unlikely that the consumer will experience a dangerously high level in fish sold at retail. The proviso concerning the susceptibility of children and other sensitive groups (e.g., pregnant women) to lower levels should, however, be kept in mind.

Fish caught by subsistence and sports anglers represent a significant component of U.S. seafood consumption, approximately 4 live pounds (or 1.6 edible pounds) per person above the commercial consumption of 15.9 pounds per capita in 1989 (NMFS, 1990). Catfish, trout, salmon, and other cultured fish have a good record as far as food-borne disease is concerned. Because all are usually eaten after cooking, it is not surprising that microbiological hazards are limited. There is less information concerning chemical residues in cultured fish, although there is no evidence of acute concern. Because these fish are raised under controlled conditions it should be possible to produce animals with very low contamination levels, equivalent to other farmed animals. There is concern about agriculture and chemical runoff and drugs in feed as discussed in previous chapters. Risks from recreationally caught fish may be higher than from commercially available seafoods because temperature control after capture is generally poor. This is true, for example, of bluefish and tuna, where poor temperature control after capture might be expected to occur more frequently in a sport fishing context. Ciguatera incidence data from Hawaii support the view that sport fishers are at high risk from reef fish consumption. The hazard to freshwater anglers and others consuming their catch from the Great Lakes and several large river systems is well recognized and arises from the egregious chemical contamination of these waters by human activities. A similar hazard exists for some marine species taken in inshore marine fishing areas of California, Washington, New England, and the Chesapeake Bay. Local authorities have issued warnings in the form of specific advisories and listing of hazards in fish and game regulations made available to recreationists. The risks of delayed disease effects, including cancer from consumption of fish containing substances such as PCBs and dioxin, are sufficiently high that an increased effort to discourage anglers from consuming contaminated fish seems warranted.

Canned fish in general seems to be among the safest of seafood items. Canning is designed to destroy dangerous microorganisms and to protect the fish from future contamination. Most canning operations are large enough to support technical staff, and tests for both sterility and the presence of toxic substances are commonplace; moreover, because canned products are stable they are available for testing over a long period of time, whereas fresh and often even frozen products must be moved quickly through trade channels.

Clearly, the highest-risk category of seafood products for the general U.S. consumer is molluscan shellfish eaten raw. Traditionally, whole clams, mussels, and oysters are consumed raw, including the intestines and other viscera. This practice exposes the consumer to all possible sources of contamination, including any potentially pathogenic microorganisms or chemicals present in the gut contents. In a few cases where risk is recognized, the viscera may be removed before eating (this procedure is followed with the Pacific razor clam to reduce risks of PSP occurrence). The hazards of contaminating pathogenic bacteria from human sewage are greatly reduced for legally harvested molluscs in commercial trade by the surveillance of water quality in growing areas under the NSSP, but are less consistent in terms of human enteric viruses and bacteria that are natural marine inhabitants. Unfortunately, the NSSP program is circumvented by infiltration of shellfish harvested illegally from closed areas. The integrity of the shellfish supply is further compromised by unregulated importation of shellfish from foreign sources. The sessile nature and filter feeding of molluscs make them likely sites for accumulation of waste chemicals, which constitute another source of potential hazard in unregulated systems. Thus, there is always some risk in consuming uncooked whole molluscan shellfish, and this practice – although of long standing – should perhaps be discouraged. Fortunately, the consumption of raw shellfish is confined to a minority of the fish-eating population, but among this group the risk of at least mild disease is quite high. Some reduction in risk may come from improved processing methods and better education of consumers.

Other risks associated with finfish and shellfish consumption are more disparate in origin. Some are associated with specific eating practices such as the consumption of the tomalley of lobsters, which can expose the eater to excessively high levels of chemicals, or the consumption of whole scallops, which can expose the consumer to PSP. Others are related to unsafe home preparation practices, including marinating, pickling, or fermenting seafoods and even improper home canning of fish. Educational materials are necessary, including handbooks, public service spots, etc., to inform consumers of some of these dangers and alert them to proper practices. Public service ads or labels may also be useful.

Risks are unevenly distributed among fish consumers. There is little risk of acute illness being contracted by people eating most fish obtained from regular commercial channels when such products are eaten after cooking. The extent of the risk due to chemical contamination is uncertain because of lack of understanding of the effects of particular chemicals and poor information on the extent of contamination. Nevertheless, there is no evidence of an urgently critical situation as far as the general population is concerned. It should be apparent from the preceding discussion that people at greatest risk of seafood-borne illness are (1) consumers of raw molluscan shellfish, (2) sports anglers who eat their catch, (3) inhabitants of tropical islands, and (4) consumers of fresh/frozen mahimahi, tuna, and bluefish. Most people who become ill from seafood-borne disease suffer mild and transient symptoms, but certain groups of people including the elderly, immunosuppressed individuals, and those with underlying chronic disease conditions may suffer severe and even life-threatening illness. Young children and pregnant women are at risk from long-term effects of ingestion of certain chemical contaminants and should be protected from eating fish from contaminated areas.

CONCLUSIONS AND RECOMMENDATIONS

The preceding analysis suggests the following conclusory notes and general recommendations.

Microbial and Natural Toxin Contaminants

The process used to set federal regulatory guidelines for microbial and natural toxin contaminants is housed solely within the Food and Drug Administration. The process used by FDA to determine safe levels of these contaminants is largely reactive. Guidelines have been set primarily on an as-needed basis. However, as a group, if effectively implemented, these guidelines could provide an adequate and appropriate safeguard for the U.S. seafood consuming public.

However, the current system for these contaminant classes is not without its problems. A large number of questions remain fundamentally unresolved under present regulations and guidelines. For example, although FDA has research efforts in place, there has been no formal response by way of explicit regulatory guidelines for either ciguatoxin or domoic acid – areas of clear and acknowledged concern in domestic and imported products. Furthermore, additional product forms and emerging processing or handling concepts necessitate continued evaluation and supplementation (e.g., *sous vide*, modified atmosphere packaging, custom smoking techniques, and further processing in the retail setting). Without more fundamental assistance from the federal government, these responsibilities will be left to states, which may lack the required financial resources and technical expertise.

Although the FDA has, in the opinion of this committee, developed a set of adequate and appropriate regulatory limits for seafood deemed injurious to public health, the agency has not sufficiently communicated those limits to either the regulated industry or the consuming public. The various tolerances, action levels, and other regulatory guidelines used by the agency to carry out its statutory responsibilities can be fully discerned only by an extensive and rather circuitous search of FDA Compliance Policy Guides, announcements in the *Federal Register*, and copies of various FDA memoranda. A more concise, comprehensive, and generally available single source for all FDA guidelines relating to seafood safety should be developed and updated on a regular basis. This information should be disseminated to industry and integrated into state regulatory programs through more routine and uniform training and education.

Residual Chemical Contaminants

An assertion that current federal regulatory guidelines are sufficient to protect consumers from residual chemical risks is rather more difficult to support. At present, FDA enforcement activities focus primarily on those 15 residual chemical contaminants for which the FDA has developed action levels. That this list is sufficiently comprehensive to ensure an acceptable level of carcinogenic or chronic health risk must be questioned. The Food and Drug Administration contends that its present surveillance program supports an assertion that other contaminants do not pose a sufficient risk in seafood to warrant a more active regulatory response. However, a systematic review of FDA, EPA, National Oceanic and Atmospheric Administration (NOAA), and state-sponsored efforts to determine contaminant levels in fish and shellfish, carried out as part of this study, suggests a range of additional elements and compounds worthy of more fundamental review. These issues are addressed in detail in Chapter 5.

The committee also notes that the development or reassessment of contaminant guidelines should take into account critical regional differences in seafood harvesting and consumption patterns. A focus on the creation of national contaminant standards (as opposed to regionally based standards, for example) could lead to a situation in which a higher than anticipated seafood risk could be characterized for critical subpopulations (e.g., pregnant women, women of childbearing age, children, and recreational fishermen). Among other things, this leads to a recommendation that regional and high-risk group consumption data be collected so that more realistic seafood risk characterizations can be developed.

The development of regulatory guidelines for seafood safety is a responsibility shared by EPA and FDA (for pesticides), and by FDA and states (for shellfish). Although a rather impressive number of interagency boards, councils, and formal understandings exists, these arrangements have not been used sufficiently to reduce the problems that result from the lack of interagency cooperation. Of particular concern are the rather important differences between EPA and FDA in their respective risk assessment methodologies. The development of an interagency structure with a single focus on seafood safety could contribute significantly toward reducing these difficulties.

Monitoring and Inspection

In general, the present monitoring and inspection program carried out by all federal agencies lacks both the frequency and the direction sufficient to ensure effective implementation of the nation's regulatory limits for seafood safety. However, the need for a renewed and redesigned seafood inspection effort is now almost universally acknowledged. This committee is not in the position to evaluate prospectively the likely success of alternative inspection models currently under consideration by Congress and the administration. However, whatever inspection does emerge from this effort should address several discrete questions and concerns.

Future efforts must recognize the importance of understanding and quantifying the source and level of contaminants in seafood harvesting areas. Existing environmental monitoring efforts are not, for the most part, designed to be of direct use in evaluating seafood safety concerns. Among other things, they lack (1) sufficient geographic scope, (2) a common methodological approach, and (3) sufficient focus on the edible portion of seafood in order to determine public health risks, as opposed to environmental health impacts. This last point is of particular importance. Save for the monitoring of harvesting waters carried out as part of the National Shellfish Sanitation Program, data evaluating contaminant levels in fish and shellfish do not consistently focus on the analysis of edible tissue. More often the focus is on whole fish, liver, or gallbladder analysis which, by design, offers insufficient insights into contaminant levels in the marketable seafood product. In addition, any expanded seafood safety effort must focus on the level of hazard at the point of capture. One strategy to mitigate such risks is for agencies, both federal and state, to more explicitly develop regulations allowing for fishing closure based on questions of public health.

There is widespread application of HACCP-based systems for ensuring control of the safety of food products. Such systems are well designed to control the safety of processing operations in which human activities can either decrease or increase risk. However, control of the intrinsic safety of the raw material may not be easily achieved.

This is a particular problem for seafoods derived from wild stocks. It is clear from analyses presented in the preceding chapters that most of the reported incidents of human disease caused by seafood in the United States derive from species of fish and shellfish that have been contaminated in the ocean and are consumed in a nonprocessed form. The Critical Control Points (CCPs) in such cases are difficult to define. In the case of molluscs, which are the single largest cause of illness, the CCP is apparently prior to harvest and involves environmental (water) testing with subsequent closure of areas. However, the system is flawed by the unreliability of tests (viruses and vibrios are not detected) and the imperfect nature of distribution controls. A second example is ciguateric fish for which the CCP should be at or before harvest, but testing methods are lacking and the legal basis for fishery control is questionable. It is easy to draw a box at the beginning of a seafood process flow diagram that says "Harvest CCP," but this does not resolve the problem.

Statistical sampling concerns are certainly an important aspect of raw material safety control in such situations (see Chapter 7). To deal with these, more information is needed on the distribution of hazards among fish and shellfish stocks, particularly of chemicals and viruses, and additional research is required along the lines noted in previous chapters.

Recreational Fishing

Any future monitoring and inspection effort must take greater account of that part of seafood caught recreationally. This fraction of the total domestic catch imposes a significant and largely unregulated risk on the consumer. Strong consideration should be given to creating a marine recreational fishing license system that is linked to the distribution of information characterizing the level and scope of potential risk from eating recreationally caught seafood. Strong consideration should also be given to the recreational closure of harvesting areas deemed to pose a threat to human health.

Public Health Monitoring

A fundamental contribution to the reasoned development of regulatory responses to seafood safety questions is the development of accurate and reliable information on seafood-borne illness. The present CDC system is useful for identifying seafood-related hazards but is inadequate to quantify and fully characterize risks that would permit the development of risk-based intervention strategies. Rather, CDC should develop an active program, founded on community-based health surveys, to better determine the level and source of seafood-borne illness in the U.S. population.

Regulation of Imported Products

One of the important differences between the regulation of domestic and imported seafood products is that, for the most part, any assurance of the quality of foreign harvesting environments and postharvest handling practices is lacking. Therefore, to further enhance the safety of imported seafood, consideration should be given to the development of agreements with foreign authorities or individual producers to ensure that imported products are produced in a manner consistent with and equivalent to domestic products. Such a system is currently in place, for example, for imported meat and poultry. The current practice of developing memoranda of understanding (MOUs) with other countries constitutes a reasonable, if initial, effort. However, given the proportion of imported seafood products, the committee suggests that the question of imported product regulation is in need of fundamental reconsideration.

The large portion of the U.S. seafood supply that is imported presents another serious problem for control. It has been proposed that HACCP-type control systems be required for imported seafoods. This would require either extranational inspections by U.S. personnel or MOUs with the exporting countries and some reliable cross-checking. Unfortunately, many seafood exporting countries probably lack the technical ability to meet this proposed requirement. Fish are often transshipped through several countries (and jurisdictions) before appearing in U.S. markets as finished products, and despite country-of-origin labeling requirements, it is difficult to identify the actual location in which animals were harvested. This implies that some type of lot testing will probably continue to be necessary for a significant proportion of imported products. The U.S. food safety authorities should make every effort, working with international agencies, to develop a system for effective identification of harvest areas for fish and shellfish in international commerce. There should also be some ongoing process to identify toxigenic areas, regions of high chemical contamination, and fecally polluted regions in parts of the world from which fish imported to the U.S. originate. Some aspects of these issues could conceivably be undertaken under the *Codex Alimentarius* process or through international programs concerned with water pollution.

Because of the large international trade in seafood and the very diversified nature of both the fish and the environments from which they come, it is essential that the United States consider hazard from a global viewpoint. There needs to be constant awareness of the health-related conditions in areas from which seafoods are imported, in terms of both environmental effects and food-borne disease. Such considerations, together with an improved data base on contaminants and rapid, effective test methods, could lead to more strongly directed sampling and testing with a high probability of success in protecting public health.

Seafood Health Advisories

The determination of seafood health advisories has been made almost exclusively by state regulatory agencies. The committee suggests that a more pronounced and consistently defined federal role in the risk characterizations leading to these advisories would be of significant benefit. A more consistent and focused effort in the determination and communication of public health risks from contaminated seafood should be developed. Without such an effort the public to whom these advisories are directed cannot make effective risk judgments. As already noted, strong consideration should be given to the development of a marine recreational licensing system that would serve, primarily, as a vehicle to communicate risks to recreational fishers.

Educational Programs

Although federal and state training and education do exist for both industry and regulatory authorities, these programs should be expanded, offered on a more routine basis, and structured for uniformity across industries and states. Furthermore, one issue in seafood education that has been consistently undervalued is the integration of food and seafood safety with continuing education for the medical and public health professions. Finally, and as noted elsewhere in this report, the value of a greatly expand public education effort focusing on proper seafood handling in the home should not be underestimated. Such programs should take advantage of existing educational networks available through cooperative extension services and other state institutions.

State Regulations and Programs

At present, states play a fundamental role in the current governance effort to regulate seafood safety in the United States. Given the diversity of our nation's harvesting waters, seafood species, and seafood processing practices, states should continue to play a prominent role in the development of seafood safety standards and inspection practices. Unlike most other food commodities with more uniform production and product forms, seafoods require more regional or local control and surveillance.

In general, the committee's evaluation of existing state regulatory programs for seafood safety suggests that states have developed, with some notable exceptions, a sufficient authority to respond reasonably to problems related to seafood safety. However, the implementation of that authority is extremely uneven. The importance of effective and well-funded seafood surveillance and inspection programs is underscored by the fact that the authority of the FDA is limited to seafood products sold in interstate commerce. For seafood both harvested and consumed within the boundaries of a single state the only controls for product safety are those imposed by the state.

State seafood regulatory programs are very dependent on federal guidance in statutes and advice, but federal rules do not always take into account the regional specificity of seafoods. The ISSC is an ongoing example of communication between federal authorities and state programs. The ISSC concept could be expanded to ensure more state involvement in federal policy in order to reflect regional considerations. Established professional organizations (e.g., AFDO) or respective state and federal officials should be better utilized in facilitating communication and decisions for more uniform and consistent surveillance.

State-based educational programs through cooperative extension services, Sea Grant College Programs, and community education offer experienced networks of expertise that have not been fully utilized to assist regulatory communication, industry compliance, and public perception and protection. These programs offer additional links to research advances in seafood safety and environmental/risk assessments. Together, these educational and research programs warrant further and direct funding considerations as a primary source of future expertise to address food safety in the United States.

Industry Initiatives

Although initiatives on the part of private industry do exist and do, in some instances, add measurably to the enhancement of seafood safety, these programs are, for the most part, designed as quality assurance and product promotion programs. However, the manner in which these programs are communicated to the consumer does not clearly distinguish between those specifically designed to enhance product safety and those with other intentions. Regulations should be developed to qualify and to affirm initiatives for seafood safety claims.

International Issues

One final recommendation relating to setting standards for seafood safety evolves out of a recognition of the importance of international trade in the seafood industry. Several countries have instituted extensive and formal regulatory standards designed to reduce health risks from seafood consumption. There is an emerging recognition within the U.S. government that the development or reevaluation of domestic regulatory guidelines must be cognizant of and take into account other such efforts. However, it should be noted that the regulatory guidelines developed by individual countries are not consistent. Indeed, for certain contaminants, regulatory limits may differ by two orders of magnitude. As more states require equivalency for domestic and imported products, it is increasingly apparent that the time has come for the international community to begin a process to minimize the existing differences in national regulatory guidelines and approaches.

NOTES

1. Surimi is a washed mince of the separated muscle tissue from fish, usually Alaskan pollock, to which cryoprotectants are added. The surimi is formed into blocks and frozen to provide material for the manufacturing of analogue products.
2. The term Memorandum of Understanding (MOU) refers to a formal agreement between a United States government agency (e.g., FDA) and another government agency (federal, state, local), or an informal agreement with a foreign government or other foreign institution. An MOU does not cover areas such as personnel, transfer of personnel or funds, or property. Formal international agreements require clearance through the Department of State (FDA, 1975).

REFERENCES

Adams, C.M., and F.J. Lawlor, III. 1989. Trends in the importation of selected fresh and frozen seafood products into the southeastern United States. Florida Sea Grant Tech. Report No. 59. 70 pp.

AFDO (Association of Food and Drug Officials). 1989. A national letter on seafood inspection mandate. September 9, 1989. Association of Food and Drug Officials, York, Pennsylvania.

AFDO/FDA (Association of Food and Drug Officials/Food and Drug Administration). 1982. Retail Food Store Sanitation Code. Association of Food and Drug Officials, York, Pennsylvania, and

Food and Drug Administration, Washington, D.C. 74 pp.

Anonymous. 1989a. "The Unicode": A dynamic food safety system. Dairy, Food and Environ. Sanitation 9:459.

Anonymous. 1989b. Aquaculture: New markets for meals, fats and oils. J. Am. Oil Chemist. Soc. 66:1531-1546.

Bennett, J.V., S.C. Holmberg, M.F. Rogers, and S.L. Solomon. 1987. Infectious and parasitic diseases. Pp. 102-114 in R.W. Amler and J.B. Dull, eds. Closing the Gap: The Burden of Unnecessary Illness. Oxford University Press, New York.

Benson, J.S. 1990. Statement Before Subcommittee on Department Operations, Research, and Foreign Agriculture, Committee on Agriculture, United States House of Representatives, February 7.

Bevan, D. 1989. Effectiveness of Canadian fish inspection in protecting consumer health. Paper presented at the Workshop on Assessing and Controlling Health Hazards from Fishery Products, Food and Nutrition Board, Institute of Medicine, National Academy of Sciences Study Center, Woods Hole, Mass., July 26. 18 pp.

Bryan, F.L. 1986. Seafood-transmitted infections and intoxications in recent years. Pp. 319-337 in D.E. Kramer and J. Liston, eds. Seafood Quality Determination. Proceedings of an International Symposium Coordinated by the University of Alaska November 10-14, 1986. Elsevier Science Publishers, Amsterdam, The Netherlands.

CDC (Centers for Disease Control). 1981a. *Salmonella* Surveillance, Annual Summary, 1978. HHS Publ. No. (CDC)81-8219. Public Health Service, U.S. Department of Health and Human Services, Atlanta, Ga. 25 pp.

CDC (Centers for Disease Control). 1981b. Annual Summary of Foodborne Disease, 1978. HHS Publ. No. (CDC)81-8185. Public Health Service, U.S. Department of Health and Human Services, Atlanta, Ga. 53 pp.

CDC (Centers for Disease Control). 1981c. Annual Summary of Foodborne Disease, 1979. HHS Publ. No. (CDC) 81-8185. Public Health Service, U.S. Department of Health and Human Services, Atlanta, Ga. 40 pp.

CDC (Centers for Disease Control). 1983a. Food-Borne Disease Outbreaks, Annual Summary 1980. HHS Publ. No. (CDC) 83-8185. Public Health Service, U.S. Department of Health and Human Services, Atlanta, Ga. 32 pp.

CDC (Centers for Disease Control). 1983b. Food-Borne Disease Outbreaks, Annual Summary 1981. HHS Publ. No. (CDC) 83-8185. Public Health Service, U.S. Department of Health and Human Services, Atlanta, Ga. 41 pp.

CDC (Centers for Disease Control). 1984. Food-Borne Disease Outbreaks, Annual summary 1983: Reported morbidity and mortality in the United States. Morbid. Mortal. Weekly Rep. (annual suppl.) 32 pp.

CDC (Centers for Disease Control). 1985a. Food-borne Disease Outbreaks, Annual Summary 1982. DHHS Publ. No. (CDC) 85-8185. Public Health Service, U.S. Department of Health and Human Services, Atlanta, Ga. 38 pp.

CDC (Centers for Disease Control). 1985b. Manual of Procedures for National Morbidity Reporting and Public Health Surveillance Archives. Public Health Service. U.S. Department of Health and Human Services, Atlanta, Ga.

CDC (Centers for Disease Control). 1989. Food-Borne Surveillance Data for All Pathogens in Fish/Shellfish for Years 1973-1987. Public Health Service, U.S. Department of Health and Human Services, Atlanta, Ga.

CEC (Commission of the European Communities). 1987a. Working document of the health conditions affecting the production and the placing on the market of live bivalve molluscs. Directorate-General for Agriculture. VI/2067/87-EN Rev. 3. 37 pp.

CEC (Commission of the European Communities). 1987b. Working paper of health conditions affecting the production and the placing on the market of fishery products. Directorate-General for Agriculture. VI/2078/87-EN Rev. 4. 33 pp.

Chorba, T.L., R.L. Berkelman, S.K. Safford, N.P. Gibbs, and H.F. Hull. 1989. Mandatory reporting of infectious diseases by clinicians. J. Am. Med. Assoc. 262:3018-3026.

DEA (Canadian Department of External Affairs). 1988. The Canada-U.S. Free Trade Agreement, 2nd ed., November 17. Ottawa.

DFO (Canadian Department of Fisheries and Oceans). 1985. Fish Inspection Act. Amendment List, December 11 and 12. Ottawa.

DFO (Canadian Department of Fisheries and Oceans). 1988. Fish Inspection Regulations, Amendment

List, June 13. Ottawa.

DFO (Canadian Department of Fisheries and Oceans). 1989. Canadian Guidelines for Chemical
Contaminants in Fish and Fish Products. Government of Canada, Ottawa.

DOC (Department of Commerce). 1970. Organization Order 25-5A, Sec. 4, October 9.

DOC (Department of Commerce). 1989. A Report to GAO: Review of Federal Food Safety and
Quality Activities. DOC/NOAA/NMFS, October. 23 pp.

FAO (Food and Agricultural Organization). 1983. Codex Alimentarius Codex Standards for Fish and
Fishery Products. Joint FAO/WHO Food Standards Programme, Vol. V, 1st ed. Food and
Agricultural Organization of the United Nations, and World Health Organization, Geneva,
Switzerland. 135 pp.

FAO (Food and Agriculture Organization). 1989. Food Safety Regulations Applied
for Fish by Major Importing Countries. FAO Fisheries Circular No. 825. Food and
Agricultural Organization of the United Nations and World Health Organization, Rome.
107pp.

FDA (Food and Drug Administration). 1975. Interagency Agreements and Memorandum of
Understanding. Staff Manual Guide IV. 2820.1. GT No. 75-34, February 19. Food and Drug
Administration, Washington, D.C., 5 pp.

FDA (Food and Drug Administration). 1985. Compliance Policy Guide, Chapter 8: Fish and Seafood.
7108.01-7108.25, 10/80 through 6/85, July 1. Food and Drug Administration, Washington,
D.C. 41 pp.

FDA (Food and Drug Administration). 1986-1987. Import Seafood Detentions Information. Food and
Drug Administrations, Washington, D.C. 51 pp.

FDA (Food and Drug Administration). 1987. Compliance Policy Guide, Chapter 41-Pesticides. 7141.01,
April 1. Food and Drug Administration, Washington, D.C.

FDA (Food and Drug Administration). 1988a. Processed Seafoods Assignment (FY 89). March 31.
Food and Drug Administration, Washington, D.C. 16 pp.

FDA (Food and Drug Administration). 1988b. Fish List: FDA Guide to Acceptable Market Names for
Food Fish Sold in Interstate Commerce. Washington, D.C. 50 pp.

FDA (Food and Drug Administration). 1988c. Summary of FY '85/86 Field Program "Lead, cadmium
and other elements in domestic shellfish" (Program 7304.004C). Pesticides and Chemical
Contaminants Program. CESAN/DCC, April 19. Division of Contaminants Chemistry, Center
for Food Safety and Applied Nutrition, Washington, D.C. 25 pp.

FDA (Food and Drug Administration). 1988d. Seafood Regulation: An Analysis of FDA Strategy.
Report of the Seafood Task Force. Food and Drug Administration, Washington, D.C. 62 pp.

FDA (Food and Drug Administration). 1989a. NSSP Shellfish Sanitation Program. Manual of
Operations. Part I: Sanitation of Shellfish Growing Areas.

FDA (Food and Drug Administration). 1989b. NSSP Shellfish Sanitation Program. Manual of
Operations. Part II: Sanitation of the Harvesting, Processing and Distribution of Shellfish.

FDA (Food and Drug Administration). 1989c. Imported Molluscan Shellfish Assignment (FY
89)--Revised. January 17. Washington, D.C. 20 pp.

FDA (Food and Drug Administration). 1990. Summary Seafood Operational Accomplishments and
Resource Expenditures, FY 1984-89, January. Program Evaluation Branch (HFC 42), Food and
Drug Administration, Rockville, Md. 15 pp.

Federal Register. 1978. Federal Trade Commission (FTC). FTC proposes prohibition. Fed. Reg.
43(December 7):57269-57284.

Federal Register. 1990. Department of Health and Human Services. Food and Drug Administration.
21 CFR Parts 109 and 509. Action levels for added poisonous or deleterious substances in
food. Fed. Reg. 55(May 21):20782-20787.

Fong, W.G., and G.M. Brooks. 1989. Regulation of chemicals for aquaculture use. Food Technol.
43:88-93.

Garrett, E.S., III. 1988. Microbiological standards, guidelines and specification and inspection of
seafood products. Food Technol. 42:90-93, 103.

Greenberg, E.V.C. 1985. The debate over fish product quality and inspection. Paper presented at the
Fourth Annual National Fishery Law Symposium, Seattle, Wash., October 11-12. 13 pp.

Griffen, N. 1986. Finding new markets for Maine fish. Seafood Leader Magazine 5:74-76.

Haddock, R.L. 1989. Letter report on food-borne disease incidence dated September 8, 1989 from Dr.
Robert L. Haddock, Territorial Epidemiologist, Department of Public Health and Social
Services, Government of Guam to Dr. Farid E. Ahmed, Project Director, Committee on

Evaluation of the Safety of Fishery Products, Institute of Medicine, National Academy of Sciences, Washington, D.C.

Hui, Y.H. 1986. United States Food Laws, Regulations and Standards, Vol. II. John Wiley & Sons, New York. 704 pp.

ICF. 1986. Preliminary Analysis of a National Seafood Inspection Program. Prepared for NMFS/NOAA/DOC by ICF, Inc., Washington D.C. December. 363 pp.

Isaac, R., and J. Delany. 1975. Toxic Element Survey: Final Report, Research and Demonstration Project 71-06. Commonwealth of Massachusetts, Department of Environmental Quality Engineering, Division of Water Pollution Control, November. 25 pp.

Johnsen, P.B. 1989. Factors influencing the flavor quality of farm-raised catfish. Food Technol. 43:94-97.

Kilara, A. 1982. Food allergies–Facts or fiction. Nutr. Letter 1:1-4.

Kvenberg, J. 1989. FDA Pathogen Surveillance Program. Paper presented at the Workshop on Assessing and Controlling Health Hazards from Fishery Products conducted by the Committee on Evaluation of Safety of Fishery Products, Food and Nutrition Board, Institute of Medicine, National Academy of Sciences Study Center, Woods Hole, Mass., July 26. 25 pp.

Lombardo, P., and N.J. Yess. 1989. FDA program on chemical contaminants in seafood. Paper presented at the 1989 Interstate Seafood Conference, Ocean City, Md., October 17-18. 9 pp.

Maine DMR (Department of Marine Resource). 1989. The Best Is Fresh from Maine. Maine Department of Marine Resources, Augusta. 2 pp.

Martin, R. 1990. Regulations. Pp. 351-380 in R.E. Martin and G.J. Flick, eds., The Seafood Industry. VanNostrand and Reinhold, New York.

Matches, J.R., E. Raghubeer, I.A. Yoon, and R.E. Martin. 1986. Microbiology of Surimi-based products. Pp. 373-387 in D.E. Kramer and J. Liston, eds. Seafood Quality Determination. Elsevier Science Publishers, Amsterdam, The Netherlands.

Morris, J.G., Jr., P. Lewin, C.W. Smith, P.A. Blake, and R. Schneider. 1982. Ciguatera fish poisoning: Epidemiology of the disease on St. Thomas, U.S. Virgin Islands. Am. J. Trop. Med. Hyg. 31:574-578.

NBCIA (National Blue Crab Industry Association). 1984. National Crabmeat Industry Pasteurization Standards. National Fisheries Institute, Arlington, Va. 8 pp.

NFPA (National Food Processors Association). 1989. The 1989 Canned Salmon Control Plan and Container Integrity Program. A voluntary cooperative agreement between participating salmon packers, U.S. Food and Drug Administration, and the National Food Processors Association in Seattle, Wash. April. 20 pp.

NMFS (National Marine Fisheries Service). 1989. Fisheries of the United States, 1988. DOC/NOAA/NMFS, U.S. Government Printing Office, Washington, D.C. 116 pp.

NMFS (National Marine Fisheries Service). 1990. Fisheries of the United States, 1989. DOC/NOAA/NMFS, U.S. Government Printing Office, Washington, D.C. 111 pp.

NOAA (National Oceanic and Atmospheric Administration). 1988a. Fishery Products Inspection Manual. Part I: Inspection. Handbook No. 25. DOC/NOAA/NMFS, October.

NOAA (National Oceanic and Atmospheric Administration). 1988b. Fishery Products Inspection Manual. Part III: Certification. Handbook No. 25. DOC/NOAA/NMFS, October.

Otwell, W.S. 1989. Regulatory status of aquaculture products. Food Technol. 43:103-105.

PBCHD (Palm Beach County Health Department). 1988. Episode Care Notes. A comprehensive report prepared by Palm Beach County Health Department. Palm Beach, Fla., May 25.

Ratcliffe, S. , and D.S. Wilt, eds. 1971. Proceedings Seventh National Shellfish Sanitation Workshop, Washington, D.C., October 20-22. 412 pp.

Redmayne, P.C. 1989. World aquaculture developments. Food Technol. 43:80-81.

Rodrick, G.E., and T.C. Cheng. 1989. Parasites: Occurrence and significance in marine animals. Food Technol. 43:98-102.

SFA (Southeastern Fisheries Association). 1990a. Product Quality Code. Southeastern Fisheries Association, Tallahassee, Fla. 1107 pp.

SFA (Southeastern Fisheries Association). 1990b. Industry and Regulatory Interface to Address Concerns for Seafood Product Quality and Safety. Southeastern Fisheries Association, Tallahassee, Fla. June., 215 pp.

Todd, E.C.D. 1989. Preliminary estimates of costs of foodborne disease in the United States. J. Food Protect. 52:595-601.

USDA (United States Department of Agriculture). 1985a. Nationwide Food Consumption Survey.

Continuing Survey of Food Intakes by Individuals. Men 19-50 Years, 1 Day. NFCS, CSFII Report No. 85-3. Nutrition Monitoring Division, Human Nutrition Information Service, United States Department of Agriculture, Hyattsville, Md. 94 pp.

USDA (United States Department of Agriculture). 1985b. Nationwide Food Consumption Survey. Continuing Survey of Food Intakes by Individuals. Women 19-50 Years and Their Children 1-5 Years, 1 Day. NFCS, CSFII, Report No. 85-1. Nutrition Monitoring Division, Human Nutrition Information Service, United States Department of Agriculture, Hyattsville, Md. 102 pp.

Ward, D.R. 1989. Microbiology of aquacultured products. Food Technol. 43:82-87.

Appendix to Chapter 8

SUMMARIES FROM GROUP MEETINGS WITH INDUSTRY AND VARIOUS STATE REGULATORY PERSONNEL

This appendix material includes summaries from group meetings with industry representatives and various state regulatory authorities responsible for some related aspect of surveillance and monitoring to ensure seafood product safety and quality. The meetings in California, Hawaii, Massachusetts, and Washington were conducted by the staff/members of the Committee on Evaluation of the Safety of Fishery Products of the National Academy of Sciences' Institute of Medicine. Summaries from meetings in Alabama, Florida, Georgia, Louisiana, Mississippi, North Carolina, Puerto Rico, South Carolina, and Texas were referenced from a similar project being conducted by the Southeastern Fisheries Association (SFA), a trade association based in Tallahassee, Florida (SFA, 1990b). The SFA project was supported by Saltonstall-Kennedy funds, project number NA 88-WC-J-06065. The SFA project was separate from, yet similar to, the work conducted by the committee.

The basic approach for each group meeting was to assemble industry and respective state regulatory representatives to discuss the current state regulatory structure and practices in addressing seafood safety in production, processing, and marketing. The open discussion format was directed to explain activities from environmental monitoring and production (harvest, culture, or import); through product and processing inspection; through further preparation in retail outlets, restaurants, or other routes; to final consumption. The objective was to illustrate authorities and programs and to record experiences, concerns, and recommendations.

Table A   Review of State Regulatory and Industry Responses (November 1, 1988) Concerning Seafood Quality and Safety

ALABAMA

Industry Character (1988)

1. Ranked 17th in total state production (22.3 million pounds) and 18th in value ($39.7 million).
2. State production primarily from warm waters with significant portion of additional product coming from out-of-state sources.
3. Most fishing vessels independently owned and operated.
4. Diverse state production, principal species including shrimp, oysters, blue crabs, and assorted finfish from nearshore and deepwater fisheries.
5. Diversity in levels and types of processing firms, to include smaller packing houses at dockside; blue crab, shrimp, and oyster processors; large shrimp canneries, and cultured catfish processors. Permitted processing firms totaled 236 in 1988.
6. Consumption includes demand from some large metropolitan regions and some seasonal tourism.
7. Aquaculture development primarily for catfish with annual production ranked third among state productions.
8. Recreational fisheries – all species.   Recreational harvest does enter commercial settings.
9. Imports play significant role as supply for processors and product for consumers, particularly in metropolitan regions.

Primary Product Safety Problems

1. Records and industry practice reflect no major concerns for seafood safety in Alabama. Any potential problem areas are being addressed by current regulatory programs (i.e., molluscan shellfish harvest). The principal concern is consumption of raw molluscan shellfish.

Primary Product Quality Problems

1. Most common violations involve GMPs.
2. Industry is concerned about the continuing and increasing use and misuse of chemicals in treatment to prolong shelf life and increase product yields without required labeling.
3. Enforcement for country of origin labeling.

Additional Problems

1. Aquaculture may introduce new species to the environment that could influence existing stocks.
2. Aquaculture may introduce cultured varieties that will be difficult to distinguish from traditionally harvested species.

Regulatory Concerns for Seafood Industry

1. In all levels of seafood industry there is some general confusion coupled with a lack of awareness of the current, pertinent seafood quality and safety regulations and regulatory authorities.

Regulatory Concerns for Their Respective Programs

1. Training for inspectors is lacking, particularly in relation to seafoods and in noncoastal counties.
2. Program effectiveness and ability to build a better-informed program is compromised by employee turnover and limited career incentives.
3. Seafood regulatory and educational efforts in Alabama must consider the significant portion of Vietnamese workers.

Industry Concerns for Regulations

1. Alabama has recently received a disproportionate amount of federal regulatory scrutiny through site- and species-specific sampling programs.
2. Regulatory authorities need to initiate more active programs to enforce proper species identification and net weights.
3. Regulations for net weights/content declarations require more clarification and increased awareness for industry compliance (i.e., water content in oysters).
4. Regulatory surveillance is primarily complaint activated and oriented.
5. County health inspections look for obviously ill workers, with little or no screening for less obvious illnesses.
6. Regulations are not apparent or easily accessible for guidance or explanations in commercial practice.
7. Regulatory surveillance, particularly federal based, should be more instructive and helpful to ensure compliance. Currently most technical guidance is provided through financially limited academic-based programs and advice (i.e., Alabama Sea Grant Program).
8. Line of authority between state and counties is not clear relative to enforcing labeling, net weight/content declarations, country of origin, etc.
9. Need more regulatory surveillance of seafood imports.
10. A better understanding of regulations would encourage more compliance.

Recommendations

1. Consider a certification program for various levels of industry that is based on voluntary participation with acknowledged credits for completion.
2. Publish a simple, usable version of all county, state, and federal seafood regulations for vessels, processors, and retailers.
3. Consider a structured, periodic training program on seafood safety and regulations for all segments of the industry and regulatory agencies.
4. Need more accessible means to note complaints in industry practice or regulatory activity without drawing regulatory attention to the complainer.

Regulatory Initiatives

None recorded.

Industry Initiatives

None recorded.

Summary

Production and processing of seafoods in Alabama are typical and modest in comparison with other coastal states around the Gulf of Mexico. Records and practice reflect a safe, reputable product, both from harvests and from well-established aquaculture. The main regulatory responsibility is in the Department of Public Health (DPH). Oyster and blue crab production and processing operations, primary in the coastal area, are monitored by a specific state program (DPH), whereas other seafoods and segments of the industry are monitored by the respective county health departments referencing DPH regulations. All agencies and industry representatives request more education and regulatory orientation.

Table B   STATE REGULATORY JURISDICTIONS RELATIVE TO SEAFOOD PRODUCT SAFETY AND QUALITY

ALABAMA

	RECREATIONAL HARVEST - Molluscan	- Non-Molluscan	COMMERCIAL HARVEST - Vessel	- Dockside	PROCESSING - Vessel, Offshore	- Molluscan	- Non-Molluscan	DISTRIBUTION	RETAIL - Store	- Mobile Unit	FOOD SERVICE
Dept. of Agriculture	X					(X)[1]	(X)[1]				
Dept. of Public Health		?	?	?	?	X (i)	(X)[2] (i)	(X) (i)			
County (Local) Health Departments			?	?	?		X (i)	X (i)	X (i)	X (i)	X (i)
Dept. of Conservation & Natural Resources Marine Res. Div.		(X)									

Key:

X - primary authority

(X) - partial authority or limited activity

? - questionable authority, not delineated or not designated

(c) - closures; (i) inspection and licensing; (m) monitoring

1. Weights and measures
2. Oysters and Blue Crabs.

347

Table C STATE REGULATORY PROGRAMS RELATIVE TO SEAFOOD PRODUCT SAFETY AND QUALITY

ALABAMA

	WATER CLASSIFICATION - Coastal Waters	Shellfish Growing Areas	DEPURATION	AQUACULTURE - Freshwater	AQUACULTURE - Saltwater	TOXINS, PRODUCT	TOXINS, ENVIRONMENT	PRODUCT SEIZURE	HEALTH REPORTING	HEALTH ADVISORS RISK COMMUNICATION	ECONOMIC FRAUD	LIVE INTRODUCTION
Dept. of Agriculture and Industries		X c m		?	?	(X)	(X)	(X)			X	
Dept. of Public Health			X	(X)	X^1	(X)		(X)	X	X	(X)	
County (Local) Health Departments									(X)	(X)	(X)	
Dept. of Conserv. & Natural Resources -Div. Marine Reso.		$(X)^3$	$(X)^3$					(X)				(X)
Dept. of Environmental Management	X			X^2	X^2		X					

Key:
X - primary authority
(X) - partial authority or limited activity
? - questionable authority, not delineated or not designated
(c) - closures; (i) inspection and licensing; (m) monitoring

1. For molluscan shellfish only.
2. Permit and monitor any discharge.
3. Primarily resource management which can relate to health concerns.

Table A Review of State Regulatory and Industry Responses (December 13, 1989)
Concerning Seafood Quality and Safety

CALIFORNIA

Industry Character (1989)

1. Ranked 4th in production and value among all seafood producing states.
2. Production includes a variety of fish [e.g., salmon, rockfishes, assorted ground fish and some tuna, traditional squid and dungeness crab landings, and limited molluscan shellfish (production limited by suitable and approved growing waters)].
3. Processing operations (approximately 85%) are concentrated around Los Angeles, including firms producing value added items (e.g., breading, smoking surimi).
4. Company owned vessels are principally the larger seiners and trawlers, but most fishing vessels are independently owned.
5. Recreational fisheries are increasing for mackerel, salmon, rockfishes, some tuna and other assorted ground species and a variety of freshwater fish.
6. Aquaculture is established for oysters, trout, catfish, tilapia, sturgeon, some crayfish, and limited abalone.
7. A substantial amount of seafood imports are consumed in California.

Primary Product Safety Problems

1. Raw molluscan shellfish consumption is a principal seafood safety concern relative to environmental contaminants.
2. The occurrence of paralytic shellfish poison (PSP) requires a continuous monitoring commitment to manage commercial and recreational harvest for molluscan shellfish.
3. Popularity of sushi (raw fish consumption) poses concern for parasitic infections.
4. High influx and establishment of ethnic populous introduces concern for particular dietary habits, product selections, and methods of preparation that require specific surveillance. Likewise, health and seafood safety advisories must be multilingual.
5. Significant recreational fishery poses increasing challenge to assure safety of fish relative to environmental contaminants per location and species. State resorts to strong dependence on contaminant and site specific fishing advisories.

Regulatory Concerns

1. Constant demand for environment and product monitoring and public advisement to assure product safety relative to contaminants is a growing multi-agency commitment that requires more interagency cooperation and better federal liaison relative to "guidelines" and "risk assessment" methods.
2. State agencies need better exposure and consumption data to assist in state-based risk assessments relative to environmental contaminants.
3. Better and more rapid analytical methods are needed for monitoring PSP and addressing "indicators" for approved shellfish growing waters. Likewise, there is an information gap for the survival and behavior of many aquatic microbial pathogens.
4. State agencies are continually frustrated by perceived delays in federal communications to immediate and recurring seafood safety problems. For example, there is a lack in understanding or existence of federal "action levels" for many environmental contaminants.
5. Some autonomy in certain local and county health and food safety related programs can hamper some interagency communications.
6. Recreational harvest can enter commercial distribution.
7. Agencies need to improve their data clearing and storage methods relative to seafood epidemiology, water quality, and seafood product safety assessments in order to better prioritize programs and to assess effectiveness of the programs.
8. In comparisons with most other states, imports represent a higher proportion of the seafoods consumed in California, yet there are no data to judge the safety of imports versus domestic sources.

Industry Concerns

1. The seafood processors should not be blamed for perceived safety problems due to environmental consequences.
2. There needs to be more coordination and consideration for consolidating of the multitude of agency efforts in assessing waters and seafood products relative to environmental contaminants.
3. Industry is often confused by the diversity of agencies and pertinent regulations. There is no single source manual or guide to clarify responsibility and regulatory requirements.
4. Many processing facilities are located on public lands, thus limiting incentive to invest in improvements requiring long-term returns.
5. Fishing (safety) advisories for commercial or recreational sectors should be subject to a central, standard authority prior to "official" release.
6. Regulatory inspectors and portions of the seafood industry need more specific, dedicated and continuous training in aquatic product quality and safety. In some instances, this concern is more evident in local settings.
7. The HACCP vogue does not address the primary seafood quality and safety violations. The primary causes are a few less scrupulous firms or individuals that are not deterred due to lack of penalties and an ineffective enforcement

of existing regulations.
8. The NMFS volunteer inspection program, taunted by some retail advertising, is primarily promotional with a perceived "safety assurance" message, yet the program is quality oriented.
9. The FDA regulatory response is often too complaint oriented.

Regulatory and Industry Initiatives

1. State has an ongoing effort, soon to be completed, for monitoring radioactivity in fish around Farallon Islands and adjacent locations.
2. New California statute will focus more attention on "Recommended Public Health Levels" for contaminants, whereby enforcement can be based on a regulatory review and judgment that can be more inclusive and conservative than current federal guidelines or action levels.
3. Trade associations are encouraging more compliance with commercial licensing and need for regulatory orientation for industry participants, particularly new entries.

Recommendations

1. Need to improve industry knowledge of pertinent regulations and regulators.
2. Need to address more interagency cooperation relative to environmental monitoring pertinent to aquatic food safety, advisories, and industry liaison.
3. Expand public education relative to seafood safety perception and advisories.

Summary

Regulatory structure and activity in California represents one of the nation's most responsive and current state-based programs to assure seafood product safety. Where problems occur they are being addressed or have been mandated for attention. The higher proportion of imports, recreational fishing, immigrants, various ethnic groups, and extensive coast pose challenging problems.

The seafood processing industry is not considered a primary culprit in any seafood safety problems. The principal concerns are environmental contaminants which involve commercial and recreational sectors.

California industry and regulatory commitments to seafood safety represent one of the most significant state efforts in the nation.

Table B STATE REGULATORY JURISDICTIONS RELATIVE TO SEAFOOD PRODUCT SAFETY AND QUALITY

CALIFORNIA

	RECREATIONAL HARVEST - Molluscan	- Non-Molluscan	COMMERCIAL HARVEST - Vessel	- Dockside	PROCESSING - Vessel, Offshore	- Molluscan	- Non-Molluscan	DISTRIBUTION	RETAIL - Store	- Mobile Unit	FOOD SERVICE
Dept. of Health Services	X m,c	(X)	X i,m,c	X i,m,c	X i	X i	X i	X i,m,c	X m[1]	X m	X m[1]
Dept. of Fish & Game	(X)	(X)	(X)	(X)							
State Water Resources Control Board	(X)	(X)	(X)	(X)							

Key:

X - primary authority

(X) - partial authority or limited activity

? - questionable authority, not delineated or not designated

(c) - closures; (i) inspection and licensing; (m) monitoring

1. Local Health agencies have primary responsibility. Department of Health Services exercises authority when local agencies fail to act.

352

Table C   STATE REGULATORY PROGRAMS RELATIVE TO SEAFOOD PRODUCT SAFETY AND QUALITY

CALIFORNIA

	WATER CLASSIFICATION - Coastal Waters	WATER CLASSIFICATION - Shellfish Growing Areas	DEPURATION	AQUACULTURE - Freshwater	AQUACULTURE - Saltwater	TOXINS, PRODUCT	TOXINS, ENVIRONMENT	PRODUCT SEIZURE	HEALTH REPORTING	HEALTH ADVISORS RISK COMMUNICATION	ECONOMIC FRAUD	LIVE INTRODUCTION
Dept. of Health Services		X i,m,c	X i	X m	X m	X i,m	(X)	X i,m	X i,m	X	X	(X) m
Dept. of Fish & Game	(X)	(X)		(X)	(X)		(X)			X		X
State Water Resources Control Board	(X)						X			(X)	(X)	
Dept. of Food & Agriculture				?	?	?	?					?

Key:
X - primary authority
(X) - partial authority or limited activity
? - questionable authority, not delineated or not designated
(c) - closures; (i) inspection and licensing; (m) monitoring

Table A   Review of State Regulatory and Industry Responses (March 29, 1988) Concerning Seafood Quality and Safety

FLORIDA

Industry Character (1988)

1. Ranked 8th in total production (182.2 million pounds) and 7th in dockside value ($169.6 million).
2. Primarily warmwater, subtropical source of production with significant imports (shrimp and warmwater species) and advanced processing.
3. Most fishing vessels independently owned and operated and few company vessels in shrimp fishery.
4. Very diverse production through finfish and shellfish; principal species shrimp, spiny lobster, stone and blue crab, grouper and snapper, tuna, oysters, scallops and clams, etc.
5. Largest number of licensed seafood processing firms per state. Over 570 firms licensed to process in 1988.
6. Consumption includes significant portion of tourist and elderly.
7. Aquaculture – initial developments with oysters, clams, catfish, tilapia, and alligators; established crawfish and soft crabs production.
8. Major recreational fisheries – all species. Recreational harvest can enter commercial settings.
9. Imports include an increasing influx of tropical, subtropical species to complement traditional species and shrimp destined for large shrimp processing firms.

Primary Product Safety Problems

1. Raw molluscan shellfish harvest, processing and consumption versus water quality "indicator" regulations relative to potential pathogens (e.g., *Vibrio vulnificus*).
2. Occurrence of ciguatera primarily as a recreational event or from imported fish and fish taken in foreign waters. Public perception is thought to exceed actual incidence.
3. Ensuring product safety for precooked, ready-to-eat items (e.g., cooked shrimp, pasteurized crabmeat).
4. Lack of funds and personnel to better address issues in a preventive rather than a reactive role.
5. Need to assess product quality and potential toxins of concern in the variety of freshwater sources.

Primary Product Quality Problems

1. General product spoilage for certain fish species.
2. Net weight or content declarations for certain frozen crustaceans, fresh shucked oysters, or shellstock.
3. Improper species identification and mislabeling.
4. Improper storage conditions, (e.g., temperature, packaging).

Additional Problems

1. Ability to distinguish gamefish versus commercial fish, and aquacultured products versus naturally harvested products.
2. Continuing concern for introduction of exotic and potentially disease-bearing species for commercial sales or aquaculture.
3. Aquaculture development versus environmental regulations for water quality.

Regulatory Concern for Seafood Industry

1. Product definitions, (e.g., gallon or pint of oysters, bushel of oysters).
2. Mislabeling of ingredients (i.e., use of sulfiting or phosphating agents).
3. Monitoring product quality at the vessel level.
4. Frozen substitution for product declared fresh (never frozen).

Regulatory Concerns for Their Respective Programs

1. No or limited seafood-specific training for agencies and inspectors, with exception of federally assisted training for regulation of molluscan shellstock harvest and processing.
2. Low salaries; for some agencies there is no geographic adjustments for cost of living.
3. Job pressure and diversity for Marine Patrol officers limits their time to address seafood harvest and quality within jurisdiction of Department of Natural Resources (DNR).
4. Lack of job advancement.
5. Excessive ratio of establishments and products to inspection staff and analytical capability.

Industry Concern for Regulations

1. Overlapping and sometimes inconsistent regulations pertinent to product quality and sanitation.
2. Clarification of product seizure, or destruction authority, particularly for Florida Marine Patrol.
3. Clarification of the food quality/safety regulatory role of DNR's Florida

Marine Patrol and Marine Fisheries Commission.

4. Clarification of vessel or processing equipment confiscation by respective authorities relative to product handling.
5. Clarification of state authority and procedures for any product reclamation.
6. Extensive product retention time and destruction during regulatory sampling, particularly by FDA with imports.
7. Ensuring product quality and safety for recreational harvest sold, legally or illegally, directly to wholesalers or to food service establishments (e.g., potential ciguatoxic fish).
8. Better and necessary full inspection and certification before licensing processing/wholesale participants.
9. Better communication or regulatory changes and reemphasis versus too many and too diverse agency meetings, particularly by Marine Fisheries Commission to warrant beneficial participation.
10. Difficulty in regulating seafood wholesale and retail mobile units.
11. Better means to orient and identify "newcomers" to the industry less familiar with regional regulations and practices.

Recommendations

1. Expand education of regulatory staff with more specific attention to seafoods.
2. Add seafood specialists to regulatory staff.
3. Establish a "complaint" system that does not result in compliance repercussions.
4. Explore utility of a Florida seafood quality "seal" program.
5. Explore the development of an industry and regulator agent "certification" program to ensure basic, necessary education and compliance with food safety.

Regulatory Initiatives

1. DNR's oyster producer "certification" training program.
2. Establishing species (frozen) library for Department of Agriculture reference in product identity.
3. Expanding academic-regulatory interface to enhance education of regulatory staff and industry.
4. Florida legislated "promotional campaign" to be administered by Agriculture and Consumer Services with potential use of Florida Seal of Quality.
5. In-state construction of new, state-of-the-art linear accelerator with partial goal to advance technology in irradiation for food safety with nonradioactive source.
6. Authorization of molluscan shellfish depuration (e.g., clams) with specific restrictions to ensure product safety.

Industry Initiatives

1. SFA Product Quality Control Code.
2. SFA Seafood Import Surveillance project.

Summary

Florida is more prone to seafood product safety problems due to its geographic setting and particular products. The industry is very diverse in product forms and levels of processing, ranging from one-man harvest-sell operations to the world's largest processing firms for shrimp and scallops. The populace contains a significant portion of at risk consumers relative to age.

Regulatory structures are equally diverse and are often perceived as redundant in jurisdiction. Despite limited funds and personnel, they have identified and are addressing all major seafood safety and quality issues. The primary safety issues are raw molluscan shellfish consumption and ciguatoxin.

Table B STATE REGULATORY JURISDICTIONS RELATIVE TO SEAFOOD PRODUCT SAFETY AND QUALITY

FLORIDA

	RECREATIONAL HARVEST - Molluscan	- Non-Molluscan	COMMERCIAL HARVEST - Vessel	- Dockside	PROCESSING - Vessel, Offshore	- Molluscan	- Non-Molluscan	DISTRIBUTION	RETAIL - Store	- Mobile Unit	FOOD SERVICE
Agric. & Consumer Services					?		X (i)	X (i)	X (i)	(X) (i)	
Health & Rehabilitative Services			X (i)	(X) (i)	?	(X) (i)	(X) (i)	(X) (i)	(X) (i)	(X) (i)	X (i)
Natural Resources	X		X (i)	(X)		X (i)	(X) (i)	(X) (i)	(X) (i)	(X) (i)	
Marine Fish. Comm.	(X)	(X)	(X)	(X)	(X)		?	?	?	?	?
Game & Fresh Water Fish Comm.[1]	(X)	X	(X) (i)	(X) (i)							

Key:
X - primary authority
(X) - partial authority or limited activity
? - questionable authority, not delineated or not designated
(c) - closures; (i) inspection and licensing; (m) monitoring

1. Freshwater fisheries

Table C STATE REGULATORY PROGRAMS RELATIVE TO SEAFOOD PRODUCT SAFETY AND QUALITY

FLORIDA

	WATER CLASSIFICATION - Coastal Waters	Shellfish - Growing Areas	DEPURATION	AQUACULTURE - Freshwater	- Saltwater	TOXINS, PRODUCT	TOXINS, ENVIRONMENT	PRODUCT SEIZURE	HEALTH REPORTING	HEALTH ADVISORS / RISK COMMUNICATION	ECONOMIC FRAUD	LIVE INTRODUCTION
Agric. & Consumer Services		X c m	X	X	(X)	X m	(X)	X		(X)	X	
Health & Rehabilitative Services						(X)		X	X	X	X	
Natural Resources			(X)		(X)	(X)	(X)	X	?	(X)	X	X
Marine Fish. Comm.				(X)		(X)	(X)					X
Game & Fresh Water Fish Comm.												X
Environmental Regulation	X m					(X)	X m			?		

Key:
X - primary authority
(X) - partial authority or limited activity
? - questionable authority, not delineated or not designated
(c) - closures; (i) inspection and licensing; (m) monitoring

Table A   Review of State Regulatory and Industry Responses (October 11, 1988) Concerning Seafood Quality and Safety

GEORGIA

Industry Character (1988)

1. Ranked 20th in total production (16.6 million pounds) and 19th in dockside value ($21.5 million).
2. Includes temperate and warmwater sources of state production with significant portion of product coming from out of state.
3. Most fishing vessels independently owned and operated, whereas few company vessels participate in the shrimp fishery.
4. Diverse state production, principal species including shrimp, blue crabs, oysters, clams, whelks, and assorted nearshore finfishes.
5. Processing firms range in size and sophistication from fully integrated shrimp breading firms to typical dockside packing houses or off-loading operations.
6. Consumption includes demand from large metropolitan regions and some tourism.
7. Aquaculture has yet to develop. Includes some progress with soft-shell blue crabs and attempts with crawfish.
8. Recreational fisheries – all species. Recreational catch can enter commercial settings.
9. Imports play significant role in meeting state demand, particularly in metropolitan regions and as a necessary source of shrimp for established processing firms.
10. There are approximately 150 seafood wholesalers and 50 processors/packers in Georgia.

Primary Product Safety Problems

1. Seafood safety is not evidenced or considered a major concern in production, processing, or retailing in Georgia.
2. In ranking problems relative to the amount of regulatory attention, raw molluscan shellfish harvest, shellfish processing and consumption, and blue crab processing are the primary concerns. Concerns for the oyster and clam harvests are controlled through a unique "closed fishery" leasing only concept. Likewise, the industry receives advisory assistance in processing through the University of Georgia Sea Grant Program.

Primary Product Quality Problems

1. Need more regulatory scrutiny for product integrity [e.g., proper species identification, net weight/content declarations, particularly for out-of-state products in metropolitan regions (retail settings)].

Additional Problems

1. Aquaculture products not yet an issue, but should evolve in compliance with Department of Agriculture regulations for product quality and safety, and with reference to species and water quality concerns of Department of Natural Resources.

Regulatory Concerns for Seafood Industry

1. Industry should request more specific training and involve a trade association.
2. Industry should establish more quality control programs with more emphasis on sanitation.

Regulatory Concern for Their Respective Programs

1. Primary limitations to providing additional and specific regulatory seafood scrutiny from vessel through retail and food service include (in priority order): funds, personnel, equipment, and training. Predictions suggest these limitations will impose more restrictions in the near future.
2. Revision and promulgation of additional regulations applicable to the seafood industry have not been adequate.
3. Seafood quality and safety are not major concerns or problems in Georgia; thus, it is difficult to justify more regulations or regulatory scrutiny.
4. Most (seafood) inspectors initially dependent on on-the-job training in industry settings.
5. There are no specific state guidelines for molluscan depuration other than reference to ISSC guidance.
6. Consider better regulatory scrutiny, routine and compliance driven, for seafood species identification, particularly in retail and food service sectors in metropolitan regions.
7. State regulations reflect dependence on federal and industry guidance (i.e., shellfish regulations in reference to ISSC-NSSP directions, and blue crab processing regulations currently referencing recommendation from the National Blue Crab Processors Association).
8. Consider mandatory education for other segments of the seafood industry as required for food service certification. Best to start on voluntary basis.
9. Inspection authority and practice begin at the dock. There is no inspection of fishing vessels, with the exception of guidelines for oyster and clam harvest as provided through the ISSC (oysters).

10. Evaluate all current regulations for any necessary change. Evaluations should include industry liaison.

Industry Concern for Regulations

1. Increase awareness and understanding of current state seafood regulations and regulators (i.e., who does what, who approves labels). More active involvement in state/federal regulatory revisions.
2. New, better-structured liaison between seafood industry and respective regulatory agencies to consider new and amended regulations, education-certification programs, etc.
3. More training and orientation for industry personnel at all levels.
4. Department of Agriculture has only one seafood specialist with statewide orientation for seafood quality and safety from vessel through retail, but most inspections are under the supervision of 20 general food inspectors.
5. Need more regulatory scrutiny of out-of-state seafoods, which constitute bulk of Georgia consumption.
6. In certain settings, NMFS's voluntary inspection service is cooperatively oriented, rather than taking a more advisory approach as in other federal inspection programs.

Recommendations

1. Initiate seafood educational/training programs for industry and for Department of Agriculture and county health inspectors (Department of Human Resources).

Regulatory Initiatives

1. Recent interagency meetings to draft plans to address future aquaculture developments.

Industry Initiatives

1. Currently planning more in-service training in seafood quality and safety for regulatory agencies and industry as provided through Georgia Sea Grant Program and Marine Extension Service.

Summary

Seafood production in Georgia is comparatively modest, yet the processing sector is well established, including large shrimp firms and blue crab processors. The retail and food service sector, particularly in large metropolitan regions, assures a traditional and increasing demand for all seafoods.

The current state regulatory scheme is well organized, with one dominant department adequately addressing most seafood safety concerns. Requests for more specific training and orientation have been noted both for the industry and for regulatory agencies. Academic programs and state agencies are experienced and poised to assist. Additional surveillance is deemed necessary for product in retail, food service, and transport from out of state.

Table B   STATE REGULATORY JURISDICTIONS RELATIVE TO SEAFOOD PRODUCT SAFETY AND QUALITY

GEORGIA	RECREATIONAL HARVEST - Molluscan	- Non-Molluscan	COMMERCIAL HARVEST - Vessel	- Dockside	PROCESSING - Vessel, Offshore	- Molluscan	- Non-Molluscan	DISTRIBUTION	RETAIL - Store	- Mobile Unit	FOOD SERVICE
Dept. of Agriculture			X	X	(X) —	X —	X —	X —	X —	X —	X —
Department of Natural Resources	X c m	X c m									
County Health (Dept. of Human Resources)									X —	X —	X —

Key:
X - primary authority
(X) - partial authority or limited activity
? - questionable authority, not delineated or not designated
(c) - closures; (i) inspection and licensing; (m) monitoring

1. Except for vessels landing shellfish (oysters and clams). No other seafood vessels are inspected.

Table C   STATE REGULATORY PROGRAMS RELATIVE TO SEAFOOD PRODUCT SAFETY AND QUALITY

GEORGIA	WATER CLASSIFICATION - Coastal Waters	WATER CLASSIFICATION - Shellfish Growing Areas	DEPURATION	AQUACULTURE - Freshwater	AQUACULTURE - Saltwater	TOXINS, PRODUCT	TOXINS, ENVIRONMENT	PRODUCT SEIZURE	HEALTH REPORTING	HEALTH ADVISORS RISK COMMUNICATION	ECONOMIC FRAUD	LIVE INTRODUCTION
Dept. of Agriculture	X		(X)	(X)	(X)	X		X		(X)	(X)	
Department of Natural Resources		X c m	(X)	(X)	(X)		(X)	X			(X)	X
County Health (Dept. of Human Resources)							(X)		X	X	(X)	

Key:
X - primary authority
(X) - partial authority or limited activity
? - questionable authority, not delineated or not designated
(c) - closures; (l) inspection and licensing; (m) monitoring

Table A   Review of State Regulatory and Industry Responses (January 2, 1990) Concerning Seafood Quality and Safety

HAWAII

Industry Character (1990)

1. Ranked 17th (21.1 million pounds) in production and 19th ($39.7 million) in value.
2. Exclusively warmwater fishery, with significant contribution from reef species.
3. No commercial shellfishing at present.
4. Seafood production primarily for fresh and frozen market, with little additional processing carried out within the state.
5. Per capita annual consumption exceeds 22 pounds with a significant proportion of seafood (~16%) consumed raw. Estimated that 94% of the residents of the island of Oahu consumed seafood during 1987.
6. Expanding exports directed at exotic and high-quality markets. The state has developed a "Hawaii Seafood" marketing label to enhance export sales of Hawaiian seafood products.
7. Recreational fishery important to overall consumption patterns and to the tourist industry.
8. Imports of traditional Hawaiian seafood products (such as mahimahi) have begun to play an increasingly important role in the market.
9. Aquaculture is an expanding industry with total industry value (production and aquaculture service sector) reaching $18.2 million in 1988.

Primary Product Safety Problems

1. State seafood safety problems are almost exclusively limited to three categories: (1) ciguatera poisoning, (2) scombroid poisoning, and (3) "hallucinogenic fish poisoning."
2. Cases of ciguatera may number in the hundreds on an annual basis. State officials report that between 1983 and 1987 there were 417 individuals involved in 127 incidents of ciguatera/hallucinogenic fish poisoning. A more recent report places the number of cases at a higher level, with trend analysis suggesting a significant worsening of the problem during the 1980s.
3. It has been suggested that as few as one-quarter of ciguatera cases are reported; 80% of the cases are attributable to recreational fishing.
4. Ciguatera limited to fish caught within reef environments. Evidence that coastal development activities may serve as a catalyst for elevated levels of ciguatoxin in adjacent areas.
5. Ongoing research has produced a simple and inexpensive stick test for ciguatera and other polyether toxins. The test is characterized as being 100% reliable for results indicating the absence of polyether toxins but may produce overly sensitive positive results.
6. The number of reported cases of scombroid poisoning has increased in recent years. However, a majority of cases have been attributed to imported

products.
7. The relative lack of industrialization and enviable water quality in commercial harvesting areas suggest the lack of a significant residual chemical problem in locally harvested seafood.

Issues in the Regulation of Seafood Safety

1. At present, there is little formal regulatory response, beyond public education, to recreationally caught fish. Further, no state agency has direct responsibility for regulating offshore vessel processors.
2. The state fisheries resource agency (Department of Land and Natural Resources, Division of Aquatic Resources) has no legal competency to regulate fisheries on the basis of human health impacts.
3. Effective management of ciguatera will require a more fundamental understanding of the temporal and spatial relationship between the occurrence and density of *Gambierdiscus toxicus* (the dinoflagellate that produces the toxin) and levels of ciguatoxin in fish.

Industry Initiatives

1. Sponsorship by the Hawaii Seafood Promotion Committee of position papers related to seafood safety. Specifically, a recent report, "The Wholesomeness of Raw Tuna: The Case Against Freezing" prepared by Dr. John Kaneko in response to recent FDA recommendations that all fish destined for raw or rare consumption be previously frozen to eliminate the potential health risk from parasites.

Recommendations

1. FDA recommendation that all seafood destined for raw or rare consumption be frozen should be reconsidered and rejected. Risk from parasites is limited to a small number of species and regulations requiring freezing should be species specific.
2. The state of Hawaii should develop a more proactive strategy to identify and regulate fishing grounds populated by ciguatoxic fish. Such a strategy should incorporate research that would allow for a more effective forecast of likely ciguatoxic areas.

Summary

Hawaii provides an unusual case in seafood safety. Good coastal water quality and the present lack of an indigenous shellfish industry mean the absence of a broad suite of seafood safety issues in evidence in much of the continental United States. However, the state does have a significant problem with ciguatera and, to a somewhat lesser degree, with scombroid poisoning, the preponderance of cases being attributable to either recreationally caught fish or imported products.

Regulatory agencies are generally knowledgeable and well trained to deal with the state's significant seafood safety issues. However, there are important gaps in the state's jurisdiction. Particularly, there is no well-defined regulatory competence to manage fisheries resources on the basis of human health.

Table B   STATE REGULATORY JURISDICTIONS RELATIVE TO SEAFOOD PRODUCT SAFETY AND QUALITY

HAWAII	RECREATIONAL HARVEST - Molluscan	- Non-Molluscan	COMMERCIAL HARVEST - Vessel	PROCESSING - Dockside	- Vessel, Offshore	- Molluscan	- Non-Molluscan	DISTRIBUTION	RETAIL - Store	- Mobile Unit	FOOD SERVICE
Dept. of Health Environmental Health Service Division											
-Food & Drug Branch	(X)			?	?	?	X	X	X	X	X
-Sanitation Branch											(X)
Department of Land & Natural Resources											
-Enforcement Division			(X)								

Key:
X - primary authority
(X) - partial authority or limited activity
? - questionable authority, not delineated or not designated
(c) - closures; (i) inspection and licensing; (m) monitoring

Table C   STATE REGULATORY PROGRAMS RELATIVE TO SEAFOOD PRODUCT SAFETY AND QUALITY

HAWAII	WATER CLASSIFICATION - Coastal Waters	WATER CLASSIFICATION -Shellfish Growing Areas	DEPURATION	AQUACULTURE -Freshwater	AQUACULTURE -Saltwater	TOXINS, PRODUCT	TOXINS, ENVIRONMENT	PRODUCT SEIZURE	HEALTH REPORTING	HEALTH ADVISORS RISK COMMUNICATION	ECONOMIC FRAUD	LIVE INTRODUCTION
Dept. of Health Environmental Health Service Division -Food & Drug Branch		X	X	X	(X)	X	(X)	X	(X)	X	X	
-Sanitation Branch									(X)	(X)	(X)	
-Epidemiology Branch							X		X	(X)	(X)	
Environmental Mgmt. Division -Clean Water Branch	X											
Dept. of Agriculture -Plant Quarantine Branch								(X)				

Key:
X - primary authority
(X) - partial authority or limited activity
? - questionable authority, not delineated or not designated
(c) - closures; (i) inspection and licensing; (m) monitoring

Table A   Review of State Regulatory and Industry Responses (May 24, 1988) Concerning Seafood Quality and Safety

LOUISIANA

Industry Character (1988)

1. Ranked 2nd in total state production (1,356.5 million pounds) and 2nd in value ($317.3 million). Production includes a substantial portion of industrial fishery products (e.g., menhaden, fish meal) and valuable traditional edible products (e.g., shrimp, oysters, blue crabs, crawfish).
2. State production centers about warm coastal and intercoastal waters supplemented by nutrient-rich flow of the Mississippi delta region. A significant portion of additional products comes from out-of-state sources.
3. Other state-based processors dependent on Louisiana's production of certain species (i.e., oysters and shrimp).
4. Most fishing vessels independently owned and operated.
5. Diversity in levels and types of processing firms include smaller packing houses at dockside; blue crab, shrimp, and oyster processors; large shrimp canneries; and cultured catfish and crawfish processors. There were more than 300 licensed seafood processors in Louisiana in 1988.
6. Consumption includes demand in some large metropolitan regions and some seasonal tourism.
7. Aquaculture is well established for crawfish and catfish and developing for other food fish.
8. Recreational fisheries – all species. Recreational catch can enter commercial settings.
9. Imports play significant role as supply for processors and product for consumers, particularly in metropolitan regions.

Primary Product Safety Problems

1. Primary seafood product safety problems in Louisiana involved the necessary regulatory attention and industry compliance concerns for production and consumption of unprocessed, raw molluscs.

Primary Product Quality Problems

1. Principal product integrity concerns in commerce are net weight declarations and species identification.

Additional Problems

1. Producers and processors contend a limited number of commercial buyers will emphasize price over quality and occasionally adjust pricing to provide outlets for inferior product.
2. The Louisiana Department of Health and Hospitals has the authority under the State Food, Drug and Cosmetic Law to inspect any vessel or vehicle carrying a commercial food product, but there are no routine vessel inspections with the exception of some molluscan shellfish harvest.
3. Industry is often unaware or confused by Louisiana Department of Agriculture versus Louisiana Department of Health inspections for quality or sanitation, despite the fact that the latter agency is mandated by law to permit, inspect, and regulate seafood processing and distribution.
4. Current regulatory distinction for cultured products (e.g., alligators, catfish, and crawfish) can be confusing. Inspections can depend on the processor's decision to receive per fee services from the Louisiana Department of Agriculture (through agreements with the USDC-NMFS volunteer Inspection Services), whereas the Louisiana Department of Health (in reference to FDA standards) still maintains concomitant authority which it may not exercise. In addition, the USDA role in assisting cultured product can add to the confusion.
5. Any attempts to initiate a state-based "quality seal" program would depend on a realistic mode of standard enforcement that could compete for financing necessary for current regulatory programs in need of more support.
6. Efforts to educate the public are difficult due to extreme product diversity.

Regulatory Concerns for Seafood Industry

1. Department of Agriculture is typically poised to address processing of a "live" harvest (e.g., red meat), yet seafoods are usually landed dead, thus initiating postmortem quality and safety concerns.
2. It is difficult to define or distinguish all seafood processors relative to the diversity in levels of product procurement and handling. Distinction based on "altering the original product form" can eliminate firms that only purchase, repack, and distribute.

Regulatory Concerns for Their Respective Programs

1. Basically, state agencies need more manpower, support funds, and analytical capability to better address seafood quality and safety.
2. There are no major concerns to warrant specific, routine vessel inspections for attributes that may compromise product safety.

Industry Concerns for Regulations

1. Basically, seafood inspections in Louisiana need to be more equitable and consistent across all segments and sizes of industry.
2. Knowledge of regulations and regulatory authority often depends on one or a few individuals' knowledge and possible opinion.
3. Seafood processors are deemed the primary target for regulatory surveillance, although they are positioned between two minimally regulated commercial segments, production and retail, which can significantly influence product quality and safety.
4. Seafood product quality and safety liabilities must be adjusted to include more responsibility setting. In general, more seafood regulatory surveillance is needed beyond production and processing.
5. Federal inspections (i.e., FDA) are focused only on faults, with no offer to advise or direct compliance.
6. State inspectors need more seafood-specific orientation and experience in their credentials and training.
7. Need clarification and more enforcement for country-of-origin labeling.
8. Methods and sources by which to register seafood quality and safety complaints from industrial settings are not obvious, encouraged, or convenient.
9. Fishery regulations promulgated to protect stocks can influence product quality and processing modes [i.e., state restrictions that require all fish be landed with head and tail intact (for size verification)].

Recommendations

1. Need better coordination and clarification of regulations, regulatory authorities, and safety criteria within and among respective agencies and industry.
2. Need to review and improve the state's current seafood quality and safety regulations. Some specific concerns cited are
   - production and processing of pasteurized blue crab meat and soft-shell crabs;
   - oyster "sell-by" dating;
   - clarify regulations and authorities for alligator production and processing; and
   - address emerging industries (e.g., soft-shell crawfish).
3. Need condensed, user friendly version of current seafood quality- and safety-related regulations and regulators.
4. Education necessary for any seafood buyer group (i.e., retailers, consumers, institutions).
5. Need to consider some forms of uniform, annual training for seafood inspectors and permitted industry participants, both general and species specific.
6. Continuing and additional seafood education available through universities (e.g., Louisiana Sea Grant Programs) would be best assisted by initiatives and

support from the respective state agencies and industry groups.

7. Need more regulatory attention directed on a probable concern basis to address vessel product quality (e.g., cleanliness, proper ice, product abuses).

8. Federal authorities need to improve efforts to interface with state regulatory authorities and respective industry participants with particular attention on assisting compliance.

9. Need more product quality and safety assurance in state-based promotional programs to address errant publicity.

Regulatory Initiatives

None identified.

Industry Initiatives

None identified.

Summary

Louisiana represents a state with very abundant and valuable seafood production, which is essential to suit the traditional demands of consumers and utility of in-state and neighboring state processors. This production includes species of primary product safety concern (i.e., molluscan shellfish and certain fish species). Regulatory ability to continue surveillance that ensures product safety will depend on future supplements for manpower with financial and analytical support. Current regulatory jurisdictions can be confusing, particularly pertinent to processing of cultured products.

Recommendations for improvements focus on general knowledge and application of existing regulations rather than any need for more regulations.

374

Table B STATE REGULATORY JURISDICTIONS RELATIVE TO SEAFOOD PRODUCT SAFETY AND QUALITY

LOUISIANA

	RECREATIONAL HARVEST - Molluscan	RECREATIONAL HARVEST - Non-Molluscan	COMMERCIAL HARVEST - Vessel	COMMERCIAL HARVEST - Dockside	PROCESSING - Vessel, Offshore	PROCESSING - Molluscan	PROCESSING - Non-Molluscan	DISTRIBUTION	RETAIL - Store	RETAIL - Mobile Unit	FOOD SERVICE
Dept. of Hlth. & Hospitals -Seafood Sanitation Unit	X (c m)	(X)	X	X	?	X i	X i	X	(X)	(X)	
-Food & Drug Unit							(X)[1]	(X)	(X)	(X)	
-Retail Food Inspt. Prog.									X i	X i	X i
Local Health Units (parish)							(X)	(X)	X i	X i	X i
Dept. of Agriculture							(X)[2]	(X)[3]	(X)[3]	(X)[3]	
Dept. of Wildlife and Fisheries	(X)	(X)									

Key:

X - primary authority

(X) - partial authority or limited activity

? - questionable authority, not delineated or not designated

(c) - closures; (i) inspection and licensing; (m) monitoring

1. FDU authority and practice primarily for food processing or manufacturing of food in which seafood may be one ingredient.

2. Established agreements with NMFS that accredit certain state inspectors to provide, through fees, the volunteer inspection services of the USDC.

3. Monitor weights and measures.

Table C STATE REGULATORY PROGRAMS RELATIVE TO SEAFOOD PRODUCT SAFETY AND QUALITY

LOUISIANA

	WATER CLASSIFICATION - Coastal Waters	WATER CLASSIFICATION -Shellfish Growing Areas	DEPURATION	AQUACULTURE - Freshwater	AQUACULTURE - Saltwater	TOXINS, PRODUCT	TOXINS, ENVIRONMENT	PRODUCT SEIZURE	HEALTH REPORTING	HEALTH ADVISORS RISK COMMUNICATION	ECONOMIC FRAUD	LIVE INTRODUCTION
Dept. of Hlth. & Hospitals -Environ. Epidemo. Sec.						X	X	X	X	X		
-Seafood Sanitation Unit		X c m	X	(X)	(X)				(X)	(X)	(X)	
-Oyster Growing Mon. Unit	X c m											
-Food & Drug Unit						(X)		(X)			(X)	
-Epidemology Sect.									X	X		
Local Health Units (parish)									(X)	(X)		
Dept. of Agriculture				(X)[1]	?	(X)[2]					(X)	
Dept. of Wildlife & Fisheries		(X)[3]										X
Dept. Environ. Quality	X						X					

Key:

X - primary authority
(X) - partial authority or limited activity
? - questionable authority, not delineated or not designated
(c) - closures; (l) inspection and licensing; (m) monitoring

1. Approves use of herbicides and pesticides.
2. Provide pesticide and heavy metal analysis per request by exporters.
3. Enforcement of closures.

Table A   Review of State Regulatory and Industry Responses (July 25, 1989) Concerning Seafood Quality and Safety

MASSACHUSETTS

Industry Character (1989)

1. Ranked 15th in production and 14th in landed value (1987).
2. Port of New Bedford ranked 1st in value landed by port (1987).
3. Primarily coldwater source production, dominant offshore finfishery with shellfishing predominantly inshore (within the territorial sea). Sea scallops and surf clams also taken offshore.
4. Diverse production with principal species including lobster, sea scallops, flounder (particularly yellowtail), cod, shrimp, bay scallop, soft- and hard-shell clams.
5. Consumption is representative of principal species, with significant recreational fishery for lobster, cod, winter flounder, bay scallops and soft-shell clams, bluefish and striped bass.
6. Seafood contributes significantly to state tourist industry.
7. Aquaculture is an emerging, rather than an established, industry in the state.
8. Imports constitute a significant portion of consumption in the state, with Canada playing a dominant role, particularly with lobster, flounder and cod (including haddock).

Primary Product Safety Problems

1. Significant organic chemical contamination of fisheries in Boston and New Bedford Harbors (principally PCBs).
2. Widespread closures of shellfish beds throughout the state. Boston Harbor beds are all either closed or restricted to commercial harvesting and depuration.
3. PSP closures are common but well controlled by regulatory closures.
4. Mercury warnings have been issued for selected inland locations.

Additional Problems

1. The impact of shellfish depuration on public health (particularly concerning reduction of virus-associated disease) is not well understood.
2. The Commonwealth has tested and embargoed a significant proportion of shellfish imported from other states (particularly Maryland).

Regulatory Concerns

1. The Commonwealth is presently experiencing a severe fiscal crisis. Funding needed for regulatory positions to perform seafood inspection and for harvesting water quality has proven difficult to secure.
2. Public health reporting is focused at the level of cities and towns. Less than one-third of Massachusetts cities and towns have fulltime health officers.
3. The regulation of shellfish harvest is controlled primarily at the level of cities and towns where level of training can be very uneven.
4. Lack of more effective federal guidance for the establishment of regulatory limits is in evidence. Massachusetts waters are contaminated with a number of chemical contaminants not addressed by existing federal limits.
5. Aquaculture is a growing industry that, at present, is not well regulated in any discreet fashion.
6. The state has established vessel-based regulations, but these regulations have not been well communicated to the industry.
7. Massachusetts does not enforce the FDA action level for mercury in marine fish.

Industry Initiatives

1. Certain seafood restaurants have established independent laboratories to determine levels of pathogens.

Summary

The Commonwealth of Massachusetts produces and imports a wide variety of fresh, fresh-frozen, and processed seafood products. Recreational harvesting for both fish and shellfish is common. Significant near-shore problems with chemical contaminants have led to a closure to the taking of all seafood within the Acushnet River estuary and to limited advisories in Quincy Bay. State fiscal problems have severely limited the ability of the Commonwealth to regulate seafood safety.

Table B STATE REGULATORY JURISDICTIONS RELATIVE TO SEAFOOD PRODUCT SAFETY AND QUALITY

MASSACHUSETTS

	RECREATIONAL HARVEST - Molluscan	RECREATIONAL HARVEST - Non-Molluscan	COMMERCIAL HARVEST - Vessel	COMMERCIAL HARVEST - Dockside	PROCESSING - Vessel, Offshore	PROCESSING - Molluscan	PROCESSING - Non-Molluscan	DISTRIBUTION	RETAIL - Store	RETAIL - Mobile Unit	FOOD SERVICE
Dept. of Public Health -Div. of Food & Drug	X		X	?	?	X –		(X)	(X)		
Dept. of Fish., Wildlife, & Environ. Law Enforcement -Div. of Marine Fisheries			X			X[1]					
-Div. of Wildlife and Law Enforcement						X[2]					
Cities and Towns -Health Agencies								(X)	X –	(X)	X –
- Shellfish Officers	X									(X)	

Key:
X - primary authority
(X) - partial authority or limited activity
? - questionable authority, not delineated or not designated
(c) - closures; (l) inspection and licensing; (m) monitoring

1. Responsible for issuing licenses.
2. Responsible for enforcement of closures.

Table C STATE REGULATORY PROGRAMS RELATIVE TO SEAFOOD PRODUCT SAFETY AND QUALITY

MASSACHUSETTS	WATER CLASSIFICATION - Coastal Waters	-Shellfish Growing Areas	DEPURATION	AQUACULTURE - Freshwater	- Saltwater	TOXINS, PRODUCT	TOXINS, ENVIRONMENT	PRODUCT SEIZURE	HEALTH REPORTING	HEALTH ADVISORS RISK COMMUNICATION	ECONOMIC FRAUD	LIVE INTRODUCTION
Dept. of Public Health -Div. of Food & Drug			X —			X		X	X	X	X	
Dept. of Fish., Wildlife, & Environ. Law Enforcement -Div. of Marine Fisheries		X¹	X		X	X	X			X	X	
-Div. of Law Enforcement		X¹										
Dept. of Envir. Protection -Div. of Water Poll. Cntl.	X	X					X —			X		
Office of Coastal Zone Management	X						X					
Cities and Towns -Health Agencies									X		(X)	
-Shellfish Officers		X¹	X¹									

Key:
X - primary authority
(X) - partial authority or limited activity
? - questionable authority, not delineated or not designated
(c) - closures; (i) inspection and licensing; (m) monitoring

1. Responsible for enforcement of closures.

Table A   Review of State Regulatory and Industry Responses (February 9, 1989)
Concerning Seafood Quality and Safety

MISSISSIPPI

Industry Character (1988)

1. Ranked 5th in total state production (336.4 million pounds) and 14th in value ($61.2 million). Production includes a significant portion of industrial, nonedible fish species.
2. State production primarily from warm waters with significant portion of additional product coming from out-of-state sources.
3. Most fishing vessels independently owned and operated.
4. Diverse state production, principal species including shrimp, oysters, blue crabs, and assorted finfish from nearshore and deepwater fisheries.
5. Diversity in levels and types of processing firms to include smaller packing houses at dockside; blue crab, shrimp, and oyster processors; large shrimp canneries; and cultured catfish processors.
6. Consumption includes some metropolitan regions and some seasonal tourism.
7. Aquaculture is well established for catfish and being developed for other food fish.
8. Recreational fisheries – all species. Recreational catch can enter commercial settings.
9. Imports play significant role as supply for processors and product for consumers, particularly in metropolitan regions.

Primary Product Safety Problems

1. Attending representative felt that Mississippi agencies and experienced firms believe that state seafood production and processing pose no significant food safety problems, with exception of customary concerns for raw molluscan shellfish.

Primary Product Quality Problems

1. Most seafood product quality problems involve out-of-state products and retail settings.
2. Most quality problems noted in processing firms deal with basic compliance with GMPs.

Additional Problems

1. Established aquaculture industry is well managed and yields safe, quality products.   Pending aquaculture bill will address more regulatory responsibility.

Regulatory Concerns for Seafood Industry

1. There is general lack of understanding of the regulations, regulatory authorities, and applications.

Regulatory Concerns for Their Respective Programs

1. Identified needs for additional regulatory/inspection personnel and funds are difficult to achieve in light of limited product safety and quality problems.
2. No specific regulations exist to direct inspection or certification of fishing vessels relative to sanitation with exception of molluscan harvest.
3. State seafood and food regulatory authority and regulations are currently adjusting to the recent and ongoing programmatic changes in which the major portion of responsibility for seafoods was placed in the Bureau of Marine Resources. The bureau is currently trying to adapt to the new assignment.

Industry Concerns for Regulations

1. Many nonspecific or flexible regulations are left to regulatory interpretation which has caused confusion.
2. It is good to recognize regional differences, but there is a need for more uniformity in regulations across counties and states.
3. Regulatory distinction is not clear for authorities dealing with general seafoods versus oysters and crabs versus shrimp in the various industry levels from vessel through processing and retail across the state.
4. There should be more permit consolidation for various seafood handling and processing operations.
5. Need more equitable regulation of imports.
6. General lack of understandable permitting process for processors versus variety of required permits.

Recommendations

1. Marketing programs need to incorporate more quality and safety in their promotional messages.
2. Initiate more training for industry and inspectors.
3. Develop a condensed, readable explanation of pertinent state regulations.

Regulatory Initiatives

1. Agencies in continuing effort to accommodate recent program changes in jurisdictions and authorities.

Industry Initiatives

None identified.

Summary

Mississippi has recently undergone major changes in regulatory responsibility for seafood quality and safety. The changes are to be more efficient, yet they are initially confusing. Most pertinent authority is now housed in the Bureau of Marine Resources, with primary emphasis on oysters. Authority of the bureau extends to distribution, whereas the Department of Health and county health programs assume responsibility for seafood safety in retail and food service. The well-established catfish processing industry has been positioned under surveillance by a separate department (Agriculture).

Despite some transitional confusion in state regulatory authority, attending industry and regulatory personnel believe there are no major seafood safety or problems in Mississippi that are not or cannot be resolved by the current regulatory scheme. The efficiency and responsiveness of current programs are restricted only by limited personnel, meager funds, and no specific seafood training.

Table B   STATE REGULATORY JURISDICTIONS RELATIVE TO SEAFOOD
PRODUCT SAFETY AND QUALITY

MISSISSIPPI

	RECREATIONAL HARVEST - Molluscan	RECREATIONAL HARVEST - Non-Molluscan	COMMERCIAL HARVEST - Vessel	PROCESSING - Dockside	PROCESSING - Vessel, Offshore	PROCESSING - Molluscan	PROCESSING - Non-Molluscan	DISTRIBUTION	RETAIL - Store	RETAIL - Mobile Unit	FOOD SERVICE
Dept. of Agriculture	X						$(X)^1$				
Dept. of Wildlife, Fish and Parks Bur. Marine Resources			?	X	?	X —	X —	X —	$(X)^2$	$(X)^2$	$(X)^2$
Bur. Fish & Wildlife		(X)	?								
Dept. of Natural Res. Bur. Pollution Cntl.											
Dept. of Health								(X)	$(X)^2$	$(X)^2$	$(X)^2$
County Health								(X)	$(X)^2$	$(X)^2$	$(X)^2$

Key:
X - primary authority
(X) - partial authority or limited activity
? - questionable authority, not delineated or not designated
(c) - closures; (i) inspection and licensing; (m) monitoring

1. catfish only
2. Regulatory responsibility is still unclear; currently in negotiation.

Table C   STATE REGULATORY PROGRAMS RELATIVE TO SEAFOOD PRODUCT SAFETY AND QUALITY

MISSISSIPPI

	WATER CLASSIFICATION - Coastal Waters	WATER CLASSIFICATION - Shellfish Growing Areas	DEPURATION	AQUACULTURE - Freshwater	AQUACULTURE - Saltwater	TOXINS, PRODUCT	TOXINS, ENVIRONMENT	PRODUCT SEIZURE	HEALTH REPORTING	HEALTH ADVISORS / RISK COMMUNICATION	ECONOMIC FRAUD	LIVE INTRODUCTION
Dept. of Agriculture		X		X	?	?						
Dept. of Wildlife, Fish and Parks Bur. Marine Resources		c m	X		?	(X)		(X)		(X)	X	(X)
Bur. Fish & Wildlife				(X)	?							(X)
Dept. of Natural Res. Bur. Pollution Cntl.	X						X					
Dept. of Health						(X)	?		X	X		
County Health									(X)	(X)		

Key:
X - primary authority
(X) - partial authority or limited activity
? - questionable authority, not delineated or not designated
(c) - closures; (i) inspection and licensing; (m) monitoring

Table A   Review of State Regulatory and Industry Responses (August 22, 1988) Concerning Seafood Quality and Safety

NORTH CAROLINA

Industry Character (1988)

1. Ranked 7th in total state production (192 million pounds) and 11th in dockside value ($78 million). A significant portion of the annual landings includes industrial, nonedible fish (i.e., menhaden).
2. State production includes temperate and some warmwater sources complemented by a significant portion of out-of-state products.
3. Most fishing vessels independently owned and operated and some traditional harvest based on shoreline and shallow-water landing (seines).
4. Diverse state production; principal edible species include shrimp, blue crab, and assorted nearshore finfish.
5. Processing firms are diversified by size and species. There were more than 130 processing firms licensed to operate in North Carolina in 1988. The most advanced processing firms produce fresh and pasteurized crabmeat.
6. Seafood consumption centers about some large metropolitan regions, plus seasonal tourism.
7. Aquaculture development is established with production of freshwater trout and emerging efforts for catfish and striped bass.
8. Recreational fisheries – all species.   Recreational harvest can enter commercial channels.
9. Imports play major role in meeting state demand, particularly in metropolitan regions.

Primary Product Safety Problems

1. Seafood safety is not considered a major problem in North Carolina, and where problems exist or recur the current regulatory agencies feel that they are addressing these issues in a cooperative and reactive manner.
2. One of the most difficult seafood safety-related issues is classification and monitoring of molluscan shellfish growing waters.

Primary Product Quality Problems

1. The most common yet easily resolved seafood product quality problem is temperature abuse.
2. Lack of some basic food quality control practice in some industry settings.
3. Fishing vessels are not inspected routinely relative to food quality and sanitation, but there are no significant or persistent problems. As problems

occur (e.g., proper use of sulfites, handling of scallops), current regulatory programs can adequately address these issues.

Additional Problems

1. North Carolina institutional buying specifications and guidelines for product quality and sanitation could be more aligned in support of its seafood industry's products and expectations. A state program for seafood marketing that emphasizes product quality and safety has been slow to develop.
2. Product safety and quality regulations for aquaculture should mesh into existing regulatory programs rather than initiating new ones.

Regulatory Concerns for Seafood Industry

1. Trade associations can be more involved in regulatory/industry training.
2. Industry, especially newcomers, need more regulatory orientation.

Regulatory Concerns for Their Respective Programs

1. Regulatory attention is often complaint directed or planned to address most-probable problems.
2. State inspectors get very limited seafood orientation outside of on-the-job training. There is a need for more orientation to seafoods and the seafood industry.
3. Inspection for retail settings is largely left up to local, county authorities, which may or may not have a specific ordinance to direct activity. Although there are no specific agreements, county (health) authorities often reference respective state regulations. More formal agreements and regulatory attention may be warranted.
4. County authorities are confronted with a troublesome turnover rate (1 of 7 inspectors per year) that can compromise effectiveness and training commitments.
5. Mobile units are difficult to monitor, but they have not presented a food safety problem.
6. Regulation for product quality and safety in interstate commerce can be complicated by lack of uniformity across states for particular seafoods (e.g., boiled versus steamed crabmeat, raw oysters, calico and bay scallops, general grade enforcements).

Industry Concern for Regulations

1. Industry and regulatory authorities should coparticipate in more training and orientations to ensure continued product quality and safety.
2. Regulatory authorities need new, improved techniques to better accommodate processing developments and changes.
3. Retail inspections for seafood concerns appear more complaint directed than routine.
4. Need more regulatory surveillance for imports.

Recommendations

1. Consider "certification" program for processors and inspectors to ensure some education from established academic/extension service programs.
2. Consider industry "internship" programs as part of the training and orientation inspectors that will deal with seafoods.
3. Start industry/regulatory-based awards program to recognize regulatory/inspector service.
4. Produce a publication to consolidate and simplify the introduction to North Carolina's seafood quality and safety requirements and concerns.
5. Improve media liaison and public advisories on seafood safety issues in North Carolina.
6. Various state regulatory programs and industry associations should increase participation in professional organizations established to foster more interstate liaison (i.e., AFDO and AFDOSS).

Regulatory Initiatives

1. Agency liaison ongoing to consider more direction and structure for inspection of retail firms.
2. Agency liaison ongoing to plan for aquaculture products in commerce.
3. Agency liaison ongoing to consider seafood promotional activity with more product quality and safety emphasis.

Industry Initiatives

None identified.

Summary

North Carolina's edible seafood production is comparatively modest and predicted to be approaching annual maximum yield. There are no major biological indications for significant increases in state commercial harvests. Imports, out-of-state production, and some aquaculture represent the future supplies to meet North Carolina's growing product demands.

North Carolina's seafood production and processing have not and are not predicted to pose any significant seafood safety problems that cannot be addressed by existing regulatory authorities and industry cooperation. Most safety and product quality issues are known and under control. The existing surveillance system provides sufficient routine monitoring for particular concerns (e.g., molluscan harvest and blue crab processing). Likewise, existing programs have the ability to respond to emerging problems and complaints. Program effectiveness can be improved through more and specific seafood training and orientation, with coparticipation by the industry.

Table B STATE REGULATORY JURISDICTIONS RELATIVE TO SEAFOOD PRODUCT SAFETY AND QUALITY

NORTH CAROLINA

	RECREATIONAL HARVEST - Molluscan	RECREATIONAL HARVEST - Non-Molluscan	COMMERCIAL HARVEST - Vessel	COMMERCIAL HARVEST - Dockside	PROCESSING - Vessel, Offshore	PROCESSING - Molluscan	PROCESSING - Non-Molluscan	DISTRIBUTION	RETAIL - Store	RETAIL - Mobile Unit	FOOD SERVICE
Dept. of Agriculture -Food & Drug Protect. Div.			(X)	(X)	?	$(X)^1$	X^1 -	X		(X)	(X)
-Div. of Aquaculture											
Dept. of Human Resources	X c m		X^2	X^2	?	X^2 -	(X)	X			
County Health		X							X -	X -	X -
Dept. Environ., Health, & Natural Resources -Div. Marine Fisheries		X									

Key:

X - primary authority

(X) - partial authority or limited activity

? - questionable authority, not delineated or not designated

(c) - closures; (l) inspection and licensing; (m) monitoring

1. Primarily finfish; mollusk & crustaceans only if cooked.
2. Limited to crustaceans (blue crab) and mollusks (oysters and clams).

Table C STATE REGULATORY PROGRAMS RELATIVE TO SEAFOOD PRODUCT SAFETY AND QUALITY

NORTH CAROLINA

	WATER CLASSIFICATION - Coastal Waters	Shellfish - Growing Areas	DEPURATION	AQUACULTURE - Freshwater	AQUACULTURE - Saltwater	TOXINS, PRODUCT	TOXINS, ENVIRONMENT	PRODUCT SEIZURE	HEALTH REPORTING	HEALTH ADVISORS / RISK COMMUNICATION	ECONOMIC FRAUD	LIVE INTRODUCTION
Dept. of Agriculture Food & Drug Protect. Div.						(X)		X	(X)	(X)	(X)	
Div. of Aquaculture				X	X					(X)		
Dept. of Human Resources		X c m	X		(X)	(X)		X	X	X	(X)	
County Health								(X)	(X)	(X)		
Dept. of Environ., Health, & Natural Resources Div. Marine Fisheries						(X)						X
Div. Environ. Mgmt.	X						X					
Wildlife Resource Comm. Div. Boating and Inland Fish.												X

Key:
X - primary authority
(X) - partial authority or limited activity
? - questionable authority, not delineated or not designated
(c) - closures; (i) inspection and licensing; (m) monitoring

Table A   Review of Regulatory and Industry Responses (November 29, 1989) Concerning Seafood Quality and Safety

PUERTO RICO

Industry Character (1989)

1. Local seafood production in Puerto Rico is modest and primarily artisanal. In 1987 the total recorded seafood landings just exceeded 2.0 million pounds, with a dockside value of $3.1 million. These figures do not account for tuna destined for major Puerto Rican-based tuna canning operations.

2. There are more than 2,000 local, nearshore commercial fishers with an average annual production of only 3,000 pounds per fisherman. Most local, nearshore commercial fishing is from small-scale and individually owned vessels, whereas most of the larger, offshore vessels fishing tuna, swordfish, etc., are company owned or based outside Puerto Rico.

3. Harvest from nearshore waters is diverse, including a typical variety of tropical and subtropical species. Principal species include snapper, grouper, grunt, tuna, mackerel, lobster, and conch. In 1987 the recorded landing for barracuda was 27.1 thousand pounds, and reported landings for oysters and clams totaled only 52 pounds. (These shellfish landings are obviously lower than actual due to limited reporting.)

4. Puerto Rican and neighboring Caribbean coastal waters do represent some current sources for certain popular fish species (e.g., swordfish, tunas, shark) destined for U.S. fresh and frozen seafood markets.

5. Local fisheries support popular recreational fishing. Recreational harvest can enter commercial settings.

6. With the exception of modern, large-scale tuna canning operations there is very little seafood processing in Puerto Rico. Large-scale tuna canning operations shipped over 500 million pounds of canned tuna to the United States in 1987.

7. The average annual Puerto Rican per capita seafood consumption is expected to exceed the average amount (~15 pounds per person) recorded for mainland U.S. consumers. The substantial influx of tourists expects seafood availability.

8. Estimates suggest that nearly 90 to 95% of the seafood consumed in Puerto Rico is purchased from other regions. In 1986, seafood shipments from the United States alone exceeded 33.5 million pounds, excluding tuna.

9. Seafoods shipped to Puerto Rico can include "true" imports originating in countries outside of the United States or as products merchandized through the mainland United States to Puerto Rico. True imports coming into Puerto Rico are subject to clearance through U.S. Customs and FDA, whereas seafoods originating in mainland U.S. ports can be reshipped to Puerto Rico without additional federal scrutiny.

10. According to previously recorded CDC data, 49% of all seafood-related illnesses are reported from four states or territories: Hawaii, Puerto Rico, the Virgin Islands, and Guam. These tropical settings include unique species, ambient temperatures, and handling difficulties that contribute to seafood quality and safety problems. Previous public health reports (via CDC) suggest ciguatera is a primary seafood safety problem in Puerto Rico.

11. Aquaculture is limited in Puerto Rico. Initial efforts are in progress for shrimp, tilapia, and some molluscan shellfish.

Primary Product Safety Problems

1. The primary seafood safety problems in Puerto Rico are typical for tropical settings (i.e., ciguatera, scombroid poisoning, and adverse microbial pathogens associated with consumption of raw molluscs).

2. Industry practices in production (harvest and culture) and retail/restaurant handling represent the primary areas of seafood product safety concern for local authorities. There is little seafood processing, with the exception of tuna canning operations that pose no significant seafood safety problems.

Primary Product Quality Problems

1. On-board handling practices by local, nearshore fishermen are suspect for seafood quality problems. Their tendency to employ traditional methods and their inability to finance new vessels or gear contribute to product quality concerns. Despite the concerns, most fishermen can usually sell all they catch because local demand exceeds supply, and in some instances, local product scrutiny lacks knowledge in quality judgments.

2. Seafood products from the mainland United States, less subject to federal scrutiny in Puerto Rico, are suspect for inferior quality.

3. In some instances, retail and restaurant personnel lack sufficient training to prevent and identify seafood quality problems.

Additional Problems

1. Regulatory and industry representatives believe that Puerto Rico's ciguatoxic reputation is exaggerated and perpetuated without sound epidemiological confirmation. This general belief does not diminish regulatory concern for ciguatera but encourages efforts to address the problem with better epidemiology, education, and development of reasonable surveillance methods. Continuing exaggerated media coverage of ciguatera on the island results in large economic losses to the already weak fishing industry of Puerto Rico.

2. Epidemiology in the Department of Health needs to improve efforts to confirm etiological agents contributing to the large number of annual cases of gastroenteritis and associated ailments. In 1988 there were over 67,000

reported cases of gastroenteritis without etiological confirmation. Efforts are seriously compromised by infrastructure in Puerto Rico and social practices/beliefs. This situation confuses any interpretation of seafood-borne illnesses. For example, local authorities are confused by conflicting reports citing incidences for ciguatera, whereas their program does not include ciguatera as a disease in weekly reports to CDC. In 1989, only three cases of ciguatera were reported. There is serious concern about the probable incidence of hepatitis as a consequence of raw mollusc consumption.

3. CODREMAR (Corporation for the Development and Administration of Marine Resources) of Puerto Rico was established in 1979 basically as a commercial development program to assist fisheries and aquaculture. Legislated structure aligned programs with the Department of Natural Resources and issued authority ranging from assessing (records access) and licensing of harvest and cultured production, to quality control. The corporation was given authority to establish, by regulation, standards for establishments, and for sanitary and quality controls of the fish harvest and the processing of fish and fishing products. It could conduct inspections, suspend rights to process, and confiscate (seafood) products in any establishment in which it was determined that public health was jeopardized. This board authority, although directed to work in agreement with other established agencies for food quality and safety, was not generally known or understood by the respective segments of the seafood industry and pertinent agencies. In practice, CODREMAR has focused primarily on the development of fisheries and aquatic product cultivation. Recent legislative considerations indicate change may be implemented by June 1990 to reorient the program and realign efforts with the Department of Agriculture.

4. Regulatory authority is shared, in part, by the Department of Consumer Affairs and the Department of Health. The Department of Health conducts inspections for public health reasons, can seize decomposed and potentially injurious foods, and can use court assistance for cease and desist action. The Department of Consumer Affairs has the authority to act against a business through issuing administrative fines and conducting hearings. These actions can be in support of the Department of Health's activities but are primarily concerned with protecting the consumer against fraud and deceit (species substitution, selling previously frozen fish as fresh fish, net weight violations, etc.). In effect, the Department of Health's complaints or actions against a seafood proprietor can be cause for the Department of Consumer Affairs to conduct an administrative hearing that could decide for cease and desist action. Distinction of authority is not always clear or understood, and can be confused by the multiple market levels unique to seafood commerce, particularly dockside sales and mobile units.

5. Despite significant attempts to educate and warn the public and industry about ciguatoxic concerns there have been no efforts to assess the success, in terms of decreased illness of these programs. In a general public forum these efforts are thought to deter tourism and business.

Regulatory Concerns for Seafood Industry

1. Local industry from production through retail generally lacks understanding of the principal authorities and pertinent regulations that ensure seafood quality and safety.
2. There is a continuing lack of knowledge and commitment among a substantial portion of local fishermen about proper onboard handling and seafood safety concerns.
3. Recreational harvest, which may or may not be licensed as a commercial event, can enter local seafood markets through channels less subject to regulatory surveillance.
4. Although local fishermen believe their knowledge of potential ciguatoxic areas provides avoidance of ciguatoxic fish, there has not been any routine confirmation by water or product sampling to "map" problematic regions for regulatory control. In 1979 the Department of Natural Resources and CODREMAR issued a notice that prohibits buying, selling, and marketing three species that can cause ciguatera: barracuda, amberjack, and black jack. This notice also says that if these species are found in the market, CODREMAR will embargo, seize, or destroy them. It is still displayed in some fishing villages and, in the past, was also used in restaurants. (Note: CODREMAR's program status is currently in question.)
5. The major portion of seafood products consumed in Puerto Rico is shipped from the United States and not subject to routine "import" surveillance by FDA authorities based in Puerto Rico. Although there are no major documented safety concerns associated with these products, product quality has been questioned. Puerto Rico, like some other U.S. territories, has been noted as a potential "dumping" ground for inferior quality. Regulatory scrutiny for this concern relies on limited local authority currently stressed by concerns for local production.

Regulatory Concerns for Their Respective Programs

1. There are no specific regulations or directed regulatory authority to routinely address seafood handling at the vessel production level.
2. The Department of Health and Department of Consumer Affairs should offer more guidance and training for all postharvest segments of the seafood industry, particularly restaurants and retailers.
3. An interdepartmental review of current regulations and regulatory activity pertinent to seafoods is warranted, but promulgation of additional and more specific regulations and surveillance would be limited by the lack of program personnel and funds.
4. Local molluscan shellfish production by harvest or cultivation is very limited, but the confirmed presence of certain microbial pathogens (e.g., viruses, *Vibrio vulnificus*), no specific monitoring and approval of harvestable waters, and associated illnesses from raw consumption warrant consideration for regulatory attention. Any regulatory initiative must realize the limited production relative to program operational costs and incorporate cost-

effective use of public and professional education.

5. Recent additions to the Department of Health's analytical capability for environmental contaminants should consider aquatic product assessments in terms of edible portions.

6. Regulatory authority for aquaculture product quality and safety is not distinct and can be confused with programs aligned to promote development of cultured production.

Industry Concern for Regulations

1. Local merchants welcome additional regulatory surveillance for seafood quality and safety, which they currently feel is limited in activity and visibility. This concern results from a combination of actual regulatory limitations and general industry confusion about responsible regulatory activity.

2. Local fishermen's concern for harvest quality and safety is compromised by limited to no available, reasonable financing to purchase new vessels and gear to allow better preservation and access to less problematic offshore resources. This economic situation compromises local efforts and incentives to resolve any quality and safety problems, while allowing resource access to more modernized non-Puerto Rican fishing competition.

3. Regulatory surveillance and liaison with the tuna canning operations are believed adequate and appreciated. This position is based on the processors' intuitive HACCP approach common for canning operations.

Recommendations

1. Develop a financial support program that allows local fishermen to invest in vessels and gear that provide better preservation of the harvest and access to offshore resources.

2. Additional, routine food quality, safety, and general sanitation training for seafood proprietors and respective regulatory authorities is strongly encouraged. A single, comprehensible publication that outlines the pertinent seafood regulations and the regulators should be the first educational objective.

3. Aquacultural development, particularly in the event of molluscan shellfish aquaculture, should be made more mindful of water quality in terms of site selection and various operating parameters that may adversely contribute to product quality and safety.

4. Research, education, and regulatory efforts must be continued to prevent seafood-borne illnesses in Puerto Rico, particularly ciguatera. Goals should include rapid, analytical methods for prevention, "targeted" education for avoidance, and considerations of regulatory positions on parameters to minimize occurrence (e.g., restrictions by species or harvest location).

5. Local trade associations (e.g., "Meat Institute") should join forces with academic-based programs (e.g., University of Puerto Rico Sea Grant College Program) to design and support seafood quality and safety training efforts

for all segments of the seafood industry and regulatory authorities. This effort could establish an industry-based seafood quality and safety advisory board to direct and attract necessary support and participation.

6. An interagency committee should be established to better communicate the responsibilities, current and planned efforts, and industry liaison pertinent to seafood quality and safety. This committee should incorporate expertise from the industry and advisory/research programs in academic institutions.

7. Because the major portion (~95%) of seafoods consumed in Puerto Rico is imported from various countries and shipped from the mainland United States, these products warrant more equivalent surveillance to ensure seafood safety and quality. This recommendation is most applicable to seafood reshipped from the mainland United States and not subject to additional clearance through customs or FDA.

Initiatives

1. The Governor of Puerto Rico has established a Food and Nutrition Committee composed of many agency representatives to prepare an advisory paper on food nutrition, quality, and safety problems in Puerto Rico. This report is due by mid-1990 and plans to include problems related to seafoods as produced and consumed in Puerto Rico.

2. Recent FDA regional programming has rearranged federal authority for Puerto Rico within the Atlanta-based jurisdiction. This arrangement is intended to direct more attention to seafood safety concerns in import surveillance and further assistance for local authorities, principally the Puerto Rico Department of Health, in addressing seafood safety of molluscan shellfish, reshipped products, and any specific issues through various levels of commerce.

3. Besides preparing and distributing publications to consumers and fishermen, the University of Puerto Rico Sea Grant College Program also offers seminars and workshops directed to the entire distribution chain, including housewives, students, fishermen, fish inspectors from the Health Department, restaurants, and supermarkets. Besides stressing proper fish handling techniques, these workshops and seminars cover an array of subjects such as hazards posed by these products to the consumer [e.g., ciguatera, contaminants in the water (especially for shellfish), parasites, scombroid poisoning, naturally toxic fish, seafood nutritional value, preparation, display techniques].

Summary

Puerto Rico is more prone to seafood product quality and safety problems due to its particular geographic setting, artisanal nearshore fisheries, and dependence on "imported" products. Local fishing activity lacks abundant nearshore seafood resources to justify financial support for vessel and gear improvements for better on-board preservation or offshore sourcing in less problematic waters. Seafood processing is limited to large tuna canning operations that maintain sufficient product quality and safety assurance programs. The per capita seafood consumption exceeds the average amount for the United States and includes tourist trade.

Regulatory programs and authority are present and can be effective in surveillance for seafood safety and quality. Their efforts are limited by lack of enough personnel and operating funds to allow more specific attention to seafoods. Industry compliance and cooperation are hampered by a clear distinction between pertinent regulations and regulatory authorities. Additional regulatory liaison and surveillance, and more industry, regulatory, and public education are requested to ensure better seafood quality and safety.

Table B   STATE REGULATORY JURISDICTIONS RELATIVE TO SEAFOOD PRODUCT SAFETY AND QUALITY

PUERTO RICO

	RECREATIONAL HARVEST - Molluscan	- Non-Molluscan	COMMERCIAL HARVEST - Vessel	- Dockside	PROCESSING - Vessel, Offshore	- Molluscan	- Non-Molluscan	DISTRIBUTION	RETAIL - Store	- Mobile Unit	FOOD SERVICE
Dept. of Health			(X)	X	X	X	X —	X —	X —	X —	X —
Dept. of Natural Resources	?	(X)									
Dept. of Consumer Affairs						(X)	(X)	(X)	(X)	(X)	(X)
Dept. of Commerce [1]							(X)	(X)	(X)	(X)	(X)
CODREMAR [2]			?	?	?	?	?				

Key:
X - primary authority
(X) - partial authority or limited activity
? - questionable authority, not delineated or not designated
(c) - closures; (l) inspection and licensing; (m) monitoring

1. Primary licensing authority.
2. Legislated authority and department alignment currently in question and changing from Natural Resources to Agriculture.

Table C   STATE REGULATORY PROGRAMS RELATIVE TO SEAFOOD PRODUCT SAFETY AND QUALITY

PUERTO RICO

	WATER CLASSIFICATION - Coastal Waters	WATER CLASSIFICATION -Shellfish Growing Areas	DEPURATION	AQUACULTURE - Freshwater	AQUACULTURE - Saltwater	TOXINS, PRODUCT	TOXINS, ENVIRONMENT	PRODUCT SEIZURE	HEALTH REPORTING	HEALTH ADVISORS RISK COMMUNICATION	ECONOMIC FRAUD	LIVE INTRODUCTION
Dept. of Health		?	?	(X)	?	X m		X	X	X	(X)	
Dept. of Natural Resources				(X)	?	(X)						X
Dept. of Agriculture					?	?						
Dept. of Consumer Affairs								?		(X)	X	
Environ. Qual. Board	X m	(X)[1]					X m					
Dept. of Commerce											(X)	
CODREMAR [2]			?	?	?						?	?

Key:

X - primary authority

(X) - partial authority or limited activity

? - questionable authority, not delineated or not designated

(c) - closures; (i) inspection and licensing; (m) monitoring

1. No current open or closed water classification.

2. Legislated authority and department alignment currently in question and changing from Natural Resources to Agriculture.

Table A   Review of State Regulatory and Industry Responses (November 10, 1988) Concerning Seafood Quality and Safety

SOUTH CAROLINA

Industry Character (1988)

1. Ranked 21st in total production (16.2 million pounds) and 20th in dockside value ($21.1 million).
2. Includes temperate and warmwater sources of state production with significant portion of product coming from out of state.
3. Most fishing vessels independently owned and operated.
4. Diverse state production; principal species include shrimp, blue crabs, oysters, and assorted nearshore finfish.
5. Most processing firms are comparatively small with majority involved in operations for picking and pasteurizing blue crab meat.
6. Consumption includes large metropolitan regions and seasonal tourism.
7. Aquaculture limited and in infancy with catfish, hybrid striped bass, clams, and soft-shell crabs.
8. Recreational fisheries – all species
9. Imports play significant role in meeting state demand, particularly in metropolitan regions.

Primary Product Safety Problems

1. Regulatory agencies and state-based industry firms believe seafood production and processing in South Carolina do not pose any major seafood product safety concerns.
2. Concerns for molluscan shellfish harvest and processing, and blue crab processing, are being adequately addressed with reference to established federal and state guidelines.

Primary Product Quality Problems

1. Product integrity in terms of proper species identification, net weight/content declarations, and use of ingredients are the principal concerns, particularly for the major portion of seafoods from out-of-state sources.

Additional Problems

1. Aquaculture could introduce additional species identification problems (e.g., cultured striped bass versus natural striped bass stocks).
2. The "25-mile line" distinguishing regulatory authorities to inspect fish handling/processing operations offers economic advantages for operations, but can be confusing if not well coordinated.

Regulatory Concerns for Seafood Industry

1. In general, industry has a poor understanding of the pertinent seafood regulations and regulators from vessel through retail.

Regulatory Concerns for Their Respective Programs

1. Need more training and orientation for regulator inspectors and less dependence on on-the-job training.
2. Employee turnover due to weak salaries and lack of career orientation hampers regulatory capability and limits justification of more significant, structured education.
3. Level of current state production and predicted decreases cannot support justification for increased regulatory emphasis, particularly in reference to primary species and limited safety problems.

Industry Concerns for Regulations

1. Want more active than reactive regulatory program, especially for product integrity (i.e., species identification and incoming product quality).
2. Need more regulatory consolidation and explanation of the pertinent regulations and regulators for product quality and safety.
3. Regulatory activity is primarily compliance oriented, particularly concerning product integrity (e.g., fresh versus frozen declaration, species identification, proper net weights). Would like to see more routine surveillance, particularly for products from out of state.
4. Need more equitable inspection of imports and products from out of state.

Recommendations

1. Plan periodic training on seafood quality and safety for all levels of industry and regulatory agencies.

Regulatory Initiatives

None identified.

Industry Initiatives

None identified.

Summary

South Carolina is not a major seafood producing and processing state, yet the seafood industry and products are a traditional and expected part of the state's economy and image. The major portion of seafood consumed comes from out-of-state sources. State production and processing of oysters and blue crabs are being adequately monitored to ensure consumer safety. Increasing product demand and operational requirements for the regulatory agencies could compromise future surveillance for product quality and safety.

The industry and respective regulatory agencies are content with the current "25-mile line" distinguishing jurisdictions for inspection of fish processing, but this economic operational agreement could be compromised by steady-state and reduced budgets.

Table B   STATE REGULATORY JURISDICTIONS RELATIVE TO SEAFOOD PRODUCT SAFETY AND QUALITY

SOUTH CAROLINA	RECREATIONAL HARVEST - Molluscan	- Non-Molluscan	COMMERCIAL HARVEST - Vessel	- Dockside	PROCESSING - Vessel, Offshore	- Molluscan	- Non-Molluscan	DISTRIBUTION	RETAIL - Store	- Mobile Unit	FOOD SERVICE
Dept. of Health and Environmental Control -Div. Shellfish Sanitation	X		?	X	(X)	X[1] (i)	X[1] (i)	(X)[1] (i)	(X)[1]	(X)[1]	(X)[1]
-Div. Food Protection								X (i)	X (i)	X (i)	X (i)
Dept. of Agriculture -Food & Cosmetic Sect.							X[1] (i)	(X)[1]			
-Consumer Serv. Div.									(X)[2]	(X)[2]	
Wildlife & Marine Resource Dept. -Div. Wildlife & Mar. Reso.		(X)									
-Div. Wildlife and Freshwater Fish		(X)									

Key:

X - primary authority

(X) - partial authority or limited activity

? - questionable authority, not delineated or not designated

(c) - closures; (i) inspection and licensing; (m) monitoring

1. 25 mile rule, Dept. of Agriculture, primarily finfish, inland from 25 mile line.
   Dept. of Health & Environ. Control, all seafoods on coast and blue crabs & oysters statewide.

2. Weights and measures.

Table C STATE REGULATORY PROGRAMS RELATIVE TO SEAFOOD PRODUCT SAFETY AND QUALITY

SOUTH CAROLINA	WATER CLASSIFICATION - Coastal Waters	Shellfish Growing Areas	DEPURATION	AQUACULTURE - Freshwater	- Saltwater	TOXINS, PRODUCT	TOXINS, ENVIRONMENT	PRODUCT SEIZURE	HEALTH REPORTING	HEALTH ADVISORS RISK COMMUNICATION	ECONOMIC FRAUD	LIVE INTRODUCTION
Dept. of Health and Environmental Control -Environ. Quality Control	X						X					
-Shellfish Sanitation Sec.		X c m	X	?	(X)	(X)	(X)	(X)	(X)	(X)	(X)	
-Preventive Health Serv.									X	X		
Dept. of Agriculture -Food & Cosmetic Sect.				(X)[1]	(X)[1]	(X)[2]		(X)			(X)	
Wildlife & Marine Resource Dept. -Div. Wildlife & Mar. Reso.					?							X
-Dept. of Wildlife and Freshwater Fish				?								X

Key:
X - primary authority
(X) - partial authority or limited activity
? - questionable authority, not delineated or not designated
(c) - closures; (i) inspection and licensing; (m) monitoring

1. Can involve processing of culture products.
2. Response usually based on complaints.

Table A Review of State Regulatory and Industry Responses (March 6, 1990) Concerning Seafood Quality and Safety

TEXAS

Industry Character (1990)

1. In 1988, dockside seafood landings in Texas ranked 14th in production (96.0 million pounds) and 5th in value ($175.7 million).
2. Primarily warmwater, nearshore fisheries from subtropical sources were supplemented with significant imports including foreign entries via ground transport from Mexico.
3. Fish vessel ownership split between individuals and company-based operations.
4. The high value for Texas seafood production is attributed to the shrimp harvest, which generates approximately 80% of the landed value. Blue crab and oyster production constitutes the next major portion of the industry, whereas finfish production is meager due to management decisions for recreational interest.
5. Most significant segment of seafood processing involves blue crabs and oysters; larger shrimp harvest supports a traditional off-loading/packing practice destined for fresh and frozen markets or further processing outside Texas.
6. Consumption includes significant portion of ethnic groups and some particular tastes (e.g., Texas consumes 40% of nation's cultured catfish production).
7. Aquaculture is in a fledgling yet developing state, with primary focus on catfish and growing interest in tilapia and crawfish. Saltwater aquaculture is not evident to date.
8. Major recreational finfish fisheries exist for near and inshore species.
9. There are strong regulatory distinction and enforcement between recreational and commercial fishing activity.
10. Imports continue to increase to suit regional demands.

Primary Product Safety Problems

1. Raw molluscan shellfish consumption constitutes most important concern for regulatory scrutiny among Texas-based seafood production and use, but it is not considered a major problem without effective controls.
2. Stronger enforcement penalties have proved effective and necessary to curb illegal harvest or bootleg activity from unapproved growing areas.
3. There is a growing concern about use of further processing in retail settings.

Primary Product Quality Problems

1. Assuring postharvest product quality and maintaining product quality in wholesale and retail settings (e.g., basic time temperature abuse).
2. Recurrent problems include initial spoilage, excessive or undeclared use of sulfites, and misuse of phosphates and net control labeling.

Additional Problems

1. There is no specific legislated authority to monitor postharvest product quality with the exception of molluscan shellfish.
2. Blue crab processing in Mexico has not evolved to a level of concern for more surveillance of ground imports (via Mexico), yet should activity increase the only regulatory recourse for Texas health authorities is reliance on limited federal screening upon entry. This situation places strong dependence on foreign government assurance that plants comply with adequate GMPs for potential ready-to-eat seafood items.
3. More routine product assessments are warranted to ensure that regional and site-specific aquatic resources do not harbor potential contaminants. Despite interagency cooperation, authorities lack sufficient allocations to support activity under the "Aquatic Life Law" that directs field sampling for routine product analysis of potential chemical contaminants. The respective health authorities rely on data from agency programs more directed to assess the water quality and consequences on aquatic life.
4. Authorities question if illegal harvest restrictions should be imposed to deter catching finfish from areas identified as potentially toxic (e.g., closures, advisories, bans), similar to the authority to halt harvest of shellfish from prohibited waters.

Regulatory Concerns for Seafood Industry

1. An ethnic related problem exists for bootleg crabmeat.
2. Principal seafood surveillance programs focus primarily on ensuring seafood safety, with concomitant inference for quality, thus leaving seafood quality assurance an industry responsibility.

Regulatory Concerns for Their Respective Programs

1. Based on home rule, counties and cities establish their own surveillance for retail and restaurant operations. They rely on help from their state-level counterparts, which can be directly involved in the absences of local authorities. This system warrants additional attention to ensure more uniform and specific activity across the retail sector, particularly in reference to seafood products and handling.
2. State health authorities do not have the mandate or support to conduct technical work (research) to assess new processing innovations (e.g., alternative crab

washing procedures). Current regulatory programs must rely on developments and verification in industry or academic settings, or from the federal government.

3. Current shellfish program, like all state programs, lacks ability to confidently trace molluscan shellfish back to the source of actual harvest, thus limiting resolution of any adverse consequence beyond the processor.

4. Current surveillance programs for seafood safety need more manpower and funds to support additional and more uniform coverage from dock, through processing, to retail sectors.

5. Although academic and federally based programs offer annual educational support for the agency staff, additional seafood-specific training is necessary particularly at county and city levels. Current programs depend on substantial amounts of on-the-job training.

6. Federal inspection activity in Texas had decreased, leaving a larger burden for state health authorities.

7. Coastal, inshore water quality assessments need to include more work with long-term trend assessments and "bioaccumulation."

8. Initial lack of interagency coordination in legislation and program development for aquaculture has confused regulatory distinction in authority for surveillance of processing cultured products.

Industry Concern for Regulations

1. There is some confusion over the respective roles and rules of the divisions within the Texas Department of Health and other agencies relative to permitting and surveillance of traditional seafood processing.

2. To avoid federal inspection, some seafood processors can cease operation, yet maintain their license to process, then resume processing once the probability of inspection is lower.

3. Licensing and permitting requirements with Texas Departments of Health, Agriculture, Parks and Wildlife, and Texas Water Commission can be confusing and discouraging for aquaculture development.

Recommendations

1. Additional emphasis and support should be directed to increase and standardize seafood quality and safety surveillance in the retail and restaurant sectors as monitored by respective county and city authorities.

2. Aquaculture development, particularly in processing sector, warrants more interagency coordination relative to pertinent product quality and safety assurances.

3. Regulatory seafood inspectors for processing through retail need additional and more uniform training in seafood processing and handling.

4. A condensed compilation of all related Texas regulations on seafood quality and seafood safety should be published for industry reference.

5. Health authorities and seafood processors should consider a "certification" program based on minimal, standardized training for inspectors, processing

      personnel, and plant managers.

  6. Additional manpower is needed for adequate surveillance of seafood processors and wholesalers.

Regulatory Initiatives

    None identified.

Industry Initiatives

    None identified.

Summary

    Texas seafood production and processing do not pose any major acute seafood safety concerns that are not being addressed by current regulatory programs. The processing sector is primarily limited to two species, blue crabs and oysters. Product quality compromised prior to processing or in wholesale retail/restaurant settings is the principal concern. Regulatory efforts at county and city level may warrant reassessment for the surveillance for seafoods in retail. The evolving aquaculture industry offers an opportunity for agencies to evaluate their roles and initiate interagency cooperation to better address cultured product quality and safety. Continuing concern for potential contaminants in edible, aquatic resources destined for commercial or recreational harvest will require sufficient funds to support established health programs and encourage additional interagency cooperation.

Table B STATE REGULATORY JURISDICTIONS RELATIVE TO SEAFOOD PRODUCT SAFETY AND QUALITY

TEXAS

	RECREATIONAL HARVEST - Molluscan	RECREATIONAL HARVEST - Non-Molluscan	COMMERCIAL HARVEST - Vessel	COMMERCIAL HARVEST - Dockside	PROCESSING - Vessel, Offshore	PROCESSING - Molluscan	PROCESSING - Non-Molluscan	DISTRIBUTION	RETAIL - Store	RETAIL - Mobile Unit	FOOD SERVICE
Dept. of Health											
-Food & Drug	X	X		(X)			X -	X	X[1] -	X[1] -	X[1] -
-Shellfish [2]	X		(X)	(X)		X -		(X)	(X)	(X)	(X)
-Public Health Promotion											
-Epidemiology											
Agriculture							(X)[3]				
Parks & Wildlife	(X)	(X)									
Water Commission											
County/City									X[1] -	X[1] -	X[1] -

Key:

X - primary authority

(X) - partial authority or limited activity

? - questionable authority, not delineated or not designated

(c) - closures; (l) inspection and licensing; (m) monitoring

1. Home rule, local county and city authority can apply in conjunction with the Department of Health.
2. Only blue crab and mollusk   3. Aquacultured products

Table C STATE REGULATORY PROGRAMS RELATIVE TO SEAFOOD PRODUCT SAFETY AND QUALITY

TEXAS	WATER CLASSIFICATION - Coastal Waters	WATER CLASSIFICATION - Shellfish Growing Areas	DEPURATION	AQUACULTURE - Freshwater	AQUACULTURE - Saltwater	TOXINS, PRODUCT	TOXINS, ENVIRONMENT	PRODUCT SEIZURE	HEALTH REPORTING	HEALTH ADVISORS / RISK COMMUNICATION	ECONOMIC FRAUD	LIVE INTRODUCTION
Dept. of Health -Food & Drug		X c m	X	X^5	X^5			X		X	X	
-Shellfish			X		$(X)^1$	X^2		X	(X)	X	(X)	
-Public Health Promotion										X	(X)	
-Epidemiology					?				X	(X)		
Dept. of Agriculture				X^4								
Parks & Wildlife		X^3 m										X
Water Commission	X			$(X)^6$	$(X)^6$	(X)	X					
County/City										(X)		

Key:

X - primary authority
(X) - partial authority or limited activity
? - questionable authority, not delineated or not designated
(c) - closures; (l) inspection and licensing; (m) monitoring

1. Shellfish & crabs
2. Aquatic Life Law, all seafood
3. Enforcement
4. Promotional
5. Shared jurisdiction of processing with Dept. of Agriculture
6. Any necessary discharge permits.

Table A Review of State Regulatory and Industry Responses (May 24, 1989) Concerning Seafood Quality and Safety

WASHINGTON

Industry Character (1989)

1. Ranked 9th in production and 6th in landed value.
2. Primarily coldwater source production and pass-through processing for Alaska and offshore vessels.
3. Principal species – salmon, halibut, albacore, tanner and dungeness crab, shrimp, and oysters.
4. Introduction of large-scale offshore processing.
5. Significant portion of seafood utilization in King County.
6. Aquaculture principal species – salmon and oysters.
7. Recreational fisheries increasing.
8. Imports constitute significant and increasing portion of commerce.

Primary Product Safety Problems

1. Molluscan shellfish safety – microbial consequences and PSP on the product and in the environment as encountered by both commercial and recreational interests.
2. Monitoring for toxic contaminants in the environment with need to increase surveillance and interprogram coordination for prevention and assessments.

Regulatory Concerns

1. Use of live tanks (wet storage) and mixed molluscan species should be addressed.
2. Need to improve epidemiology including commercial and recreational consequence.
3. Need more equitable surveillance for imports versus domestic products, and products during and from offshore processing.
4. Currently programs have experienced some poor coordination in identifying import problems, general food safety/quality concerns and species marketing and introduction.
5. There are occasional conflicts with federal program as pertains to concomitant state responsibility (e.g., state versus FDA versus NMFS on foreign certification for wholesomeness).
8. Public perception versus reality (education) for seafood safety.
9. Lack of adequate funding, staff and analytical tools, with emphasis on rapid methods.

Regulatory Initiatives

1. Statewide recreational mollusc harvest regulation.
2. Expand labeling to inform public.
3. Initiate education programs for regulatory agencies, industry, and public.

Industry Initiatives

1. Canned Salmon Control Plan.
2. Annual training/education in cooperation with academic based expertise (e.g., Sea Grant Programs).

Recommendations

1. Formalize and exercise HACCP concept in regulatory and commercial practice.
2. Improve current regulations and analytical capability.
3. Address microbiological standards for high-risk products (e.g., raw, cooked ready to eat).
4. Address safety issues for molluscan shellfish in retail (e.g., use of live tanks, tagging, and pull dates).
5. Expand education of
   - public (high-risk groups and special issues);
   - industry (consider "certification"); and
   - regulators (more and more frequent seafood training).

Summary

Washington State is not a problem area due primarily to unique features of environment, specific species involved, nature of processing (largely pass-through operations), and effective, responsible regulatory programs.

Where problems exist they have been identified and are being addressed with current capability and recommendations. The primary seafood safety concerns are molluscan shellfish consumption and specific environmental contaminants.

Washington State stands as an excellent example that regulation (inspection, surveillance) does exist and does work at the state level.

Table B   STATE REGULATORY JURISDICTIONS RELATIVE TO SEAFOOD PRODUCT SAFETY AND QUALITY

WASHINGTON	RECREATIONAL HARVEST - Molluscan	- Non-Molluscan	COMMERCIAL HARVEST - Vessel	- Dockside	PROCESSING - Vessel, Offshore	- Molluscan	- Non-Molluscan	DISTRIBUTION	RETAIL - Store	- Mobile Unit	FOOD SERVICE
Dept. of Agriculture			(X)	(X)	?		X [1]	(X)			
Dept. of Health	X		X	X		X [1]		X [1]	X [1]	X [1]	X [1]
King Co. Health Dept.						X [1]	X [1]	X [1]	X [1]	X [1]	X [1]

Key:
X - primary authority
(X) - partial authority or limited activity
? - questionable authority, not delineated or not designated
(c) - closures; (i) inspection and licensing; (m) monitoring

1. Only for mollusk.

Table C   STATE REGULATORY PROGRAMS RELATIVE TO SEAFOOD PRODUCT SAFETY AND QUALITY

WASHINGTON

	WATER CLASSIFICATION - Coastal Waters	WATER CLASSIFICATION - Shellfish Growing Areas	DEPURATION	AQUACULTURE - Freshwater	AQUACULTURE - Saltwater	TOXINS, PRODUCT	TOXINS, ENVIRONMENT	PRODUCT SEIZURE	HEALTH REPORTING	HEALTH ADVISORS RISK COMMUNICATION	ECONOMIC FRAUD	LIVE INTRODUCTION
Dept. of Agriculture		X[1] c		?	X	X m		X			X	(X)
Dept. of Health			?			X m	X m	X	X	(X)	X	
King Co. Health Dept.						X		(X)	X	(X)	X	
Dept. of Ecology	X			?	?	(X)	X m					
Dept. of Natural Reso.[2]												
Dept. of Fisheries												X

Key:
X - primary authority
(X) - partial authority or limited activity
? - questionable authority, not delineated or not designated
(c) - closures; (l) inspection and licensing; (m) monitoring

1.
2. Primarily address land management.

Appendixes

APPENDIX A

GLOSSARY OF TERMS AND ACRONYMS

Action levels Levels set to provide regulatory guidance to FDA field personnel to determine whether or not a product should be deemed adulterated and an appropriate enforcement action imposed.

ADI Acceptable daily intake.

AFDO Association of Food and Drug Officials, York, Pa.

AFDOSS Association of Food and Drug Officials of Southern States, Knoxville, Tenn.

ALAD Aminolevulinic acid dehydratase.

APA Administrative Procedures Act, administered by Food and Drug Administration.

APC Aerobic plate count (for microorganisms).

APHA American Public Health Association, Washington, D.C.

AQL Acceptable quality level (quality that has a 95% chance of acceptance).

ASP Amnesic shellfish poisoning.

BHC Benzene hexachloride (a mixture of the α, β, γ-isomers of 1,2,3,4,5,6-hexa-chlorocyclohexane, depending on the manufacturer).

BH Boston Harbor in Boston, Mass.

CAP Controlled atmosphere packaging.

CCPs Critical control points.

CDC Centers for Disease Control, Public Health Service, Atlanta, Ga.

CFR Code of Federal Regulations.

CFU Colony forming unit.

Chemically contaminated Presence of significant levels of undesirable (usually toxic) chemicals derived from natural environment or of anthropogenic origin.

CHPB Canadian Health Protection Board, Ottawa.

CNI Community Nutrition Institute, Washington, D.C.

CNS Central nervous system.

Control systems Mechanisms to reduce or eliminate risk from hazards by government, industry, or individual action.

CPG Compliance policy guidelines relating to seafood safety.

CSF Cerebrospinal fluid.

CSTE Conference of State and Territorial Epidemiologists, Albany, N.Y.

CT Cholera toxin.

CWA Clean Water Act, administered by Environmental Protection Agency.

DB Delaware Bay in Delaware.

DCC Division of Contaminants Chemistry of Food and Drug Administration Center for Food Safety and Applied Nutrition, Washington, D.C.

DCPA Dacthal pesticide.

DDE Dichlorodiphenyldichloroethane (a metabolite of DDT).

DDT Dichlorodiphenyltrichloroethane [1,1,1-trichloro-2,2-bis(p-chlorophenyl)ethane].

Deficiencies Aspects of control systems that reduce their effectiveness.

Depuration A procedure to remove pathogens from molluscan shellfish.

DFO Department of Fish and Oceans of Canada, Ottawa.

DNA Deoxyribonucleic acid.

DOC U.S. Department of Commerce.

DOD U.S. Department of Defense.

DSHS Department of Social and Health Services in Washington state.

DSP Diarrhetic shellfish poisoning.

D-value The number of minutes at the indicated temperature necessary to reduce a microbial population by 90%.

ED$_{50}$ Median effective dose; the dosage required to produce a response in 50% of a population.

EDB Ethylene dibromide.

EEC European Economic Community, headquartered in Brussels, Belgium.

ELISA Enzyme-linked immunoabsorbent assay.

EPA U.S. Environmental Protection Agency.

ESADDI Estimated safe and adequate daily dietary intake levels set by National Academy of Sciences.

FAO Food and Agriculture Organization of the United Nations, Rome, Italy.

FDA U.S. Food and Drug Administration, Public Health Service.

FEL Frank effect level for blood.

FEP Free erythrocyte protoporphyrin.

FFDCA Federal Food, Drug and Cosmetic Act, administered by Food and Drug Administration.

FMI Food Marketing Institute, Washington, D.C.

FNB Food and Nutrition Board of the National Academy of Sciences.

F-value Equivalent in minutes, at given temperature, of heat considered necessary to destroy spores or vegetative cells of a particular microorganism.

FWS U.S. Fish and Wildlife Service.

GAO U.S. General Accounting Office, Washington, D.C.

GMP Good manufacturing practices.

GNP Gross national product.

HACCP Hazard Analysis Critical Control Point.

HAV Hepatitis type A virus.

Hazard An organism, substance, or condition having the potential to cause disease.

Hazard severity *High*: may cause disability, extended sequelae, and in some cases, death. *Moderate*: may require medical intervention to avoid debilitating or life-threatening effects; rarely self-resolving. *Mild*: symptoms transitory, rarely lasting more than a few days, no sequelae; not life threatening, usually self-resolving.

Hazardous seafood Fish or shellfish, the consumption of which can lead to disease.

HCB The fully aromatic form of benzene with six chlorine molecules.

HDH Hawaii Department of Health, Honolulu.

HHS U.S. Department of Health and Human Services.
HPLC High-performance liquid chromatography.
H/R Hudson/Raritan Estuary in New York.

IAMFES International Association of Milk, Food and Environmental Sanitarians, Ames, Iowa.
ICMSF International Commission on Microbiological Specifications for Foods.
IOM Institute of Medicine of the National Academy of Sciences.
IQL Indifference quality level (quality that has a 50% chance of acceptance).
ISSC Interstate Shellfish Sanitation Conference; the organization that implements the National Shellfish Sanitation Program.

Lindane γ-isomer of 1,2,3,4,5,6-hexachlorocyclohexane, also known as BHC.
LOAEL Low-observed-adverse-effect level.
LQL Limiting quality level (quality that has a 10% chance of acceptance).

MAP Modified atmosphere packaging (a process in which air is replaced by other gases, usually CO_2).
MATC Median acceptable toxicant concentration for blood.
MMWR *Morbidity and Mortality Weekly Report,* published by Centers for Disease Control.
MOU Memorandum of understanding.
MPN Most probable number, a means for estimating bacterial densities.
MPRSA Marine Protection, Research and Sanctuaries Act, administered by Environmental Protection Agency.

NACMCF National Advisory Committee on Microbiological Criteria for Food.
NANB Non-A, non-B enteral hepatitis and unspecified hepatitis.
NAS National Academy of Sciences, Washington, D.C.
NBCIA National Blue Crab Industry Association, Division of National Fisheries Institute, Arlington, Va.
NCBP National Contaminant Biomonitoring Program of the U.S. Fish and Wildlife Service.
NETSU Northeast Technical Support Unit of Food and Drug Administration, Davisville, R.I.
NFI National Fisheries Institute, Inc., Arlington, Va.
NFPA National Food Processors Association, Seattle, Wash.
NFSPC National Fish and Seafood Promotional Council of National Oceanic and Atmospheric Administration.
NHMRC National Health and Medical Research Council of Australia, or ANHMRC.
NMFS National Marine Fisheries Service of National Oceanic and Atmospheric Administration.
NOAA National Oceanic and Atmospheric Administration.
NOAEL No-observed-adverse-effect level.
NOEL No-observed-effect level.
NPD National Purchase Dairy Panel, Inc., Schaumburg, Ill.
NPMP National Pesticide Monitoring Program of National Oceanic and Atmospheric Administration.
NRC National Research Council of the National Academy of Sciences.

NSP Neurotoxic shellfish poisoning.

NSSP National Shellfish Sanitation Program carried out by states under supervision of Food and Drug Administration.

NS&T National Status and Trends Program of National Oceanic and Atmospheric Administration.

NYSB New York Bight in New Jersey.

OAD Ocean Assessment Division of National Oceanic and Atmospheric Administration.

Organoleptic Affecting or relating to qualities such as appearance, color, odor, and texture.

PAHs Polycyclic aromatic hydrocarbons.

PCBs Polychlorinated biphenyls.

PFP Puffer fish poisoning.

PHS U.S. Public Health Service.

PHSA Public Health Service Act, administered by Food and Drug Administration.

Probit Number of standard deviations from the median of a lognormal distribution of tolerances plus five.

PSP Paralytic shellfish poisoning.

PTDI Provisional tolerance daily intake limits set by Food and Agriculture Organization/World Health Organization.

PTWI Provisional tolerance weekly intake limits set by Food and Agriculture Organization/World Health Organization.

PUFI Packed under federal inspection.

Quality Refers to palatability and organoleptic characteristics such as tenderness, juiciness, and flavor, based on the maturity, marbling, color, firmness, and texture of the product.

RBP Retinol binding protein.

RfD Reference dose.

RIA Radioimmunoassay.

Risk Probability that a person will become ill from a hazard.

Safety Probability that harm will not occur under specified conditions (the reciprocal of risk).

SD Standard deviation.

SFA Southeastern Fisheries Association, Tallahassee, Fla.

SRV Small round virus.

TBT Tri-n-butyltin.

TCBS Thiosulfate-citrate-bile salts-sucrose selective agar medium.

TCDD 2,3,7,8-Tetrachlorodibenzo-p-dioxin.

TCI The Catfish Institute, Belzoni, Miss.

TD$_{25}$ Lifetime dose estimated to produce cancer in 25% of exposed people.

TDE Or DDD [(diphenylethanedichlorophenyl(ethane), a metabolite of DDT].

Teratogen Agent causing congenital defect(s).

TMAO Trimethylamine oxide.

Tolerance Limit above which the product is deemed to be injurious.

TRF Tuna Research Foundation, Washington, D.C.

UCL Upper confidence limit.
USDA U.S. Department of Agriculture.
USF&WS U.S. Fish and Wildlife Service.

WHO World Health Organization of the United Nations, Geneva, Switzerland.
Wholesomeness The general term used to imply that the product is processed in a sanitary and healthful manner and is safe to eat.

Z-score Number of standard deviations above or below the midpoint of a standard normal or lognormal distribution; inferred from the work of a specific individual value in a data set.
Z-value The temperature difference associated with a tenfold difference in the killing rate of microorganisms.

APPENDIX B

COMMITTEE ON EVALUATION OF THE SAFETY OF FISHERY PRODUCTS AFFILIATIONS AND MAJOR RESEARCH INTERESTS

CHAIRMAN

John Liston, Ph.D.
Professor
Institute for Food Science
  and Technology
University of Washington
  Seattle, Washington
Major interests: Microbiology,
  fish toxins, and seafood policy

MEMBERS

Roger D. Anderson, Ph.D.
Retail Corporate Accounts Manager
Bee Gee Shrimp
Tampa, Florida
Major interests: Seafood safety and
  industry structure

Robert E. Bowen, Ph.D.
Associate Professor
Environmental Sciences Program
University of Massachusetts
Boston, Massachusetts
Major interests: Seafood policy,
  regulations, and international
  programs

Cameron R. Hackney, Ph.D.
Associate Professor
Department of Food Science and
  Technology
Virginia Polytechnic Institute and
  State University
Blacksburg, Virginia
Major interests: Microbiology
  and seafood technology

MEMBERS (Continued)

Dale Hattis, Ph.D.
Principal Research Associate
Center for Technology, Policy and
  Industrial Development
Massachusetts Institute of Technology
Cambridge, Massachusetts
Major interests: Risk assessment and
  environmental chemical contaminants

Marilyn B. Kilgen, Ph.D.
Distinguished Service Professor
Department of Biological Sciences
Nicholls State University
Thibodeaux, Louisiana
Major interests: Microbiology and
  virology of seafood

J. Glenn Morris, Jr., M.D., M.P.H., T.M.
Associate Professor
Department of Medicine
University of Maryland, School of
  Medicine
Baltimore, Maryland
Major interests: Public health,
  epidemiology, fish toxins, and
  microbiology

W. Steven Otwell, Ph.D.
Professor
Food Science and Human
  Nutrition Department
University of Florida
Gainesville, Florida
Major interests: Seafood technology,
  seafood regulations, and industry structure

423

MEMBERS (Continued)

Morris E. Potter, D.V.M., M.S.
Epidemiologist
Division of Bacterial Diseases
Centers for Disease Control
Atlanta, Georgia
Major interests: Epidemiology,
    microbiology, and food safety

Edward J. Schantz, Ph.D.
Professor Emeritus
Food Research Institute
University of Wisconsin
Madison, Wisconsin
Major interests: Fish toxins
    and biochemistry

David Steinman, M.A.
Consultant and Writer
Arizona Republic Newspaper
Los Angeles, California
Major interests: Public interest
    and food safety policy

Harrison M. Wadsworth, Ph.D.
Professor
School of Industrial and Systems
    Engineering
Georgia Institute of Technology
Atlanta, Georgia
Major interests: Statistical analysis
    and sampling

Richard E. Wolke, Ph.D.
Professor
Comparative Aquatic Pathology
    Laboratory
University of Rhode Island
Kingston, Rhode Island
Major interests: Marine pathology,
    parasitology, and trace-metal
    contaminants

CONSULTANTS

Judith McDowell Capuzzo, Ph.D.
Senior Scientist
Biology Department
Woods Hole Oceanographic Institute
Woods Hole, Massachusetts
Major interests: Marine contaminants
    and seafood safety

Harold Humphrey, Ph.D.
Chief, Great Lakes Health Studies Division
Michigan Department of Public Health
Lansing, Michigan
Major interests: Epidemiology, public
    health, and environmental chemical
    contaminants

Kathryn Mahaffey, Ph.D.
Science Advisor to the Director
NIEHS at University of Cincinnati
    Medical Center
Cincinnati, Ohio
Major interests: Trace-metal contaminants
    and seafood consumption

Joseph Rodricks, Ph.D.
Principal
Environ Corporation
Arlington, Virginia
Major interests: Risk management and
    assessment

INSTITUTE OF MEDICINE STAFF

Farid E. Ahmed, Ph.D.
Senior Program Officer
Food and Nutrition Board
Washington, D.C.
Major interests: Food safety, toxicology,
    risk assessment, biotechnology, environ-
    mental carcinogenesis and mutagenesis,
    and scientific communication

Index